Computer Networking and the Internet

Visit the *Computer Networking and the Internet, fifth edition* Companion Website at **www.pearsoned.co.uk/halsall** to find valuable **student** learning material including:

- Multiple choice questions to help test your learning
- Annotated links to relevant sites on the web

Web material prepared by Richard Read of Middlesex University

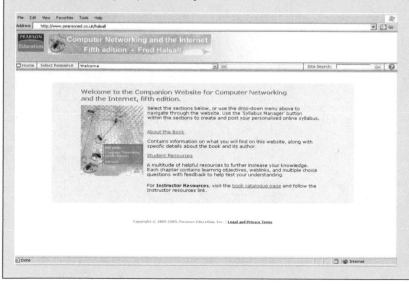

PEARSON
Education

We work with leading authors to develop the strongest educational materials in computing, bringing cutting-edge thinking and best learning practice to a global market.

Under a range of well-known imprints, including Addison Wesley, we craft high quality print and electronic publications which help readers to understand and apply their content, whether studying or at work.

To find out more about the complete range of our publishing, please visit us on the World Wide Web at: www.pearsoned.co.uk

Computer Networking and the Internet

Fifth edition

Fred Halsall

ADDISON-WESLEY

An imprint of **Pearson Education**

Harlow, England · London · New York · Reading, Massachusetts · San Francisco · Toronto · Don Mills, Ontario · Sydney
Tokyo · Singapore · Hong Kong · Seoul · Taipei · Cape Town · Madrid · Mexico City · Amsterdam · Munich · Paris · Milan

Pearson Education Limited
Edinburgh Gate
Harlow
Essex CM20 2JE
England

and Associated Companies throughout the world.

Visit us on the World Wide Web at:
www.pearsoned.co.uk

First published 1985
Fifth edition published 2005

© Pearson Education Limited 2005

ISBN 0-321-26358-8

British Library Cataloguing-in-Publication Data
A catalogue record for this book can be obtained from the British Library.

10 9 8 7 6 5 4 3 2 1
09 08 07 06 05

Typeset by 30 in New Baskerville 10/12pt
Printed and bound in the United States of America

The publisher's policy is to use paper manufactured from sustainable forests.

Contents

Supporting resources

Visit **www.pearsoned.co.uk/halsall** to find valuable online resources

Companion Website for students
- Multiple choice questions to help test your learning
- Annotated links to relevant sites on the web

For instructors
- PowerPoint slides containing all the diagrams from the text and the worked examples, that can be downloaded and used as OHTs

Also: The regularly maintained Companion Website provides the following features:

- Search tool to help locate specific items of content
- E-mail results and profile tools to send results of quizzes to instructors
- Online help and support to assist with website usage and troubleshooting

Web material prepared by Richard Read of Middlesex University

For more information please contact your local Pearson Education sales representative or visit **www.pearsoned.co.uk/halsall**

OneKey: All you and your students need to succeed

OneKey is an exclusive new resource for instructors and students, giving you access to the best online teaching and learning tools 24 hours a day, 7 days a week.

OneKey means all your resources are in one place for maximum convenience, simplicity and success.

A OneKey product is available for *Computer Networking and the Internet, fifth edition* for use with Blackboard™, WebCT and CourseCompass. It contains:

For students
- Learning objectives for each chapter
- Multiple choice questions to help test your learning
- Annotated links to relevant sites on the web
- Interactive animations of key figures

For instructors
- PowerPoint slides containing all the diagrams from the text and the worked examples, that can be downloaded and used as OHTs

For more information about the OneKey product please contact your local Pearson Education sales representative or visit **www.pearsoned.co.uk/onekey**

Preface

Objectives

Prior to the introduction of the World Wide Web, there were many different types of computer networks used to interconnect geographically distributed sets of computers. Many large corporations and businesses, for example, often used proprietary networks, each with its own protocols and networking infrastructure, while, at the same time, the Internet was used primarily to interconnect distributed sets of computers that were located at academic and research institutions around the world. Typical applications were electronic mail and more general file transfers between computers.

With the advent of the Web, however, since the Internet was the networking infrastructure used for the Web, the Internet has rapidly become the dominant computer network as people at home and at work started to use the Web. Typical applications are interactive entertainment, electronic commerce, and so on, which, of course, are in addition to the standard applications already supported by the Internet. As we can deduce from this, therefore, the subject of computer networking is now synonymous with the study of the Internet and its applications.

The combined effect of these developments means that the number of users of the Internet has expanded rapidly. To support this expansion, instead of most users accessing the Internet through an academic network, a number of different types of access network are now used. For example, most users at home and in small businesses gain access through their local switched telephone network using either a low bit rate modem or, more usually, a broadband modem. Alternatively, for cable television subscribers, access is often through a high bit rate cable modem. In practice, however, both access methods provide only a physical connection to a second network called an Internet service provider (ISP) network. This, as its name implies, provides the access point to the Internet for a set of users that fall within the field of coverage of a particular ISP network. Clearly, therefore, there are many ISPs each of which is a private, commercial company and hence access to the Internet through an ISP must be paid for.

In addition to telephone and cable networks, with the introduction of Internet-enabled mobile phones and laptops with radio interfaces, many users on the move now gain access to the Internet using a regional/national/international cellular phone network. All of these different types of access network are in addition, of course, to the conventional site networks used by large corporations and businesses. Because of the importance of the Web to their businesses, most of these site networks now use the same protocols as the Internet to facilitate interworking with it.

In many instances, the expanding range of applications supported by the Internet has come about through the technological advances in the way the user data associated with these applications is represented. For example, until relatively recently, a number of the access networks that are now used, in addition to providing their basic service such as telephony, only supported applications in which the application data was composed of text comprising strings of alphanumeric characters entered at a keyboard. As a result of the technological advances in the area of compression, however, the same access networks can now support a much richer set of applications involving multiple data types. These include, in addition to text, digitized images, photos/pictures, speech, audio and video.

As we can deduce from this brief overview, to study the technological issues relating to computer networking and the Internet requires an in-depth understanding not only of the operation of the Internet itself but also the operation of the different types of access network that are used and how they interface with the Internet. In addition, because many of the applications involve the transfer of sensitive information, the topic of security is now essential when describing the operation of the Internet. The aim of this book is to provide this body of knowledge. To do this, the book is divided into two logical parts. The first – Chapters 1 through 5 – is concerned with the fundamentals of digital transmission and communication protocols together with descriptions of the mode of operation of the different types of access network that are now used and how they interface with the global Internet. The second – Chapters 6 through 10 – describes the architecture and communication protocols used by the Internet and the applications that it supports. In addition, the second part describes the techniques that are used to ensure that all the data relating to these applications are transferred in a secure way.

The book has five appendices. In Appendix A we present descriptions of how the different types of data used in the various Internet applications are represented together with an overview of the operation of the compression algorithms that are employed with text, digitized images, photos/pictures, speech, audio and video.

As we shall explain, when transmitting digital data over a network, bit corruptions/errors are often introduced. Hence in Appendix B we describe a number of the different methods that are used to detect the presence of transmission/bit errors in a received block of data.

Normally, when a bit error within a block of data is detected, another copy of the block is requested by the receiving device. In some instances, however – for example when data is being transmitted over a radio/wireless link – the frequency of bit errors is such that the request message for a new copy of a corrupted block may also be corrupted and hence an alternative approach must be used. This involves adding significantly more what are called *error control bits*. These are added in such a way that the receiver can use them to deduce what the original data block contained. This approach is called forward error control and an introduction to this topic is given in Appendix C.

Wireless networks – that is, networks that use radio as the transmission medium – are now widely used in a number of access networks. In Appendix D, therefore, we give a short introduction to the subject of radio propagation and transmission so that the standards relating to this type of network can be understood.

As we shall see, the global Internet is composed of many thousands of networks that are organized into hierarchical layers. At the higher layers, the networks must route data through them at very high rates and are called backbone networks. In Appendix E we describe the technology that is used to achieve these very high switching rates.

Intended readership

The book has been written primarily as a course textbook for both university and college students studying courses relating to the technical issues associated with computer networking based on the Internet, its protocols and applications. Typically, the students will be studying in a computer science, computer systems, computer engineering or electronic engineering department/school. In addition, the book is suitable for computer professionals and engineers who wish to build up a working knowledge of this rapidly evolving subject. At one extreme this requires the reader to understand the techniques that are used to transmit a digital bitstream over the different types of transmission medium, such as copper wire, coaxial cable, radio and optical fiber. At the other extreme it requires an understanding of the software that is used in the different types of equipment – personal computers, workstations, laptops, mobile phones, set-top boxes, etc. – that are used to support Internet applications. The first is the domain of the electronics engineer and the second of the computer scientist. Care has been taken, however, to ensure that the book is suitable for use with courses for both types of student by ensuring that the level of detail required in each subject area is understandable by both categories of reader.

In order to achieve this goal, an introductory chapter has been included that describes the basic hardware and software techniques that are used to achieve the reliable transfer of a block/stream of digital data over a transmission channel. These include the different methods that are used to detect the presence of transmission errors – bit corruptions – in a received block/stream of data and the procedures that are followed to obtain another copy of the block/stream when this occurs. The latter form what is called a communications protocol. Hence this chapter also includes an introduction to the subject of protocols to give the reader who has no previous knowledge of this subject the necessary foundation for the later chapters that describe the operation of the different types of access networks and the protocols and applications of the Internet.

Intended usage

To the instructor

As we can see from the list of contents, the book covers a range of topics each of which is to a depth that makes it interesting and academically challenging. As a result, the book can be used for a number of different courses relating to computer networking and the Internet. Ideally, in order to obtain an in-depth technical understanding of the subject area, a set of courses should be used to collectively cover the total contents of the book from the principles of data communications through to details of the different types of access networks and the protocols and applications of the Internet. Alternatively, it can be used for one or two courses each of which covers a subset of this subject area. For example, one course may cover the basics of digital communications and an overview of the operation of the different types of access network that are used with the Internet. The second course can then cover the architecture and detailed operation of the Internet and its protocols together with its applications including the World Wide Web and the topic of security. The book is considered to be suitable for both undergraduate and taught masters courses.

As indicated earlier, all of the topics are covered to a depth that enables the reader to build up an in-depth technical understanding of the subject. Hence because of the technical nature of the subject, to help the reader to understand each topic within an area, either a worked example or a relatively detailed diagram is used to illustrate the concepts involved. This is considered to be one of the main advantages of the book over competing texts owing to the technical detail associated with many of the diagrams. Also, both the examples and diagrams are seen as being particularly useful for instructors as they can be used directly for lectures. To facilitate this, therefore, both the worked examples and all the diagrams are available to instructors in their electronic form so reducing considerably the time required to prepare a set of lectures for a course. These can be downloaded from *www.booksites.net/halsall.* In addition, each chapter has a comprehensive set of exercises that have been structured to help the student to revise the topics covered in that chapter in a systematic way.

To the student

The book has been structured to be used for self-study. Worked examples are included in most chapters and, to aid understanding of all the topics that are covered, associated with each topic is a relatively detailed diagram that illustrates the concepts involved. These you should find particularly useful since they facilitate understanding the technical details relating to the many topics covered. In addition, the comprehensive set of exercises at the end of each chapter have been structured to help you to test your knowledge and understanding of each of the topics covered in that chapter in a systematic way. In order to aid self-study, there is an exercise for each topic discussed within a section. Hence for each question within a section heading, you can relate back to the topic within that section of the book to find the answer.

Guided Tour

Acronyms: a full list is provided at the front of the book for easy reference.

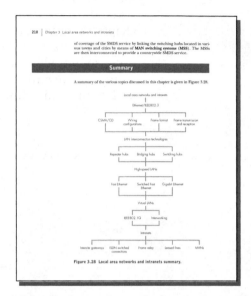

Visual Summaries at the end of each chapter help you to learn and revise key concepts at a glance.

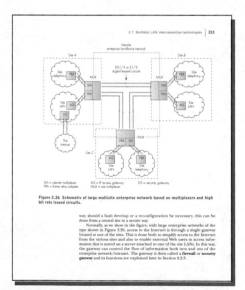

Diagrams provide a clear visual understanding of complex processes in Networking.

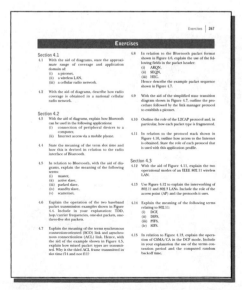

Exercises are provided for each section, to check your understanding of key topics.

Guided Tour of the Website

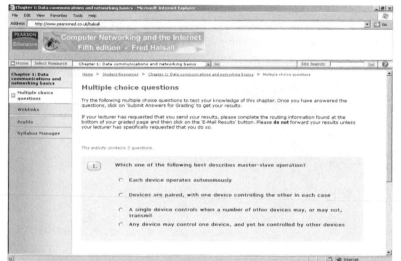

Multiple choice questions

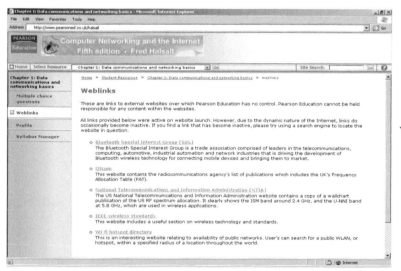

Weblinks

Acknowledgments

I should like to take this opportunity to thank various people for their help during the period I was preparing the manuscript. Firstly to Simon Plumtree and Keith Mansfield at Pearson Education for their enthusiasm and motivation that encouraged me to write the book. Secondly to my wife Rhiannon for her unwavering support, patience, and understanding while I was writing the book. Finally, to our first grandchild Annelie Grace; I promise that now I have finished writing my book, I shall take you out much more frequently. It is to Annelie and her mother Lisa that I dedicate the book.

Fred Halsall
December 2004

Acronyms

3G	Third generation		BTS	Base transceiver subsystem
			BUS	Broadcast and unknown address server
AAL	ATM adaptation layer		BWB	Bandwidth balancing
ABM	Asynchronous balanced mode			
ABR	Available bit rate		CA	Certification authority
AC	Alternating current/Authentication center		CAC	Channel access code
ACK	Acknowledgment		CAS	Channel-associated signaling
ACL	Asynchronous connectionless link		CATV	Cable television
ADC	Analog-to-digital conversion/converter		CBC	Chain block cipher
ADM	Add-drop multiplexer		CBDS	Connectionless broadband data service
ADPCM	Adaptive differential PCM		CBR	Constant bit rate
ADSL	Asymmetric DSL		CCA	Clear channel assessment
AH	Authentication header		CCD	Charge-coupled device
AMA	Active member address		CCITT	International Telegraph and Telephone
AMI	Alternate mark inversion			Consultative Committee (now ITU-T)
ANSI	American National Standards Institute		CCK	Complementary code keying
AP	Application process/program/protocol		CCS	Common-channel signaling
APC	Adaptive predictive coding		CD	Carrier detect/Collision detect
API	Application program interface		CDC	Countdown counter
ARM	Asynchronous response mode		CELP	Code-excited linear prediction
ARP	Address resolution protocol		CFI	Canonical format identifier
ARPA	Advanced Research Projects Agency		CGI	Common gateway interface
ARQ	Automatic repeat request		CID	Channel identifier
AS	Autonomous system		CIDR	Classless inter-domain routing
ASCII	American Standards Committee for		CIF	Common intermediate format
	Information Interchange		CIR	Committed information rate
ASI	Alternate space inversion		CL	Connectionless
ASK	Amplitude-shift keying		CLP	Cell loss priority
ASN.1	Abstract syntax notation one		CLUT	Color look-up table
ATM	Asynchronous transfer mode		CM	Cable modem
ATV	Advanced television		CMTS	Cable modem termination system
AVO	Audio-visual object		CO	Connection-oriented
			COFDM	Coded orthogonal FDM
BA	Behavior aggregate		COM	Continuation message
BCC	Block check character		CPE	Customer premises equipment
BER	Bit error rate/ratio		CR	Carriage return
BGCF	Breakout gateway control functions		CRC	Cyclic redundancy check
BGP	Border gateway protocol		CS	Carrier sense/Convergence sublayer
BISDN	Broadband ISDN		CSCF	Call/session control function
BOM	Beginning of message		CSCW	Computer-supported cooperative working
BPDU	Bridge PDU		CSMA	Carrier-sense multiple-access
BPSK	Binary phase shift keying		CSMA/CA	CSMA with collision avoidance
BRI	Basic rate interface		CSMA/CD	CSMA with collision detection
BS	Backspace		CTI	Computer telephony integration
BSC	Base station controller		CTS	Clear-to-send
BSS	Basic service set		CW	Contention window
BSSID	BSS identifier		DA	Destination address

DAC	Digital-to-analog conversion/converter
DBS	Digital broadcast satellite
DC	Direct current
DCE	Data circuit terminating equipment
DCF	Distributed coordination function
DCT	Discrete cosine transform
DEL	Delete
DES	Data encryption standard
DFT	Discrete Fourier transform
DHCP	Dynamic host configuration protocol
DIFS	DCF inter-frame spacing
DLC	Data link control
DLE	Data link escape (character)
DMPDU	Derived MAC PDU
DMT	Discrete multitone
DN	Distinguished name
DNS	Domain name server
DOCSIS	Data-over-cable service interface specification
DPC	Designated port cost
DPCM	Differential PCM
DPLL	Digital phase-locked line
DQDB	Distributed queue dual bus
DS	Differentiated services/Downstream
DSL	Digital subscriber line
DSLAM	Digital subscriber line access multiplexer
DSSS	Direct sequence spread spectrum
DTE	Data terminal equipment
DTMF	Dual-tone multiple frequency
DVA	Distance vector algorithm
DVB	Digital video broadcast
DVB-S/T	DVB-satellite/terrestrial
DVD	Digital versatile disk
DVMRP	Distance vector MRP
EBCDIC	Extended binary coded decimal interchange code
ECB	Electronic code book/Event control block
ECN	Explicit congestion notification
ED	End delimiter
EF	Expedited forwarding
EGP	Exterior gateway protocol
EIA	Electrical Industries Association
EIR	Equipment identity register
EMS	Enhanced message service
EOM	End of message
EOS	End of stream
ES	End system
ESC	Escape
ESP	Encryption security payload
ETX	End of text
FCS	Frame check sequence
FDD	Frequency division duplex
FDDI	Fiber distributed data interface
FDM	Frequency-division multiplexing

FF	Form feed
FHSS	Frequency-hopping spread spectrum
FIFO	First-in, first-out
FM	Frequency modulation
FN	Fiber node
FQDN	Fully-qualified DN
FRA	Frame relay adapter
FS	File separator
FSK	Frequency-shift keying
FTP	File transfer protocol
FTTB	Fiber-to-the-building
FTTC/K	Fiber-to-the-curb/kerb
FTTcab	Fiber-to-the-cabinet
FTTH	Fiber-to-the-home
GA	Grand Alliance
GB	Guard-band
GEO	Geostationary/geosynchronous earth orbit
GGSN	Gateway GPRS support node
GIF	Graphics interchange format
GLP	Gateway location protocol
GOB	Group of blocks
GOP	Group of pictures
GPRS	General packet radio service
GSM	Global system for mobile communications
GSTN	General switched telephone network
GTP	GPRS tunneling protocol
GW	Gateway
HDB3	High density bipolar 3
HDLC	High-level data link contol
HDSL	High-speed DSL
HDTV	High-definition television
HE	Headend
HEC	Header error checksum
HFC	Hybrid fiber coax
HLR	Home location register
HMAC	Hash message authentication code
HS	Home subscriber server
HTML	HyperText Markup Language
HTTP	HyperText Transfer Protocol
HTTPD	HTTP daemon
IA5	International alphabet number five
IAC	Inquiry access code
ICANN	Internet Corporation for Assigned Names and Numbers
ICMP	Internet control message protocol
IDCT	Inverse DCT
IDEA	International data encryption algorithm
IDFT	Inverse DFT
IDSL	ISDN-DSL
IEE	Institution of Electrical Engineers
IEEE	Institute of Electrical and Electronics Engineers

IETF	Internet Engineering Task Force	MA	Multiple access
IGE	International gateway exchange	MAC	Medium access control
IGMP	Internet group management protocol	MAN	Metropolitan area network
IGP	Interior gateway protocol	MAT	Multicast address table
IKE	Internet key exchange	M-bone	Multicast (Internet) backbone
IMEI	International mobile equipment identity	MCM	Multi-carrier modulation
IMG	IMS media gateway	MCU	Multipoint control unit
IMS	IP multimedia services	MD	Message digest
INIC	Internet Network Information Center	MDS	Multipoint distribution system
IP	Internet protocol	MFN	Multifrequency network
IPsec	IP security	MGCF	Media gateway control function
IS	Integrated services/ Intermediate system	MGW	Media gateway
ISDN	Integrated services digital network	MIB	Management information base
ISI	Intersymbol interference	MIDI	Music Instrument Digital Interface
ISO	International Standards Organization	MII	Media-independent interface
ISP	Internet service provider	MIME	Multipurpose Internet mail extension
ITU-T	International Telecommunications Union – Telecommunications (Sector)	MIT	Management information tree
		MMDS	Multichannel MDS
IV	Initialization vector	MMR	Modified–modified read
IWF	Interworking function	MMS	Multimedia message service
IWU	Interworking unit	MO	Managed object
IXC	Interexchange carrier	MOD	Movie on demand
		MOSPF	Multicast OSPF
JPEG	Joint Photographic Experts Group	MP3	MPEG layer 3 (audio)
		MPEG	Motion Picture Experts Group
Kc	Cipher key	MPLS	MultiProtocol Label Switching
ki	Authentication key	MRFC	Media resource function controller
		MRFP	Media resource function processor
L2CAP	Logical link control and adaptation protocol	MRP	Multicast routing protocol
LA	Location area	MS	Message store/Mobile station
LAI	Location area identification	MSC	Mobile switching center
LAN	Local area network	MSISDN	Mobile subscriber ISDN number
LAPB	Link access procedure, balanced	MSL	Maximum segment lifetime
LAPM	Link access procedure for modems	MSRN	Mobile subscriber roaming number
LCN	Logical channel number	MSS	MAN switching system
LCP	Link control protocol	MTA	Message transfer agent
LE	LAN emulation	MUX	Multiplexer
LEC	LE client		
LECS	LE configuration server	NAK	Negative acknowledgment
LED	Light-emitting diode	NAP	Network access point
LEP	LE protocol	NAPT	Network address and port translation
LES	LE server	NAV	Network allocation vector
LF	Line feed	NBS	National Bureau of Standards
LGN	Logical group number	NCP	Network control protocol
LL	Link layer	NEXT	Near-end crosstalk
LLC	Logical link control	NMOD	Near movie-on-demand
LMDS	Local MDS	NMS	Network management system
LNB/C	Low noise block/converter	NNTP	Network news transfer protocol
LPC	Linear predictive coding	NOP	No operation
LS	Link state	NPA	Network point of attachment
LWE	Lower window edge	NRM	(Unbalanced) normal response mode
LXC	Local exchange carrier	NRZ	Non-return to zero
LZ	Lempel–Ziv	NRZI	Non-return to zero inverted
LZW	Lempel–Ziv–Welsh	NSAP	Network service access point

NSDU	Network service data unit		QCIF	Quarter CIF
NSS	Network and switching subsystem		QoS	Quality of service
NT	Network termination		QPDS	Queued-packet distributed-switch
NTE	Network termination equipment		QPSK	Quadrature phase shift keying
NTSC	National Television Standards Committee			
NTU	Network termination unit		RAM	Random access meomory
NVT	Network virtual terminal		RARP	Reverse ARP
			RCU	Remote concentrator unit
OMC	Operation and maintenance center		RDN	Relative distinguished name
ONU	Optical network (termination) unit		READ	Relative element address designate
OSA	Open service access		RED	Random early detection
OSC	Open service capability		RF	Radio frequency
OSI	Open systems interconnection		RGB	Red, green, blue
OSPF	Open shortest path first		RI	Ring indication
OSS	Operation subsystem		RIP	Routing information protocol
			RNC	Radio network controller
PAL	Phase alternation line		ROM	Read only memory
PAWS	Protection against wrapped sequence (numbers)		RP	Root port
			RPC	Root path cost
PBX	Private branch exchange		RS	Record separator
PC	Personal computer		RSA	Rivest, Shamir, Adelman
PCF	Point coordination function		RSS	Radio subsystem
PCI	Protocol connection identifier		RSU	Remote switching unit
PCI	Protocol control information		RSVP	Resource reservation protocol
PCM	Pulse-code modulation		RTC	Round-trip correction
PDA	Personal digital assistant		RTCP	Real-time transport control protocol
PDH	Plesiochronous digital hierarchy		RTD	Round-trip delay
PDU	Protocol data unit		RTO	Retransmission timeout
PEL	Picture element		RTP	Real-time transport protocol
PGP	Pretty good privacy		RTS	Request to send
PHB	Per-hop behavior		RTSP	Real-time streaming protocol
PIFS	PCF inter-frame spacing		RTT	Round-trip time
PIN	Personal identity number			
PISO	Parallel in, serial out		SA	Security association/Source address
Pixel	Picture element		SAAL	Signaling AAL
PL	Physical layer		SACK	Selective ACK
PMA	Parked member address		SAP	Service access point
PMD	Physical medium dependent		SAR	Segmentation and reassembly
POP	Point of presence/Post Office Protocol		SAS	Single attach station
POTS	Plain old telephone service		SAT-IF	Satellite intermediate frequency
PPP	Point-to-point protocol		SCO	Synchronous connection-oriented link
PRI	Primary rate interface		SCP	Signaling control point
PS	Parked slave		SD	Start delimiter
PSE	Packet-switching exchange		SDD	Service discovery database
PSK	Phase-shift keying		SDH	Synchronous digital hierarchy
PSM	Protocol/service multiplexer		SDP	Session description protocol
PSTN	Public-switched telephone network		SDSL	Single-pair DSL
PTE	Path termination equipment		SET	Secure electronic transaction
PTT	Post, telephone, and telecommunications (authority)		SFD	Start-of-frame delimiter
			SFN	Single-frequency network
PVC	Permanent virtual connection		SG	Signaling gateway
			SGML	Standard Generalized Mark-up Language
QA	Queued arbitrated		SGSN	Serving GPRS support node
QAM	Quadrature amplitude modulation		SHC	Secure hash coding

SIF	Source intermediate format
SIFS	Short inter-frame spacing
SIG	Special Interest Group
SIM	Subscriber identity module
SIP	Session initiation protocol
SIP	SMDS interface protocol
SIPO	Serial in, parallel out
SMDS	Switched multimegabit data service
SMP	Standby monitor present
SMS	Short message service
SMT	Station management
SMTP	Simple mail transfer protocol
SNMP	Simple network management protocol
SNR	Signal-to-noise ratio
SOH	Start of heading
SONET	Synchronous optical network
SOS	Start of stream
SP	Space
SPF	Shortest-path first
SPI	Security parameter index
SRGP	Simple raster graphics package
SS	Standby slave
SS7	Signaling system number 7
SSL	Secure socket layer
SST	Slow start threshold
STB	Set-top box
STE	Section termination equipment
STM	Synchronous transport module
STP	Shielded twisted-pair
STS	Synchronous transport signal
STX	Start of text
SVCC	Signaling virtual channel connection
SVGA	Super VGA
SWS	Silly window syndrome
SYN	Synchronous idle
TA	Terminal adapter
TCM	Trellis coded modulation
TCP	Transmission control protocol
TCS	BIN telephony control specification binary
TCU	Trunk coupling unit
TDD	Time-division duplex
TDM	Time-division multiplexing
TE	Terminal equipment
TEI	Terminal endpoint identifier
TFTP	Trivial file transfer protocol
THT	Token hold time
TIFF	Tagged image file format
TIFF/EP	TIFF for electronic photography
TLS	Transport layer security
TRT	Token rotation time
TTRT	Target TRT

TU	Tributary unit
TUG	Tributary unit group
UA	Unnumbered acknowledgment/User agent
UART	Universal asynchronous receiver transmitter
UBR	Unspecified bit rate
UD	User database
UDB	User data buffer
UDP	User datagram protocol
UIP	User interface part
UMTS	Universal mobile telecommunications system
UNA	Upstream neighbor's address
UNI	User–network interface
U-NII	Unlicensed national information infrastructure
URI	Uniform resource identifier
URL	Uniform resource locator
US	Upstream (channel)
USRT	Universal synchronous receiver transmitter
UTP	Unshielded twisted-pair
UWE	Upper window edge
VBR	Variable bit rate
VC	Virtual connection
VCC	Virtual channel connection
VCI	Virtual channel identifier
VCR	Video cassette recorder
VDSL	Very high DSL
VG	Voice grade
VGA	Video graphics array
VLC	Variable-length code
VLR	Visitor location register
VOD	Video-on-demand
VOIP	Voice over IP
VOP	Video object plane
VPI	Virtual path identifier
VPN	Virtual private network
VT	Virtual terminal
WAN	Wide area network
WAP	Wireless Application Protocol
WEP	Wired equivalent privacy
WFQ	Weighted fair queuing
WPAN	Wireless personal area network
WTLS	Wireless transport layer security
WWW	World Wide Web
WYSIWYG	"What you see is what you get"
XHTML	Extended HTML
XID	Exchange identification
XML	Extensible Markup Language

data communications and networking basics

1.1 Overview

The rapid expansion in the geographical coverage and the range of applications supported by the Internet means that it is now the dominant network for most networked applications. As we can see in Figure 1.1, users gain access to the Internet and its applications in a variety of ways. Most users at home and in small offices, for example, gain access through, say, a personal computer (PC) that is connected to either a **telephone network** – that is, a public switched telephone network (**PSTN**) or an integrated services digital network (**ISDN**) – or, in some cases, a cable television (**CATV**) network. In practice, these provide only a physical connection to a second network called an **Internet service provider (ISP) network**. This, as its name implies, provides the access point to the Internet for such users and also support for a range of applications.

Similarly, users at work gain access through, say, a PC or workstation that is connected to either an office or a campus network – known as a **local area network** or **LAN** – or, for a large business/corporation, to an **enterprise-wide private network**. As we can see in the figure, these are composed of multiple

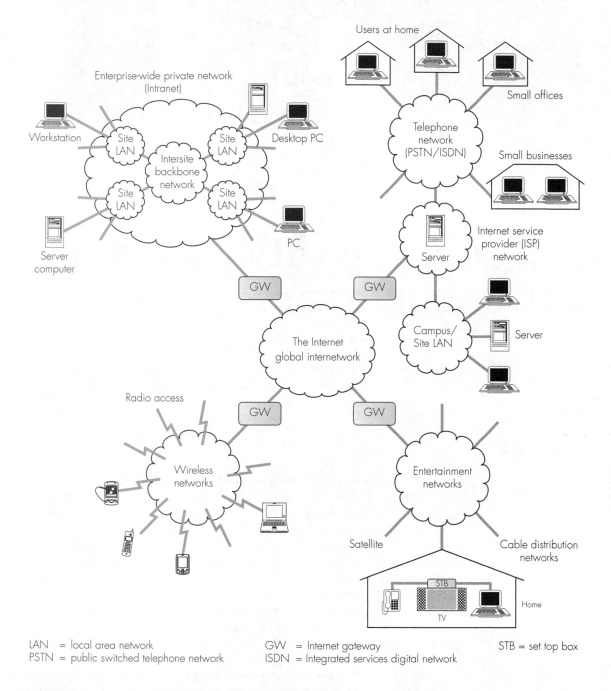

LAN = local area network
PSTN = public switched telephone network
GW = Internet gateway
ISDN = Integrated services digital network
STB = set top box

Figure 1.1 The Internet and its access networks.

site LANs that are interconnected by an inter-site backbone network. In practice, each of these networks now utilize the same operational mode and protocols as the Internet itself and hence, in the case of an enterprise network, these are known also as **intranets**.

Two more recent access networks are also shown in the figure. Users on the move, for example, can now gain access to the services of the Internet through, say, a mobile phone, a personal digital assistant (PDA) or a laptop that communicates over a radio link that is the access point to a **wireless network**. In this way, the point of attachment of the user device to the network can vary, so supporting user mobility. Secondly, in addition to providing basic radio and television broadcasts, **entertainment networks** now provide an access point to the Internet and hence access to a much richer set of applications.

In many instances, the expanding range of applications supported by the Internet has come about through the technological advances in the way the user information associated with these applications is represented. For example, until recently, the various access networks shown in the figure, in addition to providing their basic service such as telephony, only supported applications in which the user information was composed of text comprising strings of alphanumeric characters. As a result of the technological advances in the area of **compression**, however, the same access networks can now support a much richer set of applications involving multiple media types. These include not only text but digitized images, photos/pictures, speech, video and audio.

As we can conclude from this brief overview, to study the technological issues relating to the Internet and its applications requires an in-depth understanding not only of the operation of the Internet itself but also of the operation of the different types of access network and how they interface with the Internet. In addition, because many of the applications involve the transfer over a network of sensitive information, the topic of **security** is now essential when describing the structure of the information being transferred. The aim of this book is to provide this body of knowledge.

In Chapter 1, an introduction to the subjects of data communications and computer networking is given. This includes a definition of the various terms that are used and the operational characteristics of the different types of network. In addition, it presents a detailed introduction to the subject of data communications which forms the foundation of all computer networks. Chapters 2–5 are then devoted to describing the operation of the different types of access network that are used and how they interface with the global Internet. This is then followed in Chapters 6–10 by a detailed description of the protocols and applications of the Internet including a separate chapter devoted to the subject of security. There are five appendices that give an introduction to the subjects of multimedia data representation and compression, error detection methods, forward error control, radio propagation and transmission, and ATM networks.

1.2 Application and networking terminology

Before we describe the operation of the different types of access networks, it will be helpful if we first review some of the terminology used in relation to the different types of data that are used in Internet applications. Also, we describe the terminology and operational characteristics of the different types of communication channels that are provided by the various types of access network.

1.2.1 Data types and their characteristics

As we show in Figure 1.2, there are four basic types of data: text, images, video and audio. We shall discuss each separately.

Text

Essentially, there are three types of text that are used to produce pages of documents:

- **unformatted text**: this is known also as **plaintext** and enables pages to be created which comprise strings of fixed-sized characters from a limited character set;
- **formatted text**: this is known also as **richtext** and enables pages and complete documents to be created that are comprised of strings of characters of different styles, size and shape with tables, graphics and images inserted at appropriate points;
- **hypertext**: this enables Web pages to be created in the form of an integrated set of documents (each comprising formatted text) with defined linkages between them.

Images

There are two types of images:

- **computer-generated images**: more generally referred to as computer graphics or simply graphics;
- **digitized images**: these include digitized documents and digitized pictures/photos.

Ultimately, both types of image are displayed and printed in the form of a two-dimensional matrix of individual picture elements known as **pixels**. In the case of continuous-tone monochromatic images – such as a printed picture or scene – good quality black-and-white pictures can be obtained with 8 bits per pixel – that is, 256 levels of grey. For color images, each pixel may contain 8, 16, 24 or more bits to produce a good range of colors. Typical screen sizes are 640×480 (VGA) and 1024×768 (SVGA). With 8 bits per pixel the VGA format requires 307.2 kbytes to store an image and with 24 bits per pixel the SVGA format requires 2.359296 Mbytes.

Video

Most video cameras now operate digitally and generate a sequence of digitized images, each of which is called a **frame**. With broadcast television, however, the video signal is in an analog form and hence the source video signal must first be converted into a digital form. To do this, there are a number of what are called **digitization formats** used, each of which is targeted at a particular screen size. Then, to obtain a moving picture, the frames are stored/played-out at a rate determined by the digitization format that is used. For example, the raw bit rate of digital television is 162 Mbps and that for a small-screen picture phone is 40 Mbps.

Audio

All audio signals are generated in an **analog** form; that is, the signal that is generated by a microphone varies continuously with time as the amplitude of the speech/audio varies. Hence before an audio signal can be stored in a computer and integrated with the other media types, it must first be converted into a digital form. This is done using an electronic circuit called an **analog-to-digital converter (ADC).** This involves sampling the amplitude of the speech/audio signal at regular time intervals; the higher the sampling rate, the better quality is the reproduced analog signal. The reverse conversion is done using a circuit called a **digital-to-analog converter** (**DAC**) and the reproduced signal is played out via speakers. In the case of a speech signal – as used in telephony – a typical sampling rate is 8 kHz with 8 bits per sample. This yields a digital signal of 64 kbps, which is the bit rate used in telephone networks. For CD-quality audio, however, a common sampling rate is 44.1 kHz with 16 bits per sample, which produces a bit rate of 705.6 kbps or, for stereo, 1.411 Mbps.

As we can deduce from these figures – and especially those for video and audio – the raw transmission bit rate required of a communications channel far exceeds the available capacity of most network types. Hence, as we show in Figure 1.2, in almost all Internet applications the source signals are first compressed using a suitable **compression algorithm**. As an introduction to the subject, we discuss various compression algorithms in Appendix A.

As we show in the figure, the flow of data associated with the different applications can be either continuous or block-mode. In the case of **continuous data**, this means that the data stream is generated by the source continuously in a time-dependent way. In general, therefore, continuous data is passed directly to the destination as it is generated and, at the destination, the data stream is played out directly as it is received. This mode of operation is called **streaming** and, since continuous data is generated in a time-dependent way, it is also known as **real-time data**. With continuous data, therefore, the bit rate of the communications channel that is used must be compatible with the rate at which the (compressed) source data is being generated. Two examples of media types that generate continuous streams of data in real time are audio and video.

In terms of the bit rate at which the source data stream is generated, this may be at either a **constant bit rate** (**CBR**) or a **variable bit rate** (**VBR**). With audio, for example, the digitized audio stream is generated at a constant bit rate. In the case of video, however, although the individual pictures/frames that make up the video are generated at a constant rate, after compression the amount of data associated with each frame varies. In general, therefore, the data stream associated with compressed video is generated at fixed time intervals but the resulting bit rate is variable.

In the case of **block-mode data**, the source data comprises one or more blocks of data that is/are created in a time-independent way, for example, a

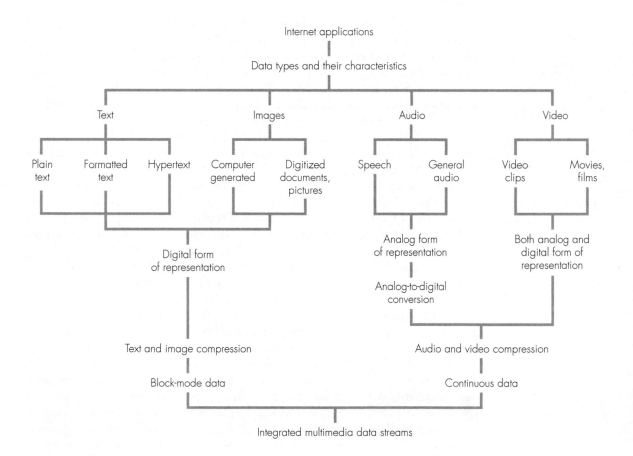

Figure 1.2 Data types used in Internet applications.

block of text representing an e-mail, a two-dimensional matrix of pixel values that represents an image, and so on. Normally, therefore, block-mode data is created in a time-independent way and is often stored at the source in, say, a file. Then, when it is requested, the blocks of data are transferred across the network to the destination where they are again stored and subsequently output/displayed at a time determined by the requesting application program. This mode of operation is known as **downloading** and, as we can deduce from this, with block-mode data the bit rate of the communications channel need not be constant but must be such that, when a block is requested, the delay between the request being made and the contents of the block being output at the destination is within an acceptable time interval. This is known as the **round-trip delay** (**RTD**) and, for human–computer interaction, ideally should be no more than a few seconds.

1.2.2 Data communications and networking terminology

A selection of the terms relating to data communications and computer networking is shown in Figure 1.3. In terms of the communication modes and channels that are provided by the various network types these are illustrated in Figure 1.4. As we show in the figure, the transfer of the data streams associated with an application can take place in one of five modes:

- **simplex**: this means the data associated with the application flows in one direction only. An example is the transmission of photographic images from a deep-space probe at predetermined times since this involves just a unidirectional flow of data from the probe to an earth station;

- **half-duplex**: this means that data flows in both directions but alternately. This mode is also known as **two-way alternate** and an example is a user making a request for some data from a remote server and the latter returning the requested data;

- **duplex**: this means that data flows in both directions simultaneously. It is also known as **two-way simultaneous** and an example is the two-way flow of digitized speech associated with a telephony application;

- **broadcast**: this means that the data output by a single source device is received by all the other devices – computers, and so on – that are connected to the same network. An example is the broadcast of a television program over a cable network as all the television receivers that are connected to the network receive the same set of programs;

- **Multicast**: this is similar to a broadcast except that the data output by the source is received by only a specific subset of the devices that are connected to the network. The latter form what is called a **multicast group** and an example application is videoconferencing, which involves a predefined group of terminals/computers connected to a network exchanging integrated speech and video streams.

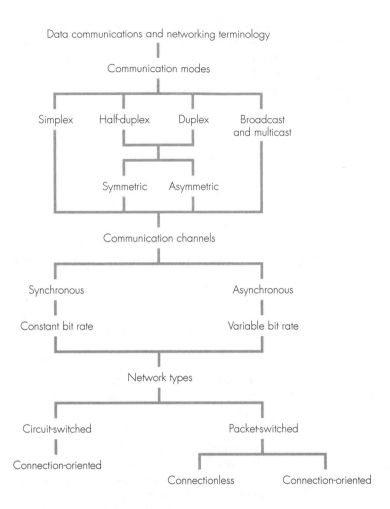

Figure 1.3 Data communications and networking terminology.

In the case of half-duplex and duplex communications, the bit rate associated with the flow of data in each direction can be either equal or different; if the flows are equal, the data flow is said to be **symmetric**, and if the flows are different, **asymmetric**. For example, a video telephone call involves the exchange of an integrated digitized speech and video stream in both directions simultaneously and hence a symmetric duplex communications channel is required. Alternatively, in an application involving a browser (program) and a Web server, a low bit rate channel from the browser to the Web server is required for request and control purposes and a higher bit rate channel from the server to the subscriber for the transfer of, say, the requested Web page. Hence for this type of application, an asymmetric half-duplex communications channel is sufficient.

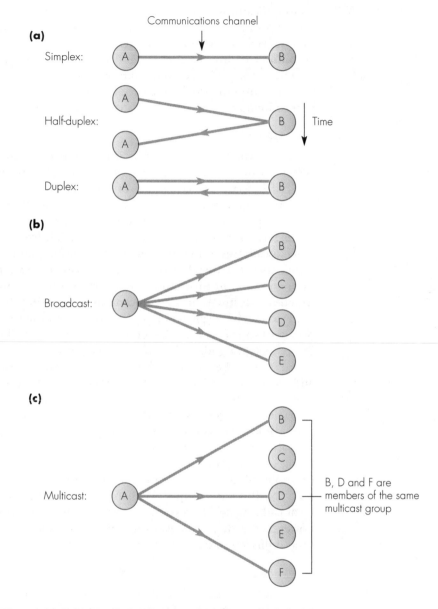

Figure 1.4 Communication modes: (a) unicast; (b) broadcast; (c) multicast.

1.2.3 Network types

In the same way that there are two types of data stream associated with the different media types – continuous and block-mode – so there are two types of communications channel associated with the various network types: one that operates in a time-dependent way known as **circuit-mode** and the other in a time-varying way known as **packet-mode**. The first is known as a **synchronous communications channel** since it provides a constant bit rate service at a specified rate. The second is known as an **asynchronous communications channel** since it provides a variable bit rate service, the actual rate being determined by the (variable) transfer rate of packets across the network.

Circuit-switched

A circuit-switched network is shown in Figure 1.5 and, as we can see, it comprises an interconnected set of **switching offices/exchanges** to which the subscriber terminals/computers are connected. This type of network is known as a **circuit-switched network** and, prior to sending any data, the source must first set up a connection through the network. Each subscriber terminal/computer has a unique network-wide number/address associated with it and, to make a call, the source first enters the number/address of the intended communication partner. The local switching office/exchange then uses this to set up a connection through the network to the switching office/exchange to which the destination is connected and, assuming the destination is free and ready to receive a call, a message is returned to the source indicating that it can now start to transfer/exchange data. Finally, after all the data has been transferred/exchanged, either the source or the destination requests for the connection to be cleared. The bit rate associated with the connection is fixed and, in general, is determined by the bit rate that is used over the access circuits that connect the source and destination terminal/computer to the network.

The messages associated with the setting up and clearing of a connection are known as **signaling messages**. As we can deduce from the above, with a circuit-switched network there is a time delay while a connection is being established. This is known as the **call/connection setup delay** and two examples of networks that operate in this way are a PSTN and an ISDN. With a PSTN, the call setup delay can range from a fraction of a second for a local call through to several seconds for an international call. With an ISDN, however, the delay ranges from tens of milliseconds through to several hundred milliseconds.

Packet-switched

As we see in Figure 1.6, there are two types of packet-switched network: **connection-oriented** (**CO**) and **connectionless** (**CL**). The principle of operation of a connection-oriented network is shown in Figure 1.6(a) and, as we can see, it comprises an interconnected set of **packet-switching exchanges** (**PSEs**). This type of network is known as a **packet-switched network** and, as with a circuit-switched network, each terminal/computer that is connected to the network has a unique network-wide number/address associated with it. With a connection-oriented network, as the name implies, prior to sending any data, a connection is first set up through the network using the addresses

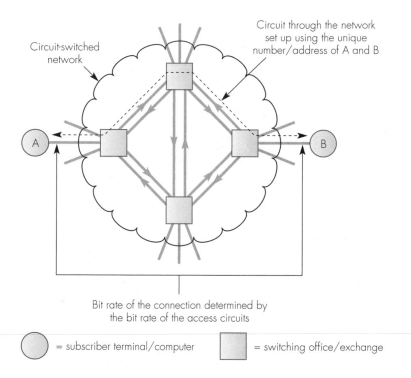

Circuit through the network
set up using the unique
number/address of A and B

Circuit-switched
network

A

B

Bit rate of the connection determined by
the bit rate of the access circuits

= subscriber terminal/computer   = switching office/exchange

Figure 1.5 Circuit-switched network schematic.

of the source and destination terminals. However, in a packet-switched network, the connection/circuit that is set up utilizes only a variable portion of the bandwidth of each link and hence the connection is known as a **virtual connection** or, more usually, a **virtual circuit** (**VC**).

To set up a VC, the source terminal/computer sends a *call request* control packet to its local PSE which contains, in addition to the address of the source and destination terminal/computer, a short identifier known as a **virtual circuit identifier** (**VCI**). Each PSE maintains a table that specifies the outgoing link that should be used to reach each network address and, on receipt of the *call request* packet, the PSE uses the destination address within the packet to determine the outgoing link to be used. The next free identifier (VCI) for this link is then selected and two entries are made in a **routing table**. The first specifies the incoming link/VCI and the corresponding outgoing link/VCI; the second, in order to route packets in the reverse direction, is the inverse of these, as we show in the example in the figure. The *call request* packet is then forwarded on the selected outgoing link and the same procedure is followed at each PSE along the route until the destination terminal/computer is reached.

(a)

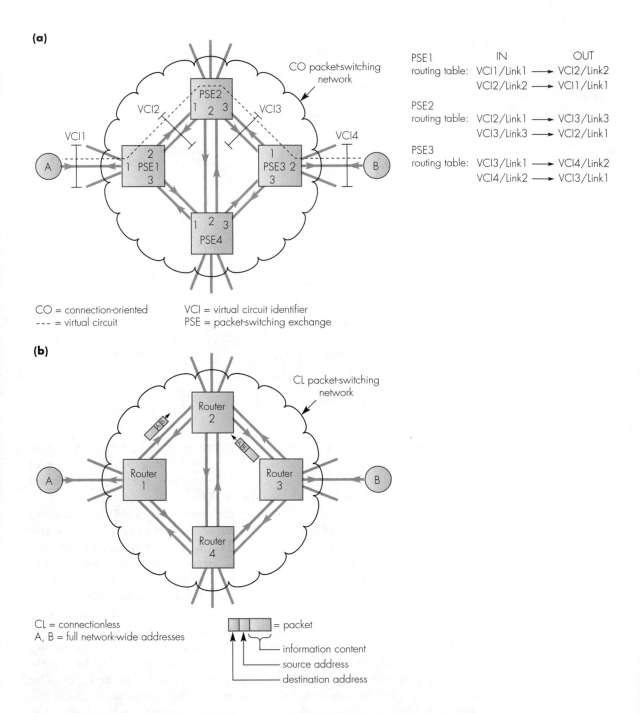

Figure 1.6 Packet-switching network principles: (a) connection-oriented; (b) connectionless.

Collectively, the VCIs that are used on the various links form the virtual circuit and, at the destination, assuming the call is accepted, a *call accepted* packet is returned to the source over the same route/virtual circuit. The data transfer phase can then start but, since a VC is now in place, only the VCI is needed in the packet header instead of the full network-wide address. Each PSE first uses the incoming link/VCI to determine the outgoing link/VCI from the routing table. The existing VCI in the packet header is then replaced with that obtained from the routing table and the packet is forwarded on the identified outgoing link. The same procedure is followed to return data in the reverse direction and, when all the data has been transferred/exchanged, the VC is cleared and the appropriate VCIs are released by passing a *call clear* packet along the VC.

In contrast, with a connectionless network, the establishment of a connection is not required and the two communicating terminals/computers can communicate and exchange data as and when they wish. In order to do this, however, as we show in Figure 1.6(b), each packet must carry the full source and destination addresses in its header in order for each PSE to route the packet onto the appropriate outgoing link. In a connectionless network, therefore, the term **router** is normally used rather than packet-switching exchange.

In both network types, as each packet is received by a PSE/router on an incoming link, it is stored in its entirety in a memory buffer. A check is then made to determine if any transmission/bit errors are present in the packet header – that is, the signal that is used to represent a binary 0 is corrupted and is interpreted by the receiver as a binary 1 and vice versa – and, if an error is detected, the packet is simply discarded. The service offered by a connectionless network is said, therefore, to be a **best-effort service**. If no errors are detected then the addresses/VCIs carried in the packet header are read to determine the outgoing link that should be used and the packet is placed in a queue ready for forwarding on the selected outgoing link. All packets are transmitted at the maximum link bit rate. With this mode of operation, however, it is possible for a sequence of packets to be received on a number of incoming links all of which need forwarding on the same outgoing link. Hence a packet may experience an additional delay while it is in the output queue for a link waiting to be transmitted. Clearly, this delay will be variable since it depends on the number of packets that are currently present in the queue when a new packet arrives for forwarding. This mode of operation is known as (packet) **store-and-forward** and, as we can see, there is a packet store-and-forward delay in each PSE/router. The sum of the store-and-forward delays in each PSE/router contributes to the overall transfer delay of the packet across the network. The mean of this delay is known as the **mean packet transfer delay** and the variation about the mean the **delay variation** or **jitter**.

An example of a packet-switched network that operates in the connectionless mode is the Internet, which we shall describe in some detail in Chapter 6. Two examples of networks that operate in the connection-oriented mode are the international X.25 packet-switching network and asynchronous transfer mode (ATM) networks. The X.25 network is used primarily for the transfer of large files containing text and binary data between large computers that belong to a collection of banks for interbank transfers. In contrast, ATM networks have been designed from the outset to support high data transfer rates. This is achieved by using high bit rate interconnecting links and, once a virtual circuit has been set up, a very small fixed-sized packet of 53 bytes is used to transfer the data over the link. Each small packet is known as a **cell** and includes a short 5-byte header that enables cells to be switched at the very high link bit rates that are used. It is for this reason that ATM networks are also known as **fast packet-switching networks** or sometimes **cell-switching networks**. Because of the very high switching rates of ATM switches, they are used extensively in the core networks of both the PSTN/ISDN and the Internet and many wireless networks.

1.2.4 Network QoS

The operational parameters associated with a digital communications channel through a network are known as the **network Quality of Service (QoS) parameters** and collectively they determine the suitability of the channel in relation to its use for a particular application. In practice, the QoS parameters associated with a circuit-switched network are different from those associated with a packet-switched network and hence we shall discuss each separately.

Circuit-switched network

The QoS parameters associated with a constant bit rate channel that is set up through a circuit-switched network include:

- the bit rate,
- the mean bit error rate,
- the transmission delay.

The mean **bit error rate** (**BER**) of a digital channel is the probability of a binary bit being corrupted during its transmission across the channel over a defined time interval. Hence, for a constant bit rate channel, this equates to the probability of a bit being corrupted in a defined number of bits. A mean BER of 10^{-3}, therefore, means that, on average, for every 1000 bits that are transmitted, one of these bits will be corrupted. In some applications, providing the occurrence of bit errors is relatively infrequent, their presence is acceptable while in other applications it is imperative that no residual bit errors are present in the received data. For example, if the application involves speech, then an occasional bit error will go unnoticed but in an application involving the transfer of, say, financial information, it is essential that the received information contains no errors. Hence with such applications, prior to transmission the source data is normally divided into blocks the maximum size of which is determined by the mean BER of the communications channel.

For example, if the mean BER of the channel is 10^{-3}, then the number of bits in a block must be considerably less than 1000 otherwise, on average, every block will contain an error and will be discarded. Normally, however, bit errors occur randomly and hence, even with a block size of, say, 100 bits, blocks may still contain an error but the probability of this occurring is considerably less. In general, if the BER probability is P and the number of bits in a block is N, then, assuming random errors, the probability of a block containing a bit error, P_B, is given by:

$$P_B = 1 - (1-P)^N$$

which approximates to $N \times P$ if $N \times P$ is less than 1.

In practice, most networks – both circuit-switched and packet-switched – provide an **unreliable service** which is also known as a **best-try** or **best-effort** service. This means that any blocks containing bit errors will be discarded either within the network – packet-switched networks – or in the network interface at the destination – both packet-switched and circuit-switched networks. Hence if the application dictates that only error-free blocks are acceptable, it is necessary for the sending terminal/computer to divide the source information into blocks of a defined maximum size and for the destination to detect when a block is missing. When this occurs the destination must request that the source send another copy of the missing block. The service offered is then said to be a **reliable service**. Clearly, this will introduce a delay so the retransmission procedure should be invoked relatively infrequently, which dictates a small block size. This, however, leads to high overheads since each block must contain the additional information that is associated with the retransmission procedure. Normally, therefore, the choice of block size is a compromise between the increased delay resulting from a large block size – and hence retransmissions – and the loss of transmission bandwidth resulting from the high overheads of using a smaller block size.

Example 1.1

Derive the maximum block size that should be used over a channel which has a mean BER probability of 10^{-4} if the probability of a block containing an error – and hence being discarded – is to be 10^{-1}.

Answer:

$$P_B = 1 - (1-P)^N$$

Hence $0.1 = 1 - (1-10^{-4})^N$ and $N = 950$ bits

Alternatively, $P_B = N \times P$

Hence $0.1 = N \times 10^{-4}$ and $N = 1000$ bits

The **transmission delay** associated with a channel is determined not only by the bit rate that is used but also by delays that occur in the terminal/computer network interfaces (known as **codec delays**), plus the propagation delay of the digital signals as they pass from the source to the destination across the network. This is determined by the physical separation of the two communicating devices and the velocity of propagation of a signal across the transmission medium. In free space, for example, the latter is equal to the speed of light $(3 \times 10^8 \text{ m s}^{-1})$ while it is a fraction of this in physical media, a typical value being $2 \times 10^8 \text{ m s}^{-1}$.

Notice that the propagation delay in each case is independent of the bit rate of the communications channel and, assuming the codec delay remains constant, is the same whether the bit rate is 1 kbps, 1 Mbps, or 1 Gbps.

Packet-switched network

The QoS parameters associated with a packet-switched network include:

- the maximum packet size,
- the mean packet transfer rate,
- the mean packet error rate,
- the mean packet transfer delay,

Example 1.2

Determine the propagation delay associated with the following communication channels:

(i) a connection through a private telephone network of 1 km,

(ii) a connection through a PSTN of 200 km,

(iii) a connection over a satellite channel of 50 000 km.

Assume that the velocity of propagation of a signal in the case of (i) and (ii) is $2 \times 10^8 \text{ m s}^{-1}$ and in the case of (iii) $3 \times 10^8 \text{ m s}^{-1}$.

Answer:

Propagation delay T_p = physical separation/velocity of propagation

(i) $\quad T_P = \dfrac{10^3}{2 \times 10^8} = 5 \times 10^{-6} \text{ s}$

(ii) $\quad T_P = \dfrac{200 \times 10^3}{2 \times 10^8} = 10^{-3} \text{ s}$

(iii) $\quad T_P = \dfrac{5 \times 10^7}{3 \times 10^8} = 1.67 \times 10^{-1} \text{ s}$

- the worst-case jitter,
- the transmission delay.

In a packet-switched network, although the rate at which packets are transferred across the network is influenced strongly by the bit rate of the interconnecting links, because of the variable store-and-forward delays in each PSE/router, the actual rate of transfer of packets across the network is also variable. Hence the **mean packet transfer rate** is a measure of the average number of packets that are transferred across the network per second and, coupled with the packet size being used, determines the equivalent mean bit rate of the channel.

The **mean packet error rate** or **PER** is the probability of a received packet containing one or more bit errors. It is the same, therefore, as the block error rate associated with a circuit-switched network which we derived in the previous section. Hence it is related to both the maximum packet size and the worst-case BER of the transmission links that interconnect the PSEs/routers that make up the network.

We defined the meaning of the term "mean packet transfer delay" in Section 1.2.3 when we described the operation of packet-mode networks. It is the summation of the mean store-and-forward delay that a packet experiences in each PSE/router that it encounters along a route and the term "jitter" is the worst-case variation in this delay. As we just explained, the transmission delay is the same whether the network operates in a packet mode or a circuit mode and includes the codec delay in each of the two communicating computers and the signal propagation delay.

1.2.5 Application QoS

The network QoS parameters define what the particular network being used provides rather than what the application requires. The application itself, however, also has QoS parameters associated with it. In an application involving images, for example, the parameters may include a minimum image resolution and size, while in an application involving video, the digitization format and refresh rate may be defined. The application QoS parameters that relate to the network include:

- the required bit rate or mean packet transfer rate,
- the maximum startup delay,
- the maximum end-to-end delay,
- the maximum delay variation/jitter,
- the maximum round-trip delay.

For applications involving the transfer of a constant bit rate stream, the important parameters are the required bit rate/mean packet transfer rate, the end-to-end delay, and, equally important, the delay variation/jitter since this can cause problems in the destination decoder if the rate of arrival of the bitstream is variable. For interactive applications, however, the **startup delay** defines the amount of time that elapses between an application making a request to start a session and the confirmation being received from the application at the destination – a server, for example – that it is prepared to accept the request. Hence this includes, in addition to the time required to establish a network connection – if this is required – the delay introduced in both the source and the destination computers while negotiating that the session can take place. As we saw earlier in Section 1.2.1, the round-trip delay is important because, for human–computer interaction to be successful, the delay between a request for some information being made and the start of the information being received/displayed should be as short as possible and, ideally, should be less than a few seconds.

As we can see from the above, for applications that involve the transfer of a constant bit rate stream, a circuit-switched network would appear to be most appropriate since, firstly, the call setup delay is often not important and secondly, the channel provides a constant bit rate service of a known rate. Conversely, for interactive applications, a connectionless packet-switched network would appear to be most appropriate since with this there is no network call setup delay and any variations in the packet transfer delay are not important.

An example application that illustrates the benefits of a packet-switched network over a circuit-switched network is the transfer of a large file of data from a server computer connected to the Internet to a client PC/workstation in a home. As we showed earlier in Figure 1.1, access to the Internet from home can be by means of a PSTN (with a modem), an ISDN connection, or a cable modem. In the case of a PSTN and an ISDN, these operate in a circuit-switched mode and provide a constant bit rate channel of in the order of 28.8 kbps (PSTN with modem) and 64/128 kbps (ISDN). In contrast, cable modems operate in a packet mode and, as we shall see later in Section 5.2.1, the modems in each of the homes in a cable region time-share the use of a single high bit rate channel/circuit. A typical bit rate of the shared channel is 27 Mbps and the number of concurrent users of the channel may be several hundred. Hence, assuming 270 concurrent users, each user would get a mean data rate of 100 kbps.

With this type of application, however, the main parameter of interest is not the mean data/bit rate but the time to transmit the complete file. With a PSTN and an ISDN, this is directly related to the channel bit rate and the size of the file. With a cable modem, however, although they time-share the use of the 27 Mbps channel, when they gain access to it, the file transfer takes place at the full rate. Hence assuming the file size is 100 Mbits, the minimum time to transmit the file using the different Internet access modes is:

PSTN and 28.8 kbps modem:	57.8 minutes
ISDN at 64 kbps:	26 minutes
ISDN at 128 kbps:	13 minutes
cable modem at 27 Mbps:	3.7 seconds

In the case of a cable modem, if other transfer requests occur during the time the file is being transmitted, then the completion time of each transfer request will increase as they share the use of the channel. Nevertheless, with this type of application, the probability of multiple users requesting a transfer in this short window of time is relatively low.

In many instances, however, this does not mean that the alternative network types cannot be used. For interactive applications, for example, the call setup delay with an ISDN network – and a PSTN for local calls – is very fast and, for many applications, quite acceptable. Similarly, for constant bit rate applications, providing the equivalent mean bit rate provided by the network is greater than the input bit rate and the maximum jitter is less than a defined value, then a packet-switched network can be used. To overcome the effect of jitter a technique known as **buffering** is used, the general principles of which are shown in Figure 1.7.

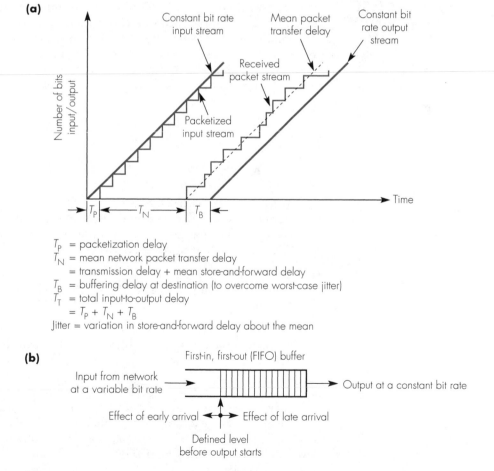

T_P = packetization delay
T_N = mean network packet transfer delay
   = transmission delay + mean store-and-forward delay
T_B = buffering delay at destination (to overcome worst-case jitter)
T_T = total input-to-output delay
   = $T_P + T_N + T_B$
Jitter = variation in store-and-forward delay about the mean

Figure 1.7 Transmission of a constant bit rate stream over a packet-switched network: (a) timing schematic; (b) FIFO buffer operation.

As we show in the figure, the effect of jitter is overcome by retaining a defined number of packets in a memory buffer at the destination before playout of the information bitstream is started. The memory buffer operates using a first-in, first-out (FIFO) discipline and the number of packets retained in the buffer before output starts is determined by the worst-case jitter and the bit rate of the information stream. However, as we show in part (a) of the figure, when using a packet-switched network for this type of application, an additional delay is incurred at the source as the information bitstream is converted into packets. This is known as the **packetization delay** and adds to the transmission delay of the channel. Hence in order to minimize the overall input-to-output delay, the packet size used for an application is made as small as possible but of sufficient size to overcome the effect of the worst-case jitter.

Example 1.3

A packet-switched network with a worst-case jitter of 10 ms is to be used for a number of applications each of which involves a constant bit rate information stream. Determine the minimum amount of memory that is required at the destination and a suitable packet size for each of the following input bit rates. It can be assumed that the mean packet transfer rate of the network exceeds the equivalent input bit rate in each case.

(i)   64 kbps

(ii) 256 kbps

(iii) 1.5 Mbps.

Answer:

(i)   At 64 kbps, 10 ms = 640 bits
Hence choose a packet size of, say, 800 bits with a FIFO buffer of 1600 bits – two packets – and start playout of the bitstream after the first packet has been received.

(ii) At 256 kbps, 10 ms = 2560 bits
Hence choose a packet size of, say, 2800 bits with a FIFO buffer of 4800 bits.

(iii) At 1.5 Mbps, 10 ms = 15000 bits
Hence choose a packet size of, say, 16 000 bits with a FIFO buffer of 32 000 bits.

Notice that if the computed packet size exceeds the network maximum packet size, then the equivalent number of packets must be sent before playout starts. For example, if the maximum network packet size was 8000 bits, then for case (iii) above playout would not start until two packets have been received and the FIFO buffer should hold four packets.

In order to simplify the process of determining whether a particular network can meet the QoS requirements of an application, a number of standard application **service classes** have been defined. Associated with each service class is a specific set of QoS parameters and a network can either meet this set of parameters or not. Also, for networks that support a number of different service classes – the Internet for example – in order to ensure the QoS parameters associated with each class are met, the packets relating to each class are given a different **priority**. It is then possible to treat the packets relating to each class differently.

For example, as we shall see in Chapter 6, in the Internet, packets relating to multimedia applications involving real-time streams are given a higher priority than the packets relating to applications such as e-mail. Typically, packets containing real-time streams such as audio and video are also more sensitive to delay and jitter than the packets containing textual information. Hence during periods of network congestion, the packets containing real-time streams are transmitted first. Packets containing video are more sensitive to packet loss than packets containing audio and hence are given a higher priority.

1.3 **Digital communications basics**

Associated with all the access networks that are used to support Internet applications is a standard network interface to which all the end systems/hosts/stations that are attached to the network must adhere. Hence in each end system is a **network interface card** (**NIC**) – consisting of hardware controlled by associated software – that performs the related network interface functions. In this section we describe these functions.

In the last section we found that, in general, the integrated information stream generated by the various applications is a series of blocks of binary data of varying size. In some instances, the application involves a dialog using these blocks while in others it involves the transfer of a stream of blocks. In terms of the network interface, however, the data relating to the different applications that is to be transferred over the network is treated simply as a string of one or more blocks containing what is referred to as (network) user data.

Although the various networks that are used operate in different ways, the physical and link layers of both the network interface standards and the internal network standards have a number of common features associated with them. So before we describe the operation of the various networks and their interfaces, we shall discuss in this section the basic principles associated with digital communications that are common for all networks.

The access lines (and the internal transmission lines used within the various networks) all use bit-serial transmission. In general, therefore, the signal output by the NIC simply varies between two voltage levels ($+V$ and $-V$ for example) at a rate determined by the transmission bit rate. This mode of transmission is known as **baseband transmission** and is illustrated in Figure 1.8(a).

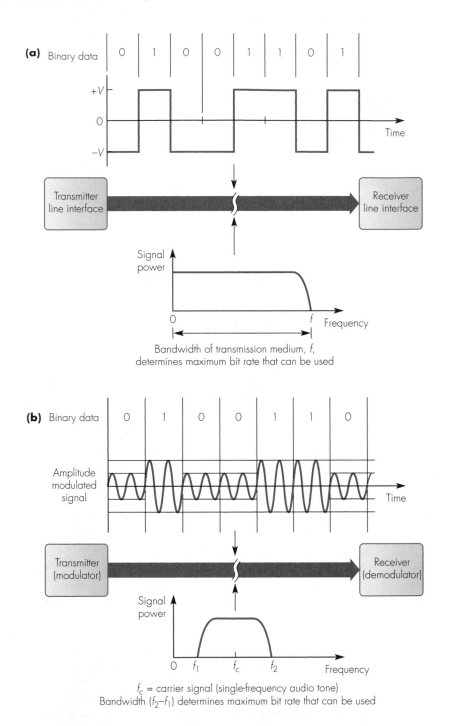

Figure 1.8 Modes of transmission: (a) baseband transmission; (b) modulated transmission.

Thus with networks that provide a digital interface, such as a LAN and an ISDN, baseband transmission is also used over the access lines to the network. With networks such as a PSTN, however, analog transmission is used over the access lines since, as we shall expand upon in Section 2.2.1, the presence of a transformer in the speech path means a DC signal – for example a long string of binary 0s or 1s – will not be discernible. The bandwidth used over these lines is that of a speech signal and is from 200 Hz through to 3400 Hz. Hence as we show in Figure 1.8(b), prior to transmitting the baseband signal output by the NIC, it is necessary first to convert this signal into an analog signal within the same bandwidth that is used for speech. This is done, for example, by modulating – also known as mixing or multiplying – a single-frequency audio signal/tone – chosen from within the bandwidth used for a speech signal and known as the **carrier signal** – by the binary signal to be transmitted. This mode of transmission is known as **modulated transmission** and the unit that performs the modulation and demodulation functions is a **modem**.

We shall describe modems and this mode of transmission further in Section 2.2.2. It should be noted, however, that even though modulated transmission is sometimes used over the access lines to the network – and also within the various types of broadcast entertainment networks – normally, the output from the NIC within each end system is a baseband signal.

When transmitting any type of electrical signal over a transmission line, the signal is **attenuated** (decreased in amplitude) and **distorted** (misshapen) by the transmission medium. Also, present with all types of transmission medium is an electrical signal known as **noise**. The amplitude of the noise signal varies randomly with time and adds itself to the electrical signal being transmitted over the line. The combined effect is that at some stage, the receiver is unable to determine from the attenuated received signal with noise whether the transmitted signal was a binary 1 or 0. An example showing the combined effect of attenuation, distortion, and noise on a baseband signal is shown in Figure 1.9.

In practice, the level of signal impairment is determined by:

■ the type of transmission medium,
■ the length of the transmission medium,
■ the bandwidth of the medium,
■ the bit rate of the data being transmitted.

We shall discuss the characteristics of the different types of transmission media in the following subsection.

As we can see in Figure 1.9, the received signal is at its peak amplitude in the centre of each **bit cell period**. Hence in order for the receiving electronics to determine the signal level (and hence bit) present on the line during each bit cell period, it endeavors to sample the received signal at the center of each bit cell. When the receiver is doing this, it is said to be in **bit**

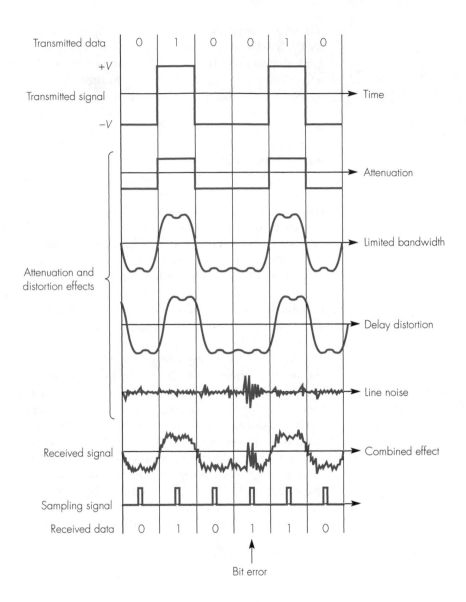

Figure 1.9 Sources of signal impairment.

synchronism with the incoming bitstream. However, although the receiver knows the nominal bit rate being used by the transmitter to transmit the bit-stream, the receiver electronics operates quite independently of the transmitter, with the effect that the receiver clock used to sample the signal will be slightly different from that used at the transmitter. In practice, therefore, sampling the signal present on the line at the correct time instant is a non-trivial task.

Achieving bit synchronism is only the initial step in achieving the reliable transfer of information over a transmission line. Most of the bit synchronization methods that are used take a variable number of bits before bit synchronism is achieved. Hence in order to interpret the received bitstream on the correct character/byte boundaries, the receiver electronics must also be able to determine the start of each new character/byte and, where appropriate, the start and end of each block of characters/bytes. Again, when the receiver is doing this, it is said to be in **character/byte synchronism** and **block/frame synchronism** respectively. In practice, there are two alternative types of baseband transmission – asynchronous and synchronous – and each uses different methods to achieve the three levels of synchronization. We describe the methods used with asynchronous transmission in Section 1.3.3 and those used with synchronous transmission in Section 1.3.4.

As we showed in Figure 1.9, if the amplitude of the received signal falls below the noise signal level, then the received signal may be incorrectly interpreted and, if it is, a transmission/bit error will result. To allow for this possibility, additional bits are added to each transmitted block to enable the receiver to determine – to high probability – when transmission errors are present in a received block. We describe a selection of the methods that are used to detect the presence of transmission errors in Appendix B.

In some applications, the loss of occasional blocks of information from the received bitstream can be tolerated and hence blocks that are found to contain transmission errors are simply discarded. In other applications, however, the loss of a block is unacceptable and it then becomes necessary for the receiver to request another copy of those blocks that contain errors. This involves the receiver sending what are called error control messages back to the transmitter. This is done in one of two ways and depends on whether the network interface offers a best-effort service or a reliable service. If the service offered is best-effort, both the network and link layers simply discard blocks in error and the error recovery procedure is carried out as part of the transport protocol in the two communicating end systems. If a reliable network service is offered, then the error recovery is part of the link protocol. We discuss link protocols in Section 1.4 and a practical example in Section 1.4.9. We shall defer the discussion of transport protocols until Chapter 7.

1.3.1 Transmission media

The transmission of an electrical signal requires a transmission medium which, normally, takes the form of a transmission line. In some cases, this consists of a pair of conductors or wires. Common alternatives are a beam of light guided by a glass fiber and electromagnetic waves propagating through free space. The type of transmission medium is important, since the various types of media have different bandwidths associated with them which, in turn, determines the maximum bit rate that can be used. We discuss the more common types of transmission media in the following subsections.

Twisted-pair lines

As the name implies, a twisted-pair line is composed of a pair of wires twisted together. The proximity of the signal and ground reference wires means that any interference signal is picked up by both wires, reducing its effect on the difference signal. Furthermore, if multiple twisted pairs are enclosed within the same cable, the twisting of each pair within the cable reduces crosstalk. A schematic of two types of twisted-pair line is shown in Figure 1.10(a).

Twisted-pair lines are suitable, with appropriate line driver and receiver circuits that exploit the potential advantages gained by using such a geometry, for bit rates in order of 1 Mbps over short distances (less than 100 m) and lower bit rates over longer distances. More sophisticated driver and receiver circuits enable bit rates of tens of Mbps to be achieved over similar distances. Such lines, known as **unshielded twisted pairs** (**UTPs**), are used extensively in telephone networks and (with special integrated circuits) in many local area networks. With **shielded twisted pairs** (**STPs**), a protective screen or shield is used to reduce further the effects of interference signals. This was introduced by IBM and is shown in Figure 1.10(b). It is more rigid than UTP and hence is more difficult to install. For this reason, UTP is the most widely used cable in networking applications.

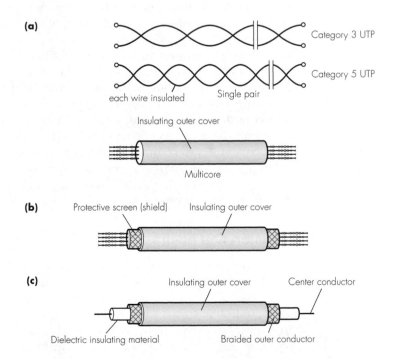

Figure 1.10 Copper wire transmission media: (a) unshielded twisted pair (UTP); (b) shielded twisted pair (STP); (c) coaxial cable.

Coaxial cable

The main limiting factors of a twisted-pair line are its (electrical) **capacity** and a phenomenon known as the **skin effect**. As a result of these, as the bit rate (and hence frequency) of the transmitted signal increases, the current flowing in the wires tends to flow only on the outer surface of the wire, thus using less of the available cross-section. This increases the electrical resistance of the wires for higher-frequency signals, leading to higher attenuation. In addition, at higher frequencies, more signal power is lost as a result of radiation effects. Hence, for applications that demand a high bit rate over long distances, coaxial cable is often used as the transmission medium.

Coaxial cable minimizes both these effects. Figure 1.10(c) shows the signal and ground reference wires as a solid center conductor running concentrically (coaxially) inside a solid (or braided) outer circular conductor. Ideally the space between the two conductors should be filled with air, but in practice it is normally filled with a dielectric insulating material with a solid or honeycomb structure.

The center conductor is effectively shielded from external interference signals by the outer conductor. Also only minimal losses occur as a result of electromagnetic radiation and the skin effect because of the presence of the outer conductor. Coaxial cable can be used with either baseband or modulated transmission, but typically 10 Mbps over several hundred meters – or much higher with modulation – is perfectly feasible. As we shall see in Section 5.2, coaxial cable is used extensively in cable television (CATV) networks.

Optical fiber

While the geometry of coaxial cable significantly reduces the various limiting effects, the maximum signal frequency, and hence the bit rate that can be transmitted using a solid (normally copper) conductor, although very high, is limited. This is also the case for twisted-pair cable. **Optical fiber cable** differs from both these transmission media in that it carries the transmitted bitstream in the form of a fluctuating beam of light in a glass fiber, rather than as an electrical signal on a wire. Light waves have a much wider bandwidth than electrical waves, enabling optical fiber cable to achieve transmission rates of hundreds of Mbps. It is used extensively in the core transmission network of PSTNs, ISDNs and LANs and also CATV networks.

Light waves are also immune to electromagnetic interference and crosstalk. Hence optical fiber cable is extremely useful for the transmission of lower bit rate signals in electrically noisy environments, in steel plants, for example, which employ much high-voltage and current-switching equipments. It is also being used increasingly where security is important, since it is difficult physically to tap.

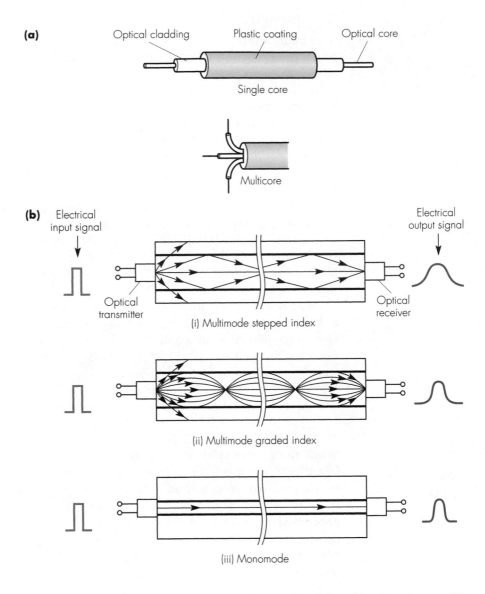

Figure 1.11 Optical fiber transmission media: (a) cable structures; (b) transmission modes.

As we show in Figure 1.11(a) an optical fiber cable consists of a single glass fiber for each signal to be transmitted, contained within the cable's protective coating, which also shields the fiber from any external light sources. The light signal is generated by an optical transmitter, which performs the conversion from a normal electrical signal as used in a NIC. An optical receiver is used to perform the reverse function at the receiving end. Typically, the transmitter uses a **light-emitting diode** (**LED**) or **laser diode** (**LD**) to perform the conversion operation while the receiver uses a light-sensitive **photodiode** or **photo transistor**.

The fiber itself consists of two parts: an optical core and an optical cladding with a lower refractive index. Light propagates along the optical fiber core in one of three ways depending on the type and width of core material used. These transmission modes are shown in Figure 1.11(b).

In a **multimode stepped index fiber** the cladding and core material each has a different but uniform refractive index. All the light emitted by the diode at an angle less than the critical angle is reflected at the cladding interface and propagates along the core by means of multiple (internal) reflections. Depending on the angle at which it is emitted by the diode, the light will take a variable amount of time to propagate along the cable. Therefore the received signal has a wider pulse width than the input signal with a corresponding decrease in the maximum permissible bit rate. This effect is known as **dispersion** and means this type of cable is used primarily for modest bit rates with relatively inexpensive LEDs compared to laser diodes.

Dispersion can be reduced by using a core material that has a variable (rather than constant) refractive index. As we show in Figure 1.11(b), in a **multi-mode graded index fiber** light is refracted by an increasing amount as it moves away from the core. This has the effect of narrowing the pulse width of the received signal compared with stepped index fiber, allowing a corresponding increase in maximum bit rate.

Further improvements can be obtained by reducing the core diameter to that of a single wavelength (3–10 μm) so that all the emitted light propagates along a single (dispersionless) path. Consequently, the received signal is of a comparable width to the input signal and is called **monomode fiber**. It is normally used with LDs and can operate at hundreds of Mbps.

Alternatively, multiple high bit rate transmission channels can be derived from the same fiber by using different portions of the optical bandwidth for each channel. This mode of operation is known as **wave-division multiplexing** (**WDM**) and, when using this, bit rates in excess of tens of Gbps can be achieved.

Satellites

All the transmission media we have discussed so far have used a physical line to carry the transmitted data. However, data can also be transmitted using electromagnetic (radio) waves through free space as in **satellite** systems. A collimated **microwave beam**, onto which the data is modulated, is transmitted to the satellite from the ground. This beam is received and retransmitted (relayed) to the predetermined destination(s) using an on-board circuit known as a **transponder**. A single satellite has many transponders, each covering a particular band of frequencies. A typical satellite channel has an extremely high bandwidth (500 MHz) and can provide many hundreds of high bit rate data links using a technique known as **time division multiplexing** (**TDM**). We shall describe this in Section 5.3 but, essentially, the total available capacity of the channel is divided into a number of subchannels, each of which can support a high bit rate link.

Satellites used for communication purposes are normally **geostationary**, which means that the satellite orbits the earth once every 24 hours in synchronism with the earth's rotation and hence appears stationary from the ground. The orbit of the satellite is chosen so that it provides a line-of-sight communication path to the transmitting station(s) and receiving station(s). The degree of the collimation of the microwave beam retransmitted by the satellite can be either coarse, so that the signal can be picked up over a wide geographical area, or finely focused, so that it can be picked up only over a limited area. In the latter case the signal power is higher, allowing smaller-diameter receivers called **antennas** or **dishes** to be used. Satellites are widely used for data transmission applications ranging from interconnecting different national computer communication networks to providing high bit rate paths to link communication networks in different parts of the same country. They are also used in entertainment applications for the broadcast of TV programs.

A typical satellite system used for TV broadcast applications is shown in Figure 1.12(a). Only a unidirectional transmission path is used with the up and down channels operating at different frequencies. For data communication applications, however, a more common configuration involves a central hub ground station that communicates with a number of ground stations distributed around the country. Each ground station has a small antenna associated with it – typically 1 meter in diameter – which, in addition to receiving the signal transmitted by the hub station, allows the station to transmit back to the hub. Such ground stations are known as **very small aperture terminals** or **VSATs**. Typically, as we show in Figure 1.12(b), the computer associated with each VSAT communicates with a central computer connected to the hub. Normally, the central site broadcasts to all VSATs at a high bit rate of 0.5–2 Mbps while in the reverse direction each VSAT transmits at a lower bit rate of up to 64 kbps.

To communicate with a particular VSAT, the central site broadcasts the message with the identity of the intended VSAT at the head of the message. For applications that require VSAT-to-VSAT communication, all messages are first sent to the central site – via the satellite – which then broadcasts them to the intended recipients. With the next generation of higher-powered satellites it will be possible for the routing to be carried out on board the satellite without passing through a central site. Direct VSAT-to-VSAT communication is then possible.

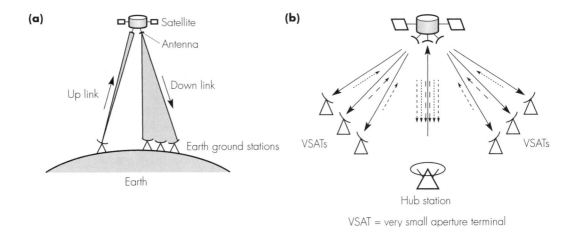

Figure 1.12 Satellite systems: (a) broadcast television; (b) data communications.

Terrestrial microwave

Terrestrial microwave links are widely used to provide communication links when it is impractical or too expensive to install physical transmission media, for example across a river or perhaps a swamp or desert. As the collimated microwave beam travels through the earth's atmosphere, it can be disturbed by such factors as manufactured structures and adverse weather conditions. With a satellite link, on the other hand, the beam travels mainly through free space and is therefore less prone to such effects. Nevertheless, line-of-sight microwave communication through the earth's atmosphere can be used reliably for the transmission of relatively high bit rates over distances in excess of 50 km.

Radio

Radio transmission using lower-frequency radio waves (cf. microwaves) is also used for the transmission of digital information in place of fixed-wire links over large distances.

Modulated transmission is used and example applications include mobile telephony and more general mobile data applications. However, since radio/wireless networks now form an important part of the Internet, a more detailed explanation of radio transmission is given in Appendix D.

Signal propagation delay

As we saw in Section 1.2.4, there is always a short but finite time delay for a signal (electrical, optical, or radio) to propagate (travel) from one end of a transmission medium to the other. This is known as the **propagation delay**, T_p, of the medium. At best, signals propagate (radiate) through the medium at the speed of light ($3 \times 10^8\,\mathrm{m\,s^{-1}}$). The speed of propagation for twisted-pair wire or coaxial cable is a fraction of this figure. Typically, it is in the region of

$2 \times 10^8 \, \text{m s}^{-1}$, that is, a signal will take $0.5 \times 10^{-8} \, \text{s}$ to travel $1 \, \text{m}$ through the medium. Although this may seem insignificant, in some situations the resulting delay is important.

As we explain later in Section 1.4.1, in many instances, on receipt of each block of data, an acknowledgment of correct (or otherwise) receipt is returned to the sender. An important parameter of a transmission link, therefore, is the **round-trip delay** associated with the link, that is, the time delay between the first bit of a block being transmitted by the sender and the last bit of its associated acknowledgment being received. Clearly, this is a function not only of the time taken to transmit the frame at the link bit rate – known as the transmission delay, T_x – but also of the propagation delay of the link, T_p. The relative weighting of the two times varies for different types of link and hence the two times are often expressed as a ratio a such that:

$$a = \frac{T_p}{T_x}$$

where $\quad T_p = \dfrac{\text{physical separation } S \text{ in meters}}{\text{velocity of propagation } V \text{ in meters per second}}$

and $\quad T_x = \dfrac{\text{number of bits to be transmitted } N}{\text{link bit rate } R \text{ in bits per second}}$

We can conclude from Example 1.4:

- If a is less than 1, then the round-trip delay is determined primarily by the transmission delay.
- If a is equal to 1, then both delays have equal effect.
- If a is greater than 1, then the propagation delay dominates.

Furthermore, in the third case it is interesting to note that, providing blocks are transmitted contiguously, there will be:

$$10 \times 10^6 \times 1.67 \times 10^{-1} = 1.67 \times 10^6 \, \text{bits}$$

in transit between the two end systems at any one time, that is, the sending system will have transmitted 1.67×10^6 bits before the first bit arrives at the receiving system. Such links are said, therefore, to have a large **bandwidth/ delay product**, where bandwidth relates to the bit rate of the link and delay to the propagation delay of the link. We shall discuss these implications further in Section 1.4.2.

As we have explained, thermal noise is present in a line even when nothing is being transmitted. In addition, there are other noise signals present that are caused by electrical activity external to the transmission line. We identified one source of this, crosstalk, in Section 1.3.1 when we discussed

Example 1.4

A 1000-bit block of data is to be transmitted between two computers. Determine the ratio of the propagation delay to the transmission delay, a, for the following types of data link:

(i)   100 m of twisted-pair wire and a transmission rate of 10 kbps,
(ii)   10 km of coaxial cable and a transmission rate of 1 Mbps,
(iii) 50 000 km of free space (satellite link) and a transmission rate of 10 Mbps.

Assume that the velocity of propagation of an electrical signal within each type of cable is $2 \times 10^8 \, \mathrm{m\,s^{-1}}$, and that of free space $3 \times 10^8 \, \mathrm{m\,s^{-1}}$.

Answer:

(i) $T_p = \dfrac{S}{V} = \dfrac{100}{2 \times 10^8} = 5 \times 10^{-7} \, \mathrm{s}$

$T_x = \dfrac{N}{R} = \dfrac{1000}{10 \times 10^3} = 0.1 \, \mathrm{s}$

$a = \dfrac{T_p}{T_x} = \dfrac{5 \times 10^{-7}}{0.1} = 5 \times 10^{-6}$

(ii) $T_p = \dfrac{S}{V} = \dfrac{10 \times 10^3}{2 \times 10^8} = 5 \times 10^{-5} \, \mathrm{s}$

$T_x = \dfrac{N}{R} = \dfrac{1000}{1 \times 10^6} = 1 \times 10^{-3} \, \mathrm{s}$

$a = \dfrac{T_p}{T_x} = \dfrac{5 \times 10^{-5}}{1 \times 10^{-3}} = 5 \times 10^{-2}$

(iii) $T_p = \dfrac{S}{V} = \dfrac{5 \times 10^{-7}}{3 \times 10^8} = 1.67 \times 10^{-1} \, \mathrm{s}$

$T_x = \dfrac{N}{R} = \dfrac{1000}{10 \times 10^6} = 1 \times 10^{-4} \, \mathrm{s}$

$a = \dfrac{T_p}{T_x} = \dfrac{1.67 \times 10^{-1}}{1 \times 10^{-4}} = 1.67 \times 10^3$

twisted-pair transmission lines. Crosstalk is caused by unwanted electrical coupling between adjacent lines. This coupling results in a signal that is being transmitted in one line being picked up by adjacent lines as a small but finite (noise) signal.

There are several types of crosstalk but in most cases the most limiting impairment is **near-end crosstalk** or **NEXT**. This is also known as **self-crosstalk** since it is caused by the strong signal output by a transmitter circuit being coupled (and hence interfering) with the much weaker signal at the input to the local receiver circuit. As we showed in Figure 1.9, the received signal is normally significantly attenuated and distorted and hence the amplitude of the coupled signal from the transmit section can be comparable with the amplitude of the received signal.

Special integrated circuits known as **adaptive NEXT cancelers** are now used to overcome this type of impairment. A typical arrangement is shown in Figure 1.13. The canceler circuit adaptively forms an attenuated replica of the crosstalk signal that is coupled into the receive line from the local transmitter and this is subtracted from the received signal. Such circuits are now used in many applications involving UTP cable, for example, to transmit data at high bit rates.

1.3.2 Transmission control schemes

There are two types of transmission control scheme used to transmit the serial bitstream relating to an application over a transmission line. These are called asynchronous transmission and synchronous transmission. We shall describe each separately.

Asynchronous transmission

With asynchronous transmission, each character or byte that makes up a block/message is treated independently for transmission purposes. Hence it can be used both for the transfer of, say, single characters that are entered at a keyboard, and for the transfer of blocks of characters/bytes across a low bit rate transmission line/channel.

The most widely used character set is the **American Standard Code for Information Interchange (ASCII)**. The complete set of characters is shown in tabular form in Figure 1.14. The table includes the binary codewords used to represent each character entered at a keyboard plus some additional characters.

As we can see, each character is represented by a unique 7-bit binary codeword. The use of 7 bits means that there are 128 alternative characters and the codeword used to identify each character is obtained by combining the corresponding column (bits 7–5) and row (bits 4–1) bits together. Bit 7 is the most significant bit and hence the codeword for uppercase M, for example, is 1001101.

In addition to all the normal alphabetic, numeric and punctuation characters – collectively referred to as **printable characters** – the total ASCII character set also includes a number of **control characters**. These include:

■ **format control characters**: BS (backspace), LF (line feed), CR (carriage return), SP (space), DEL (delete), ESC (escape) and FF (form feed);

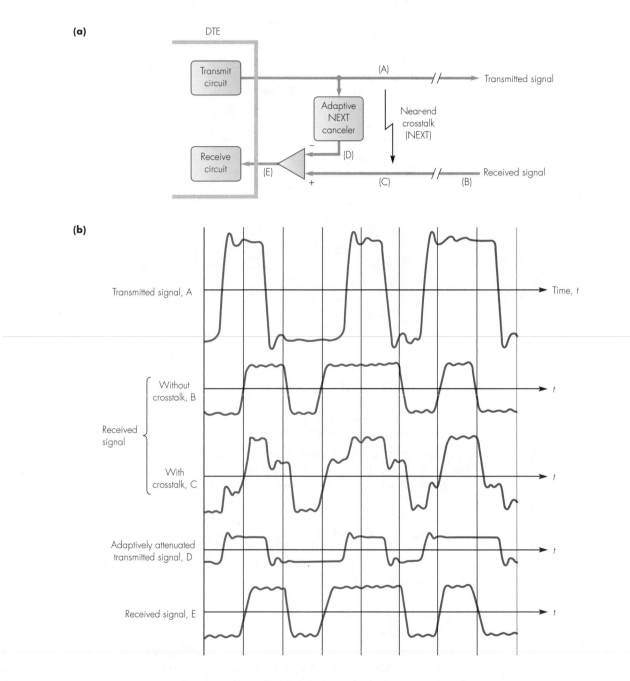

Figure 1.13 Adaptive NEXT cancelers: (a) circuit schematic; (b) example waveforms.

Bit positions 7	0	0	0	0	1	1	1	1
6	0	0	1	1	0	0	1	1
5	0	1	0	1	0	1	0	1
4 3 2 1								
0 0 0 0	NUL	DLE	SP	0	@	P	\	p
0 0 0 1	SOH	DC1	!	1	A	Q	a	q
0 0 1 0	STX	DC2	"	2	B	R	b	r
0 0 1 1	ETX	DC3	#	3	C	S	c	s
0 1 0 0	EOT	DC4	$	4	D	T	d	t
0 1 0 1	ENQ	NAK	%	5	E	U	e	u
0 1 1 0	ACK	SYN	&	6	F	V	f	v
0 1 1 1	BEL	ETB	'	7	G	W	g	w
1 0 0 0	BS	CAN	(	8	H	X	h	x
1 0 0 1	HT	EM	)	9	I	Y	i	y
1 0 1 0	LF	SUB	*	:	J	Z	j	z
1 0 1 1	VT	ESC	+	;	K	[	k	{
1 1 0 0	FF	FS	,	<	L	\	l		
1 1 0 1	CR	GS	–	=	M	]	m	}
1 1 1 0	SO	RS	.	>	N	^	n	~
1 1 1 1	SI	US	/	?	O	—	o	DEL

Figure 1.14 The ASCII character set.

- **information separators:** FS (file separator) and RS (record separator);
- **transmission control characters**: SOH (start of heading), STX (start of text), ETX (end of text), ACK (acknowledge), NAK (negative acknowledge), SYN (synchronous idle) and DLE (data link escape).

Within end systems – computers, etc. – all data is transferred between the various circuits and subsystems in a word or byte parallel mode. Consequently, since all transfers that are external to the system are carried out bit-serially, the transmission control circuit on the network interface card (NIC) must perform the following functions:

- parallel-to-serial conversion of each character or byte in preparation for its transmission on the line;
- serial-to-parallel conversion of each received character or byte in preparation for its storage and processing in the receiving end system;
- a means for the receiver to achieve bit, character, and frame synchronization;
- the generation of suitable error check digits for error detection and the detection of such errors at the receiver should they occur.

As we show in Figure 1.15(a), parallel-to-serial conversion is performed by a **parallel-in**, **serial-out** (**PISO**) **shift register**. This, as its name implies, allows a complete character or byte to be loaded in parallel and then shifted out bit-serially. Similarly, serial-to-parallel conversion is performed by a **serial-in**, **parallel-out** (**SIPO**) **shift register**, which executes the reverse function.

To achieve bit and character synchronization, we must set the receiving transmission control circuit (which is normally programmable) to operate with the same characteristics as the transmitter in terms of the number of bits per character and the bit rate being used.

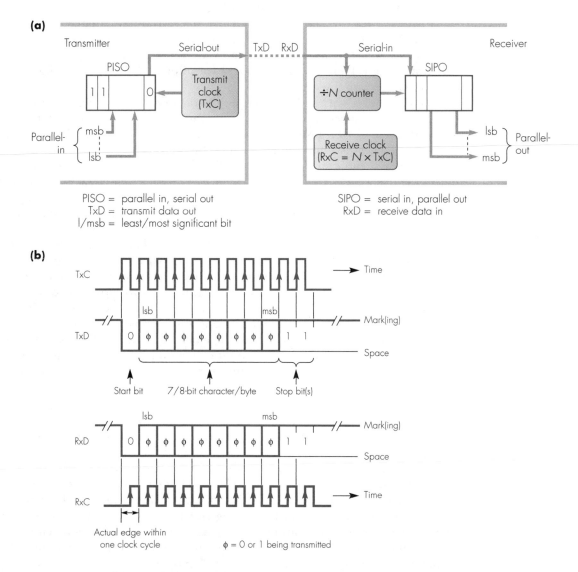

Figure 1.15 Asynchronous transmission: (a) principle of operation; (b) timing principles.

Bit synchronization

In asynchronous transmission, the receiver clock (which is used to sample and shift the incoming signal into the SIPO shift register) runs asynchronously with respect to the incoming signal. In order for the reception process to work reliably, we must devise a scheme whereby the local (asynchronous) receiver clock samples (and hence shifts into the SIPO shift register) the incoming signal as near to the center of the bit cell as possible.

To achieve this, each character/byte to be transmitted is encapsulated between a *start bit* and one or two *stop bits*. As we show in Figure 1.15(b), the start bit is a binary 0 (and known as a *space*) and the stop bit a binary 1 (and known as a *mark*). When transmitting a block comprising a string of characters/bytes, the start bit of each character/byte immediately follows the stop bit(s) of the previous character/byte. When transmitting random characters, however, the line stays at the stop/1 level until the next character is to be transmitted. Hence between blocks (or after each character), the line is said to be *marking* (time).

The use of a start and stop bit per character/byte of different polarities means that, irrespective of the binary contents of each character/byte, there is a guaranteed $1 \rightarrow 0$ transition at the start of each new character/byte. A local receiver clock of N times the transmitted bit rate ($N = 16$ is common) is used and each new bit is shifted into the SIPO shift register after N cycles of this clock. The first $1 \rightarrow 0$ transition associated with the start bit of each character is used to start the counting process. Each bit (including the start bit) is sampled at (approximately) the center of each bit cell. After the first transition is detected, the signal (the start bit) is sampled after $N/2$ clock cycles and then subsequently after N clock cycles for each bit in the character and also the stop bit(s). Three examples of different clock rate ratios are shown in Figure 1.16.

Remembering that the receiver clock (RxC) is running asynchronously with respect to the incoming signal (RxD), the relative positions of the two signals can be anywhere within a single cycle of the receiver clock. Those shown in the figure are just arbitrary positions. Nevertheless, we can deduce from these examples that the higher the clock rate ratio, the nearer the sampling instant will be to the nominal bit cell center. Because of this mode of operation, the maximum bit rate normally used with asynchronous transmission is 19.2 kbps.

Character synchronization

As we indicated above, the receiving transmission control circuit is programmed to operate with the same number of bits per character and the same number of stop bits as the transmitter. After the start bit has been detected and received, the receiver achieves character synchronization simply by counting the programmed number of bits. It then transfers the received character/byte into a local **buffer register** and signals to the controlling device (a microprocessor, for example) on the NIC that a new character/byte has been received. It then awaits the next line signal transition that indicates a new start bit (and hence character) is being received.

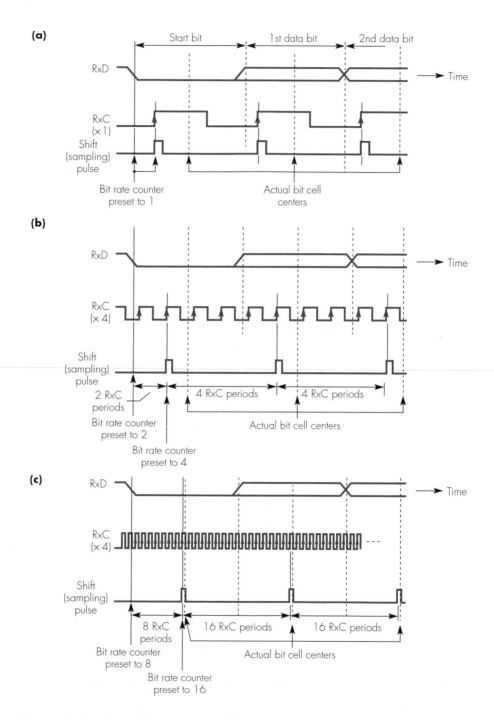

**Figure 1.16 Examples of three different receiver clock rate ratios:
(a)×1; (b)×4; (c)×16.**

Example 1.5

A block of data is to be transmitted across a serial data link. If a clock of 19.2 kHz is available at the receiver, deduce the suitable clock rate ratios and estimate the worst-case deviations from the nominal bit cell centers, expressed as a percentage of a bit period, for each of the following data transmission rates:

(i) 1200 bps

(ii) 2400 bps

(iii) 9600 bps

Answer:

It can readily be deduced from Figure 1.16 that the worst-case deviation from the nominal bit cell centers is approximately plus or minus one half of one cycle of the receiver clock.

Hence:

(i) At 1200 bps, the maximum RxC ratio can be × 16. The maximum deviation is thus ± 3.125%.

(ii) At 2400 bps, the maximum RxC ratio can be × 8. The maximum deviation is thus ± 6.25%.

(iii) At 9600 bps, the maximum RxC ratio can be × 2. The maximum deviation is thus ± 25%.

Clearly, the last case is unacceptable. With a low-quality line, especially one with excessive delay distortion, even the second may be unreliable. It is for this reason that a × 16 clock rate ratio is used whenever possible.

Frame synchronization

When messages comprising blocks of characters or bytes – normally referred to as **information frames** – are being transmitted, in addition to bit and character synchronization, the receiver must be able to determine the start and end of each frame. This is known as frame synchronization.

The simplest method of transmitting blocks of printable characters is to encapsulate the complete block between two special (nonprintable) transmission control characters: STX (start-of-text), which indicates the start of a new frame after an idle period, and ETX (end-of-text), which indicates the end of the frame. As the frame contents consist only of printable characters, the receiver can interpret the receipt of an STX character as signaling the start of a new frame and an ETX character as signaling the end of the frame. This is shown in Figure 1.17(a).

Although the scheme shown is satisfactory for the transmission of blocks of printable characters, when transmitting blocks that comprise strings of bytes (for example, the contents of a file containing compressed speech or video), the use of a single ETX character to indicate the end of a frame is not sufficient. In the case of a string of bytes, one of the bytes might be the same as an ETX character, which would cause the receiver to terminate the reception process abnormally.

To overcome this problem, when transmitting this type of data the two transmission control characters STX and ETX are each preceded by a third transmission control character known as **data link escape** (**DLE**). The modified format of a frame is then as shown in Figure 1.17(b).

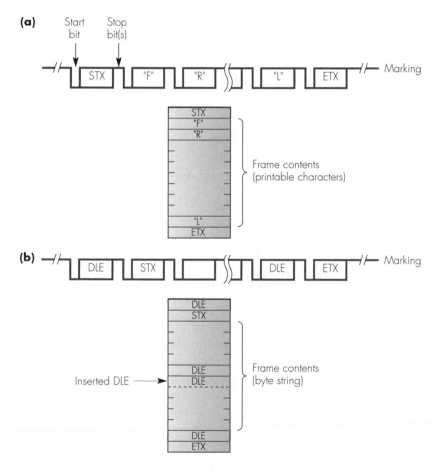

Figure 1.17 Frame synchronization with different frame contents: (a) printable characters; (b) string of bytes.

Remember that the transmitter knows the number of bytes in each frame to be transmitted. After transmitting the start-of-frame sequence (DLE-STX), the transmitter inspects each byte in the frame prior to transmission to determine if it is the same as the DLE character pattern. If it is, irrespective of the next byte, a second DLE character (byte) is transmitted before the next byte. This procedure is repeated until the appropriate number of bytes in the frame have been transmitted. The transmitter then signals the end of the frame by transmitting the unique DLE-STX sequence.

This procedure is known as **character** or **byte stuffing**. On receipt of each byte after the DLE-STX start-of-frame sequence, the receiver determines whether it is a DLE character (byte). If it is, the receiver then processes the next byte to determine whether that is another DLE or an ETX. If it is a DLE, the receiver discards it and awaits the next byte. If it is an ETX, this can reliably be taken as being the end of the frame.

Synchronous transmission

The use of an additional start bit and one or more stop bits per character or byte means that asynchronous transmission is relatively inefficient in its use of transmission capacity, especially when transmitting messages that comprise large blocks of characters or bytes. Also, the bit (clock) synchronization method used with asynchronous transmission becomes less reliable as the bit rate increases. This results, firstly, from the fact that the detection of the first start bit transition is only approximate and, secondly, although the receiver clock operates at N times the nominal transmit clock rate, because of tolerances there are small differences between the two that can cause the sampling instant to drift during the reception of a character or byte. We normally use synchronous transmission to overcome these problems. As with asynchronous transmission, however, we must adopt a suitable method to enable the receiver to achieve bit (clock) character (byte) and frame (block) synchronization. In practice, there are two synchronous transmission control schemes: character-oriented and bit-oriented. We shall discuss each separately but, since they both use the same bit synchronization methods, we shall discuss these methods first.

Bit synchronization

Although we often use the presence of a start bit and stop bit(s) with each character to discriminate between asynchronous and synchronization transmission, the fundamental difference between the two methods is that with asynchronous transmission the receiver clock runs asynchronously (unsynchronized) with respect to the incoming (received) signal, whereas with synchronous transmission the receiver clock operates in synchronism with the received signal.

As we have just indicated, start and stop bits are not used with synchronous transmission. Instead each frame is transmitted as a contiguous stream of binary digits. The receiver then obtains (and maintains) bit synchronization in one of two ways. Either the clock (timing) information is embedded into the transmitted signal and subsequently extracted by the receiver, or the receiver has a local clock (as with asynchronous transmission) but this time it is kept in synchronism with the received signal by a device known as a **digital phase-lock-loop** (**DPLL**). As we shall see, the DPLL exploits the $1 \rightarrow 0$ or $0 \rightarrow 1$ bit transitions in the received signal to maintain bit (clock) synchronism over an acceptably long period. Hybrid schemes that exploit both methods are also used. The principles of operation of both schemes are shown in Figure 1.18.

Clock encoding and extraction The alternative methods of embedding timing (clock) information into a transmitted bitstream are shown in Figure 1.19. The scheme shown in part (a) is called **Manchester encoding** and that in part (b) **differential Manchester encoding**.

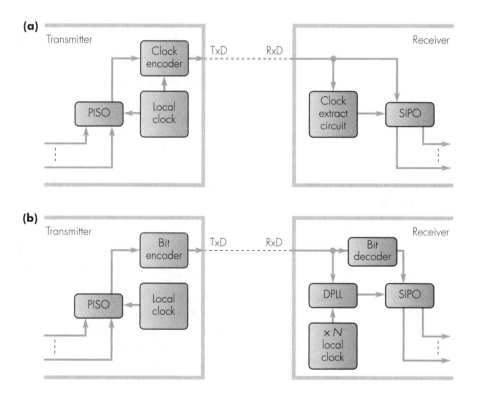

Figure 1.18 Alternative bit/clock synchronization methods with synchronous transmission: (a) clock encoding; (b) digital phase-lock-loop (DPLL).

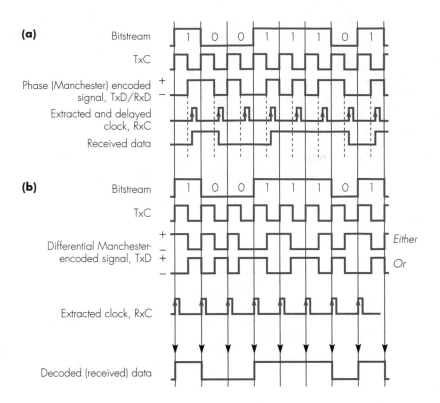

Figure 1.19 Synchronous transmission clock encoding methods: (a) Manchester; (b) differential Manchester.

As we can see, with Manchester encoding each bit is encoded as either a low-high signal (binary 1) or a high-low signal (binary 0), both occupying a single bit-cell period. Also, there is always a transition (high-low or low-high) at the center of each bit cell. It is this that is used by the clock extraction circuit to produce a clock pulse that is then delayed to the center of the second half of the bit cell. At this point the received (encoded) signal is either high (for binary 1) or low (for binary 0) and hence the correct bit is sampled and shifted into the SIPO shift register.

The scheme shown in Figure 1.19(b) is differential Manchester encoding. This differs from Manchester encoding in that although there is still a transition at the center of each bit cell, a transition at the start of the bit cell occurs only if the next bit to be encoded is a 0. This has the effect that the encoded output signal may take on one of two forms depending on the assumed start level (high or low). As we can see, however, one is simply an inverted version of the other and this is the origin of the term "differential". As we show later in Figure 2.12(c), and explain in the accompanying text, a differential driver circuit produces a pair of differential signals and the differential receiver operates by determining the difference between these two signals. For example, if the two signals each vary between $+V$ and $-V$, then the difference would be $+2V$ and $-2V$. The extracted clock is generated at the start of each bit cell. At this point the received (encoded) signal either changes – for example, from $+2V$ to $-2V$ or from $-2V$ to $+2V$ in which case a binary 0 is shifted into the SIPO – or remains at the same level, in which case a binary 1 is shifted into the SIPO.

The two Manchester encoding schemes are **balanced codes** which means there is no mean (DC) value associated with them. This is so since a string of binary 1s (or 0s) will always have transitions associated with them rather than a constant (DC) level. This is an important feature since it means that the received signal can be **AC coupled** to the receiver electronics using a transformer. The receiver electronics can then operate using its own power supply since this is effectively isolated from the power supply of the transmitter.

Digital phase-lock-loop An alternative approach to encoding the clock in the transmitted bit stream is to utilize a stable clock source at the receiver which is kept in time synchronism with the incoming bit stream. However, as there are no start and stop bits with a synchronous transmission scheme, we must encode the information in such a way that there are always sufficient bit transitions $(1 \rightarrow 0$ or $0 \rightarrow 1)$ in the transmitted waveform to enable the receiver clock to be resynchronized at frequent intervals. One approach is to pass the data to be transmitted through a **scrambler**, which randomizes the transmitted bitstream so removing contiguous strings of 1s or 0s. Alternatively, the data may be encoded in such a way that suitable transitions will always be present.

The bit pattern to be transmitted is first differentially encoded as shown in Figure 1.20(a). We refer to the resulting encoded signal as a **non-return-to-zero-inverted** (**NRZI**) waveform. With NRZI encoding the signal level (1 or 0) does not change for the transmission of a binary 1, whereas a binary 0 causes a change. This means that there will always be bit transitions in the incoming signal of an NRZI waveform, providing there are no contiguous streams of binary 1s. On the surface, this may seem no different from the normal NRZ waveform but, as we shall describe later, if a bit-oriented scheme with zero bit insertion is used, an active line will always have a binary 0 in the transmitted bitstream at least every five bit cells. Consequently, the resulting waveform will contain a guaranteed number of transitions, since long strings of 0s cause a transition every bit cell. This enables the receiver to adjust its clock so that it is in synchronism with the incoming bitstream.

The circuit used to maintain bit synchronism is known as a digital phase-lock-loop and is shown in Figure 1.20(b). A crystal-controlled oscillator (clock source), which can hold its frequency sufficiently constant to require only very small adjustments at irregular intervals, is connected to the DPLL. Typically, the frequency of the clock is 32 times the bit rate used on the data

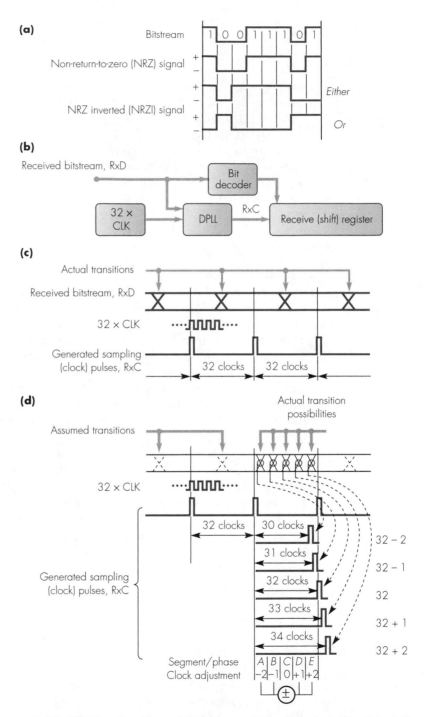

Figure 1.20 DPLL operation: (a) bit encoding; (b) circuit schematic; (c) in phase; (d) clock adjustment rules.

link and is used by the DPLL to derive the timing interval between successive samples of the received bitstream.

Assuming the incoming bitstream and the local clock are in synchronism, the state (1 or 0) of the incoming signal on the line will be sampled (and hence clocked into the SIPO shift register) at the center of each bit cell with exactly 32 clock periods between each sample. This is shown in Figure 1.20(c).

Now assume that the incoming bitstream and local clock drift out of synchronism because of small variations in the latter. The sampling instant is adjusted in discrete increments as shown in Figure 1.20(d). If there are no transitions on the line, the DPLL simply generates a sampling pulse every 32 clock periods after the previous one. Whenever a transition ($1 \rightarrow 0$ or $0 \rightarrow 1$) is detected, the time interval between the previously generated sampling pulse and the next is determined according to the position of the transition relative to where the DPLL thought it should occur. To achieve this, each bit period is divided into five segments, shown as A, B, C, D, and E in the figure. For example, a transition occurring during segment A indicates that the last sampling pulse was too close to the next transition and hence late. The time period to the next pulse is therefore shortened to 30 clock periods. Similarly, a transition occurring in segment E indicates that the previous sampling pulse was too early relative to the transition. The time period to the next pulse is therefore lengthened to 34 clock periods. Transitions in segments B and D are clearly nearer to the assumed transition and hence the relative adjustments are less (−1 and +1 respectively). Finally a transition in segment C is deemed to be close enough to the assumed transition to warrant no adjustment.

In this way, successive adjustments keep the generated sampling pulses close to the center of each bit cell. In practice, the widths of each segment (in terms of clock periods) are not equal. The outer segments (A and E), being further away from the nominal center, are made longer than the three inner segments. For the circuit shown, a typical division might be $A = E = 10$, $B = D = 5$, and $C = 2$. We can readily deduce that in the worst case the DPLL requires 10 bit transitions to converge to the nominal bit center of a waveform: 5 bit periods of coarse adjustments (±2) and 5 bit periods of fine adjustments (±1). Hence when using a DPLL, it is usual before transmitting the first frame on a line, or following an idle period between frames, to transmit a number of characters/bytes to provide a minimum of 10 bit transitions. Two characters/bytes each composed of all 0s, for example, provide 16 transitions with NRZI encoding. This ensures that the DPLL generates sampling pulses at the nominal center of each bit cell by the time the opening character or byte of a frame is received. We must stress, however, that once in synchronism (lock) only minor adjustments normally take place during the reception of a frame.

We can deduce from Figure 1.20(a) that with NRZI encoding the maximum rate at which the encoded signal changes polarity is one half that of Manchester encoding. If the bit period is T, with NRZI encoding the maximum rate is $1/T$, whereas with Manchester encoding it is $2/T$. The maximum rate is known as the **modulation rate**. The highest fundamental frequency component of each scheme is $1/T$ and $2/T$ respectively. This means that, for the same data rate, Manchester encoding requires twice the transmission bandwidth of an NRZI encoded signal, that is, the higher the modulation rate, the wider is the required bandwidth.

The effect of this is that Manchester and differential Manchester encoding are both used extensively in applications such as LANs. As we shall expand upon in Chapter 3, LANs operate in a single office or building and hence use relatively short cable runs. This means that even though they operate at high bit rates – for example 10 Mbps and multiples of this – the attenuation and bandwidth of the transmission medium are not generally a problem. In contrast, as we shall expand upon in Chapter 2, in networks such as an ISDN twisted-pair cable is often used with relatively high bit rates and over distances of several kilometers. Hence encoding schemes such as NRZI are used with each bit represented by a full-width pulse. We shall describe a number of examples of each scheme in later chapters.

Character-oriented

As we indicated at the beginning of the subsection on synchronous transmission, there are two types of synchronous transmission control scheme: character-oriented and bit-oriented. Both use the same bit synchronization methods. The major difference between the two schemes is the method used to achieve character and frame synchronization.

Character-oriented transmission is used primarily for the transmission of blocks of characters, such as files of ASCII characters. Since there are no start or stop bits with synchronous transmission, an alternative way of achieving character synchronization must be used. To achieve this the transmitter adds two or more transmission control characters, known as **synchronous idle** or **SYN** characters, before each block of characters. These control characters have two functions. Firstly, they allow the receiver to obtain (or maintain) bit synchronization. Secondly, once this has been done, they allow the receiver to start to interpret the received bitstream on the correct character boundaries – **character synchronization**. The general scheme is shown in Figure 1.21.

Part (a) shows that frame synchronization (with character-oriented synchronous transmission) is achieved in just the same way as for asynchronous transmission by encapsulating the block of characters – the frame contents – between an STX-ETX pair of transmission control characters. The SYN control characters used to enable the receiver to achieve character synchronization precede the STX start-of-frame character. Once the receiver has obtained bit synchronization it enters what is known as the **hunt mode**. This is shown in Figure 1.21(b).

When the receiver enters the hunt mode, it starts to interpret the received bitstream in a window of eight bits as each new bit is received. In this way, as each bit is received, it checks whether the last eight bits were equal to the known SYN character. If they are not, it receives the next bit and repeats the check. If they are, then this indicates it has found the correct character boundary and hence the following characters are then read after each subsequent eight bits have been received.

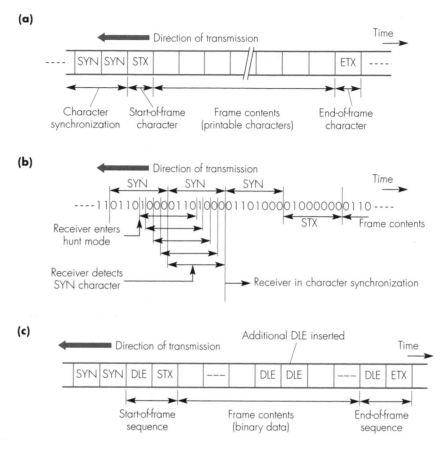

Figure 1.21 Character-oriented synchronous transmission: (a) frame format; (b) character synchronization; (c) data transparency (character stuffing).

Once in character synchronization (and hence reading each character on the correct bit boundary), the receiver starts to process each subsequently received character in search of the STX character indicating the start of the frame. On receipt of the STX character, the receiver proceeds to receive the frame contents and terminates this process when it detects the ETX character. On a point-to-point link, the transmitter normally then reverts to sending SYN characters to allow the receiver to maintain synchronism. Alternatively, the above procedure must be repeated each time a new frame is transmitted.

Finally, as we can see in Figure 1.21(c), when binary data is being transmitted, data transparency is achieved in the same way as described previously by preceding the STX and ETX characters by a DLE (data link escape) character and inserting (stuffing) an additional DLE character whenever it detects a DLE in the frame contents. In this case, therefore, the SYN characters precede the first DLE character.

Bit-oriented

The need for a pair of characters at the start and end of each frame for frame synchronization, coupled with the additional DLE characters to achieve data transparency, means that a character-oriented transmission control scheme is relatively inefficient for the transmission of binary data. Moreover, the format of the transmission control characters varies for different character sets, so the scheme can be used only with a single type of character set, even though the frame contents may be pure binary data. To overcome these problems, a more universal scheme known as **bit-oriented transmission** is now the preferred control scheme as it can be used for the transmission of frames comprising either printable characters or binary data. The main features of the scheme are shown in Figure 1.22(a). It differs mainly in the way the start and end of each frame are signaled.

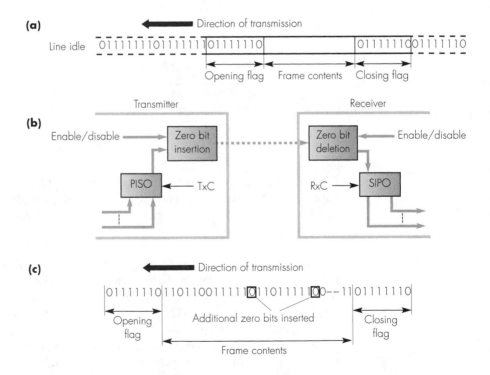

Figure 1.22 Bit-oriented synchronous transmission: (a) framing structure; (b) zero bit insertion circuit location; (c) example transmitted frame contents.

The start and end of a frame are both signaled by the same unique 8-bit pattern 01111110, known as the **flag byte** or **flag pattern**. We use the term "bit-oriented" because the received bitstream is searched by the receiver on a bit-by-bit basis both for the start-of-frame flag and, during reception of the frame contents, for the end-of-frame flag. Thus in principle the frame contents need not necessarily comprise multiples of eight bits.

To enable the receiver to obtain and maintain bit synchronism, the transmitter sends a string of **idle bytes** (each comprising 01111111) preceding the start-of-frame flag. Recall that with NRZI encoding the 0 in the idle byte enables the DPLL at the receiver to obtain and maintain clock synchronization. On receipt of the opening flag, the received frame contents are read and interpreted on 8-bit (byte) boundaries until the closing flag is detected. The reception process is then terminated.

To achieve data transparency with this scheme, we must ensure that the flag pattern is not present in the frame contents. We do this by using a technique known as **zero bit insertion** or **bit stuffing**. The circuit that performs this function is located at the output of the PISO register, as shown in Figure 1.22(b). It is enabled by the transmitter only during transmission of the frame contents. When enabled, the circuit detects whenever it has transmitted a sequence of five contiguous binary 1 digits, then automatically inserts an additional binary 0 digit. In this way, the flag pattern 01111110 can never be present in the frame contents between the opening and closing flags.

A similar circuit at the receiver located prior to the input of the SIPO shift receiver performs the reverse function. Whenever a zero is detected after five contiguous 1 digits, the circuit automatically removes (deletes) it from the frame contents. Normally the frame also contains additional error detection digits preceding the closing flag which are subjected to the same bit stuffing operation as the frame contents. An example stuffed bit pattern is shown in Figure 1.22(c).

1.4 Protocol basics

In Appendix B we describe the different methods that are used to detect the presence of transmission errors. Also, as we explained in Section 1.3, in most cases any blocks/frames that are received containing errors are simply discarded by the link layer. It is then left to the transport layer in each of the two communicating end systems to detect any missing blocks and, if necessary, to request that another copy of these is retransmitted. However, in a small number of cases the error recovery procedure is performed in the link layer; for example, in the link layer associated with a line leased from a PSTN. In this section we describe the basic principles associated with the error control procedure that is used and we then use this to explain how a protocol is specified.

1.4.1 Error control

The transmission control circuit associated with most NICs performs both the transmission control and error detection functions. The link layer protocol then builds on these basic functions to provide the required link layer service. In some networks – for example LANs and the Internet – frames received with errors are simply discarded. In others – for example wireless LANs – the receiving link protocol checks the received frame for possible transmission errors and then returns a short control message/frame either to acknowledge its correct receipt or to request that another copy of the frame is sent. This type of error control is known as **automatic repeat request** (**ARQ**) and the aim of all ARQ schemes is to provide a *reliable* link layer service. In this context, "reliable" means that the two peer link layer protocols will communicate with each other in order to deliver a sequence of blocks that is submitted to the sending link layer protocol. Thus

- the blocks will be delivered by the receiving link layer protocol in the same sequence as they were submitted and with no duplicate copies of any of the blocks;
- to a high probability, each block will be free of any bit errors.

The most basic type of ARQ scheme is **idle RQ** and so we shall start by explaining this. We then identify the limitations of idle RQ and explain how these are overcome in the **continuous RQ** scheme. In practice, there are two types of continuous RQ: selective repeat and go-back-N, both of which we describe. We then return to the idle RQ scheme to explain how the error control part of a protocol is specified.

1.4.2 Idle RQ

In order to discriminate between the sender (source) and receiver (destination) of data frames – more generally referred to as information or **I-frames** – the terms **primary** (**P**) and **secondary** (**S**) are used respectively. The idle RQ protocol operates in a half-duplex mode since the primary, after sending an I-frame, waits until it receives a response from the secondary as to whether the frame was correctly received or not. The primary then either sends the next frame, if the previous frame was correctly received, or retransmits a copy of the previous frame if it was not.

The secondary informs the primary of a correctly received frame by returning a (positive) **acknowledgment** or **ACK-frame**. Similarly, if the secondary receives an I-frame containing errors, then it returns a **negative acknowledgment** or **NAK-frame**. Three example frame sequences illustrating various aspects of this basic procedure are shown in Figure 1.23. The following points should be noted when interpreting the sequences:

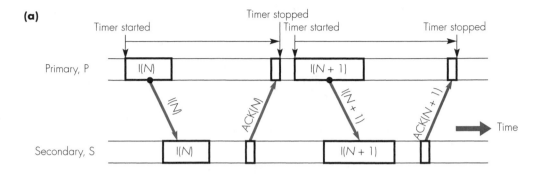

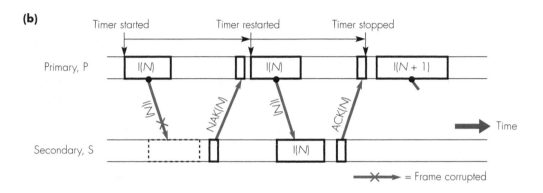

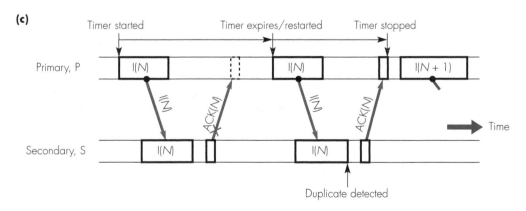

**Figure 1.23 ARQ error control scheme: (a) error free; (b) corrupted I-frame;
(c) corrupted ACK-frame.**

- P can have only one I-frame outstanding (awaiting an ACK/NAK-frame) at a time.

- When P initiates the transmission of an I-frame it starts a timer.

- On receipt of an error-free I-frame, S returns an ACK-frame to P and, on receipt of this, P stops the timer for this frame and proceeds to send the next frame – part (a).

- On receipt of an I-frame containing transmission errors, S discards the frame and returns a NAK-frame to P which then sends another copy of the frame and restarts the timer – part (b).

- If P does not receive an ACK- (or NAK-) frame within the timeout interval, P retransmits the I-frame currently waiting acknowledgment – part (c). However, since in this example it is an ACK-frame that is corrupted, S detects that the next frame it receives is a duplicate copy of the previous error-free frame it received rather than a new frame. Hence S discards the duplicate and, to enable P to resynchronize, returns a second ACK-frame for it. This procedure repeats until either an error-free copy of the frame is received or a defined number of retries is reached in which case the network layer in P would be informed of this.

As we show in the figure, in order for S to determine when a duplicate is received, each frame transmitted by P contains a unique identifier known as the **send sequence number N(S)** (*N*, *N*+1, and so on) within it. Also, S retains a record of the sequence number contained within the last I-frame it received without errors and, if the two are the same, this indicates a duplicate. The sequence number in each ACK- and NAK-frame is known as the **receive sequence number N(R)** and, since P must wait for an ACK- or NAK-frame after sending each I-frame, the scheme is known also as **send-and-wait** or sometimes **stop-and-wait**. Alternatively, since only a single frame is being transferred at a time, only two sequence numbers are required. Normally, just a single bit is used and this alternates between 0 and 1. Hence the scheme is known also as the **alternating bit protocol** and an example application is in the Bluetooth wireless network that we describe later in Section 4.2 of Chapter 4.

Link utilization

Before considering the error procedures associated with the two types of continuous RQ scheme, we shall first quantify the efficiency of utilization of the available link capacity with the idle RQ scheme. The efficiency of utilization *U* is a ratio of two times, each measured from the point in time when the transmitter starts to send a frame. It is defined as:

$$U = \frac{T_{ix}}{T_t}$$

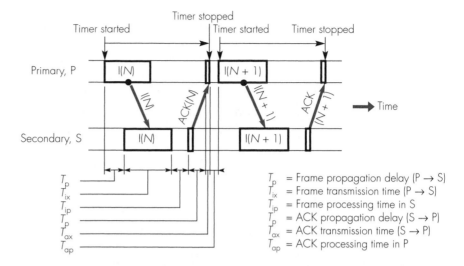

Figure 1.24 Idle RQ link utilization.

where T_{ix} is the time for the transmitter to transmit a frame and T_t equals T_{ix} plus any time the transmitter spends waiting for an acknowledgment.

To quantify the link utilization with idle RQ, a frame sequence diagram with the various component times identified is given in Figure 1.24. In practice, in most cases for which the idle RQ protocol is adequate, the time to process an I-frame T_{ip} and its associated ACK-frame T_{ap} are both short compared with their transmission times T_{ix} and T_{ax}. Also, since an ACK-frame is much shorter than an I-frame, T_{ax} is negligible compared with T_{ix}. Hence the minimum total time before the next frame can be transmitted is often approximated to $T_{ix} + 2T_p$ where T_p is the signal propagation delay of the link. An approximate expression for U is thus:

$$U = \frac{T_{ix}}{T_{ix} + 2T_p}$$

or:

$$U = \frac{1}{1 + 2T_p / T_{ix}}$$

As we described earlier in the subsection on Signal propagation delay, the ratio T_p / T_{ix} is often given the symbol a and hence:

$$U = \frac{1}{1 + 2a}$$

In Example 1.4 we saw that a can range from a small fraction for low bit rate links of modest length to a large integer value for long links and high bit rates. For these two extremes, U varies between a small fraction and near unity (100%).

Example 1.6

A series of 1000-bit frames is to be transmitted using an idle RQ protocol. Determine the link utilization for the following types of data link assuming a transmission bit rate of (a) 1 kbps and (b) 1 Mbps. Assume that the velocity of propagation of the first two links is $2 \times 10^8 \, \mathrm{m\,s^{-1}}$ and that of the third link $3 \times 10^8 \, \mathrm{m\,s^{-1}}$. Also the bit error rate is negligible.

(i)   A twisted-pair cable 1 km in length

(ii) A leased line 200 km in length

(iii) A satellite link of 50 000 km.

Answer:

The time taken to transmit a frame T_{ix} is given by:

$$T_{ix} = \frac{\text{Number of bits in frame, } N}{\text{Bit rate, } R, \text{ in bps}}$$

At 1 kbps:

$$T_{ix} = \frac{1000}{10^3} = 1\,\mathrm{s}$$

At 1 Mbps:

$$T_{ix} = \frac{1000}{10^6} = 10^{-3}\,\mathrm{s}$$

$$T_p = \frac{S}{V} \quad \text{and} \quad U = \frac{1}{1 + 2a}$$

(i) $T_p = \dfrac{10^3}{2 \times 10^8} = 5 \times 10^{-6}\,\mathrm{s}$

    (a) $a = \dfrac{5 \times 10^{-6}}{1} = 5 \times 10^{-6}$ and hence $(1 + 2a) \cong 1$ and $U = 1$

    (b) $a = \dfrac{5 \times 10^{-6}}{10^{-3}} = 5 \times 10^{-3}$ and hence $(1 + 2a) \cong 1$ and $U = 1$

(ii) $T_p = \dfrac{200 \times 10^3}{2 \times 10^8} = 1 \times 10^{-3}\,\mathrm{s}$

    (a) $a = \dfrac{1 \times 10^{-3}}{1} = 1 \times 10^{-3}$ and hence $(1 + 2a) \cong 1$ and $U = 1$

    (b) $a = \dfrac{1 \times 10^{-3}}{10^{-3}} = 1$ and hence $(1 + 2a) > 1$ and $U = \dfrac{1}{1 + 2} = 0.33$

$$(iii) \; T_p = \frac{50 \times 10^6}{3 \times 10^8} = 0.167\,s$$

$$(a) \;\; a = \frac{0.167}{1} = 0.167 \text{ and hence } (1+2a) > 1 \text{ and } U = \frac{1}{1+0.334} = 0.75$$

$$(b) \;\; a = \frac{0.167}{10^{-3}} = 167 \text{ and hence } (1+2a) > 1 \text{ and } U = \frac{1}{1+334} = 0.003$$

The results are summarized in Figure 1.25 from which we can make some interesting observations. Firstly, for relatively short links for which a is less than 1, the link utilization is (to a good approximation) 100% and is independent of the bit rate. This means that an idle RQ protocol is perfectly adequate for short links and modest bit rates. Examples are networks based on modems and an analog PSTN. Secondly, for longer terrestrial links, the link utilization is high for low bit rates (and hence low values of a) but falls off significantly as the bit rate (and hence a) increases. Thirdly, the link utilization is poor for satellite links, even at low bit rates. We can conclude that an idle RQ protocol is unsuitable for such applications and also for those that involve high bit rate terrestrial links which include all of the networks that are used for multimedia.

1.4.3 Continuous RQ

With a continuous RQ error control scheme, link utilization is much improved at the expense of increased buffer storage requirements. As we shall see, a duplex link is required for its implementation. An example illustrating the transmission of a sequence of I-frames and their returned ACK-frames is shown in Figure 1.26. You should note the following points when interpreting the operation of the scheme:

- P sends I-frames continuously without waiting for an ACK-frame to be returned.

- Since more than one I-frame is awaiting acknowledgment, P retains a copy of each I-frame transmitted in a **retransmission list** that operates on a FIFO queue discipline.

- S returns an ACK-frame for each correctly received I-frame.

- Each I-frame contains a unique identifier which is returned in the corresponding ACK-frame.

- On receipt of an ACK-frame, the corresponding I-frame is removed from the retransmission list by P.

(a)

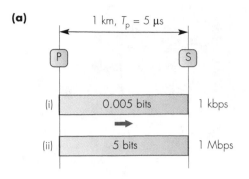

(b)

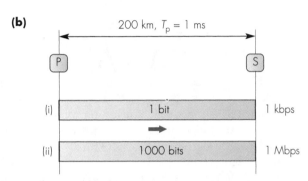

(c)

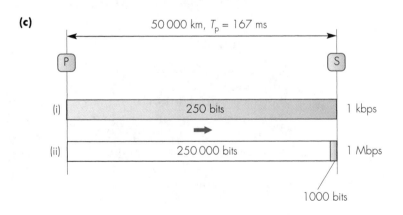

Figure 1.25 Effect of propagation delay as a function of data transmission rate; parts correspond to Example 1.6.

- Frames received free of errors are placed in the **link receive** list to await processing.
- On receipt of the next in-sequence I-frame expected, S delivers the information content within the frame to the upper network layer immediately it has processed the frame.

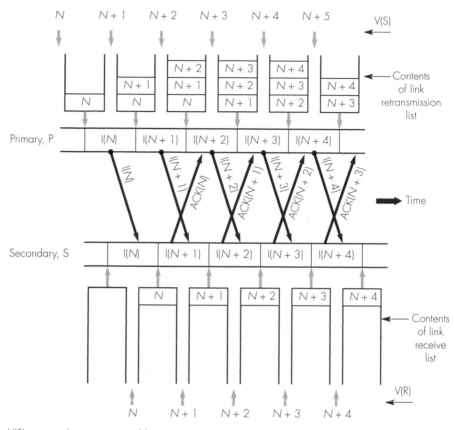

Figure 1.26 Continuous RQ frame sequence without transmission errors.

To implement the scheme, P must retain a send sequence variable V(S), which indicates the send sequence number N(S) to be allocated to the next I-frame to be transmitted. Also, S must maintain a receive sequence variable V(R), which indicates the next in-sequence I-frame it is waiting for.

The frame sequence shown in Figure 1.26 assumes that no transmission errors occur. When an error does occur, one of two retransmission strategies may be followed:

■ S detects and requests the retransmission of just those frames in the sequence that are corrupted – selective repeat.

■ S detects the receipt of an out-of-sequence I-frame and requests P to retransmit all outstanding unacknowledged I-frames from the last correctly received, and hence acknowledged, I-frame – go-back-N.

Note that with both continuous RQ schemes, corrupted frames are discarded and retransmission requests are triggered only after the next error-free frame is received. Hence, as with the idle RQ scheme, a timeout is applied to each frame transmitted to overcome the possibility of a corrupted frame being the last in a sequence of new frames.

Selective repeat

Two example frame sequence diagrams that illustrate the operation of the selective repeat retransmission control scheme are shown in Figure 1.27. The sequence shown in part (a) shows the effect of a corrupted I-frame being received by S. The following points should be noted when interpreting the sequence:

■ An ACK-frame acknowledges all frames in the retransmission list up to and including the I-frame with the sequence number the ACK contains.

■ Assume I-frame $N+1$ is corrupted.

■ S returns an ACK-frame for I-frame N.

■ When S receives I-frame $N+2$ it detects I-frame $N+1$ is missing from V(R) and hence returns a NAK-frame containing the identifier of the missing I-frame $N+1$.

■ On receipt of NAK $N+1$, P interprets this as S is still awaiting I-frame $N+1$ and hence retransmits it.

■ When P retransmits I-frame $N+1$ it enters the **retransmission state**.

■ When P is in the retransmission state, it suspends sending any new frames and sets a timeout for the receipt of ACK $N+1$.

■ If the timeout expires, another copy of I-frame $(N+1)$ is sent.

■ On receipt of ACK $N+1$ P leaves the retransmission state and resumes sending new frames.

■ When S returns a NAK-frame it enters the retransmission state.

■ When S is in the retransmission state, the return of ACK-frames is suspended.

■ On receipt of I-frame $N+1$, S leaves the retransmission state and resumes returning ACK-frames.

■ ACK $N+1$ acknowledges all frames up to and including frame $N+4$.

■ A timer is used with each NAK-frame to ensure that if it is corrupted (and hence NAK $N+1$ is not received), it is retransmitted.

The sequence shown in Figure 1.27(b) shows the effect of a corrupted ACK-frame. The following points should be noted:

■ Assume ACK N is corrupted.

■ On receipt of ACK-frame $N+1$, P detects that I-frame N is still awaiting acknowledgment and hence retransmits it.

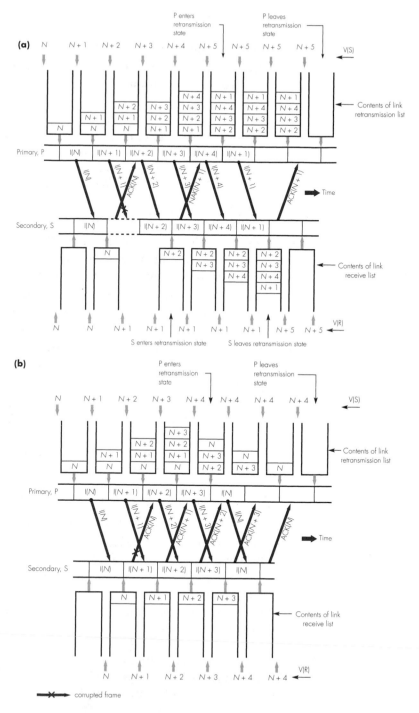

Figure 1.27 Selective repeat: (a) effect of corrupted I-frame; (b) effect of corrupted ACK-frame.

- On receipt of the retransmitted I-frame N, S determines from its received sequence variable that this has already been received correctly and is therefore a duplicate.

- S discards the frame but returns an ACK-frame to ensure P removes the frame from the retransmission list.

Go-back-N

Two example frame sequence diagrams that illustrate the operation of the go-back-N retransmission control scheme are shown in Figure 1.28. The sequence shown in part (a) shows the effect of a corrupted I-frame being received by S. The following points should be noted:

- Assume I-frame $N+1$ is corrupted.

- S receives I-frame $N+2$ out of sequence.

- On receipt of I-frame $N+2$, S returns NAK $N+1$ informing P to go back and start to retransmit from I-frame $N+1$.

- On receipt of NAK $N+1$, P enters the retransmission state. When in this state, it suspends sending new frames and commences to retransmit the frames waiting acknowledgment in the retransmission list.

- S discards frames until it receives I-frame $N+1$.

- On receipt of I-frame $N+1$, S resumes accepting frames and returning acknowledgments.

- A timeout is applied to NAK-frames by S and a second NAK is returned if the correct in-sequence I-frame is not received in the timeout interval.

The frame sequence shown in Figure 1.28(b) shows the effect of a corrupted ACK-frame. Note that:

- S receives each transmitted I-frame correctly.

- Assume ACK-frames N and $N+1$ are both corrupted.

- On receipt of ACK-frame $N+2$, P detects that there are two outstanding I-frames in the retransmission list (N and $N+1$).

- Since it is an ACK-frame rather than a NAK-frame, P assumes that the two ACK-frames for I-frames N and $N+1$ have both been corrupted and hence accepts ACK-frame $N+2$ as an acknowledgment for the outstanding frames.

In order to discriminate between the NAK-frames used in the two schemes, in the selective repeat scheme a NAK is known as a **selective reject** and in the go-back-N scheme a **reject**.

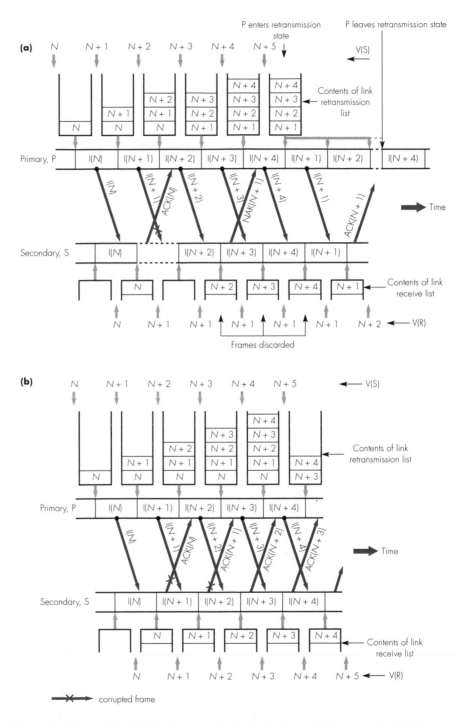

**Figure 1.28 Go-back-N retransmission strategy: (a) corrupted I-frame;
(b) corrupted ACK-frame.**

1.4.4 Flow control

Error control is only one component of a data link protocol. Another important and related component is flow control. As the name implies, it is concerned with controlling the rate of transmission of frames on a link so that the receiver always has sufficient buffer storage resources to accept them prior to processing.

To control the flow of frames across a link, a mechanism known as a **sliding window** is used. The approach is similar to the idle RQ control scheme in that it essentially sets a limit on the number of I-frames that P may send before receiving an acknowledgment. P monitors the number of outstanding (unacknowledged) I-frames currently held in the retransmission list. If the destination side of the link is unable to pass on the frames sent to it, S stops returning acknowledgment frames, the retransmission list at P builds up and this in turn can be interpreted as a signal for P to stop transmitting further frames until acknowledgments start to flow again.

To implement this scheme, a maximum limit is set on the number of I-frames that can be awaiting acknowledgment and hence are outstanding in the retransmission list. This limit is the **send window**, K for the link. If this is set to 1, the retransmission control scheme reverts to idle RQ with a consequent drop in transmission efficiency. The limit is normally selected so that, providing the destination is able to pass on or absorb all frames it receives, the send window does not impair the flow of I-frames across the link. Factors such as the maximum frame size, available buffer storage, link propagation delay, and transmission bit rate must all be considered when selecting the send window.

The operation of the scheme is shown in Figure 1.29. As each I-frame is transmitted, the **upper window edge** (**UWE**) is incremented by unity. Similarly, as each I-frame is acknowledged, the **lower window edge** (**LWE**) is incremented by unity. The acceptance of any new message blocks, and hence the flow of I-frames, is stopped if the difference between UWE and LWE becomes equal to the send window K. Assuming error-free transmission, K is a fixed window that moves (slides) over the complete set of frames being transmitted. The technique is thus known as "sliding window".

The maximum number of frame buffers required at S is known as the **receive window**. We can deduce from the earlier frame sequence diagrams that with the idle RQ and go-back-N schemes only one buffer is required. With selective repeat, however, K frames are required to ensure frames are delivered in the correct sequence.

1.4.5 Sequence numbers

Until now, we have assumed that the sequence number inserted into each frame by P is simply the previous sequence number plus one and that the range of numbers available is infinite. Defining a maximum limit on the number of I-frames being transferred across a link not only limits the size of the link retransmission and receive lists, but also makes it possible to limit the

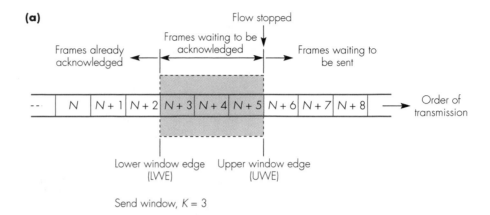

Figure 1.29 Flow control principle: (a) sliding window example; (b) send and receive window limits.

range of sequence numbers required to identify each transmitted frame uniquely. The number of identifiers is a function of both the retransmission control scheme and the size of the send and receive windows.

For example, with an idle RQ control scheme, the send and receive windows are both 1 and hence only two identifiers are required to allow S to determine whether a particular I-frame received is a new frame or a duplicate. Typically, the two identifiers are 0 and 1; the send sequence variable is incremented modulo 2 by P.

With a go-back-N control scheme and a send window of K, the number of identifiers must be at least $K+1$. We can deduce this by considering the case when P sends a full window of K frames but all the ACK-frames relating to them are corrupted. If only K identifiers were used, S would not be able to determine whether the next frame received is a new frame – as it expects – or a duplicate of a previous frame.

With a selective repeat scheme and a send and receive window of K, the number of identifiers must not be less than $2K$. Again, we can deduce this by considering the case when P sends a full window of K frames and all subsequent acknowledgments are corrupted. S must be able to determine whether any of the next K frames are new frames. The only way of ensuring that S can deduce this is to assign a completely new set of K identifiers to the next window of I-frames transmitted, which requires at least $2K$ identifiers. The limits for each scheme are summarized in Figure 1.30(a).

(a)

Protocol	Maximum number of frame identifiers
Idle RQ	2
Selective repeat	$2K + 1$
Go-back-N	$K + 1$

(b)

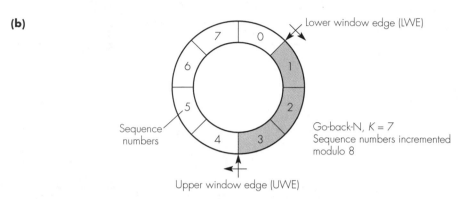

Figure 1.30 Sequence numbers: (a) maximum number for each protocol; (b) example assuming eight sequence numbers.

In practice, since the identifier of a frame is in binary form, a set number of binary digits must be reserved for its use. For example, with a send window of, say, 7 and a go-back-N control scheme, three binary digits are required for the send and receive sequence numbers yielding eight possible identifiers: 0 through 7. The send and receive sequence variables are then incremented modulo 8 by P and S respectively. This is illustrated in Figure 1.30(b).

1.4.6 Layered architecture

The frame sequence diagrams that we showed earlier provide a qualitative description of the error control (and flow control) components of a link layer protocol that is based on an idle RQ scheme – Figure 1.23 – and a continuous RQ scheme – Figures 1.26–1.28. In practice, however, it is not possible to describe fully the operation of all aspects of a protocol using just this method. Normally, therefore, the operation of a protocol is specified in a more formal way and, in order to gain an insight into how this is done, we shall specify the error control component of the idle RQ error control scheme.

Before we do this, we revisit the subject of layering, which involves decoupling each protocol layer one from another and defining a formal interface between them. Assuming an idle RQ scheme, a suitable layered architecture for the link layer is as shown in Figure 1.31. As we have described, the service provided to the network layer in the source is to transfer in a reliable way a series of blocks of information to the network layer in the destination. Also, depending on the BER probability of the line, a maximum block size will be specified that ensures a good percentage of I-frames transmitted will be free of errors.

As we show in Figure 1.31, in order to decouple the network and link layers in each system, we introduce a queue between them. Each queue is simply a data structure that implements a first-in, first-out (FIFO) queuing discipline. Elements are added to the tail of the queue and are removed from the head.

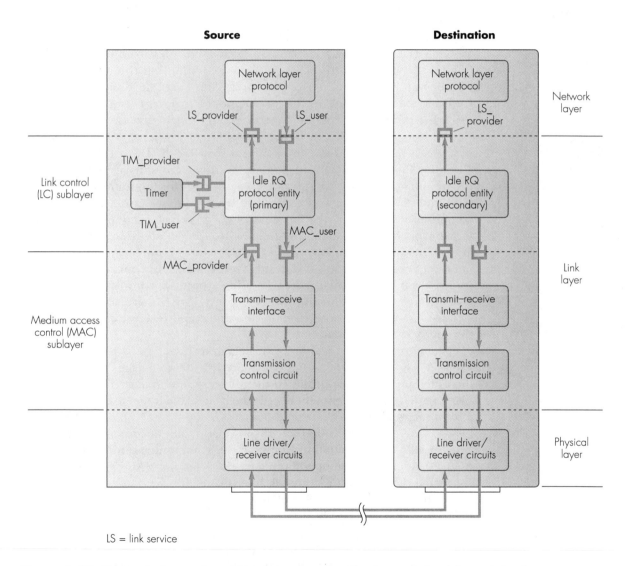

LS = link service

Figure 1.31 Example layered architecture showing the layer and sublayer interfaces associated with the idle RQ protocol.

Normally, the user service primitive(s) associated with a layer is/are passed between layers using a data structure known as an **event control block** (**ECB**). This has the primitive type in the first field and an array containing the user data in a second field. For example, whenever the network layer protocol wishes to send a message block – the contents of a data structure – it first obtains a free ECB, sets the primitive type field to L_DATA.request, writes the address pointer of the data structure in the user data field, and inserts the ECB at the tail of the link layer (LS_user) input queue ready for reading by the idle RQ primary.

When the idle RQ protocol software is next run, it detects the presence of an entry (ECB) in the LS_user queue, reads the entry from the head of the queue, and proceeds to create an I-frame containing the send sequence number and the contents of the user data field. It then initiates the transmission of the frame to the secondary protocol using the services provided by the transmission control circuit. Normally, as we show in the figure, associated with the latter is a piece of low-level software that, in practice, is part of the **basic input-output software** (**BIOS**) of the computer. Assuming bit-oriented transmission, as the frame contents are being output, the transmission control circuit generates the CRC for the frame and adds the start and end flags. As we can deduce from this, therefore, the link layer comprises two sublayers: the **link control** (**LC**) – which is concerned with the implementation of the error and flow control procedures that are being used and is independent of the type of transmission control mode – and the **medium access control** (**MAC**) **sublayer** – which is concerned with the transmission of preformatted blocks using a particular transmission control mode which may vary for different networks. The physical layer comprises suitable bit/clock encoding circuits, line driver and receiver circuits, and the plug and socket pin definitions.

At the destination, assuming the received frame is error free, the MAC sublayer passes the frame contents to the LC sublayer using a MAC_DATA. indication primitive in an ECB and the MAC_provider queue. The LC sublayer then uses the send sequence number at the head of the frame to confirm it is not a duplicate and passes the frame contents – the message block – up to the network layer in an ECB using the LS_provider output queue with the primitive type set to L_DATA.indication. It then creates and returns an ACK-frame to P using a MAC_DATA.request primitive in an ECB and the MAC_user queue.

When the destination network layer protocol is next run, it detects and reads the ECB from the LS_provider queue and proceeds to process the contents of the message block it contains according to the defined network layer protocol. At the sending side, assuming the ACK-frame is received free of errors, the MAC sublayer passes the frame to the LC sublayer primary, which frees the memory buffer containing the acknowledged I-frame and checks the LS_user input queue for another waiting ECB. If there is one, the procedure is repeated until all queued blocks have been transferred. Note that the LS_user queue and the retransmission list are quite separate. The first is used to hold new message blocks waiting to be transmitted and the second to hold frames – containing blocks – that have already been sent and are waiting to be acknowledged.

We can conclude that the adoption of a layered architecture means that each layer performs its own well-defined function in relation to the overall communications task. Each layer provides a defined service to the layer immediately above it. The service primitives associated with the service are each implemented by the layer protocol communicating with a peer layer protocol in the remote system. Associated with the protocol are protocol data units (PDUs) – for example, I-frame, ACK-frame, and so on in the case of the link layer – and these are physically transferred using the services provided by the layer immediately below it.

1.4.7 Protocol specification

Irrespective of the specification method that is used, we model a protocol as a **finite state machine** or **automaton**. This means that the protocol – or, more accurately, the **protocol entity** – can be in just one of a finite number of defined **states** at any instant. For example, it might be idle waiting for a message to send, or waiting to receive an acknowledgment. Transitions between states take place as a result of an incoming event, for example, a message becomes ready to send, or an ACK-frame is received. As a result of an incoming event, an associated **outgoing event** is normally generated, for example, on receipt of a message, format and send the created I-frame on the link, or on receipt of a NAK-frame, retransmit the waiting I-frame.

Some incoming events may lead to a number of possible outgoing events. The particular outgoing event selected is determined by the computed state of one or more **predicates** (boolean variables). As an example, predicate P1 may be true if the N(R) in a received ACK-frame is the same as the N(S) in the I-frame waiting to be acknowledged. Hence, if P1 is true, then free the memory buffer in which the I-frame is being held; if it is false, initiate retransmission of the frame.

An incoming event, in addition to generating an outgoing event (and possibly a change of state), may also have one or more associated **local** or **specific actions**. Examples include *start a timer* and *increment the send sequence variable.*

We shall now expand upon all of these aspects of the specification of a protocol by considering the specification of the error control procedure associated with the idle RQ protocol. To simplify the description, we shall consider only a unidirectional flow of I-frames – from the source to the destination. In most applications, however, a two-way flow is needed and both sides require a primary and a secondary.

All finite state machines – and hence protocol entities – operate in an atomic way. This means that once an incoming event has started to be processed, all processing functions associated with the event, including the generation of any outgoing event(s), local (specific) actions, and a possible change in state, are carried out in their entirety (that is, in an indivisible way) before another incoming event is accepted.

To ensure this happens, the various incoming (and outgoing) event interfaces are decoupled from the protocol entity itself by means of queues. As we showed earlier in Figure 1.31, there is an additional pair of queues between the protocol entity and the transmit–receive procedure that controls the particular transmission control circuit being used. Similarly, there is a pair of queues between the protocol entity and the timer procedure. Normally, the latter is run at regular (tick) intervals by means of an **interrupt** and, if a timer is currently running, its current value is decremented by the tick value. If the value goes to zero, a **timer expired** message is returned to the protocol entity via the appropriate queue.

The role of the transmit–receive procedure is simply to transmit a preformatted frame passed to it or to receive a frame from the link and queue the frame for processing by the protocol entity. This procedure may also be run as a result of an interrupt, but this time from the transmission control circuit. Also, although in principle only a single input and output queue is necessary to interface the primary and secondary to their respective network layers, in practice a pair of queues is necessary at each interface in order to handle the duplex flows of primitives.

To simplify the specification procedure, we give each of the various incoming events, outgoing events, predicates, specific actions, and states associated with each protocol entity an abbreviated name. Prior to specifying the protocol, the various abbreviated names are listed and all subsequent references are made using these names. For the error control component of the idle RQ protocol, the list of abbreviated names for the primary is as shown in Figure 1.32.

Since each protocol entity is essentially a sequential system, we must retain information that may vary as different incoming events are received. This information is held in a number of **state variables**. Examples, for the primary, are the send sequence variable $V(S)$ – Vs in the specification – which holds the sequence number to be allocated to the next I-frame to be transmitted; the PresentState variable, which holds the present state of the protocol entity; and RetxCount, which is a count of the number of erroneous frames received. Typically, if either RetxCount or ErrorCount reaches its maximum limit then the frame is discarded, an error message is sent to the network layer above and the protocol (entity) reinitializes.

The three most common methods that are used for specifying a communication protocol are **state transition diagrams**, **extended event–state tables**, and high-level structured programs. In many instances, we define a protocol as a combination of these coupled with time sequence diagrams to illustrate the user service primitives associated with the protocol.

The formal specification of the primary is shown in Figure 1.33. In part (a) a state transition diagram is used, in part (b) an extended event–state table, and in part (c) structured pseudocode.

Incoming events

Name	Interface	Meaning
LDATAreq	LS_user	L_DATA.request service primitive received
ACKRCVD	MAC_provider	ACK-frame received from S
TEXP	TIM_provider	Wait-ACK timer expires
NAKRCVD	MAC_provider	NAK-frame received from S

States

Name	Meaning
IDLE	Idle, no message transfer in progress
WTACK	Waiting an acknowledgment

Outgoing events

Name	Interface	Meaning
TxFrame	MAC_user	Format and transmit an I-frame
RetxFrame	MAC_user	Retransmit I-frame waiting acknowledgment
LERRORind	LS_provider	Error message: frame discarded for reason specified

Predicates

Name	Meaning
P0	N(S) in waiting I-frame = N(R) in ACK-frame
P1	CRC in ACK/NAK-frame correct

Specific actions

[1] = Start_timer using TIM_user queue
[2] = Increment Vs
[3] = Stop_timer using TIM_user queue
[4] = Increment RetxCount
[5] = Increment ErrorCount
[6] = Reset RetxCount to zero

State variables

Vs	= Send sequence variable
PresentState	= Present state of protocol entity
ErrorCount	= Number of erroneous frames received
RetxCount	= Number of retransmissions for this frame

Figure 1.32 Abbreviated names used in the specification of the idle RQ primary.

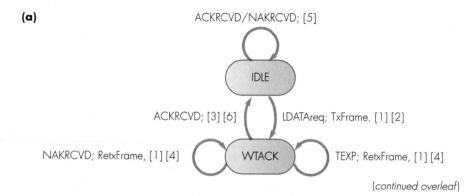

(continued overleaf)

Figure 1.33 Specification of idle RQ primary in the form of: (a) a state transition diagram; (b) an extended event–state table; (c) pseudocode.

(b)

Incoming event / Present state	LDATAreq	ACKRCVD	TEXP	NAKRCVD
IDLE	1	0	0	0
WTACK	4	2	3	3

0 = [5], IDLE (error condition)
1 = TxFrame, [1] [2], WTACK
2 = P0 and P1: [3] [6], IDLE
    P0 and NOT P1: RetxFrame, [1] [4], WTACK
    NOT P0 and NOT P1: [5], IDLE
3 = RetxFrame, [1] [4], WTACK
4 = NoAction, WTACK

(c)
```
program IdleRQ_Primary;
const    MaxErrCount;
         MaxRetxCount;
type     Events = (LDATAreq, ACKRCVD, TEXP, NAKRCVD);
         States = (IDLE, WTACK);
var      EventStateTable = array [Events, States] of 0..4;
         PresentState : States;
         Vs, ErrorCount, RetxCount : integer;
         EventType : Events;
procedure          Initialize;      }      Initializes state variables and contents of EventStateTable
procedure          TxFrame;
procedure          RetxFrame;       }      Outgoing event procedures
procedure          LERRORind;
procedure          Start_timer;     }      Specific action procedures
procedure          Stop_timer;
function  P0 : boolean;  } Predicate functions
function  P1 : boolean;

begin    Initialize;
         repeat   Wait receipt of an incoming event
                  EventType := type of event
                  case EventStateTable [EventType, PresentState] of
                  0: begin      ErrorCount := ErrorCount + 1; PresentState = IDLE;
                          if(ErrorCount = MaxErrCount) then LERRORind end;
                  1: begin      TxFrame; Start_timer; Vs := Vs + 1; PresentState := WTACK end;
                  2: begin      if(P0 and P1) then begin Stop_timer; RetxCount := 0; PresentState := IDLE
end;
                          else if (P0 and NOTP1) then begin      RetxFrame; Start_timer;
                                              RetxCount := RetxCount + 1;
                                              PresentState := WTACK end;
                          else if (NOTP0 and NOTP1) then begin PresentState := IDLE; ErrorCount := ErrorCount +
1 end;
                                          if (ErrorCount = MaxErrorCount) then begin LERRORind; Initialize; end;
                                  end;
                  3: begin RetxFrame; Start_timer; RetxCount := RetxCount + 1; PresentState := WTACK;
                          if (RetxCount = MaxRetxCount) then begin LERRORind; Initialize; end;
                          end;
                  4: begin NoAction end;
                  until Forever;
         end.
```

Figure 1.33 Continued.

Using the state transition diagram method, the possible states of the protocol entity are shown in ovals with the particular states written within them. **Directional arrows** (also known as **arcs**) indicate the possible transitions between the states, with the incoming event causing the transition and any resulting outgoing event and specific actions written alongside. If, for example, an L_DATA.request (LDATAreq) is received from LS_user interface, then the frame is formatted and output to the MAC_user interface (TxFrame), a timer is started for the frame [1], the send sequence variable incremented [2], and the WTACK state entered. Similarly, if an ACK-frame is received with an N(R) equal to the N(S) in the waiting frame and the CRC is correct, then the timer is stopped [3] and the transitions can be interpreted in a similar way.

Although state transition diagrams are useful for showing the correct operation of a protocol, because of space limitations it is not always practicable to show all possible incoming event possibilities including error conditions. Hence most state transition diagrams are incomplete specifications. Moreover, with all but the simplest of protocols, we need many such diagrams to define even the correct operation of a protocol. It is for these reasons that we use the extended event–state table and the structured program code methods.

Using the extended event–state table method – as we see in part (b) of the figure – we can show all the possible incoming events and protocol (present) states in the form of a table. For each state, the table entry defines the outgoing event, any specific action(s), and the new state for all possible incoming events. Also, if predicates are involved, it defines the alternative set of action(s). Clearly, the extended event–state table is a far more rigorous method since it allows for all possible incoming-event, present-state combinations. A basic event–state table has only one possible action and next-state for each incoming-event/present-state combination. It is the presence of predicates – and hence possible alternative actions/next states – that gives rise to the use of the term "extended" event–state table.

When we are interpreting the actions to be followed if predicates are involved, we must note that these are shown in order. Hence the action to be followed if the primary is in the WTACK state and an ACK-frame is received (ACKRCVD), is first to determine if P0 and P1 are both true. If they are, then carry out specific action [3] and [6] and enter the IDLE state. Else, determine if {P0 and NOTP1} is true, and so on. If neither condition is true then an error is suspected and the actions are shown.

A feature of the extended event–state table is that it lends itself more readily to implementation in program code than a state transition diagram. We can see this by considering the pseudocode specification of the idle RQ primary in Figure 1.33(c). In the figure this is shown as a program but in practice it is implemented in the form of a procedure or function so it can be included with the other protocol layers in a single program. However, this does not affect the basic operation of the program shown.

When each program (layer) is first run, the Initialize procedure is invoked. This performs such functions as initializing all state variables to their initial values and the contents of the EventStateTable array to those in the extended event–state table. The program then enters an infinite loop waiting for an incoming event to arrive at one of its input queues.

The incoming event that causes the program to run is first assigned to EventType. The current contents of PresentState and EventType are then used as indices to the EventStateTable array to determine the integer – 0, 1, 2, 3, or 4 – that defines the processing actions associated with that event. For example, if the accessed integer is 2, this results in the predicate functions P0 and P1 being invoked and, depending on their computed state (true or false), the invocation of the appropriate outgoing event procedure, coupled with any specific action procedures(s) as defined in the specification; for example, starting or resetting the timer, and updating PresentState.

We have simplified the pseudocode to highlight the structure of each program and hence the implementation methodology. No code is shown for the various outgoing event procedures nor for the predicate functions. In practice, these must be implemented in an unambiguous way using the necessary steps listed in the specification.

1.4.8 User service primitives

As we explained in the last section, to initiate the transfer of a block of information across the transmission line/link, the source network layer uses an ECB with a L_DATA.request primitive and the block of information within it. Similarly, the destination link layer (protocol), on receipt of an error-free I-frame containing the block of information, also uses an ECB to pass the block to the network layer with a L_DATA.indication primitive within it.

Example 1.7	Use the frame sequence diagram shown earlier in Figure 1.23 and the list of abbreviated names given in Figure 1.34(a) to specify the operation of the idle RQ secondary using (i) a state transition diagram, (ii) an extended event–state table, (iii) pseudocode.

Answer:

The specification of the idle RQ secondary in each form is given in Figure 1.34(b), (c), and (d) respectively. Note that just two state variables are needed for the secondary: the receive sequence variable – shown as V_r in the specification – which holds the sequence number of the last correctly received I-frame, and ErrorCount which keeps a record of the number of erroneous I-frames received. Again, if ErrorCount reaches a defined maximum limit an error message – LERRORind – is output to the network layer in an ECB.

(a) **Incoming events**

Name	Interface	Meaning
IRCVD	MAC_provider	I-frame received from P

States

Name	Meaning
WTIFM	Waiting a new I-frame from P

Outgoing events

Name	Interface	Meaning
LDATAind an	LS_provider	Pass contents of received I-frame to user AP with L_DATA.indication primitive
TxACK(X)	MAC_user	Format and transmit an ACK-frame with N(R) = X
TxNAK(X)	MAC_user	Format and transmit a NAK-frame with N(R) = X
LERRORind	LS_provider	Issue error message for reason specified

Predicates

Name	Meaning
P0	N(S) in I-frame = Vr
P1	CRC in I-frame correct
P2	N(S) in I-frame = Vr − 1

Specific actions

[1] = Increment Vr
[2] = Increment ErrorCount

State variables

Vr = Receive sequence variable
ErrorCount = No. of erroneous frames received

(b)

IRCVD⁻; TxNAK (WTIFM) IRCVD⁺; LDATAind, TxACK, [1] [2]

(c)

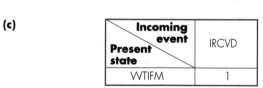

Incoming event / Present state	IRCVD
WTIFM	1

1 = NOT P1: TxNAK, [2]
P1 and P2: TxACK
P0 and P1: LDATAind, TxACK, [1]

(continued overleaf)

Figure 1.34 Specification of idle RQ secondary: (a) abbreviated names; (b) state transition diagram; (c) extended event–state table; (d) pseudocode.

```
(d)    program IdleRQ_Secondary;
       const.    MaxErrorCount;
       type      Events = IRCVD;
                 States = WTIFM;
       var       EventStateTable = array [Events, States] of 1;
                 EventType : Events;
                 PresentState : States;
                 Vr, X, ErrorCount : integer;
       procedure              Initialize;      }         Initializes state variables and contents of EventStateTable
       procedure              LDATAind;
       procedure              TxACK(X);        |
       procedure              TxNAK(X);                   Outgoing event procedures
       procedure              LERRORind;
       function  P0 : boolean;
       function  P1 : boolean;     |           Predicate functions
       function  P2 : boolean;

       begin    Initialize;
                repeat    Wait receipt of incoming event; EventType := type of event;
                          case EventStateTable[EventType, PresentState] of
                          1 : X := N(S) from I-frame;
                              if (NOTP1) then TxNAK(X);
                              else if(P1 and P2) then TxACK(X);
                              else if(P0 and P1) then begin LDATAind; TxACK(X); Vr := Vr + 1; end;
                              else  begin                        ErrorCount := ErrorCount + 1; if (ErrorCount =
       MaxErrorCount) then
                                        begin LERRORind; Initialize; end;
                                  end;
                     until Forever;
       end.
```

Figure 1.34 Continued.

Finally, for the error and flow control schemes we have outlined in the previous sections to function correctly, we have assumed that both communicating link protocols have been initialized so that they are ready to exchange information. For example, both sides of the link must start with the same send and receive sequence variables before any information frames are transmitted. In general, this is known as the initialization or **link setup** phase and, after all data has been exchanged across a link, there is a **link disconnection** phase. Since the link setup and disconnection phases are not concerned with the actual transfer of user data, they are collectively referred to as **link management**. The two link management functions are also initiated by the network layer (protocol) using an ECB and the set of primitives that we show in Figure 1.35(a). Since the primitives shown are in the same sequence as they are issued, this form of representing the various user service primitives associated with a protocol is known as a **time sequence diagram**. Note that to avoid the diagram becoming too cluttered, we have left off the two error indication primitives.

On receipt of an **L_CONNECT.request** primitive, the link protocol entity at the source initializes all state variables and then creates a **link SETUP** frame (known as a **protocol data unit**(PDU)). This is sent to the correspondent (peer) link protocol entity in the destination using the selected transmission mode. On receipt of the SETUP frame, the destination initializes

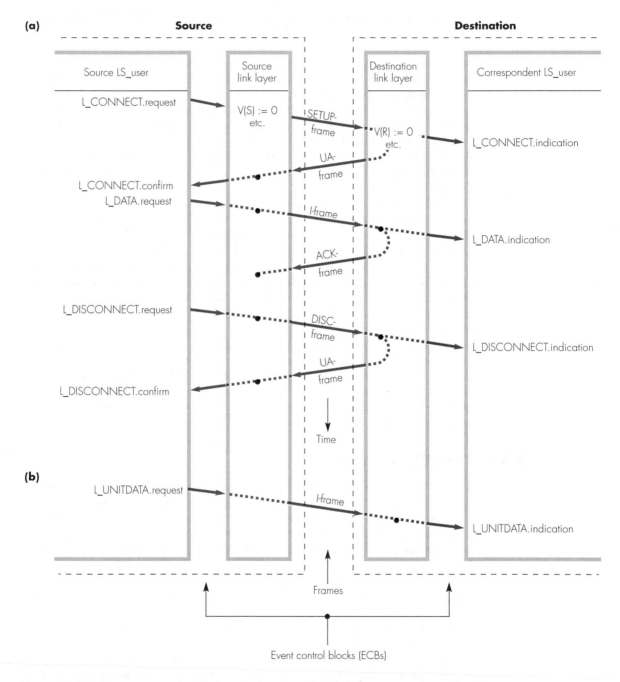

Figure 1.35 Time sequence diagram showing the link layer service primitives: (a) connection-oriented (reliable) mode; (b) connectionless (best-effort) mode.

its own state variables and proceeds by sending an **L_CONNECT.indication** primitive to the correspondent LS_user and an acknowledgment frame back to the source.

Since this acknowledgment does not relate to an I-frame, it does not contain a sequence number. It is known, therefore, as an **unnumbered acknowledgment** or **UA-frame**. On receipt of this UA-frame, the source protocol entity issues the **L_CONNECT.confirm** primitive to the LS_user and the link is now ready for the transfer of data using the L_DATA service. Finally, after all data has been transferred, the setup link is released using the L_DISCONNECT service, which is also a confirmed service. The corresponding frame, known as a **disconnect** or **DISC frame**, is acknowledged using a UA-frame.

This mode of operation of the link layer is known as the connection-oriented mode and, as we have explained, it provides a reliable service. As we indicated at the start of Section 1.4, however, in many applications this mode of operation is not used and instead the simpler best-effort service is used in which the link layer protocol at the destination simply discards any frames received with errors. The two user service primitives associated with this mode are shown in Figure 1.35(b).

Since it is not necessary to set up a logical connection prior to sending blocks of information, this mode of operation is known as the connectionless mode and, in order to discriminate between the data transfer service associated with the two modes, as we show in the figure, the two service primitives used are **L_UNITDATA.request** and **L_UNITDATA.indication**. Also, since in the connectionless mode no retransmissions are used, no sequence numbers are required. Note, however, that the differences between the two modes occur only at the link control layer.

1.4.9 The HDLC protocol

To conclude this section, we describe selected aspects of a practical example of a link layer protocol known as the **high-level data link control** (**HDLC**) protocol. This is an international standard that has been defined for use with a number of different network configurations and types. These include duplex point-to-point links as used over the access circuits associated with an ISDN, and half-duplex multidrop/broadcast links as used in some LANs. Hence there is the original HDLC protocol and a number of variants of it, each of which uses slightly different fields in the frame header and also a different link control layer. Examples include the **link access procedure D-channel** (**LAPD**) which is used with an ISDN and the **logical link control** (**LLC**) which is used with LANs.

In HDLC, the frames sent by the primary to the secondary are known as **commands**, and those from the secondary to the primary as **responses**. Also, when the link control layer is operating in a connection-oriented (reliable) mode, all error and flow control frames are known as **supervisory frames** and the various frames that are used to set up and disconnect a logical link are known as **unnumbered frames**. A standard format is used for all frames, however, and this is shown in Figure 1.36(a).

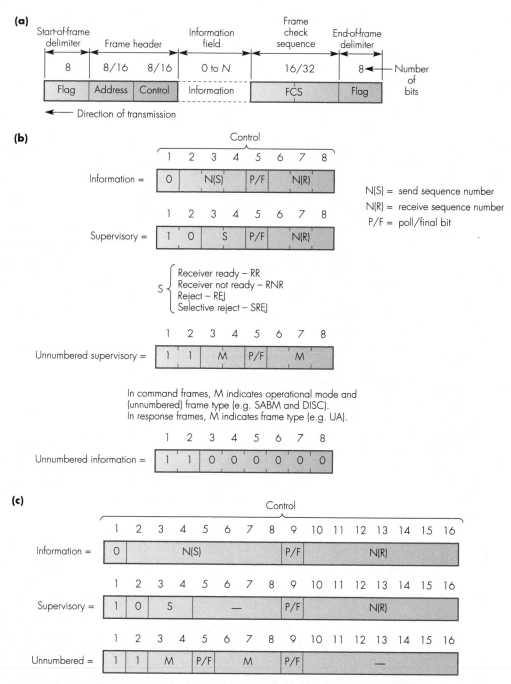

Note: With the indicated direction of transmission, all control field types are transmitted bit 8/16 first.

Figure 1.36 HDLC frame format and types: (a) standard/extended format; (b) standard control field bit definitions; (c) extended control field bit definitions.

As we can see, HDLC is based on a bit-oriented transmission control scheme with flags to indicate the start and end of each frame together with zero bit insertion and deletion to ensure the flag pattern (01111110) does not occur within the bitstream between the flags. The frame check sequence (FCS) is a 16-bit CRC that is computed using the generator polynomial:

$$x^{16} + x^{12} + x^5 + 1$$

The CRC is first generated using the procedure we describe in Appendix B but an additional step is taken to make the check more robust. This involves adding sixteen 1s to the tail of the dividend (instead of zeros) and inverting the remainder. This has the effect that the remainder computed by the receiver is not all zeros but the bit pattern 0001 1101 0000 1111.

The various control field bit definitions are shown in Figure 1.36(b). The S-field in supervisory frames and the M-field in unnumbered frames are used to define the specific frame type. The send and receive sequence numbers – N(S) and N(R) – are used in conjunction with the error and flow control procedures.

The **P/F bit** is known as the **poll/final bit**. A frame of any type is called a **command frame** if it is sent by the primary station and a **response frame** if it is sent by a secondary station. The P/F bit is called the poll bit when used in a command frame and, if set, indicates that the receiver must acknowledge this frame. The receiver acknowledges this frame by returning an appropriate response frame with the P/F bit set; it is then known as the final bit.

The use of three bits for each of N(S) and N(R) means that sequence numbers can range from 0 through 7. This, in turn, means that a maximum send window of 7 can be selected. Although this is large enough for many applications, those involving very long links (satellite links, for example) or very high bit rates require a larger send window if a high link utilization is to be achieved. The extended format uses seven bits (0 through 127), thereby increasing the maximum send window to 127. This is shown in Figure 1.36(c).

The address field identifies the secondary station that sent the frame, and is not needed with point-to-point links. However, with multipoint links, the address field can be either eight bits – normal mode – or multiples of eight bits – extended mode. In the latter case, bit 1 of the least significant address octet(s) is/are set to 0 and bit 1 in the last octet is set to 1. The remaining bits form the address. In both modes, an address of all 1s is used as an all-stations broadcast address.

Unnumbered frames are used both to set up a logical link between the primary and secondary and to inform the secondary of the mode of operation to be used. For example, the set asynchronous balanced mode (SABM) command frame – indicated by the M-bits in the control field – is used to set up a logical link in both directions when a duplex point-to-point link is being used. Other examples are the DISC-frame (which is used to disconnect the link) and the UA-frame, which is a response frame and is sent to acknowledge receipt of the other (command) frames in this class. Also, when operating in the connectionless (best-effort) mode, no acknowledgment information is required. Hence all information is transmitted in **unnumbered information** (**UI**) frames with the control field set to 11000000.

The four supervisory frames are used to implement a continuous RQ error control scheme and have the following functions:

- receiver ready (RR): this has the same function as the ACK-frame in Figures 1.27 and 1.28;

- reject (REJ): this has the same function as the NAK-frame in the go-back-N scheme;

- selective reject (SREJ): this has the same function as the NAK-frame in the selective repeat scheme;

- receiver not ready (RNR): this can be used by the secondary to ask the primary to suspend sending any new I-frames.

Each RR (ACK) frame contains a receive sequence number – $N(R)$ – which acknowledges correct receipt of all I-frames awaiting acknowledgment up to and including that with an $N(S)$ equal to $N(R) - 1$. This is slightly different from what we used earlier in the frame sequence diagrams in Figures 1.27 and 1.28 in which $N(R)$ acknowledged I-frames up to $N(S)$. This is because in HDLC the receive sequence variable $V(R)$ is incremented before the ACK-frame is returned rather than after as we used in the earlier figures.

A summary of the various service primitives and frame types (protocol data units) associated with HDLC is given in Figure 1.37(a). In practice, there are more unnumbered frames associated with HDLC than are shown in the figure but, as mentioned earlier, the aim is simply to highlight selected aspects of HDLC operation. To reinforce understanding further, a (simplified) state transition diagram for HDLC is given in Figure 1.37(b). The first entry alongside each arc is the incoming event causing the transition (if any); the second entry is the resulting action. Note that a state transition diagram shows only the correct operation of the protocol entity; normally it is accompanied by a more complete definition in the form of an extended event–state table and/or pseudocode.

(a)

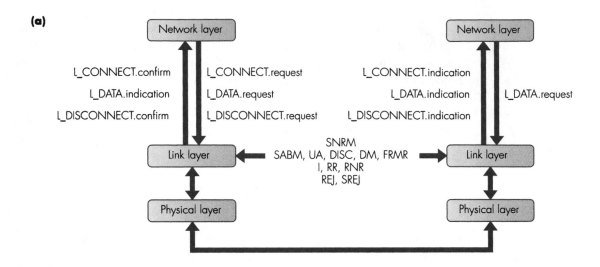

(b)

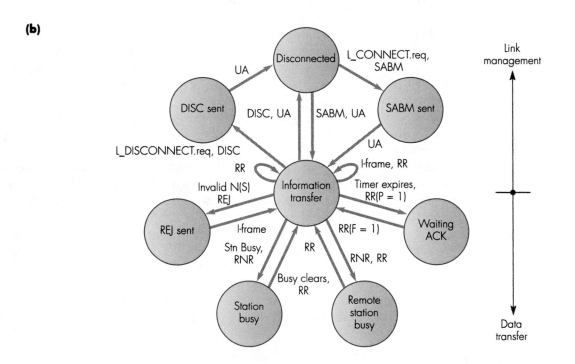

Figure 1.37 HDLC summary: (a) service primitives; (b) state transition diagram (ABM).

1.5 Protocol stacks

As we showed in Figure 1.37 of the previous section, the HDLC link layer protocol built on the underlying data transmission services of the physical layer to provide either a reliable or a best-effort service to transfer frames containing user data over a data link. The figure also showed how the HDLC protocol provided these services through a set of user service primitives. As we can deduce from this, therefore, the link layer protocol offers a defined set of user service primitives – part (a) – and implements these services by exchanging a sequence of frame types – called **protocol data units (PDUs)** – with the same link layer protocol in a remote system using the services provided by the underlying physical layer. Also, both the type and sequence of the PDUs that are exchanged are determined by the link layer protocol – part (b). This general arrangement is known as **layering** and is shown in diagrammatic form in Figure 1.38(a).

As we shall see, there are a number of protocol layers involved in data transfers over the Internet. Each layer performs a well-defined function in the context of the overall communication subsystem. The protocol used at each layer is chosen to meet the needs of a particular application/network combination. The two peer communicating protocol entities within each layer operate according to the specified protocol to implement the required function of the layer. This is achieved by adding appropriate **protocol control information (PCI)** to the head of the data being transferred. In the case of the HDLC protocol, for example, the PCI includes send and receive sequence numbers. The complete PDU is then transferred to the peer protocol entity in the remote system using the services provided by the layer below. The latter simply treats the PDU as user data, adds its own PCI to this to create a new PDU and proceeds to transfer the new PDU to the same peer layer in the remote system again using the services provided by the layer below.

1.5.1 The Internet protocol stack

As its name implies, the link layer protocol is concerned only with the transfer of user data – a PDU of the layer protocol immediately above it in practice – over a point-to-point physical link. Hence when communicating over a network, this is the physical link that connects the source end system/station to the nearest access point of the network; for example, an access gateway in the case of the Internet. A separate instance of the protocol is then needed to transfer the PDU over each physical link connecting the switches/routers that make up the network and also over the link connecting the remote access gateway to the destination end system/station. As we can deduce from

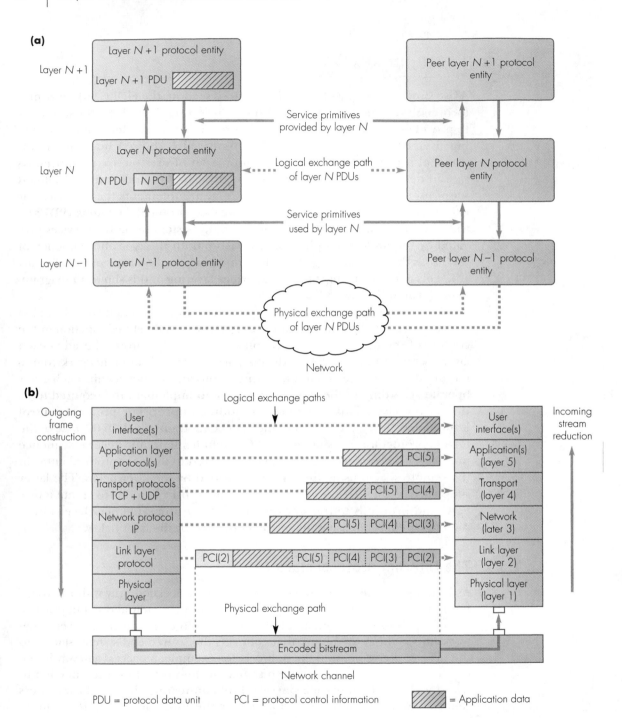

(a)

Layer N +1 — Layer N +1 protocol entity / Layer N +1 PDU

Service primitives provided by layer N

Layer N — Layer N protocol entity / N PDU / N PCI

Logical exchange path of layer N PDUs

Peer layer N protocol entity

Service primitives used by layer N

Layer N −1 — Layer N −1 protocol entity

Peer layer N −1 protocol entity

Physical exchange path of layer N PDUs

Network

(b)

Outgoing frame construction

Logical exchange paths

Incoming stream reduction

User interface(s)

Application layer protocol(s)

Transport protocols TCP + UDP

Network protocol IP

Link layer protocol

Physical layer

User interface(s)

Application(s) (layer 5)

Transport (layer 4)

Network (later 3)

Link layer (layer 2)

Physical layer (layer 1)

PCI(5)

PCI(5) PCI(4)

PCI(5) PCI(4) PCI(3)

PCI(2) PCI(5) PCI(4) PCI(3) PCI(2)

Physical exchange path

Encoded bitstream

Network channel

PDU = protocol data unit   PCI = protocol control information   = Application data

Figure 1.38 Protocol stacks: (a) layer interactions and terminology; (b) the Internet protocol stack.

this, therefore, an additional protocol is needed to route the PDU over the total network. This is the role of the **network layer** and, in the case of the Internet, the protocol is called the **Internet protocol (IP)**.

The IP provides a connectionless best-effort service that involves the formatting of the PDU to be transferred into **packets**, each of which has the unique network-wide address of both the source and destination end systems in the header of each packet/PDU. As with the link and physical layers below it, the network protocol – IP – is not concerned with the content of the packet being transferred but simply with how the total packet – header/PCI plus the PDU/data being transferred – is routed over the total network.

As we indicated in the introduction to this chapter, the Internet supports a wide range of applications. These include e-mail, Web access, telephony and so on. E-mail and Web access require a reliable connection-oriented service while for telephony a best-effort service is more appropriate. Clearly, therefore, since the IP only provides a best-effort service, an additional protocol/layer is needed to support both types of application. This is the role of the **transport layer**, which provides applications with a network-independent data interchange service.

To support both service types, there are two transport protocols in the transport layer: the **transmission control protocol (TCP)**, which provides a reliable service, and the **user datagram protocol (UDP)**, which provides a best-effort service. The PDUs relating to both protocols are all transferred over the network/Internet using the IP network layer protocol. In addition, since there are multiple applications, the transport layer is also responsible for directing the flow of application PDUs to the related application in the **application layer**.

The application layer provides the user, through a suitable interface, with access to the range of Internet applications. Associated with each application is a specific **application protocol** that provides the user with the corresponding service. The complete set of protocols is then called the **protocol stack** of the Internet or, more usually, the **TCP/IP protocol stack**. This is shown in diagrammatic form in Figure 1.38(b). As you can deduce from this, the name is derived from the two protocols that form the core of the Internet protocol stack.

Summary

A summary of the topics discussed in this chapter is given in Figure 1.39.

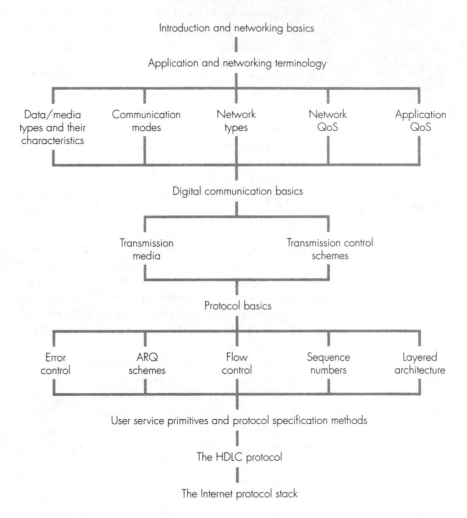

Figure 1.39 Introduction and networking basics summary.

Exercises

Section 1.2

1.1 State the basic form of representation of:
   (i)   text,
   (ii) an image,
   (iii) audio,
   (iv) video.
   State the form of representation that is used when all are integrated together and give your reason.

1.2 State the meaning of the term "bits per second" in relation to digitized audio and video.

1.3 What is the meaning of the term "compression" and why is compression used?

1.4 Describe the meaning of the following terms relating to the different types of data used in data communications:
   (i)   block-mode,
   (ii) continuous,
   (iii) streaming,
   (iv) constant bit rate,
   (v)   variable bit rate.

1.5 With the aid of diagrams, explain the meaning of the following operational modes of a communication channel:
   (i)   simplex,
   (ii) half-duplex,
   (iii) duplex,
   (iv) broadcast,
   (v)   multicast,
   (vi) asymmetric and symmetric.

1.6 With the aid of a diagram explain the principle of operation of a circuit-mode network. Include in your explanation the need for signaling (messages) and the overheads of the connection setup delay associated with this.

1.7 With the aid of diagrams, explain the principle of operation of a connection-oriented packet-mode network. Include in your explanation the need for a virtual connection/circuit, a virtual circuit identifier, and a routing table.

1.8 In relation to a connectionless packet-mode network, explain the meaning of the following terms:
   (i)   best-effort service,
   (ii) store-and-forward delay,
   (iii) mean packet transfer delay,
   (iv) jitter.

1.9 Identify and explain the meaning of the key QoS parameters associated with the following network types:
   (i)   circuit-switched,
   (ii) packet-switched.

1.10 Define the BER probability of a transmission line/channel. How does this influence the maximum block size to be used with the line/channel?

1.11 Define the transmission delay of a transmission line/channel. First identify the individual sources of delay that contribute to this.

1.12 Identify and explain the meaning of the key parameters associated with application QoS.

1.13 With the aid of a diagram, explain the meaning of the following terms relating to packet-switched networks:
   (i)   packetization delay,
   (ii) mean packet transfer delay,
   (iii) jitter.

   Hence describe how the effects on a constant bit rate stream of packetization delay and jitter can be overcome by buffering.

1.14 A Web page of 10 Mbytes is being retrieved from a Web server. Assuming negligible delays within the server and transmission network, quantify the time to transfer the page over the following types of access circuit:
   (i)   a PSTN modem operating at 56 kbps,
   (ii) an aggregated ISDN basic rate access line of 128 kbps,
   (iii) a primary rate ISDN access line of 1.5 Mbps,

(iv) a high-speed modem operating at 1.5 Mbps,
(v) a cable modem operating at 27 Mbps.

1.15 Discuss the term "application service classes". Include in your discussion how packets belonging to different classes are treated within the network.

Section 1.3

1.16 With the aid of the diagrams shown in Figure 1.8(a) and (b), explain the basic principles of the following transmission modes:
(i) baseband,
(ii) modulated.

1.17 With the aid of the waveform set shown in Figure 1.9, explain why the receiver samples the incoming signal as near to the center of each bit cell period as possible and, in some instances, bit errors occur.

Section 1.3.1

1.18 Explain why twisted-pair cable is preferred to non-twisted-pair cable. What are the added benefits of using shielded twisted-pair cable?

1.19 With the aid of diagrams, explain the differences between the following transmission modes used with optical fiber:
(i) multimode stepped index,
(ii) multimode graded index,
(iii) monomode,
(iv) wave-division multiplexing.

1.20 State the meaning of the following relating to satellite systems:
(i) microwave beam,
(ii) transponder,
(iii) geostationary.

1.21 With the aid of diagrams, explain the operation of a satellite system that is used in
(i) TV broadcast applications, and
(ii) data communication applications.

1.22 The maximum distance between two terrestrial microwave dishes, d, is given by the expression:

$$d = 7.14 \sqrt{Kh}$$

where h is the height of the dishes above ground and K is a factor that allows for the curvature of the earth. Assuming $K = 4/3$, determine d for selected values of h.

1.23 Explain the terms "signal propagation delay" and "transmission delay". Assuming the velocity of propagation of an electrical signal is equal to the speed of light, determine the ratio of the signal propagation delay to the transmission delay, a, for the following types of data link and 1000 bits of data:
(i) 100 m of UTP wire and a transmission rate of 1 Mbps,
(ii) 2.5 km of coaxial cable and a transmission rate of 10 Mbps,
(iii) a satellite link and a transmission rate of 512 kbps.

1.24 With the aid of sketches, explain the effect on a transmitted binary signal of the following:
(i) attenuation,
(ii) limited bandwidth,
(iii) delay distortion,
(iv) line and system noise.

1.25 With the aid of a diagram and associated waveform set, explain the meaning of the term "adaptive NEXT canceler" and how such circuits can improve the data transmission rate of a line.

Section 1.3.2

1.26 Explain the difference between asynchronous and synchronous transmission.
Assuming asynchronous transmission, one start bit, two stop bits, one parity bit, and two bits per signaling element, derive the useful information transfer rate in bps for each of the following signaling (baud) rates:
(i) 300,
(ii) 600,
(iii) 1200,
(iv) 4800.

1.27 With the aid of a diagram, explain the clock (bit) and character synchronization methods used with an asynchronous transmission control scheme. Use for example purposes a receiver clock rate ratio of ×1 and ×4 of the transmitter clock.

1.28 With the aid of the diagrams shown in Figure 1.17, explain how frame synchronization is achieved with an asynchronous transmission control scheme, assuming the data being transmitted is
(i) printable characters,
(ii) binary bytes.

1.29 With the aid of the diagrams shown in Figure 1.18 relating to bit/clock synchronization with synchronous transmission, explain how synchronization is achieved using
(i) clock encoding,
(ii) DPLL.

1.30 With the aid of the waveform sets shown in Figure 1.19, explain
(i) the Manchester and
(ii) the differential Manchester clock encoding methods.
Why do both methods yield balanced codes?

1.31 (i) Explain under what circumstances data encoding and a DPLL circuit may be used to achieve clock synchronization. Also, with the aid of a diagram, explain the operation of the DPLL circuit.
(ii) Assuming the receiver is initially out of synchronization, derive the minimum number of bit transitions required for a DPLL circuit to converge to the nominal bit center of a transmitted waveform. How may this be achieved in practice?

1.32 Assuming a synchronous transmission control scheme, explain how character and frame synchronization are achieved:
(i) with character-oriented transmission,
(ii) with bit-oriented transmission.

1.33 Explain what is meant by the term "data transparency" and how it may be achieved using:
(i) character stuffing,
(ii) zero bit insertion.

Section 1.4

1.34 With the aid of frame sequence diagrams and assuming an idle RQ error control procedure with explicit retransmission, describe the following:
(i) the factors influencing the minimum time delay between the transmission of two consecutive information frames,
(ii) how the loss of a corrupted information frame is overcome,
(iii) how the loss of a corrupted acknowledgment frame is overcome.

1.35 A series of information frames with a mean length of 100 bits is to be transmitted across the following data links using an idle RQ protocol. If the velocity of propagation of the links is $2 \times 10^8 \text{ m s}^{-1}$, determine the link efficiency (utilization) for each type of link:
(i) a 10 km link with a BER of 10^{-4} and a data transmission rate of 9600 bps,
(ii) a 500 m link with a BER of 10^{-6} and a data transmission rate of 10 Mbps.

1.36 With the aid of frame sequence diagrams, describe the difference between an idle RQ and a continuous RQ error control procedure. For clarity, assume that no frames are corrupted during transmission.

1.37 With the aid of frame sequence diagrams, describe how the following are overcome with a selective repeat error control scheme:
(i) a corrupted information frame,
(ii) a corrupted ACK frame.

1.38 Repeat Exercise 1.37 for a go-back-N scheme.

1.39 Discriminate between the send window and receive window for a link and how they are related with:
(i) a selective repeat retransmission scheme,
(ii) a go-back-N control scheme.

1.40 With the aid of frame sequence diagrams, illustrate the effect of a send window flow control limit being reached. Assume a send window of 2 and a go-back-N error control procedure.

1.41 Assuming a send window of K, deduce the minimum range of sequence numbers (frame

identifiers) required with each of the following error control schemes:
(i)   idle RQ,
(ii) selective repeat,
(iii) go-back-N.

Clearly identify the condition when the maximum number of identifiers is in use.

1.42 With the aid of Figure 1.31, explain the meaning of the following terms:
(i)   layered architecture,
(ii) interlayer queues,
(iii) local event,
(iv) user services,
(v)   used services.

1.43 Using the abbreviated names listed in Figure 1.32, show how the idle RQ primary can be specified in the form of:
(i)   a state transition diagram,
(ii) an extended event–state table,
(iii) a high-level pseudocode program.

1.44 With the aid of a time sequence diagram, show a typical set of link layer service primitives, assuming the link layer provides
(i)   a reliable service, and
(ii) a best-effort service.

1.45 In relation to the HDLC frame format shown in Figure 1.36, explain the meaning and use of the following terms:
(i)   supervisory frames,
(ii)   unnumbered frames,
(iii) poll/final bit,
(iv)   command and response frames,
(v)   extended control field bit definitions,
(vi)   piggyback acknowledgment,
(vii) unnumbered information frame.

Section 1.5

1.46 With the aid of a diagram, explain the meaning of the following terms:
(i)   protocol data unit,
(ii) protocol control information,
(iii) layering,
(iv) protocol stack.

1.47 In relation to the Internet protocol stack, with the aid of a diagram explain briefly the role of the following protocol layers:
(i)   physical layer,
(ii) data link control layer,
(iii) network layer,
(iv) transport layer,
(v)   application layer.

telephone networks and modems

2.1 Introduction

The basic service provided by telephone networks is of course telephony. The service is available worldwide with the effect that the two subscribers can be located anywhere in the world where there is a telephone network. To provide this service, the telephone network operates in a connection-oriented, circuit-switched mode. This means that, when the called subscriber number has been entered, a dedicated (speech) channel is set up through the network. Also, when the telephone handset is replaced, the reserved channel is released. Its duration and the distance between the two subscribers then determine the cost of the call. It is also possible to arrange for a channel to be set up permanently between two subscribers. This is then called a **leased line** but with this, of course, the cost is very much higher.

As we shall see, the telephone network is hierarchical with, at the lowest level, a very large number of local exchanges/end offices to which the subscriber access lines – for example within a town – are terminated and, at the highest level, a much smaller set of national exchanges/offices. The former switch a relatively low volume of calls while the latter switch a much larger volume. The speech relating to a call that is transmitted over the access line is represented in either an analog form or a digital form. Once within the switching network, however, all transmissions are digital. Hence by using a technique called multiplexing, the digital signals relating to a number of calls – 24/30 being common – are transmitted using either a high bit rate line or a portion of a higher bit rate line. When analog transmission is used over the access lines, the total network is known as a **public switched telephone network** (**PSTN**) and, when digital transmission is used, an **integrated services digital network** (**ISDN**).

As we can deduce from this, with the advent of optical fiber, a PSTN/ISDN contains a large volume of transmission bandwidth. Hence to exploit this, portions of the high bit rate lines are used also by a **telecommunications operating company** (**telco**) to create what are called **Internet service provider** (**ISP**) **networks**. In addition, the same lines can be leased from the provider and used to create independent ISP networks. It is for this reason that telephone networks form an integral part of the (public) Internet and hence it is useful to build up a more detailed understanding of the operation of these networks and how the transmission bandwidth is used to create ISP networks.

Both a PSTN and an ISDN use circuit switching and are composed of three hierarchical networks:

- a relatively large number of **local access and switching networks**: these connect subscribers within a localized area to their nearest local exchange (LE) or end office (EO) and are concerned with the transmission and switching of calls within their own area;

- one or more **interexchange trunk/carrier networks**: these are national networks concerned with the transmission and switching of calls between different regional and national exchanges/offices;

- an interconnected set of **international networks**: associated with each national network is an international gateway exchange (IGE) and collectively these are concerned with the transmission and switching of calls internationally between the different national networks.

This general architecture is shown in Figure 2.1.

In some countries, the total national network is owned and managed by a single operator. In most countries, however, the various parts of the network are privately owned and managed by a number of operators. In some cases, the total local access and switching network is owned by a single operator and the various interexchange trunk networks are each owned by different operators. In others, there is one set of operators that own and run different parts of the local access network – known as **local exchange carriers** (**LXCs**) – and a different set of operators that run their own interexchange trunk networks – **interexchange carriers** (**IXCs**). Nevertheless, the same basic architecture that we show in Figure 2.1 can be used to explain the principle of operation of this type of network. In practice, the overall network consists of three interrelated systems – transmission, switching, and signaling – and hence we shall describe their operation under these headings.

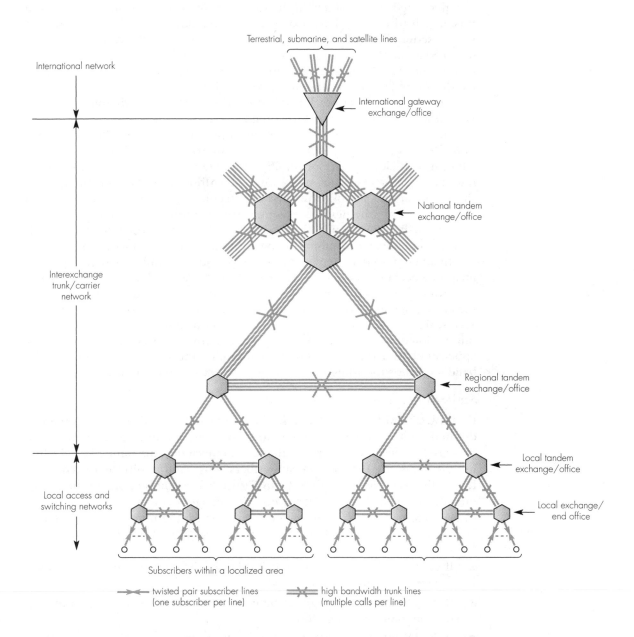

Figure 2.1 General architecture of a national circuit-switched network.

Transmission system

Each subscriber within a localized area is connected to an LE/EO in that area by a dedicated circuit which, in the case of most homes and small offices, is a twisted-pair wire cable. This is known as the **customer line** or, more generally, the **subscriber line** (**SL**) as it is used exclusively by that subscriber. In the case of a PSTN, analog transmission is used over each subscriber line, which means that all the signals relating to a call are analog signals within a bandwidth of 200 Hz through to 3.4 kHz. With an ISDN, digital transmission is used over the subscriber line, which is then known as a **digital subscriber line** (**DSL**) since all the signals relating to a call are digital.

In customer premises that contain a **private branch exchange** (**PBX**), multiple calls can be in progress concurrently, so a digital subscriber line with a bit rate sufficient to support multiple simultaneous calls is used. Typical bit rates are 1.5 Mbps (supporting 24 calls) or 2 Mbps (30 calls) – or multiples of these. A similar set of transmission circuits interconnects the various exchanges within the network except, since the number of simultaneous calls can be much larger, optical fiber cables are used which operate at very high bit rates and hence can support many thousands of simultaneous calls.

In addition to telephony, a PSTN also provides a number of digital services including fax and access to the Internet. In order to do this, **modems** are used to convert the digital signals associated with these applications into and from the analog signals used over the subscriber line. In the case of fax and Internet access, since these involve a switched connection similar to that used for telephony, low bit rate modems of up to 56 kbps are used. In addition, for applications over the Internet that do not utilize the switching network, **broadband modems** supporting up to and in excess of 1.5 Mbps are used.

Switching system

Each LE/EO within a local area has sufficient switching capacity to support a defined number of simultaneous calls/connections. In some instances, the calls are between two subscribers that are connected to the same LE/EO while in others they are between two subscribers connected to different exchanges. In the first case, as we can see from Figure 2.1, a connection can be set up directly by the LE/EO without any other exchanges being involved. In all other cases, however, additional exchanges are involved; the number is determined by the location of the LE/EO to which the called subscriber is connected.

- If the LE/EO is within the same local area, the connection involves just the two interconnected LEs/EOs.
- If the LE/EO is in a neighboring local area, the connection is through a local tandem exchange/office.
- If the LE/EO is in a different region, the connection is either through a pair of neighboring regional tandem exchanges/offices, or through one or more additional higher-level national tandem exchanges/offices.

■ If the LE/EO is in a different country, the connection is through the complete set of exchanges in each country including the two international gateway exchanges involved.

As we can deduce from the interconnection structure illustrated in Figure 2.1, within the total switching network, there are a number of alternative paths/routes between any two exchanges. The additional lines are provided both to increase capacity and to improve the resilience of the total network to exchange and/or line failures.

Signaling system

As we indicated earlier, both PSTNs and ISDNs operate in a circuit-switched mode. This means that, prior to a call taking place, a connection through the network between the two subscribers must be set up and, on completion of the call, the connection is closed down. The setting up and closing down of connections is carried out by the transfer of a defined set of control messages – known as **signaling messages** – between the calling and called subscriber and their respective LE/EO and also between the various exchanges that are involved.

The signaling messages used over the subscriber line are different from those used within the core transmission and switching (trunk) network. In the case of an analog subscriber line, the signaling messages are analog signals such as single-frequency audio tones. With a digital line, the signaling messages are also digital and, because an ISDN can support two (or more) calls simultaneously, the signaling messages are allocated a dedicated portion of the bandwidth/bit rate of the line. Within the trunk network, however, the signaling messages relating to both types of network are digital and use a common format and signaling protocol.

As we have stated, public circuit-switched networks comprise three interrelated systems: transmission systems, switching systems and signaling systems. Hence in the remainder of this chapter we shall describe the underlying principles associated with each of these systems. However, because our main aim is to build up an understanding of how a PC/workstation gains access to the Internet, we shall limit our coverage to the mode of operation of the two types of access network and the essential features of the transmission system that is used within the core trunk network. As we shall see, high bandwidth lines leased from a telco are used extensively within the Internet to provide high bit rate point-to-point links both between and within the networks that make up the Internet. In addition, since modems provide the user interface to public circuit-switched networks, we shall also discuss the principle of operation of the different types of low bit rate and high bit rate (broadband) modem.

2.2 Transmission systems

As we explained in the last section, the transmission system comprises two parts: that used in the local access network and that used in the trunk network. The type of transmission used in the local access network can be either analog (PSTN) or digital (ISDN). Also, although all-digital transmission (and switching) is used in the trunk network, for historical reasons, two different types of digital transmission system are used: one is called the **plesiochronous digital hierarchy** (**PDH**) and the other the **synchronous digital hierarchy** (**SDH**), the latter also known as the **synchronous optical network** or **SONET**. We shall discuss the operation of each type of system separately.

2.2.1 Analog subscriber lines

As we mentioned in the introduction to the chapter, each subscriber line comprises a single twisted-pair wire that connects the subscriber network termination to a **line termination unit** (**LTU**) in the LE/EO. In practice, the cable used has a number of twisted-pairs within it and, for a home or small business that requires more than one user to be active at a time, more than one twisted-pair can be allocated to it. The complete cable linking the subscriber premises to the LE/EO is made up of multiple cable sections with a combined length of up to about 5 miles (8 km) depending on the telecommunications operating company (telco). In order to enable new customers to be added and faults on individual lines to be located, each subscriber line within a localized area is terminated at a **junction box**. Normally, this is located within a few hundred yards/meters of the customer premises within that area and, inside the box, the individual wire pair from each subscriber premises is joined to a second pair within a larger cable containing multiple pairs.

In addition, for cable lengths greater than a mile (1.5 km), the individual pairs within these cables are joined to a third set of pairs within an even larger cable. This is done in a roadside cabinet known as a **cross-connect**. Typically, the cable from a junction box to a cross-connect contains in the order of 50 pairs and that from a cross-connect to the LE/EO several hundred pairs.

Telephone basics

The various components that are present in a telephone are shown in Figure 2.2(a).

A d.c. voltage of 48 V is permanently applied to the subscriber line by the LTU and, when the handset is lifted, contacts in the *cradle switch unit* close which causes a current to flow from the LTU to the handset. This flow of current is detected by the LTU and, as a result, it applies a pair of

(a)

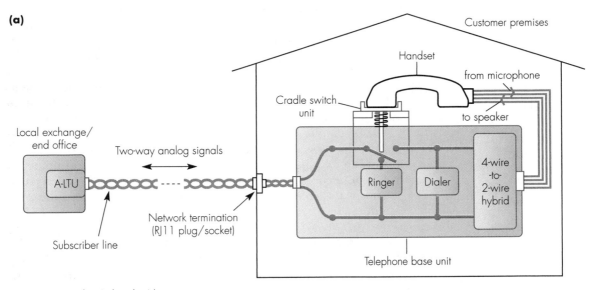

A-LTU = analog (subscriber) line termination unit

(b)

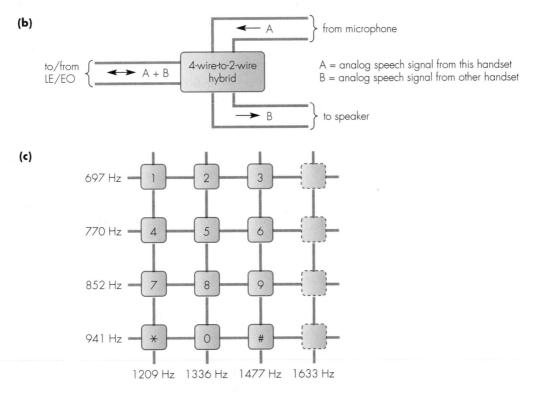

Figure 2.2 Analog subscriber line principles: (a) telephone components; (b) 4-wire to 2-wire hybrid; (c) dual-tone multifrequency keypad.

low-frequency tones – collectively known as dial-tone – to the line. On hearing this, the subscriber proceeds to enter the number of the called party using the telephone keypad, which is connected to the *dialer*.

As we show in Figure 2.2(c), when each key on the keypad is pressed, a pair of (single-frequency) tones is applied to the line by the dialer; for example, pressing the digit 5 causes two tones to be applied, one of frequency 770 Hz and the other of 1336 Hz. This type of dialing is called **dual-tone multi-frequency (DTMF) keying**. At the exchange end, a bank of filters – each of which detects just one of the tones – is used to determine the string of dialed digits that have been entered by the subscriber. The called number is then passed to the exchange *control processor*, which proceeds to initiate the setting up of a connection through the switching network to the called party.

The *ringer circuit* is connected across the subscriber line before the *cradle switch unit* and, to alert the called subscriber of an incoming call, the LTU of the called party applies a series of short bursts of a pair of low frequency (*ringing*) *tones* to the line. The lifting of the handset by the called subscriber causes a current to flow as before and, in response, the LTU removes the ringing tone. Both subscribers are aware of this, and the conversation then starts.

As we indicated earlier, all transmission and switching within the trunk network is performed digitally. Hence as the analog speech signal from the calling subscriber is received at the LE/EO, it is immediately sampled and converted into a (PCM) digital signal as we describe in Appendix A. Similarly, the received digital signal from the called subscriber is converted back into an analog form for onward transmission over the subscriber line. However, since the subscriber line comprises only a single pair of wires, this means that the same pair of wires must be used to transfer the two analog speech signals associated with the call. Hence in order for each subscriber not to hear their own voice when speaking, a unit called a **4-wire to 2-wire hybrid** is present in each telephone, the principle of which is shown in Figure 2.2(b).

Essentially, the output from the microphone in the handset (A) is passed to the subscriber line for onward transmission to the other party but, simultaneously, within the hybrid the same signal is subtracted from the combined signal received from the line (A + B). This means that only the signal received from the other party (B) is fed to the speaker in the handset. In practice, the hybrid is a transformer and, since a transformer will not pass a DC signal, it is the presence of the transformer that dictates the use of an analog signal. In addition, imperfections in the hybrid transformer often result in an attenuated version of the received signal – that is, from the distant subscriber – being coupled into the line from the microphone. Hence this signal is returned to the distant subscriber handset as if it was from the local subscriber but with a delay equal to twice the signal propagation delay time between the two subscribers. This is known as the **echo signal** and, providing it is received within less than 24 ms, it is not discernible to the remote subscriber. Above this value it is necessary to introduce a circuit known as an **echo canceler** to remove the echo signal.

Finally, the connection is closed down when either subscriber replaces the handset, the loss of current flow to the handset being detected by the related LTU, which, in turn, initiates the clearing of the network connection.

Remote concentrator units

The distance between the subscriber premises and the LE/EO is limited by the attenuation that occurs in the subscriber line. Hence in order to provide a connection to subscribers who are beyond the maximum allowable distance, a device known as a **remote concentrator unit** (**RCU**) is used. The general layout of the access network is then as shown in Figure 2.3.

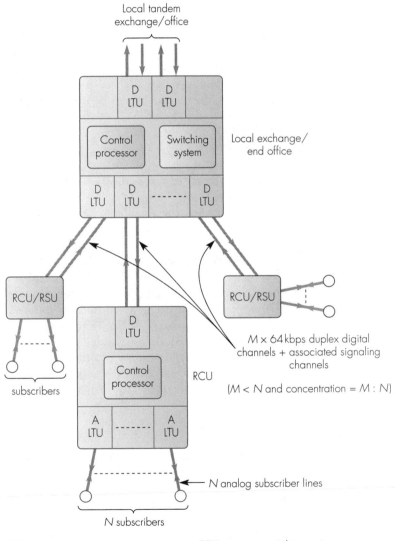

Figure 2.3 Access network structure with remote concentrator/ switching units.

Each subscriber line connected to an RCU is terminated by an LTU, which performs a similar set of functions to those carried out by an A-LTU within an LE/EO. However, although the subscriber line used to connect each subscriber to the RCU operates using analog transmission, the circuit that connects the RCU to the LE/EO operates in a digital mode. The two speech signals associated with a call are digitized to produce a corresponding pair of 64 kbps (PCM – pulse code modulation) digital signals. Hence, in theory, the digital circuits that are used to link the RCU to the LE/EO must each operate at a bit rate that supports $N \times 64$ kbps where N is the number of subscriber lines connected to the RCU. Normally, however, the number of calls that take place concurrently, M, is much less than N. Hence in order to reduce the bit rate of the digital circuit, the bit rate is made equal to $M \times 64$ kbps rather than $N \times 64$ kbps. This is the origin of the term **concentration** and is expressed as $N{:}M$, a typical figure being 8:1. Also, because RCUs effectively replace multiple (twisted-pair) subscriber lines, they are known as **pair-gain systems**.

In addition to the digitized speech signals associated with each (active) call, the signaling information (dialed digits) associated with a call must also be passed to the LE/EO in a digital form. Normally, therefore, as we shall expand upon in Section 2.2.3, a portion of the bandwidth of the digital line is used to exchange the signaling messages associated with all of the currently active calls. As we show in the figure, this bandwidth is used to produce a channel known as the **signaling channel**.

To perform the various signaling functions associated with each call – off-hook detection, dial-digit collection, ringing, and so on – an RCU has a separate control processor within it that communicates with the control processor within the LE/EO to set up and release connections. Hence by adding some additional processing functions, it is also possible to allow the processor within an RCU to set up calls between any two subscribers who are connected directly to it rather than through the LE/EO. The RCU is then known as a **remote switching unit** (**RSU**) and, as we can deduce from Figure 2.3, the effect of using RCUs and RSUs is that each LE/EO can then operate with all-digital transmission and switching similar in principle to the various tandem exchanges used in the trunk network.

2.2.2 PSTN modems

As we explained in Section 1.3.1, in order to transmit a digital signal over an analog subscriber line, modulated transmission must be used; that is, the electrical signal that represents the binary bitstream output by the source (digital) device must first be converted into an analog signal that is compatible with a (telephony) speech signal. As we indicated earlier, the range of signal frequencies that a public circuit-switched network passes is from 200 Hz through to 3400 Hz. This means that an analog subscriber line will not pass the low-frequency signals that could occur if, for example, the bitstream to be transmitted is made up of a very long string of binary 1s or 0s. For this reason, it is not possible simply to apply two voltage levels to the telephone line, since zero output will be obtained for both levels if the binary stream is all 1s or all 0s. Instead, we must convert the binary data into a form compatible with a speech signal at the sending end of the line and reconvert this signal back into its binary form at the receiver. The circuit that performs the first operation is known as a **modulator**, and the circuit performing the reverse function a **demodulator**. Since the two communicating devices normally both send and receive data, the combined device is known as a **modem**.

Using modems, data can be transmitted through the network either by setting up a switched path through the network as with a normal telephone call, or by leasing a **dedicated** (or **leased**) **line** from the network operator. Since leased lines bypass the normal switching equipment (exchange) in the network and are set up on a permanent or long-term basis, they are economically justifiable only for applications having a high utilization factor. An added advantage of a leased line is that its operating characteristics can be more accurately quantified than for a short-term switched circuit, making it feasible to operate at higher bit rates. Figure 2.4 shows the two alternative operating modes.

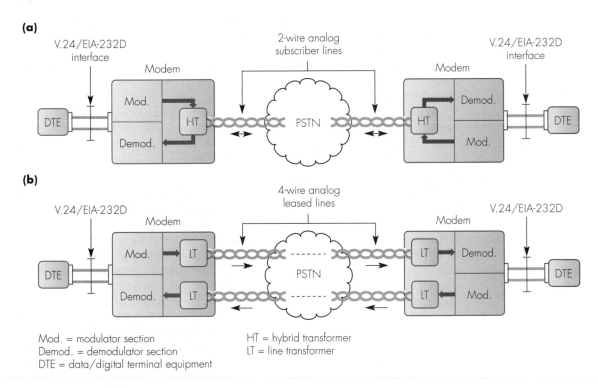

Figure 2.4 Modem operating alternatives: (a) 2-wire switched connections; (b) 4-wire leased circuits.

As we can see, in the case of a switched connection, the two analog signals that carry the transmitted and received bitstreams must share the use of the single twisted-pair subscriber line. Hence, as in a telephone, a hybrid transformer is used. In the case of a leased circuit, however, normally a 4-wire – two pairs – line is used. We shall explain the principle of operation of the modem and the terminal interface to the modem separately.

Modem principles

Three basic types of modulation are used: amplitude, frequency and phase. Since binary data is to be transmitted, in the simplest modems just two signal levels are used. The signal then switches (shifts) between these two levels as the binary signal changes (keys) between a binary 1 and 0. The three basic modulation types are known, therefore, as **amplitude shift keying (ASK)**, **frequency shift keying (FSK)** and **phase shift keying (PSK)** respectively. The essential components that make up the modulator and demodulator sections of a modem are shown in Figure 2.5(a) and example waveforms relating to the three modulation types in Figure 2.5(b).

With ASK, the amplitude of a single-frequency audio tone is keyed between two levels at a rate determined by the bit rate of the transmitted binary signal. The single-frequency audio tone is known as the **carrier signal** (since it effectively carries the binary signal as it passes through the network) and its frequency is chosen to be within the band of frequencies that are allowed over the access circuit. The amount of bandwidth required to transmit the binary signal is then determined by its bit rate: the higher the bit rate, the larger the required bandwidth.

With FSK, the amplitude of the carrier signal remains fixed and its frequency is keyed between two different frequency levels by the transmitted binary signal. The difference between these two frequencies is known as the frequency shift and the amount of bandwidth required is determined by the bit rate and the frequency shift.

With PSK, the amplitude and frequency of the carrier remain fixed and transitions in the binary signal being transmitted cause the phase of the carrier to change. As we can see in the figure, two types of PSK are used. The first uses two fixed carrier signals with a 180° phase difference between them to represent a binary 0 and 1. Since one signal is simply the inverse of the other, it is known as **phase-coherent PSK**. The disadvantage of this scheme is that a reference carrier signal is required at the receiver against which the phase of the received signal is compared. In practice, this requires more complex demodulation circuitry than the alternative **differential PSK**. With this scheme, phase shifts occur at each bit transition irrespective of whether a string of binary 1 or 0 signals is being transmitted; a phase shift of 90° relative to the current signal indicates a binary 0 is the next bit while a phase shift of 270° indicates a binary 1. As a result, the demodulation circuitry need determine only the magnitude of each phase shift rather than its absolute value. In practice, PSK is the most efficient modulation scheme in terms of the amount of bandwidth it requires and hence is the one used in modems that provide a bit rate in excess of 4.8 kbps.

(a)

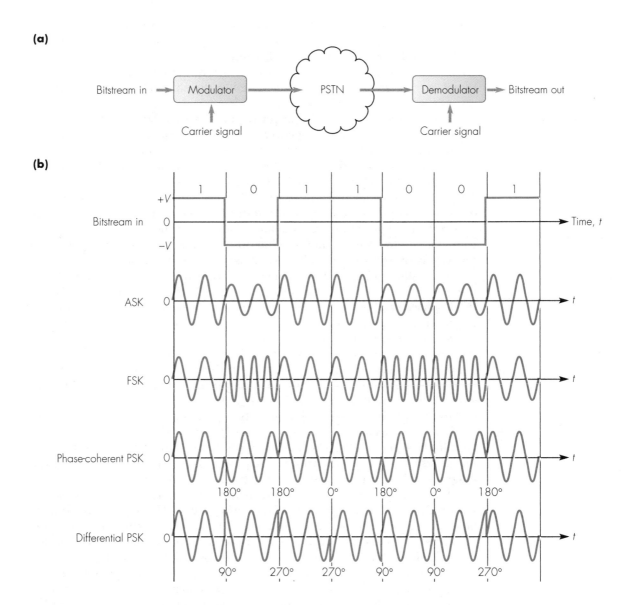

(b)

Figure 2.5 Modem principles: (a) modulator/demodulator schematic; (b) waveforms of basic modulation methods.

Multilevel modulation

As we can deduce from Figure 2.5, with the basic modulation methods just two different signal changes are used – in either amplitude, frequency, or phase – to represent the binary bitstream being transmitted. This means, therefore, that the maximum rate of change of the transmitted signal – that is, the **baud rate** – is equal to the bit rate of the input bitstream. Since the bandwidth of the access circuit is fixed, however, in order to obtain higher bit rates multiple signal levels are used. Hence instead of the transmitted signal changing at the same rate as the input bitstream, it changes at a lower rate; that is, for a given baud rate – determined by the channel bandwidth – the bit rate is two or more times this.

For example, with PSK, if four phase changes are used – 0°, 90°, 180°, 270° – this enables each phase change to represent a pair of bits from the input bitstream, as we show in Figure 2.6(a). This means, therefore, that the bit rate is twice the baud rate and, because this scheme uses four phases, it is known as **quadrature PSK** (**QPSK**) or 4-PSK. Higher bit rates are achieved using larger numbers of phase changes. In practice, however, there is a limit to how many different phases can be used, as the reducing phase differences make it progressively more prone to the noise and phase impairments introduced during transmission. In order to minimize the number of phase changes required, two separate carriers are used, each of which is separately modulated.

As we show in Figure 2.6(b), the two carriers have the same frequency but there is a 90° phase difference between them. They are known, therefore, as the **in-phase carrier** (**I**) and the **quadrature carrier** (**Q**). The two modulated carriers are transmitted concurrently and, as we show in the figure, with just a single phase change per carrier – 0–180° and 90–270° – there are four combinations of the two modulated signals, which means that each combination can represent two bits from the input bitstream. This type of modulation is known as **quadrature amplitude modulation** (**QAM**) and, because there are four combinations, **4-QAM**.

In order to increase the bit rate further, a combination of ASK and PSK is used. This means that as well as the I and Q carriers changing in phase, their amplitude also changes. The complete phase diagram showing all the possible combinations of amplitude and phase is known as the **constellation diagram** and an example is shown in Figure 2.6(b). As we can see, this uses 16 combinations of two amplitude and two phase changes per carrier and is known therefore as **16-QAM** or sometimes QAM-16. This type of modem can be used, for example, to transmit data at a bit rate of 9600 bps over a line that supports 2400 baud. Because of the structure of the constellation diagram, this type of modulation is called **trellis coded modulation** (**TCM**).

Larger numbers of combined phase and amplitude changes are used but, as we indicated earlier, this means that the probability of bit errors occurring increases as each received symbol – in phase and amplitude – is sampled. Hence to detect when errors are present in the received bitstream, the higher bit rate modems – that is, with 32 or higher symbols/places in the trellis – insert additional parity bits into the bitstream at periodic intervals for error detection purposes. For example, a modem with 32 points in the trellis – and hence five bits per symbol – inserts an additional parity bit after every fourth data bit. Normally, modems operate in a duplex mode – two-way simultaneous – which is done by using two separate carrier frequencies.

As we can see from the above, there are many combinations of the different modulation schemes. Hence for each application, it is essential that both modems utilize the same bit rate and modulation method. For this reason the ITU-T has defined a set of international standards for modems. These are known as the **V-series** set of standards and a selection of these is given in Figure 2.7. In this way, a person who buys a modem that adheres to, say, the V.29 standard, can readily use it to communicate with a V.29-compatible modem from a possibly different manufacturer.

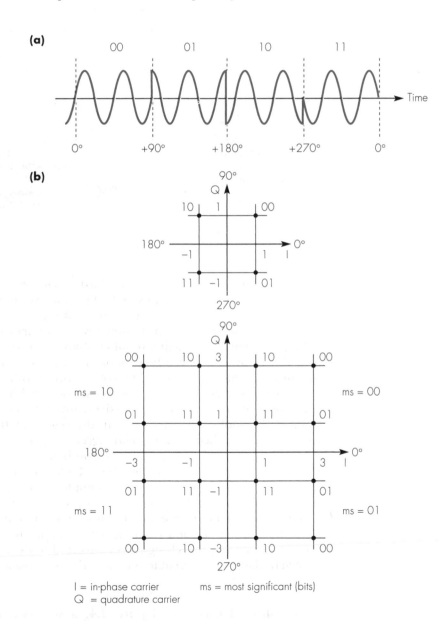

Figure 2.6 Multilevel modulation: (a) 4-PSK using a single carrier; (b) 4-QAM and 16-QAM using two carriers, one at 90° (Q) out of phase with the other (I).

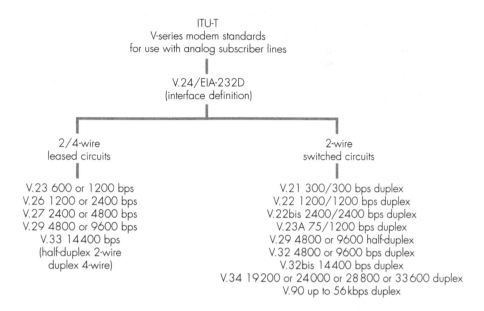

Figure 2.7 A selection of ITU-T V-series modem standards.

As we can see, some of the standards relate to modems to be used with leased circuits and others with switched circuits/connections. Also most of the modems can operate at more than one rate. Hence once a connection has been set up and prior to transmitting any user information, the two communicating modems go through a **training phase** to determine the highest of the available bit rates that can be supported by the connection. This is done by one modem sending a standard bitstream and the other measuring the BER of the received stream. Normally, the lowest available bit rate is selected first and the rate is then increased progressively until the measured BER reaches a defined threshold. Typically this is in the region of 10^{-5} and 10^{-6} and, once this has been reached, both modems agree to operate at this rate.

The choice of operating bit rate – and hence baud rate – is transparent to the user and the only observable effect of a lower bit rate is a slower response time in an interactive application, for example, or an inferior speech/video quality in an interpersonal application. Also, it should be remembered that the analog signal output by the modulator is converted into an equivalent digital signal for transmission and switching within the trunk network in just the same way that an analog speech signal is converted. Indeed, whether the source is speech or data is transparent to the network transmission and switching systems.

V.24/EIA-232D interface standard

As we showed earlier in Figure 2.4, a standard interface is used for connecting the serial part of a data terminal equipment (DTE) – a computer for example – to a PSTN modem. This is defined in ITU-T Recommendation **V.24** which is the same as the EIA standard **EIA-232D**, the latter being the latest version of the earlier RS-232A, B, and C standards. In the standards documents the modem is referred to as the **data circuit-terminating equipment** (**DCE**) and a diagram indicating the position of the interface in relation to two communicating DTEs/DCEs is shown in Figure 2.8(a).

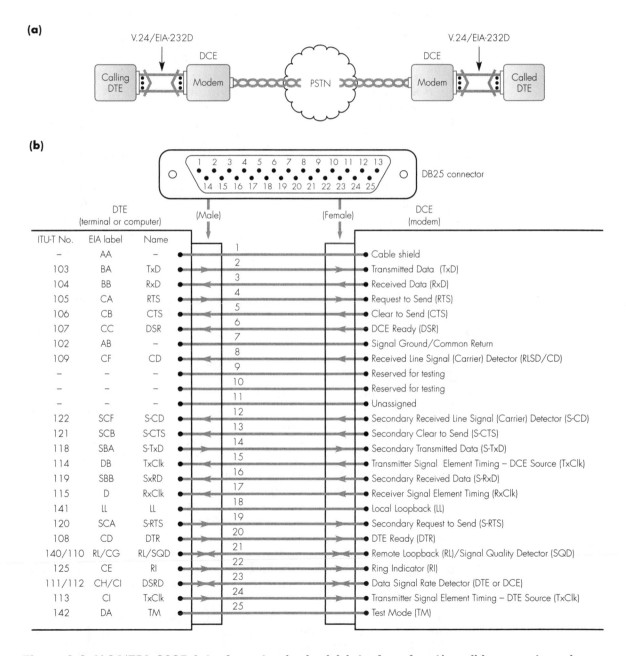

Figure 2.8 V.24/EIA-232D interface standards: (a) interface function; (b) connector, pin, and signal definitions.

The connector used between a DTE and a modem is a 25-pin connector of the type shown in Figure 2.8(b). It is defined in standard ISO 2110 and is known as a **DB25 connector**. Also shown is the total set of signals associated with the interface together with their names and pin assignments. In most cases, however, only a subset of the signals are required.

The transmit data (TxD) and receive data (RxD) lines are used by the DTE to transmit and receive data respectively. The other lines collectively perform the timing and control functions associated with the setting-up and clearing of a switched connection through the PSTN and with performing selected test operations. The second (secondary) set of lines allows two data transfers to take place simultaneously over the one interface.

The timing control signals are concerned with the transmission (TxClk) and reception (RxClk) of the data on the corresponding data line. As we explained in Section 1.3.3, data is transmitted using either an asynchronous or a synchronous transmission mode. In the asynchronous mode, the transmit and receive clocks are both generated by an independent clock source and fed directly to the corresponding pins of the DTE. In this mode, only the transmit and receive data lines are connected to the modem. In the synchronous mode, however, data is transmitted and received in synchronism with the corresponding clock signal and these are normally generated by the modem. The latter is then known as a **synchronous modem** and, when the signaling (baud) rate is less than the data bit rate – that is, multiple signal levels are being used – the transmit and receive clocks generated by the modem operate at the appropriate fraction of the line signaling rate.

We can best see the function and sequence of the various call-control lines by considering the setting-up and clearing of a call. Figure 2.9 shows how a connection (call) is first set up, some data is exchanged between the two DTEs in a half-duplex (two-way alternate) mode and the call is then cleared. We assume that the calling DTE is a user at a personal computer and its modem has automatic dialing facilities. Typically the called DTE is a server computer and its modem has automatic answering facilities. Such facilities are defined in **Recommendation V.25**. When a DTE is ready to make or receive data transfer requests, it sets the data terminal ready (DTR) line on and the local modem responds by setting the DCE ready (DSR) line on.

A connection is established by the calling DTE sending the telephone number of the modem (line) associated with the called DTE. On receipt of the ringing tone from its local switching office/telephone exchange, the called modem sets the ring indicator (RI) line to on and the called DTE responds by setting the request-to-send (RTS) line on. In response, the called modem sends a carrier signal – the data tone for a binary 1 – to the calling modem to indicate that the call has been accepted by the called DTE and, after a short delay to allow the calling modem to prepare to receive data, the called modem sets the clear-to-send (CTS) line on to inform the called DTE that it can start sending data. On detecting the carrier signal, the calling modem sets the carrier detect (CD) line on. The connection is now established and the data transfer phase can begin.

(a)

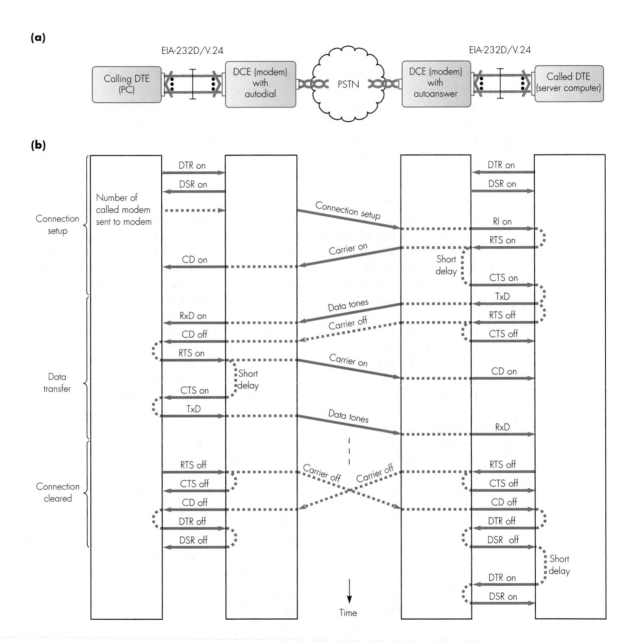

(b)

Figure 2.9 V.24/EIA-232D connection setup, two-way alternate data transfer and connection clearing sequences.

Typically, the called DTE (computer) starts by sending a short invitation-to-send message over the setup connection. When this has been sent, it prepares to receive the response from the calling DTE by setting the RTS line off and, on detecting this, the called modem stops sending the carrier signal and sets the CTS line off. At the calling side, the removal of the carrier signal is detected by the calling modem and, in response, it sets the CD line off. In order to send its response message, the calling DTE (PC) sets the RTS line on and, on receipt of the CTS signal from the modem, starts to send the message. This procedure then repeats as messages are exchanged between the two DTEs. Finally, after the complete transaction has taken place, the call is cleared. This is accomplished by both DTEs setting their RTS lines off, which, in turn, causes the two modems to switch their carriers off. This is detected by both modems and they set their CD lines off. Both DTEs then set their DTR lines off and their modems respond by setting the DSR lines off thereby clearing the call. Typically, the called DTE (the server computer) then prepares to receive a new call by resetting its DTR line on after a short delay.

We have described the use of a half-duplex switched connection to illustrate the meaning and use of some of the control lines available with the standard. In practice, however, the time taken to change from the receive to the transmit mode in the half-duplex mode – known as the **turnaround time** – is not insignificant. It is preferable to operate in the duplex mode whenever possible, even when half-duplex working is required. In the duplex mode, both RTS lines are permanently left on and both modems maintain the CTS line on and a carrier signal to the remote modem.

When two DTEs are communicating and a fault develops, it is often difficult to ascertain the cause of the fault – the local modem, the remote modem, the communications line, or the remote DTE. To help identify the cause of faults, the interface contains three control lines: the local and remote loopback (LL and RL) and the test mode (TM). Their function is shown in Figure 2.10(a): in (i) a local loopback test is used and in (ii) a remote loopback.

The DTE (modem) always sets its DSR line on when it is ready to transmit or receive data. To perform a test on its local modem, the DTE sets the LL line on and, in response, the modem internally connects the output from the modulator circuit back to the input of the demodulator circuit. It then sets the TM line on and, when the DTE detects this, it transmits a known test (data) pattern on its TxD line and simultaneously reads the data from its RxD line. If the received data is the same as the test data, then the DTE assumes the local modem is working satisfactorily. If it is not – or no signal is present at all – then the local modem is assumed faulty.

If the local modem is deemed to be working correctly, then the DTE proceeds to test the remote modem by this time setting the RL control line on. On detecting the RL line going on, the local modem sends a predefined command to the remote modem, which, in turn, performs a remote loopback as shown. The remote modem then sets its TM line on to inform the remote DTE that it is involved in a test – and hence cannot transmit data – and returns an acknowledgment command back to the modem originating the test. The modem, on receipt of this, sets its TM line on and, on detecting this, the local DTE starts to transmit the test data pattern. Again, if this data is

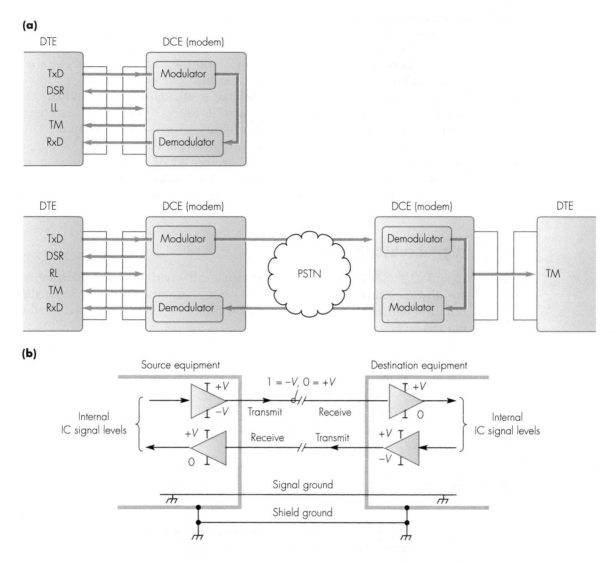

Figure 2.10 V.24/EIA-232D interface: (a) local and remote loopback tests; (b) V.28/RS.232A signal levels.

received correctly, then both modems are assumed to be working correctly and the fault lies with the remote DTE. Alternatively, if the received data is badly corrupted then the remote modem is assumed to be faulty or, if no signal is received at all, then the PSTN line is assumed faulty.

The V.24/EIA-232D interface uses either a flat-ribbon or a multiple-wire cable that includes a single ground reference wire. However, because of the short distances – less than a few centimeters – between neighboring integrated circuits within a computer, the signal levels used to represent binary data are of very low power and, as a result, cannot be used directly for transferring signals outside the computer. Hence, as we show in Figure 2.10(b), associated with each signal line of the V.24/EI-232D interface is a matching **line driver** and **line receiver** circuit.

The electrical signal levels are defined in standards **V.28/RS.232A**. The signals used on the lines are symmetric with respect to the ground reference signal and are at least 3V: +3V for a binary 0 and –3V for a binary 1. In practice, the actual voltage levels used are determined by the supply voltages applied to the interface circuits, ±12V or even ±15V not being uncommon. The transmit line driver circuits convert the low-level signal voltages used within the equipment to the higher voltage levels used on the connecting lines. Similarly, the line receiver circuits perform the reverse function.

2.2.3 Digital subscriber lines

In an ISDN, all the signals associated with a call – both the two speech signals and the associated signaling messages – are transmitted over the subscriber line in a digital form. An ISDN has a number of different subscriber line interfaces:

- a basic rate interface (BRI) that provides two independent 64 kbps duplex channels;
- a primary rate interface (PRI) that provides either 23 or 30 independent 64 kbps duplex channels;
- a primary rate interface that provides a single duplex channel of $p \times 64$ kbps where p can be 1–23 or 1–30.

We shall discuss each interface separately.

Basic rate interface

The basic rate interface – and the associated **network termination unit** (**NTU**) – allows for two calls of 64 kbps duplex to be in progress concurrently. Hence, since the two calls can be set up independently – that is, the second call can be set up while the first is in progress – an additional duplex channel of 16 kbps is used for the exchange of the signaling messages relating to the two calls. This arrangement is known as **out-of-band signaling**. Each 64 kbps user channel is known as a **bearer** or **B-channel** and the 16 kbps signaling channel the **D-channel**. Hence the combined bit rate associated with this interface is 2B+D or 144 kbps duplex. Two examples of an NTU associated with an ISDN BRI are shown in Figure 2.11.

As we show in Figure 2.11(a), in the first example the NTU has two digital ports and two analog ports associated with it. The two analog ports are provided to enable the subscriber to utilize existing analog equipment such

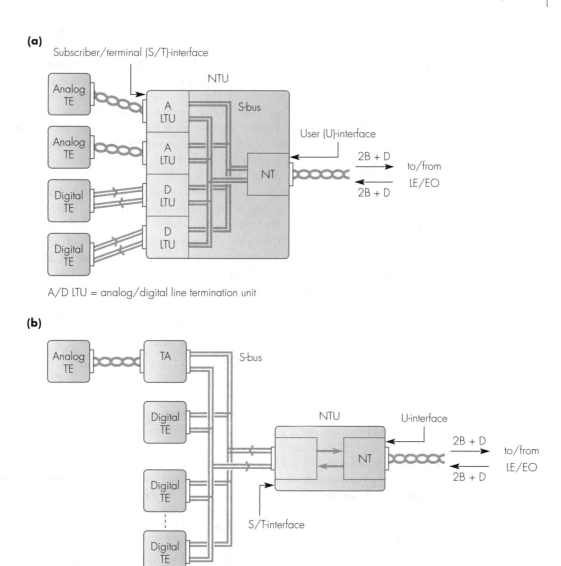

Figure 2.11 ISDN network termination alternatives: (a) 4-port NTU; (b) S-bus NTU.

as an analog phone, a fax machine, or a PC with modem. The two digital ports are provided to enable newer digital equipment with an ISDN interface to be used. In the case of the two analog ports, the conversion of the analog signals into and from their digital form is performed within the NTU. This means that the subscriber can use any mix of the four ports with any two active at one time.

As we show in Figure 2.11(b), a second mode of working is also used that allows from one up to eight devices to (time) share the use of the two B-channels. This mode of working is defined in **ITU-T Recommendation I.430**. In this mode the NTU has a single port associated with it to which is connected a duplex bus known as the subscriber or **S-bus**. The various terminal equipments (TEs) then gain access to the bus – and hence B-channels – using a defined interface and associated protocol. In the case of an existing analog TE, a device known as a **terminal adaptor** (**TA**) must be used to convert the analog signals associated with the TE into and from the digital signals used over the S-bus.

The S-bus must support the duplex flow of two (64 kbps) B-channels and the 16 kbps D-channel together with the contention resolution logic for time-sharing the use of the D-channel. To achieve this, the bitstream in each direction is divided into a stream of 48-bit frames each of which contains 16 bits for each of the two B-channels and 4 bits for the shared D-channel multiplexed in the order 8B1, 1D, 8B2, 1D, 8B1, 1D, 8B2, 1D. The remaining 12 bits are then used for various functions including:

- the start-of-frame synchronization pattern;
- contention resolution of the shared D-channel;
- the activation and deactivation of the interface of each TE;
- DC balancing.

The duration of each 48-bit frame is 250 microseconds, which yields a bit rate of 192 kbps in each direction. As we show in Figure 2.12, an 8-pin connector is used to connect each user TE to the NTU. This is defined in the **ISO 8877** standard and is known as a **RJ45**. The relatively high bit rate and physical separations associated with the S-bus mean that **differential line driver and receiver circuits** must be used. As we show in the figure, this requires a separate pair of wires for each of the transmit and receive signals. This type of signal is defined in standards **V.11/RS-422A**.

A differential transmitter produces twin signals of equal and opposite polarity for every binary 1 or 0 signal to be transmitted. As the differential receiver is sensitive only to the difference between the two signals on its two inputs, noise picked up by both wires will not affect receiver operation. Differential receivers, therefore, are said to have good **common-mode rejection** properties. A derivative of the RS-422A, the **RS-423A/V.10**, can be used to accept single-ended (**unbalanced**) voltages output by an EIA-232D interface with a differential receiver.

An important parameter of any transmission line is its **characteristic impedance** (Z_0) because a receiver absorbs all of the received signal power only if the line is terminated by a resistor equal to Z_0. If this is not the case, **signal reflections** occur which further distort the received signal. Normally, therefore, lines are terminated by a resistor equal to Z_0, with values from 50 to 200 ohms being common.

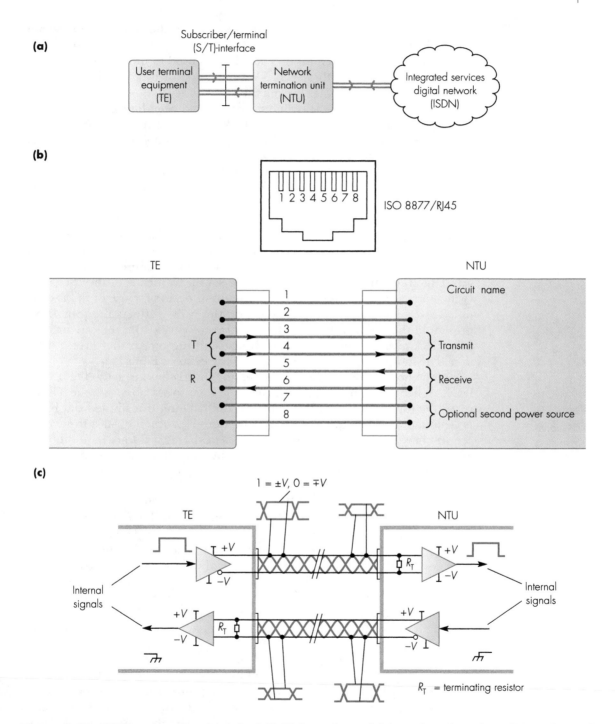

Figure 2.12 ISDN subscriber/terminal (S/T)-interface: (a) interface location; (b) socket, pin, and signal definitions; (c) signal levels.

The line code used over the S-bus is known as **alternate space inversion** (**ASI**), the principle of which is shown in Figure 2.13(a). As we can see, this is a three -level code: +V, 0, and –V. The 0 level is used to indicate the transmission of a binary 1 and either +V or –V a binary 0: for every 0 bit transmitted, the line signal changes polarity from the last 0-bit level; that is, either from +V to –V or vice versa. This type of line signal is called **pseudoternary**.

At the start of each 48-bit frame is the 2-bit frame synchronization pattern of +V, –V. The line signal then changes according to the transmitted bitstream with the first 0-bit encoded as –V. As we can deduce from the figure, however, the line signal will not be balanced if, overall, the number of 0 bits is odd. Hence, since each TE is connected to the bus by means of a transformer, the polarity of the various DC balancing bits present in each frame is chosen so that the mean DC level of the line is always zero.

Although the bus can have up to four to eight TEs connected to it, only two can be active at any point in time. A scheme is required, therefore, to enable all the TEs to contend for access to the two B-channels in a controlled way. However, since the two calls must be set up by means of the D-channel (which is shared by all the TEs) the contention occurs for use of the D-channel. To resolve any possible contention, the NTU reflects the four D-bits present in the (48-bit) frame it is currently receiving (from the one or more TEs) back in the frame it is currently transmitting out in the reverse direction. The four reflected bits are known as the **echo** or **E-bits**.

When no TE is using the D-channel, the four D-bits are set to the 0 signal level. Hence prior to sending a request message to set up a call, the TE first reads the four E-bits from the frame currently being transmitted out by the NTU and only if they are all at the 0 level does it proceed to start to send the request message in the four D-channel bits in the next frame. In addition, to allow for the possibility of one or more other TEs starting to send a request message at the same time, each TE that is trying to send a message monitors the (reflected) E-bits in the frame currently being received to check that these are the same as the D-bits that it has just transmitted. If they are the same, then it continues to send the remaining bits in the message; if they are different, then it stops transmitting and tries again later. The principle of the scheme is shown in Figure 2.13(b) and, as we can see, because of the line code used, the winner of a contention will always be the TE whose message contains a 0 bit when the other(s) contains a 1 bit. Also, in the event of both B-channels being in use when a (successful) new request is made, then a busy response message will be returned to the requesting TE. If the call can be accepted, however, then an acceptance message will be returned and the signaling procedure continues.

The interface between the NTU and the subscriber line is known as the **U-interface** and this is defined in **ITU-T Recommendation G.961**. As we showed earlier in Figure 2.11, as with an analog subscriber line, a single pair of wires is used to connect the subscriber NTU to the LE/EO. This means, therefore, that both the transmitted and received digital bitstream of 144 kbps (2B + D) must be transmitted over the same pair of wires simultaneously.

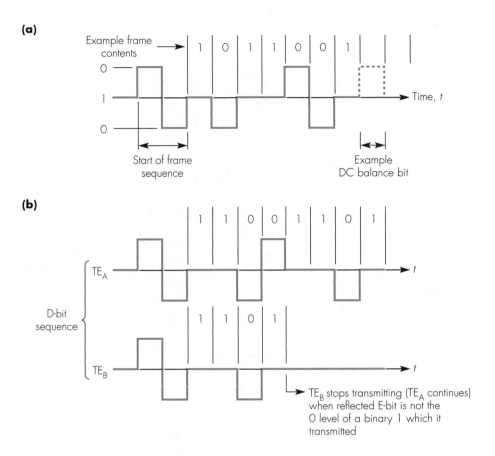

Figure 2.13 ISDN basic rate access S-bus line code principles: (a) alternate space inversion (ASI) line code; (b) example of contention resolution.

Hence in order for the receiver part of the NTU to receive only the incoming digital bitstream, an electronic version of the hybrid transformer used with an analog line is incorporated into the NTU, as we show in Figure 2.14(a).

As we can see, in addition to the hybrid, the network termination includes a circuit known as an **adaptive echo canceler**. In practice, the hybrids present at each end of a subscriber line – there is also one in the line termination unit at the LE/EO – are not perfect and, as a result, an attenuated version of the transmitted signal (A) is echoed back from the remote hybrid and hence is passed to the receiver part of the NTU together with the wanted received signal (B). Essentially, the adaptive echo canceler circuit estimates the magnitude of the attenuated version of its own transmitted signal – that is, the echo signal – and subtracts this from the combined signal output by the hybrid.

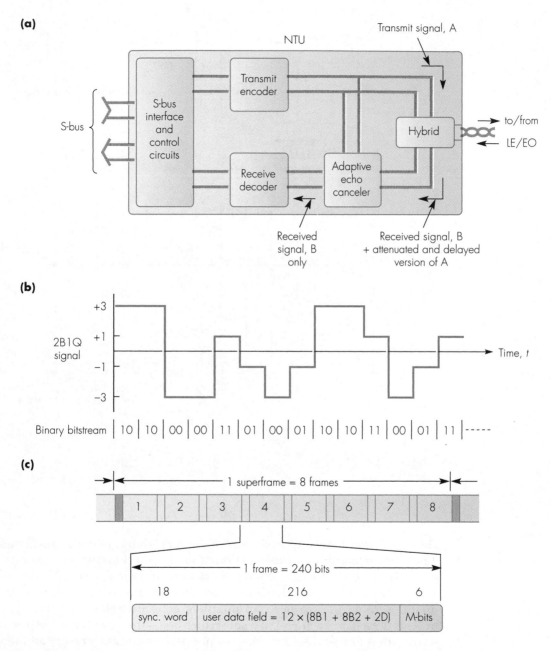

Figure 2.14 ISDN subscriber line principles: (a) NTU schematic; (b) 2B1Q line signal example; (c) frame and superframe format.

In order for the distance from the LE/EO to the subscriber NTU to be as large as possible, the line code used over the subscriber line is a four-level code known as **two binary, one quaternary** (**2B1Q**), the principles of which are shown in Figure 2.14(b). As we can deduce from the example bitstream shown in the figure, with this code the maximum rate of change of the line signal – the baud rate – is half the bit rate. As a result, the bandwidth required for this code is half that required for a two level bipolar code.

The total 2B + D bitstream is divided into a sequence of frames of 240 bits the format of which is shown in Figure 2.14(c). As we can see, each frame consists of:

- an initial 18-bit *synchronization word* comprising the quaternary symbol sequence of +3+3−3−3+3+3−3−3 ... to enable the receiver to determine the start of each frame;
- the *user data* field comprising a set of 12 groups of 18 bits, 8 bits for each of the two B-channels and 2 bits for the D-channel (multiplexed in the order 8B1, 8B2, 2D);
- a 6-bit field that relates to a separate M-channel that is used for maintenance messages and for other purposes.

A further structure known as a **superframe** which comprises eight frames is then defined by inverting the symbols in the synchronization word of the first frame. The resulting 48 M-bits are then used to carry a number of fields including a 12-bit CRC that is used to monitor the quality of the line.

Primary rate interface

In the case of a **primary rate interface** (**PRI**), only a single TE can be connected to the NTU. As we explained in the introduction, however, the TE can be a PBX, for example, which, in turn, supports multiple terminals each operating at 64 kbps or a reduced number of terminals operating at a higher bit rate. To provide this flexibility, the transmitted bitstream contains a single

---

Example 2.1

Deduce the bit rate and baud rate of the subscriber line of an ISDN basic rate access circuit assuming the 2B1Q line code and the frame format shown in Figure 2.14(c).

Answer:

Each 240-bit frame comprises $12 \times 8 = 96$ bits per B-channel. Hence, since this is equivalent to a bit rate of 64 kbps, the total bit rate is $64 \times 240/96 = 160$ kbps.

Since there are two bits per signal element, the signaling rate = 80 kbaud.

D-channel which is used by the TE to set up the required call(s). The number of 64 kbps channels present in the bitstream is either 23 or 30 depending on the type of interface being used. These correspond to the 1.544 Mbps interface and 2.048 Mbps interface respectively. Since each operates in a different way, we shall discuss them separately.

1.544 Mbps interface

The line code used with this interface is known as **alternate mark inversion (AMI)** with **bipolar and eight zeros substitution (B8ZS)**. The principle of both coding schemes is shown in Figure 2.15(a).

As we can see, AMI is a three-level code: +V, 0, and –V. The 0 level is used to indicate the transmission of a binary 0 and either +V or –V a binary 1: for every 1 bit transmitted, the line signal changes polarity from the last 1 bit level; that is, either from $+V$ to $-V$ or vice versa. Normally, as we explained in Section 1.3.3, a DPLL is used to obtain clock/bit synchronization. The disadvantage of AMI on its own, therefore, is that a long string of binary 0s will have no associated signal transitions. Consequently, the DPLL may lose bit synchronization whenever a string of 0s is present.

To overcome this limitation, the additional B8ZS coding scheme is used. As we can see, when B8ZS is used with AMI, the line code is the same as that with AMI on its own except that when a string of eight 0 bits is detected in the string these are encoded as 000VB0VB prior to transmission, where V is a violation (same polarity) transition and B a normal (opposite polarity) transition. With B8ZS present, therefore, the maximum string of 0 bits that can be present is seven, which is acceptable for the DPLL. We note also that both AMI and the combined scheme produce differential signals, which allows longer cable lengths to be used with transformers at each end.

The transmitted bitstream is divided into a sequence of 193-bit frames the format of which is shown in Figure 2.15(b). As we can see, each frame comprises a single **framing** or **F-bit** followed by 24 8-bit time slots. The duration of each frame is 125 microseconds and hence each of the 8-bit time slots forms a 64 kbps channel. Also, 193 bits every 125 μs produces a bit rate of 1.544 Mbps. Normally, one of the time slots – and hence 64 kbps channels – is used as a signaling (D) channel and the messages carried over this relate to the setting up and closing down of the calls carried over the remaining 23(B) channels. The 23 time slots are used either singularly or in groups to provide the required bit rate.

In order for the receiver to detect the start of each frame using a single bit, a group of 24 frames – known as a **multiframe** – is defined. The F-bits from frames 4, 8, 12, 16, 20, and 24 are set to the bit sequence 0, 0, 1, 0, 1, 1 respectively and this is then known as the **frame alignment signal (FAS)**. Six of the remaining 18 F-bits are then used for a 6-bit CRC that is used to monitor the quality of the line.

(a)

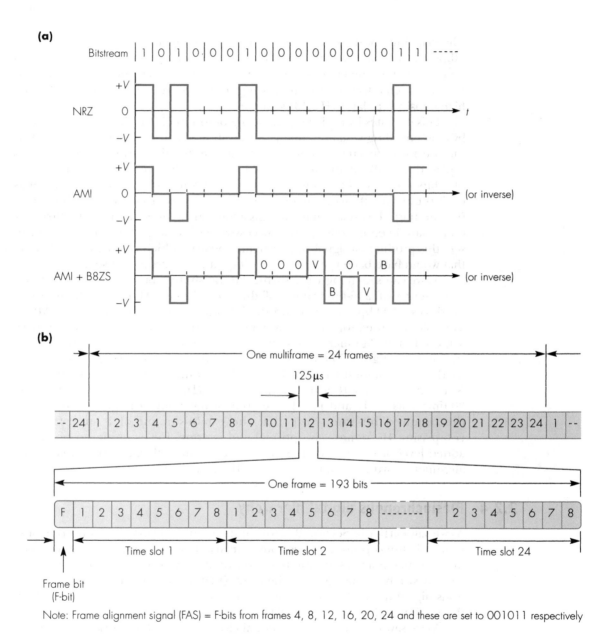

(b)

Note: Frame alignment signal (FAS) = F-bits from frames 4, 8, 12, 16, 20, 24 and these are set to 001011 respectively

Figure 2.15 ISDN 1.544 Mbps primary rate interface principles: (a) line code; (b) frame and multiframe structure.

2.048 Mbps interface

The principles of the line code and the framing structure used with the 2.048 Mbps interface are shown in parts (a) and (b) of Figure 2.16 respectively. As we can see, the line code is also AMI but the additional coding scheme used to obtain signal transitions when strings of 0 bits are being transmitted is the **high density bipolar 3** (**HDB3**) scheme.

This operates by replacing any string of four 0 bits by three 0 bits followed by a bit encoding violation; that is, a transition which is of the same polarity as the previous transition. Hence, as we can see, the first string of four 0 bits is replaced by 000V. With this basic rule, however, the presence of a long string of 0 bits would lead to a mean DC level being introduced into the signal as each set of four 0 bits is encoded in the same way. To overcome this, when transmitting a bitstream that contains a long string of 0 bits, after the first four 0 bits have been encoded, each successive set is changed to B00V. As we can see, this produces a signal of alternating polarity which removes the DC level that would have been present so allowing transformers to be used.

As we can see in Figure 2.16(b), the transmitted bitstream is divided into a sequence of 256-bit frames of duration 125 µs. Hence each time slot produces a 64 kbps channel and the bit rate of the bitstream is 2.048 Mbps. Time slot 0 is used for frame alignment and other maintenance functions. To achieve frame alignment, the contents of time slot 0 in alternate frames is as shown in the figure. The remaining bits – shown as × in the figure – are then used to carry a 4-bit CRC for line quality monitoring and other functions. Normally, time slot 16 is used as a signaling (D) channel and the remaining 30 time slots (1–15 and 17–31) are used either singly or in groups to provide the required bit rate. Note that the establishment of a superframe – comprising 16 frames – is optional and is done, for example, to obtain an added level of line quality monitoring. To achieve this, an additional frame alignment word is present in time slot 16 of frame 0.

2.2.4 Plesiochronous digital hierarchy

As we saw earlier in Section 2.1, within the trunk network digital transmission (and switching) is used throughout. For historical reasons, two types of transmission system are used, one based on what is known as the plesiochronous (nearly synchronous) digital hierarchy (PDH) and the other on a synchronous digital hierarchy (SDH). We shall explain the principles of the PDH in this section and those of the SDH in the next section.

As we saw in Figure 2.1, a national circuit-switched network is made up of a hierarchy of digital transmission and switching systems. And as we explained in the previous two sections, in terms of transmission systems, multiplexing starts within the access network where, typically, the 64 kbps channels derived from the 24/32 time slots are multiplexed together. At higher levels in the hierarchy, however, the transmission systems must support progressively larger numbers of channels/simultaneous calls. Hence this also is carried out in a hierarchical way by progressively multiplexing together multiple lower-level multiplexed streams.

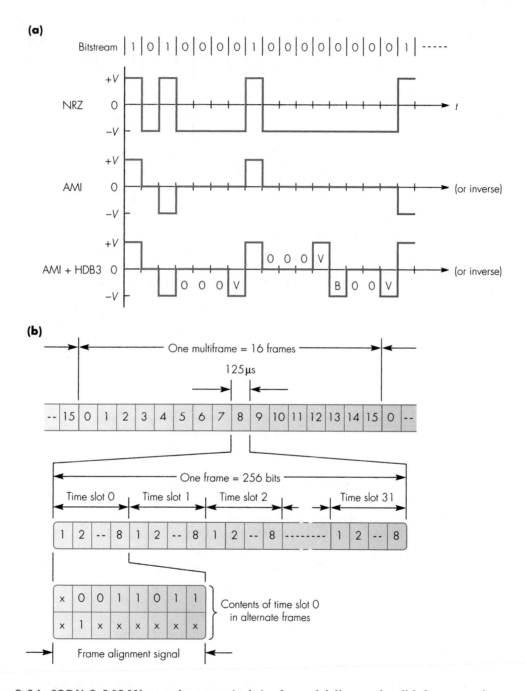

Figure 2.16 ISDN 2.048 Mbps primary rate interface: (a) line code; (b) frame and multiframe structure.

The early multiplexers used in the trunk network operated in an analog mode and the newer digital multiplexers were introduced in an incremental way as these were upgraded. As a result, although all the replacement digital multiplexers operate at nominally the same bit rates, small variations in the timing circuits used in each multiplexer mean that, in practice, there are small differences in their actual bit rates. Hence when multiplexing together two or more lower-order multiplexed streams, steps have to be taken to compensate for the small differences in the timing of each stream. To overcome such differences, an output (multiplexed) bit rate that is slightly higher than the sum of the combined input bit rates is used. Any bits in the output bitstream that are not used are filled with what are called **justification bits**. The resulting set of higher-order multiplexed rates form the plesiochronous digital hierarchy.

The two alternative primary rate access circuits we described in the last section – 1.544 and 2.048 Mbps – form what is called the **primary multiplex group** of a related PDH. In the case of the 1.544 Mbps multiplex this is called a **DS1** or **T1** circuit and in the 2.048 Mbps multiplex an **E1 circuit**. Each is at the lowest level of the related hierarchy and hence all of the higher-level multiplexed groups contain multiples of either 24 or 32 64 kbps channels. The bit rate and derivation of the two sets of multiplexed groups are summarized in parts (a) and (b) of Figure 2.17.

As we explained in the last section, both primary multiplex groups are derived using what is called **byte interleaving** since the multiplexed stream comprises an 8-bit byte from each channel. This is done since a PCM sample of a speech signal is 8 bits and hence it is convenient electronically to multiplex together the complete set of 8-bit samples from each channel. In contrast, when multiplexing a number of primary-rate groups together, since each bitstream is independent of the others and arrives at the multiplexer bit serially, the various higher-level multiplex groups are formed using **bit interleaving**; that is, as each bit from each group arrives – 1 bit per group – they are transmitted out immediately in the output bitstream.

In the same way that additional bits (to the user data bits) are required in each primary multiplex group for framing and maintenance purposes, so additional bits are present in the various higher-level bitstreams for framing – to enable the corresponding receiving multiplexer to interpret the received bitstream on the correct multiplexed group boundaries – and maintenance. Hence the bit rates of all the higher-level multiplexed streams shown in Figure 2.17 contain additional bits for framing and maintenance purposes. For example, an E2 circuit contains the bitstreams from four 2.048 Mbps E1 circuits. Hence, since $4 \times 2.048 = 8.192$ Mbps and the actual bit rate is 8.448 Mbps, 0.256 Mbps are used. The various bit rates shown in the figure are often abbreviated to 1.5, 3, 6, 44, 274, 565 and 2, 8, 34, 140, 565 respectively.

(a)

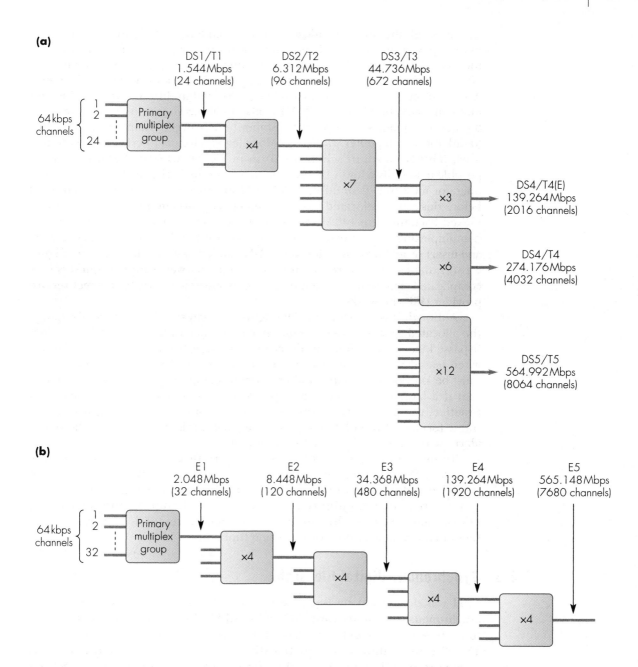

Figure 2.17 Plesiochronous digital hierarchies: (a) 1.544 Mbps derived multiplex hierarchy; (b) 2.048 Mbps derived multiplex hierarchy.

Although the use of justification bits at each level in the hierarchy does not in itself pose a problem, their presence means that we cannot identify precisely the start of a lower-level multiplex bitstream within a higher-order stream. The effect of this is best seen by considering a typical operational requirement. Assume three switching centers/exchanges located in different towns/cities are interconnected by 140 Mbps (PDH) trunk circuits as shown in Figure 2.18(a). A business customer, with sites located somewhere between them, makes a request to link the sites together with, say, 2 Mbps leased circuits to create a private network. This is shown in schematic form in Figure 2.18(b). Because it is not possible to identify a lower bit rate channel from the higher-order bitstream, the operator must fully demultiplex the 140 Mbps stream down to the 2 Mbps level before this can be allocated to the customer. This stream must then be remultiplexed back into the 140 Mbps stream for onward transmission. This type of demultiplexing/multiplexing operation is performed by a device called a **drop-and-insert** or **add-drop multiplexer** (**ADM**) and, as we can deduce from Figure 2.18(c), the equipment required to meet this relatively simple request is very complicated. The same procedure is used extensively to create **Internet service provider** (**ISP**) networks.

Although it is not shown in the figure, at each switching office/exchange the allocated 2 Mbps leased circuit must be similarly identified and the switch bypassed in order to form a direct link between the customer sites. Hence when leased circuits are provided for customers in this way, careful records must be kept of the circuits and equipment being used for each customer so that if a fault is reported, appropriate remedial action can be taken. In practice, the provision of only basic performance monitoring within the frame formats of the PDH means that normally, it is the customer who has to alert the provider of the occurrence of faults.

To overcome these limitations, the more flexible synchronous digital hierarchy (SDH) is now used for all new installations. As we shall explain below, in addition to providing a more flexible transmission network which can be readily reconfigured to meet ever changing and expanding requirements, SDH equipment can be configured remotely and has a richer set of maintenance and error reporting functions.

2.2.5 Synchronous digital hierarchy

SDH was developed by Bellcore in the United States under the title of **synchronous optical network** (**SONET**). All SDH equipment is synchronized to a single master clock. The basic transmission rate defined in the SDH is 155.52 Mbps – abbreviated to 155 Mbps – and is known as a **synchronous transport module level 1** signal or simply **STM-1**. Higher rates of **STM-4** (622 Mbps) and **STM-16** (2.4 Gbps) are also defined. In the SONET hierarchy the term **synchronous transport signal** (**STS**) or sometimes **optical circuit** (**OC**) is used to define the equivalent of an STM signal. In SONET the lower rate of 51.84 Mbps forms the first-level signal – **STS-1/OC-1**. An STM-1 signal is produced by multiplexing three such signals together and hence is equivalent to an STS-3/OC-3 signal.

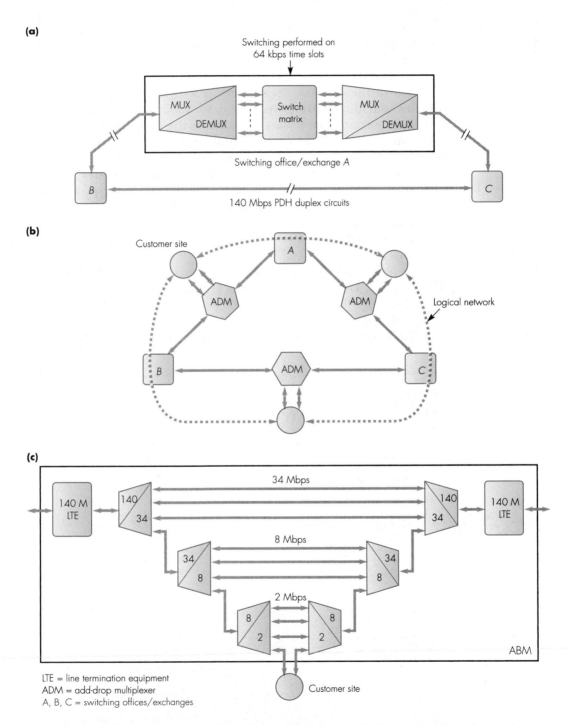

(a)

Switching performed on
64 kbps time slots

MUX
DEMUX

Switch
matrix

MUX
DEMUX

Switching office/exchange A

B

C

140 Mbps PDH duplex circuits

(b)

Customer site

A

ADM

ADM

Logical network

B

ADM

C

(c)

34 Mbps

140 M
LTE

140
34

140
34

140 M
LTE

8 Mbps

34
8

34
8

2 Mbps

8
2

8
2

ABM

LTE = line termination equipment
ADM = add-drop multiplexer
A, B, C = switching offices/exchanges

Customer site

**Figure 2.18 Private network provision with a PDH transmission network: (a) existing
network; (b) modified network; (c) ADM principles.**

As with the PDH, the STM-1 signal consists of a repetitive set of frames which repeat with a period of 125 microseconds. The information content of each frame can be used to carry multiple 1.5/2/6/34/45 or 140 Mbps PDH streams.

Each of these streams is carried in a different **container** which also contains additional **stuffing bits** to allow for variations in actual rate. To this is added some control information known as the **path overhead** which allows such things as the bit error rate (BER) of the associated container to be monitored on an end-to-end basis by network management. The container and its path overhead collectively form a **virtual container** (**VC**) and an STM-1 frame can contain multiple VCs either of the same type or of different types. Some example multiplexing alternatives are shown in Figure 2.19. Note that the first digit of the lowest-level container – and hence VC – is a 1 and the second digit indicates whether it contains a 1.5 Mbps PDH signal (1) or 2 Mbps (2).

The higher-order transmission rates are produced by multiplexing multiple STM-1 (STS-3/OC-3) signals together. For example, an STM-16 (STS-48/OC-48) signal is produced by multiplexing either 16 STM-1 (STS-3/OC-3) signals or four STM-4 (STS-12/OC-12) signals. To provide the necessary flexibility for each higher-order signal, in addition to the overheads at the head of each

SONET	SDH	Bit rate (Mbps)
STS-1/OC-1		51.84
STS-3/OC-3	STM-1	155.52
STS-9/OC-9		466.56
STS-12/OC-12	STM-4	622.08
STS-18/OC-18		933.12
STS-24/OC-24		1244.16
STS-36/OC-36		1866.24
STS-48/OC-48	STM-16	2488.32

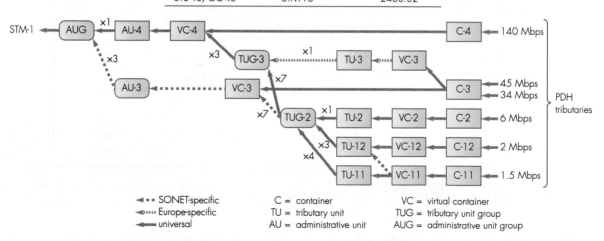

Figure 2.19 SDH/SONET multiplexing hierarchy and terminology.

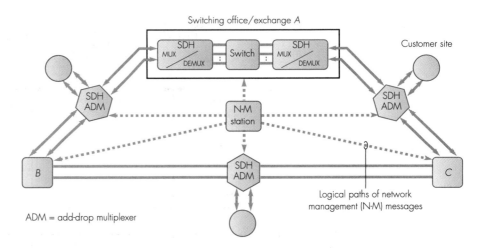

Figure 2.20 Service provision with SDH equipment using network management.

lower-level STM frame, a pointer is used to indicate the position of the lower-level STM frame within the higher-order frame.

All SDH equipment has software associated with it known as a **network management** (**NM**) **agent** and the communication channels in the overhead bytes of each VC are used by this to report any malfunctions of sections, lines, or paths to a central network management station. They are also used for the latter to download commands to change the allocation of the payload field associated with each STM-1 frame. For example, SDH ADMs can be configured – and reconfigured – remotely to provide any desired bandwidth mix without the need for demultiplexing. The general principle is shown in Figure 2.20. Redundant (standby) links are used between each pair of SDH multiplexers and these can be brought into service using commands received from a remote network management station. Again, this is used extensively in the creation of ISP networks.

2.3 Access network signaling

The basic operations associated with the setting up and closing down of a connection over the access network are shown in diagrammatic form in Figure 2.21. The steps involved are:

■ **call setup**: this includes the dialing, ringing, and answer stages;

■ **information interchange:** this is concerned with the exchange of information – speech/data – between the two subscribers;

■ **call clearing:** this results in the disconnection/release of the connection and can be initiated by either subscriber.

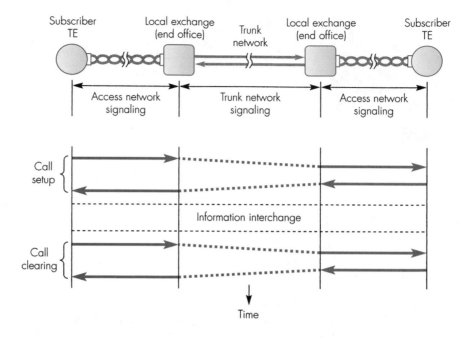

Figure 2.21 Signaling system components.

In practice, these basic operations are carried out differently over the two types of access network. We shall explain each separately.

2.3.1 Analog access circuits

We explained the basic features of an analog access circuit in the text associated with Figure 2.2. As you may recall, most signaling operations involve the transmission of one or more single-frequency audio tones. A selection of these is shown in Figure 2.22(a) and an example of their use in the setting up and clearing of a call/connection is given in Figure 2.22(b).

As we can see, in this example the call is successful and a connection would be set up. If the called subscriber line was busy, however, then the busy tone would be returned to the calling subscriber who would then replace the handset.

In the case of a modem, the same call setup and clearing sequences are followed by the incorporation of appropriate circuits within the modem. In addition, some modems – for example the V.32 – use an error detection and correction protocol during the information interchange phase in order to achieve a more reliable transfer of information. This is known as **link access procedure for modems** (**LAPM**) and these modems transmit the source

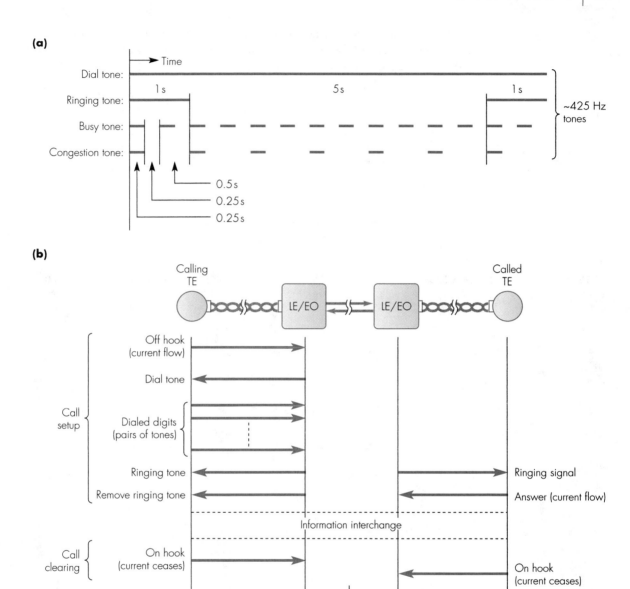

Figure 2.22 Analog access signaling: (a) a selection of the signals used; (b) sequence of signals exchanged to set up and clear a call.

information in frames using bit-oriented synchronous transmission and an HDLC-based error correcting protocol, the principles of which we explained in the last chapter. The applicability of LAPM is shown in Figure 2.23(a).

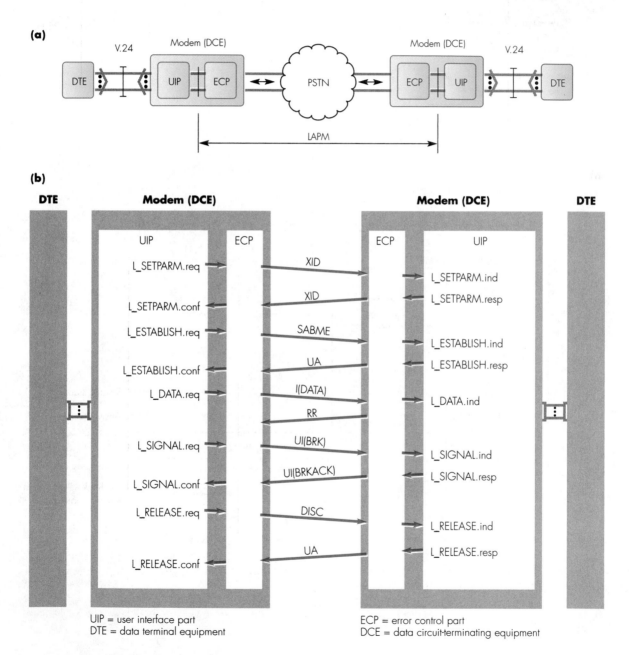

UIP = user interface part
DTE = data terminal equipment

ECP = error control part
DCE = data circuit-terminating equipment

Figure 2.23 LAPM: (a) operational scope; (b) user service primitives and corresponding frame types.

Each modem comprises two functional units: a **user** (DTE) **interface part** (**UIP**) and an **error correcting part** (**ECP**). The LAPM protocol is associated with the latter while the UIP is concerned with the transfer of single characters/bytes across the local V.24 interface and with the interpretation of any flow control signals across this interface.

The UIP communicates with the ECP using a defined set of service primitives, as shown in the time sequence diagram in Figure 2.23(b). The different HDLC frame types used by the LAPM protocol entity to implement the various services are also shown.

Before establishing a (logical) link, the originating and responding ECPs must agree on the operational parameters to be used with the protocol. These parameters include the maximum number of octets in I-frames, the acknowledgment timer setting, the maximum number of retransmission attempts, and the window size. Default values are associated with each of these, but if they are not used, the originating UIP must issue an L_SET-PARM.request primitive with the desired operational parameter values. The values are negotiated when the two ECPs exchange two special unnumbered frames – known as **exchange identification** (**XID**) – one as a command and the other as a response.

Once the operational parameters have been agreed, a link can then be set up when the UIP issues an L_ESTABLISH.request primitive. This, in turn, results in an SABM (normal) or SABME (extended) supervisory frame being sent by the ECP. The receiving ECP then issues an L_ESTABLISH.indication primitive to its local UIP and, on receipt of the response primitive, the receiving ECP returns a UA-frame. On receipt of this frame, the originating ECP issues a confirm primitive and the (logical) link is now set up. Data transfer can then be initiated using the L_DATA service.

Typically, the UIP first assembles a block of data, comprising characters or bytes received over the V.24 interface, then passes the complete block to the ECP using an L_DATA.request primitive. The ECP packs the data into the information field of an I-frame as a string of octets and transfers this using the normal error correcting procedure of the HDLC protocol. The receiving ECP then passes the (possibly error corrected) block of data to its local UIP which transfers it a character (byte) at a time bit-serially across the local V.24 interface.

If a flow control (break) condition is detected during the data transfer phase – for example, an X-OFF character is received or the DTR line becomes inactive – then the UIP stops outputting data to the local DTE and immediately issues an L_SIGNAL.request primitive to its local ECP. The local ECP then informs the distant ECP to (temporarily) stop sending any more data by sending a BRK (break) message in an unnumbered information (UI) frame. Recall that this, as the name implies, does not contain sequence numbers since it bypasses any error/flow control mechanisms. The receiving ECP then issues an L_SIGNAL.indication primitive to its local UIP and acknowledges receipt of the break message by returning a BRKACK message in another UI-frame. The UIP then initiates the same flow control signal across its own V.24 interface.

Finally, after all data has been transferred, the link is cleared when the originating UIP issues an L_RELEASE.request primitive. Again this is a confirmed service and the associated LAPM frames are DISC and UA.

2.3.2 ISDN digital access circuits

As we explained in Section 2.2.3, there are two alternative physical interfaces to an ISDN: basic rate and primary rate, the latter being either 1.544 Mbps or 2.048 Mbps. The basic rate interface provides a separate 16 kbps D-channel for signaling – in addition to the two 64 kbps user B-channels – and the two alternative primary rate interfaces include a 64 kbps signaling channel. Since both interfaces are digital, the setting up and clearing of calls/connections is carried out by the exchange of (signaling) messages over the respective D-channel. This mode of operation is called **channel associated signaling (CAS)**.

The signaling system associated with an ISDN digital access circuit is known as **digital subscriber signaling number one (DSS1)** and its composition is shown in Figure 2.24. Since the signaling messages must be received free of any transmission (bit) errors, a reliable data link protocol known as **link access procedure D-channel (LAPD)** is used to control their transfer over the interface. This is based on the HDLC protocol and is defined in **ITU-T Recommendation Q.921**. The format of the actual signaling messages and the protocol that is used to control their transfer are defined in **ITU-T Recommendation Q.931**. We shall describe the basic features of both protocols separately.

Q.921 (LAPD)

Two types of service have been defined for use with LAPD. A time sequence diagram showing the two sets of service primitives is shown in Figure 2.25. As we can see, both an unacknowledged (connectionless) and an acknowledged (connection-oriented) service are supported. The connection-oriented

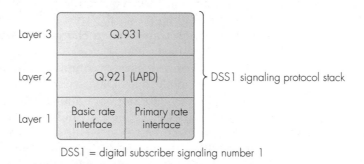

Figure 2.24 ISDN digital access signaling protocol set.

service is used to transfer call setup messages between an item of user equipment — a telephone or a DTE – and the local exchange. The associated protocol incorporates error control. The connectionless service is used for the transfer of management-related messages and the associated protocol uses a best-effort unacknowledged approach.

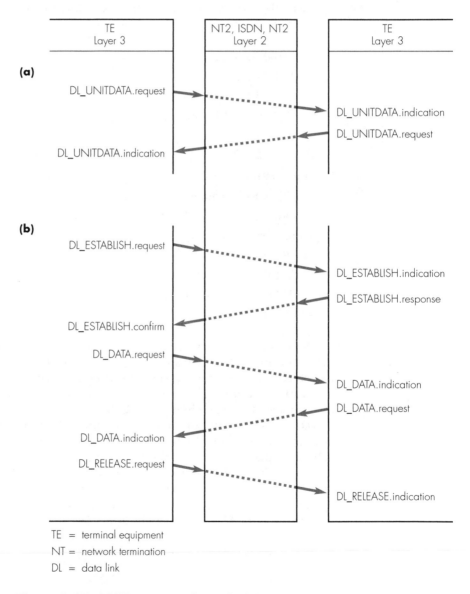

Figure 2.25 LAPD user service primitives: (a) connectionless; (b) connection-oriented.

As we explained earlier in Section 2.2.3, multiple items of terminal equipment can time-share the use of the access circuit. However, all the layer 3 signaling messages are sent to a specific terminal equipment using the address field in the header of each LAPD frame.

Q.931

The Q.931 protocol is concerned with the sequence of the signaling messages (packets) that are exchanged over the D-channel to set up a call. An abbreviated list of the message types used is as follows:

- call establishment:
  - ALERTing
  - CALL PROCeeding
  - CONnect ACKnowledge
  - SETUP
  - Others;
- information transfer:
  - USER INFOrmation
  - Others;
- call clearing:
  - DISConnect
  - RELEASE
  - RELease COMPlete
  - Others.

Some of these messages have local significance (TE/LE) while others have end-to-end significance (TE/TE). However, all the messages are transferred across the interface in layer 2 (LAPD) I-frames. An example illustrating the use of some of these messages in setting up a conventional telephone call is shown in Figure 2.26(a).

During the setting up of a conventional telephone call over a PSTN, it is assumed that the called telephone operates in a standard way and hence the call setup phase involves only the setting up of a connection through the network. With an ISDN, however, since it was designed to support a range of services, it is necessary not only to set up a connection but also to establish an agreed set of operational parameters for the call between the two TEs. To do this, the call SETUP message, in addition to the address/number of the called TE – required to set up a network connection – also includes the proposed operational parameters for the call.

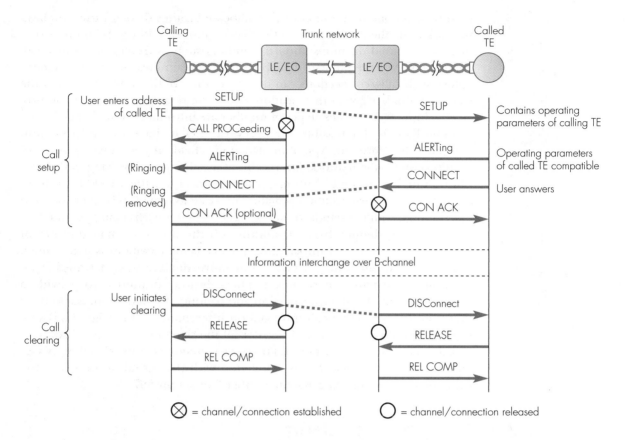

Figure 2.26 ISDN layer 3 signaling: example message sequence to set up a conventional telephone call.

2.4 Trunk network signaling

In early networks, channel associated signaling over PCM circuits was also used within the core trunk network. As the range of services supported by the network increased, so a more flexible form of signaling was introduced. For example, with a basic telephony service, a standard phone number is used which includes a country (if required), area, and local part. Then, when all calls use only these numbers, each exchange in the switching hierarchy can readily select one of a number of preallocated routes through the switching network using the various parts of the dialed number/address. With the advent of services based on non-standard numbers such as free-phone and local-charge, however, the number dialed does not contain these same parts. Hence before such calls/connections can be set up, the LE/EO must first obtain the standard number giving the location where the related service is being provided. However, since these types of number are introduced and changed quite frequently, it is not feasible for every LE/EO to have this information. Normally, therefore, this type of information is held only at a small number of locations within the network. On receipt of a call request involving, say, a free-phone number, prior to setting up the connection, the LE/EO sends an appropriate address-resolution signaling message to one of these locations and this responds with the standard number where the service is being provided.

As we can deduce from this, although the use of a small number of locations for this type of information means its management is made much easier, as a consequence, a faster and more flexible way of transferring signaling information is required. The solution adopted is to provide a separate network for the transmission and routing of signaling messages from that used for the actual call information interchange. This (signaling) network is then used to route and transfer all the signaling messages relating to all calls. This mode of working is known as **common channel signaling** (**CCS**) and the protocol stack that is associated with the signaling network, the **common channel signaling system number 7** or simply **SS7**.

2.5 Broadband modems

As we saw in Section 2.2.2, the access network of a PSTN, in addition to supporting the plain old telephone service (POTS) for which it was designed, now supports a number of additional services. For example, a range of low bit rate data applications such as fax are supported by means of low bit rate – less than 56 kbps – modems. Also, as we saw in Section 2.2.3, twisted-pair lines in the PSTN access network are used as the access lines for an ISDN. Bit rates of between 144 kbps (basic rate) and 1.544/2.048 Mbps (primary rate) over several miles/kilometers are obtained using baseband transmission. The access line is then known as a digital subscriber line (DSL). In the case of a basic rate line, this is called an **ISDN DSL** (**IDSL**) and, in the case of a primary rate line, a **high-speed DSL** (**HDSL**). An IDSL uses a single pair and an HDSL two pairs. In addition there is a simpler version of HDSL which operates over a single pair. This is known as **single-pair DSL** (**SDSL**) and bit rates of up to 1.544/2.048 Mbps are supported depending on line length.

Both the basic rate and the primary rate lines of an ISDN are symmetric; that is, they operate with an equal bit rate in both directions. However, with most interactive applications the information flow is asymmetric and involves a low bit rate channel from the subscriber for interaction purposes and a high bit rate channel in the downstream direction for the return of the requested information. For example, a V.90 modem provides a 33.6 kbps channel from the subscriber and a 56 kbps channel downstream to the subscriber.

In addition, many telecommunication operating companies (telcos) have introduced additional types of DSL technologies to meet these same requirements over the twisted-pair lines used in most PSTN access networks. Unlike the various DSL technologies associated with an ISDN, these have been designed to enable the signals associated with the existing telephony services to coexist with those associated with the newer high-speed interactive services on the same twisted-pair line. Two types are used: the first is known as **asymmetric DSL** (**ADSL**) and the second as **very-high-speed DSL** (**VDSL**). In the case of ADSL, the high-speed asymmetric channel is designed to coexist with the existing analog telephony service. In the case of VDSL, the high-speed channel, in addition to operating at a higher bit rate than that of an ADSL, can operate in either an asymmetric or a symmetric mode and is designed to coexist with either analog telephony or basic-rate ISDN services. In this section we discuss both these technologies.

2.5.1 ADSL

The standard relating to ADSL was produced by the ANSI in 1995 and is defined in **T1.413**. It was defined originally to meet the requirements of broadcast-quality video-on-demand (VOD) service. Hence the standard allows for a bit rate of up to 8 Mbps in the downstream direction – that is, from the local exchange/end office (LE/EO) to the customer premises – and up to 1 Mbps in the upstream direction. In practice, however, high-speed access to the Internet proved to be more popular than VOD. As a result, since the bit rate and QOS requirements associated with Internet applications are less than those of VOD, a variant of the original ADSL standard known as **ADSL-Lite** (or sometimes **G-Lite**) has been defined. This has been developed within the ITU and is defined in standard **G.992.2**. It provides a downstream bit rate of up to 1.5 Mbps and an upstream bit rate of up to 384 kbps. As with ADSL, the actual bit rates achievable depend on the length and quality of the line. Nevertheless, the lower bit rates associated with ADSL-Lite means that it can be used over longer distances and with poorer-quality lines than ADSL. In addition, as we shall see, ADSL-Lite can be used with a passive network termination at the customer premises rather than the active termination that is required with ADSL.

Access network architectures

As we saw in Section 2.2.1, in the earliest PSTN access networks the transmission lines used were made up entirely of interconnected sections of unshielded cable containing multiple twisted-pair wires. Over a period of time, however, sections of these cables have been replaced with optical fiber cable. The architecture of a typical modern PSTN access network is as shown in Figure 2.27.

As we can see, the amount of twisted-pair cable used varies from zero with **fiber-to-the-home** (**FTTH**) and **fiber-to-the-building** (**FTTB**), short (less than 300 yards/meters) drop cables with **fiber-to-the-kerb/curb** (**FTTK/C**), one or two cable sections with **fiber-to-the-cabinet** (**FTTCab**), and all twisted-pair for direct-to-building cable runs of up to 2.5 miles (4 km). Hence, since the objective of ADSL is to provide high-speed interactive services over the twisted-pair portion of the access line, ADSL is designed on the assumption that the maximum length of twisted-pair cable is less than 2.5 miles (4 km).

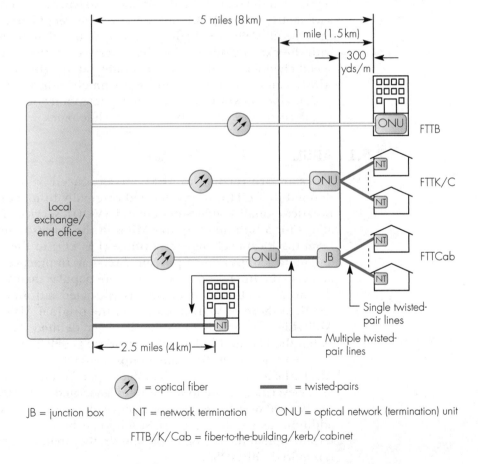

Figure 2.27 Typical modern access network architecture.

Connection alternatives

The lower frequency band up to 4 kHz of the bandwidth available with a (single) twisted-pair line is used for analog telephony (POTS). So in order for the two ADSL/ADSL-Lite signals to coexist with the POTS signal on the same line, modulated transmission must be used to take the signals away from the lower frequency band. In the case of ADSL, the two signals are transmitted in the frequency band from 25 kHz through to 1.1 MHz and, for ADSL-Lite, the upper frequency is limited to 500 kHz. The components that are used to deliver both services over the same access line are shown in Figure 2.28. The arrangement shown in part (a) relates to a typical ADSL installation and that in part (b) to an ADSL-Lite installation. In both cases it is assumed that the access line is all twisted-pair and this terminates in the LE/EO. With the various fiber access alternatives, the same line termination arrangement is located in the **optical network (termination) unit (ONU)**.

As we can see in part (a), with an ADSL installation the network termination (NT) at each customer premises is the same as that used in the LE/EO. This comprises an electrical circuit known as a **POTS splitter** and its role is to separate out the POTS and ADSL signals. This is done by means of two filters, a low-pass filter from 0–4 kHz that passes only the POTS signal and a high-pass filter from 25 kHz–1.1 MHz that passes only the forward and return ADSL signals. As we can see, having separated out the POTS signal, the existing customer wiring and connection sockets can be used to connect telephones to the NT. In the case of the ADSL signals, normally the ADSL modem is located within the NT and new wiring is used to connect the customer equipment to the NT. This can be a PC or the TV set-top box depending on the service that is being provided. Alternatively, the ADSL modem can be located within the customer equipment and the latter is then connected directly to the output of the high-pass filter.

As we can see in part (b), with an ADSL-Lite installation the existing (passive) NT and twisted-pair wiring is used. The telephone handsets are attached directly to this as they are responsive only to the low-frequency speech signal. The equipment using the ADSL-Lite line – typically a PC for Internet access – can also be attached to this same wiring. Integrated within the equipment (PC), however, is a high-pass filter and the ADSL-Lite modem. The advantage of this approach is the much simplified NT as it avoids the use of a POTS splitter and filters. Also, the existing wiring and sockets can be used to provide access to both services. To use the fast-access Internet service, the customer simply purchases and installs the line-termination board containing the high-pass filter and ADSL-Lite modem into the PC and informs the telco that they wish to use the fast-access Internet service. The telco then connects the customer line to the newer NT equipment at the LE/EO to provide this service without the need to install any new wiring or visit the customer premises.

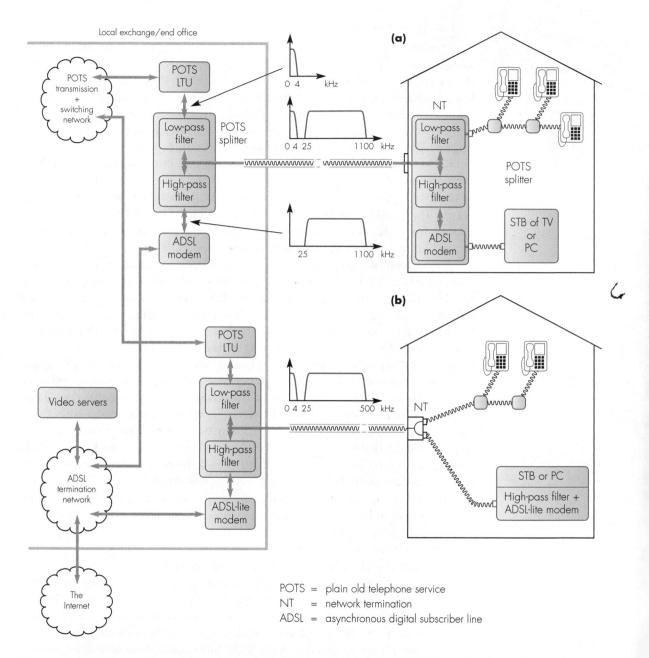

Figure 2.28 Connection alternatives: (a) ADSL with active NT; (b) ADSL-Lite with passive NT.

The disadvantage of this approach is that, in some instances, since the ADSL-Lite signal is carried over the whole in-house wiring, some interference can be experienced with the basic telephony service when the high bit rate service is being used concurrently. The main cause of the interference arises from the higher-frequency components in the ADSL-Lite signal being down-converted by some telephony handsets into speech-frequency signals and hence heard. This is one of the reasons why the upper frequency used with ADSL-Lite is limited to 500 kHz. In addition, if the existing in-house wiring is poor, then interference may also arise owing to external effects such as radio broadcasts. So in instances where interference is obtained, it is often necessary to install a low-pass filter into the sockets to which telephones are connected.

Modulation method

In the ANSI T1.413 standard, the modulation method used with ADSL modems is called **discrete multitone** (**DMT**). With this, the bitstream to be transmitted is divided into fixed-length blocks. The bits in each block are then transmitted using multiple carriers, each of which is separately modulated by one or more bits from the block. With this application, the number of carriers is either 256 or 512. However, as we show in Figure 2.29, those carriers that lie in the lower part of the frequency spectrum that are reserved for telephony are not used. Also, because with twisted-pair wire the level of attenuation associated with each carrier increases as a function of frequency, a non-linear allocation of bits per carrier is used. Typically, the lower-frequency carriers are modulated using multiple bits per carrier – for example 8-QAM – and the higher-frequency carriers use progressively fewer bits down to one bit (PSK), the number of bits per carrier being chosen so that optimum use is made of each carrier.

In addition, because of the relatively high levels of noise present on the lines – caused by the various telephony functions such as ringing, radio frequency signals from other lines, and lightning effects – in order to improve the raw bit error rate (BER) probability of each line, a forward error correction (FEC) scheme similar to that used with satellite and (and terrestrial) broadcast channels is used. As we will show in Section 5.3.2, this involves the bitstream to be transmitted being segmented into 188-byte blocks each of which has 16 FEC bytes appended to it. Byte interleaving is then used to overcome longer noise bursts, the principles of which we will show in Figure 5.18(a) and (b).

Duplex transmission

The ADSL baseband signal comprises a duplex bitstream of up to 8 Mbps in the downstream direction and up to 1 Mbps in the return direction. In the case of ADSL-Lite the bit rates are up to 1.5 Mbps downstream and up to 384 kbps upstream. In both cases, however, since a single twisted-pair line is used, a scheme must be employed to enable both bitstreams to be

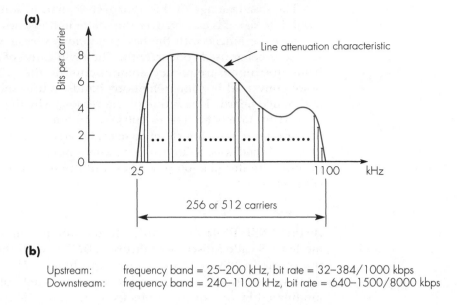

(b)

Upstream: frequency band = 25–200 kHz, bit rate = 32–384/1000 kbps
Downstream: frequency band = 240–1100 kHz, bit rate = 640–1500/8000 kbps

Figure 2.29 Example DMT frequency usage: (a) bits per carrier allocation, (b) duplex frequency usage.

transmitted over the line simultaneously. In the case of both ADSL variants this is achieved using a technique known as **frequency division duplex (FDD)**. With this the bitstream in each direction is transmitted concurrently using a different portion of the allocated bandwidth and hence set of carriers. An example set of frequencies is given in Figure 2.29(b).

2.5.2 VDSL

Very-high-speed digital subscriber line (VDSL) is the most recent technology for providing high bit rates over existing unshielded twisted-pair access lines. It is intended for use over the twisted-pair section of fiber-to-the-kerb/curb installations with the VDSL modem located in the same cabinet as the ONU. As we saw in Figure 2.27, the maximum length of the twisted-pair section is set at 300 yards/meters and hence higher bit rates than those with ADSL can be achieved. Bit rates can be up to 20 Mbps in each direction when used in a symmetric configuration or up to 52 Mbps in an asymmetric configuration with a return path of up to 1.5 Mbps.

The technical details of VDSL are currently being decided but the modulation scheme is likely to be DMT. As we saw earlier, it is intended that the higher bit rate service should share the use of the access line with both POTS and basic rate ISDN. Hence the amount of bandwidth available for the higher bit rate service is less than that of an equivalent ADSL configuration.

The duplexing method is likely to be based on **time-division duplexing (TDD)**. Using TDD, instead of both the downstream and upstream signals being transmitted simultaneously by allocating each signal its own portion of the line bandwidth – as is the case with FDD – alternate time intervals are allocated for each direction of transmission. This approach means that the duration of each time interval can be varied to meet the particular configuration required. Also, since the whole of the usable frequency spectrum is used in both directions, filters are not required. As with ADSL, an active network termination is used in the customer premises.

2.6 Internet service providers

As we indicated earlier, access to the (public) Internet is through an ISP. The ISP site is located remotely from the user and, as we can conclude from the earlier sections, twisted-pair lines that make up the telephone (PSTN/ISDN) access network provide four alternative ways of communicating with an ISP:

- a pair of low bit rate modems over both access lines;
- a combination of a pair of low bit rate modems and one or more high bit rate digital circuits;
- digital circuits over both access lines;
- a pair of broadband modems.

We shall study the access protocols used with each alternative in the following subsections.

2.6.1 Home and small office users

As we show in Figure 2.30, in the case of a user at home or in a small office, access to an ISP can be implemented in two ways. In the first, access to the ISP is through two pairs of low bit rate modems: one pair to transmit the (digital) messages relating to a session/call over the user access line and a second pair to transmit the same set of messages over the called line providing the link to the ISP. Both pairs of modems have autodial/answer facilities and, at the start of each session, the subscriber/user initiates the set up of a physical path across the total network to the called (telephone) number of the ISP. Once this is in place, the user is then able to communicate with the ISP directly and, at the end of the session, clear down the physical path across the network.

The disadvantage of this method is that the use of two pairs of modems within the total path across the network means that the distance covered is double that of a single twisted-pair. Hence the effects of noise and other signal impairments are doubled and, because of this, the bit rate of each modem is limited to 33.6 kbps (V.34bis).

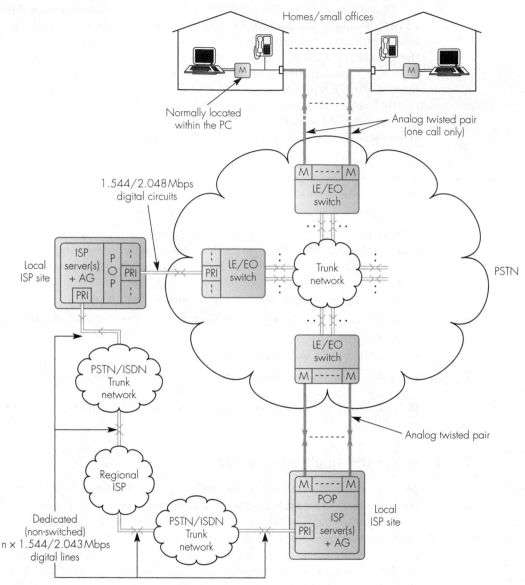

AG = access gateway   LE/EO = local exchange/end office   M = modem   POP = point of presence   ISP = Internet service provider

Figure 2.30 Internet access method for homes and small offices using low bit rate modems.

As we show in the figure, to overcome this restriction, instead of using a second pair of modems over each of the access lines to the ISP, a single high bit rate digital circuit is used. As we saw in Section 2.2.3, this is called a primary rate circuit, and it can support multiple independent channels each operating at up to 64 kbps. The signaling messages relating to the use of each channel for call setup and clearing are carried in a separate 64 kbps channel.

The use of a primary rate circuit in this way has two advantages. First, the removal of the second pair of modems on each access path to the ISP site means that the bit rate of the pair of modems over the user access lines can be increased to 56 kbps (V.90). Second, the physical connection to the ISP site is much simplified. A primary rate circuit provides a duplex link and the two bitstreams relating to a session are carried in the same assigned 64 kbps channel in each direction. However, since with most interactive applications a session involves, say, a short request message from the user for some information and a much larger response message from the server, to maximize the use of the available bandwidth, a V.90 modem supports a 33.6 kbps channel from the user and a 56 kbps channel in the reverse direction from the server. Each of these is then carried in the assigned 64 kbps channels.

Typically, the equipment at the ISP site comprises either a bank of low bit rate modems – one for each active subscriber/session – or one or more primary rate interface terminations. The bitstreams on the various lines/channels are then processed and broken down into the packets/messages relating to each session in an item of equipment called a **point of presence** (**POP**). The latter then relays the packets to an application – e-mail for example – running in a server at the site. The packets that need forwarding to the Internet are then passed to a second gateway that relays them out over a high bit rate circuit linking the ISP site to the nearest interior gateway – also referred to as an edge router – within the Internet. As we can see in the figure, this link is provided by a dedicated (non-switched) circuit in the PSTN/ISDN trunk network that is set up by the telcom provider and leased to the ISP. The bandwidth of the circuit is $n \times 1.544/2.048$ Mbps where n is determined by the amount of transmission bandwidth that is needed.

We outlined how this is done in Sections 2.2.4 and 2.2.5. Essentially, an add-drop multiplexer is installed at both the ISP site and the site where the (Internet) interior gateway is located. An unused circuit of the desired bandwidth is selected from the trunk cable that passes both sites. If, however, the trunk cable passes through an intermediary switching office/exchange, then the allocated high-bandwidth circuit is identified and the switch bypassed in order to form a direct link between the two sites.

2.6.2 Business users

As we indicated in the last section, a V.90 modem provides a 33.6 kbps channel from the user and a 56 kbps channel to the user. These, however, are the maximum rates, and in many instances poor quality lines mean that the actual operating rates are often lower than these. Hence, as we illustrate in Figure 2.31, many businesses choose to gain access to their ISP site using the digital circuits provide by an ISDN.

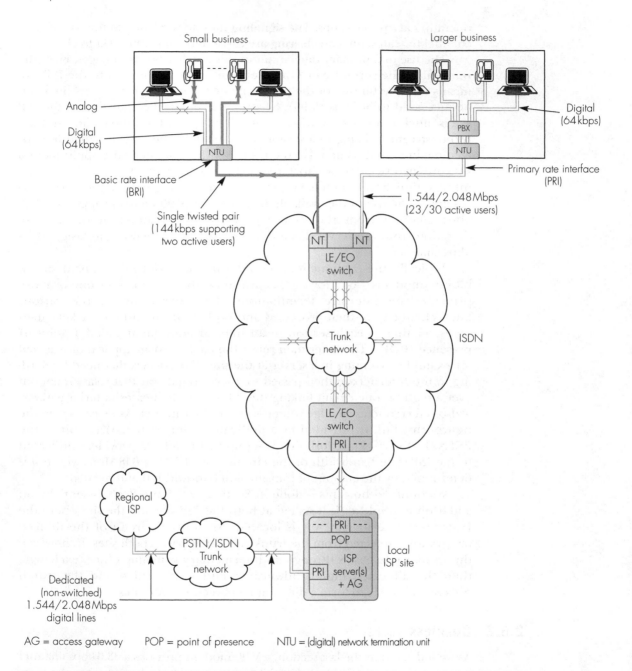

Small business

Larger business

Analog

Digital
(64 kbps)

Digital
(64 kbps)

PBX

NTU

NTU

Basic rate interface
(BRI)

Primary rate interface
(PRI)

Single twisted pair
(144 kbps supporting
two active users)

1.544/2.048 Mbps
(23/30 active users)

NT   NT

LE/EO
switch

Trunk
network

ISDN

LE/EO
switch

PRI

Regional
ISP

PSTN/ISDN
Trunk
network

PRI

POP

Local
ISP site

ISP
server(s)
+ AG

PRI

Dedicated
(non-switched)
1.544/2.048 Mbps
digital lines

AG = access gateway   POP = point of presence   NTU = (digital) network termination unit

Figure 2.31 Internet access method for small and large businesses using ISDN access circuits.

In the first example, a small business is using a basic rate interface (BRI), in which, as we showed earlier in Figure 2.11, the network termination unit (NTU) provides two 64 kbps duplex channels that can be time-shared between either four or eight user devices. In the case of older analog equipment such as an analog phone, a fax machine or a PC with a modem, the analog-to-digital conversion is carried out within the NTU. All transmissions from the NTU over the subscriber line are then in a (duplex) digital form with an aggregate bit rate of 144 kbps in both directions.

In the second example, a larger business has opted to use an ISDN-enabled private branch exchange (PBX). Typically, this will support multiple terminals – phones or PCs for example – each operating at 64 kbps, or, alternatively, a number of higher bit rate channels operating at multiples of 64 kbps. The NTU in this case provides a primary rate interface (PRI) that supports either 23 or 30 active channels which can be time-shared between all the users at the site.

The signaling messages used to set up and clear all the 23/30 channels are carried over a separate 64 kbps channel. At the LE/EO, the signaling messages are then used to switch each individual user channel to the required LE/EO and from there to the ISP. Again, to support a greater number of user channels this is done using additional primary rate circuits. The functionality of the POP and server is the same as in the first example.

2.6.3 Broadband modems

We explained the operation of ADSL and VDSL modems in Section 2.5. As we saw, an ADSL modem supports both an analog telephone channel and a high bit rate digital channel. In practice, as we show in Figure 2.32, typical bit rates are up to 384 kbps from the user and up to 1.5 Mbps to the user. Hence, although the term broadband is normally used to indicate multiples of these rates, ADSL modems are also referred to as broadband modems.

The signal output by the modem at the user side is transmitted over a single twisted-pair line and is terminated at the LE/EO side by a device known as a **splitter**. This comprises two filters: a low pass (LP) filter to separate out the telephony signal and a high pass (HP) filter to separate out the high bit rate digital channel. The telephony signal is passed to the LE/EO switch in the normal way. The output of the HP filter is terminated by a piece of equipment called an ADSL **digital subscriber line access multiplexer** (**DSLAM**). This is composed of a bank of ADSL modems and a multiplexer/demultiplexer, the operation of which we described in Section 2.2.4.

The bitstreams output by each ADSL modem are then multiplexed together and transmitted to the ISP site using a leased circuit of $n \times$ 1.544/2.048 Mbps where n is the number of streams. Normally, broadband modems are *always on*, which means that a dedicated (non-switched) channel in the trunk circuit must be used to link the LE/EO to the ISP site. At the site, the incoming bitstream is first demultiplexed into separate streams. The

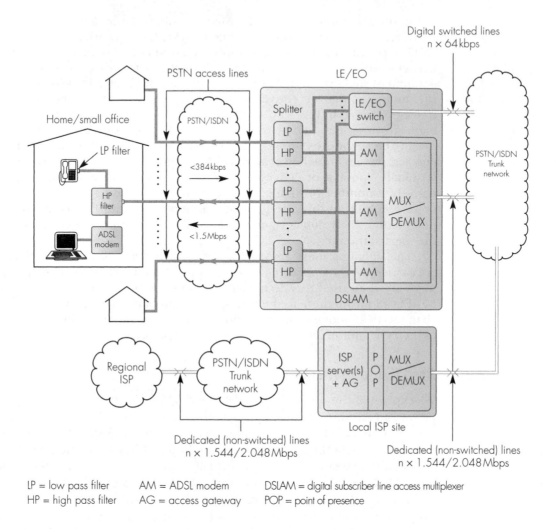

Figure 2.32 Internet access method with broadband modems.

POP then converts each stream into a stream of packets and then relays them on either to a local server at the site or to the output gateway. A similar high bit rate dedicated line is then used to link the ISP site to an interior gateway within the Internet.

The same arrangement is used with VDSL modems except a VDSL DSLAM is used. We outlined the operation of a VDSL modem in Section 2.5.2 and, as we saw, these modems operate at a much higher bit rate than ADSL. However, this is achieved only over access lines that contain a significant amount of optical fiber as we showed in Figure 2.27. Hence this restricts their use to such lines.

A final point in relation to broadband modems is that they are very easy to install and, since the telephone channel is unaffected, they provide one of the best solutions for deploying a high bandwidth link directly to the home/office.

2.6.4 The PPP link layer protocol

As we indicated earlier, the various schemes we considered in the last three sections are concerned solely with providing a direct point-to-point physical link between, say, a PC and a server within an ISP, and between the ISP access gateway and an interior gateway within the Internet. Hence a link layer protocol is needed to transfer frames of data over the various links, and an agreed network layer protocol is needed to transfer Internet packets over them.

In order to avoid the proliferation of many different protocols, the IETF has defined a standard link layer protocol to meet these requirements. This is called the **point-to-point protocol** (**PPP**) and is defined in RFC 1661/2/3 and RFC 2153. The PPP is based on the HDLC protocol we studied earlier in Section 1.4.6. To give the PPP the necessary flexibility to operate over various types of link, it has a number of features that enable it to be used in these and other applications. For example, it can operate in either the connection-oriented (reliable) or connectionless (best-effort) mode and with a variety of different types of network layer protocol. The latter feature is necessary if, for example, the protocol used over the access network link is different from the IP protocol used within the Internet.

To give it the necessary flexibility, the PPP is composed of two protocol entities: a **link control protocol** (**LCP**) and a **network control protocol** (**NCP**) In a specific application, the NCP used in both systems is selected from a set of such protocols, one for each type of network layer protocol. For example, there is an IP-NCP, an IPX-NCP and so on. The general scheme is illustrated in Figure 2.33(a) and the composition of the PPP in part (b). A state transition diagram showing the operation of the LCP and its interaction with the NCP is then illustrated in part (c). An introduction to state transition diagrams was given earlier in Section 1.4.6.

The user interface part (UIP) of the PPP is similar to that used with the LAPM protocol we showed earlier in Figure 2.23. Essentially, this issues a set of request–response service primitives that are converted by the LCP and NCP into corresponding protocol messages/PDUs. At the start of a session, the logical link between the two communicating entities – the PC and ISP for example – is in the *dead* state. On receipt of a trigger to establish a link – for example the receipt of a carrier detect signal by an ISP modem – the UIP proceeds to issue a set of service primitives first to the LCP to negotiate and establish a link with the desired options and, once this has been done, to the NCP to configure the two network layer protocols. The LCP options include whether the bit encodings are to be bit-oriented or byte-oriented, the transmission mode is to be asynchronous or synchronous, and the error control scheme is to be reliable or best-effort, all of which we described in some detail in the last chapter.

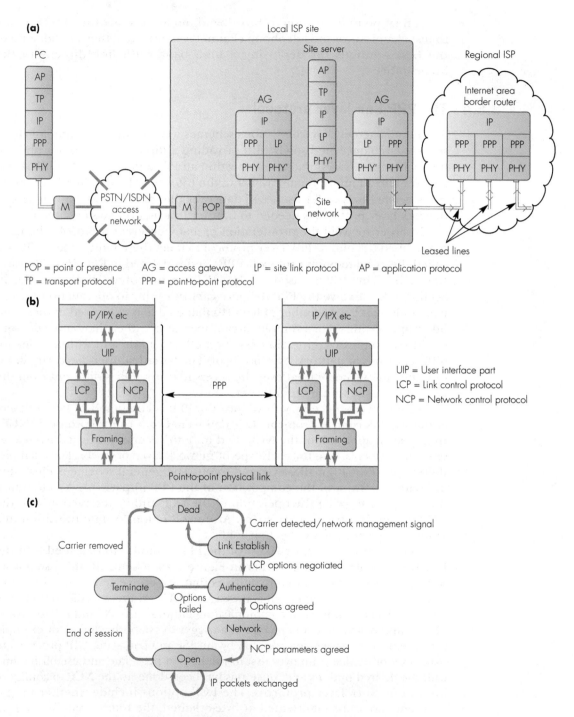

POP = point of presence   AG = access gateway   LP = site link protocol   AP = application protocol
TP = transport protocol   PPP = point-to-point protocol

Figure 2.33 The PPP protocol: (a) the location of the PPP in relation to the other protocols; (b) the composition of the PPP; (c) a state transition diagram of the PPP.

Once the LCP options have been agreed, the link is said to be *authenticated* and the NCP is then configured. For example, in the case of a PC communicating over a switched telephone circuit with modems, the block of IP addresses allocated to the ISP is much less than the number of ISP subscribers. Hence to maximize the use of these addresses each PC only receives an IP address at the start of a session and, once the session is over, the IP address is returned to the ISP.

To do this, the NCP first determines if a free IP address is available. If not, the NCP aborts the session and the LCP terminates the link. If an IP address is available, then the NCP in the ISP sends a message containing the free IP address to the NCP in the PC. This is then passed to the IP in the network layer of the PC by the UIP. The link then enters the *open* state and the exchange of (IP) packets relating to the session – e-mail, Web browsing, etc. – can start. When the session finishes, the NCP in the PC sends a message to the NCP in the ISP to release the IP address. The LCP is then informed and this proceeds to terminate the logical link and, when this has been done, the UIP commands the modem to close down the physical link.

A similar procedure is followed for the two other cases involving switched connections. In the case of broadband modems, however, since these are always on, then the PC must be allocated a permanent IP address. Clearly, this requires a significantly larger number of IP addresses. We shall study this issue in Chapter 6 when we describe the different mechanisms that are used for allocating IP addresses in the Internet.

PPP frame format

The general format of all frames used with the PPP is shown in Figure 2.34(a). Although the HDLC protocol is bit-oriented, in the PPP all frames are made up of an integral number of bytes/octets encapsulated by the opening and closing flag byte of 01111110. To achieve data transparency with the different types of synchronous transmission lines, zero bit insertion and deletion is used, the operation of which we described in Section 1.3.8.

In the case of asynchronous transmission lines, all characters are made equal to 8 bits and a form of character/byte stuffing is used, the principle of which we described in Section 1.3.3. In this application, however, in addition to flag bytes, a number of different characters/bytes are transmitted transparently. These include all the 32 control characters in the ASCII character set we identified in Figure 1.14. The list of bytes/characters and their codes is given in Figure 2.34(b).

As we can see, the escape byte/character used is 01111101 – 7D (hex) – and, whenever this is inserted, the sixth bit of the following byte/character is complemented. This rule is also used to transfer a byte/character that is equal to the escape byte.

Since the PPP is intended for use over point-to-point lines, the *address* field has no role to play. Hence it is always set to all binary 1s. Also, since in most applications all information is transferred over the line in the

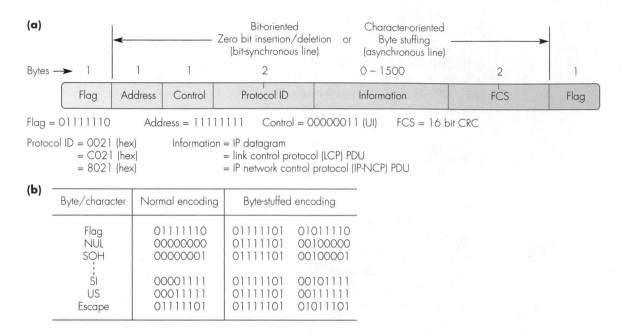

Figure 2.34 The point-to-point protocol (PPP): (a) frame format; (b) byte stuffing principle.

connectionless mode, as we explained in Section 1.3.8, the default value in the *control* field is 03 (hex), which is the code used to indicate an unnumbered information (UI) frame. The default length of the *protocol* ID field is two bytes. It is used to indicate the type of packet – and hence network layer protocol – that is present in the *information* field. For example, a value of 0021 (hex) is used to indicate that an IP packet/datagram is present.

As we indicated earlier, associated with the LCP are a number of messages – protocol data units (PDUs) – and, when one is present in the information field, the value in the *protocol* ID field is C021 (hex). For example, when transferring only IP datagrams over a line, an LCP *request* message can be sent to propose the use of a reduced frame header with no address or control fields and just a single byte for the protocol field. The other side then responds by returning either an *accept* message or a *reject* message in which case the default values must be used.

The default maximum size of the information field is 1500 bytes, although a different maximum size can be negotiated using LCP request–response messages. The *FCS* field is used to detect the presence of transmission errors in the frame and, as we explained in Section 1.3.8, it is based on a CRC. The FCS has a default length of 16 bits but a length of 32 bits can be negotiated using the LCP.

2.6.5 ISP networks and the Internet

As we showed in Figure 2.30 and the subsequent figures, Internet service providers (ISPs) are companies that enable users at home and in small businesses to gain access to the (public) Internet and its services. Typically, the local ISP site has a limited number of (Internet) servers that support, say, e-mail and Web access. A user at home, for example, can then communicate directly with these. However, if the addressed server is not located within the local ISP then the packet must be routed to a different site.

As we show in Figure 2.35, routing packets to their destination across the Internet can involve three levels called **tiers**. At the lowest level – **tier 3** – are the local ISP sites and campus and business LANs. In the case of a local ISP site, when an IP packet is received with a destination (IP) address that does

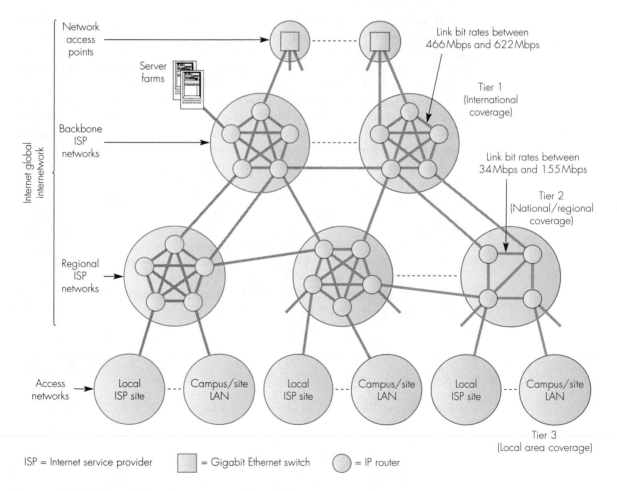

Figure 2.35 The public Internet architecture.

not belong to the set of addresses managed by the local ISP, the packet is passed directly to the router in the higher-level **regional ISP network** to which the local ISP is connected. Regional ISP networks – **tier 2** – are composed of a set of routers interconnected by high bandwidth leased lines. Each router serves a number of local ISPs, site LANs, etc. within its area of coverage. Typically, this is a city and its surrounding area and the area of coverage of the whole regional network can be that of a small country or a segment of a larger country.

As we shall see later in Chapter 6 when we discuss routing within the Internet in more detail, on receipt of a packet, the router is able to use the destination IP address in the packet header to route the packet either to a different router within the same regional network or, if the packet is addressed to a different regional network, to a higher-level router in one of the **backbone ISP networks – tier 1**. Collectively, these span the world and can route packets at very high rates.

If the packet is addressed to a computer – server/PC, etc. – that is accessible by a regional network connected to the same backbone, then the packet is forwarded to this. If this is not the case, then the packet is passed to a different backbone network using one of a set of what are called **network access points** (**NAP**). Each NAP serves a number of backbone networks and the choice of NAP to use is based on the services each offers and their cost. Typically, a NAP is a gigabit Ethernet switch. As we shall see in Section 3.4.3 of the next chapter, each line connecting a router to the switch operates at 10 Gbps and the switch is able to route packets between lines at a comparable rate.

Finally, it should be mentioned before leaving this topic that the above assumes a strictly hierarchical structure. In practice, however, because the networks at the different layers are operated by a number of different companies, private agreements are reached between them – normally on cost grounds – to provide direct links between selected routers in the same peer networks. This practice is called **private peering**. Also, there are large legacy regional/national networks still in use that do not operate using the IP protocol. Hence to provide the users of these networks with access to the services of the Internet requires additional mechanisms. We shall discuss these and other related topics later in Chapter 6.

Summary

A summary of the topics discussed in this chapter is given in Figure 2.36.

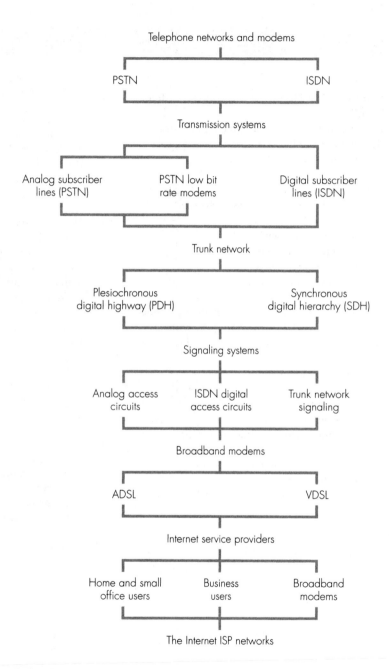

Figure 2.36 Telephone networks and modems summary.

Exercises

Section 2.1

2.1 With the aid of Figure 2.1, describe the role of the following:
(i) the local access and signaling networks,
(ii) the interexchange trunk/carrier networks,
(iii) the international network.

2.2 Explain the meaning of the following terms relating to the total transmission system:
(i) analog subscriber line,
(ii) digital subscriber line,
(iii) low bit rate modems,
(iv) high bit rate access lines,
(v) interexchange trunk lines.

2.3 With the aid of examples, identify the switching exchanges involved in providing the following types of call between two subscribers connected to:
(i) the same LE/EO,
(ii) different LE/EOs within the same region,
(iii) different regions,
(iv) different countries.
Why are alternative lines/paths present?

2.4 State the role of the signaling system
(i) over the access lines,
(ii) over the interexchange trunk lines.

Section 2.2

2.5 Explain the meaning of the following terms relating to the analog access network of a PSTN:
(i) junction box,
(ii) cross-connect,
(iii) maximum cable length.

2.6 With the aid of the diagrams in Figure 2.2 explain the roles of the following:
(i) cradle switch unit,
(ii) ringer circuit,
(iii) dialer,
(iv) 4-wire to 2-wire hybrid,
(v) dual-tone multifrequency keypad,

(vi) echo signal,
(vii) echo canceler.

2.7 With the aid of Figure 2.3, explain the role of a remote concentrator unit in the access network of a PSTN. Include in your explanation the meaning of the terms "concentration" and "pair-gain". How is a remote switching unit different from a remote concentrator unit?

2.8 With the aid of Figure 2.4, explain the following modem operating modes:
(i) 2-wire switched connections,
(ii) 4-wire leased circuits.
What is the advantage of the latter and when is it used?

2.9 With the aid of the schematic diagram and waveform sets shown in Figure 2.5, explain the principle of operation of the three basic types of modulation used in modems. Include the role of the carrier signal and the difference between phase-coherent PSK and differential PSK.

2.10 With the aid of the diagrams shown in Figure 2.6, explain the operation of the following multilevel modulation schemes:
(i) single-carrier 4-PSK,
(ii) two-carrier 4-QAM,
(iii) two-carrier 16-QAM.

2.11 Assuming an input bit rate of 56 kbps, derive the line signaling rate in baud for each of the three modulation schemes identified in Exercise 2.9.

2.12 Explain the meaning of the term "training phase" and how the bit rate for a connection is established.

2.13 Identify the subset of lines from the V.24/EIA-232D interface that are used to carry out the setting up of a connection through the PSTN and the exchange of some data. With the aid of the time sequence diagram in Figure 2.9, explain how these are used.

2.14 With the aid of the two modem connections shown in Figure 2.10(a), explain how
(i) a local loopback test, and
(ii) a remote loopback test are carried out.

2.15 Explain why line driver and receiver circuits must be used to connect a modem to the serial port of a computer. Describe the operation of such circuits.

2.16 With the aid of the two diagrams shown in Figure 2.11, explain the operation of the following ISDN network termination alternatives:
(i) a 4-port NTU,
(ii) an S-bus NTU.
Include in your explanation the meaning of the term "out-of-band" and how the use of the two B-channels is shared between the attached terminal equipments.

2.17 With the aid of the schematic diagrams shown in Figure 2.12, describe the operation of a differential line driver and receiver circuit and why these are used. Include the meaning of the term "common mode rejection" and "characteristic impedance".

2.18 In relation to the line signals shown in Figure 2.13, explain how
(i) the DC balancing bits associated with each transmitted frame ensure the mean DC level of the line is always zero, and
(ii) contentions for use of the shared signaling channel are resolved.

2.19 With the aid of Figure 2.14(a), explain how the NTU supports duplex transmission over a single twisted-pair. Include in your explanation the operation of the adaptive echo canceler.

2.20 Explain why a 4-level code is used over the twisted-pair access line from an NTU. Also explain how the code works.

2.21 With the aid of the frame structure shown in Figure 2.14(c), explain the framing structure used over the access line. Include the use of the synchronization word.

2.22 With the aid of the waveform set and frame format details relating to the 1.544 Mbps primary rate interface shown in Figure 2.15, explain

(i) the AMI line code and why this is supplemented with the B8ZS code,
(ii) the frame structure used and why a superframe is defined for use with this.

2.23 With the aid of the waveform set and frame format details relating to the 2.048 Mbps primary rate interface in Figure 2.16, explain
(i) the operation of the HDB3 line code,
(ii) the frame structure, including how the start of each frame is determined.

2.24 Explain the meaning of the following terms relating to the plesiochronous digital hierarchies:
(i) justification bits,
(ii) primary multiplex,
(iii) DS1/T1 and E1,
(iv) byte interleaving,
(v) bit interleaving.

2.25 With the aid of the schematic diagrams shown in Figure 2.18, explain how a portion of a higher bit rate stream in a PDH can be derived and used using an add-drop multiplexer. Identify the disadvantages of this approach.

2.26 In relation to the SDH/SONET, explain the meaning of the terms:
(i) container,
(ii) virtual container,
(iii) path,
(iv) line,
(v) section,
(vi) fixed stuff,
(vii) concatenation.

2.27 With the aid of Figure 2.20, explain how a lower bit rate portion of a higher bit rate stream is derived using a SDH/SONET add-drop multiplexer.

Section 2.3

2.28 With the aid of a diagram, discriminate between access networking signaling and trunk network signaling.

2.29 In relation to the diagrams shown in Figure 2.22 relating to analog access signaling:
(i) state the use of the congestion tone signal,
(ii) state how the exchange determines a wrongly keyed number and its response to this.

2.30 With the aid of the time sequence diagram shown in Figure 2.23(b), explain how
(i) error correction and
(ii) flow control
are achieved during the information transfer phase.

2.31 With the aid of the signaling protocol set identified in Figure 2.24, explain the role of:
(i) LAPD (Q.921),
(ii) Q.931.

2.32 In relation to the LAPD/Q921 protocol, state the roles of the service access point identifier and terminal endpoint identifier in the frame header. Explain the uses of the various control fields.

2.33 In relation to the Q.931 protocol:
(i) give examples of the information present in the SETUP message,
(ii) explain the role of the protocol discriminator field in the message header.

2.34 Explain the meaning of the term "channel associated signaling" and give an example of its use.

2.35 Explain the meaning of the term "common channel signaling" and how it is different from channel associated signaling.

Section 2.5

2.36 State the meaning, bit rate, and use of the following PSTN high-speed access technologies:
(i) IDSL,
(ii) HDSL,
(iii) SDSL,
(iv) ADSL-Lite,
(v) ADSL,
(vi) VDSL.

2.37 With the aid of the schematic diagram of a typical modern access network architecture shown in Figure 2.27, state the length of twisted-pair cable with each of the following:
(i) FTTH,
(ii) FTTK/C,
(iii) FTTCab,
(iv) direct-to-building.
Hence state the maximum length of twisted-pair cable that can be used with ADSL.

2.38 With the aid of the access network architecture shown in Figure 2.28(a), describe how the POTS and high-speed interactive services are provided with an ADSL installation. Include the role of the low-pass and high-pass filters in the POTS splitter and the ADSL modem.

2.39 With the aid of the access network architecture shown in Figure 2.28(b), describe how the POTS and high-speed interactive services are provided with an ADSL-Lite installation. Include in your description the advantages of using a passive network termination (NT) and one of the potential drawbacks of this.

2.40 In relation to the discrete multitone (DMT) modulation method used with ADSL modems, state:
(i) the number of carriers per symbol that are used,
(ii) the reason why multilevel modulation is not used with all carriers,
(iii) how duplex transmission is obtained.

2.41 State the following for a VDSL installation:
(i) the type of access network and the location of the VDSL modem,
(ii) typical bit rates,
(iii) how duplex transmission is obtained.

Section 2.6

2.42 State the role of an ISP. List the four ways of accessing a local ISP.

2.43 With the aid of a diagram, explain how a user at home or in a small office gains access to the Internet using low bit rate modems. Clearly identify the location of the modems involved and the role of the point-of-presence (POP) module.

2.44 With the aid of a diagram, explain how users in small and large businesses gain access to the Internet using both basic rate and primary rate ISDN connections. What are the benefits of this over low bit rate modems?

2.45 With the aid of a diagram, describe how a user at home or in a small business gains access to the Internet using a broadband modem. Clearly identify the equipment required in the LE/EO of the users and how a telephony service is concurrently supported.

2.46 In relation to the point-to-point protocol (PPP), with the aid of diagrams, explain:
   (i)   a typical application domain involving a local ISP site,
   (ii) the component parts of the PPP,
   (iii) a state transition diagram of the PPP.

2.47 Produce a sketch of the component networks that make up the public Internet. Clearly identify the geographical scope of each network type and the interconnections between layers.

local area networks and intranets

3.1 Introduction

As we saw in the last chapter, when a person is at home access to the Internet is through an Internet service provider (ISP). The ISP is located remotely from the subscribers and access to it is obtained using a PSTN/ISDN access network and either a low bit rate modem or, in many instances, a broadband modem. In the case of low bit rate modems, the cost of a session is determined by normal telephone charges; that is, by the duration of the session and the distance from the home to the ISP site. In the case of broadband modems, normally the connection to the ISP is permanent and the subscriber then pays a regular monthly subscription. This mode of access is also used in small offices and businesses.

In the case of a person in a large business/enterprise, in addition to accessing the Internet, he/she needs to communicate with other members of the business/enterprise. In the case of a large enterprise, this may involve multiple sites that are physically distributed around a single country or, with the largest enterprises/corporations, around the world.

To provide a telephony service at a site, a private branch exchange (PBX) that is similar to a (small) LE/EO is used. To provide a data communications service, a (private) site network is used which, because of its physical scope, is called a local area data network or simply a **local area network** or **LAN**. Examples are a campus, a hospital complex and a large office building.

For a large multi-site enterprise, normally the PBXs at each site are interconnected together using leased lines so extending the telephony service to the whole enterprise. Similarly, the site LANs are also interconnected using portions of the bandwidth of the same leased lines. The total network is then known as an **enterprise network** and these provide each member of the enterprise with a communication facility for both telephony/voice and data.

In the case of telephony, each PBX, in addition to the leased-line connections to the other sites, also has a connection to a LE/EO owned by a public telecommunications provider. In this way, a member of the enterprise can also speak to clients/customers, etc., in other businesses and enterprises. Similarly, in the case of data communications, the enterprise network has a connection to the Internet/ISP through an access gateway, so enabling the staff at each site to send e-mail, access the Web, and so on, and to enable other organizations to access Web sites maintained by the enterprise. In the past, many large enterprises/corporations used proprietary protocols in their networks. Increasingly, however, these have been replaced with the Internet protocols. For this reason, therefore, large multi-site enterprise networks that use the Internet protocols are called **intranets**.

As we have just indicated, LANs are used to interconnect distributed communities of end systems – referred to as **stations** in the context of LANs – including multimedia PCs, workstations, servers, and so on. Typically, these are physically distributed around an office, a single building, or a localized group of buildings, all of which belong to a single company/enterprise. The international standards body responsible for LANs is the IEEE and all the different LAN types are part of the IEEE 802 series. They operate using a shared, high bit rate transmission network to which all stations are attached and the information frames relating to all sessions transmitted. To ensure the transmission bandwidth is shared fairly between all of the attached stations, a number of different **medium access control** (**MAC**) methods are used. These include **carrier-sense multiple-access with collision detection** (**CSMA/CD**) and **control token**, both of which have a defined maximum number of attached stations and length of transmission medium associated with them. As we shall see, in practice the maximum distance is relatively small and hence most LANs of this type comprise multiple (LAN) **segments** that are interconnected together using either electrical **repeaters** or devices known as **bridges** and high bit rate **switches**.

An example of a LAN that operates using the CSMA/CD MAC method is **Ethernet** and one that operates using a control token is **Token ring**. Ethernet LANs are defined in IEEE802.3 and Token ring LANs in IEEE802.5. However, IEEE802.3 LANs are now the dominant LAN type, primarily because the

CSMA/CD MAC method can operate at the much higher bit rates that have become possible owing to the advances in transmission technology over the past few years.

All the IEEE802.3 LANs utilize fixed wiring such as coaxial cable, twisted-pair wire and, more recently, optical fiber as the transmission medium. However, the advent of sophisticated pocket PCs and notebook computers means that, in addition to operating solely as portable devices, they often need to communicate with computers that are attached to a wired LAN. To facilitate this, a number of wireless LANs have been developed. The one that is compatible with IEEE802.3 LANs is defined in IEEE802.11. However, since wireless LANs use radio as the transmission medium, we shall defer studying them until the next chapter where we describe the various types of wireless access networks. In this chapter, therefore, we shall limit our discussion to the operation of the various IEEE802.3 LANs and the methods that are used to create both small and large single-site LANs and multi-site enterprise networks and intranets.

Ethernet/IEEE802.3 networks are used extensively in technical and office environments. As we shall see, Ethernet has gone through many phases of development since its first introduction and, in general, the same basic MAC method is still used. All frame transmissions between all the stations that are attached to the same LAN segment take place over a shared high bit rate transmission cable. The CSMA/CD MAC method is then used to share the use of the transmission bandwidth of the cable in an equitable way. We describe this in some detail in Section 3.2.

More recently, higher bit rate versions of the older LAN types – now known as **legacy LANs** – have become available. To obtain the higher network throughputs that are required with multimedia applications, the central **hubs** associated with the earlier LANs have been upgraded to operate at much higher bit rates. We explain the different LAN interconnection technologies in Section 3.3. Also, as we shall explain, the older hubs operate in a half-duplex mode and support only a single frame transfer at a time. Hence the newer hubs operate in a duplex mode and allow the frames relating to multiple sessions to be transmitted concurrently. Examples include **fast Ethernet** hubs, **Ethernet switching** hubs, and **Gigabit Ethernet**, all of which we describe in Section 3.4. In addition, to improve security and obtain higher throughput, **virtual LANs** have been defined and these are described in Section 3.5.

In terms of the link layer protocol associated with LANs, the various LAN types all use a standard link control sublayer and there is a different MAC sublayer for each of the LAN types. We describe the structure and the user services offered by each sublayer in Section 3.6. Finally, we describe the different interconnection methods that are used to create large enterprise-wide networks in Section 3.7.

3.2 Ethernet/IEEE802.3

Ethernet/IEEE803.2 networks are used extensively in technical and office environments. Also, as we indicated earlier, Ethernet has gone through many phases of development since its first introduction but, in general, the same basic MAC method is still used. All frame transmissions between all the stations that are attached to the same LAN segment take place over a shared high bit rate transmission cable. The CSMA/CD MAC method is then used to share the use of the transmission bandwidth of the cable in an equitable way.

3.2.1 CSMA/CD

Since all the stations are attached directly to the same cable/bus, it is said to operate in a **multiple access** (**MA**) **mode.** To transmit a block of data, the source station first encapsulates the data in a frame with the address of the destination station and its own address in the frame header and an FCS field at the tail of the frame. The bus operates in the **broadcast mode**, which means that every frame transmitted is received by all the other stations that are attached to the bus. Hence as each of the other stations receives the frame, it first checks that the frame is free of errors using the FCS and, if it is, it compares the destination address in the header with its own address. If they are different, the station simply discards the frame; if they are the same, the frame contents are passed up to the link control sublayer for processing together with the address of the source station.

With this mode of operation, two (or more) stations may attempt to transmit a frame over the bus at the same time. Because of the broadcast mode, this will result in the contents of the two (or more) frames being corrupted and a **collision** is said to have occurred. Hence in order to reduce the possibility of a collision, prior to sending a frame the source station first determines whether a signal/frame is currently being transmitted on the bus. If a signal – known as the **carrier** – is **sensed** (**CS**), the station defers its own transmission until the current frame transmission is complete and only then does it attempt to send its own frame. Even so, in the event of two (or more) stations waiting to send a frame, both will start to transmit their frame simultaneously on detecting that the transmission of the current frame is complete. When this happens, however, it is necessary for the two (or more) stations involved, to detect a collision has occurred before each has finished transmitting its own frame. In practice, because of the possibly large signal propagation delay of the bus and the high transmission bit rate used (10 Mbps), this is not as straightforward as it might seem.

A station detects that a collision has occurred by simultaneously monitoring the signal that is present on the cable all the time it is transmitting a frame. Then, if the transmitted and monitored signals are different, a collision is assumed to have occurred – **collision detected (CD)**. As we show in Figure 3.1, however, a station can experience a collision not just at the start of a frame but after it has transmitted a number of bits. The worst-case time delay – and hence maximum number of bits that have been transmitted – before detecting that a collision has taken place is known as the **collision window** and occurs when the two colliding stations are attached to opposite extremities of the bus, as we show in the figure.

In the figure, station A has determined that no transmission is in progress and hence starts to transmit a frame – part (i). As we explained in Chapter 1, in the section on signal propagation delay, irrespective of the bit rate being used, the first bit of the frame will take a small but finite time to propagate over the transmission medium determined by the length of the cable, l, and the signal propagation velocity, v. The maximum length of cable is set at 2.5 km. Hence, assuming a v of 2×10^8 m s^{-1}, the worst-case signal propagation delay time, T_p, going from one end of the cable to the other, is given by:

$$T_p = l/v = 2.5 \times 10^3 \ / \ 2 \times 10^8 = 12.5 \,\mu s$$

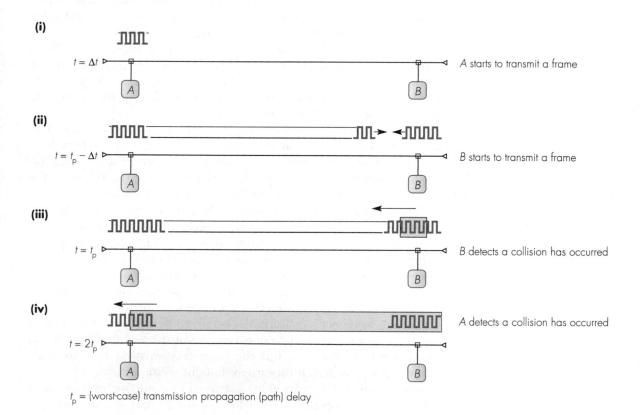

t_p = (worst-case) transmission propagation (path) delay

Figure 3.1 CSMA/CD worst-case collision detection.

Now assume that, just prior to the first bit of the frame arriving at its interface, station *B* determines the transmission medium is free and starts to transmit a frame – part (ii).

As we show, after *B* has transmitted just a few bits, the two signals collide – part (iii) – and the collision signal then continues to propagate back to station *A* – part (iv). Hence the worst-case time before station *A* detects that a collision has occurred, $2T_p$, is 25 µs. In addition, as we shall expand upon later, in order to transmit the signal over this length of cable, the cable is made up of five 500 m *segments*, all interconnected together by means of four devices called **repeaters**. Each repeater introduces a delay of a few microseconds in order to synchronize to each new frame. Hence the total worst-case time is set at 50 µs or, assuming a bit rate of 10 Mbps, after *A* has transmitted:

$$10 \times 10^6 \times 50 \times 10^{-6} = 500\,\text{bits}$$

A safety margin of 12 bits is then added to this and the minimum frame size is set at 512 bits or 64 bytes/octets which takes 51.2 µs to transmit. This is called the **slot time** and ensures that station *A* will have detected a collision before it has transmitted its smallest frame. Also, to ensure that the collision signal persists for sufficient time for it to be detected by *A*, on detecting the collision, *B* continues to send a random bit pattern for a short period. This is known as the **jam sequence** and is equal to 32 bits.

After detecting a collision, the two (or more) stations involved then wait for a further random time interval before trying to retransmit their corrupted frames. As we shall explain later, the maximum frame size including a four-byte CRC is set at 1518 bytes and hence a collision will occur if two (or more) stations create a frame to send during the time another station is currently transmitting a maximum sized frame. This is equal to a time interval of:

$$1518 \times 8/10 \times 10^6 = 1.2144\,\text{ms}$$

Clearly, the probability of this occurring increases with the level of traffic (number of frames) being generated and the maximum throughput of the LAN occurs when this limit is reached. Hence if a second collision should occur when a station is trying to send a frame, this is taken as a sign that the cable is currently overloaded. To avoid further loading the cable, therefore, the time interval between trying to retransmit a frame is increased exponentially after each new attempt is made using a process known as **truncated binary exponential backoff**.

When a collision first occurs, each station waits for a random time of either 0 or 1 slot time before attempting to retransmit its frame. Clearly, if both stations select the same number then a second collision will occur the probability of which is 0.5. In the event of a second collision occurring, the degree of randomness is increased by each station waiting for one of 0, 1, 2 or 3 slot times. Hence the probability of a collision occurring is now halved to

0.25. In the event of a third collision, each station waits for one of 0, 1, 2, 3, 4, 5, 6, 7 or 8 slot times, so again halving the probability of a collision occurring to 0.125.

As we can deduce from this, after n successive collisions a random number of slot times between 0 and $2n - 1$ is selected. This continues for up to 10 collisions after which the random number of slot times selected remains fixed at between 0 and 1023. The number 10 is known as the backoff limit. As we can deduce from the operation of the algorithm, it ensures that only a small delay is incurred when the cable/LAN is lightly loaded and the access time increases in a controlled way as the load increases. As we explain later in Section 3.6.2, in the event of a set number of attempts to send a frame failing – called the **attempt limit** – then the sending LLC sublayer is informed that the transmission of the frame has failed owing to excessive collisions.

Finally, it should be noted that the CSMA/CD access method is only concerned with sharing the physical transmission medium in an equitable way. It does not guarantee that a frame that does not incur a collision arrives at its intended destination free of errors. This is the role of the FCS at the tail of the frame and, if bit errors are detected by the FCS, the frame is discarded.

3.2.2 Wiring configurations

There are a number of different types of cable that have been used with Ethernet. These are listed in historical order:

- **10Base5**: thick-wire (0.5 inch diameter) coaxial cable with a maximum segment length of 500 m.
- **10Base2**: thin-wire (0.25 inch diameter) coaxial cable with a maximum segment length of 185 m;
- **10BaseT**: hub (star) topology with twisted-pair drop cables of up to 100 m;
- **10BaseF**: hub (star) topology with optical fiber drop cables of up to 2 km.

Although different types of cable are used, they all operate using the same CSMA/CD MAC method.

At the time the first Ethernet installations were carried out, the only transmission medium available that could operate at 10 Mbps was coaxial cable. Initially, thick-wire coaxial cable was installed since this can be used in relatively long lengths of up to 500 m before the transmitted/broadcast signal needs to be repeated. As we explained in Section 1.3.1, this involves the attenuated signal received at the extremity of the cable segment being amplified and restored to its original form before it is retransmitted – repeated – out onto the next cable segment. Up to five cable segments – and hence four repeaters – can be used in this way. Hence the maximum length of cable the signal propagates is 2.5 km plus four repeaters, which is the origin of the slot-time figure used in the standard.

The disadvantage of thick-wire coax is that it is relatively difficult to bend and hence install. To overcome this, thin-wire coax was used but, because of the increased (electrical) resistance associated with it, the maximum length of cable for each segment is reduced to 185 m.

More recently, as we explained in Section 1.3.2, with the arrival of inexpensive adaptive crosstalk canceler circuits to overcome near-end crosstalk (NEXT), it is possible to obtain bit rates of tens of Mbps over unshielded twisted-pair cable of up to 100 m in length. Also, it was found that, in a vast majority of offices, the maximum length of cable used for telephony to reach each desktop from the wiring closet was less than 100 m. Hence unshielded twisted-pair (UTP) cable – as used for telephony – became the standard for use with Ethernet. The configuration used for each segment is shown in Figure 3.2(a).

Since the cable forms a physical bus, both thick and thin wire coaxial cable installations involve the cable passing near to each attached station. As we can see in the figure, however, with twisted-pair cable a star configuration is used with the hub located in the wiring closet and each station connected to it by means of twisted-pair drop cables. Initially, category three (CAT3) UTP cable was used as for telephony. Each cable contains four separate twisted-pairs. In the case of Ethernet, just two pairs are used: one pair for transmissions from the station to the hub and the second pair for transmissions in the reverse direction. More recently, higher bit rate versions of the basic Ethernet have been introduced that use the higher-quality category five (CAT5) unshielded twisted-pair (UTP) cable. Also, as we shall see later in Section 3.3, optical fiber is now used extensively to interconnect hubs together since, in many instances, this is over larger distances than those possible with twisted-pair cables.

To emulate the broadcast mode of working associated with CSMA/CD, as we show in Figure 3.2(b), the repeater electronics within the hub repeats and broadcasts out the signal received from each of the input pairs onto all of the other output pairs. Hence the signal output by any of the stations is received by all the other stations and, as a result, the carrier sense function simply involves the MAC unit within each station determining whether a signal is currently being received on its input pair. Similarly, the collision detection function involves the station determining if a signal arrives on its input pair while it is transmitting a frame on the output pair.

Because of their mode of operation, this type of hub is called a **repeater hub** and typical numbers of attached stations – and hence sockets – are from 8 through to 16. Above this number multiple hubs are stacked together and are connected by repeaters or, as we shall explain in Section 3.3, bridges or switches. In the case of repeaters, the maximum length of cable between any two stations – including the 100 m drop cables – must not exceed 1.5 km. To achieve this coverage/distance, however, normally it is necessary to use a central hub to which each twisted-pair hub is connected by means of optical fiber cables.

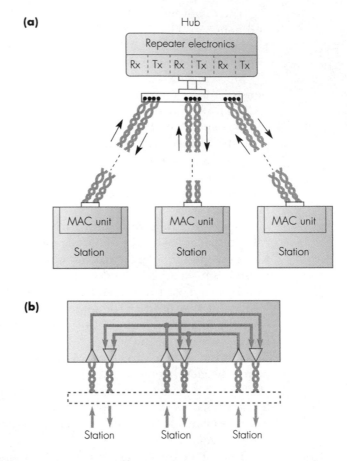

Figure 3.2 Hub configuration principles: (a) topology; (b) repeater schematic.

3.2.3 Frame format and operational parameters

The format of a frame and the operational parameters of a CSMA/CD network are shown in Figure 3.3. The *preamble* field is sent at the head of all frames. Its function is to allow the receiving electronics in each MAC unit and repeater to achieve bit synchronization before the actual frame contents are received. The preamble pattern is a sequence of seven bytes, each equal to the binary pattern 10101010. All frames are transmitted on the cable using Manchester encoding. Hence, as we explained in Section 1.3.3, the preamble results in a periodic waveform being received by the receiver electronics in each station, which acts as a reference clock. The *start-of-frame delimiter* (*SFD*) is the single byte 10101011 that immediately follows the preamble and signals the start of a valid frame to the receiver.

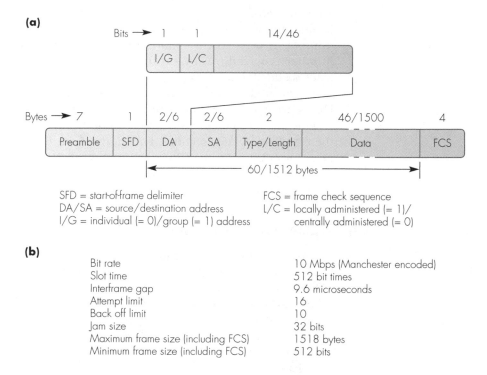

SFD = start-of-frame delimiter
DA/SA = source/destination address
I/G = individual (= 0)/group (= 1) address

FCS = frame check sequence
L/C = locally administered (= 1)/
centrally administered (= 0)

(b)

Bit rate	10 Mbps (Manchester encoded)
Slot time	512 bit times
Interframe gap	9.6 microseconds
Attempt limit	16
Back off limit	10
Jam size	32 bits
Maximum frame size (including FCS)	1518 bytes
Minimum frame size (including FCS)	512 bits

Figure 3.3 Ethernet/IEEE802.3 characteristics: (a) frame format; (b) operational parameters.

The *destination* and *source addresses* – also known as **MAC addresses** because they are used by the MAC sublayer – specify the identity of the hardware interface of both the intended destination station(s) and the originating station, respectively. Each address field can be either 16 or 48 bits, but for any particular LAN installation the size must be the same for all stations. The first bit in the destination address field specifies whether the address is an **individual address** (= **0**) or a **group address** (= **1**). If an individual address is specified, the transmitted frame is intended for a single destination. If a group address is specified, the frame is intended either for a logically related group of stations (group address) or for all other stations connected to the network (**broadcast** or **global address**). In the latter case, the address field is set to all binary 1s and, for a group address, the address specifies a previously agreed group of stations. The type of grouping is specified in the second bit and can be locally administered (= 1) or centrally administered (= 0). Group addresses are used for multicasting and the MAC unit/circuit associated with each station in the multicast group is then programmed to read all frames with this group address at its head.

With the original Ethernet standard, the two-byte *type* field immediately follows the address fields and indicates the network layer protocol that created the information in the data field. With the more recent IEEE802.3 format, the next two bytes are used as a *length indicator* which indicates the number of bytes in the data field. If this value is less than the minimum number required for a valid frame (minimum frame size), a sequence of bytes is added, known as **padding**. The maximum size of the data field – normally referred to as the **maximum transmission unit** (**MTU**) – is 1500 bytes. Hence to enable the same field to act as a type field, any value greater than 1500 is interpreted as indicating a frame type. We shall illustrate the use of the type field in later sections. Finally, the *frame check sequence* (*FCS*) field contains a four-byte (32-bit) CRC value that is used for error detection. Note that with the original Ethernet standard, the end of a frame is detected when signal transitions end.

3.2.4 Frame transmission and reception

The frame transmission sequence is summarized in Figure 3.4(a). When a frame is to be transmitted, the frame contents are first encapsulated by the MAC unit into the format shown in Figure 3.3(a). To avoid contention with other transmissions on the medium, the MAC unit first monitors the carrier sense signal and, if necessary, defers to any passing frame. After a short additional delay (known as the **interframe gap**) to allow the passing frame to be received and processed by the addressed station(s), transmission of the frame is initiated.

As the bitstream is transmitted, the transmitter simultaneously monitors the received signal to detect whether a collision has occurred. Assuming a collision has not been detected, the complete frame is transmitted and, after the FCS field has been sent, the MAC unit awaits the arrival of a new frame, either from the cable or from the link control layer within the station. If a collision is detected, the transmitter immediately turns on the collision detect signal and enforces the collision by transmitting the jam sequence to ensure that the collision is detected by all other stations involved in the collision. After the jam sequence has been sent, the MAC unit terminates the transmission of the frame and schedules a retransmission attempt after a short randomly computed interval.

Figure 3.4(b) summarizes the frame reception sequence. The MAC unit first detects the presence of an incoming signal and switches on the carrier sense signal to inhibit any new transmissions from this station. The incoming preamble is used to achieve bit synchronization and, when the start-of-frame delimiter has been detected, with an IEEE802.3 LAN, the length indicator is read and used to determine the number of bytes that follow. The frame contents including the destination and source addresses are then received and loaded into a frame buffer to await further processing. The received FCS field is first compared with the computed FCS and, if they are equal, the frame content is further checked to ensure it contains an integral number of bytes and that it is neither too short nor too long. If any of these checks fail then the frame is discarded. If all checks pass, then the destination address is read

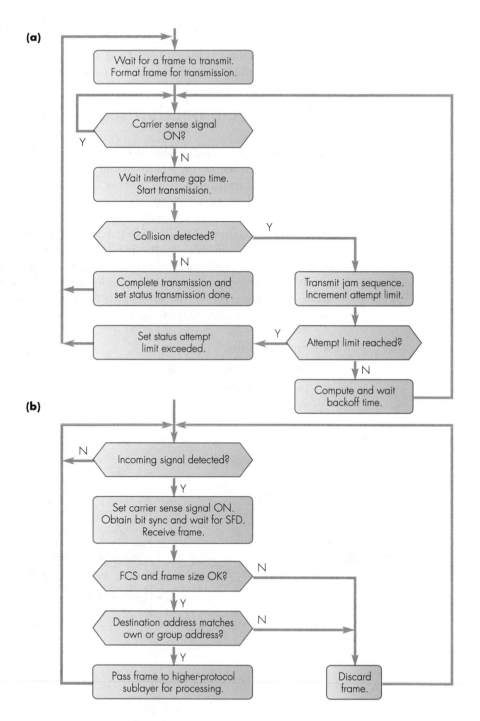

**Figure 3.4 CSMA/CD MAC sublayer operation: (a) transmit;
(b) receive.**

from the head of the frame and, if the frame is intended for this station – that is, the address of the station is the same as that in the frame or, if it is a group address, the station is a member of the specified group – the frame contents are passed to the link control layer for processing.

3.3 LAN interconnection technologies

In general, within a small business/site, the basic communications requirement – in addition to telephony – is to enable a number of users, each with a desktop PC/workstation, to access a server computer that is used as, say, a print server and an e-mail server for the site. To achieve the latter function, the server is connected to the Internet through an Internet service provider that also provides access to the Web. As we explained in Section 2.6 and illustrate in Figure 3.5, the connection to the ISP can be by means of either a broadband modem or, if higher throughput is required, a primary rate leased line.

With a larger business that requires multiple hubs, to enable all users to access the site server(s), the hubs must be interconnected together. This can be done in three alternative ways:

■ repeater hubs,
■ bridging hubs,
■ switching hubs.

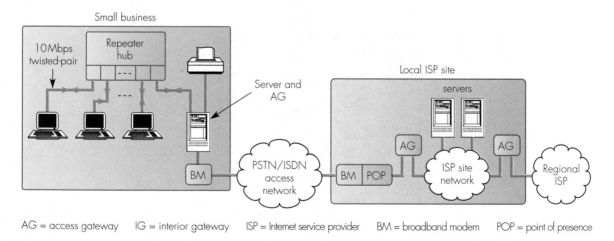

AG = access gateway   IG = interior gateway   ISP = Internet service provider   BM = broadband modem   POP = point of presence

Figure 3.5 Access to the Internet for a small business.

3.3.1 Repeater hubs

A repeater hub, in addition to repeating each frame received at each of its input ports out onto all of its other ports, also repeats each frame it receives out to a higher level repeater if one is present. Hence, as we can deduce from the example network topology shown in Figure 3.6, each frame transmitted by a member of any of the workgroups is repeated to all the other segments – and hence stations – in the total network. This means, therefore, that in terms of the available bandwidth, the network behaves like a single LAN segment. In many instances, however, there is no necessity for the frames generated within a workgroup to be transmitted beyond the hub/segment on which they are attached. Bridging hubs were introduced therefore to limit the forwarding of frames to those that are intended for a different segment/workgroup.

3.3.2 Bridging hubs

The function of a bridging hub is similar to a repeater hub in that it is used for interconnecting a set of repeater hubs. However, when a bridging hub is used, all frames received from a lower-level hub are first buffered (stored) and error checked before they are repeated (forwarded). Moreover, only those frames that are free of errors and addressed to a station that is attached to a different repeater hub/segment from the one on which the frame was received are forwarded. Consequently, all frames that are addressed to another member of the same workgroup are not forwarded and hence do

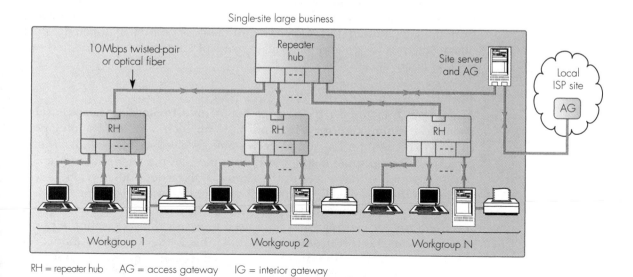

Figure 3.6 Access to the Internet for a single-site large business using repeater hubs only.

not load the rest of the network, so increasing significantly the overall network throughput.

The presence of a bridging hub in a path between two communicating stations is transparent to the two stations and their associated repeater hubs. For this reason, bridging hubs are also known as **transparent bridges** and are often abbreviated to simply bridges. All routing decisions are made exclusively by the bridge(s). Moreover, a bridge automatically initializes and configures itself (in terms of its routing information) in a dynamic way after it has been put into service. A schematic of a bridge is shown in Figure 3.7(a) and a simple bridged LAN in Figure 3.7(b).

A LAN segment is physically connected to a bridge through a **bridge port**. A basic bridge has just two ports whereas a **multiport bridge** has a number of connected ports (and hence segments). In practice, each bridge port comprises the MAC integrated circuit chipset associated with the particular type of LAN segment – Ethernet – together with some associated port management software. The software is responsible for initializing the chipset at start-up – chipsets are all programmable devices – and for buffer management. Normally, the available memory is logically divided into a number of fixed-size units known as buffers. Buffer management involves passing a free buffer (pointer) to the chipset ready for receiving a new frame and passing the pointer of a full buffer to the chipset for onward transmission (forwarding).

Every bridge operates in the **promiscuous mode**, which means it receives and buffers all frames received on each of its ports. When a frame has been received at a port and put into the assigned buffer by the MAC chipset, the port management software prepares the chipset for a new frame and then passes the pointer of the memory buffer containing the received frame to the **bridge protocol entity** for processing. Since two (or more) frames may arrive concurrently at the ports and two or more frames may need to be forwarded from the same output port, the passing of memory pointers between the port management software and the bridge protocol entity software is carried out via a set of queues.

Frame forwarding (filtering)

As we show in Figure 3.7(b), a bridge maintains a **forwarding database** (also known as a **routing directory**) that indicates, for each port, the outgoing port (if any) to be used for forwarding each frame received at that port. If a frame is received at a port that is addressed to a station on the segment (and hence port) on which it was received, the frame is discarded; otherwise it is forwarded via the port specified in the forwarding database. The normal routing decision involves a simple look-up operation: the destination address in each received frame is first read and then used to access the corresponding port number from the forwarding database. If this is the same as the port on which it was received, the frame is discarded, else it is queued for forward transmission on the segment associated with the accessed port. This process is also known as **frame filtering**.

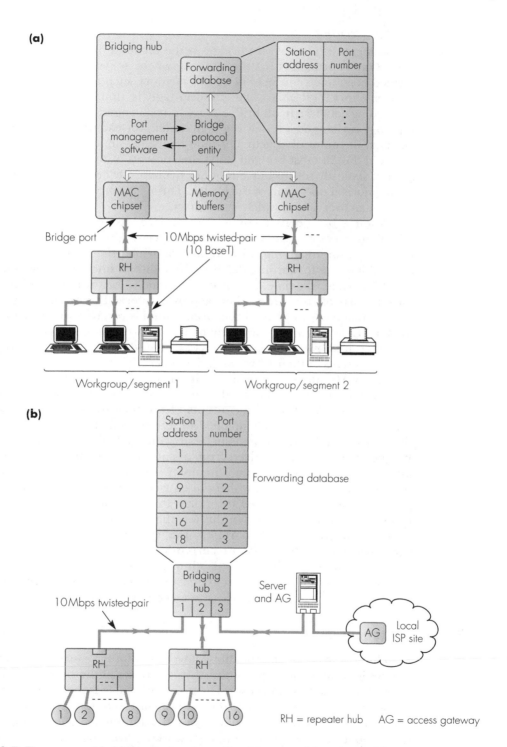

Figure 3.7 Transparent bridging hub schematic: (a) general topology; (b) multiport bridge example.

Bridge learning

A problem with transparent bridges is the creation of the forwarding database. One approach is for the contents of the forwarding database to be created in advance and held in a fixed memory, such as programmable read-only memory (PROM). The disadvantage is that the contents of the forwarding database in all bridges have to be changed whenever the network topology is changed – a new segment added, for example – or when a user changed the point of attachment (and hence segment) of his or her station. To avoid this, in most bridged LANs the contents of the forwarding database are not statically set up but rather are dynamically created and maintained during normal operation of the bridge. This is accomplished using a learning process, an overview of which is as follows.

When a bridge first comes into service, its forwarding database is initialized to empty. Whenever a frame is received, the *source address* within it is read and the incoming port number on which the frame was received is entered into the forwarding database. In addition, since the forwarding port is not known at this time, a copy of the frame is forwarded on all the other output ports of the bridge. This action is referred to as **flooding** since it ensures that a copy of each frame transmitted is received on all segments in the total LAN. During the learning phase this procedure is repeated for each frame received by the bridge. In this way, all bridges in the LAN rapidly build up the contents of their forwarding databases.

The MAC address associated with a station is fixed at the time of its manufacture. If a user changes the point of attachment to the network of his or her PC/workstation, the contents of the forwarding database in each bridge must be periodically updated to reflect such changes. To accomplish this, an **inactivity timer** is associated with each entry in the database. Whenever a frame is received from a station within the predefined time interval, the timer expires and the entry is removed. Whenever a frame is received from a station for which the entry has been removed, the learning procedure is again followed to update the entry in each bridge with the (possibly new) port number. In this way the forwarding database in a bridge is continuously updated to reflect the current LAN topology and the addresses of the stations that are currently attached to the segments it interconnects. The inactivity timer also limits the size of the database since it contains only those stations that are currently active. This is important since the size of the database influences the speed of the forwarding operation.

3.3.3 Switching hubs

Switching hubs – normally abbreviated to switches – are very similar to bridges in so much as they use the MAC addresses at the head of each frame for routing/switching purposes. The main difference is that a bridge discards frames that come from the same workgroup/segment whereas a switch switches/routes all the frames it receives. In addition, in order to improve the throughput rate, switches use duplex working over the cables that connect lower-level hubs to the switch. An example of a site network configuration using a switching hub is shown in Figure 3.8.

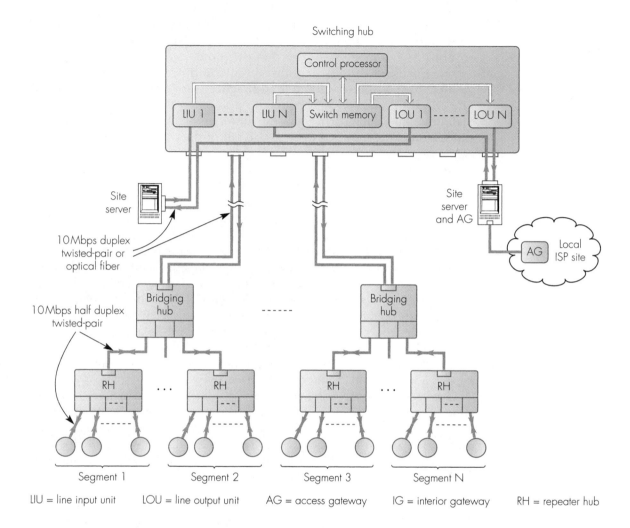

Switching hub

Figure 3.8 Example network configuration using a switching hub.

As we can see, lower-level hubs are connected to the switch by means of a pair of (duplex) cables that, typically, are implemented as UTP (or STP) cables or, for longer cable runs, dual multimode fiber cables. Also, with a switching hub CSMA/CD is not used and instead all lower-level hubs can transmit and receive frames concurrently. However, since repeater hubs operate in the half-duplex (repeating) mode, these cannot be connected directly to the switch and instead, bridging hubs must be used. Also, in order to obtain a high level of throughput, the two servers are connected directly to the switch by means of duplex cables.

Because each lower-level hub can transmit frames simultaneously, a frame may be received at multiple input ports of the switch – and hence require processing – simultaneously. Similarly, two or more frames may require the same output line simultaneously. Hence associated with each input and output line is a memory buffer that can hold several fames waiting to be either processed (input) or transmitted (output). The frames – memory pointers to the start of the frame in practice – are stored in a FIFO queue. The control processor then reads the pointer to the frame at the head of each input queue in turn, obtains the destination MAC address from its head, and transfers the frame pointer to the tail of the required output queue to await transmission.

In order to retain the same connectionless mode of operation, when the switch is first brought into service – and subsequently at periodic intervals – the control processor enters a learning state similar to that used in transparent bridges. Hence when in the learning state, the switch simply initiates the onward transmission of a copy of each frame received from an input line onto all output lines. Prior to doing this, however, the control processor reads the source address from the head of the frame and keeps a record of this, together with the input port number of the port number on which the frame was received, in a routing table. The contents of the routing table are then subsequently used to route each received frame to specific output port. As we can deduce from this, there is a store-and-forward delay associated with a switch. Also, as with a bridge, the FCS at the tail of each frame is used to check for the presence of transmission errors prior to the frame being forwarded and corrupted frames are discarded.

Alternatively, some switches do not use a store-and-forward mode of operation and instead, providing the required output line is available, the switch starts to forward the frame as soon as the destination MAC address has been received. A switch that operates in this way is called a **cut-through switch**. However, since there is no provision for a frame to be stored, the frame is discarded if the required output line is busy.

3.4 High-speed LANs

As the application of LANs has become more diverse, so the demands on them in terms of information/data throughput have increased. As we have just described, by using a combination of bridges and a high bit rate backbone, the throughput of the total LAN is determined by the maximum throughput of each LAN segment. As we explained in Section 3.2, the maximum throughput of an Ethernet LAN is only a fraction of the 10 Mbps bit rate that is used. Hence in order to meet the higher throughput requirements of the newer multimedia applications, a number of high-speed LAN types have been developed. These include three variations of the basic Ethernet LAN: **Fast Ethernet**, **Switched Fast Ethernet**, and **Gigabit Ethernet**.

3.4.1 Fast Ethernet

The aim of Fast Ethernet was to use the same shared, half-duplex transmission mode as Ethernet but to obtain a $\times 10$ increase in operational bit rate over 10BaseT while at the same time retaining the same wiring systems, MAC method, and frame format. As we explained in Section 3.2.2, when using hubs with unshielded twisted-pair (UTP) cable, the maximum length of drop cable from the hub to a station is limited to 100 m by the driver/receiver electronics. Assuming just a single hub, this means that the maximum distance between any two stations is 200 m and the worst-case path length for collision detection purposes is 400 m plus the repeater delay in the hub. Clearly, therefore, a higher bit rate can be used while still retaining the same CSMA/CD MAC method and minimum frame size of 512 bits. In the standard, the bit rate is set at 100 Mbps over existing UTP cable.

Line code

The major technological hurdle to overcome with Fast Ethernet was how to achieve a bit rate of 100 Mbps over 100 m of UTP cable. Category 3 UTP cable – as used for telephony, and the most widely installed – contains four separate twisted-pair wires. To reduce the bit rate used on each pair, all four pairs are used to achieve the required bit rate of 100 Mbps in each direction. Hence the standard is also known as **100Base4T**.

With the CSMA/CD access control method, in the absence of contention for the medium, all transmissions are half-duplex, that is, either station-to-hub or hub-to-station. In a 10BaseT installation, just two of the four wire pairs are used for data transfers, one in each direction. Collisions are detected when the transmitting station (or hub) detects a signal on the receive pair while it is transmitting on the transmit pair. Since the collision detect function must also be performed in 100Base4T, the same two pairs are used for this function. The remaining two pairs are operated in a bidirectional mode, as shown in Figure 3.9(a).

The figure shows that data transfers in each direction utilize three pairs – pairs 1, 3, and 4 for transmissions between a station and the hub and pairs 2, 3, and 4 for transmissions between the hub and a station. Transmissions on pairs 1 and 2 are then used for collision detection and carrier sense purposes as with 10BaseT. This means that the bit rate on each pair of wires need only be $100/3 = 33.33$ Mbps.

If we use Manchester encoding, a bit rate of 33.33 Mbps requires a baud rate of 33.33 Mbaud, which exceeds the 30 Mbaud limit set for use with such cables, as above this, unacceptably high levels of crosstalk are obtained. To reduce the baud rate, a three-level (**ternary**) **code** is used instead of straight (two-level) binary coding. The code used is known as **8B6T**, which means that, prior to transmission, each set of eight binary bits is first converted into six ternary (three-level) symbols. From the example shown in Figure 3.9(b), we can deduce that this yields a symbol rate of:

$$\frac{100 \times 6/8}{3} = 25\,\text{Mbaud}$$

which is well within the set limit.

The three signal levels used are +V, 0, –V, which are represented simply as +, 0, –. The codewords are selected such that the line is DC balanced, that is, the mean line signal is zero. This maximizes the receiver's discrimination of the three signal levels since these are then always relative to a constant 0 (DC) level. To achieve this, we exploit the inherent redundancy present in the use of six ternary symbols. The six ternary symbols means that there are 729 (3^6)

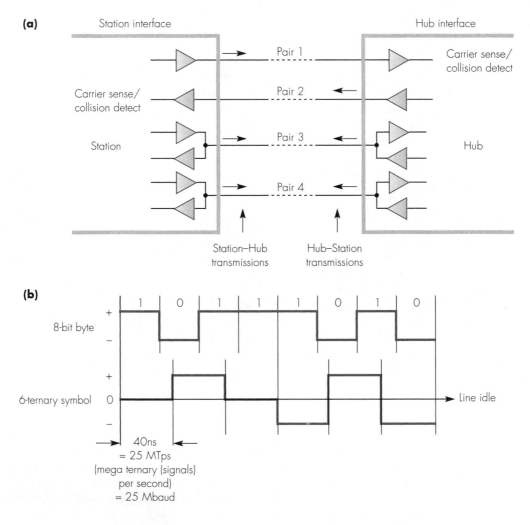

Figure 3.9 100Base4T: (a) use of wire pairs; (b) 8B6T encoding.

possible codewords. Since only 256 codewords are required to represent the complete set of 8-bit byte combinations, the codes used are selected, firstly, to achieve DC balance and secondly, to ensure all codewords have at least two signal transitions within them. This is done so that the receiver DPLL maintains clock synchronization.

To satisfy the first condition, we choose only those codewords with a combined weight of 0 or +1 and 267 codes meet this condition. To satisfy the second condition, we eliminate those codes with fewer than two transitions – five codes – and also those starting or ending with four consecutive zeros – six codes. This leaves the required 256 codewords, the first 128 of which are listed in Table 3.1.

DC balance

As we have just indicated, all the codewords selected have a combined weight of either 0 or +1. For example, the codeword $+--+00$ has a combined weight of 0 while the codeword $0+++--$ has a weight of +1. Clearly, if a string of codewords each of weight +1 is transmitted, then the mean signal level at the receiver will move away rapidly from the zero level, causing the signal to be misinterpreted. This is known as **DC wander** and is caused by the use of transformers at each end of the line. The presence of transformers means there is no path for direct current (DC).

To overcome this, whenever a string of codewords with a weight of +1 is to be sent, the symbols in alternate codewords are inverted prior to transmission. For example, if a string comprising the codeword $0+++--$ is to be sent, then the actual codewords transmitted will be $0+++--$, $0---++$, $0+++--$, $0---++$, and so on, yielding a mean signal level of 0. At the receiver, the same rules are applied and the alternative codewords will be reinverted into their original form prior to decoding. The procedure used for transmission is shown in the state transition diagram in Figure 3.10(a).

To reduce latency during the decoding process, the six ternary symbols corresponding to each encoded byte are transmitted on the appropriate three wire pairs in the sequence shown in Figure 3.10(b). This means that the sequence of symbols received on each pair can be decoded independently. Also, the frame can be processed immediately after the last symbol is received.

End-of-frame sequence

The transmission procedure adopted enables further error checking to be added to the basic CRC. We can deduce from the state transition diagram in Figure 3.10(a) that the running sum of the weights is always either 0 or +1. At the end of each frame transmission – that is, after the four CRC bytes have been transmitted – one of two different **end-of-stream** (**EOS**) codes is transmitted on each of the three pairs. The code selected effectively forms a checksum for that pair. The principle of the scheme is shown in Figure 3.10(c).

In this figure, we assume the last of the four CRC bytes (CRC-4) is on pair 3. The next codeword transmitted on pair 4 is determined by whether the running

Table 3.1 First 128 codewords of 8B6T codeword set.

Data byte	Codeword	Data byte	Codeword	Data byte	Codeword	Data byte	Codeword
00	-+00-+	20	-++-00	40	-00+0+	60	0++0-0
01	0-+-+0	21	+00+--	41	0-00++	61	+0+-00
02	0-+0-+	22	-+0-++	42	0-0+0+	62	+0+0-0
03	0-++0-	23	+-0-++	43	0-0++0	63	+0+00-
04	-+0+0-	24	+-0+00	44	-00++0	64	0++00-
05	+0--+0	25	-+0+00	45	00-0++	65	++0-00
06	+0-0-+	26	+00-00	46	00-+0+	66	++00-0
07	+0-+0-	27	-+++--	47	00-++0	67	++000-
08	-+00+-	28	0++-0-	48	00+000	68	0++-+-
09	0-++-0	29	+0+0--	49	++-000	69	+0++--
0A	0-+0+-	2A	+0+-0-	4A	+-+000	6A	+0+-+-
0B	0-+-0+	2B	+0+--0	4B	-++000	6B	+0+--+
0C	-+0-0+	2C	0++--0	4C	0+-000	6C	0++--+
0D	+0-+-0	2D	++00--	4D	+0-000	6D	++0+--
0E	+0-0+-	2E	++0-0-	4E	0-+000	6E	++0-+-
0F	+0--0+	2F	++0--0	4F	-0+000	6F	++0--+
10	0--+0+	30	+-00-+	50	+--+0+	70	000++-
11	-0-0++	31	0+--+0	51	-+-0++	71	000+-+
12	-0-+0+	32	0+-0-+	52	-+-+0+	72	000-++
13	-0-++0	33	0+-+0-	53	-+-++0	73	000+00
14	0--++0	34	+-0+0-	54	+--++0	74	000+0-
15	--00++	35	-0+-+0	55	--+0++	75	000+-0
16	--0+0+	36	-0+0-+	56	--++0+	76	000-0+
17	--0++0	37	-0++0-	57	--+++0	77	000-+0
18	-+0-+0	38	+-00+-	58	--0+++	78	+++--0
19	+-0-+0	39	0+-+-0	59	-0-+++	79	+++-0-
1A	-++-+0	3A	0+-0+-	5A	0--+++	7A	+++0--
1B	+00-+0	3B	0+--0+	5B	0--0++	7B	0++0--
1C	+00+-0	3C	+-0-0+	5C	+--0++	7C	-00-++
1D	-+++-0	3D	-0++-0	5D	-000++	7D	-00+00
1E	+-0+-0	3E	-0+0+-	5E	0+++--	7E	+---++
1F	-+0+-0	3F	-0+-0+	5F	0++-00	7F	+--+00

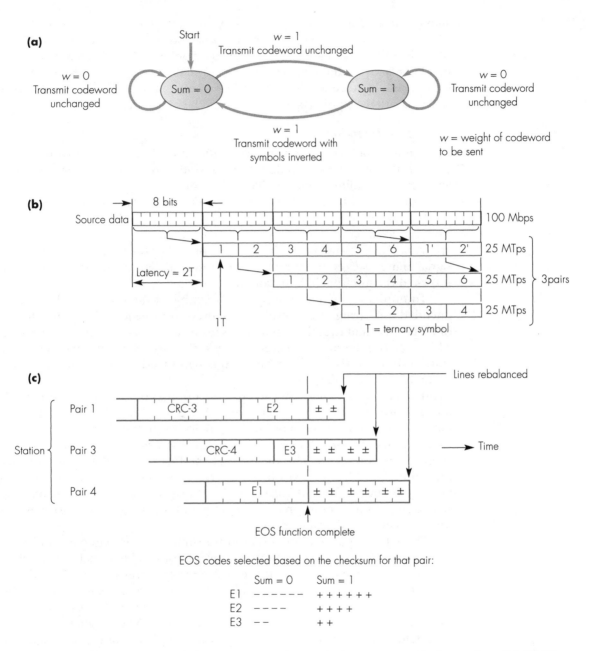

Figure 3.10 100Base4T transmission detail: (a) DC balance transmission rules; (b) 8B6T encoding sequence; (c) end of stream encoding.

sum of the weights on that pair – referred to as the checksum – is 0 or +1. The EOS function is complete at the end of this codeword and the lengths of the other two EOS codes are reduced by two or one times the latency, that is, 4T or 2T. This means the receiver can detect reliably the end of a frame since all signals should cease within a short time of one another. This allows for very small variations in propagation delay on each pair of wires.

Collision detection

An example station–hub transmission without contention is shown in Figure 3.11(a). Recall that a station detects a collision by detecting a signal on pair 2 while it is transmitting and, similarly, the hub detects a collision by the presence of a signal on pair 1. However, as Figure 3.11(a) shows, the strong (unattenuated) signals transmitted on pairs 1, 3, and 4 from the station side each induce a signal into the collision detect – pair 2 – wire. This is near-end crosstalk (NEXT) and, in the limit, is interpreted by the station as a (collision) signal being received from the hub. The same applies for transmissions in the reverse direction from hub to station.

To minimize any uncertainty the preamble at the start of each frame is encoded as a string of two-level (as opposed to three-level) symbols, that is, only positive and negative signal levels are present in each encoded symbol. This increases the signal-level amplitude variations, which, in turn, helps the station/hub to discriminate between an induced NEXT signal and the preamble of a colliding frame.

The preamble pattern on each pair is known as the **start of stream** (**SOS**) and is made up of two two-level codewords, SOS-1 and SFD. The complete pattern transmitted on each of the three pairs is shown in Figure 3.11(b) and, as we can see, the SFD codeword on each pair is staggered by sending only a single SOS-1 on pair 4. This means that the first byte of the frame is transmitted on pair 4, the next on pair 1, the next on pair 3, and so on. An acceptable start of frame requires all three SFD codes to be detected, and the staggering of them means that it takes at least four symbol errors to cause an undetectable start-of-frame error.

On detecting a collision, a station transmits the jam sequence and then stops transmitting. At this point, the station must be able to determine when the other station(s) involved in the collision cease transmitting in order to start the retry process. In practice, this is relatively easy since, in the nontransmitting (idle) state with 8B6T encoding, a zero signal level is present on the three data wires. This means that there is no induced NEXT signal in the collision detect wire, which, in turn, enables the completion of the jam sequence from the hub side to be readily determined. Also, to improve the utilization of the cable, the interframe gap time is reduced from 9.6 μs to 960 ns.

100BaseX

In addition to the 100Base4T standard, a second Fast Ethernet standard is available which is known as **100BaseTX**. Unlike 100Base4T, which was

(a)

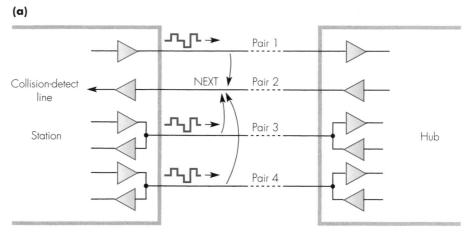

NEXT = near-end crosstalk

(b)

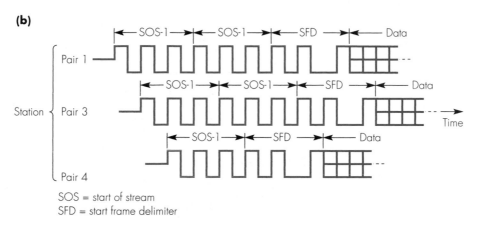

SOS = start of stream
SFD = start frame delimiter

Figure 3.11 Start-of-frame detail: (a) effect of NEXT; (b) preamble sequence.

designed for use with existing category 3 UTP cable, 100BaseTX was designed for use with the higher quality category 5 cable now being used in most new installations. In addition, it is intended for use with STP. The use of various types of transmission media is the origin of the "X" in the name.

Each different type of transmission medium requires a different physical sublayer. The first to be developed was that for use with multimode optical fiber cable. It uses a bit encoding scheme known as 4B5B (sometimes written 4B/5B) and is known as **100BaseFX**. A schematic diagram showing the physical interface to the fiber cable is shown in Figure 3.12(a).

Each interface has its own local clock. Outgoing data is transmitted using this clock while incoming data is received using a clock that is frequency and phased locked to the transitions in the incoming bitstream. As we shall see,

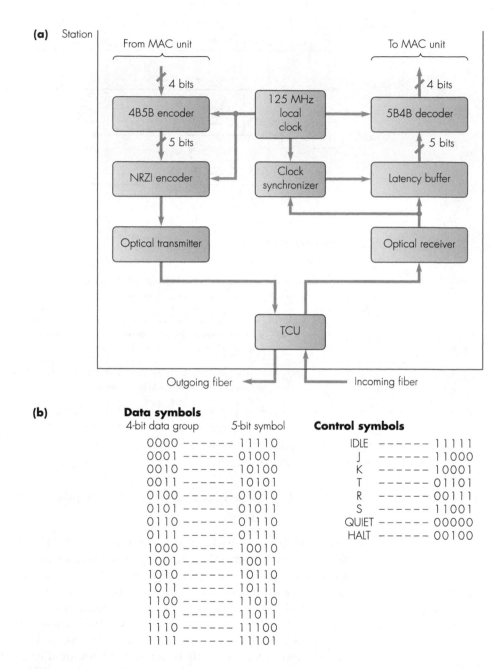

(b)

Data symbols

4-bit data group	5-bit symbol
0000	11110
0001	01001
0010	10100
0011	10101
0100	01010
0101	01011
0110	01110
0111	01111
1000	10010
1001	10011
1010	10110
1011	10111
1100	11010
1101	11011
1110	11100
1111	11101

Control symbols

IDLE	11111
J	11000
K	10001
T	01101
R	00111
S	11001
QUIET	00000
HALT	00100

Figure 3.12 100BaseFX: (a) physical interface schematic; (b) 4B/5B codes.

all data is encoded prior to transmission so that there is a guaranteed transition in the bitstream at least every two bit-cell periods. This ensures that each received bit is sampled/clocked very near to the bit cell center.

All data to be transmitted is first encoded prior to transmission using a **4 of 5 group code**. This means that for each four bits of data to be transmitted, a corresponding five-bit codeword/symbol is generated by what is known as a **4B5B encoder**. The five-bit symbols corresponding to each of the 16 possible four-bit groups are shown in Figure 3.12(b). As we can see, there is a maximum of two consecutive zero bits in each symbol. The symbols are then shifted out through a further NRZI encoder, the operation of which we described in the subsection on synchronous transmission in Chapter 1. This produces a signal transition whenever a 1 bit is being transmitted and no transition when a 0 bit is transmitted. In this way, there is a guaranteed signal transition at least every two bits.

The use of five bits to represent each of the 16 four-bit groups means that there are a further 16 unused combinations of the five bits. Some of these combinations/symbols are used for other (link) control functions such as indicating the start and end of each transmitted frame. A list of the link control symbols is shown in Figure 3.12(b).

The cable comprises two fibers, one of which is used for transmissions between the station and hub and the other for transmissions between the hub and the station. As with 100 Base4T, collisions are detected if a (colliding) signal is present on the receive fiber during the time the station is transmitting a frame. However, because of the additional cost of both the electrical-to-optical conversion circuits and the associated optical plugs and sockets that are required per port, the cost of the MAC unit associated with the NIC is higher than that used with 100Base4T. Hence the most popular type of Fast Ethernet is 100Base4T, and 100BaseFX is used primarily when longer drop cables are required.

3.4.2 Switched Fast Ethernet

As we explained at the start of Section 3.4.1, Fast Ethernet uses the same shared, half-duplex transmission mode as Ethernet. Hence in applications that involve access to, say, large enterprise Web servers, even though the server can handle multiple transfers concurrently, the overall access time and throughput experienced by the various stations using the server is limited by the shared access circuit connecting the server (station) to the hub.

In order to allow multiple access/transfers to be in progress concurrently, two developments have been made: the first, the introduction of a switched hub architecture, and the second, duplex working over the circuits that connect the stations to the hub. The resulting type of hub is known as a **Fast Ethernet switch**.

Switch architecture

The general architecture of a switching hub is shown in Figure 3.13. As we can see, each station is connected to the hub by means of a pair of (duplex) lines that, typically, are implemented as dual UTP (or STP) cables or dual multimode fiber cables. Recall from the last section, each UTP (and STP) cable contains four separate twisted pairs. In the case of 100Base4T, three pairs are used to transmit the 100 Mbps bitstream – in a half-duplex mode – and the fourth pair is used to perform the carrier sense and collision detection functions. As we described earlier in Section 3.3.3, with a switching hub CSMA/CD is not used and instead all stations can transmit and receive frames concurrently. Hence, as with 100Base4T, three pairs in each cable are used collectively to transmit frames (at 100 Mbps) in each direction.

In the case of dual multimode fiber cables, as we described earlier, each fiber is used to transmit at 100 Mbps over several kilometers, one in each direction of transmission. Since the 4B5B coding scheme is used, the line signaling rate is 125 Mbaud. In addition, an active signal is maintained on each fiber continuously by transmitting an idle symbol during the idle period between frames. This ensures the receiver DPLL can maintain clock synchronism between successive frame transmissions.

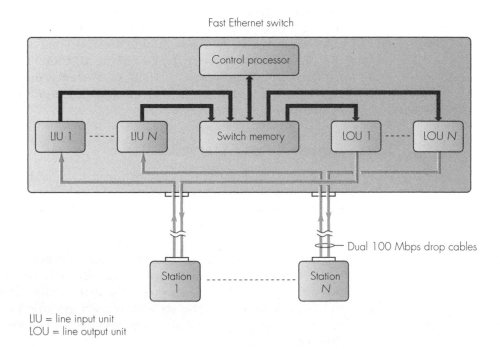

LIU = line input unit
LOU = line output unit

Figure 3.13 Fast Ethernet switch schematic.

Flow control

As we can see from the above with a store-and-forward switch, under heavy load conditions it is possible for all the frame buffers within the switch to become full. At this point, therefore, the control processor must discard any new frame(s). Alternatively, an optional feature associated with switched hubs is to incorporate flow control into the switch. When using flow control, should the control processor find that the level of memory in use reaches a defined threshold, it initiates the transmission of what is called a **Pause** frame on all of its input ports.

On receipt of a Pause frame, the attached station must then stop sending any further frames to the switch until either a defined time has expired or it receives a notification from the switch that the overload condition has passed. Having sent a Pause frame, the control processor monitors the level of memory in use and, when this falls below a second level, it sends out a **Continue** frame on all input ports to inform the attached stations that they can now resume sending new frames.

The two control frames are normal Ethernet frames with a defined code in the *type* field of the frame header. The first two bytes of the data field then give the command – Pause/Continue – and, in the case of the Pause command, succeeding bytes are then used to indicate the duration of the pause in multiples of the minimum frame transmission time. For fast Ethernet (100 Mbps), this is 5.12 μs and the maximum pause duration is 336 ms.

Network configurations

An example network configuration that includes a Fast Ethernet switching hub is shown in Figure 3.14. As we can see, in order to obtain a high level of throughput, the two servers are connected directly to the switch by means of duplex 100 Mbps lines. All the end-user stations then gain access to the servers through either a 10BaseT or a 100Base4T hub. As we explained in the last section, both these types of hub operate in the half-duplex repeating mode. Hence the duplex uplink port connecting each hub to the switch is through a bridging hub, since this has bridging circuitry within the hub to temporarily buffer all frame transfers to and from the switch and to perform the CSMA/CD MAC protocol associated with the shared medium hub ports. The switch also automatically configures the operating speed of each of its ports to be either 10 or 100 Mbps.

3.4.3 Gigabit Ethernet

As the name implies, the drop cables associated with Gigabit Ethernet hubs operate at 1000 Mbps (1 Gbps). The standard is defined in IEEE802.3z and has been introduced to meet the throughput demands of an increasing number of servers that hold files containing multimedia information; examples include Web pages comprising very high resolution graphics, motion video and general audio. The hub can be either a simple repeater hub – that

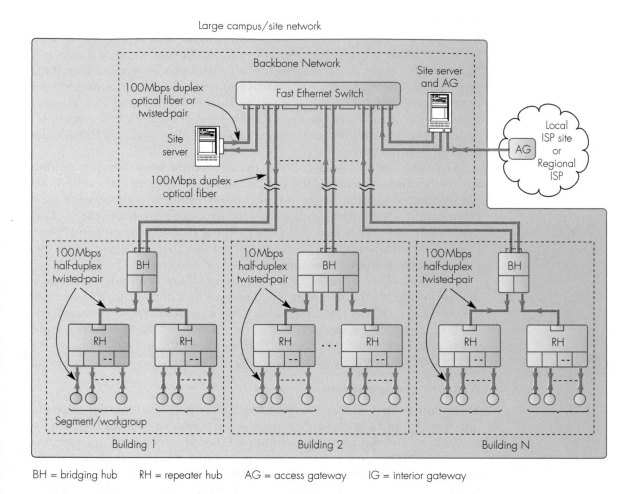

BH = bridging hub   RH = repeater hub   AG = access gateway   IG = interior gateway

Figure 3.14 Example network configuration for a large site/campus using a mix of repeater hubs, bridging hubs and a Fast Ethernet switch.

is, one that has no memory associated with it and operates in the half-duplex mode – or a switched hub that operates in the duplex mode.

Repeater hub

An example application of a repeater hub is to distribute the output of a powerful supercomputer (performing, say, 3D scientific visualizations) to a localized set of workstations. The main issue when operating in the half-duplex – CSMA/CD – mode is to ensure that the round-trip delay between any two stations – the slot time – exceeds the time required to transmit the smallest allowable frame of 512 bits. The time to transmit a 512-bit frame at 1 Gbps is $0.512\,\mu s$. However, with a maximum cable length of 2.5 km, the signal propagation delay would still be 12.5 μs. Hence, as we computed earlier in Section 3.2.1, the slot time would still be in the order of 50 μs. Hence at 1 Gbps, the minimum frame size to detect a collision would be 50 000 bits or 6250 bytes.

Clearly, this is not acceptable and the maximum length of drop cable has to be reduced significantly. The initial maximum length was set at 25 m which, with a hub topology, means that the worst-case signal propagation distance is then 4×25 or 100 m. Hence, assuming the velocity of propagation of a signal through the transmission medium is, say, $2 \times 10^8 \, m \, s^{-1}$, the worst-case time – the slot time – is $100/2 \times 10^8 \, s = 0.5 \, \mu s$, which is the same as the time to transmit a 512-bit frame at 1 Gbps.

The choice of 25 m, however, was rejected by the standards committee as being too small and, after much debate and lobbying, the maximum length of drop cable was set at 200 m. This has a nominal slot time of $800/2 \times 10^8 \, s = 4 \, \mu s$ and, to ensure the sender is still transmitting when a collision/noise-burst is detected, the minimum frame size must be in excess of $4 \times 10^{-6} \times 1 \times 10^9 = 4000$ bits or 500 bytes. The standard has set 512 bytes as the minimum frame size compared with the existing 64 bytes.

When a frame of less than 512 bytes is being transmitted – determined by the length indicator in the frame header – the sending MAC interface hardware adds padding bytes to extend the frame to 512 bytes. The receiving MAC interface then removes the added parity bytes before passing the frame (memory pointer) to the required output MAC interface.

This procedure is known as **carrier extension** and, as we can deduce from the foregoing, the link utilization can be as low as 12.5%. Hence, in addition, a second scheme known as **frame bursting** is used. This allows the sending station to transmit a set of smaller frames – should these be queued and awaiting transmission – in a single block. Again, if necessary, padding bytes are added to ensure the total block size is greater than 512 bytes.

Switching hub

As with a Fast Ethernet switch, CSMA/CD is not used and instead duplex transmission is used using two separate cables. Each frame is transmitted – by a lower level hub or station – and, on arrival at the switch MAC interface port, the frame is first stored/buffered and then processed before it is queued for onward transmission at the required output MAC interface port. Hence, since CSMA/CD is not used, the length of the drop cables is determined solely by the attenuation characteristics of the transmission cable that is used.

Cabling

In relation to cabling, repeating hubs can use either category 5 UTP cable with a drop cable length of up to 100 m (1000Base4T) or STP cable providing the length of the drop cable is limited to 25 m (1000BaseCX). In the case of a switching hub – used as a backbone for example – optical fiber cable is used that supports drop cable lengths of up to 550 m using multimode fiber (1000BaseSX) or up to 5 km using monomode fiber (1000BaseLX).

Signal encoding

The signal encoding scheme used has the same aims as those of Fast Ethernet, which we studied in detail in Section 3.4.1. However, two new encoding schemes have been selected for use with the two types of cable. The scheme selected for use with fiber cable is called 8B/10B; that is, each 8-bit byte – in the bitstream – is encoded into a 10-bit symbol. Hence, since the line bit rate is 1 Gbps, the line signaling rate is extended to 1.25 Gbaud. The use of 10-bit symbols means there are 1024 different symbols available to represent each of the 256 different 8-bit bytes. The choice of symbol for each byte is such that no symbol has more than four of the same bit – 0 or 1 – in a row and no more than six 0s or six 1s. In this way each symbol has enough signal transitions to ensure the receiver clock stays in synchronism with the incoming bitstream. In addition, in order to keep the mean DC level of the bitstream near to zero – so maximizing the amplitude of the signal transitions at the receiver – because there are more than 256 codewords that meet the above conditions, many of the 256 bytes have two alternative codewords assigned to them. Then, when these bytes are present in the byte stream, the codeword chosen is such that the number of 0 or 1 bits in the overall encoded bitstream is equalized.

As we indicated earlier, there is also a new encoding scheme used with the 1000Base4T twisted-pair cable. Since category 5 UTP cable has four twisted-pairs within it, all four pairs are used to transmit each byte, two bits per pair. There are four combinations of two bits: 00, 01, 10 and 11. The pair of bits that are to be transmitted on each pair is represented by one of five different voltage levels, the fifth level indicating that the bits on the four pairs form either a data byte or a control byte such as a start-of-frame and end-of-frame delimiter. In this way, eight bits are transmitted every clock cycle, which reduces the line signaling rate from 1 Gbaud to 125 Mbaud.

Flow control

As with Fast Ethernet, a flow control scheme is used based on the use of the Pause and Continue control frames. This is the same as that used with Fast Internet, which we described in Section 3.4.2. The only difference is the minimum frame size, which, at 1 Gbps, is 0.512 μs. As we explained, this is also the minimum pause time and larger pauses are multiples of this up to 33.6 ms.

Network configurations

This can be the same as that shown in Figure 3.14 with Fast Ethernet, the only difference being the replacement of the Fast Ethernet switch with a Gigabit Ethernet switch. Alternatively, multiple Fast Ethernet switches can be used each with a gigabit uplink to the Gigabit Ethernet switch.

Further developments

A standard is also available for 10-gigabit Ethernet. This is known as **IEEE802.3ae** and demonstrates the constantly increasing demands for higher bandwidths with multimedia applications involving, for example, streamed audio and video. In addition to being used for higher bit rate LANs, however, the maximum distance supported by the new standard is up to 40 km (24 miles) – 10GBase-E (extended) – using single-mode fiber. This means that it can be used in new application domains such as **metropolitan area networks** (**MANs**) that we shall discuss later in Section 3.7.5.

3.5 Virtual LANs

As we saw in the network configuration shown in Figure 3.14, with a LAN composed of hierarchical hubs, each workgroup – for example, within an office or department – can be physically separated from all the other workgroups. In practice, however, this is not always possible. For example, in a college/university department often a member of staff is responsible for managing the accounts relating to research grants, general teaching and research funding. Hence to do this, he/she needs access to the finance department LAN to, say, check on payments from grants, salaries of research staff, purchases, etc. However, since the servers that are attached to the finance department LAN hold sensitive information, for security reasons it is necessary for the PC/workstation of the member of staff responsible for financial matters to be attached to the finance department LAN even though the PC is physically located/attached to the department LAN.

Clearly, one approach is to relocate the member of staff to the finance office. In many instances, however, financial matters are only part of his/her job description and hence it is preferable for him/her to be located locally within the department but logically linked to the finance department LAN. To overcome this type of problem, therefore, the IEEE has produced a standard that allows a machine that is physically attached to one LAN to be a member of a workgroup associated with a different LAN. The total LAN is then known as a **virtual LAN** or **VLAN** and the standard is defined in **IEEE 802.1Q**. In this section we shall describe the operation of VLANs and identify the advantages that they can bring.

3.5.1 IEEE802.1Q

As we indicated earlier in Figure 3.3 and explained in the accompanying text, the *type* field in the original Ethernet specification was replaced with a *type/length* field when the IEEE 802.3 standard was introduced. Since that time, however, all subsequent standards have retained the same frame format. The approach adopted with the VLAN standard, however, was to introduce a new frame format.

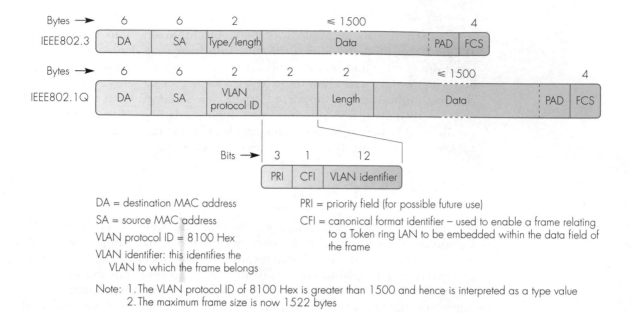

DA = destination MAC address
SA = source MAC address
VLAN protocol ID = 8100 Hex
VLAN identifier: this identifies the
    VLAN to which the frame belongs

PRI = priority field (for possible future use)
CFI = canonical format identifier – used to enable a frame relating
    to a Token ring LAN to be embedded within the data field of
    the frame

Note: 1. The VLAN protocol ID of 8100 Hex is greater than 1500 and hence is interpreted as a type value
      2. The maximum frame size is now 1522 bytes

Figure 3.15 IEEE802.1Q frame format and field descriptions.

Frame format

The new frame format – together with descriptions of the various fields – is shown in Figure 3.15.

As we can see, the new frame format has two new two-byte fields. Following the source and destination MAC address fields is the existing *type/length* field. This is set to 8100Hex and, since this is greater than 1500, it is interpreted as a type value and 8100Hex indicates the **VLAN protocol ID**.

The next two-byte field is composed of three subfields. The first is a three-bit **priority (PRI)** field and has been introduced to enable (future) frames to be assigned a priority value in order to define the sequence in which frames are transmitted. For example, a frame carrying real-time speech/video could be given a higher priority than a frame carrying a string of textual information. Although this may seem an attractive feature, as we shall see in Chapter 6, it is already present in the header of IP packets.

The second subfield is called the **canonical format identifier (CFI)** and is used to enable a frame relating to a Token ring LAN to be embedded within the data field of the frame. Token ring LANs are still found in some legacy networks and hence this feature allows such frames to be transmitted within the total VLAN network.

The third subfield is a 12-bit **VLAN identifier**. As we shall see, each workgroup is allocated a separate VLAN ID and each frame transmitted by members of the same workgroup has the same identifier in this field.

The next two-byte field is then a new *length* field and this indicates the number of bytes in the data field.

Frame forwarding

In order to explain the frame forwarding operation associated with a VLAN network, consider the simple LAN topology shown in Figure 3.16. It is based on bridging hubs with both the lowest tier of three hubs and the single hub in the upper tier all being IEEE802.1Q compliant. Also, all the stations that are attached to the total network have network interface cards (NICs) that are compliant; that is, they generate and process frames that are in the new format. This means that each station is assigned a specific VLAN identifier that indicates the VLAN to which the station belongs and, since this is done when the station is first initialized, it can be readily changed should modifications to the current workgroups become necessary.

In the standard, each PC/server can be identified by either its port number, its MAC address or, in some instances, its (Internet) IP address. As we shall see in Chapter 6, the IP address is found within the data field of the MAC frame and hence can lead to problems should alternative network address formats from IP be present. Also, since the port number associated with a station changes whenever a PC/server is relocated, this also can create problems. Hence in most cases each PC/server is identified by its MAC address.

As we showed in Figure 3.7 and explained in the accompanying text, at startup a bridge learns the port number to which each PC/server is attached by reading the source (MAC) address in the header of each frame received at a port before the frame is forwarded out onto all the other ports. The port number, together with the related MAC address, is then entered into the routing table of the bridge.

The same procedure is followed with an IEEE802.1Q compliant bridging hub with the addition that the VLAN identifier in the header of each frame is also entered into the routing table. Similarly, during the learning phase, a copy of the frame is forwarded to the hub at the higher level and this in turn creates its own routing table. As an example, the routing tables of the four bridges are as shown in Figure 3.16.

Once the learning phase has been carried out, the routing of frames between and within each VLAN can then start. For example, assuming a PC with a MAC address of 52 sends a frame to, say, a server with a MAC address of 57, since the VLAN identifier is the same for both the PC and the server, hub BH1 carries out the routing of the frame directly without any further transmissions. If now a PC with a MAC address of 58 and a VLAN identifier of G sends a frame to, say, a server with a MAC address of 67, BH1 first forwards the frame to BH0. The latter then consults its routing table and, after determining that the server with a MAC address of 67 is also a member of VLAN G, it forwards the frame out on port 2.

In this way, frames are routed not just on their MAC address but also on their VLAN identifier and, because of this, the load on the total network is significantly reduced by including the VLAN identifier. Also, if a frame has a

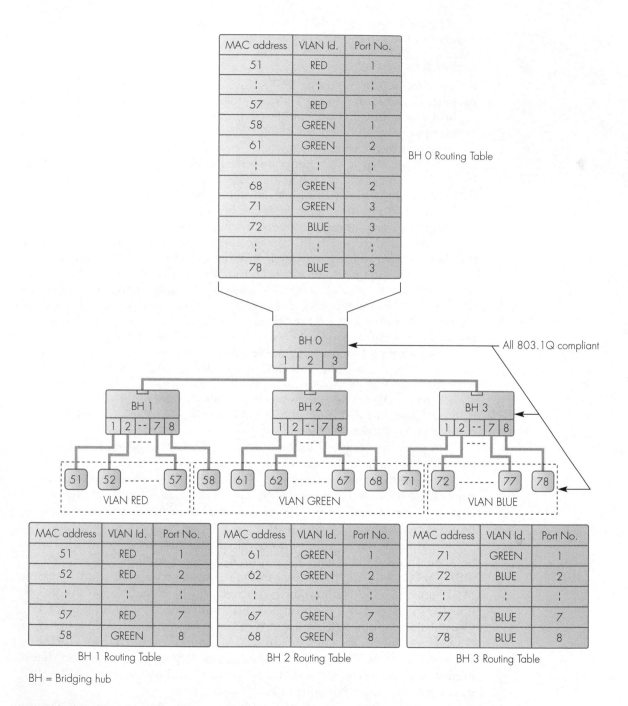

Figure 3.16 Example VLAN configuration and routing tables when all devices are IEEE802.1Q compliant.

VLAN identifier that is different from that in the routing table, then the frame is discarded, so improving the security of the network. Note also that the same procedure holds for both broadcast and multicast frames

Interworking

Problems arise when interworking between IEEE802.1Q compliant stations/hubs/switches and one or more legacy devices because the latter have no knowledge of VLAN identifiers. For example, assume the four hubs in the example network configuration shown in Figure 3.16 are all compliant but all the stations have legacy NICs. In this case the frames received at each bridge port have no VLAN identifier and hence the routing of frames can only be based on their MAC address.

To overcome this problem, therefore, the routing tables in bridging hubs BH1, 2 and 3 have to be entered by network management software within each hub. Once this has been carried out, each lower-level bridge, on receipt of a legacy frame at one of its ports, reformats the frame into the new format with the related VLAN identifier obtained from the routing table.

Once this has been done, bridge BH0 is unaware of the legacy frames and hence learns and routes frames as in the previous example. Then, on receipt of a (reformatted) frame by a lower-level bridge, the bridge first determines the required output port number using the destination MAC address and VLAN identifier from its routing table. It then proceeds to reformat the frame into the legacy format and forwards this to the station that is attached to the port number obtained from its routing table. The same procedure is followed if the upper-level hub was a switch but, in this case, the routing table of the switch must be entered by network management.

Clearly, there are a number of other potential problems that can arise when interworking between the old and new frame formats and compliant and non-compliant devices. However, as PCs and servers are upgraded, the newer devices will now have an IEEE802.1Q compliant NIC. The same applies for hubs and switches. Indeed, the most recent devices such as gigabit switching hubs are already compliant and, after a period of time, VLAN will become the standard mode of working in many application domains.

3.6 LAN protocols

As we have learnt, there is a range of different types of Ethernet LAN, each of which uses a different transmission mode and transmission medium. In the context of our reference model, however, these differences only manifest themselves at the physical layer. The link control sublayer – known as the **logical link control (LLC) sublayer** in the context of LANs – then offers a standard link layer service to the network layer above it.

As we have seen, the various protocol standards associated with LANs are all part of the **IEEE 802 series**. The framework used for defining the various standards is shown in Figure 3.17(a) and a selection of the protocols that we have described in the previous sections are listed in Figure 3.17(b).

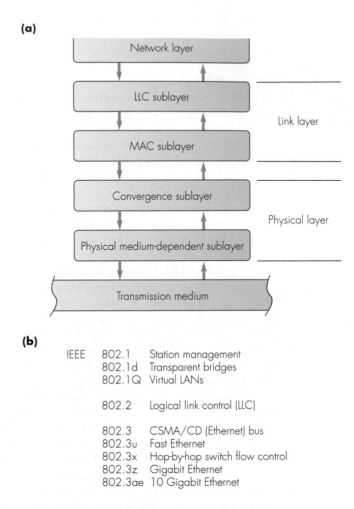

Figure 3.17 LAN protocols: (a) protocol framework; (b) examples.

3.6.1 Physical layer

To cater for the different types of media and transmission bit rates, the physical layer has been divided into two sublayers: the **physical medium-dependent (PMD) sublayer** and the (physical) **convergence sublayer (CS)**. To facilitate the use of different media types, a **media-independent interface (MMI)** has been defined for use between the convergence and PMD sublayers. The role of the convergence sublayer is then to make the use of different media types and bit rates transparent to the MAC sublayer.

The set of signals associated with both interfaces for the different types of Ethernet (802.3) are shown in Figure 3.18.

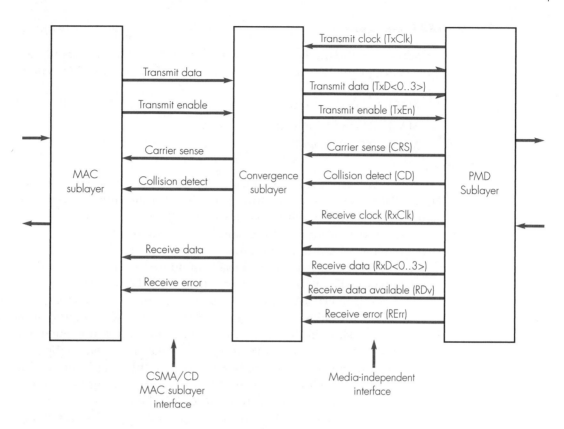

Figure 3.18 Fast Ethernet media-independent interface.

As we explained in Section 1.4.1, at bit rates in excess of 10 Mbps it is not possible to use clock encoding – for example Manchester – because the resulting high line signal transition (baud) rate would violate the limit set for use over UTP cable. Instead, bit encoding and a DPLL are used and, to ensure the transmitted signal has sufficient transitions within it, the encoding schemes use one or more groups of four bits in each transmitted symbol, for example, one 4-bit group when 4B5B coding is used (100BaseSX), and two 4-bit groups when 8B/10B coding is used (1000BaseSX). Hence to accommodate this, all transfers over the MII are in 4-bit nibbles. The other control lines are concerned with the reliable transfer of these nibbles over the interface. The major functions of the convergence sublayer, therefore, are to convert the transmit and receive serial bitstream at the MAC sublayer interface into and from 4-bit nibbles for transfer across the MII, and, when half-duplex transmission is being used, to relay the carrier sense and collision detect signals generated by the PMD sublayer to the MAC sublayer.

3.6.2 MAC sublayer

Irrespective of the mode of operation of the MAC sublayer, a standard set of user service primitives is defined for use by the LLC sublayer. These are:

> MA_UNITDATA.request
>
> MA_UNITDATA.indication
>
> MA_UNITDATA.confirm

A time sequence diagram illustrating their use is shown in Figure 3.19. For a CSMA/CD LAN, the confirm primitive indicates that the block of data associated with the request has been successfully (or not) transmitted.

Each service primitive has parameters associated with it. The MA_UNIT-DATA.request primitive includes the required destination MAC address (this may be an individual, group, or broadcast address) and a service data unit (containing the data to be transferred – that is, the LLC PDU).

The MA_UNITDATA.confirm primitive includes a parameter that specifies the success or failure of the associated MA_UNITDATA.request primitive. However, as we show in the figure, the confirm primitive is not generated as a result of a response from the remote LLC sublayer but rather by the local MAC entity. If the parameter indicates success, this simply shows that the MAC protocol entity (layer) was successful in transmitting the service data unit onto the network medium. If unsuccessful, the parameter indicates why the transmission attempt failed. As an example, with a CSMA/CD bus, "excessive collisions" may be a typical failure parameter.

3.6.3 LLC sublayer

The LLC protocol is based on the high-level data link control (HDLC) protocol that we described earlier in Section 1.4.9. It therefore supports both a connectionless (best-effort) and a connection-oriented (reliable) mode. In almost all LAN networks, however, only the connectionless mode is used. Hence, since this operational mode adds only minimal functionality, when the older Ethernet MAC standard is being used – see the discussion on frame formats in Section 3.2.3 – the LLC sublayer is often not present. Instead, the network layer – for example the Internet protocol (IP) – uses the services provided by the MAC sublayer directly.

When the newer IEEE802.3 MAC standard is being used, the LLC sublayer is present. However, since it operates in the connectionless mode, the only user service primitive is L_DATA.request and all data is transferred in an unnumbered information (UI) frame. The interactions between the LLC and MAC sublayers are as shown in Figure 3.20.

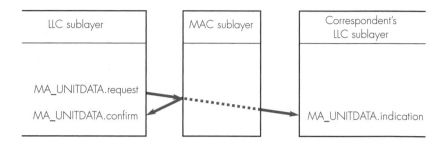

Figure 3.19 MAC user service primitives for CSMA/CD.

The L_DATA.request primitive has parameters associated with it. These are a specification of the source (local) and destination (remote) addresses and the user data (service data unit). The latter is the network layer protocol data unit (NPDU). The source and destination addresses are each a concatenation of the MAC sublayer address of the station and an additional service access point (SAP) address. In theory, this can be used for interlayer routing purposes within the protocol stack of the station. In applications such as the Internet, however, this feature is not used and both the destination SAP (DSAP) and the source SAP (SSAP) are set to AA (hex). In addition, two further fields are added. Collectively, the two fields form what is called the **subnet access protocol (SNAP)** header. The first is a three-byte field known as the *organization (org) code* – in which, with the Internet, all three bytes are set to zero – and a two-byte *type* field. This is the same as that used in the original Ethernet standard and indicates the network layer protocol that created the NPDU.

A more detailed illustration of the interactions between the LLC and MAC sublayers is shown in Figure 3.21. The LLC sublayer reads the destination and source LLC service access point addresses (DSAP and SSAP) – from the two address parameters in the **event control block** (**ECB**) associated with the L_DATA.request service primitive – and inserts these at the head of an LLC PDU. It then adds an 8-bit *control* (*CTL*) field – set to 03 (hex) to indicate it is an unnumbered information (UI) frame – the three-byte org code and the type field, followed by the network layer protocol data unit in the user data field. The resulting LLC PDU is then passed to the MAC sublayer as the user data parameter of an MA_UNITDATA.request primitive in a MAC ECB. Other parameters include the MAC sublayer destination and source addresses (DA and SA) and the number of bytes (length indicator) in the user data field.

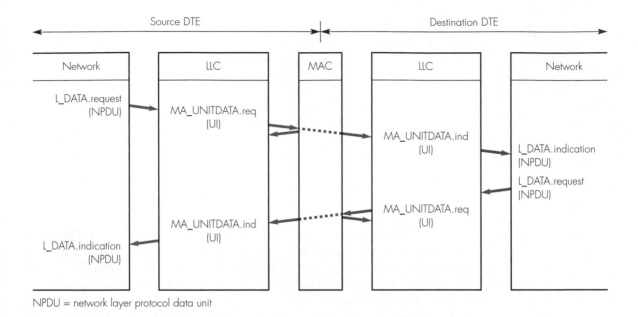

NPDU = network layer protocol data unit

Figure 3.20 LLC/MAC sublayer interactions.

On receipt of the request, the MAC protocol entity creates a frame ready for transmission on the link. In the case of a CSMA/CD network, it creates a frame containing the preamble and SFD fields, the DA and SA fields, an I-field, and the computed FCS field. The complete frame is then transmitted bit serially onto the cable medium using the CSMA/CD MAC method.

A similar procedure is followed in the NIC of the destination station except that the corresponding fields in each PDU are read and interpreted by each layer. The user data field in each PDU is then passed up to the layer/sublayer immediately above together with the appropriate address parameters.

3.6.4 Network layer

The most popular protocol stack used within LANs is **Novell NetWare**. Hence it is common for all the stations connected to a site LAN to communicate using this stack. The network layer protocol associated with this is a connectionless protocol known as the **internet packet exchange (IPX)** protocol and, as its name implies, it can route and relay packets over the total LAN. There is no LLC sublayer associated with the stack and hence the IPX protocol communicates directly with the MAC sublayer.

The protocol stack used within the Internet is TCP/IP and the network layer protocol associated with this stack is a connectionless protocol known as the Internet protocol (IP). Hence, as we will show later in Figure 8.9, it is common for server machines such as e-mail servers that need to communicate

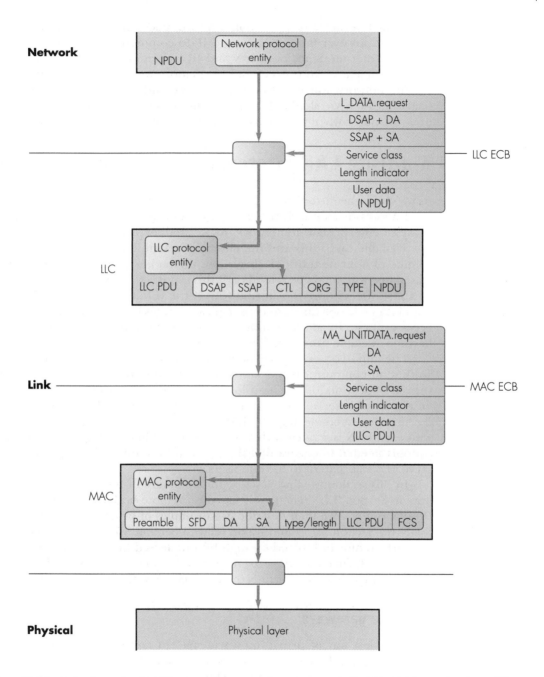

Figure 3.21 Interlayer primitives and parameters.

across the Internet, to support both protocol stacks, IPX to communicate with client stations over the site LAN, and IP to communicate with other servers over the Internet. Since both IPX and IP are connectionless protocols, they use a single packet to transfer all information over the related network with the full network address of both the source and destination stations in the packet header. We shall defer further discussion of network layer protocols until Chapter 6 when we discuss the operation of the Internet protocol.

3.7 Multisite LAN interconnection technologies

As we saw in the introduction to this chapter, in multisite enterprise networks, the LANs associated with the different sites are interconnected together to form an enterprise-wide network. As we shall explain, various technologies are available to do this and the choice of technology is determined by the volume of intersite traffic. If this is low, then a low bit rate – up to 56 kbps – leased line with modems is used or, if this is not sufficient, one or more leased 64 kbps ISDN channels. Alternatively, if the volume of traffic is high, then high bit rate leased lines are used, typical bit rates being 1.5 or 2 Mbps or multiples of these. In addition, a number of high bit rate switched services have become available from some telecom providers.

The aim of an enterprise network is to provide an integrated structure so that all communications across the total enterprise are transparent to the site/location of the employee's PCs/workstations and the various enterprise-wide servers. Hence providing a physical link between sites is only the first step in connecting the LANs at the various sites together. Associated with each LAN is a gateway that provides the additional higher-level protocol support needed to ensure that the physical location of the application-level services is transparent to the end users.

In this section, we first describe the operation of the typical intersite gateways in Section 3.7.1. The first is based on remote bridges and the second on IP/IPX routers. We then describe two examples of switched services: switched ISDN (in Section 3.7.2) and frame relay in Section 3.7.3. A typical enterprise network architecture based on high bit rate leased lines is then described in Section 3.7.4. Finally, we describe in Section 3.7.5 how the two Gigabit Ethernet products are being used for LAN interconnection within towns and cities.

3.7.1 Intersite gateways

The simplest way of providing a transparent connection between sites is to use a **remote bridge** as the intersite gateway. Normally, such bridges are connected directly to the LAN backbone on one port and to the intersite line/network termination on the other. A similar bridge is then used at each site. An example network architecture is shown in Figure 3.22.

As we explained in Section 3.3, the 48-bit MAC addresses used in LANs to route frames are built into the MAC chipset at the time of its manufacture and each contains a unique address. In practice, therefore, it is possible to treat the interconnected set of site LANs as a single LAN and use just the MAC addresses at the head of each frame for routing.

As we have just explained, various schemes are used to set up connections between sites. Irrespective of the scheme used, however, there is a separate connection set up between each site and hence each pair of LANs. Thus even though each remote bridge has only two physical ports, logically, they behave like multiport bridges with a separate link to each of the other remote bridges. A remote bridge performs the basic learning and forwarding/filtering functions. Hence after the learning phase, it can route all subsequent frames over their appropriate intersite link. Normally, the protocol used over each (point-to-point) intersite link is the PPP with the LAN frame in the information field.

As we show in Figure 3.22, an alternative (and more flexible) way of providing a transparent connection between sites is to use an IP/IPX router as the gateway. Routers are used when either the site LANs are of different types and/or the intersite communications facility is itself a network and requires routing. In both these cases, MAC addresses cannot be used for routing

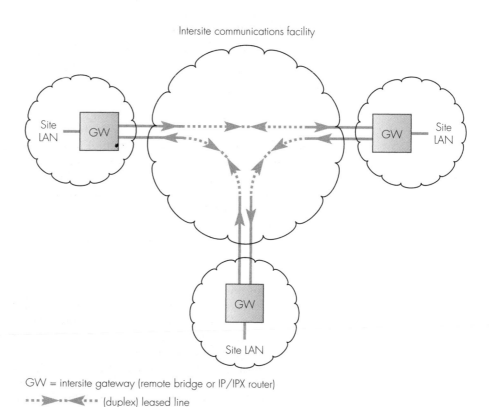

GW = intersite gateway (remote bridge or IP/IPX router)

$\cdots\blacktriangleright\cdot\blacktriangleleft\cdots$ (duplex) leased line

Figure 3.22 Example enterprise network architecture.

purposes as they only have local significance to a particular site. Hence routing must be carried out at the network layer using either IP or IPX. In practice, since each site requires access to the Internet, in many instances the intersite network is the Internet and hence the network protocol is IP.

As we explained in Section 3.6.4, both IP (as used with the Internet) and IPX (as used with Novell NetWare) are connectionless protocols and all information is transferred over the intersite communications facility in self-contained packets. At the head of each packet is the (enterprise-wide) network address of both the source station and the destination station. As we shall expand upon in Chapter 6 when we discuss the operation of the Internet, each network address comprises a network identifier, which identifies uniquely each site network (LAN) within the context of the total enterprise, and a station identifier, which identifies each station at that site. All routing over the intersite network is then carried out using these network addresses. It is for this reason that, when the IP protocol is used, the enterprise network is known also as an **intranet**. We shall defer further discussion of how the routing is carried out until Section 6.6 when we describe the operation of the IP protocol in some detail.

3.7.2 ISDN switched connections

As we explained in Section 2.3.2, a basic rate interface to an ISDN offers two separately switched 64 kbps digital channels. Also, with an ISDN, the connection setup time of a channel is only a fraction of a second. Hence for small enterprises, one solution is to set up (and close down) a channel on demand. For medium-sized enterprises, although the same approach is often acceptable, multiple 64 kbps channels are required to meet the intersite bandwidth requirements. As we explained in Section 2.2.3, to meet this type of requirement a service known as **ISDN multirate** is available from some telecom providers that allows the user to request the bandwidth of a call to be any multiple of 64 kbps. The service is known also as switched $p \times 64$ where p can be up to either 23 or 30 depending on the provider. In order to use the multiple channels as a single high bit rate channel, however, it is necessary to use a device called an **inverse multiplexer**. The general scheme is shown in Figure 3.23(a).

We introduced the concept of multiplexing in Section 2.2.4 as a means of transmitting multiple low bit rate – 64 kbps – digitized voice signals over a single high bit rate line. In contrast, inverse multiplexing is used to derive a single high bit rate channel using multiple lower bit rate channels. For example, an inverse multiplexer can be used to derive a single 384 kbps channel from six independent 64 kbps channels.

At the sending side, the inverse multiplexer first sets up the appropriate number of 64 kbps channels to the required destination. It then proceeds to segment the high bit rate digital stream output by the user equipment – for example a remote bridge – ready for transmission over the multiple low bit rate channels. At the receiving side, once the multiple channels have been

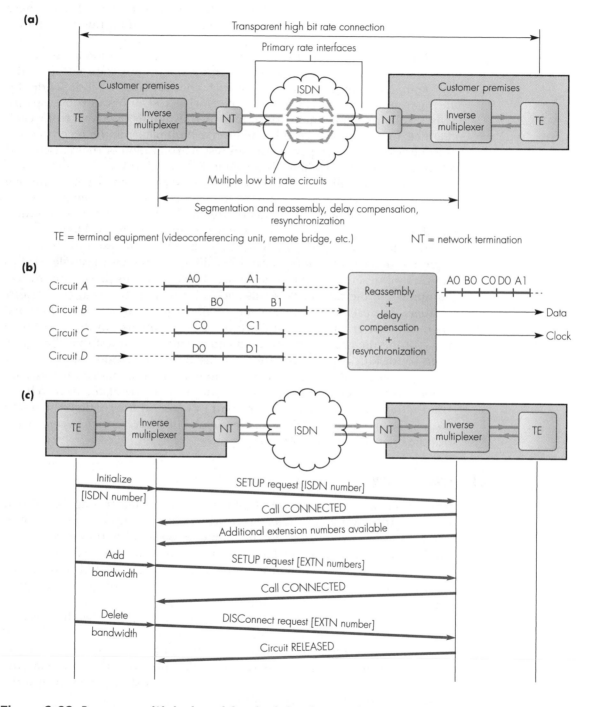

Figure 3.23 Inverse multiplexing: (a) principle of operation; (b) reassembly schematic; (c) bonding protocol.

set up, the inverse multiplexer accepts the bitstreams received from these channels and reassembles them back into a single high bit rate channel for onward transmission to the receiving terminal equipment.

Hence the function of the inverse multiplexers, in addition to call setup, is to make the segmentation and reassembly operations transparent to the user equipment. In practice, because each channel is set up independently, they may all traverse the ISDN trunk network across different routes/paths. This results in small time differences in the signals received from each channel. To compensate for this, the inverse multiplexer at the receiving side must perform delay compensation and resynchronization of the reassembled bitstream. The general scheme is shown in Figure 3.23(b).

To obtain a similar service to that provided by switched $p \times 64$, inverse multiplexers are available that enable the user terminal equipment to set up and clear multiple 64 kbps circuits on demand. The technique is known as **bonding** and the principles of the scheme are shown in Figure 3.23(c).

In order to set up the high bit rate channel – in response to a user request – the inverse multiplexer at the calling side requests a single 64 kbps channel to be set up to the remote site. Once this is in place, the inverse multiplexer at the called side sends back a list of available local (extension) numbers. The calling multiplexer sets up the required number of additional channels – one at a time – and the two user equipments can then exchange data. During the call, a user terminal equipment can request that the aggregated bandwidth available is either increased or decreased by setting up or clearing channels dynamically. For example, if the terminal equipments are remote bridges then the aggregate bandwidth can be regulated to match the data traffic being exchanged at any point in time. An international standard has now been defined in **ITU-T recommendation H.221**, which is concerned with the operation of this type of equipment.

3.7.3 Frame relay

Frame relay was initially defined as a service provided through an ISDN. Subsequently a number of telecom providers have set up networks to offer just a frame relay service. As the name implies, with frame relay, the multiplexing and routing of frames is performed at the link layer. Moreover, the routing of frames is very straightforward so the channel bit rate can be high, typical rates being up to 34 or 45 Mbps. A schematic diagram of a typical public frame relay network is shown in Figure 3.24.

The customer first informs the service provider of the sites that need to be interconnected. The provider then creates a set of permanent virtual connections that interconnect all the sites by setting up appropriate routing table entries in each frame relay node. The provider then informs the network manager at each site of the identifier that should be put into the header of a frame to reach each of the other sites.

All frames are multiplexed together onto the link connecting the **customer interface equipment** (**CIE**) to its nearest node. Logically, this

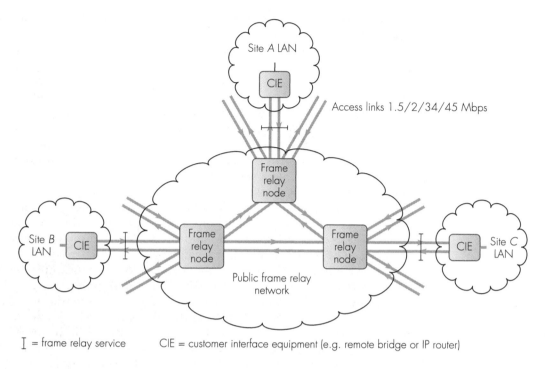

I = frame relay service   CIE = customer interface equipment (e.g. remote bridge or IP router)

Figure 3.24 Public frame-relay network schematic.

appears to the customer equipment like a set of point-to-point connections between itself and all the other sites, each identified by the corresponding identifier.

The identifier is known as the **data link connection identifier** (**DLCI**) and is put into the header of each frame. It is then used by the network to route (relay) the frame to its intended destination.

Frame relay networks employ traffic monitoring and policing. A traffic contract is agreed between the customer and the network operator for each permanent virtual connection, which depends on a certain average rate that also allows for a level of burstiness in this rate. The traffic generated by the customer is then monitored and, if the average or peak (burst) rates are exceeded, frames may be discarded.

The format of each frame is based on that used in the HDLC protocol and is shown in Figure 3.25(a). It comprises a two-byte (extended) address header with no control field owing to the lack of any error control. In addition to the DLCI, the header contains the **forward explicit congestion notification** (**FECN**) **bit**, the **backward explicit congestion notification** (**BECN**) **bit** and the **discard eligibility** (**DE**) **bit**. These are used for controlling congestion within the network.

The DLCI, like the VCI in packet-switched networks, has only local significance on a specific network link and therefore changes as a frame traverses the links associated with a virtual path. When the virtual path is first set up, an entry is made in the routing table of each frame relay node along the route of the incoming link/DLCI and the corresponding outgoing link/DLCI to reach the intended destination of the frame. An example set of entries is shown in Figure 3.25(b) and the related routing of each frame is illustrated in Figure 3.25(c).

When a frame is received, the frame handler within each node simply reads the DLCI from within the frame and combines this with the incoming link number to determine the corresponding outgoing link and DLCI. The new DLCI is written into the frame header and the frame is queued for forwarding on the appropriate link. The order of relayed frames is thus preserved and their routing is very fast.

Since multiple frame transfers can be in progress concurrently over each link within the network, during periods of heavy traffic an outgoing link may become temporarily overloaded, resulting in its queue starting to build up. This is known as **congestion** and the additional congestion control bits in each frame can be used to alleviate this condition.

Whenever the frame handler relays a frame to a link output queue, it checks the size of the queue. If this exceeds a defined limit, the frame handler signals this condition to the two end users involved in the transfer. This is done in the forward direction by setting the FECN bit in the frame header. In the backward direction, it is done by setting the BECN bit in the header of all frames which are received on this link. If the condition persists, the frame handler also returns a special frame called a **consolidated link layer management** (**CLLM**) frame to all CIEs that have routes (paths) involving the affected link. Such frames are simply relayed by each intermediate frame relay node in the normal way.

When the frame handler in an edge frame relay node receives an indication of network congestion, it temporarily reduces its frame forwarding rate until there are no further indications of congestion. If the overload increases, however, the frame relay node must start to discard frames. In an attempt to achieve fairness, the DE bit in the frame header is used since this is set by the frame handler in each edge frame relay node whenever the rate of entry of frames into the network exceeds the peak rate agreed at subscription time.

To implement this scheme, associated with each permanent virtual connection is a parameter called a **committed information rate** (**CIR**) which is used by the service provider to dedicate a specific amount of transmission bandwidth to the connection. This is measured in units of bits per second and is always less than the bit rate of the access line to the CIE. The cost of the frame relay service is determined by the allocated CIR and, to ensure the customer complies with this rate, the edge frame relay node measures the rate of entry of frames from the CIE over repetitive time intervals. Hence, since the CIR is measured in bits per second and assuming a time interval of 1 s, then the CIR equates to a specific number of frames per measured interval. Then, if the number of frames received in an interval is less than the CIR, all the frames are marked as high priority (DE = 0). However, any additional frames that are received within a measured interval are marked as low priority (DE = 1) and hence may be discarded during heavy load conditions.

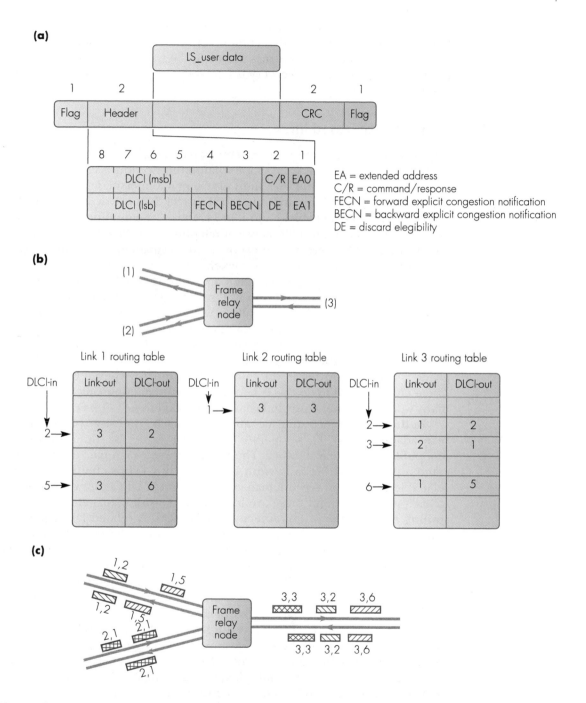

Figure 3.25 Frame relay principles: (a) frame format; (b) frame routing; (c) frame relay schematic.

To minimize the possibility of wrongly delivered frames, the CRC at the tail of each frame is used to detect bit errors in the frame header (and information) fields. Then, if an error is detected, the frame is discarded. With the frame relay service, error recovery is left to the higher protocol layers in the end-user stations.

3.7.4 High bit rate leased lines

A typical large multisite enterprise network based on high bit rate leased lines is illustrated in Figure 3.26. As we explained in Section 3.1, in addition to LAN (data) traffic, the network must also support intersite telephony traffic. Typically, the leased lines are either DS1/T1 (1.5 Mbps) or E1 (2 Mbps) or higher such as DS3 (44 Mbps) and E3 (34 Mbps). The multiple 64 kbps channels these contain are divided between telephony (for PBX interconnection) and data (for LAN interconnection) on a semipermanent basis using network management within each site multiplexer.

In the case of telephony, although a 64 kbps channel is used by the PBX for each call, it is now common to use each 64 kbps channel of the intersite leased circuit for more than one call. As we indicated earlier in Section 1.2.1, there is now a range of compression algorithms/circuits available that provide good quality voice communication using 32, 16 or 8 kbps. This means that two, four or eight calls can be multiplexed into a single 64 kbps channel giving a substantial saving in the number of channels required between sites. The technique used to do this is known as **subrate multiplexing** and is particularly worthwhile over costly international leased lines.

In the case of data traffic, a common approach is to use a (private) **frame relay adapter** (**FRA**). These operate in a similar way to the frame relay nodes in a public frame relay network. The traffic between each pair of sites is allocated a portion of the bandwidth – number of 64 kbps channels – of the related leased line by network management. A set of DLCIs are then assigned to each path/route and these are loaded by network management into the routing tables of the interconnected set of FRAs. A related DLCI for each path is also passed to the router at each site and, once the set of IP addresses associated with each path have been learnt by the router, it writes the appropriate DLCI in the header of each frame prior to passing the frame to its local FRA. The role of the FRA is then to relay each frame received from the router using the preassigned entries in its routing table and the corresponding set of aggregated channels.

Although not shown, there is a single network management station for the total network and all the devices shown in the figure have network management (agent) software within them. Normally, the management station is connected to one of the site multiplexers and a single 64 kbps channel of the intersite leased circuits is then used to transfer management-related messages to/from the management station and all the other network devices. The messages include configuration information to all devices – routing table entries, bandwidth allocations, and so on – and fault reports from the devices. In this

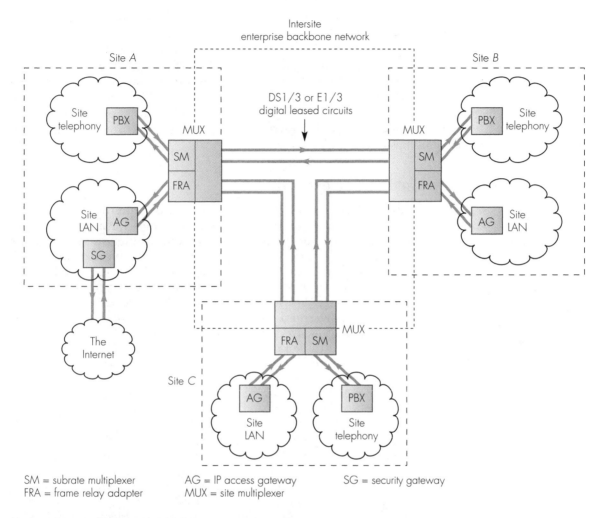

Figure 3.26 Schematic of large multisite enterprise network based on multiplexers and high bit rate leased circuits.

way, should a fault develop or a reconfiguration be necessary, this can be done from a central site in a secure way.

Normally, as we show in the figure, with large enterprise networks of the type shown in Figure 3.26, access to the Internet is through a single gateway located at one of the sites. This is done both to simplify access to the Internet from the various sites and also to enable external Web users to access information that is stored on a server attached to one of the site LANs. In this way, the gateway can control the flow of information both into and out of the enterprise network/intranet. The gateway is then called a **firewall** or **security gateway** and its functions are explained later in Section 9.2.3.

Finally, although most private networks are run and managed by the enterprise to which they belong, a number of telecom providers now offer the option for an equivalent private network to be set up within the provider's network. This is then known as a **virtual private network** (**VPN**). These offer the same set of services to the private network but are managed and operated by the telecom provider. In general, VPNs are more expensive than private networks but they have the advantage that the enterprise need not then be involved in the recruitment of staff who are not concerned with the core business of the enterprise.

3.7.5 Metropolitan area networks

Metropolitan area networks (MANs) have been installed by a number of network providers to meet the demand from customers for a switched high-speed LAN interconnection facility. Prior to the introduction of MANs, the only way of interconnecting a set of LANs that belong to different companies/enterprises was by means of high bit rate leased lines. The disadvantage of this approach is the large number of leased lines that are required and, for each additional site, a new set of lines must be put in place. Initially, the LANs were all distributed around a large town or city but later the service was extended to cover multiple towns and cities.

As we indicated at the end of Section 3.4.3, 1 and 10 Gigabit Ethernet switches are now being used in MANs and a typical network architecture is shown in Figure 3.27(a).

As we can see, a single switch can cover a distance of up to 40 km (24 miles). At each site/customer premises is an access gateway that is provided by the network operator. In a public network, the service provided is known as the **switched multimegabit data service** (**SMDS**) or sometimes the **connectionless broadband data service** (**CBDS**) which is the name used by the ITU-T. The access gateway is called a **SMDS edge gateway** and, on one port, the gateway is connected to, say, the site Fast Ethernet switch and on the other port to the MAN 1/10 Gigabit Ethernet switch.

In such networks the various sublayer functions/protocols shown in part (b) of the figure are known as **SMDS interface protocols** (**SIP**). The SIP level 3 protocol is called the MAC convergence protocol and the SIP level 2 and 1 protocols relate to the MAC and PHY layers used by the SMDS switch. Since not all LANs use the same frame format, the initial MAC PDU to be sent is first encapsulated by the MAC convergence protocol into a standard form by adding a header and a trailer to it. The new header includes the source and destination network-wide addresses of the SMDS edge routers involved and the trailer is an optional FCS of the new expanded frame. The new frame is then sent over the SMDS network to the edge router specified by the destination (SMDS) address in the frame header and from there to the station specified in the destination address field in the original MAC frame.

Note that the cost of the service is determined by the volume of data transferred. Hence, in general, the cost of the service is less than that of using leased lines. Note also that in the example shown in the figure the relaying operation takes place at the MAC sublayer and hence the SMDS edge gateway

(a)

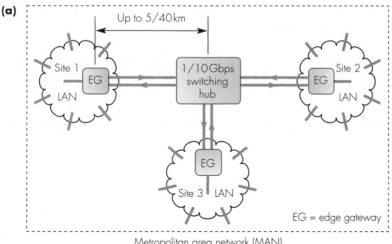

Metropolitan area network (MAN)

(b)

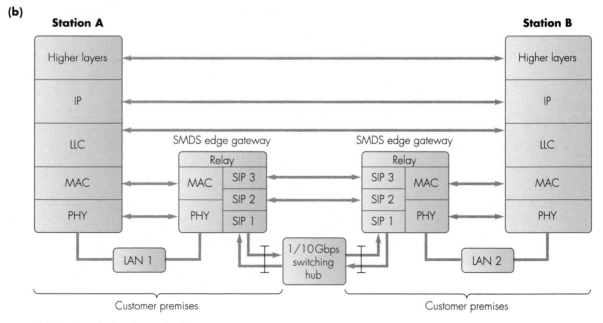

SMDS = Switched multimegabit data service
SIP n = SMDS interface protocol 1–3
I = SMDS network addresses

Figure 3.27 (a) Metropolitan area network schematic; (b) SMDS internetworking protocol architecture.

is acting as a bridge. It is also possible to perform the relaying function at the network (IP) layer in which case the edge gateway acts as a router. Finally, as we indicated earlier, a number of network providers have extended the area of coverage of the SMDS service by linking the switching hubs located in various towns and cities by means of **MAN switching systems** (**MSS**). The MSSs are then interconnected to provide a countrywide SMDS service.

Summary

A summary of the various topics discussed in this chapter is given in Figure 3.28.

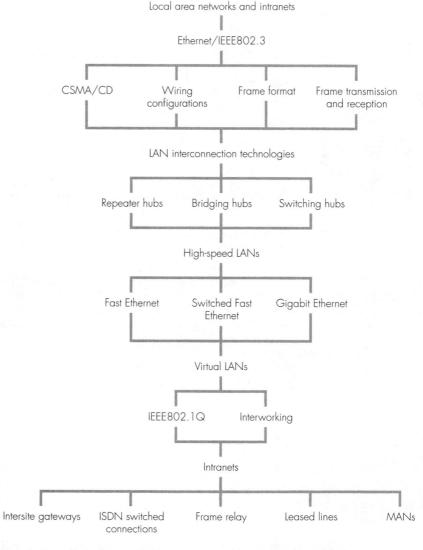

Figure 3.28 Local area networks and intranets summary.

Exercises

Section 3.1

3.1 What is the meaning of the term "enterprise network"? Describe the factors that determine when such networks are created. Also explain the meaning of the term "intranet".

Section 3.2

3.2 Explain the meaning of the following terms relating to the CSMA/CD medium access control method:
(i) multiple access,
(ii) broadcast mode,
(iii) collision,
(iv) carrier sense.

3.3 With the aid of Figure 3.1, explain the meaning of the term "slot time" and how this is derived. State how the slot time determines the maximum throughput of the LAN.

3.4 State the use of a jam sequence with the CSMA/CD MAC method and explain why a truncated binary exponential process is used. Explain the operation of this process.

3.5 Explain the origin of the hub configuration as is now used for Ethernet LANs. Also, with the aid of a diagram, explain how the broadcast mode of operation is achieved.

3.6 Two UTP hubs to which user stations are attached are each connected to a third hub by optical fiber cable in order to gain access to a server that is attached to the third hub. Derive the maximum length of optical fiber cable that can be used.

3.7 With the aid of the frame format shown in Figure 3.3(a), explain:
(i) the clock encoding method used and how the start of a new frame is detected,
(ii) how each station that receives a frame determines from the destination address whether the frame contents are intended for it.
(iii) the use of the type/length field.

3.8 Explain the meaning and use of:
(i) an interframe gap,
(ii) a backoff limit,
(iii) an attempt limit.
Hence, with the aid of flow diagrams, describe the transmit and receive procedures followed by the CSMA/CD MAC sublayer.

Section 3.3

3.9 How is a bridge different from a repeater? What are the advantages and disadvantages of each?

3.10 With the aid of the bridge architecture shown in Figure 3.7(a), explain the operation of a bridge including the meaning of the terms:
(i) promiscuous mode,
(ii) forwarding database,
(iii) bridge learning.

3.11 With the aid of Figure 3.7(b), explain how the entries in the two forwarding databases would be built up assuming the following message exchanges: 1 to/from 3, 1 to/from 10, 2 to/from 4, 2 to/from 13.

3.12 Discriminate between a repeater hub, a bridging hub, and a switching hub.

3.13 With the aid of a diagram, describe how a repeater hub and a broadband modem can be used by a single-site small business to provide central services at the site and access to the Internet.

3.14 With the aid of a diagram, describe how a single-site large business can provide central services at the site and access to the Internet using only repeater hubs. State the limitations of this approach.

3.15 Explain how a switching hub learns the set of MAC addresses that belong to each of its ports.

3.16 Describe how a cut-through switching hub differs from a store-and-forward switching hub.

Section 3.4

3.17 Derive the slot time in bits for a Fast Ethernet hub operating with drop cables of up to 100 m and a bit rate of 100 Mbps. State the implications of your answer in relation to that of a 10BaseT hub.

3.18 With the aid of the wiring configuration of a 100Base4T hub shown in Figure 3.9(a), explain how the carrier sense and collision detection functions associated with CSMA/CD are carried out.

3.19 State why the 8B6T encoding scheme is used for transmissions over each twisted-pair wire with 100Base4T. Also explain why a DC balancing scheme is required.

3.20 With the aid of Figures 3.10 and 3.11, explain:
    (i)   how DC balance is maintained,
    (ii) the latency associated with the 8B6T encoding sequence,
    (iii) how additional error detection is obtained by sending one of two different end-of-stream codes,
    (iv) how the start-of-stream code used gives a more reliable collision detection.

3.21 With the aid of Figure 3.13 explain the operation of a Fast Ethernet switch. Include in your explanation how duplex working is achieved.

3.22 Produce a sketch of a three-tier network configuration composed of repeater hubs, bridging hubs, and a Fast Ethernet switching hub. State why each type of hub needs to be at the particular level in the hierarchy and where central services including Internet access are provided.

3.23 With the aid of the interface schematic of 100BaseFX shown in Figure 3.12(a), explain the meaning/use of the:
    (i) latency buffer,
    (ii) clock synchronizer,
    (iii) 4B/5B encoder/decoder.

3.24 Explain the flow control procedure associated with a Fast Ethernet switch. Include in your explanation the use of the Pause and Continue frames and how these are recognized.

3.25 In relation to a Gigabit Ethernet repeater hub, determine:
    (i)   the slot time,
    (ii) the maximum length of drop cable.

3.26 In relation to a Gigabit Ethernet repeater hub, explain the meaning of the terms padding bytes, carrier extension, and frame bursting.

3.27 What is the maximum length of drop cable when duplex working is used with a Gigabit Ethernet switch?

3.28 Describe the signal encoding scheme used with Gigabit Ethernet with each of the following cable types:
    (i)   optical fiber,
    (ii) category 5 UTP.

Section 3.5

3.29 Explain the benefits of a virtual LAN (VLAN) and state its major disadvantage.

3.30 In the frame format for VLANs a new field is present in the frame header comprising three subfields. Explain the role of each subfield.

3.31 Using the example shown in Figure 3.16, explain the frame forwarding procedure in a VLAN. Clearly identify the role of the VLAN identifier and the learning procedure associated with this.

Section 3.6

3.32 With the aid of the protocol framework shown in Figure 3.17, explain the role of the following sublayer protocols:
    (i)   PMD,
    (ii) convergence,
    (iii) MAC,
    (iv) LLC.

3.33 With the aid of the interlayer parameters shown in Figure 3.21, explain the meaning/use of:
(i) the DSAP and SSAP,
(ii) SNP including the ORG and type fields,
(iii) CTL.

Section 3.7

3.34 With the aid of the diagram of an enterprise network shown in Figure 3.22, explain how intersite communications are carried out using the following types of intersite gateway:
(i) remote bridge,
(ii) IP/IPX router.

3.35 With the aid of the diagrams shown in Figure 3.23, state the role and describe the operation of an inverse multiplexer. Include in your description the principles of the delay compensation and resynchronization procedures.

3.36 With the aid of the network schematic shown in Figure 3.24, explain how a public frame relay network can be used to create an enterprise network. Hence use the frame format and routing principles shown in Figure 3.25 to explain how frames are relayed/routed between all the network sites. Include in your

explanation the role of the following fields in each frame header:
(i) DLCI,
(ii) FECN, BECN and DE bits.
Explain the term "committed information rate (CIR)" and how this features in the congestion control scheme in the frame relay network.

3.37 With the aid of the network schematic shown in Figure 3.26, explain how both telephony (via a PBX) and data (via a remote bridge or router) are extended to cover an entire enterprise. Include in your explanation the role and operation of:
(i) a subrate multiplexer,
(ii) a frame relay adapter.
Can the latter also be used for telephony?
Why is only one firewall/security gateway used?

3.38 Explain the role of a metropolitan area network and how this differs from that of an interconnected set of LANs using leased lines.

3.39 In relation to the metropolitan area network shown in Figure 3.27, explain the role of the SMDS edge gateway. State the use of the three SMDS interface protocols.

wireless networks

4.1 Introduction

Unlike wired/fixed networks that require a physical connection to a network termination point, the user devices associated with wireless networks – mobile phones, personal digital assistants (PDAs), notebook computers, pocket PCs, laptops, etc. – communicate with the network by radio transmissions. In some instances, wireless networks are used to replace existing wired (local area) networks. In most cases, however, they are used to provide mobility to the subscribers of the network.

There is a range of different types of wireless network each tailored to a particular application domain. They can be categorized according to the range of radio coverage involved and three examples are shown in diagrammatic form in Figure 4.1.

Ad-hoc piconets

Within a piconet – also known as a **wireless personal area network (WPAN)** – one device acts as a master and there can then be up to seven active slave devices. All slaves must be located within a radius of 10 m of the master. Hence a piconet covers a small area such as a room or an office. They are used, for example, to set up a spontaneous ad-hoc conference involving multiple, say, laptop/notebook computers in a conferencing room. Also, they are

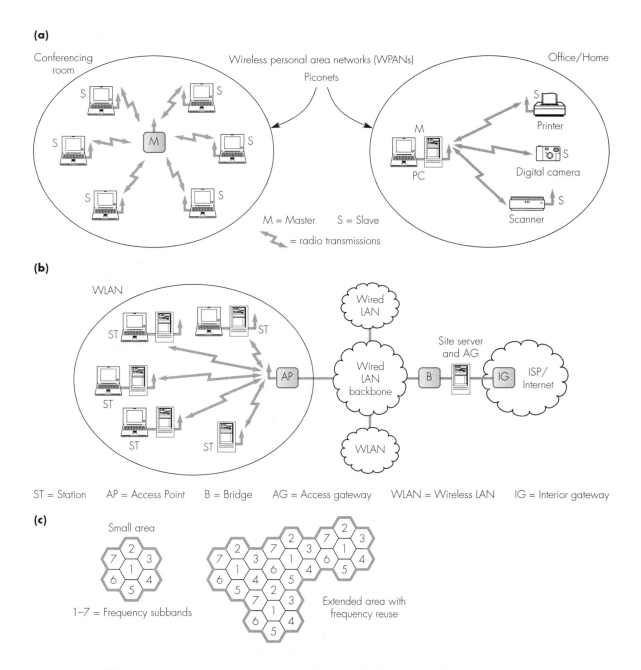

Figure 4.1 Wireless networks: (a) piconets/wireless PANs; (b) wireless LAN; (c) cellular/mobile radio networks.

used for the interconnection of multiple devices such as a personal computer, a printer, a scanner, a digital camera, etc., that are distributed around an office or home. They use short-range radio transmissions between the various devices to communicate and transfer data. A schematic diagram illustrating this mode of operation is shown in Figure 4.1(a) and an example of such a network standard is **Bluetooth**.

Normally, the computer shown in the figure will contain a **system unit** and, within each of the peripherals, a **slave unit**. Both the system and slave units contain a **radio transceiver** – radio transmitter/receiver – and all transmissions/data transfers are controlled by the system unit. Typical maximum data transfer rates are between 400 and 700 kbps depending on whether the transfer is symmetric or asymmetric.

Wireless local area networks

Wireless local area networks (**WLANs**) are now used extensively to enable a number of computers – both fixed and portable – to communicate with, say, a shared server computer or a fixed network access point such as a bridge. All devices within the WLAN have a radio modem within them with a typical maximum range of coverage of 100 m. Hence the range of coverage of a single WLAN is that of a large office or laboratory. Then, as we can see in Figure 4.1(b), to achieve wider coverage such as a campus, multiple WLANs can be interconnected together using, for example, high bandwidth wired LAN technology.

The use of radio instead of fixed-wire cables provides more flexibility when changes are made to the location of desks, etc. WLANs are also common in older buildings where installing cables can be difficult. As we can see in the figure, associated with each WLAN network is a unit called an **access point** (**AP**) and all communications take place between the various wireless nodes – called stations – and the AP. The AP then controls all radio transmissions within its network and, in addition, all communications with the AP of the other networks over the establishment-wide backbone network. There are now a number of WLAN types all of which have been standardized under the IEEE802.11 banner. Typical data rates range from 11 Mbps for IEEE802.11(b) to 54 Mbps for IEEE802.11(a).

Cellular radio networks

Unlike the two previous types of wireless network – WPAN and WLAN – cellular radio networks have a typical coverage of a whole country, or of a wider area providing the neighboring countries have adopted a compatible radio network. They have been designed from the outset to enable a person with a compatible handset to make a call – involving voice, text messages, photo/images and video – when he/she is away from their home or office. The handsets are called **mobile phones** and, because of this, cellular radio networks are known also as **mobile phone networks**.

The early wide area radio networks used a single high-powered transmitter to cover an area such as a town or city and this supported a rudimentary telephone service. The strict limits set on the power of radio transmissions, however, meant that this mode of working could not be used to cover a wider area than a single town or city. As a result, it was not until the first cellular radio network was introduced in the US in the early 1980s that mobile phone networks started to take off.

With cellular networks, the desired area of coverage of the total network is divided into a large number of small areas called **cells**. Associated with each cell is a low-power radio transmitter that is sufficient to cover only that cell. The total radio bandwidth that has been allocated for the network is first divided into a number of **frequency subbands**. Then, to ensure there is no radio interference between adjacent cells, the frequency subbands are allocated in the manner shown in Figure 4.1(c).

In the example shown in the figure, seven subbands are used and, as we can see, each cell is surrounded by cells that use a different frequency subband. In addition, the use of small cells means that only low-power radio transmissions are used by handsets which, in turn, means that only small-sized batteries are required and hence smaller handsets. Also, as we can see, the same set of frequency subbands can be used repeatedly until the required area of coverage is reached. This technique is known as **frequency reuse** and, since radio bandwidth is an expensive resource, it is this that makes such networks financially viable.

In this chapter we shall study the operation of these three different types of wireless network and how each provides access to the Internet.

4.2 Bluetooth

The Bluetooth standard is an open standard published by an industry-based association called the **Bluetooth Special Interest Group** (**SIG**). It is intended for use in ad-hoc piconets and two example applications are shown in Figure 4.2.

In part (a) of the figure, the piconet is being used to connect several peripheral devices that are distributed around an office to a personal computer using radio – wireless – transmissions in place of fixed wiring. In part (b), with the aid of a Bluetooth-enabled mobile phone, for example, the mobile phone is acting as a bridge between a laptop computer and the Internet. The laptop can then access e-mail and surf the Web. It is for this reason that most portable devices now have a Bluetooth interface built-in during their manufacture.

The standard does not just specify details of the radio interface. Rather, it specifies a complete range of protocols and components that can be used by application designers. However, to ensure compatibility between devices supporting the same service, the standard includes a range of what are called **application profiles** each of which represents a default solution for a specific

(a)

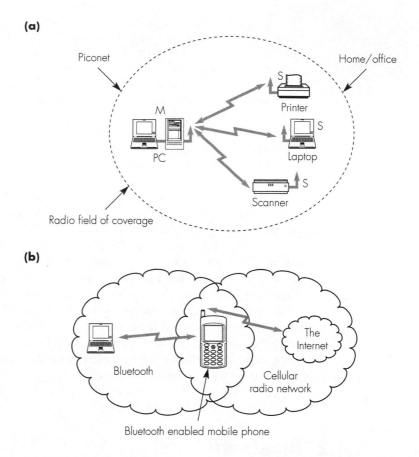

(b)

Figure 4.2 Bluetooth applications: (a) connection of peripheral devices to a computer; (b) Internet access via a mobile phone.

application. The applications include cordless handsets and the associated mobile phone attachments, PC cards supporting LAN access using the PPP protocol, Bluetooth interfaces for mobile phone handsets, and many others.

4.2.1 Radio interface

In order to be able to operate worldwide, the portion of the radio spectrum that is used is in what is called the **industrial, scientific and medical (ISM) band**. This operates at 2.4 GHz and its appeal is that no license is required for its use. The transmission scheme used is known as **frequency-hopping spread spectrum (FHSS)** with **time division duplex (TDD)**. A detailed discussion of radio frequency transmission is outside the scope of this book but an introduction to the subject is given in Appendix D. In addition, since a basic understanding of the radio interface is necessary to explain the operation of a piconet, we shall give a brief explanation of it here.

Essentially, Bluetooth uses 79 separate carrier frequencies within the ISM band, each of which is equally spaced at 1 MHz intervals. Hence it requires an overall bandwidth of 80 MHz. The modulation bit rate is 1 Mbps and each carrier is used to transmit a single bit from the bitstream using conventional **frequency shift keying** (**FSK**), the principles of which we described earlier in Section 2.2.2. In addition, in order to minimize interference from other users of the ISM band, the set of 79 individual carrier frequencies are not used linearly but instead in a pseudo-random order hopping from one frequency to another at a rate of 1600 hops per second. Hence the time between hops is 625 μs. This is referred to as the **slot time** and all transmissions within the piconet take place in one, three or five consecutive slot time intervals.

The clock of the master provides the system timing for the piconet. Each Bluetooth device has a separate 48-bit address that is assigned to each radio transceiver during the manufacturing process. The pseudo-random sequence used for transmissions is then determined by the device address of the master. Before a slave can communicate with the master it has to synchronize to the hopping sequence of the master. To do this, the master sends its clock and device address to each slave in turn and, after adjusting its internal clock to synchronize with the clock of the master and using the device address to determine the pseudo-random sequence the master is using, each slave becomes an active member of the piconet. In this way, each piconet has a unique hopping sequence and all the active slave devices in a piconet hop to the same carrier frequency of the master in synchronism.

There are three classes of Bluetooth radio transceivers:

- **Power class 1**: this has a maximum power of 100 mW with a typical range of up to 100 m (without any obstacles).
- **Power class 2**: this has a maximum power of 2.5 mW with a typical range of 10 m.
- **Power class 3**: this has a maximum power of 1 mW with a typical range of between 1 and 2 m.

In most Bluetooth applications – within a piconet, for example, and device-to-device communications – a range of 10 m is adequate and hence Power class 2 is the most widely used.

4.2.2 Configurations and terminology

As we indicated earlier, a Bluetooth device can be either a master or a slave and any of the devices within a piconet can be the master. However, the device that establishes the piconet automatically becomes the master and all the other devices then become slaves. There can be up to seven **active slave** (**AS**) devices active at a time within a single piconet. In addition, as we show in Figure 4.3(a), a device may be a **standby slave** (**SS**) or a **parked slave** (**PS**). Devices in the standby mode cannot participate in the piconet. A parked

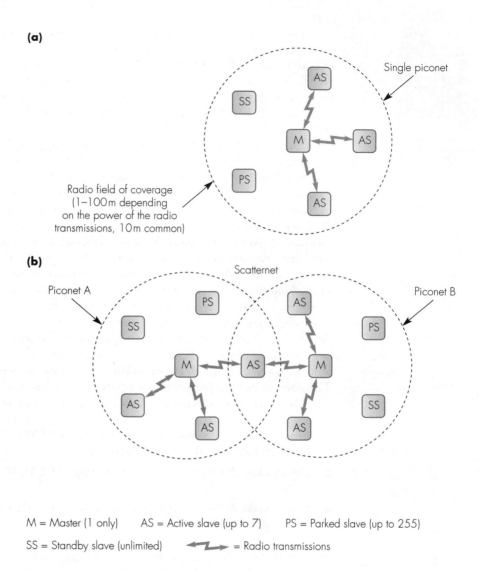

Figure 4.3 Bluetooth configurations and terminology: (a) single piconet; (b) scatternet.

slave, however, cannot actively participate in the piconet but is known by the master and can be reactivated by it. Typically, these are devices that the master has switched to a low-power state in order to save the power in the batteries of the device.

All parked slaves have an 8-bit **parked member address** (**PMA**) and there can be up to 255 such devices. If there are already seven active slaves, then a parked slave must wait until one of the active slaves switches to the parked mode before it can become active. All active slaves have a 3-bit **active member address** (**AMA**) and this is used by the master both to send blocks of data – referred to as **packets** in the standard – to a specific slave and to identify the slave that has sent a response packet. All communications are via the master and slave-to-slave communications are prohibited.

In order to utilize the 80 MHz of bandwidth in an efficient way, multiple piconets can be present in a room/office at the same time. In addition, multiple piconets can be interconnected together to provide a wider area of coverage. The resulting configuration is then known as a **scatternet** and a simple example is shown in Figure 4.3(b).

As we can see, in this example one of the active slave devices is located in the region of the two overlapping piconets. However, since each piconet has a different pseudo-random hopping sequence, both piconets can operate concurrently. Hence the slave can become a member of either piconet but not both at the same time. To change its membership, the slave first informs its current master that it will be unavailable for a specified time. It then proceeds to synchronize with the master of the other piconet in the described way.

In practice, creating more piconets in the same area leads to a degradation in the performance of each piconet. This is because the probability of the same carrier frequency being used at the same time increases so resulting in the respective bit in the bitstream being corrupted.

4.2.3 Baseband packet transmissions

As we indicated earlier, all the active slave devices within each piconet synchronize to the master and hop to the same carrier frequency in synchronism. Also, the hop rate is 1600 hops per second and hence the time between hops is 625 µs. This is known as the slot time and all transmissions take place in one, three or five consecutive slot time intervals. A technique called time division duplex (TDD) is then used to control the order of transmissions: the master always sends in the first set of one, three or five time slots – the header of the packet containing the active member address (AMA) of the slave – and the addressed slave then responds in the next set of one, three or five time slots. To illustrate this, the transmission of a sequence of one-slot packets is shown in Figure 4.4(a) and the example shown in part (b) shows a sequence involving one, three or five-slot packets.

As we can see in part (a), in the first example there is just a single slave and this is exchanging one-slot packets with the master. Note, however, that the second packet sent by the master comprises only a header and no payload field. This occurs, for example, when a control packet is being sent.

In the second example, it is assumed that the master is communicating with three slaves. The master first sends a one-slot packet to slave 1 and this replies with a one-slot packet. The master then sends a three-slot packet to slave 2 and this again replies with a one-slot packet. Finally, the master sends a five-slot packet to slave 3 and this also replies with a one-slot packet. Note that

(a)

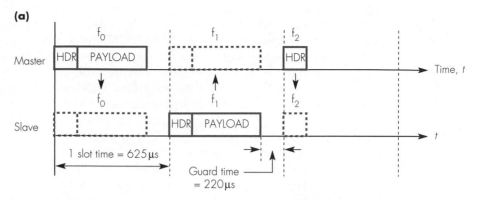

f_0, f_1, f_2 = a sequential set of pseudo-random hop/carrier frequencies   HDR = Packet header

Note: The guard time is used to ensure there are no corruptions between the end of one frame and the start of the next

(b)

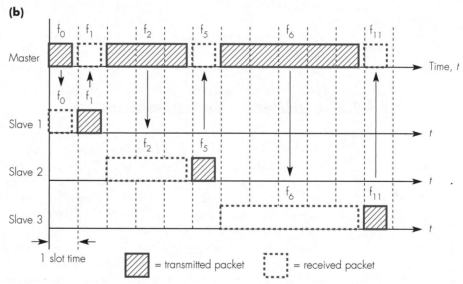

Note: All transmissions from the master use even-frequency slots and those from the slave odd-frequency slots

Figure 4.4 Piconet packet transmission examples: (a) one-slot packets; (b) one-, three- and five-slot packets.

when the master is sending a multiple-slot packet, both the master and the slave use the next in-sequence hop/carrier frequency to transmit/receive the whole packet. However, the next packet sent by the slave is always in the correct hop-sequence frequency for the time slot.

Bluetooth supports two types of service – called links in the standard – a **synchronous connection-oriented link (SCO)** and an **asynchronous connectionless link (ACL)**. An SCO link is intended for speech/audio applications and an ACL for general data applications. The SCO link provides a 64 kbps duplex connection by the master reserving a pair of consecutive single slots at constant time intervals. The standard allows for three consecutive calls to be in progress concurrently. The data associated with ACL applications are then transmitted in the remaining free slots. Only one ACL link between the master and a slave can be in progress at a time and the maximum data rates are 433.9 kbps (symmetric) and 723.3/57.6 kbps asymmetric. A simple example illustrating the transmission of mixed SCO and ACL packets is shown in Figure 4.5.

4.2.4 Baseband packet formats

The format of each packet is shown in Figure 4.6 and, as we can see, the first field in the packet is the **access code**. This is used for clock synchronization and identification purposes. Three different codes have been identified:

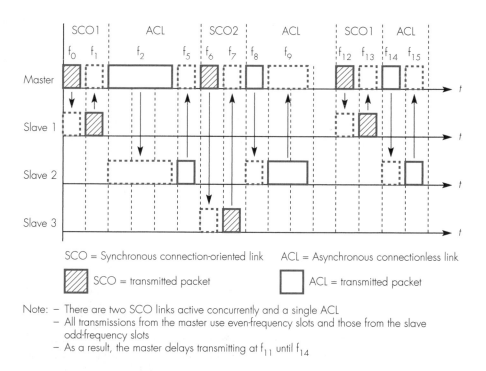

Figure 4.5 **An example showing the transmission of mixed packet types.**

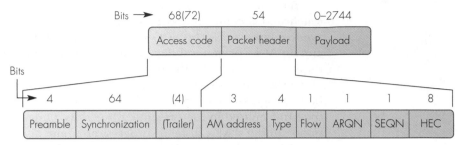

Access codes:
    – Channel access code : used to identify the piconet,
    – Device address code : used by the master to page the (slave) device,
    – Inquiry access code : used to find address of a neighboring device.
Packet header:
    – AM address : identifies one of the 7 active slaves (0 indicates the master),
    – Type : packet type indicates the structure/contents in the payload,
    – Flow : used for flow control with the ACL mode (stop = 0, resume = 1),
    – ARQN : used to indicate the type of acknowledgment (1 = ACK, 0 = NAK),
    – SEQN : a modulo-2 packet sequence number (0, 1, 0, 1, ...),
    – HEC : error check on the header field (1/3 forward error correcting code)
Payload : 0–343 bytes which includes an additional 1 or 2 byte header (1 byte for 1-slot packets and 2 bytes for 3- and 5-slot packets) and a 2-byte CRC that is used for error detection purposes.

Figure 4.6 Bluetooth packet format and field descriptions.

- **Channel access code** (**CAC**): this is derived from the 48-bit address of the master and is used to identify the piconet.
- **Device address code** (**DAC**): this is derived from the (slave) device address and is used by the master to page the device.
- **Inquiry access code** (**IAC**): this is used to find the address of a neighboring device.

We shall describe the use of these later in Section 4.2.7.
    The **packet header** is composed of five subfields:

- **AM address**: this is the 3-bit active member address and identifies one of the seven active slaves; the zero value is used to indicate a broadcast packet from the master.
- **Type**: this indicates the packet type and is determined by the structure of the **payload** field. For example, varying levels of forward error correction (FEC) are available for use with both SCO packets and ACL packets and the *type* field indicates the division of the payload field into data bits and either 0, 1/3 or 2/3 FEC bits. An introduction to the subject of forward error control is given in Appendix D.
- **Flow**: this is used with the ACL mode to provide a simple flow control scheme, stop sending = 1 and resume = 0.

■ **SEQN**: this is the sequence number of the packet based on a simple modulo-2 scheme (0, 1, 0, 1, ...) and is used with ACL traffic.

■ **ARQN**: this is used in conjunction with the SEQN for an automatic repeat request (ARQ) error control scheme, the operation of which we described in Section 1.4.2. The ARQN bit indicates the type of acknowledgment: 1 = ACK and 0 = NAK.

■ **HEC**: this is an 8-bit error check on the header field. The whole 18-bit header is then further protected by a 1/3 rate FEC that makes up the 54-bit packet header.

The contents of the payload field vary and depend on the type of service/link – SCO and ACL – and the degree of FEC that is used. With an SCO link, the payload is 30 bytes in length and the degree of FEC can be 0, 2/3 or 1/3; that is, the amount of user data can be 30, 20 or 10 bytes respectively. With an ACL, the payload can be from 0 to 343 bytes. This includes a one or two-byte (payload) header – one byte for one-slot packets and two bytes for three- and five-slot packets – plus a two-byte CRC at the tail. The header is composed of an *identifier* (service access point) for the logical link control protocol – which sits immediately above the baseband protocol – a *flow control* field, and a *length* field that indicates the number of data bytes in the payload.

In addition to the SCO and ACL packets, there are a number of control packets. These include:

■ **Poll packets**: these are used by the master to poll slaves.

■ **Hopping synchronization packets**: these are sent by the master to a slave to enable it to synchronize to the clock of the master and its hopping sequence.

■ **Acknowledgment packets** (ACK and NAK) for use with the IdleRQ/ARQ error control scheme.

4.2.5 Error control

An example showing the operation of the ARQ error control scheme that is used with ACL packets is illustrated in Figure 4.7. As we can see, the first packet is received without errors and hence an ACK with the same SEQN is returned. The second packet received, however, is found to have (bit or burst) errors and hence the slave returns a NAK with a SEQN = 1, which indicates it is still waiting to receive an error-free copy of the previously transmitted packet with SEQN = 1. Hence the master sends another copy of this which, in the example, is received free of errors and the slave therefore returns an ACK packet with a SEQN = 1. This time, however, it is the ACK that is corrupted and, as a result, the master sends another copy of the packet. On receipt of this, the slave detects that the packet is a duplicate as it is expecting a packet with a SEQN = 0. Hence to overcome this, the slave discards the

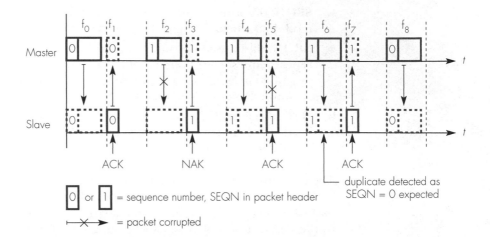

Figure 4.7 **Example packet sequence with ARQ error control scheme.**

received packet and returns an ACK packet to the master. The master then sends the next in-sequence packet. Further discussion of the ARQ scheme is given in Section 1.4.2.

The HEC at the tail of the packet header and the CRC at the tail of the payload are both used to detect errors in a packet. In general, however, wireless/radio links are more prone to errors than fixed-wire links and it is for this reason that forward error correction (FEC) is used also. Indeed, all but one of the SCO packets rely on FEC since an ARQ scheme is inappropriate for use with synchronous links. With an audio/speech service, for example, a few residual bit errors can be tolerated. In most cases, however, when transmitting data, the presence of bit errors must be detected: hence the presence of a FEC and a CRC. The various levels of FEC are then used to reduce the probability of (residual) bit errors being present in a packet. An introduction to FEC is given in Appendix C.

4.2.6 The link manager protocol and establishing a piconet

The link manager protocol is responsible for link set-up between devices and also a number of management functions of devices including security – authentication and encryption – synchronization, power control, and parameter negotiation. A simplified state transition diagram showing the various (baseband) states of a Bluetooth device and the possible transitions between states is shown in Figure 4.8.

In general, Bluetooth devices rely on a battery for their power and hence can only be in the active state for a set period of time. Each device that is currently switched on but is not a member of a piconet is in the **standby mode**. This is the minimum-power state in which only the device clock is running.

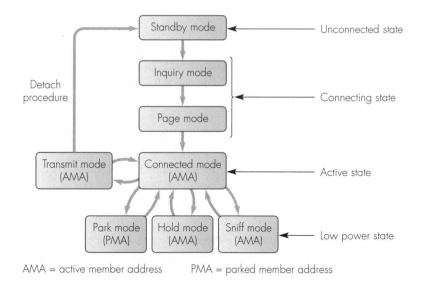

AMA = active member address   PMA = parked member address

Figure 4.8 A simplified state transition diagram of a Bluetooth device.

When in this mode, the device may establish a piconet using first the **inquiry mode** and then the **page mode**. Devices only respond to inquiry and page packets, however, if the device is in the inquiry scan mode or page scan mode respectively.

To establish a piconet, the user of a device starts the inquiry procedure by broadcasting a packet containing an **inquiry access code** (**IAC**). This is common to all Bluetooth devices and is broadcast over 32 carrier frequencies – called the **wake-up carriers** – in turn. Normally, devices in the standby mode enter the inquiry mode at periodic intervals to listen for an IAC packet on any of the wake-up carriers. Then, if a device detects an IAC packet, it responds by returning a message/packet containing its device address, class of device, and the timing information required by the master to set up a connection with it. At this point the device becomes a slave and the master first derives the channel access code (CAC) and then enters the page mode.

While in the page mode, the master, after making contact with all the slave devices, proceeds to set up connections to each device thereby creating a piconet. First, based on the device addresses that it has received, the master uses each of these to compute the corresponding device address code (DAC) of each slave which it needs to page each slave device individually. The master then computes the pseudo-random hopping sequence for the piconet using its own device address and informs each slave of this. Each device then answers by synchronizing with the clock of the master and locking into the hopping sequence it has received. All the devices then enter the connected mode.

The **Active state** is composed of the *connected* and *transmit* modes and the **Low-power state** comprises three modes: *Park, Hold* and *Sniff*. When in the Active state, a slave communicates with the master by listening, receiving and transmitting over SCO and ACL links using the 3-bit active member address (AMA) allocated to it. The three low-power modes in decreasing power order are:

- **Sniff**: the device keeps its AMA and continues to listen but not at every other slot time. Also, the master allocates a reduced number of slots for transmissions to slaves.
- **Hold**: the device keeps its AMA but suspends any further ACL transmissions. However, a slave may still exchange SCO packets. It is used, for example, when the master is establishing a connection with a slave device that is joining the piconet.
- **Park**: the device releases its AMA – allowing another device to become active – and is allocated a parked member address (PMA). The device is still a member of the piconet and, at preset – called beacon – intervals, resynchronizes with the master. All messages/packets are broadcast to all parked slaves.

Also, as we show in the figure, a device can re-enter the standby mode by invoking the *detach procedure*.

4.2.7 L2CAP

The **logical link control and adaptation protocol** (**L2CAP**) is a data link control protocol that operates on top of the baseband layer in the same way as the link manager protocol. It supports only ACL links – audio and speech applications using SCO links operate directly on top of the baseband layer – using three different types of logical channels:

- **Connectionless**: these are unidirectional channels and are used, for example, for broadcasts between a master and its slaves.
- **Connection-oriented**: these are bi-directional and support a defined quality of service (QoS) in each direction. The QoS parameters include average/peak data rate, maximum burst size, latency and jitter, all of which we described earlier in Section 1.2.5.
- **Signaling**: these are also bi-directional and are used to exchange signaling messages between the master and a slave using the L2CAP protocol.

Each channel type is identified by a **channel identifier** (**CID**): CID = 1 for signaling, CID = 2 for connectionless, and CIDs of 64 or greater are assigned dynamically at each end of a connection-oriented channel to identify the connection and hence the recipient of the packet data. A different packet format is then used with each channel type and these are shown in Figure 4.9.

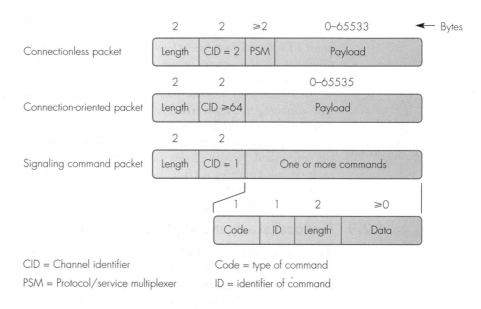

Figure 4.9 L2CAP packet types and their format.

For connection-oriented and signaling packets, the CID in the packet header is used to identify the intended higher-layer protocol at the receiving side. In the case of connectionless packets, an additional field called the **protocol/service multiplexer** (**PSM**) is used. The payload field can be up to 64 kbytes.

However, as we saw in Section 4.2.4, the maximum packet size of the underlying baseband protocol layer is significantly smaller than this. Hence, since L2CAP accepts a block of up to 64 kbytes from the upper layers, the L2CAP has to perform a segmentation and reassembly function. For example, a one-slot packet has a maximum payload field of 340 bytes and hence it would take 189 packets to send the block of 64 kbytes.

The payload of the signaling packets contains one or more *commands*, each of which has its own *code* and an *ID* to relate a reply to an earlier request. For example, there is a connection request and response, disconnection request and response, command reject, etc.

4.2.8 Service discovery protocol

As part of its brief, Bluetooth devices should be able to operate with other devices in an ad-hoc fashion. To do this, it is necessary for a device to be able to determine what services are available on each of the devices within its radio coverage. This is the role of the service discovery protocol (SDP) which, in turn, uses the services offered by the L2CAP.

The SDP operates in a client-server mode with a *service discovery database* (*SDD*) maintained by the server. The SDD contains a number of *service records*, each of which contains attributes of the service. For example, one of the attributes is the *service record handle* which identifies uniquely each service record within the database.

The SDP supports two basic functions: searching for services and browsing. The *searching function* is used by a client device to search for a specific service. The *browsing function* is used by a client to discover what services are supported. Then, once a particular service has been identified, its attributes can be requested by the client using the *service record handle*. The attributes include information such as how to connect to the service using the various protocols that make up the particular application profile.

4.2.9 Protocol stack and application profiles

As we show in Figure 4.10(a), the various protocols that we have studied in the previous subsections form what is called the **core specification** of Bluetooth. In addition, as we indicated in the introduction to this section, there are a number of application profiles. Each profile is composed of a protocol stack that collectively represents the default solution for a specific application. A small collection of the applications for which profiles have been written are listed in Figure 4.10(b).

The **RFCOMM** protocol emulates a serial line/port and is also called a **cable replacement protocol**. The protocol emulates the EIA-232 – formerly RS-232 – interface standard we explained in Section 2.2.2. It supports multiple serial ports over a single physical channel. It is used in a number of profiles. For example, it is used to obtain LAN and Internet access. With this profile, multiple data terminals – laptops, pocket PCs, etc. – use a LAN access point (AP) as a wireless connection to a LAN and the Internet. The full LAN/Internet protocol stack is used. The link control protocol is PPP and this communicates directly with the RFCOMM layer.

The **telephony control specification binary** (**TCS BIN**) protocol is a bit-oriented protocol that has been designed to connect to three different telephony services:

■ a cordless phone at home or in an office connecting to a PSTN or an ISDN;
■ in an intercom application involving two telephones connected directly (walkie talkie);
■ a mobile phone connecting to a cellular phone network.

The **AT command** protocol is used to enable a mobile phone or a (cordless) modem to communicate with a PC to provide dial-up networking – to the Internet for example – without the need for a physical connection. The AT-commands are needed to control the mobile phone or modem and a second stack – for example, PPP over RFCOMM – is used to transfer the (application) payload data.

(a)

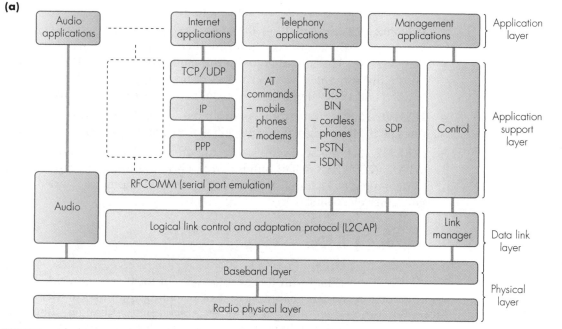

TCS BIN = telephony control protocol specification – binary   AT = attention   RFCOMM = radio frequency communications

(b)

Example application profiles:
- cordless telephony within the home;
- intercomm between two devices;
- headset: hands-free voice communication;
- serial port (emulation): includes dial-up networking, fax, LAN and Internet access using the LLC and PPP protocols respectively;
- object exchange (OBEX) : a means to exchange objects such as business cards and pictures;
- personal area networking (interconnection of peripherals to a PC);
- LAN and Internet access;
- 3G handsets.

Figure 4.10 Bluetooth applications: (a) protocol stack; (b) example profiles.

4.2.10 IEEE802.15

The Bluetooth standard is now well established and most portable devices now have a Bluetooth interface built in. However, the IEEE also has a working group for wireless personal area networks (WPANs) that has similar goals to Bluetooth. The standard goes under the title of IEEE802.15 and the working group for this is divided into four subgroups, each focused on a different aspect of the standard. These are:

- **IEEE802.15.1**: this subgroup is concerned only with the lower layers of Bluetooth and works with the Bluetooth SIG.

- **IEEE802.15.2**: as we shall see in the next section, the most popular standard for wireless LANs – in terms of current installations – is IEEE802.11b. This also operates in the same ISM band as Bluetooth. Hence this subgroup is concerned with the coexistence of WPANs and WLANs and to develop algorithms and protocols to achieve this.

- **IEEE802.15.3**: this subgroup is working on a standard providing data rates of 20 Mbps or greater while still working at low power.

- **IEEE802.15.4**: this subgroup is working on a standard for low-rate WPANs (LR-WPANs). The aim is extremely low power consumption and low complexity. Example applications are home automation and consumer electronics.

4.3 Wireless LANs

A major cost associated with the various types of local area network (LANs) we described in the last chapter is that of installing the physical wire cables. Moreover, if the layout of the interconnected computers changes, then a cost similar to the initial installation cost can be incurred as the wiring plan is changed. This is one of the reasons why wireless LANs – that is, LANs that do not use physical wires as the transmission medium – have been developed.

A second reason is the widespread deployment of handheld devices – PDAs, pocket PCs, etc. – and portable computers – notebooks, laptops, etc. Advancing technology means that such devices are rapidly becoming comparable in computing power to many desktop computers. Although the primary reason for using these devices is portability, they often have to communicate with other computers. These may be other portable computers or, more likely, a server that is attached to a wired LAN. Examples are a handheld terminal in a retail store communicating with a back-of-store computer to update stock records or, in a hospital, a nurse with a notebook computer accessing a patient record held in a database on a large server.

In addition, wireless LANs are now being used extensively by many public telecom providers in airport terminals, train and bus stations, shopping malls, etc., for access to the Internet. To discriminate between these and those used in offices and campuses, they are called **public wireless LANs**.

As we indicated in the last chapter, Ethernet/IEEE802.3 is now the dominant standard for local area networking. Hence the IEEE standards committee for wireless LANs decided from the outset that the new standard should be able to interwork with the existing IEEE802.3 standards above the MAC sublayer. The standard for wireless LANs is **IEEE802.11** and has the colloquial name of **WiFi** (wireless fidelity).

The standard defines two alternative operational modes: one using a radio base station – which is part of a unit called an **access point** (**AP**) in the standard – and the other without an AP. A schematic diagram illustrating the two alternative modes is shown in Figure 4.11.

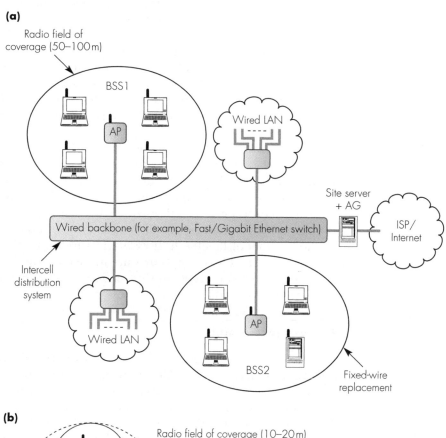

(a)

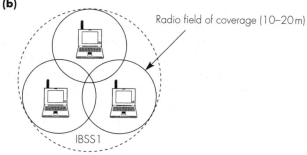

(b)

AP = access point – includes a radio base station and a network interface to the wired backbone network

AG = access gateway

BSS = basic service set

IBSS = independent BSS

Figure 4.11 IEEE802.11 operational modes: (a) infrastructure; (b) ad-hoc.

As we can see, in part (a) an AP is used and in part (b) it is absent. The first is called an **infrastructure wireless LAN** and the second an **ad-hoc wireless LAN**. In the case of an infrastructure LAN, all communications take place between the AP and the wireless devices – normally referred to as stations in the context of LANs – but not directly between the wireless stations. Also, the AP, in addition to performing the medium access control function, acts as a bridge to either another wireless LAN or, more likely, a fixed-wire LAN. The main application of infrastructure wireless LANs, therefore, is for fixed-wire replacement.

In contrast, in an ad-hoc wireless LAN each wireless station/device communicates directly with the other devices so removing the necessity of having a central AP. This means, however, that each device must implement the medium access control function. Typical applications of ad-hoc wireless LANs are in conference/meeting rooms to enable people to exchange data, for example. It should be noted, however, that although this is a similar application to that of Bluetooth, IEEE802.11 wireless LANs operate at much higher bit rates than Bluetooth so they are more compatible with the higher bit rates of the fixed-wire LANs. In this section we shall describe selected aspects of both types of wireless LAN.

4.3.1 Wireless media

The IEEE802.11 standard supports two types of wireless media: radio and infrared optical signals. However, since in this application domain the range of coverage of optical signals is much less than that of radio waves, most wireless LANs use radio-frequency waves as the wireless media. Hence, as we did at the beginning of our description of Bluetooth, in the remainder of this subsection we shall simply list the main transmission and modulation schemes that are used in each standard. Then, in the following subsections, we shall study the different types of medium access control (MAC) algorithms that are used. As we indicated earlier, however, a more detailed introduction to the alternative radio transmission methods is given in Appendix D.

In the same way that there are multiple 802.3 standards – Ethernet, Fast Ethernet, etc. – so there are a number of standards associated with 802.11. In terms of the radio frequency, most use the ISM band at 2.4 GHz since this is available worldwide and no license is required for its use. The transmission and modulation schemes and transmission bit rates of the main standards are as follows:

■ **802.11 DSSS**: this operates in the ISM band at 2.4 GHz and offers two alternative bit rates: 1 Mbps and 2 Mbps. Each bit is transmitted as 11 **chips** using a type of binary phase shift keying (BPSK) modulation for 1 Mbps and a type of quadrature phase shift keying (QPSK) modulation for 2 Mbps. The baud/signaling rates, therefore, are 1 Mbaud and 2 Mbaud respectively.

- **802.11 FHSS**: this also operates in the ISM band at 2.4 GHz and offers the same two operating bit rates of 1 Mbps and 2 Mbps. It uses 79 **hopping channels**, each with a bandwidth of 1 MHz. The modulation schemes used are based on frequency shift keying (FSK). For 1 Mbps each bit is mapped to one of the hopping channel frequencies and at 2 Mbps two bits are mapped to each frequency.

- **802.11a OFDM**: this operates in the **US unlicensed national information infrastructure** (**U-NII**) band at 5 GHz and provides a bit rate of up to 54 Mbps. Fifty-two orthogonal subcarrier frequencies are used, 48 for information frames and four for synchronization functions. Each subcarrier is modulated using BPSK (up to 9 Mbps), QPSK (up to 18 Mbps), 16-QAM (up to 36 Mbps) and 64-QAM (up to 54 Mbps). Forward error correction (FEC) – the principles of which we describe in Appendix C – is used also at coding rates of 1/2, 2/3 or 3/4.

- **802.11b HR-DSSS**: this operates in the ISM band at 2.4 GHz and provides bit rates of 1, 2, 5.5 and 11 Mbps with a maximum user data rate of 6 Mbps. The two lower bit rates use the same 11-chip Barker sequence as DSSS and the same modulation methods. The two higher rates – 5 and 11 Mbps – use a new scheme called 8-chip **complementary code keying** (**CCK**). With this standard, to minimize interference, three non-overlapping channels are chosen during installation of the access points.

- **802.11g OFDM**: this operates in the ISM band at 2.4 GHz and provides a bit rate of 54 Mbps. It uses the same OFDM modulation scheme as 802.11a plus forward error correction.

At the time of writing – this is a very fast moving area – the most popular standard in terms of installations is 802.11b and almost all current portable devices have an IEEE802.11b network interface built in. However, since 802.11g operating in the 2.4 GHz band has arrived, the higher bit rate it offers may be a factor when installing a new network.

4.3.2 MAC sublayer protocol

As we saw earlier in part (b) of Figure 4.11, the various types of IEEE802.11 infrastructure LANs have been designed to interwork with existing fixed-wire Ethernet LANs. The applications running on a wireless station, therefore, are unaware of whether the physical medium is fixed-wiring or radio. A schematic diagram showing how this is achieved is shown in Figure 4.12.

As we can see, the LLC sublayer within the AP performs the relaying function; that is, the contents of a MAC frame received from a mobile device over the radio network are simply relayed by the LLC to the MAC sublayer associated with the fixed-wire network for onward transmission over the wired LAN. Similarly, a response frame from the server computer is relayed in the same way. The main difference is that the mobile device may experience a slightly longer delay in receiving a response frame relative to that of a device attached to the fixed-wire network.

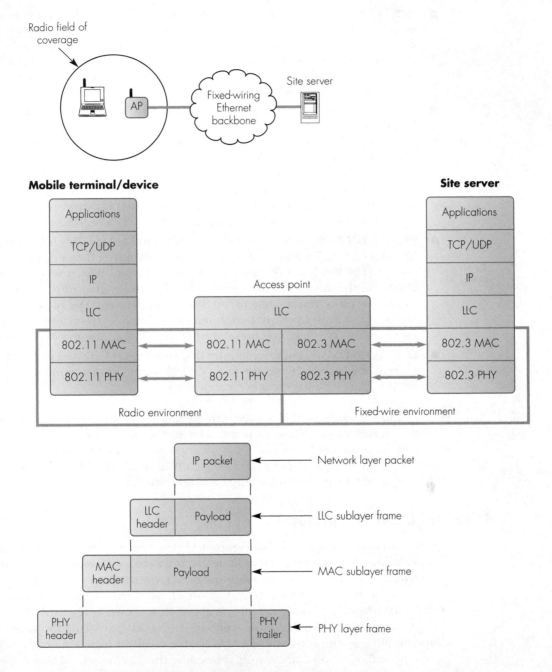

Figure 4.12 IEEE802.11/802.3 interworking schematic.

As we shall expand upon later, since radio transmissions have a worse bit error rate probability than transmissions over fixed wiring, the maximum frame size over the wireless network must be proportionately less than that used over the fixed-wire network. As a result, each frame must first be segmented into a number of small fragments for transmission over the radio link. Hence, since there are time overheads associated with transmitting each frame fragment, this leads to slightly longer response times.

There are two types of service provided by the MAC sublayer: an **asynchronous data service** – best-effort, variable-delay – and a **time-bounded service**. The first is mandatory for use in both types of network – ad-hoc and infrastructure – and the second is optional and is intended for use in infrastructure networks. The first is called the **distributed coordination function** (**DCF**) and the second the **point coordination function** (**PCF**) which requires an AP to control access to the (shared) radio medium. We shall discuss each service separately.

For all the access methods, there are several parameters that are used to control the waiting time before a station can access the medium. The values of the parameters depend on the type of modulation being used by the physical layer. They are defined in relation to a **slot time**. This is derived from the propagation delay of the medium and delays in the transmitter, and is $20\,\mu s$ for DSSS and $50\,\mu s$ for FHSS. In all cases, the medium is idle if a signal called the **clear channel assessment** (**CCA**) is present. The three most important time parameters are shown in Figure 4.13(a) and are:

- **Short inter-frame spacing** (**SIFS**): this is the shortest waiting time – and hence highest priority – and is used with control messages such as data acknowledgments (described later). For DSSS SIFS is $10\,\mu s$ and for FHSS it is $28\,\mu s$.

- **DCF inter-frame spacing** (**DIFS**): this is the longest waiting time – and hence lowest priority – and is used with the asynchronous data service. It is defined as SIFS plus two time slots.

- **PCF inter-frame spacing** (**PIFS**): this is a waiting time between SIFS and DIFS – and hence medium priority – and is used with the time-bounded service. PIFS is SIFS plus one slot time.

Distributed coordination function (DCF)

The use of DCF is mandatory in both ad-hoc and infrastructure LANs and hence we shall describe it first. The medium access control method used in DCF is called **carrier-sense multiple-access with collision avoidance** (**CSMA/CA**). There are two alternative operational modes of CSMA/CA: the first is referred to as DCF with CSMA/CA and the second DCF with RTS/CTS extension. We shall describe each separately.

(a)

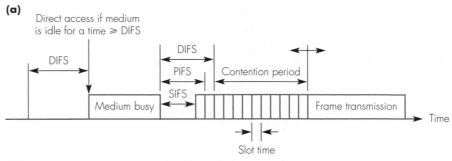

SIFS = short inter-frame waiting time (and hence highest priority)
DIFS = longest inter-frame waiting time (and hence lowest priority)
PIFS = a waiting time between SIFS and DIFS (and hence medium priority)

(b)

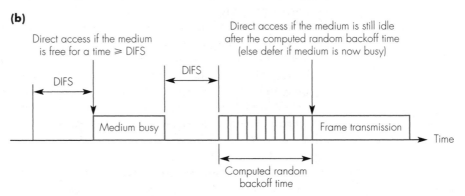

DCF = Distributed coordination function
CSMA/CA = Carrier sense multiple access with collision avoidance

Figure 4.13 Operation of the basic DCF with CSMA/CA in the broadcast mode: (a) definition of the timing parameters; (b) use of random backoff.

DCF with CSMA/CA

When a station has a data frame to transmit, the MAC unit senses the medium and, if it is idle – that is, the CCA signal is detected – it proceeds to wait for the duration of DIFS and then transmits the complete frame. This means that only a short access delay is incurred under light traffic conditions. If the medium is busy, the MAC unit defers for the duration of DIFS and then enters a contention phase for use of the medium with any other waiting stations.

To do this, each competing station computes a random backoff time – measured in slot times – that is within a time interval called the **contention window** (**CW**). The station then waits for this time while, at the same time, it continues to sense the medium. If the medium goes busy before the computed backoff time expires, then the station has lost this cycle and must wait until the medium goes idle again before retrying. However, if the medium is still idle when the backoff time expires, the station can transmit the frame immediately. This procedure is illustrated in Figure 4.13(b).

This basic procedure is unfair since any new station coming into contention during the time a frame is being transmitted has the same chance of transmitting a frame in the next cycle as the stations that lost out in the previous cycle. Hence to overcome this, each station has a count-down counter – called the **backoff timer** – into which the computed backoff time is loaded. Then, if a station does not gain access to the medium in the first cycle, when the line becomes busy – that is, the winner starts to transmit its frame – the station stops its backoff timer. It then waits for the medium to become idle again and, after the DIFS period, it starts to count down the backoff timer again. Then, if the counter reaches zero and the medium is still idle, the station can transmit its frame immediately. However, if the medium becomes busy before the counter expires, the station stops the counter again at its current value and defers to the new winning station. The same procedure is then repeated until the frame is transmitted.

As we can deduce from this, the scheme is strongly influenced by the maximum duration of the contention window. If the window is too small, the computed random values can be too small – and hence cause too many collisions. If it is too high, unnecessarily long delays are incurred. To overcome this, the window value held in all stations tries to adapt to the number of stations trying to send a frame. It starts with a low value – number of slot times – and each time a collision occurs – detected by the receipt of a corrupted frame – each station doubles its maximum window size. In the event of prolonged heavy load conditions the procedure repeats until a defined maximum window size is reached. The algorithm is called **binary exponential backoff** and is the same as that used with the CSMA/CD access control method we described earlier in Section 3.2.1 of the previous chapter.

Radio is a broadcast medium and hence each frame transmitted is received by all the other stations. The standard, however, in addition to the scheme we have just described for use in the broadcast mode, also supports a scheme that operates in the unicast mode: that is, each data frame transmitted is processed only by the station specified in the destination MAC address in the frame header. An example frame transmission is shown in Figure 4.14.

In part (a) it is assumed that the sending station, after waiting for the DIFS period and detecting that the medium is still idle, proceeds to transmit the frame, and that it is received free of errors by the addressed destination station. In response, the station generates an **acknowledgment (ACK) control frame** and sends this immediately after the SIFS period, which, since this is less than DIFS, is before any other station can access the medium. The sender must then compete in the normal way before it can send the next frame.

In part (b), it is assumed that the frame from the sender is corrupted. This is detected by the medium being idle after the SIFS period has expired –

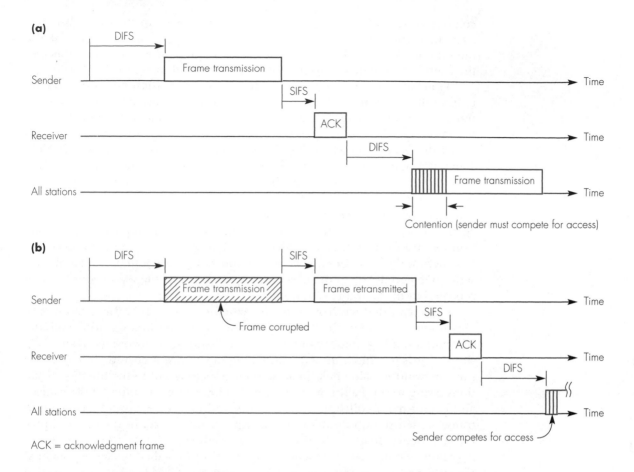

Figure 4.14 Operation of basic DCF with CSMA/CA in the unicast mode: (a) successful frame transmission; (b) retransmission procedure.

and hence an ACK frame has not been sent by the receiver. On detecting this, the sender immediately retransmits another copy of the frame and, in the example, this is received free of errors and hence is acknowledged by the receiver as in part (a). There is a limit set on the number of retransmission attempts – the **attempt limit** – and, if this is reached, the MAC sublayer stops sending any further frames and returns a *failure status* to the LLC sublayer.

DCF with RTS/CTS extension

The RTS/CTS extension is used to overcome a phenomenon that can arise with radio transmissions. It is called the **hidden station problem.** It is caused by the fact that the power of the radio transmissions may vary from one station to another since it is a function of the current charge of the station's battery. This has the effect that not all of the stations are within radio contact of each other. The problem is best described by considering the example shown in Figure 4.15(a).

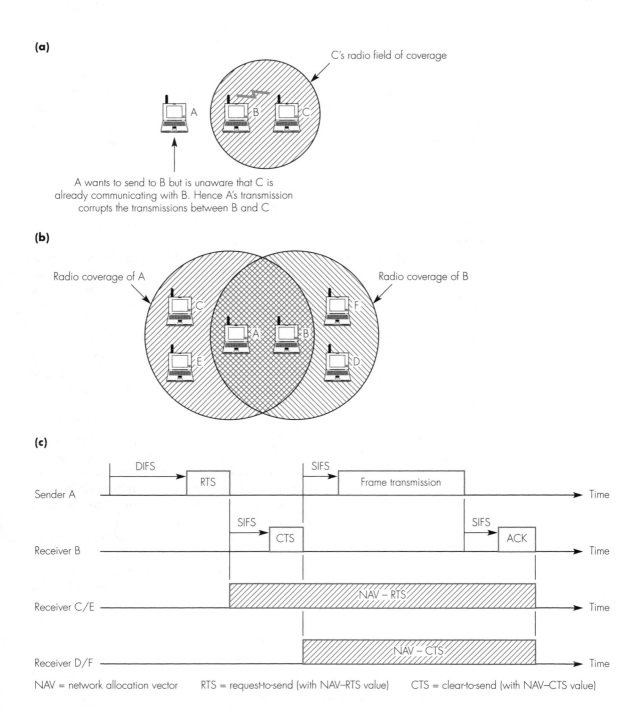

Figure 4.15 DCF with RTS/CTS extension: (a) hidden station problem; (b) example network configuration; (c) associated timing diagram.

In this example, station A wants to send a frame to station B but, as we can see, A is unaware that B is already communicating with C. Hence when A senses the medium, it detects the medium is idle and proceeds to transmit its frame to B so corrupting the current communication between B and C.

To overcome this problem, the standard defines an extension to the basic CSMA/CA method that involves the use of two control frames: a **request-to-send** (**RTS**) and a **clear-to-send** (**CTS**). The extension is optional but each station must be able to react correctly if it receives either a RTS or a CTS frame. To explain how the scheme works, consider the example shown in Figure 4.15(b).

In this, A wants to send a data frame to B. C is within radio coverage of A and D is within coverage of B but not A. E is also within the field of coverage of A, and F is within the coverage of B. The operation of the scheme is illustrated in Figure 4.15(c).

Station A first waits for the duration of DIFS – assuming the medium is idle – and then sends a RTS control frame to B. This has a standard format and includes the destination MAC address of B – the intended recipient – and the computed time duration of the whole transmission from the time the RTS is sent up to the end of the ACK frame. On receipt of the RTS with a MAC address of B within it, B waits for the duration of SIFS and then sends a CTS frame back to A. On receipt of this, A waits for SIFS and then transmits the waiting data frame to B. This is error checked by B and, if no errors are present, it waits for SIFS and then returns an ACK control frame to A so completing the transfer.

However, since C is within radio coverage of A, C also receives the RTS but in this case it determines that it is not the intended recipient of the forthcoming data frame. Hence to avoid any possible collisions, on receipt of the RTS, C sets a parameter called the **network allocation vector** (**NAV**). As we show in the figure, this is equal to the time duration contained within the RTS frame and specifies how long the station should defer from trying to send a new frame. The same procedure is followed by E.

In the case of station B, since D is within its field of coverage, D also receives the CTS frame transmitted by B. This also has a duration value within it but in this case it is the original NAV minus the time to return the CTS frame. Hence station D sets this value into its own NAV to ensure it defers for the appropriate time. The same procedure is followed by F. As we can deduce from this, essentially, the scheme reserves the medium for the duration of a single sender's transmission and hence it is called also a **virtual reservation scheme**.

Frame fragmentation

As we indicated earlier, the radio frequencies used with the various types of wireless LAN are in the ISM band and, in most cases, at 2.4 GHz. This is done because no license is required for its use and it is available worldwide. However, for the same reasons, there are many other users of this band.

Examples are high-power radio frequency heating equipment and microwave ovens. Amateur radio operators are allowed to use these bands also, often at high power levels. As a result, the radio medium is very susceptible to co-channel interference effects. This has the effect that the bit error rate (BER) of the transmission medium – see Appendix B – can be several orders of magnitude higher than that of fixed wiring. Hence, for a given frame length, the probability of a frame being corrupted is much higher for a radio link. As we indicated earlier, the maximum length of an Ethernet frame with a wired link can be up to 1522 bytes or 12 176 bits. This means that with a wireless link and the same frame size almost every frame would have bit errors and hence be discarded. For this reason, therefore, with wireless LANs a much shorter frame size is used.

The MAC sublayer, on receiving a LLC frame for transmission, first divides it into multiple small fragments. Each fragment has a sequence number in the frame header and a FCS at its tail and, on receipt of an error-free fragment, it is acknowledged using an ACK frame with the same sequence number within it. Then, to overcome the effect of a corrupted frame/fragment, the IdleRQ/ARQ error control scheme we described in Section 1.4.2 is used. At the receiver side, the MAC sublayer reassembles the fragments back into the original LLC frame using the sequence number in each frame header. The actual frame size used is adjusted dynamically according to the current bit error rate of the medium. A time sequence diagram illustrating the sequence of frames transmitted to transfer a frame comprising just two fragments is shown in Figure 4.16. The example assumes the same network configuration as in Figure 4.15(b).

As we can see, the sending station (A) sends the first fragment using the same procedure as that for the transmission of a single frame that we showed earlier in Figure 4.15(c). In this case, however, the fragment frame also contains a duration value that includes the time the sender expects to wait for the ACK for the first fragment plus the computed overall time to send the second fragment. The receiver of fragment 1 (B) replies directly after SIFS by returning an ACK 1 frame with a duration value equal to the overall time to transmit fragment 2. Similarly, if fragment 2 was not the last fragment then it would include a duration value equal to the overall time to send the third fragment. However, in this example, since fragment 2 is the last fragment, A does not reserve the medium. On receipt of fragment 2, B returns an ACK 2 after SIFS but again without a duration value.

As we can conclude from the timing diagram, the two fragments – called a **fragment burst** – are sent from A to B without contention from the other four stations. Note also that if ACK 1 was not received at its expected time, then A would resend fragment 1 ahead of fragment 2. As we explained in Section 1.4.1, the sequence numbers present in both fragment and ACK frames are used to detect duplicates.

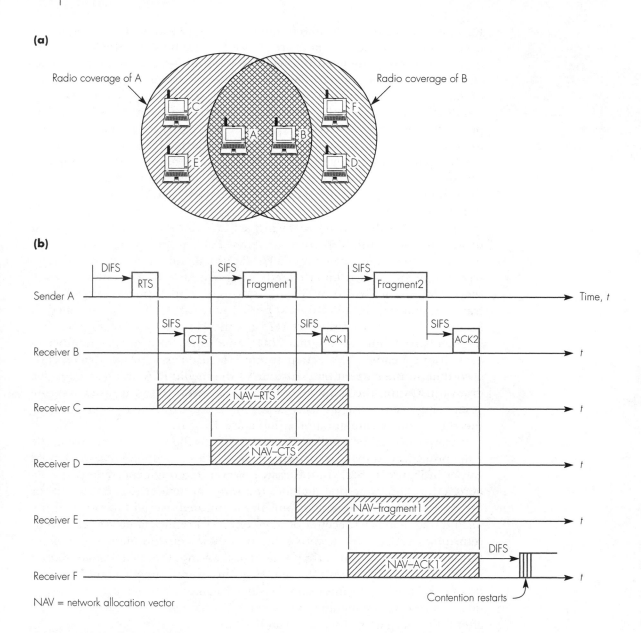

(a)

(b)

NAV = network allocation vector

Figure 4.16 DCF fragmentation example: (a) network configuration; (b) associated timing diagram.

PCF with polling

Although the two versions of DCF we have just studied achieve an orderly use of the radio medium, the resulting access delay experienced by stations will be variable. This is the only operational mode of ad-hoc networks and is also mandatory for use in infrastructure networks. In addition, however, there is a time-bounded service that can be used in infrastructure networks called the point coordination function (PCF). This operates alongside DCF and requires an access point (AP) to control access to the (shared) radio medium.

Recall that when an AP is present, all frames are transmitted via the AP; that is, to send a data frame, the frame is first sent by the mobile station to the AP and the AP then forwards it to the intended recipient station. In this way, the AP controls all access to the medium. As we shall see, this is achieved by the use of a polling sequence involving the source station and a subsystem within the AP called the **point coordinator**. Recall also that in the DCF mode, only one station is entitled to respond after the SIFS period as we showed in Figure 4.16. If the station does not respond, then after the PIFS period has expired, since PIFS is shorter than DIFS, the point coordinator can seize the medium before any waiting mobile stations.

At periodic intervals of between 10 and 100 seconds, the point coordinator broadcasts a **beacon frame**. This is a management frame and contains a set of operational parameters relating to the bit rates and modulation scheme currently in use within the cell and for clock and time synchronization. Synchronized clocks are needed for coordination of the hopping sequence with FHSS, for example, and for coordination of the PCF. The frame also includes an invitation to any new mobile stations to register with the point coordinator. Typically, a response is received when a station within the cell first becomes active and the response frame from the station includes its identity and capabilities. The latter include the bit rates that it supports, whether it can support the PCF mode, the polling-rate required and its power management capabilities. The point coordinator can then either reject the station or, if it is accepted, the station must proceed to authenticate itself before it can send any data. Authentication is necessary because rogue stations can readily intercept (and corrupt) all transmissions within a cell.

To do this, the point coordinator sends a second management frame called a **challenge frame** to determine whether the station knows the secret key of the authentication scheme being used. This is assigned to the station by the network manager and the station proves that it knows the secret key by using it to encrypt the received challenge frame. On receipt of a correctly encrypted frame the coordinator admits the station to the current list of authenticated stations. The station is then said to be *associated*. The station then goes through a similar sequence before shutting down and leaving the cell.

An example frame sequence for contention-free access using the PCF polling scheme is shown in Figure 4.17. In the example it is assumed that four stations are in the authenticated list held by the coordinator. Note that a poll message is a data frame with or without a data field.

The point coordinator divides the overall access time into time periods called **superframes**. Each superframe is composed of a contention-free period during which the PCF mode operates and a contention period during

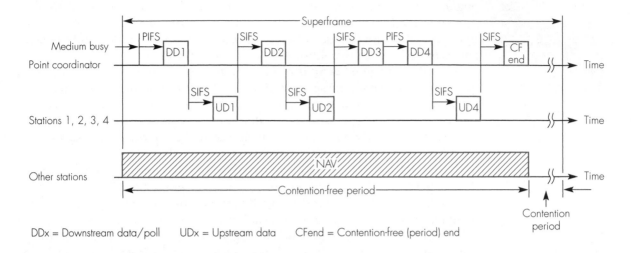

DDx = Downstream data/poll   UDx = Upstream data   CFend = Contention-free (period) end

Figure 4.17 PCF with polling.

which the two DCF modes operate. At the end of a superframe, the point coordinator, on detecting the medium has now become idle – indicating the last frame in the contention period of the previous superframe has been transmitted – waits for PIFS and, since this is less than DIFS, it starts a new superframe by sending a poll message to station 1. This is shown in the figure as downstream data (DD1) and, after SIFS, station 1 replies by sending its data upstream to the coordinator (UD1).

This procedure then repeats for stations 2 and 3 but this time station 3 has no data to send when it is polled. Hence the coordinator, on detecting that no data has been returned after the SIFS period, waits for an additional time slot – to become PIFS – and sends a new poll to station 4 together with any waiting data it may have. Station 4 responds by sending UD4 and, since this is the last station in its polling list, the coordinator waits for SIFS and then broadcasts a CFend management frame to signal that the contention-free period is over and the contention period can start. Note that when in the PCF mode, the coordinator sets the NAV signal ON for the duration of the contention-free period.

MAC frame formats

There are three different classes of MAC frame: data, control and management. All data frames have the format shown in part (a) of Figure 4.18, control frames have the format shown in part (b), and management frames have a similar format to data frames except they have only three address fields. We conclude this section with a brief description of the various fields.

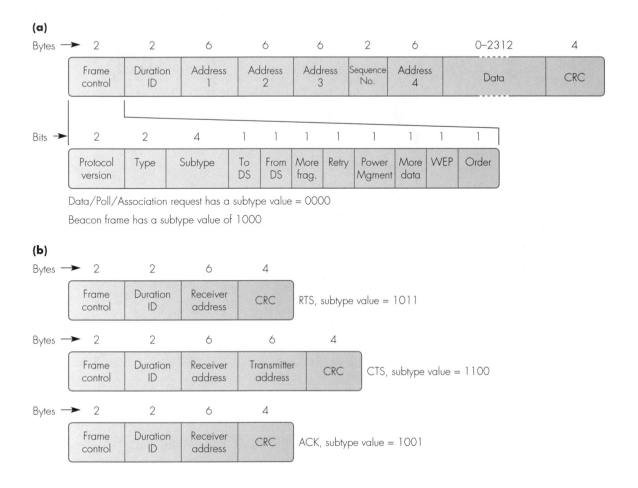

Figure 4.18 MAC frame formats: (a) data and management frames; (b) control frames.

- **Frame control**: this is composed of 11 subfields:
  - *Protocol version*: this allows two versions of the protocol to operate in the same cell at the same time.
  - *Type*: data (=10), control (=01), management (=00).
  - *Subtype*: example subtypes are beacon (=1000), association request (=0000), user data (=0000, with a *type* field=10), RTS (= 1011), CTS (=1100), ACK (=1001).
  - *ToDS/FromDS*: indicates whether the frame is going to or coming from the intercell distribution system (Fast/Gigabit Ethernet, for example). Also, to determine the role of the four 48-bit MAC addresses in the frame header as we show in Figure 4.19.

To DS	From DS	Address 1	Address 2	Address 3	Address 4	Notes
0	0	DA Address of the wireless station/device receiving the frame	SA Address of the wireless station/device sending the frame	BSSID The BSSID of the cell	—	Ad-hoc and single-cell infrastructure LANs
0	1	DA Address of the receiving station within the BSSID	BSSID BSSID/AP address of the cell receiving the frame from the DS	SA Address of the mobile/static station sending the frame	—	Frame sent via the DS to the AP within the cell identified by the BSSID
1	0	BSSID Address of destination BSSID/AP attached to the DS	SA Address of the wireless station sending the frame	DA Address of the wireless station receiving the frame	—	Frame sent via the DS to an AP within a different cell identified by the BSSID
1	1	RA Address of the receiving AP within the DS	TA Address of the transmitting AP within the DS	DA Address of the wireless station receiving the frame	SA Address of the wireless station sending the frame	For frames sent between two APs/cells over the DS

DA = destination address   SA = source address   BSSID = basic service set identifier

RA = receiver AP address   TA = transmitter AP address   DS = distribution system

Figure 4.19 Address fields and their usage.

- *More fragments*: this is set to 1 in all data and management frames if another fragment of the frame is to follow.
- *Retry*: this is set to 1 if the frame is a retransmission of an earlier frame.
- *Power management*: this is set after the successful transmission of a frame: 1 indicates the station goes into power-save mode, 0 indicates the station is still active.
- *More data*: this is set to 1 if either the station or the point coordinator has more data to send after this frame.
- *Wired equivalent privacy* (*WEP*): this indicates that the standard security mechanism of 802.11 is applied.
- *Order*: if this is set to 1 the received frames must be processed in order.

- **Duration/ID:** this indicates – in units of a microsecond – how long the frame and its acknowledgment will occupy the medium. It is used also for setting the duration of NAV.
- **Address 1 to 4:** As we showed earlier in Figure 4.11, in an ad-hoc network all communications are between a pair of wireless stations/devices so just the source and destination MAC addresses are needed. However, in an

infrastructure wireless LAN there may be a number of wireless cells – each called a basic service set (BSS) – each of which has a BSS identifier (BSSID) and an access point (AP) that controls access to the radio medium within that cell. In addition, each AP is attached to the intercell distribution system (DS) to enable a mobile station within a cell to communicate with a station (mobile or static) anywhere within the total LAN. Hence in addition to the MAC addresses of the sending and receiving stations (mobile or static), for communication between cells, the MAC addresses of the two APs that are involved in routing over the distribution system – wired backbone switch for example – are required. To determine which addresses go into the four address fields, the four combinations of the ToDS and FromDS bits are used. The four alternatives and their use are summarized in Figure 4.19.

■ **Sequence control**: as we showed in the example illustrated in Figure 4.16, the acknowledgment scheme used may produce duplicates of frames/fragments. Hence the value in the sequence control field of both data and ACK frames is used to hold a sequence number.

■ **Data**: the data field in a data frame may carry 0–2312 bytes and these are transferred transparently from a sender to one or more receivers.

■ **Checksum**: a 48-bit CRC.

4.4 Cellular radio networks

Cellular radio networks provide a similar set of services to traditional wired networks such as a PSTN and an ISDN. However, the subscriber handsets associated with cellular radio networks communicate with the network by radio transmissions rather than transmissions over fixed wiring. In addition, a cellular radio network supports **mobility**; that is, the subscriber can make calls from anywhere within the field of coverage of the network and also whilst the subscriber is on the move.

The earlier generations of the current networks were used primarily for voice calls, basic data services and interworking with existing networks such as a PSTN, an ISDN and a packet-switched data network (PSDN) such as the international X.25 network. With the most recent generation of networks, however, a significant number of calls now involve data such as text with the **short message service** (**SMS**). In practice, SMS messages are sent using spare capacity in the signaling network and this also is the only way of reaching a mobile phone from within the network. For this reason, the SMS is used also for updating the software of the mobile phone and for the provision of what are called **push services** in which a subscriber can receive unprompted messages. These may relate to the latest stock prices or follow the progress of a ball game. More recently, multimedia such as text, images, photos, audio and video clips have become available with first the **enhanced message service (EMS)** and later the **multimedia message service (MMS)**. Access to the Internet is also an important service provided by the latest networks.

In the following subsections we shall first present a short overview of how voice and basic data services are provided. As a model, we shall use a second-generation, all-digital network called the **global system for mobile communications (GSM)**. We will then describe how the GSM network has been developed into a third-generation network that is now able to support the much richer set of multimedia services including direct access to the Internet.

4.4.1 Functional architecture of GSM

As we show in Figure 4.20, the functional architecture of a GSM network is composed of three subsystems: the radio subsystem (RSS), the network and switching subsystem (NSS) and the operation subsystem (OSS). We shall describe the essential features of each subsystem separately.

Radio subsystem

This is concerned with the operation of the various items of equipment that make up the radio part of the network. We shall outline the role of each item separately.

- **Mobile station (MS):** the MS is the user device such as a mobile phone. Perhaps the most important module within this is the **subscriber identity module (SIM)** since it holds all the user-specific data required by the network and, without it, only emergency calls can be made.

  The SIM holds information such as a **personal identity number (PIN)** – this is used to unlock the MS, an **international mobile equipment identity (IMEI)** – this is the global identity of the MS, and an **authentication key (ki)** – this is required to enable the user to be authenticated by the network. In addition, while the MS is logged on to the network, it stores operational data such as the **cipher key (Kc)** being used and the **location area identification (LAI)**.

- **Base transceiver subsystem (BTS):** this contains all the radio equipment that enables a MS to make calls. This includes radio masts and antennas together with the associated transmitter and receiver amplifiers. Typical user data rates are 9.6 kbps and 14.4 kbps.

- **Base station controller (BSC):** the main functions of the BSC – also known as **radio network controllers (RNC)** in some networks – are to allocate frequencies to the individual BTSs within the base station subsystem and to implement the handover procedure as a MS moves from one cell – and hence BTS – to another within the same subsystem.

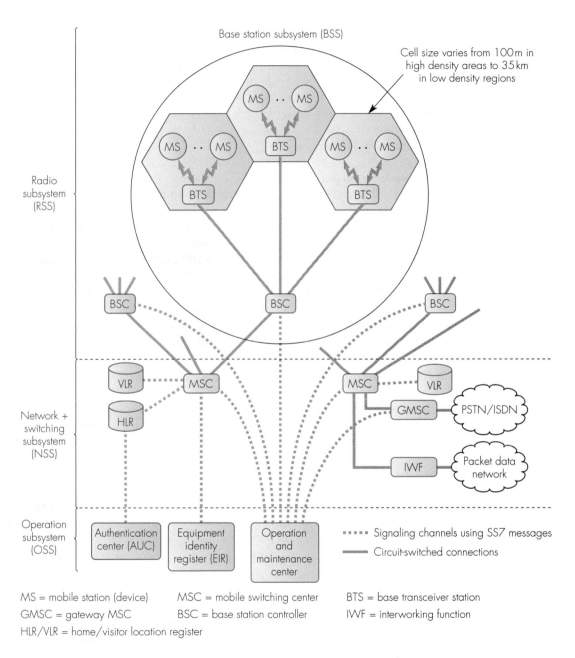

Base station subsystem (BSS)

Cell size varies from 100 m in
high density areas to 35 km
in low density regions

Radio
subsystem
(RSS)

Network +
switching
subsystem
(NSS)

Operation
subsystem
(OSS)

..... Signaling channels using SS7 messages

——— Circuit-switched connections

MS = mobile station (device)   MSC = mobile switching center   BTS = base transceiver station
GMSC = gateway MSC   BSC = base station controller   IWF = interworking function
HLR/VLR = home/visitor location register

Figure 4.20 Functional architecture of a 2G GSM voice/data network.

Network and switching subsystem (NSS)

This connects the radio subsystem to the standard fixed networks such as a PSTN and an ISDN. In addition, it implements the higher-level handover procedure as a MS moves from one base station subsystem to another. It also has procedures for the location of a MS worldwide, charging, accounting, and roaming of users/MSs between different network providers in different areas/countries. We shall describe the role of each item of equipment that makes up the NSS separately.

- **Mobile switching center** (**MSC**): in practice, these are high throughput digital ISDN switches. The MSC carries out the setting up of connections to a set of BSCs within a particular geographical area and also to other MSCs. In addition, selected MSCs have a connection to a **gateway MSC** (**GMSC**) that acts as the interface to other fixed networks such as a PSTN and an ISDN. Similarly, they have connections to an **interworking function** (**IWF**) that acts as the interface to a packet-switched data network. All connections are set up using the common channel signaling system number 7 (SS7) which we introduced earlier in Section 2.4. In addition, SS7 is used also to establish and release calls/connections within the NSS and supports functions such as multi-party calls, number portability, reverse charging, etc.

- **Home location register** (**HLR**): this is a database that is used to hold all user-related information. This includes charging and accounting, static information such as the mobile subscriber ISDN number (MSISDN) – used to enable the subscriber to communicate with a subscriber attached to a fixed network – the international mobile subscriber identity (IMSI) we introduced earlier, and the set of subscribed services of the user. The HLR also contains dynamic information such as the current **location area** (**LA**) of the MS, the **mobile subscriber roaming number** (**MSRN**), the current MSC and visitor location register (VLR). As soon as any of this information changes, the information in the HLR is updated so that the HLR always contains the current information relating to each subscriber.

- **Visitor location register** (**VLR**): this is also a database and one is attached to every MSC. It holds information relating to each MS that is currently in the location area of the MSC. The information held includes the IMSI, MSISDN and HLR address. Then, when a new MS comes into the location area, the VLR copies all relevant information for the user from the HLR. In this way, frequent updates of the HLR – which might include long-distance signaling – are avoided.

Operation subsystem (OSS)

The functions of the OSS relate to network operation and maintenance. It comprises three entities, each of which communicates with other entities using SS7 signaling messages. We shall describe each entity separately.

- **Operation and maintenance center** (**OMC**): this monitors and controls all the other network entities using SS7. Typical functions include traffic monitoring, status reports from the network entities, subscriber and security management, accounting and billing.

- **Authentication center** (**AC**): this contains the algorithms for authentication and also the keys for encryption. These are used to compute the values that are required for authentication in the HLR. Because of its role, it is often located in a reserved part of the HLR.

- **Equipment identity register** (**EIR**): this is a database for all device identifiers registered with the network. If an MS is stolen, providing it has a valid SIM then anyone can use it. To overcome this, a blacklist of stolen devices is held in the EIR and, once reported, usage of the MS is blocked.

4.4.2 Functional architecture of GSM/GPRS

As we showed in Figure 4.20, the early networks were developed primarily to provide a telephony service for mobile users and the associated data service relied on a connection-oriented packet-switched network. As we have indicated in several sections of the first three chapters, the Internet operates using a connectionless packet mode and access to it is through an access gateway/router. Hence the first step towards providing an enhanced data service – in particular, access to the Internet and the applications that it supports – is to provide an end-to-end connectionless packet mode service.

As we show in Figure 4.21, to achieve this, an extension to the GSM system called the **general packet radio service** (**GPRS**) was introduced. GPRS provides an end-to-end connectionless packet service that includes packet-mode transfers over the radio access network and an IP-based packet-switched core network. The various components that make up the radio access network – base station and radio network subsystems – are shared dynamically between the traffic relating to both circuit-mode and packet-mode services. In the case of the latter, with the new GPRS channels, bandwidth is allocated dynamically in both the uplink and downlink directions according to demand. The maximum data rate that can be allocated is 171.2 kbps. However, when the traffic enters the core switching network, it is separated out into that relating to circuit-mode services – the **GSM circuit-switched domain** – and that relating to packet-mode services – the **GPRS packet-switched domain**.

We have discussed the elements that make up the circuit-switched domain in the previous subsection. In the case of the packet-switched domain, however, the packet data is passed to an IP gateway called the **serving GPRS support node** (**SGSN**). The packet is then transferred across the internal IP-based network to the gateway with the Internet. This is called the **gateway GPRS support node** (**GGSN**). The packet transfer is carried out by using the **GPRS tunneling protocol** (**GTP**). We shall explain the tunneling

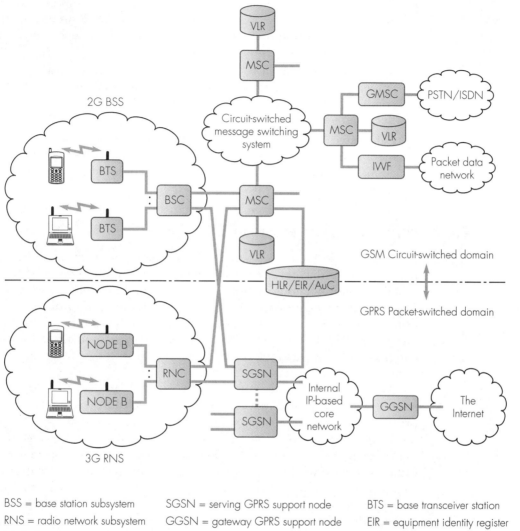

Figure 4.21 Functional architecture of a GSM/GPRS network.

BSS = base station subsystem   SGSN = serving GPRS support node   BTS = base transceiver station
RNS = radio network subsystem   GGSN = gateway GPRS support node   EIR = equipment identity register
Node B = transceiver station   AuC = authentication center   RNC = radio network controller

operation in IP networks in Section 6.6.7 when we describe the IP protocol. Essentially, the SGSN encapsulates the packet inside a second packet with a header that has the necessary information to route the packet to the GGSN over the internal IP network. The IP address in the original packet is then used to route the packet across the Internet to the addressed recipient.

4.4.3 Functional architecture of UMTS

The architecture shown in Figure 4.22 is based on one type of what are called **third generation (3G) wireless networks**. It is called the **universal mobile telecommunications system (UMTS)**. This is being developed by a number of operators and telecommunication companies that are already using the widely deployed second-generation GSM network and its more data-oriented derivative, the GSM/GPRS network.

The first release of UMTS is already deployed. The more recent release, however, in addition to providing a radio interface that supports a high-speed downlink that is an order of magnitude greater than that of GPRS, is concerned with – amongst other things – providing **IP multimedia services (IMS)** and the establishment of multimedia sessions. A session can involve either real-time or asynchronous (multimedia) data. An example of a real-time multimedia session is the display of a requested video clip since with this the audio and video need to be synchronized for simultaneous presentation to the user. An example of an asynchronous multimedia session is the multimedia message service (MMS), which is an enhancement of the short message service (SMS) that uses only text.

As we can see in the figure, at the center of the overall architecture is an IP-based core network to which a number of other networks are attached through IP gateways. In practice, the core network is based on GPRS, which, as we have seen, provides an end-to-end connectionless packet-mode service that includes packet-mode transfers over the radio access network and a packet-switched core network. The major difference between the GSM/GPRS architecture and the UMTS architecture, however, is the removal of the circuit-switched domain. In the new architecture there is just a single IP-based packet-switched core network over which all services are provided.

To establish a real-time IMS session, a separate IP multimedia subsystem is used. Currently, this also utilizes the GPRS network for packet transport but in the future this will be replaced by an all IP network/Internet based on the IPv6 protocol. Because of this new structure, as we can see, a number of new network elements/servers are needed, each of which supports a particular service. For example, the **call/session control function (CSCF)** is concerned with the initiation of multimedia sessions between two subscribers. However, a major difference is that instead of using the traditional circuit-mode mobile switching centers and the telecommunication protocols associated with a PSTN/ISDN, the IETF's **session initiation protocol (SIP)** is used. This is the preferred protocol of the IETF for providing interpersonal communication services, of which an IMS session is an example. SIP is defined in RFCs 2543 and 3261 and more details can be found later in Section 8.6.1 when we discuss Internet telephony.

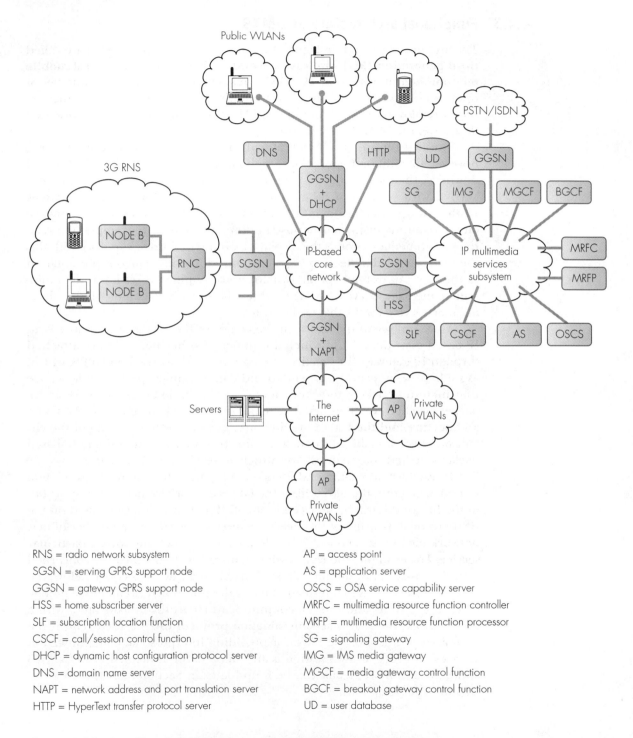

RNS = radio network subsystem
SGSN = serving GPRS support node
GGSN = gateway GPRS support node
HSS = home subscriber server
SLF = subscription location function
CSCF = call/session control function
DHCP = dynamic host configuration protocol server
DNS = domain name server
NAPT = network address and port translation server
HTTP = HyperText transfer protocol server

AP = access point
AS = application server
OSCS = OSA service capability server
MRFC = multimedia resource function controller
MRFP = multimedia resource function processor
SG = signaling gateway
IMG = IMS media gateway
MGCF = media gateway control function
BGCF = breakout gateway control function
UD = user database

Figure 4.22 Functional architecture of a 3G UMTS network.

To support interworking with a PSTN and an ISDN – for example for voice calls – four network elements are involved: the **IMS media gateway** (**IMG**), the **media gateway control function** (**MGCF**), the **signaling gateway** (**SG**), and the **breakout gateway control functions** (**BGCF**). For example, the IMG performs the translation of signals encoded in one format to another and the translation of SIP messages into/from ISDN signaling messages.

The **home subscriber server** (**HSS**) is similar to the HLR used in GSM. It is a database that holds information like subscription and location details and, for example, is queried by a CSCF during the set-up of a session. The **media resource function processor** (**MRFP**) and **controller** (**MRFC**) support multiparty multimedia conferencing and playing announcements.

The **open service access** (**OSA**) server and **open service capability** (**OSC**) server have been introduced to enable subscribers to choose between service providers. A third-party provider uses the basic IP multimedia services provided by the IMS subsystem to provide innovative new services to those supported by the provider.

Finally, as we show in the figure, the latest release of UMTS, in addition to the provision of IP-based multimedia services, also provides interworking between public wireless LANs and the services provided by the Internet. To support interworking, an additional set of network elements/servers are needed. These are shown in the figure attached to the IP-based core network. The role of a number of these are described in later chapters. However, a brief explanation of how they are used in this application follows.

It is assumed that the mobile devices/stations operating within each of the three public wireless LANs shown in the figure want to access a server that is attached to the Internet for, say, Web browsing. The **dynamic host configuration protocol** (**DHCP**) server – see Section 6.6.3 – is needed to configure the IP stack of a mobile station. Similarly, the **domain name server** (**DNS**) – see Section 9.2 – is needed to resolve an Internet domain name into a corresponding IP (network) address.

The **network and address and port translation** (**NAPT**) server – see Section 6.4.4 – located in the GGSN gateway linking the Internet to the internal IP backbone network is present to enable the operator of a WLAN to use locally managed (private) IP addresses within the WLAN while, at the same time, access the services available over the Internet.

The **HyperText transfer protocol** (**HTTP**) server provides local application services. For example, one approach to authentication and authorization of a user is to use the services of the HTTP server. When the user of a wireless station within a public WLAN starts his/her browser, the first request entered is redirected to the HTTP server. Then, in response, what is called a **landing Web page** is sent and displayed on the screen of the station. In this, the user is prompted to enter his/her username and password and, if these are accepted, his/her credit card details to pay for the session. Normally, all the details of each user/subscriber – username, etc. – are stored in a **user database** (**UD**) that is accessed by the HTTP server.

Summary

A summary of the topics discussed in this chapter is given in Figure 4.23.

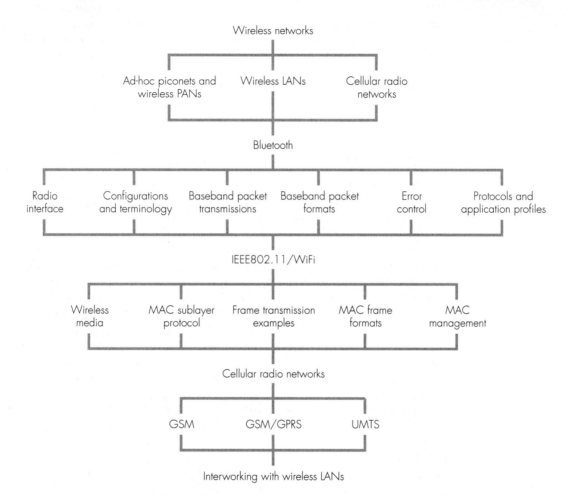

Figure 4.23 Wireless networks summary.

Exercises

Section 4.1

4.1 With the aid of diagrams, state the approximate range of coverage and application domain of:
(i)   a piconet,
(ii) a wireless LAN,
(iii) a cellular radio network.

4.2 With the aid of diagrams, describe how radio coverage is obtained in a national cellular radio network.

Section 4.2

4.3 With the aid of diagrams, explain how Bluetooth can be used in the following applications:
(i)   connection of peripheral devices to a computer,
(ii) Internet access via a mobile phone.

4.4 State the meaning of the term slot time and how this is derived in relation to the radio interface of Bluetooth.

4.5 In relation to Bluetooth, with the aid of diagrams, explain the meaning of the following terms:
(i)   master,
(ii) active slave,
(iii) parked slave,
(iv) standby slave,
(v)   scatternet.

4.6 Explain the operation of the two baseband packet transmission examples shown in Figure 4.4. Include in your explanation: TDD, hop/carrier frequencies, one-slot packets, one-three-five slot packets.

4.7 Explain the meaning of the terms synchronous connection-oriented (SCO) link and asynchronous connectionless (ACL) link. Hence, with the aid of the example shown in Figure 4.5, explain how mixed packet types are transmitted. Why is the third ACL frame transmitted in slot time f14 and not f11?

4.8 In relation to the Bluetooth packet format shown in Figure 4.6, explain the use of the following fields in the packet header:
(i)   ARQN,
(ii) SEQN,
(iii) HEC.
Hence describe the example packet sequence shown in Figure 4.7.

4.9 With the aid of the simplified state transition diagram shown in Figure 4.7, outline the procedure followed by the link manager protocol to establish a piconet.

4.10 Outline the role of the L2CAP protocol and, in particular, how each packet type is fragmented.

4.11 In relation to the protocol stack shown in Figure 4.10, outline how access to the Internet is obtained. State the role of each protocol that is used with this application profile.

Section 4.3

4.12 With the aid of Figure 4.11, explain the two operational modes of an IEEE 802.11 wireless LAN.

4.13 Use Figure 4.12 to explain the interworking of 802.11 and 802.3 LANs. Include the role of the access point (AP) and the protocols it uses.

4.14 Explain the meaning of the following terms relating to 802.11:
(i)   DCF,
(ii) DIFS,
(iii) PIFS,
(iv) SIFS.

4.15 In relation to Figure 4.13, explain the operation of CSMA/CA in the DCF mode. Include in your explanation the use of the terms contention period and the computed random backoff time.

4.16 With the aid of the two sets of frame transmissions shown in Figure 4.14, explain the retransmission procedure followed in the DCF mode with CSMA/CA.

4.17 State the meaning of the term hidden station. Hence, with the aid of the example shown in Figure 4.15, explain how this is overcome in the DCF with RTS/CTS extension mode. Clearly state the role of the two types of NAV frames.

4.18 With the aid of the example frame sequence shown in Figure 4.16, explain the fragmentation procedure used in the DCF mode. State the use of the four NAV frames. Show how the sequence changes if fragment 1 was corrupted.

4.19 Use the example shown in Figure 4.17 to explain the PCF with polling mode of operation. State clearly the role of the point coordinator and how it controls access to the transmission medium. Explain also the term superframe.

4.20 Explain the role of the following 802.11 frame types:
   (i)   beacon frame,
   (ii) challenge frame.

4.21 In relation to the MAC frame formats shown in Figure 4.18, explain the meaning of the following terms:
   (i)   duration ID,
   (ii) ToDS and FromDS.

4.22 With the aid of Figure 4.19, explain why four address fields are required in the header of each data and management frame. State the source and destination stations for each of the four entries in the table.

Section 4.4

4.23 With the aid of the functional architecture of a 2G GSM network shown in Figure 4.20, explain the role of the following units in the radio subsystem:
   (i)   mobile station including the use of the PIN and the IMEI,
   (ii) base transceiver subsystem,
   (iii) base station controller.

4.24 With the aid of the functional architecture of a 2G GSM network shown in Figure 4.20, explain the role of the following units in the network and switching subsystem:
   (i)   mobile switching center,
   (ii) gateway MSC,
   (iii) home location register,
   (iv) visitor location register,
   (v)   interworking function.

4.25 With the aid of the functional architecture of a 2G GSM network shown in Figure 4.20, explain the role of the following units in the operations subsytem:
   (i)   authentication center,
   (ii) equipment identity register,
   (iii) operation and maintenance center.

4.26 With the aid of Figure 4.21, identify and explain the role of the additional GPRS subsystem that is present in a GSM/GPRS network.

4.27 With the aid of Figure 4.22, identify the unit(s) involved and explain how the following services are supported:
   (i)   IP multimedia sessions,
   (ii) interworking with a PSTN/ISDN,
   (iii) interworking with a public wireless LAN.

chapter 5

entertainment networks

5.1 Introduction

Entertainment applications include movie/video-on-demand, broadcast television, and interactive television. The bit rate requirements for the (compressed) audio and video associated with these applications are determined by the bandwidth of the transmission channel to be used. Typical bit rates are:

VCR-quality video with sound: 1.5 Mbps (MPEG-1)

Broadcast-quality video with sound: 4/6/8 Mbps (MPEG-2, Main)

Normally, the user interaction channel need only be a low bit rate channel of tens of kilobits per second. Hence the communications requirement to provide these services is an asymmetric channel consisting of a high bit rate (1.5/4/6/8 Mbps) channel from the service provider to the subscriber and a low bit rate return channel for interaction purposes.

In terms of the networks that are used, interactions with a video server – for movie/video-on-demand – can be through either a cable network or a satellite/terrestrial broadcast network. Each can also provide interactive television with, in the case of satellite and terrestrial broadcast networks, the user interaction channel provided through a separate network such as a PSTN.

With a PSTN, the modems we described in Section 2.2.2 provide only a relatively low bit rate switched channel of up to 56 kbps. In addition to these, however, as we described in Section 2.5, high-speed modems are available which provide a non-switched asymmetric channel that can support applications such as high-speed access to the Internet. In the case of cable networks, in addition to the modems used to support broadcast television, high-speed (cable) modems are also available that provide high-speed access to the Internet and other packet-based services. In this chapter we describe the principle of operation of the different types of broadcast television networks and how interactive services are provided with these networks.

5.2 Cable television networks

Essentially, a basic cable TV network is a television distribution facility. A set of TV programs is received from satellite and/or terrestrial broadcasts and the cable network is then used to distribute this set of programs to subscriber premises. Early cable television networks – of which there are still many in existence – are based entirely on coaxial cable. These were designed to distribute broadcast television (and radio) programs that are received at a central site to customer premises geographically distributed around an area such as a town or city. Such networks are known as **community antenna television (CATV) networks** and the basic elements of this type of network are shown in Figure 5.1.

A shared-medium, tree-and-branch architecture is used with, at the root, the various antennas and associated equipment located in a unit called the **cable headend (HE)**. Each branch of the tree is implemented using a single coaxial cable. With this type of network, the electrical signals associated with each television (and radio) program are analog. Hence in order to transmit multiple TV programs concurrently, modulated transmission is used with each program/channel allocated a fixed portion of the cable bandwidth. The electrical signals of the complete set of TV programs are then multiplexed together onto the cable for distribution to all the network termination points. This technique is known as **frequency division multiplexing (fdm)**.

At each branch node in the cable distribution network, a **trunk splitter** is used to ensure the same set of signals propagate on each branch. Each home passed has a **subscriber tap** attached to the cable and this forms the connection point to the distribution cable. A separate **drop cable** is used to connect the tap to the subscriber network termination unit located in the customer premises. The distance from the cable headend to the remotest customer/subscriber premises can be up to tens of miles/kilometers. So to compensate for signal attenuation, a large number of **trunk** and **distribution amplifiers** are required to ensure that the signal received at each subscriber termination is of an acceptable quality with a defined minimum signal-to-noise ratio.

A broadcast analog TV signal comprises the video signal and the sound/audio signal. The video signal is made up of the luminance and two

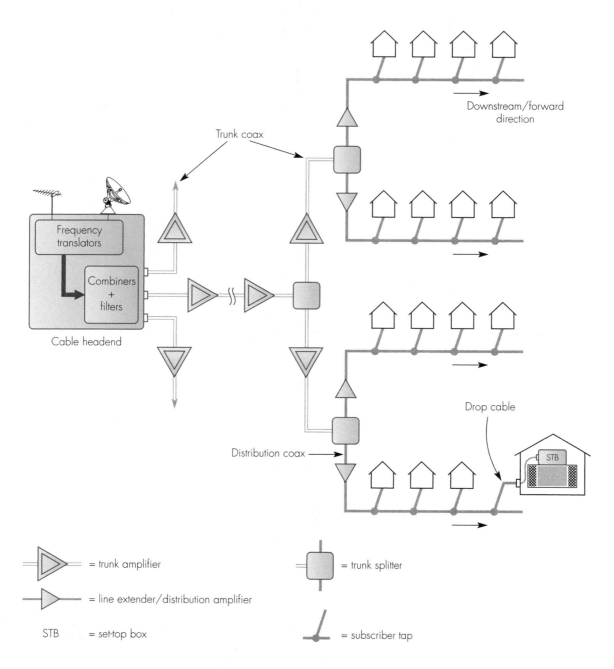

Figure 5.1 Early analog CATV distribution network and components.

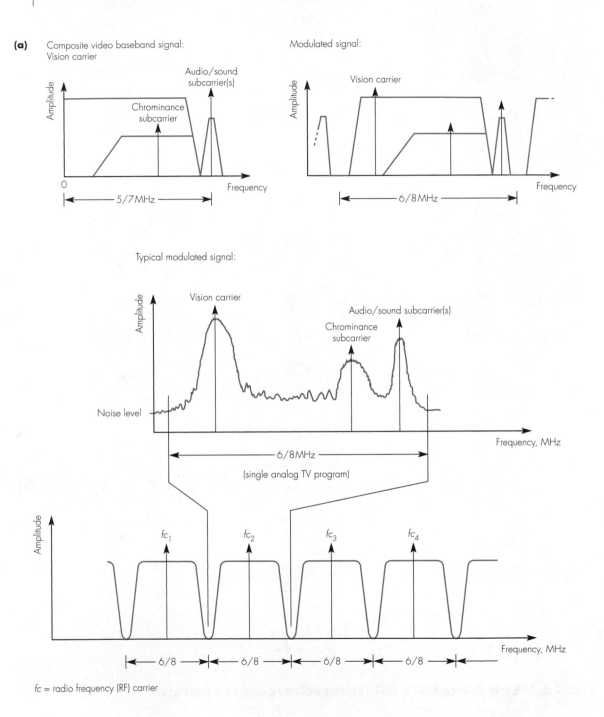

(a)

Composite video baseband signal:
Vision carrier

Modulated signal:

Typical modulated signal:

fc = radio frequency (RF) carrier

Figure 5.2 Analog CATV principles: (a) analog TV bandwidth requirements; (b) distribution cable bandwidth utilization.

(b)

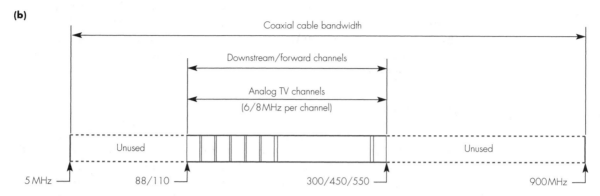

Note: Normally, the band of frequencies from 88–110 MHz are used for radio broadcasts.

Figure 5.2 Continued.

chrominance signals and collectively these are transmitted using a separate (single-frequency) carrier for each signal. A typical broadcast analog TV signal is shown in Figure 5.2(a).

The bandwidth used for each TV program/channel in the cable systems of different countries varies. Nevertheless, the same principles apply. Each channel is allocated an appropriate amount of the cable bandwidth – 6 MHz in North America and 8 MHz in Europe – which ensures the signals relating to the two neighboring channels are cleanly separated (by filters) and do not interfere. Associated with each channel is a separate (radio frequency) carrier signal, which is separated by 6/8 MHz from the carrier signals of its neighbors. The analog signal of the TV program allocated to that channel is then used to amplitude-modulate the channel carrier signal. The resulting signal is first filtered – to limit the signal bandwidth to 6/8 MHz – and then combined with the signals of all the other channels. The combined signal is then transmitted onto the distribution cable at the cable headend and hence is received by the set-top box of each subscriber. As the subscriber selects a particular program, so the related channel frequency band – and hence carrier signal – is selected. The corresponding carrier signal is then used to demodulate the received signal to obtain the original analog TV signal for that channel.

As we show in Figure 5.2(b), when modulated transmission is used, the bandwidth of a coaxial cable is in the order of 5 MHz through to 900 MHz. In practice, however, the number of channels supported – and hence bandwidth used – is significantly less than this. As we indicated earlier, because of the relatively large area covered by each trunk cable, there may be up to 20 or 30 trunk amplifiers used in each cable run. Each amplifier causes a level of deterioration of the signal as it also amplifies any noise signals introduced by crosstalk and other (external) transmissions. Normally, therefore, the bandwidth used in early cable systems is limited to 88/110 MHz at the low end through to 300, 450 or 550 MHz at the upper end, the actual upper frequency being determined by the size of – and hence number of amplifiers used in – the distribution network.

5.2.1 HFC networks

The advent of digital television and the increasing demand for interactive multimedia services – for interactive TV and high-speed access to the Internet for example – has resulted in many operators of cable networks upgrading their networks to support these newer applications. As we indicated in the previous section, even though there is plenty of unused bandwidth in the existing coaxial cable networks, the amount of usable bandwidth is limited by the number of amplifiers required. This is especially the case in the trunk network and hence in the upgraded networks the main trunk (coaxial) cables have been replaced with optical fiber cables. The resulting network is called **a hybrid fiber coax (HFC) network** and is illustrated in Figure 5.3(a).

As we can see, optical fiber is used in the main trunk network and coaxial cable is limited to the local distribution network. The retention of coaxial cable in this part of the network is done for cost reasons. The number of lines in the distribution network is much larger than the number in the trunk network and hence the cost of upgrading the distribution network to fiber is considerably higher. The fiber used in the trunk network comprises multiple (fiber) trunk cables each terminated in a unit known as a **fiber node (FN)**. Each performs the optical-to-electrical conversion and serves a number of separate coaxial distribution cables. Each distribution cable provides cable services to between 125 and 500 homes distributed over an area of approximately 3 miles/5 kilometers. Typically, therefore, a single FN serves between 500 and 2000 homes and the total network may comprise many FNs.

The use of fiber cable in the trunk network means that the signal attenuation is much reduced so removing the necessity of having a large number of amplifiers in each trunk line. As a result, a much wider portion of the available bandwidth of the coaxial distribution network can be used. A typical utilization is shown in Figure 5.3(b).

As we can see, the bandwidth utilization of the earlier all-coax networks has been extended at both the low and high ends of the available frequency spectrum. To enable existing analog broadcast services to continue to be provided unchanged, the bandwidth from 50/88/100 MHz through to 550 MHz is reserved for such services. Either side of this band is a **guard band (GB)** of 50 MHz at the upper end and 8/10 MHz at the lower end. This is necessary to ensure that the new services are cleanly separated – by means of filters – from the existing services. The additional frequency band in the **downstream/forward direction** from 600 MHz to 860/862 MHz is used for the newer digital services. These include digital TV, video-on-demand and near video-on-

(a)

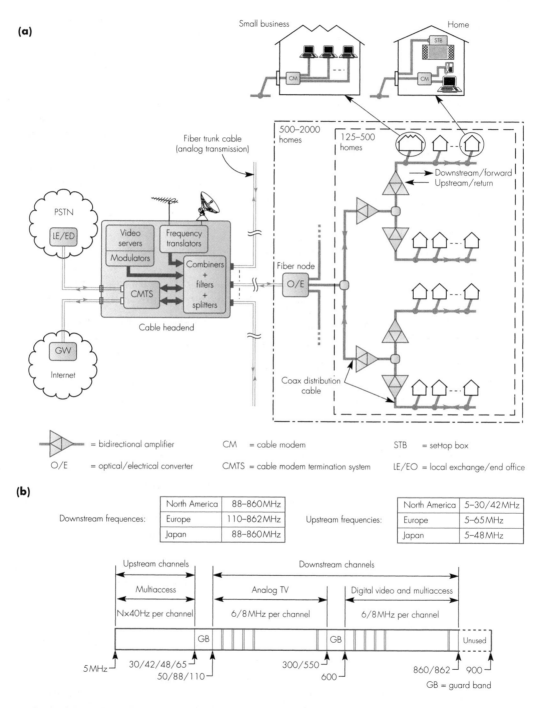

Figure 5.3 Hybrid fiber coax network principles: (a) distribution network and components; (b) cable bandwidth utilization.

demand, and the forward path of a range of two-way communication channels for high-speed Internet access, dedicated high bit rate digital circuits – for LAN interconnection for example – and, in some instances, packet-based telephony.

Although the newer services are all digital, modulated (analog) transmission must be used over the cable distribution network in order to be compatible with the existing analog TV transmissions. All transmissions over the coaxial cable distribution network, therefore, are in an analog form and analog transmission is also used over the fiber cable. Hence, since the signals associated with the newer services are all digital, modems similar to those used with a PSTN are needed to convert the source digital bitstream into (and from) an analog signal for transmission over the distribution network. Because the frequencies used are in the radio frequency spectrum, they are known as **RF modems** and even though radio frequencies are involved, they use a similar modulation scheme to that used in higher bit rate PSTN modems. As we saw earlier in Figure 2.6(c) (and explained in the accompanying text), a multilevel modulation scheme known as QAM is used. In the case of RF modems, however, 64 or even 256 different amplitude and phase combinations are used. These produce usable bit rates in the order of:

64-QAM: 6 MHz band = 27 Mbps, 8 MHz band = 38 Mbps

256-QAM: 6 MHz band = 36 Mbps, 8 MHz band = 50 Mbps

As we can deduce from these values, each additional 6/8 MHz band in the downstream direction can be used to transmit either multiple MPEG-2 (6 Mbps) digital TV programs – or proportionately more MPEG-1 (1.5 Mbps) video programs – or one or more high bit rate data channels. The specific use of the channels is determined by the services to be supported and hence is decided by the cable operator. However, if two-way services are to be supported – interactive TV, video-on-demand, Internet access, and so on – then a related channel in the **upstream/return direction** is required from the subscriber to the cable headend. As we show in Figure 5.3(b), this is achieved by using the lower band of frequencies from 5 MHz through to 30/42/48/65 MHz, the specific upper frequency being determined by the current usage of the cable.

In order to obtain an upstream/return channel, the existing amplifiers in the distribution network are changed to **dual/bidirectional amplifiers**, one to amplify the signals in the downstream frequency bands and the other to amplify the signals in the upstream band. In the case of the fiber trunk network, dual-fiber cable is used, one fiber for the transmission of the downstream signals and the other for the upstream signals. In addition, new subscriber network termination units are required containing **bandsplitting filters** to separate the upstream from the downstream channels.

In some HFC networks, a portion of the upstream bandwidth is already used for the transmission of TV signals (from, say, a camera at a local event to the cable headend for distribution) and hence not all of the bandwidth is available for the newer digital services. Also, in the coaxial cable part of the network, the lower band of frequencies can be of relatively poor quality owing to the ingress of noise from external transmissions and crosstalk from the signals in the various downstream channels. So in order to obtain reliable operation, a more robust modulation scheme is used. This is either QPSK or 16-QAM. Normally, the return channels are not restricted to 6/8 MHz bands and typical bands and example bit rates are:

160 kHz:	320 kbps	1.28 MHz:	2.56 Mbps
320 kHz:	640 kbps	2.56 MHz:	5.12 Mbps
640 kHz:	1.28 Mbps	5.12 MHz:	10.24 Mbps

To support applications such as LAN interconnection and telephony, the forward and return channels are of the same bit rate. Hence symmetric bidirectional communication channels are required. For the various interactive applications, however, the bit rate of the interaction (upstream) channel need only be a fraction of that of the downstream channel. With entertainment applications such as video-on-demand, for example, the traffic in the upstream channel consists mainly of the commands entered by the user at the remote control. Similarly, with Internet access, short commands are used to initiate searching and information retrieval. Hence asymmetry ratios from 10:1 to as high as 100:1 are common.

In some interactive TV applications, the interaction channel is via a PSTN and hence a channel in the upstream direction is required for this. In the case of Internet access, a single high bit rate channel in the downstream direction is used with a lower bit rate channel in the upstream direction for interaction purposes. Each PC/workstation in all the homes/businesses attached to the cable shares the use of each of these channels in a similar way to the stations attached to a LAN. The channels are known as **multiaccess channels** and we describe aspects of their operation in the next section.

5.2.2 Cable modems

As we have indicated, in a cable network all transmissions are either to or from the cable headend rather than between two attached stations as is the case in a LAN. For high-speed Internet access, each pair of channels – one in the downstream direction and the other in the upstream direction – provides a two-way communications path between a station – also referred to as a **customer premises equipment** (**CPE**) – in a home or business and a server attached to the Internet. As we showed in Figure 5.3(a), each station is attached to the cable through a **cable modem** (**CM**). This performs the modulation of the bits in a packet sent by a station for transmission in the upstream channel and the demodulation of the bits in a packet received from the downstream channel. In addition, some CMs support packet-based (IP) telephony. Typically therefore, the telephony interface within the CM is based on the H.323 standard. This is concerned with the creation and exchange of call setup and clearing – signaling – messages/packets and the packetization/depacketization of voice samples.

At the cable headend is a unit called a **cable modem termination system** (**CMTS**). This is used to control the transmissions to all the CMs attached to the distribution network and to relay packets to and from the related network – the Internet or a PSTN. Figure 5.4 shows the essential components of a CMTS.

As we shall explain below, in addition to (IP) packets relating to Internet access and telephony, the CMTS uses IP packets to communicate with each CM in order to configure and manage the CM. Typically, therefore, as we see in the figure, a Fast Ethernet switch is used to relay incoming/outgoing packets to their related interface. This is either a local server (for configuration and management), an access gateway (for Internet access), or an H.323 gateway (for access to a PSTN).

In the downstream direction, each packet is simply broadcast over the assigned downstream channel and hence is received by all the attached CMs. In the upstream direction, however, since the attached CMs must compete for the use of the upstream channel, a suitable medium access control (MAC) protocol must be used to ensure that each CM gains access to the channel in a fair way. In a cable network, since a CM cannot receive the transmissions made by a CM that is nearer to the CMTS than itself, MAC protocols such as CSMA/CD and control token cannot be used. So instead, access to the upstream channel is controlled by the CMTS. In practice, there are a number of different schemes that can be used. In the remaining part of this section we describe the principle of operation of just one of these – the **data-over-cable service interface specification** (**DOCSIS**), which is very similar to the **IEEE802.14** standard.

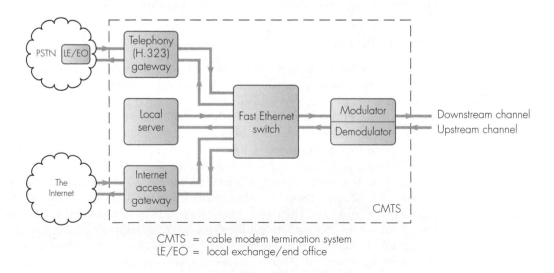

CMTS = cable modem termination system
LE/EO = local exchange/end office

Figure 5.4 Cable modem termination system schematic.

Protocol stack

A schematic diagram showing the protocol stack associated with the CMTS and CM that is used for Internet access is given in Figure 5.5.

Each CM has an integral repeater hub – for example, 10BaseT – within it, and all the stations – there can be more than one at a site – are attached to the hub by, for example, individual twisted-pair drop cables. Alternatively, the CM may have an AP within it and the various stations form a wireless LAN. Hence each CM has its own 48-bit MAC address – which is used for identification purposes by the CMTS during the configuration and management phase – and an additional set of MAC addresses, one for each station attached to the CM. Normally, the latter are acquired by the CM when each station becomes active.

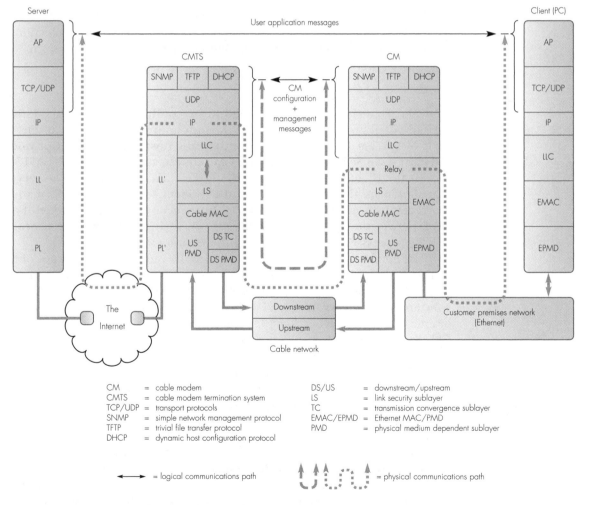

Figure 5.5 CMTS/CM protocol stacks.

The aim is to make the presence of the cable network – and hence CM and CMTS – transparent to the IP layer in a station that is communicating with a remote server attached to the Internet. To achieve this, forwarding of IP packets through the CM is carried out at the MAC sublayer and hence the CM acts as a bridge. In the case of the CMTS, although bridging can optionally be used, normally the forwarding operation is performed at the IP layer with the CMTS acting as an Internet access gateway for all the stations – through their related CMs – that are attached to the cable network. Hence, as we explain in Section 6.6.2, the ARP in the IP layer of the CMTS acts as a proxy ARP for all the attached stations. The IP layer must also support the ICMP (see Section 6.6.9) and IGMP (see Section 6.6.7) protocols. In addition, as we show in the figure, each CM attached to the cable network has additional higher-level protocols above the MAC sublayer. These enable each CM to be configured at start-up once the basic MAC-level transmission structure has been established – DHCP and TFTP – and to be remotely managed – SNMP. We describe the operation of DHCP in Section 6.8.4 and a selection of the Internet application protocols including TFTP and SNMP in various sections of Chapter 8.

Configuration and management

All CMs are diskless and hence need to be configured at start-up. This is carried out in two phases. First, since the only address a CM knows at start-up is its MAC (hardware) address, the **dynamic host configuration protocol (DHCP)** – see Section 6.8.4 – in the CM requests the DHCP in the CMTS to send it the IP address of itself and the CMTS, and the name of the servers that supply the time-of-day and hold the modem configuration information. On receipt of this information, the CM proceeds to obtain the time-of-day (ToD) from the ToD server and, using the **trivial file transfer protocol (TFTP)** – see Section 8.5 – the configuration information.

The configuration information includes the public encryption key of the CM and the QoS parameters of the packet flows the CM can support. Examples include best-effort flows associated with Internet access and the constant bit rate flows associated with telephony. We expand upon the subject of encryption later in Section 10.2. Essentially, however, the public key of the CM is used by the CMTS to send the private/secret key that is to be used by the **link security (LS)** sublayer of the CM to encrypt/decrypt the payload of each link layer frame sent/received from the cable. Once it has done this, the CM sends a request message to the CMTS to formally register and obtain permission to start to relay frames. The CMTS responds by assigning a unique **service identifier (SID)** to the CM and also one or more **service flow identifiers (SFID)**, one for each type of packet flow the CM can support. The CM can then start to relay frames to/from the stations attached to its **customer premises network (CPN)** interface.

As we shall expand upon in Section 8.7, the simple network management protocol (SNMP) is used to enable a management process in the CMTS – or another remote system – to read and change a set of operational parameters that are maintained by the CM. It is also used by the CM to report fault conditions should they arise. Normally, the CMTS displays this information on a computer screen and, should a fault be reported, the network manager can readily determine the location of the CM and the fault that is present.

Cable MAC

As we indicated earlier, all transmissions on the upstream channel – that is, from each CM to the CMTS – are controlled by the cable MAC in the CMTS. Hence when a CM wishes to transmit a frame – containing an IP packet in its payload – the cable MAC in the CM first sends a *Request* (*REQ*) message to the cable MAC in the CMTS that indicates the amount of bandwidth that is required to transmit the frame. On receipt of the REQ message, the CMTS responds by returning a *Grant* message that indicates the amount of bandwidth that has been allocated to the CM.

All transmissions on the upstream channel are scheduled to occur in fixed time intervals of 4 ms. Hence, during a transmission interval, the CMTS may receive a number of requests for a portion of the bandwidth in the next transmission interval. A bandwidth allocation algorithm is used to ensure that requests are granted in a fair way. For example, if the waiting frame contains speech samples then it may be allocated a portion of the bandwidth ahead of, say, a frame containing best-effort data traffic. Once this has been carried out, the CMTS divides the subsequent transmission interval into a number of variable-length (time) intervals each with the SID of the requesting CM that can use it. This information is then broadcast on the related downstream channel during the current transmission interval in what is called an *upstream bandwidth allocation MAP* management message.

For each requesting CM, the corresponding entry in the allocation MAP message gives the duration of time it can transmit. If the time duration for a CM has been set to zero, this indicates the request is still pending and the CM must wait for the next transmission interval. Also, since a CM can have only a single outstanding request (per SID) at a time, this blocks the CM from making a new request.

Because of the relatively wide area of coverage of HFC networks, as we saw in Section 1.2.4, the signal propagation delay over the cable can be relatively large. Hence the precise time each requesting CM receives the allocation MAP varies and depends on the physical distance the CM is from the cable headend. To ensure each CM times its frame transmission with those from all of the other requesting CMs, firstly, all CMs must be in time synchronism with the master clock in the CMTS and secondly, in order for the transmitted frames to arrive at the CMTS in their expected time intervals, each CM must know the round-trip propagation delay time between itself and the CMTS. The procedure used to enable a CM to determine this is known as **ranging** and both time synchronization and ranging must be carried out during the initialization phase of the CM prior to the transmission of any frames containing IP packets.

Time synchronization

To ensure all CMs have a common time reference, the CMTS maintains a 32-bit binary counter that is clocked using its master clock of 10.24 MHz. The CMTS then broadcasts a *SYNC management message* that contains the current state of this counter on the downstream channel at periodic (10 ms) intervals. The counter value in the SYNC message is known as the *SYNC time-stamp* and is used by each CM to synchronize its own time reference to this value. The general principle is shown in Figure 5.6.

The upstream channel bitstream is divided in *time* into a stream of numbered **minislots**. The duration of each minislot is a power-of-two multiple of 6.25 μs such that the number of bytes per minislot is equal to 16. For example, assuming a bandwidth of 640 kHz is being used for the upstream

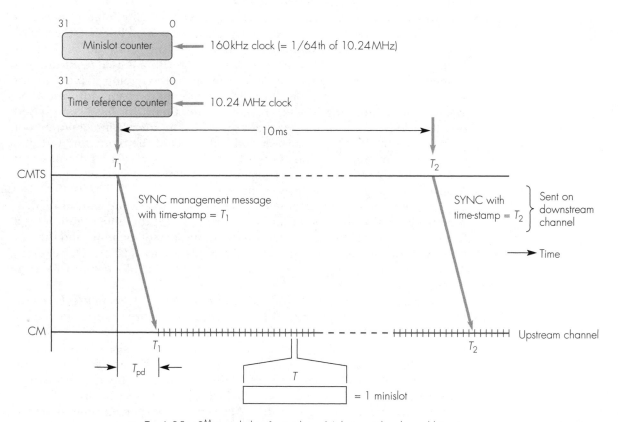

- $T = 6.25 \times 2^M$μs such that 1 minislot = 16 bytes at the channel bit rate
- Minislot N begins at time-stamp reference $N \times T \times 64$
- T_{pd} = propagation delay CMTS to CM

Figure 5.6 Cable MAC time synchronization principles.

channel, as we indicated earlier, a typical bit rate is 1280 kbps. Hence each 6.25 µs interval contains $1280 \times 10^3 \times 6.25 \times 10^{-6}$ = 8 bits. Therefore the time duration of a minislot, T, is 6.25×16 µs and hence the power-of-two multiple, M, is 4.

All frame transmissions in each transmission interval – including frames containing request and timing messages – start at a defined (numbered) minislot and the bandwidth allocation MAP uses units of minislots. The CMTS uses a second 32-bit counter to number each minislot. This is clocked at 6.25 µs intervals, which is equal to a clocking rate of 160 kHz. Hence, since this is 1/64th of the CMTS master clock of 10.24 MHz, there is always a fixed relationship between the contents of the minislot counter and the broadcast SYNC time-stamp: the least significant 0 to $(25 - M)$ bits of the minislot counter are the same as the most significant $(6 + M)$ to 31 bits of the SYNC time-stamp.

Ranging

Once a CM is in time synchronism, it invokes the ranging procedure to determine its **round-trip correction (RTC) time**; that is, how much earlier the CM should start transmitting a frame relative to a given minislot number in the bandwidth allocation MAP. As we indicated earlier, this ensures that the transmissions from all the CMs in a transmission interval arrive at the CMTS as if all the CMs were colocated with the CMTS. The principle behind the ranging procedure is shown in the time sequence diagram in Figure 5.7.

At periodic (typically 2 ms) intervals, the CMTS includes in the bandwidth allocation MAP it is transmitting, a reserved time interval – transmission opportunity – known as an *initial maintenance (IM) region*. This is present to enable a new CM to carry out the ranging procedure. Once the CM is in time synchronism, it searches each MAP it receives from the downstream channel for an IM region and, when it finds one, it immediately transmits a *Ranging Request (RNG-REQ)* message with its own (physical layer) fixed delay within it. The duration of this region is such that it can compensate for the worst-case round-trip propagation delay between a CM and the CMTS.

On receipt of the RNG-REQ message, since the CMTS knows the time offset from the start of the current transmission interval to the start of the IM region, the CMTS can estimate the round-trip propagation delay from the CM to the CMTS and back again by the time delay the RNG-REQ message is received relative to the start of the IM region. The CMTS responds by returning a *Ranging Response (RNG-RSP)* message in the downstream channel that contains the initial computed timing offset – including the CM fixed delay – to be used by the CM. On receipt of this, the CM first proceeds to locate another IM region in the next MAP it receives. It then sends a second RNG-REQ message to the CMTS but this time earlier than the start of the IM region – as seen by the CMTS – by a time equal to the initial RTC that it received in the RNG-RSP message. If this arrives at the CMTS at the start of the IM region, then the estimated RTC is correct and the CMTS returns a second RNG-RSP message containing a *Ranging Successful* notification within it.

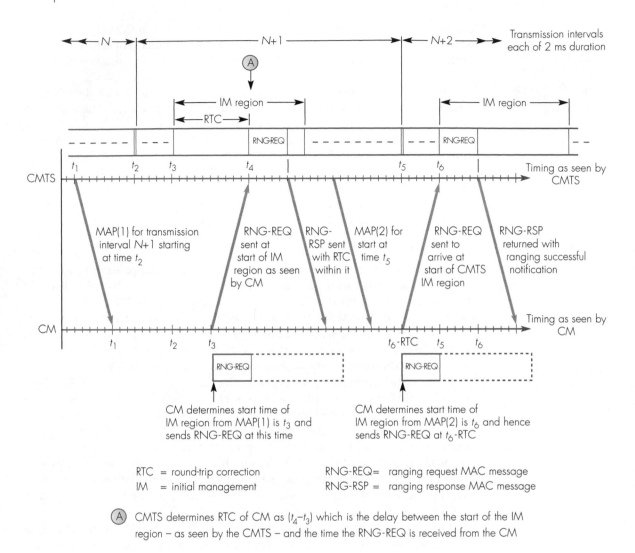

Figure 5.7 Cable MAC ranging procedure principles.

Alternatively, if the arrival of the second RNG-REQ is still later than the start of the IM region, a further REQ/RSP message interchange takes place using a revised RTC time that is indicated in the second RNG-RSP message. This procedure continues until the precise RTC is known and the CM receives a successful notification.

Once a notification success has been received, the CM can then proceed to send frames containing IP packets using the request/grant cycle outlined earlier. First the CM carries out the configuration operation we described in the previous section and this concludes with the CM being registered and allocated a service identifier (SID). It is at this point that the CM can start to relay frames – containing IP packets – to and from the stations that are attached to the hub ports of the CM.

Frame transmission

As we indicated earlier, all transmissions over the upstream channel are controlled by the CMTS using the bandwidth allocation MAP. Prior to sending a frame (containing an IP packet), the CM sends a bandwidth Request (REQ) message to the CMTS indicating the number of minislots required to transmit the frame. The CMTS then responds by including in the next allocation MAP it broadcasts on the downstream channel, a Grant message containing the SID of the CM and the number of minislots within the next transmission interval the CM can use.

Since the Request message must also be sent to the CMTS over the upstream channel, each bandwidth allocation MAP includes a reserved region – similar to the IM region used to send a Ranging Request message – to enable a CM to send a Request message during the current transmission interval. This is called the *REQ region* and, since there may be a number of CMs waiting to send a Request message, a contention resolution procedure must be used to enable each competing CM to share the use of the request region in an equitable way.

Each REQ region can support the transmission of multiple Request messages. Also, as we shall expand upon later, each Request message is 6 bytes long and includes the SID of the CM making the request and the number of minislots requested. The contention algorithm is based on a truncated binary exponential backoff algorithm similar to that used with Ethernet. In the header of each bandwidth allocation MAP is a pair of fields relating to the algorithm, one called the *data backoff start* (*DBS*) and the other the *data backoff end* (*DBE*). Each is a power-of-two value and, in the case of the DBS, a value of 2, for example, indicates a backoff value in the range 0–3, a value of 3, 0–7 and so on. The range is known as the **backoff window** and must always be less than the value derived from the DBE. The latter is known, therefore, as the **maximum backoff window**.

When a CM wishes to make a request, on receipt of the next MAP, it first reads the DBS value from the MAP and proceeds to compute a random number within the derived backoff window. This indicates the number of request opportunities (6-byte slots) from the start of the REQ region the CM must defer – and hence not use – before transmitting its own Request message. For example, if the computed random number from the current backoff window is 3 and the REQ region can support six requests, then the CM must defer from using the first three request opportunities/slots before transmitting its own request. Alternatively, if the computed random number is 8, the CM must defer from using all six request slots and wait for the next REQ region. On determining this from the MAP, the CM must then defer from using a further two slots before sending its request.

Once a CM has sent a request, it must then wait for a data *Grant* message in a subsequent MAP containing the SID of the CM and the number of minislots allocated. Providing this is received, then the Request message was received successfully by the CMTS and no collision occurred. If a Grant is not received, then the CM must try again. It first doubles its current backoff window and, providing the size of the new window is less than the maximum backoff window, the CM proceeds to compute a new random number within the limits of the new window. A maximum retry limit of 16 is used and, if this or the maximum backoff window is reached, the CM discards the frame.

This mode of operation is known as the **reservation access mode** and an example transmission sequence illustrating this is given in Figure 5.8. In this example it is assumed that the REQ region contains four request slots, the random number generated from the initial backoff window is 2, and the Request message is successfully received by the CMTS. Note that each transmission made by the CM is sent earlier than its allocated time by the round-trip correction time computed during the ranging procedure.

Frame formats

All cable MAC frames have a standard 6-byte header the format of which is shown in Figure 5.9(a). The *frame control* (*FC*) field identifies the type of MAC header and consists of three subfields. The *FC-TYPE* indicates whether the MAC frame contains a user data frame – containing an IP packet – or a cable MAC frame. For the latter, the *FC-PARM* identifies the type of MAC frame; for example, a Request message/frame or a MAC management frame such as a time synchronization frame. The *EHDR-ON* is a single bit and is set to 1 if an extension header is present. We shall give an example of the use of extension headers in the next subsection.

The *MAC-PARM* field in a REQ frame indicates the number of minislots requested or, if an extension header is present, it indicates the number of bytes in the extension header. The *LEN/SID* is either the sum of the number of bytes in the extension header (if present) and the number of bytes following the HCS field or, in a REQ frame, the SID of the requesting CM. The *HCS* is a 16-bit CRC that is used to detect transmission errors in the MAC header. It is used to ensure the integrity of the header fields and, in the contention mode, whether a collision has occurred.

Two example MAC frame types are shown in Figure 5.9(b). The first is the format of a MAC frame containing a user data frame. As we saw in Figure 3.3, for an Ethernet/IEEE 802.3 LAN the length of a frame – including a 4-byte FCS – can be from 64 to 1518 bytes and the *LEN* field in the MAC header indicates the number of bytes in the actual frame being transferred. The second example is the format of a REQ frame and, since this consists of the header only, the *SID* indicates the 14-bit SID of the CM making the request. The *MAC-PARM* contains the number of minislots that are being requested.

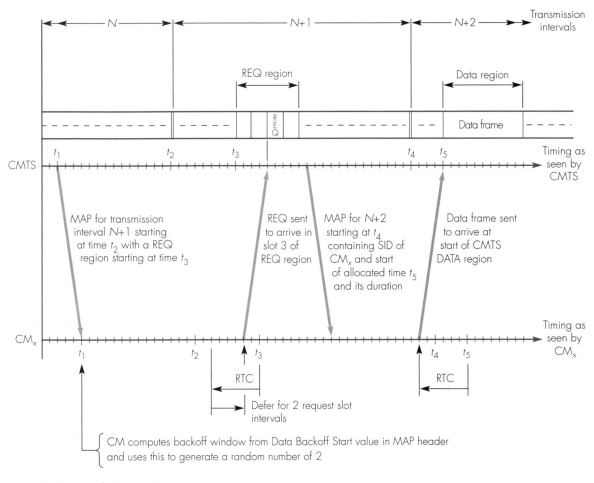

RTC = round-trip correction

Figure 5.8 Cable MAC reservation access mode of transmission.

Fragmentation

During periods of heavy traffic on the upstream channel, a grant message may specify a smaller number of minislots than have been requested by the CM to transfer the user data frame. When this happens, the MAC layer within the CM automatically fragments/splits the user data frame into a number of smaller fragments for transmission over the cable. At the CMTS, the peer MAC layer then reassembles the fragments to form the initial frame before forwarding this to the Internet gateway.

In order for the cable MAC in the CMTS to determine that a received MAC frame contains a fragment of a larger frame, an extension header is used. The format of each fragment header is shown in Figure 5.10(a) and an example is given in Figure 5.10(b).

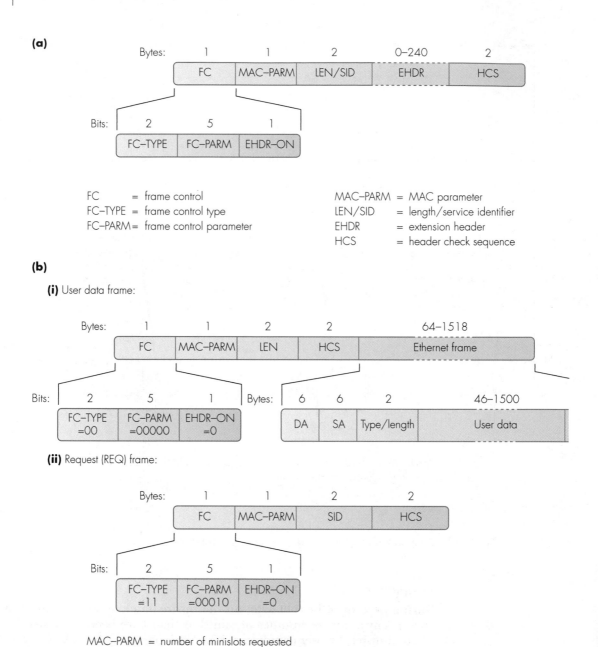

Figure 5.9 Cable MAC frame formats: (a) header field definitions; (b) two example frame types.

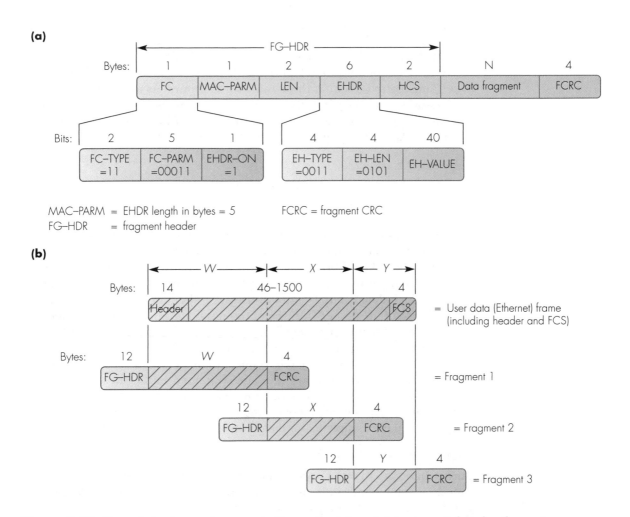

Figure 5.10 User data frame fragmentation principles: (a) fragment header format; (b) example fragmentation overheads.

In general, the EHDR field may contain multiple variable-length fields each of which is defined in a type-length-value (TLV) format. In the case of a fragment EHDR, however, only a single fixed-length field is present. The 4-bit *EH-TYPE* is set to 3, which indicates the MAC frame contains a data fragment. The 4-bit *EH-LEN* is set to 5 and the following 5-byte (40-bit) *EH-VALUE* field then contains a number of fixed-length subfields. These include the 14-bit SID of the CM carrying out the fragmentation, a 1-bit *first fragment* and a 1-bit *last fragment* – each of which is set to 1 for the first and last fragment respectively – and a 4-bit *fragment sequence number*. This is initialized to zero and is incremented by one for each fragment that is sent. Collectively these fields enable the peer cable MAC in the CMTS to reassemble the fragments into the initial user data frame. The 4-byte FCRC is a 32-bit CRC of the fragment. Note that the initial user data frame to be fragmented includes the various (Ethernet) header fields and the original FCS.

In the example shown in Figure 5.10(b), it is assumed that the initial user data frame has to be sent in three cable MAC frames. As we can see, the overhead associated with each of these frames is 16 bytes and hence it is assumed that the first grant message contains sufficient minislots to send $W + 16$ bytes, the second $X + 16$ bytes and the third $Y + 16$ bytes.

Piggyback requests

Also present in the extension header (EHDR) field of each fragment is an 8-bit *REQ* (request) subfield. This plays the same role as the Request message we described earlier. The difference is that there is no contention involved in sending the subsequent request message(s) for the additional minislots that are required to send the remainder of the user data (Ethernet) frame.

When the cable MAC in the CM prepares the first fragment of a larger frame, it computes the number of minislots required to send the remainder of the frame including the 16 bytes of overhead. It then includes this value in the REQ subfield of the frame. This type of request is known as a **piggyback request** since it is being sent in the same frame as the current fragment of data being transferred. As we can deduce from this, this procedure leads to a shorter wait time relative to sending a separate request message. Again, if the number of minislots allocated in the grant message contained in the subsequent bandwidth allocation MAP is less than the number requested, then a further level of fragmentation must be carried out using the same procedure as before. This is repeated until the complete user data frame has been transferred.

Request/data regions

During periods when the upstream channel is lightly loaded, the CMTS may include in each bandwidth allocation MAP it transmits a *Request/Data region*. This is similar to a REQ region except that in addition to Request messages, a CM can also attempt to send a short user data frame. As with a REQ region, this is a contention region and hence the data frame may be corrupted by a simultaneous transmission of a request or data frame from another CM. In order for the CM to know whether a collision has occurred, if the data frame is received without errors, the CMTS returns a *Data Acknowledge* message (containing the SID of the CM) in the next MAP it transmits. In order for the cable MAC in the CM to know the maximum time to wait for an acknowledgment, the CMTS includes in each MAP it transmits an ACK field which indicates the start time of the transmission region that any acknowledgment messages in the MAP relate. If this is later than the time the data message was sent, then a collision is assumed and the CM must try again.

QoS support

The reservation access mode described in the preceding subsections is intended for the transfer of user data frames containing IP packets relating to the best-effort service. Hence all the packets have the same priority value in the type-of-service (ToS) field in the packet header. An additional feature is also included in the cable MAC, however, to enable frames containing packets that have a high priority to be transmitted before frames containing a lower priority packet.

As we saw in Section 1.2.5, the relative priority of a packet is determined by the service class associated with the application/call. There are a number of different service classes each determined by a set of QoS parameters. These may include, for example, a defined worst-case end-to-end delay, jitter, and throughput requirement. In the context of the cable MAC, each service class has a related **service flow** and, for each service flow, the CMTS endeavors to schedule transmissions so that the agreed QoS parameters associated with each service class are met. As we can deduce from this, there are a number of different service flows each of which maps to a related packet priority. Hence packets containing a particular priority value are   transmitted according to the rules associated with the related service flow.

Each service flow is characterized by a separate **service flow identifier** and, for applications involving duplex flows – such as telephony – a separate service flow is set up in both the CMTS-to-CM and CM-to-CMTS directions. Also, for applications requiring asymmetric communication channels – that is, the class of service associated with the information flow is different for each direction – the service flow in each direction can be different.

In order to ensure that the agreed QoS parameters associated with each service flow are met, in the upstream direction, a number of additional transmission opportunities are provided by the CMTS for these flows on receipt of the related request from a CM. These include:

- **unsolicited grant**: these are intended for use for service flows involving packets containing real-time information. The CMTS, on receiving the appropriate request message from a CM, reserves in the allocation MAP specific fixed-sized transmission opportunities that are repeated at periodic intervals. The frequency and duration of the intervals is determined by the type of service flow. The CMTS stops generating intervals when it detects they are not being used;

- **real-time polling**: these also involve the CMTS reserving periodic transmission opportunities and are intended for real-time traffic flows such as voice-over-IP (Internet telephony). The CMTS periodically polls/invites each CM with an active service flow to make a bandwidth request at intervals of about 1 ms. The related transmission opportunities cease when the CM fails to respond to a poll;

- **unsolicited grant with activity detection**: the packetization process associated with voice-over-IP sometimes exploits the silence periods between talk spurts by ceasing to send packets during these periods. This service is intended for use with this type of application. All the time packets associated with this flow are being transmitted by a CM, the

CMTS continues to provide periodic transmission opportunities for it. Immediately the CMTS detects these are not being used, however, it stops providing them. Then, when the CM detects the flow of packets resumes – and hence the service flow becomes active – it sends a request message to the CMTS asking for the unsolicited periodic transmission opportunities to be resumed. Normally, the CMTS, after it stops providing transmission opportunities, provides a specific request opportunity for this CM/SID at similar periodic intervals;

■ **non-real-time polling**: this service is intended for use with non-real-time applications that involve the transfer of large volumes of data; for example large file transfers. With the basic reservation access mode, during periods of heavy loading such transfers may take unacceptably long times to complete. Hence by using non-real-time polling, the CMTS periodically polls/invites CMs to make a bandwidth request at intervals of about 12 s. Such requests always receive some reserved transmission opportunities even during periods of heavy traffic when contention requests are receiving minimal transmission opportunities.

DS TC sublayer

The MAC frames exchanged between the CMTS and a CM have the same basic structure in both the downstream and the upstream channels. In the downstream direction, however, in order to utilize similar receiving hardware to that used for a digital TV channel, the channel bitstream is divided by the transmission control (TC) sublayer into a stream of 188-byte packets. This is the packet format used by the transport multiplexer to transmit multiple digital TV programs over a single high bit rate channel. Each packet is made up of a 4-byte header and a 184-byte payload. The first byte of the header is for synchronization purposes and enables all the receivers to determine the start of each new packet. A second 13-bit field in the header (known as the *payload identifier (PID)*) is then used to identify the type of contents in the payload and, if this is data relating to Internet access, it is set to 1FFE (hex). Hence if the total channel bandwidth is being used for Internet access, all packets will contain this value in the packet identifier field. Alternatively, if the channel is being used to transmit both Internet data and digital TV programs, then only those packets containing Internet data will have this PID.

The 184-byte payload field of each packet is used to transfer the cable MAC frames. However, since a packet may contain either multiple short frames or a portion of a long frame, in order to use the available bandwidth efficiently, it is necessary for each receiver to be able to determine the start and end of each frame. Also, since there may be unused bits/bandwidth between successive frames, a means of detecting when these are present is required.

To determine the start of a frame within a packet, the first byte following the 4-byte packet header is used as a *pointer* (offset) to the first byte of a new frame should one start within the current packet. If a new frame does not start within a packet, however, and the packet contains, say, a portion of a packet that straddles multiple packets, then the first byte is not used as a pointer. For each CM to determine if a pointer byte/field is present, a single bit in the 4-byte packet header called the *payload unit start indicator* (*PUSI*) bit is set to 1. Idle periods between frames are indicated by the presence of one or more *stuff-bytes,* which have the reserved bit pattern of FF (hex). The *frame control* (*FC*) field at the head of each frame cannot be equal to this. Hence, since the length of each frame can be determined from the fields in the (MAC) frame header, each CM can readily determine the start and end of each frame. Three examples are given in Figure 5.11.

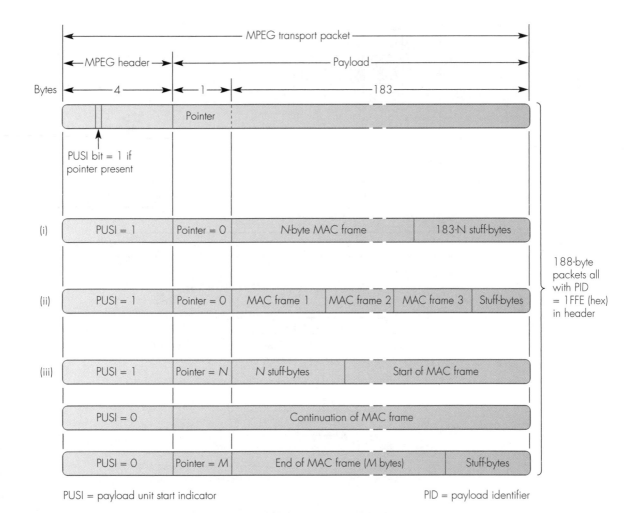

Figure 5.11 Downstream transmission convergence sublayer: examples showing the packing of MAC frames into 188-byte MPEG transport packets.

The first assumes the start of the frame immediately follows the pointer byte and just a single frame is present in the packet. The second assumes multiple short frames are packed into a single packet and the third, a single long frame spans multiple packets.

DS/US PMD sublayers

A schematic diagram showing typical packet flows in both the downstream and upstream channels is given in Figure 5.12.

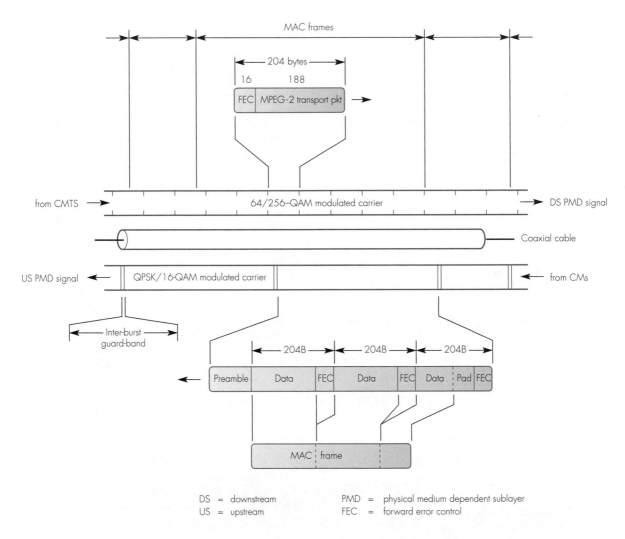

Figure 5.12 DS/US PMD sublayer: example packet flows and their overheads.

In the downstream direction, the signal is continuous and is the allocated carrier for the channel modulated by the bitstream using either 64 or 256-QAM. As we explained in the previous subsection, the bitstream is divided into a contiguous stream of 188-byte MPEG-2 transport packets each with a 4/5-byte header.

In the upstream direction, the signal is the allocated carrier modulated by the bitstream using either QPSK or 16-QAM. The bitstream in this direction, however, is made up of variable-length bursts of bits/frames each sent by a different CM. Hence in order for the PMD sublayer in the CMTS to be able to receive reliably each frame, a *guard-band* between each frame comprising several symbols at the start and end of each frame is present. Also, in order for the receiving electronics to achieve clock/symbol synchronization and determine the start of each frame, a *preamble* sequence of up to 1024 bits precedes each frame starting at the allocated minislot boundary. This is sent as either 512 (QPSX) or 256 (16-QAM) symbols and terminates with a defined symbol pattern. This is followed by the bits in the (MAC) frame and, since the length of a frame can be determined from the fields in the frame header, no end-of-frame sequence is required.

In addition, as we show in the figure, a forward error control (FEC) scheme is optionally used with both the downstream and upstream channels in order to reduce the probability of the received bitstream containing transmission/bit errors. We discuss the principles of such schemes in Appendix C. The scheme used is based on an (n, k, t) Reed–Solomon (RS) code where k is the number of bytes in the original block of data, n the number of bytes in the block after coding, and t the number of bytes in a block that the code will correct. Normally, in order to exploit the use of the same hardware as is used for digital TV, the block size used in both channels, k, is 188 bytes. This has 16 bytes of FEC and hence $n = 188 + 16 = 204$ bytes. This code has a minimum *Hamming distance*, d, of 17 bytes and hence will correct up to 8 bytes in each block. This code is written as an RS $(204, 188, t = 8)$ code and, in practice, is a shortened version of the RS $(255, 239, t = 8)$ code. The FEC bytes are computed by adding 51 zero bytes before the 188 bytes prior to computing the FEC.

Cable intranets

The network architecture we showed earlier in Figure 5.3 is an example of a typical regional HFC cable network. The CMTS in the cable headend provides a single point of access to the Internet and the cable operator acts as an Internet service provider (ISP) for its CM subscribers. Many cable operators, however, have multiple regional networks. Hence, in terms of Internet access, these operators have many thousands of subscribers. In such cases, instead of providing multiple single access points to the Internet, the cable operator creates its own intranet with all the regional headends linked together using high bit rate digital circuits. The general scheme is shown in Figure 5.13.

As we can see, each regional network is similar to a site LAN in a large enterprise intranet. As we saw in Figure 5.4, in the CMTS is a Fast Ethernet switch and, connected to this, there are a number of additional local servers that provide various services on behalf of its local community of subscribers, for example, an e-mail server, some local Web servers, and one or more cache servers that are used to retain copies of popular Web pages.

When part of an intranet, however, also connected to the switch is a router that forms the interface with other sites. In this way, all communications between subscribers that are connected to the different regional

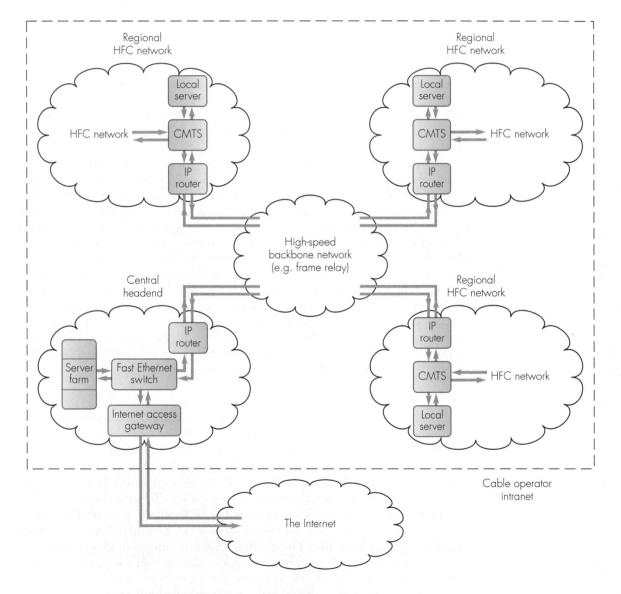

Figure 5.13 Cable operator intranet principles.

networks of the operator are via the intranet and hence are carried out at high speed. Also, a single high-speed backbone connection with the public Internet can be used so increasing the speed of access to external servers.

5.2.3 MMDS and LMDS

In areas with low subscriber densities or where laying cable is difficult, an alternative to coaxial cable is to use terrestrial microwave broadcast transmissions. As we show in Figure 5.14(a) and (b), two alternatives are available, one called the **multichannel multipoint distribution system** (**MMDS**) and the other the **local multipoint distribution system** (**LMDS**). Both use ommidirectional transmitters and, within their area of coverage, provide a similar range of services to those provided with a coaxial cable distribution network. The main difference between the two systems is the area of coverage of the transmissions and the number of channels supported. The main features of both systems are summarized in Figure 5.14(c).

As we can see, a typical MMDS operates in the 2.15–2.7 GHz frequency band. Normally, it has a relatively wide area of coverage with a direct connection between the transmitter and the cable headend. Multiple 6/8 MHz downstream channels are supported, which are used for either analog TV broadcasts or, with suitable modems, digital broadcasts. The latter include digital TV and, together with the upstream (return) channel, interactive services including access to the Internet.

An LMDS operates in a higher frequency band – typically between 27 and 30 GHz – as it is intended for local distribution with an area of coverage of up to 5 km from the transmitter. Normally, the transmitter has a direct connection to a fiber node in an HFC network. Hence an LMDS effectively replaces the coaxial cable part of an HFC network. A similar bandwidth to coax is supported and hence a similar range of services to an HFC network.

As we can see in Figure 5.14, LMDS has 850 MHz of bandwidth available in the downstream direction and 150 MHz in the upstream direction. Hence with appropriate modulation schemes, this can readily support the services provided by a coaxial cable distribution network within a localized area. As with coaxial cable, the services include the distribution of television services to the home and also interactive services including Internet access. In addition, if the transmitter is located within a town or city, then it can be used to provide Internet access in the same way as a public wireless LAN. For this reason, therefore, it is considered to be a competitor of IEEE802.11. There is a standard for this called **IEEE802.16**. Because of its function, it is called **broadband wireless** or sometimes **wireless local loop** or by the colloquial name of WiMax. We shall limit our discussion here to how the services associated with the IEEE802.16 standard are provided.

5.2.4 IEEE802.16

As with the other wireless standards, IEEE802.16 is concerned mainly with the data link and physical layers. As we can see from the protocol stack shown in Figure 5.15(a), both layers are made up of a number of sublayers.

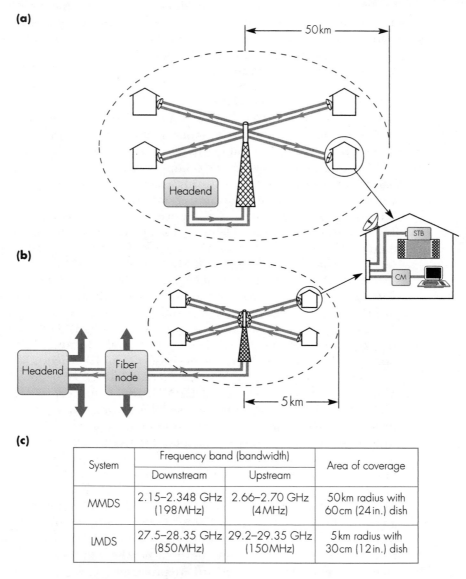

M/LMDS = multichannel/local multipoint distribution system

(c)

System	Frequency band (bandwidth)		Area of coverage
	Downstream	Upstream	
MMDS	2.15–2.348 GHz (198 MHz)	2.66–2.70 GHz (4 MHz)	50 km radius with 60 cm (24 in.) dish
LMDS	27.5–28.35 GHz (850 MHz)	29.2–29.35 GHz (150 MHz)	5 km radius with 30 cm (12 in.) dish

Figure 5.14 M/LMDS principles: (a) MMDS schematic; (b) LMDS schematic; (c) typical operating parameters.

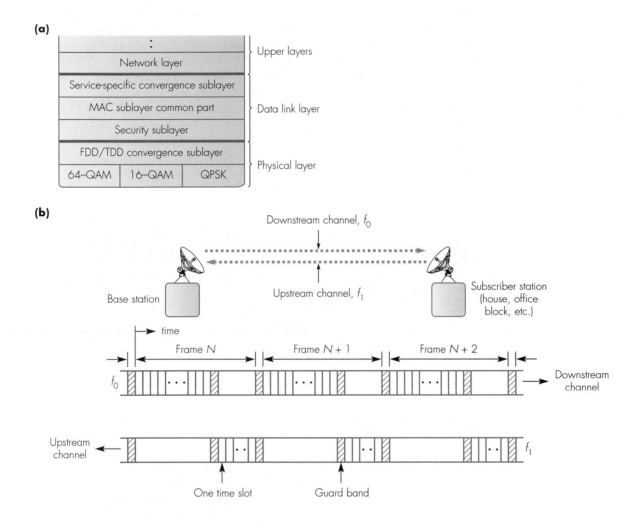

Figure 5.15 IEEE802.16: (a) protocol stack; (b) FDD/TDD schematic.

Radio interface

The received power of a radio signal is inversely proportional to the square of the distance from the transmitter and hence the received power falls off sharply with distance. As a result, three different modulation schemes are used. For subscribers that are close to a base station – and hence in a region with a high signal-to-noise ratio – 64-QAM is used giving the highest bit rate. For those subscribers that are outside this range, 16-QAM is used. Then, for subscribers that are beyond this range, the more robust QPSK is used. The available bit rate in each area is determined by the amount of bandwidth that is allocated to providing the services. For example, assuming an allocated bandwidth of 8 MHz, 64-QAM provides 6 bits per baud/Hz and hence 48 Mbps; 16-QAM provides 4 bits per baud and hence 32 Mbps; and QPSK 2 bits per baud and hence 16 Mbps. The actual bit rate required is determined by the density of the subscriber premises in the area of coverage and, in the case of a city, for example, multiples of this bandwidth are required.

At frequencies in the tens of gigahertz band, the signals travel in near straight lines. Hence to cover a circular area it is necessary for the transmitter to use multiple dishes as we showed in Figure 5.14(b). Each dish covers a single sector and has its own set of subscribers. Typically, a single transmitter has six dishes/sectors and, because of the mode of transmission, very little interference occurs between neighboring sectors.

Baseband transmission

In the standard, the available bandwidth is divided using a combination of **frequency division duplexing (FDD)** and **time division duplexing (TDD)**. FDD is used to establish a half duplex – two-way alternate – communications channel with transmissions from the base station to the subscriber stations using one frequency – called the **downstream channel** – and a second frequency for transmissions from each subscriber station to the base station – called the upstream channel. TDD is then used to divide the available bandwidth in each direction in a way that can support all of the applications/services that are currently being used. A schematic diagram illustrating the principles of the FDD/TDD scheme is shown in Figure 5.15(b).

As we can see, the overall transmission bandwidth is made up of a stream of fixed-sized **time slots**. The number of bits in each time slot is determined by the bit rate of the channel. The stream of time slots is then divided up into a series of **frames**. TDD is then used to divide the stream of time slots to create a downstream channel and an upstream channel. Between each frame in the upstream and downstream directions is a **guard band** that is used to change the carrier frequency from that used by the base station to that used by a subscriber station and vice versa. Each frame is then subdivided into a number of **subframes** and it is these that are used to transmit the data relating to the applications that are currently running.

All the services supported by the base station are connection-oriented. Hence at the start of each session the subscriber must first establish a connection. This involves going through an authentication procedure and, if this is successful, a **connection identifier** is allocated to the connection. As we shall see later, four classes of service are supported and, at connection setup time, the class of service required – and hence the bandwidth – is agreed. Once this has been carried out, the exchange of data relating to the application can start. The data relating to each application is carried in a MAC frame that has in its header the allocated connection identifier.

For transmissions in the downstream direction, the base station knows the bandwidth requirements of all the applications that are currently running and hence it can readily map the data/MAC frames relating to the applications onto the set of subframes – and hence time slots – that make up each frame. In the upstream direction, however, each subscriber operates independently of one another and hence the use of the upstream bandwidth is also managed by the base station. To do this, the first two subframes in each frame in the downstream direction are used to hold what are called the **downstream map** and the **upstream map** respectively. Essentially, these inform each station of what is currently present in each subframe/time slot and which subframes/time slots are free. In addition, although in Figure 5.15(b) all frames are composed of the same number of time slots, the number of time slots in each direction is not fixed and changes with time to meet the bandwidth requirements in each direction.

Data link layer

As we can see from the protocol stack, the data link layer is composed of three sublayers:

- **Security sublayer**: this involves first, mutual authentication using the RSA public-key algorithm and second, the encryption of the payload using DES with cipher block chaining or triple DES, all of which we describe in Chapter 10;

- **MAC sublayer common part**: as we indicated earlier, four classes of service are supported each of which is connection-oriented. These are:
  - **constant bit rate**: this is used for Internet telephony, for example, and hence comprises a string of packets each containing a number of uncompressed 8-bit speech samples that are generated at a constant rate of 8 kbytes per second. These are then carried in the payload of a MAC frame;
  - **real-time variable bit rate**: this is used for the transmission of compressed multimedia, for example, which, as we described in Section 1.2.1, is comprised of a string of blocks of data of variable length. Clearly, therefore, this type of service requires varying amounts of transmission bandwidth. This is determined by the base station polling the subscriber station at regular intervals to request the amount of bandwidth that is needed;
  - **non-real time variable bit rate**: this is used for bulk data transfers such as the contents of a large file or a Web page. In this case, the base station polls the subscriber station at varying time intervals to determine the amount of bandwidth that is needed. Alternatively, since there may be a number of subscribers requiring the same service concurrently – for example using the Internet – then if a subscriber station does not respond to a number of successive polls, the subscriber station is assigned to a multicast group of similar subscribers. Then, when the multicast group is polled, the members

of the group must compete for the service by letting any of the subscriber stations request bandwidth;

■ **best effort**: with this service polling is not used and instead all subscribers must compete for bandwidth. Selected subframes in the upstream map are marked by the base station as available for best effort traffic. A subscriber station can then make a request for the use of the subframe by returning a **bandwidth request** frame in the upstream channel. Then, if the subscriber station is successful, this will be indicated in the next downstream map. Clearly, requests for a subframe may collide and in this case the binary exponential backoff algorithm – see Section 3.2.1 – is used to ensure the subframe is used in a controlled way during periods of heavy usage;

■ **service-specific convergence sublayer**: although four classes of service are supported, this sublayer is present to form a single interface to the network layer above.

Frame formats

Although there are a number of frame types, there are just two types of frame header. Their format is shown in Figure 5.16(a) and the meaning and use of each field in the header is shown in part(b). Note that the format of control frames is the same as that of data frames except that there is no payload field with control frames.

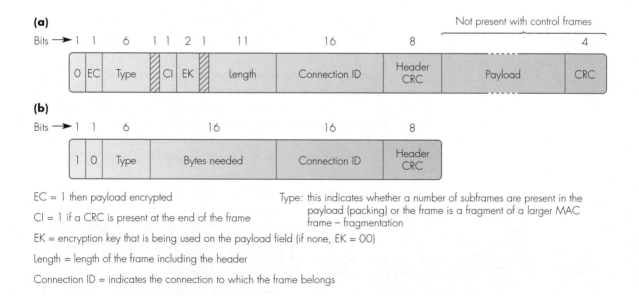

EC = 1 then payload encrypted

CI = 1 if a CRC is present at the end of the frame

EK = encryption key that is being used on the payload field (if none, EK = 00)

Length = length of the frame including the header

Connection ID = indicates the connection to which the frame belongs

Type: this indicates whether a number of subframes are present in the payload (packing) or the frame is a fragment of a larger MAC frame – fragmentation

Figure 5.16 IEEE802.16 frame formats: (a) generic frame format; (b) bandwidth request frame.

The second type of frame header is for bandwidth request frames. In this case the frame contains an additional field: *bytes needed* – and hence bandwidth – for the particular connection/application given in the *connection ID* field. In practice, there are two forms of bandwidth allocation: per connection and per subscriber station. In the first case, each request for bandwidth is treated separately by the base station. In the second, the subscriber station may support all the users in, say, a large office block and hence in this case the bandwidth request relates to the aggregated bandwidth of all the currently active users in the block. It is then the responsibility of the subscriber station to utilize the allocated bandwidth in whatever way suits the subscriber distribution network.

5.3 Satellite television networks

Satellite networks have been used for many years to deliver broadcast television direct to the home. Initially, the signals relating to all the TV programs were analog but these have now been complemented with digital TV. Also, as with cable networks, in addition to broadcast television, various interactive data services are now supported. In this section we discuss the operation of, firstly, a direct-to-home broadcast TV system, secondly, the principles behind digital TV over satellite, and thirdly, how interactive services are provided.

5.3.1 Broadcast television principles

The basic requirement of an entertainment satellite network is to broadcast a set of TV programs from a program source to the set-top boxes of a large number of subscribers who are physically distributed over a wide geographical area. Figure 5.17(a) shows how this is achieved.

The orbital period of a satellite varies according to its distance above the earth's surface. Satellites used for TV broadcasting, however, are **geosynchronous,** which means that the satellite orbits the earth once every 24 hours – slightly less than this in practice – in time synchronism with the rotation of the earth. To achieve this, the orbit must be circular and, since the earth rotates around its polar axis, the satellite's orbit must be around the earth's polar axis. A circular orbit is then obtained if the orbit is in the equatorial plane and at an (average) altitude above the equator of approximately 36 000 km/ 22 300 miles. At this height, the effect of the centrifugal force due to the rotation of the satellite is negated by the terrestrial attraction of the satellite by the earth. Also, from a point on the earth's surface, the satellite appears stationary and hence is known as a **geostationary earth orbit** (**GEO**) – or simply geostationary – satellite.

GEO satellite positioning

The satellite is first launched to an altitude of 36 000 km/22 300 miles above the equator and on-board motors are then used to ensure the orbit is circular

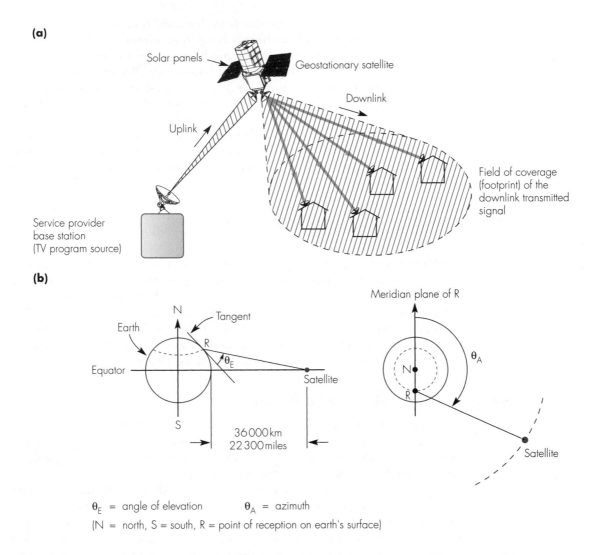

(a)

Solar panels

Geostationary satellite

Downlink

Uplink

Field of coverage
(footprint) of the
downlink transmitted
signal

Service provider
base station
(TV program source)

(b)

Meridian plane of R

N

Tangent

Earth

R

θ_E

Equator

Satellite

S

36 000 km
22 300 miles

N

R

θ_A

Satellite

θ_E = angle of elevation θ_A = azimuth

(N = north, S = south, R = point of reception on earth's surface)

**Figure 5.17 Geostationary satellite principles: (a) broadcast network schematic;
(b) positioning details.**

and in its assigned position relative to a point on the earth's surface. The on-board motors are also used at periodic intervals during the satellite's operational lifetime to effect small corrections that maintain the satellite's position to within 0.2° of its assigned position. In general, therefore, the useful lifetime of a satellite is determined by the quantity of propellant used to perform these maneuvers. The main power source for the on-board electronic equipment comes from large solar panels but this has to be complemented by batteries to overcome the loss of power from the panels during periods when the satellite is eclipsed by the earth.

Since the latitude of a satellite is $0°$, the position of a satellite is defined by its longitude relative to the Greenwich meridian. As we show in Figure 5.17(b), the position relative to a point on the earth is defined by the elevation and azimuth of the satellite. The **elevation** is the angle between the line from the satellite to the point of reception, R, and the tangent to the earth's surface at R. The **azimuth** is the angle between the N–S plane passing through R and the line from the satellite to R measured relative to the north pole.

Frequency allocations

As we saw in Figure 5.2, the bandwidth of an analog TV signal – including guard bands – is either 6 or 8 MHz. As we show in Figure 5.18, with the earliest satellites used for commercial analog television broadcasts, the signal of each TV program is frequency modulated onto a separate carrier which results in a basic channel bandwidth of 36 MHz. A satellite supports multiple channels and these are combined to form the signal that is transmitted from the base-station to the satellite using frequency division multiplexing. Typically, 24 channels are used with a guard band of 4 MHz between adjacent channels.

In order to avoid the signal received from the base-station on the uplink interfering with the signal transmitted by the satellite on the downlink, a separate frequency band is used for transmissions in the uplink and downlink directions. This means that each channel is allocated a separate carrier signal in both the uplink and downlink directions with the same fixed spacing between channels.

Antenna designs

Owing to the large distance traveled, the signal received from the transmitter is extremely weak. Hence it is essential to receive as much of the transmitted signal as possible. This is achieved by using a parabolic dish made of a reflecting material. Like light, microwaves travel in straight lines and are reflected by metallic surfaces. Hence as we show in part (i) of Figure 5.19(a), the incident waves received from the transmitter are all focused at the focal point of the dish. Moreover, since the distance travelled by all the waves is the same, they all arrive at the focal point in-phase and their energy, therefore, is additive.

Located at the focal point of the dish is a unit known as a **low-noise block converter** (**LNB/C**). This consists of a low-noise amplifier and a frequency downconverter. As we saw in Figure 5.18, the frequency of the uplink signal with early satellite systems is in the range 5.925 through to 6.425 GHz. Since this exceeds the bandwidth of a coaxial cable, prior to passing the received signal to the on-board electronics for frequency conversion, the received signal is first amplified in the LNB/C and then downconverted into a lower frequency band. This is called the **satellite intermediate frequency** (**SAT-IF**) and, with early systems, is 950 MHz. It is this signal that is then passed to the on-board electronics by means of a coaxial cable.

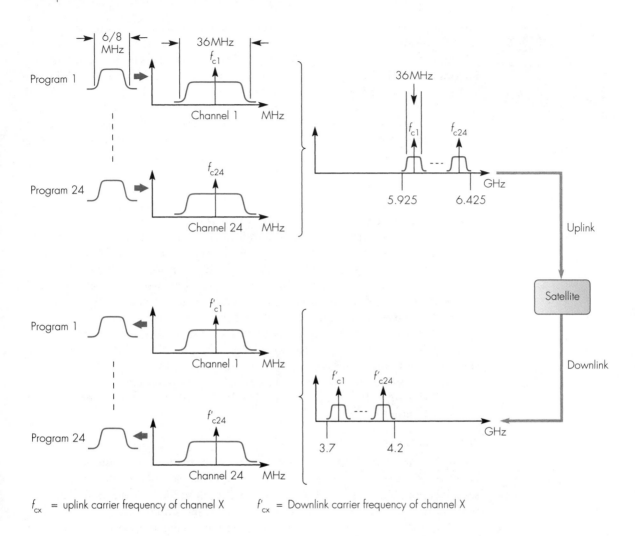

f_{cx} = uplink carrier frequency of channel X f'_{cx} = Downlink carrier frequency of channel X

Figure 5.18 Frequency bands used with early satellite systems.

The antenna design shown in part (i) of Figure 5.19(a) is called a **prime focus antenna** since the LNB/C is located in the center of the dish at its focal point. The disadvantage of this design is the LNB/C inhibits the direct waves in the center of the dish from being collected. Clearly this reduces the efficiency of the antenna and, for small dishes, the fall in efficiency can be significant. To overcome this effect, the reflector used with more modern antennas is a portion of a larger parabolic mirror. This type of design is known as an **offset focus antenna** and its principle of operation is shown in part (ii) of Figure 5.19(a). As we can see, with this design the LNB/C is attached to the bottom of the dish and hence out of the way of the incoming waves. This has the effect of increasing significantly the antenna's efficiency.

(a)

(i) prime focus antenna:

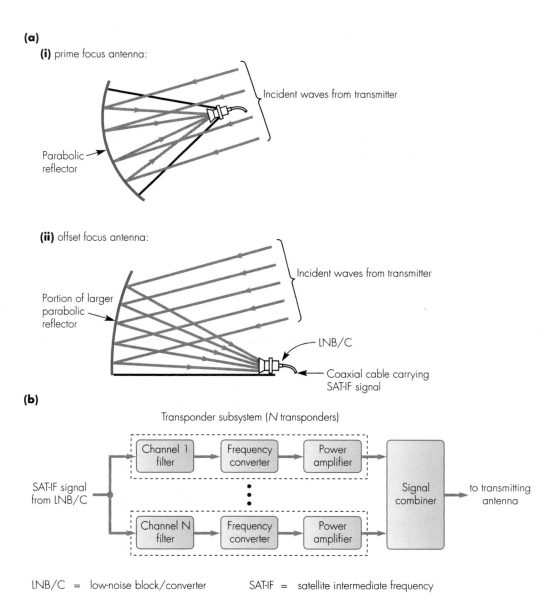

(ii) offset focus antenna:

(b)

Figure 5.19 continued below.

LNB/C = low-noise block/converter   SAT-IF = satellite intermediate frequency

Figure 5.19 Satellite components: (a) two antenna designs; (b) on-board transponder subsystem.

Transponder subsystem

The signal output by the LNB/C is passed to an electronic module within the satellite. This is known as the transponder subsystem and its composition is shown in Figure 5.19(b).

Microwave power amplifiers are only linear over a limited frequency band which dictates that each channel signal is amplified separately prior to its transmission. As we can see in the figure, the individual modulated channel signals are first separated out using filters. Each is then frequency-shifted to its allocated (downlink) frequency band and then amplified. The resulting signals are then combined to form the downlink signal that is broadcast over a defined area known as the satellite's field of coverage or **footprint**. An antenna – satellite dish – on each subscriber premises is then used to receive the broadcast signal.

The signal received by the antenna is first down-shifted in the LNB/C and then passed to the set-top box over a coaxial cable. Electronic circuitry within the STB demodulates the received signal by first filtering out each channel signal. The corresponding carrier signal for each channel is then used to recover the signal of the related TV program that has been selected by the subscriber.

As we saw in Section 1.3.2, satellites use frequencies in the microwave frequency band since these propagate through free space in straight lines and can be focussed into a beam of a defined width. In the uplink direction a narrow beam width is used to ensure the maximum amount of energy in the signal transmitted by the base-station is received by the satellite's receiving antenna. Conversely, a wide beam width is used in the downlink direction to ensure the signal is received by all the antennas within the satellite's footprint. The size of the dish required to receive the signal broadcast by the satellite is determined by the output power of the satellite's transmitter – which is influenced by the number of transponders – and its area of coverage. Most early systems use a single satellite and, in many instances, cover a wide geographical area with the effect that dishes of between 1 and 4 meters are required. With later systems, however, multiple satellites are used to cover a similar area and hence dishes as small as 45 cm (15 in.) are common. With such dishes, interference-free reception can be obtained if the satellites have orbital positions with a spacing of in the order of 10°.

For most early commercial analog television broadcasts, the frequency bands used are within what is called the **C-band** of the microwave frequency range. As we saw in Figure 5.18, with this band the frequency range of the uplink channels is from 5.925 to 6.425 GHz and that of the downlink channels from 3.7 to 4.2 GHz. Typical channel bandwidths of 40 MHz – including a guard-band – are used. With microwaves, however, it is possible to use the same frequency band twice using both horizontally polarized and vertically polarized transmissions. Hence the total 500 MHz of available bandwidth can support up to 24 active channels and hence transponders.

Normally, in order to improve reliability, most transponder subsystems contain a number of spare transponders (and other units) to replace any that may become defective. A *command and telemetry subsystem* is then used to send commands to the satellite to switch spare units into service should this be necessary. Typically, a satellite has to be replaced after 10 to 12 years of service.

5.3.2 Digital television

Since all satellite transmissions are within an allocated frequency band (within the microwave frequency spectrum), modulated transmission must also be used for the transmission of a digital TV program. As with cable TV, therefore, the bitstream containing the multiplexed set of (digital) TV programs is passed through a (microwave) modem to convert it into an analog signal within the allocated frequency band. However, in order to obtain the same bit error rate probability as that obtained with a cable distribution network, a more robust modulation scheme must be used. Hence instead of 64 or 256-QAM with 6/8 bits per symbol (signal element), the modulation scheme used is QPSK (4-QAM) which, as we saw in Figure 2.6, has just 2 bits per symbol.

For most digital TV transmissions, the frequency band used is in what is called the **Ku band,** which covers the frequency range from 10.7 through to 14.5 GHz. In the downlink direction, the lowest part of the band from 10.7 through to 11.7 GHz is used mainly for newer analog TV transmissions. For digital TV, example downlink bands are 12.2 through to 12.7 GHz for the North American **digital broadcast satellites** (**DBS**) and 11.7 through to 12.5 GHz for the European **digital video broadcasting-satellites** (**DVB-S**). The DBS system uses three orbital positions with 9° spacing, each allowing full coverage to be obtained. Each position is used by a separate service provider which then uses a number of satellites – normally three – to obtain interference-free reception with small dishes. Typically, the allocated bandwidth is used to provide 32 channels of 24 MHz each supporting a symbol rate of 20 Mbaud. Hence, with QPSK, this gives a typical channel bit rate of 40 Mbps.

The DVB-S system uses two orbital positions with 6.2° spacing, each of which allows full coverage to be obtained. Each position is used by a separate satellite operator which uses two satellites to obtain interference-free reception with small dishes. With this system, the typical allocated bandwidth is used to provide 40 channels of 33 MHz, each supporting a symbol rate of 27.5 Mbaud which, with QPSK, gives a bit rate of 55 Mbps.

Channel interface

A schematic diagram showing the individual blocks associated with each channel interface is given in Figure 5.20(a). Most satellite digital TV transmissions now use the standard, MPEG-2 transport stream multiplex. The (multiplexed) bitstreams of multiple TV programs are multiplexed together into a single bitstream that is made up of a contiguous stream of 188-byte packets, each comprising a 4-byte header and a 184-byte payload. As we indicated earlier, satellite channels are more susceptible to transmission (bit) errors than cable networks. Hence in addition to using a more robust modulation scheme, a more rigorous forward error control scheme is applied to each 188-byte packet. This involves the addition of check bytes derived using a Reed–Solomon code – as optionally used with cable networks – byte interleaving, and convolutional encoding of the resulting bitstream.

The RS check bytes are added primarily to detect burst errors and the same coding scheme as is optionally used in cable networks is used. As we saw in Section 5.2.1, this is an RS (204, 188) code and the 16 check bytes that are appended to each 188-byte packet enable up to 8 bytes in error in each 204-byte block to be identified and corrected.

Very long error bursts in a block – that is, greater than 8 bytes – can be broken down into smaller bursts by using a technique known as **interleaving**. Essentially, this involves rearranging the order of transmission of the bytes in each 204-byte block so that an error burst longer than 8 bytes will affect no more than 8 sequential bytes in the original 204-byte block. The principle is shown in Figure 5.20(b).

Prior to transmission each 204-byte block output by the RS coder is fragmented into twelve 17-byte subblocks. The transmitted byte sequence is then the first byte from each of the twelve subblocks, followed by the second byte in each subblock, and so on. The reverse operation is then performed at the receiver to reorder the bytes into their original sequence. In this way, should an error burst of, say, 12 bytes occur within a block during its transmission, this will affect only every seventeenth byte in the original 204-byte block and hence be detected and corrected by the RS decoder.

In addition to burst errors, satellite transmissions are susceptible to randomly distributed single bit errors. To minimize the effect of such errors, the bitstream output by the byte interleaver is passed through a **convolutional encoder**, the principles of which are described in Appendix C. A typical encoder used with digital TV broadcasts is shown in Figure 5.20(c).

Essentially, the bitstream output by the byte interleaver is passed through a 7-bit shift register and, for each new bit entering the shift register, two separate XOR operations are performed on the new contents of the register. The pair of bits produced by the two XOR operations are then the two bits that are transmitted for this input bit; that is, for each input bit two bits are transmitted. As we explain in Appendix C, for each type of encoder there is only a limited number of possible pairs of output bits for each new input bit. These are known by the convolutional decoder in the receiver and, for each pair of bits it receives, the decoder computes the *Hamming distance* – see Appendix C – between the pair of bits it has received and all the known possible pairs. This procedure is repeated for each new pair of bits the decoder receives and, after a predefined number of pairs, the decoder selects the sequence with the smallest Hamming distance as being the most likely sequence of (pairs of) bits that were transmitted. It then replaces each pair of bits in this sequence with the corresponding bitstream that would have produced this sequence.

Since two bits are output for every bit input into the encoder, it is known as a **rate 1/2** convolutional encoder. Hence for every 204-byte block output by the interleaver, 408 bytes are transmitted. It is also possible to operate such encoders at a higher rate by deleting selected bits from the bitstream produced by the encoder. The technique used is called **puncturing** and example rates are 2/3 – three output bits for every two input bits – 3/4, 5/6 and 7/8. This has the

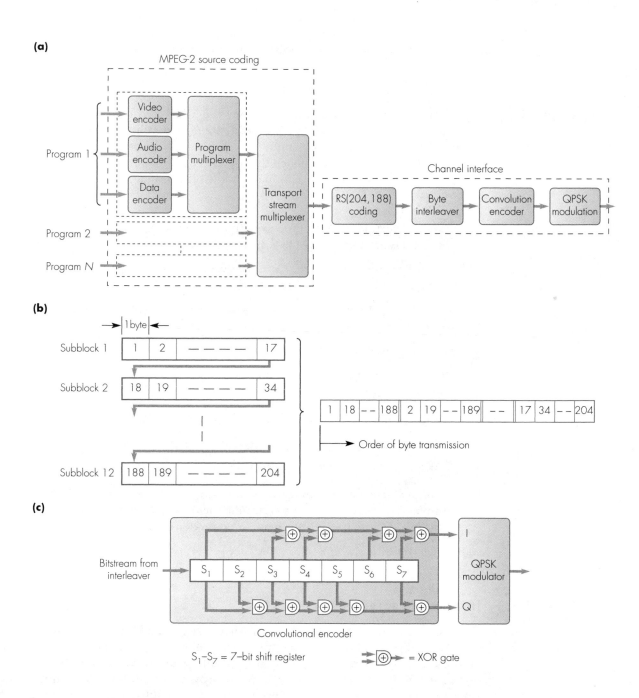

Figure 5.20 Satellite digital television channel interface: (a) schematic; (b) interleaver principle; (c) convolutional encoder.

effect, however, of reducing the error correction properties of the code and hence the rate used is a compromise between the level of error correction required and the amount of transmission overheads that are acceptable.

Example 5.1

A digital satellite channel interface uses the MPEG-2 transport stream multiplex, an RS (204, 188) block code, a rate 3/4 convolutional encoder, and QPSK modulation. Determine the number of overhead bits associated with the interface and hence the useful bit rate that is obtained with a channel that operates at (i) 20 Mbaud and (ii) 27.5 Mbuad.

Answer:

MPEG-2 transport stream multiplex comprises a stream of 188-byte packets each of which has a 4-byte header.

With an RS (204, 188) code, for each 188-byte block the RS encoder adds 16 error check bytes.

With a rate 3/4 convolutional encoder, for each 204-byte block the encoder adds 68 bytes of overhead.

Hence total overhead per 184-byte block = 4 + 16 + 68 = 88 bytes.

With QPSK, each symbol = 2 bits and hence raw bit rates are

(i) 40 Mbps and (ii) 55 Mbps.

   Hence useful bit rate with a raw bit rate of:

(i) 40 Mbps = 40 × 184/272 = 27.1 Mbps

(ii) 55 Mbps = 55 × 184/272 = 37.2 Mbps

The usage of each channel is determined by the service provider. Examples are multiple 4 Mbps channels for digital TV broadcasts and multiple 1.5 Mbps channels for near video-on-demand.

5.3.3 Interactive services

As we saw in Figure 5.3 and the accompanying text, in addition to the transmission of direct-to-home analog and digital television broadcasts, satellite networks are also used to support a range of interactive services. As we saw in the figure, the satellite network is used to provide a high bit rate channel from the service provider to the set-top box of each subscriber. As we have just seen, a single satellite channel can be used to broadcast data at rates of up to 6/8 Mbps if a single TV channel is used or up to 27/37 Mbps with a full transponder channel. Hence applications that involve the transmission of the same data to all of the subscribers concurrently can readily be supported. In some instances only local interaction with the STB is required whilst in others a facility is needed to enable the subscriber to interact with the remote information source. Typically, this is a remote server computer attached to the Internet. Hence the most popular way of providing an interaction channel is through either a PSTN (with modems) or an ISDN.

There are many applications that can exploit this type of facility and, for description purposes, they can be divided into a number of categories determined by the level of interactivity involved:

- **local interaction**: as we saw in Figure 5.20(a), each MPEG-2 program multiplexer, in addition to the audio and video associated with the (TV) program, also supports an optional data channel. This is used for a variety of purposes, for example to transmit information about the players in a ball game that is being broadcast. Typically, as this is received, it is stored in the STB and the subscriber can then locally interact with the STB to have selected information displayed on the TV screen while the game is being played.

  In other applications of this type, the data is not associated with a particular TV program but is from, say, a server that is located at the base station of the service provider and has a direct connection to the Internet. Examples of this are electronic newspapers and magazines. Typically, therefore, the data that is broadcast occupies a separate TV channel. This again is stored in the STB and subsequently can be accessed interactively by the subscriber and displayed on the TV screen. Normally, such channels are controlled by **conditional access**, that is, the broadcast bitstream has been scrambled (randomized) and requires a key to be unscrambled. Another example in this category is **pay-per-view**. The local interactions in these cases involve the subscriber inserting a *smart card* into a slot in the STB;

- **anonymous response to broadcasts**: with this category, a low bit rate interaction channel is involved, which, typically, is a PSTN. Examples are when a subscriber votes in a talent contest that is being broadcast or responds to an opinion poll. The subscriber simply calls one of a given set of telephone numbers and the call is logged;

- **purchase requests**: typically, this is in response to a product or service that is being offered via a TV broadcast. For such services the subscriber must interact with a remote location in order to enter credit card details and address information, for example. Normally, this is through a PSTN or ISDN and a call center.

Summary

A summary of the topics discussed in this chapter is given in Figure 5.21.

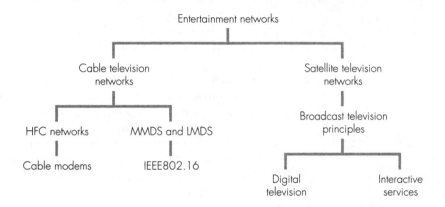

Figure 5.21 Entertainment networks summary.

Exercises

Section 5.1

5.1 List the bit rate requirements for the (compressed) audio and video associated with the following entertainment applications:
(i) movie/video-on-demand,
(ii) interactive television.
State the reason why a return channel is needed with these applications and hence the bit rate of this channel.

5.2 State the minimum bit rate requirements of a high-speed modem that provides an asymmetric channel over PSTN access lines to support
(i) VCR-quality, and
(ii) broadcast quality
movie/video-on-demand.
Give another application for this type of channel.

Section 5.2.1

5.3 With the aid of the schematic diagram of a CATV distribution network shown in Figure 5.1, explain the meaning/use of the following:
(i) cable headend,
(ii) trunk and distribution coax,
(iii) trunk and distribution amplifiers,
(iv) trunk splitter,
(v) subscriber tap.

5.4 With the aid of the frequency usage diagrams shown in Figure 5.2, state for both an NTSC system and a PAL system,
(i) the bandwidth required for the baseband composite video signal with sound,
(ii) the bandwidth required for the modulated video and audio signals,

(iii) the meaning and use of frequency division multiplexing,

(iv) the role of the frequency translators, filters, and combiner in the cable headend,

(v) how a subscriber selects a particular TV program,

(vi) the range of frequencies of the coaxial cable bandwidth that are used.

5.5 In relation to the hybrid fiber coax network shown in Figure 5.3, explain the meaning/ use of the following:
(i) a fiber node and the number of homes each serves,
(ii) bidirectional distribution amplifiers,
(iii) the utilization of the cable bandwidth in the downstream and upstream directions including the use of guard-bands and bandsplitting filters.

5.6 Explain the role of an RF modem including the modulation schemes used and the bandwidth available with a single 6/8 MHz band. State the additional applications (to broadcast TV) that these channels are used for.

5.7 In relation to the utilization of the upstream channel bandwidth in an HFC network, explain why the available cable bandwidth is divided into smaller subbands than those used for the downstream channels. Why are more robust modulation schemes used? Give some examples of typical bands and their bit rates.

Section 5.2.2

5.8 In relation to the multiaccess channels available with an HFC cable distribution network, use Figures 5.3 and 5.4 to explain the role of the following:
(i) cable modem,
(ii) cable modem termination system including the role of the Fast Ethernet switch.

5.9 In relation to the protocol stack used in a CM and the CMTS shown in Figure 5.5, state:
(i) why a CM has an integral (Ethernet) repeater hub within it,
(ii) the role of the cable MAC layer,

(iii) the role of the SNMP, TFTP, and DHCP protocols.

5.10 With the aid of the protocol stack shown in Figure 5.5, describe the role of the following protocols during the configuration and management phases of a CM:
(i) the DHCP and the information obtained,
(ii) the TFTP and the information obtained,
(iii) the SNMP.

5.11 In relation to the utilization of the (shared) upstream channel bandwidth, explain in outline how the cable MAC in a CM obtains bandwidth to send a frame. Include in your explanation the role of:
(i) the request and grant messages,
(ii) the service identifier of the CM,
(iii) the bandwidth allocation MAP,
(iv) time synchronization and ranging.

5.12 With the aid of the timing diagram shown in Figure 5.6, explain the principle of operation of the cable MAC time synchronization procedure. Include the meaning/use of:
(i) the SYNC management message,
(ii) the SYNC time-stamp,
(iii) the minislot and the power-of-two multiple associated with it,
(iv) the relationship between the minislot counter and the SYNC time-stamp.

5.13 In relation to the timing diagram relating to the cable MAC ranging procedure shown in Figure 5.7, explain:
(i) how the CM side determines when to send the first RNG-REQ message and the contents of the message,
(ii) how the CMTS side computes the RTC of the CM from the received message and informs the CM side of this,
(iii) how the returned RTC value is confirmed.

5.14 With the aid of the timing diagram relating to the cable MAC reservation access mode procedure shown in Figure 5.8, explain how the procedure works. Include in your explanation:
(i) the need for a contention resolution procedure,

(ii)   the use of the DBS and DBE fields in the bandwidth allocation MAP and the meaning of the term "backoff window",

(iii)   an example computation performed by the CM,

(iv)   how a collision is detected by the CM and the actions it takes.

5.15   In Figure 5.9, state the meaning and role of the various header fields.

5.16   With the aid of the fragment header frame format and example shown in Figure 5.10, explain the fragmentation procedure carried out by a CM to transmit a user data frame that requires more minislots than have been granted. Include in your explanation the use of the EH-TYPE, EH-LEN, and EH-VALUE fields in each fragment header.

5.17   State the role of the following additional procedures relating to the cable MAC protocol:

(i)   piggyback requests,

(ii)   request/data regions,

(iii)   QoS support including the use of un-solicited grant, real-time polling, unsolicited grant with activity detection, and non-real-time polling.

5.18   With the aid of the packet formats shown in Figure 5.11, describe the operation of the downstream transmission convergence (DSTC) sublayer. Include in your description the meaning/use of

(i)   the MPEG transport packet format,

(ii)   the use of the payload identifier (PID) and PUSI bit in the packet header,

(iii)   how the DSTC in the CM determines the length of a MAC frame,

(iv)   stuff-bytes.

5.19   With the aid of the two schematic packet flows shown in Figure 5.12, describe the principle of operation of the downstream and upstream transmission convergence sublayers. In relation to the upstream direction,

include the meaning/use of

(i)   a guard-band,

(ii)   a preamble sequence,

(iii)   the forward error control field.

5.20   With the aid of the network topology shown in Figure 5.13, explain the motivation for cable operating companies linking their regional HFC networks together to form an intranet. Describe the principle of operation of a cable intranet.

Section 5.2.3

5.21   State the application domains of a multi-channel (M) and a local (L) multipoint distribution system (MDS). Hence, with the aid of the schematic diagrams shown in Figure 5.14, explain the principle of operation and operating frequencies of both systems.

Section 5.2.4

5.22   As we show in Figure 5.15(a), the physical layer of IEEE802.16 provides three alternative modulation schemes. Explain why this is so.

5.23   With the aid of the diagram shown in Figure 5.15(b), explain the operation of the FDD/TDD transmission scheme. Include the meaning of the terms time slots, frames, sub-frames and guard band.

5.24   Explain the use of the following fields in the 802.16 frame header:

(i) type,

(ii) connection ID.

5.25   Explain how the transmission bandwidth over the cable is managed in:

(i) the downstream direction,

(ii) the upstream direction.

5.26   State and describe the service types supported by the 802.16 MAC sublayer. Give an example application of each service type.

Section 5.3

5.27   With the aid of the network schematic shown in Figure 5.17(a), explain the principle of operation of a geostationary satellite broadcast TV network. Include the meaning of the terms:
(i)   geosynchronous,
(ii)   geostationary earth orbit (GEO).

5.28   In relation to a satellite's position, use the diagrams shown in Figure 5.17(b) to explain the meaning of
(i)   angle of elevation,
(ii)   azimuth.

5.29   With the aid of the frequency bands shown in Figure 5.18 relating to early analog TV transmissions, state:
(i)   the bandwidth of each modulated TV channel,
(ii)   the guard-band between adjacent channels,
(iii) why different frequency bands are used for the uplink and downlink.

5.30   Describe the principle of operation of a satellite dish including the role of the low-noise block/converter (LNB/C). With the aid of Figure 5.19(a), state the difference and advantages of an offset-focus antenna compared with a prime-focus antenna.

5.31   With the aid of the block schematic diagram shown in Figure 5.19(b), state the meaning/use of the following:

(i)   satellite intermediate frequency,
(ii)   transponder subsystem,
(iii) channel filter,
(iv)   frequency converter,
(v)   power amplifier,
(vi)   signal combiner,
(vii) command and telemetry subsystem.

5.32   With the aid of the block schematic diagrams of the (baseband) satellite digital channel interface shown in Figure 5.20, explain the role of:
(i)   the RS coding block,
(ii)   the byte interleaver,
(iii) the convolutional encoder including the meaning of puncturing,
(iv)   QPSK modulation.

5.33   State the following for the downlink of the DBS and DVB-S digital TV transmissions:
(i)   the allocated bandwidth,
(ii)   the number of channels and the bandwidth per channel,
(iii) the symbol rate and raw bit rate of a channel,
(iv)   the useful bit rate per channel,
(v)   typical applications of this.

5.34   Explain briefly the following forms of interactivity with satellite broadcast transmission. State an application in each case:
(i)   local interaction,
(ii)   anonymous response,
(iii) purchase request.

the Internet protocol

6.1 Introduction

As we saw in Chapter 1, the Internet is a global network that supports a variety of interpersonal and interactive multimedia applications. A user gains access to these applications by means of an end system – normally referred to as a host – which, typically, is a multimedia PC or a workstation that is attached to an access network. As we showed in Figure 1.1, the Internet comprises a large number of access networks that are interconnected together by means of a global internetwork. Associated with each access network – ISP network, wireless network, intranet, enterprise network, site/campus LAN, and so on – is an **access gateway** and the global internetwork consists of an interconnected set of regional, national, and international networks all of which are interconnected together using high bit rate lines and devices known as **switching gateways** or simply **routers**.

The Internet operates in a packet-switched mode and Figure 6.1 shows the protocol stack associated with it. In the figure, we assume the network interface card in all hosts that are attached to an access network communicate with other hosts using the TCP/IP protocol stack. In practice, this is not always the case. Nevertheless, any end system (host) that communicates directly over the Internet does so using the TCP/IP protocol stack.

In general, the various access networks have different operational parameters associated with them in terms of their bit rate, frame format, maximum frame size, and type of addresses that are used. For example, in the

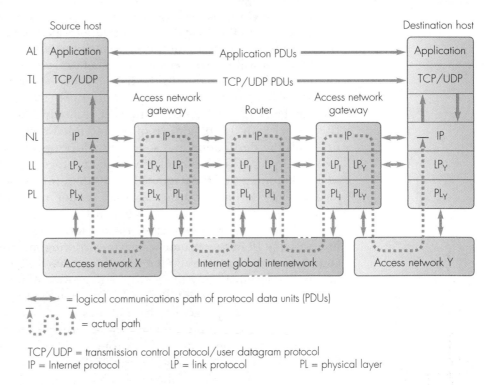

Source host
Destination host

AL Application ←━━━━━ Application PDUs ━━━━━→ Application

TL TCP/UDP ←━━━━━ TCP/UDP PDUs ━━━━━→ TCP/UDP

Access network gateway   Router   Access network gateway

NL IP — IP IP IP — IP

LL LP$_X$ LP$_X$ LP$_I$ LP$_I$ LP$_I$ LP$_I$ LP$_Y$ LP$_Y$

PL PL$_X$ PL$_X$ PL$_I$ PL$_I$ PL$_I$ PL$_I$ PL$_Y$ PL$_Y$

Access network X   Internet global internetwork   Access network Y

←━━→ = logical communications path of protocol data units (PDUs)

⊔ = actual path

TCP/UDP = transmission control protocol/user datagram protocol
IP = Internet protocol   LP = link protocol   PL = physical layer

Figure 6.1 Internet networking components and protocols.

case of a site/campus LAN, as we saw in Chapters 3 and 4, a wireless LAN uses a different bit rate, frame format, and maximum frame size from an Ethernet LAN. This means, therefore, that since bridges can only be used to interconnect LAN segments of the same type, they cannot be used to perform the network interconnection function. Hence instead, the routing and forwarding operations associated with an access gateway and router are performed at the network layer. In the TCP/IP protocol stack the network layer protocol is the **Internet protocol** (**IP**) and, as we show in Figure 6.1, in order to transfer packets of data from one host to another, it is the IP in the two hosts, together with the IP in each access gateway and router involved, that perform the routing and other harmonization functions that are necessary.

The IP in each host (that communicates directly over the Internet) has a unique Internet-wide address assigned to it. This is known as the host's **Internet address** or, more usually, its **IP address**. Each IP address has two parts: a **network number/identifier** (**netid**) and a **host number/identifier** (**hostid**). The allocation of netids is centrally managed by the **Internet Corporation for Assigned Names and Numbers** (**ICANN**) and each access network has a unique netid assigned to it. For example, each campus/site LAN is assigned a single netid. The IP address of a host attached to an access network then contains the unique netid of the access network and a unique hostid. As with netids, hostids are centrally allocated but this time by the local administrator of the access network to which the host is attached.

The IP provides a connectionless best-effort service to the transport layer above it which, as we show in the figure, is either the transmission control protocol (TCP) or the user datagram protocol (UDP). Hence when either protocol has a TCP/UDP PDU to transfer, it simply passes the PDU to its local IP together with the IP address of the intended recipient. The (source) IP first adds the destination and source IP addresses to the head of the PDU, together with an indication of the source protocol (TCP or UDP), to form what is known as an **IP datagram**. The IP then forwards the datagram to its local gateway. At this point the datagram is often referred to as a **packet** and hence the two terms are used interchangeably.

Each access gateway is attached to an internetwork router and, at regular intervals, the IP in these routers exchange routing information. When this is complete, each router has built up a **routing table** which enables it to route a packet/datagram to any of the other networks/netids that make up the Internet. Hence, on receipt of a packet, the router simply reads the destination netid from the packet header and uses the contents of its routing table to forward the packet on the path/route through the global internetwork first to the destination internetwork router and, from there, to the destination access gateway. Assuming the size of the packet is equal to or less than the maximum frame size of the destination access network, on receipt of the packet, the destination gateway reads the hostid part of the destination IP address and forwards the packet to the local host identified by the hostid part. The IP in the host then strips off the header from the packet and passes the block of information contained within it – known as the **payload** – to the peer transport layer protocol indicated in the packet header.

If the size of the packet is greater than the maximum frame size – that is, the **maximum transmission unit** (**MTU**) – of the destination access network, the IP in the destination gateway proceeds to divide the block of data contained in the packet into a number of smaller blocks each known as a **fragment**. Each fragment is then forwarded to the IP in the destination host in a separate packet the length of which is determined by the MTU of the access network. The destination IP then reassembles the fragments of data from each received packet to form the original submitted block of data and passes this to the peer transport layer protocol indicated in the packet header.

As we shall see in the following sections, the above is just a summary of the operation of the IP and, in practice, in order to perform the various functions we have just described, the IP uses a number of what are known as **adjunct protocols**. These are identified in Figure 6.2 and a summary of the role of each protocol is as follows:

- The **address resolution protocol** (**ARP**) and the **reverse ARP** (**RARP**) are used by the IP in hosts that are attached to a broadcast LAN (such as an

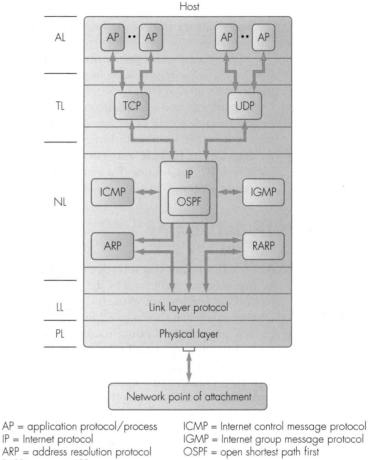

Figure 6.2 IP adjunct protocols.

Ethernet) to determine the physical (MAC) address of a host or gateway given its IP address (ARP) and, in the case of the RARP, the reverse function.

- **The open shortest path first** (**OSPF**) protocol is an example of a routing protocol used in the global internetwork. Such protocols are present in each internetwork router and are utilized to build up the contents of the routing table that is used to route packets across the global internetwork.

- The **Internet control message protocol** (**ICMP**) is used by the IP in a host or gateway to exchange error and other control messages with the IP in another host or gateway.

- The **Internet group management protocol** (**IGMP**) is used with multicasting to enable a host to send a copy of a datagram to the other hosts that are part of the same multicast group.

In this chapter we explain the operation of the different parts of the IP and each of the adjunct protocols in some detail. Also, we describe the structure of the Internet global internetwork in more detail as this influences the overall routing strategy and routing protocols that are used. Currently, the most widely used version of the IP is version 4 and hence most of the chapter is devoted to this. In a longer time span, however, this will be replaced by version 6. Hence we describe the main features of this and how it differs and interoperates with version 4. We shall defer discussion of the two transport layer protocols until the next chapter.

6.2 IP datagrams

As we indicated in the introduction, the IP is a connectionless protocol and all user data is transferred in the payload part of what is known as a datagram or packet. The header of each datagram contains a number of fields, the formats of which are shown in Figure 6.3.

The *version* field contains the version of the IP used to create the datagram and ensures that all systems – gateways, routers, and hosts – that process the datagram/packet during its transfer across the Internet to the destination host interpret the various fields correctly. The current version number is 4 and hence the IP is referred to as **IP version 4** or simply **IPv4**.

The header can be of variable length and the *intermediate header length* (*IHL*) field specifies the actual length of the header in multiples of 32-bit words. The minimum length (without options) is 5. If the datagram contains options, these are in multiples of 32 bits with any unused bytes filled with **padding** bytes. Also, since the IHL field is 4 bits, the maximum permissible length is 15.

The *type of service* (*TOS*) field allows an application protocol/process to specify the relative priority (precedence) of the application data and the preferred attributes associated with the path to be followed. It is used by each gateway and router during the transmission and routing of the packet to transmit packets of higher priority first and to select a line/route that has the specified attributes should a choice be available. For example, if a route with a minimum delay is specified then, given a choice of routes, the line with the smallest delay associated with it should be chosen. We shall discuss the use of the TOS field further in Section 6.7.

The *total length* field defines the total length of the initial datagram including the header and payload parts. This is a 16-bit field and hence the maximum length is 65 535 (64K – 1) bytes and, as we explain in the next section, should the contents of the initial datagram need to be transferred

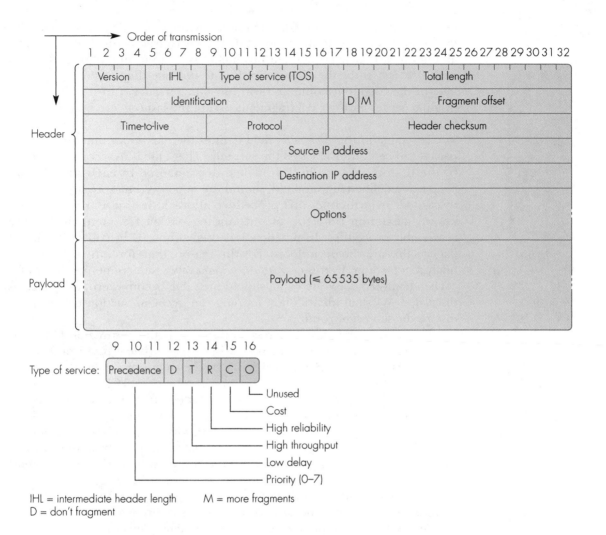

Figure 6.3 IP datagram/packet format and header fields.

in multiple (smaller) packets, then the value in *total length* is used by the destination host to reassemble the payload contained within each smaller packet – known as a fragment – into the original payload. In addition, each smaller packet contains the same value in the *identification* field to enable the destination host to relate each received packet fragment to the same original datagram.

The next three bits are known as *flag bits* of which two are currently used. The first is known as the *don't fragment* or *D-bit*. It is set by a source host and is examined by routers. A set D-bit indicates that the packet should be transferred in its entirety or not at all. The second is known as *more fragments* or *M-bit* and this also is used during the reassembly procedure associated with data transfers involving multiple smaller packets/fragments. It is set to 1 in all but the last packet/fragment in which it is set to 0. In addition, the *fragment offset* is used by the same procedure to indicate the position of the first byte of the fragment contained within a smaller packet in relation to the original packet payload. All fragments except the last one are in multiples of 8 bytes.

The value in the *time-to-live* field defines the maximum time for which a packet can be in transit across the Internet. The value is in seconds and is set by the IP in the source host. It is then decremented by each gateway and router by a defined amount and, should the value become zero, the packet is discarded. In principle, this procedure allows a destination IP to wait a known maximum time for an outstanding packet fragment during the reassembly procedure. In practice, it is used primarily by routers to detect packets that are caught in loops. For this reason, therefore, the value is normally a hop count. In this case, the *hop count* value is decremented by one by each gateway/router visited and, should the value become zero, the packet is discarded. We shall identify how looping can occur in Section 6.6 when we discuss the subject of routing.

The value in the *protocol* field is used to enable the destination IP to pass the payload within each received packet to the same (peer) protocol that sent the data. As we showed in Figure 6.2, this can be an internal network layer protocol such as the ICMP, or a higher-layer protocol such as TCP or UDP.

The *header checksum* applies just to the header part of the datagram and is a safeguard against corrupted packets being routed to incorrect destinations. It is computed by treating each block of 16 bits as an integer and adding them all together using 1s complement arithmetic. As we show in the example in Figure B.2(b) in Appendix B, the checksum is then the complement (inverse) of the 1s complement sum.

The *source address* and *destination address* are the Internet-wide IP addresses of the source and destination host respectively.

Finally, the *options* field is used in selected datagrams to carry additional information relating to:

- *security:* the payload may be encrypted, for example, or be made accessible only to a specified user group. The *security* field then contains fields to enable the destination to decrypt the payload and authenticate the sender;

- *source routing:* if known, the actual path/route to be followed through the Internet may be specified in this field as a list of gateway/router addresses;

- *loose source routing:* this can be used to specify preferred routers in a path;

- *route recording:* this field is used by each gateway/router visited during the passage of a packet through the Internet to record its address. The resulting list of addresses can then be used, for example, in the source routing field of subsequent packets;

■ *stream identification:* this, together with the source and destination addresses in the datagram header, enables each gateway/router along the path followed by the packet to identify the stream/flow to which the packet belongs and, if necessary, give the packet precedence over other packets. Examples include streams containing samples of speech or compressed video;

■ *time-stamp:* if present, this is used by each gateway/router along the path followed by the packet to record the time it processed the packet.

6.3 Fragmentation and reassembly

As we explained in Section 6.1, if the size of a packet is greater than the MTU of the destination access network – or an intermediate network in the global internetwork – the IP in the destination gateway – or intermediate router – divides the data received in the packet into a number of smaller blocks known as fragments. Each fragment is then forwarded to the IP in the destination host in a separate packet the length of which is determined by the MTU of the access/intermediate network. The IP in the destination host then reassembles the fragments of data from each received packet to form the original submitted block of data. It then passes this to the peer transport layer protocol indicated in the protocol field of the packet header.

To see how the various fields in each packet header are used to perform this function, consider the transport protocol in a host that is attached to a legacy LAN – such as a token ring – transferring a block of 7000 bytes – including the transport protocol header – over the Internet to the transport protocol in a host that is attached to an Ethernet LAN. Let us assume that the MTU associated with the token ring LAN is 4000 bytes and that of the Ethernet LAN 1500 bytes, and also that the header of each IP datagram requires 20 bytes. The steps taken to transfer the complete block of 7000 bytes are shown in Figure 6.4(a).

Since the header of each datagram requires 20 bytes, the maximum usable data in each token ring frame is 4000 − 20 = 3980 bytes. Similarly, that in each Ethernet frame is 1500 − 20 = 1480 bytes. However, all fragments of user data (except the last one) must be in multiples of 8 bytes. So we shall have to limit the maximum user data in each packet transferred over the token ring to 3976 bytes. In the case of the Ethernet, 1480 is divisible by 8 and so this value can be used unchanged.

To transfer the block of 7000 bytes over the token ring LAN requires two datagrams, one with 3976 bytes of user data and the second 7000 − 3976 = 3024 bytes. The values for the various fields associated with the fragmentation and reassembly procedures in each datagram header are given in Figure 6.4(b).

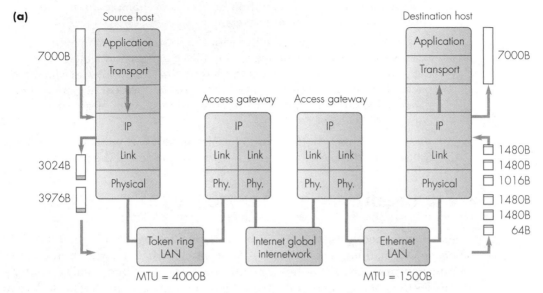

Note: All values shown are the amounts of user data in each packet/frame in bytes

(b) *Token ring LAN:*

	(i)	(ii)
Identification	20	20
Total length	7000	7000
Fragment offset	0	497
(User data)	3976	3024
M-bit	1	0

(c) *Ethernet LAN:*

	(i)	(ii)	(ili)	(iv)	(v)	(vi)
Identification	20	20	20	20	20	20
Total length	7000	7000	7000	7000	7000	7000
Fragment offset	0	185	370	497	682	867
(User data)	1480	1480	1016	1480	1480	64
M-bit	1	1	1	1	1	0

Figure 6.4 Fragmentation and reassembly example: (a) Internet schematic; (b) packet header fields for token ring LAN; (c) Ethernet LAN.

The value in the *identification* field is the same in all fragments and is used by the destination IP to relate each fragment to the same original block of information. In the example, we assume a value of 20 has been allocated by the IP in the source host.

The *total length* is the number of bytes in the initial datagram including the 20-byte header. However, since we have subtracted 20 from the maximum user data value associated with each LAN, we have shown this as 7000. Note that this is the same in all the datagram fragments and hence the destination IP can readily determine when all fragments have been received. The *fragment offset* then indicates the position of the user data in each fragment – in multiples of 8 bytes – relative to the start of the initial datagram. Finally, the *more fragments* (*M*) *bit* is 1 in each fragment and 0 in the final fragment.

We assume that the two datagrams/packets created by the source IP are transferred over the global internetwork unchanged and, on reaching the access gateway attached to the Ethernet LAN, the smaller maximum user data value of 1480 bytes means that both packets must be further fragmented. As we show in Figure 6.4(c), both packets must be fragmented into three smaller packets, the first into two maximum sized packets of 1480 bytes and a further packet containing $3976 - 2(1480) = 1016$ bytes, and the second containing two maximum sized packets and a further packet containing $3024 - 2(1480) = 64$ bytes. The IP in the destination host then reassembles the user data in each of the six packets it receives into the original 7000-byte block of information and delivers this to the peer transport protocol.

As we explained, the *time-to-live* field in each packet header – and fragment header – is present to avoid packets endlessly looping around the Internet (normally as a result of routing table inconsistencies) and also to set a maximum limit on the time a host needs to wait for a delayed/corrupted/ discarded datagram fragment. Hence although the use of fragmentation would appear to be relatively straightforward, there are drawbacks associated with its use. For example, as we shall explain in Section 7.3.2, with the TCP transport protocol, if an acknowledgment of correct receipt of a submitted block is not received within a defined maximum time limit, the source TCP will retransmit the complete block. Thus, as we can deduce from the example in Figure 6.4, it only needs one of the six datagram fragments to be delayed or discarded to trigger the retransmission of the complete 7000-byte block. As a result, therefore, most TCP implementations avoid the possibility of fragmentation occurring by limiting the maximum submitted block size – including transport protocol header – to 1048 bytes or, in some instances, 556 bytes. Alternatively, as we shall expand upon in Section 6.7, it is possible for the source IP, prior to sending any transport protocol (user) data, to determine the MTU of the path to be followed through the Internet. Then, if this is smaller than the submitted user data, the source IP fragments the data using this MTU. In this way, no further fragmentation should be necessary during the transfer of the packets through the global internetwork.

6.4 IP addresses

Each host, gateway and router has a unique Internet-wide IP address assigned to it that comprises a netid and hostid part. In the case of a host/computer, the netid identifies the network to which it is attached and the hostid then identifies the host on this network. In the case of an access gateway and router, however, each network interface of the gateway/router has a different netid assigned to it.

Over the lifetime of the Internet five different schemes have been used for assigning IP addresses. In general, as the number of Internet users has expanded, the aim of each scheme has been to utilize the 32-bit address space in a more efficient way. A brief summary of each scheme is helpful in order to follow their development.

- **Class-based addresses**: this was the first scheme that was used to assign addresses in the early Internet. It involved dividing the overall address space into five address classes: A, B, C, D and E. Each of the first three address classes – A, B and C – then has a defined boundary between the netid and hostid part of the address space. As we shall see, Class D is used for multicasting and class E is reserved.

- **Subnetting**: this was the first approach to utilizing the address space in a more efficient way. In the case of a large campus or company, for example, in the past it was not uncommon to have a number of different types of LAN at the same site, each of which had a different frame format and, more importantly, maximum frame length. Some examples of legacy LANs are token ring, token bus, FDDI and others. As a result, since MAC bridges do not support fragmentation, they can only be used to interconnect LANs of the same type. Hence IP routers were often used instead. As we saw earlier, with a router each LAN has to have its own netid so increasing the number of IP addresses required at each site. To overcome this, subnetting was introduced and, as we shall see, with subnetting only a single IP address is required at each site.

- **Classless addresses**: this is a more recent development and involves exploiting the full address space in a more efficient way than the use of class-based addresses. With this type of addressing, the network part of an IP address can be any number bits rather than being constrained to the fixed class boundaries and, as a result, this leads to a more efficient use of the total address space.

- **Network address translation**: this is the most recent development. The aim of the NAT scheme is for each access network to be allocated just a single IP address and this is then used by all the hosts when communicating outside of their local access network. For communications within the access network, however, every host is assigned its own (private) address.

- **IPv6**: this is a completely new version of IP – the current version is IPv4 – and was developed to overcome the limited address space – and other limitations – of IPv4. Hence it is the ideal solution. In practice, however, at this point in time, IPv4 is still the dominant protocol in the current Internet and the use of IPv6 is being introduced in an incremental way.

In the following subsections, we shall study the first four schemes in more detail. In the case of IPv6, however, we shall study this in a separate section since it is clearly the scheme of the future.

6.4.1 Class-based addresses

In order to have some flexibility when assigning netids, the original class-based addressing scheme – also known as **classful addressing** – was to divide the 32-bit address space into five different address formats. Each format is called an **address class** and, as we show in Figure 6.5, classes A, B and C are used for unicast; that is, for communications between a pair of host interfaces.

Each of these classes is intended for use with a different size of network, for example, at one extreme a large national network and at the other a small site LAN. The class to which an address belongs can be determined from the position of the first zero bit in the first four bits. The remaining bits then specify the netid and hostid parts with the boundary separating the two parts located on byte boundaries to simplify decoding.

Class A addresses have 7 bits for the netid and 24 bits for the hostid; class B addresses have 14 bits for the netid and 16 bits for the hostid; and class C addresses have 21 bits for the netid and 8 bits for the hostid. Class A addresses are intended for use with networks that have a large number of attached hosts (up to 2^{24}) while class C addresses allow for a large number of networks each with a small number of attached hosts (up to 256). An example of a class A network is a large national network and an example of a class C network is a small site LAN.

Netids and hostids comprising either all 0s or all 1s have special meaning:

■ An address with a hostid of all 0s is used to refer to the network in the netid part rather than a host.

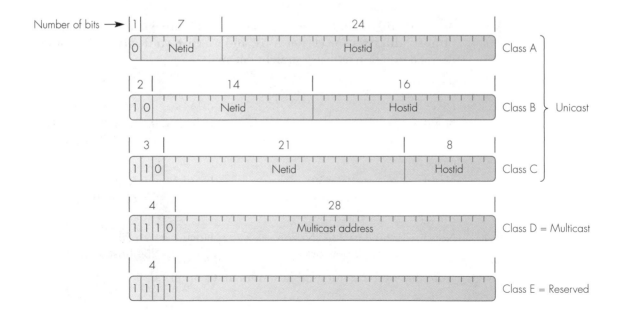

Figure 6.5 IP address formats.

■ An address with a netid of all 0s implies the same network as the source network/netid.

■ An address of all 1s means broadcast the packet over the source network.

■ An address with a hostid of all 1s means broadcast the packet over the destination network in the netid part.

■ A class A address with a netid of all 1s is used for test purposes within the protocol stack of the source host. It is known, therefore, as the **loopback address.**

To make it easier to communicate IP addresses, the 32 bits are first broken into four bytes. Each byte is then converted into its equivalent decimal form and the total IP address is represented as the four decimal numbers with a dot (period) between each. This is known as the **dotted decimal notation** and some examples are as follows:

00001010 00000000 00000000 00000000 = 10.0.0.0.
= class A, netid 10

10000000 00000011 00000010 00000011 = 128.3.2.3
= class B, netid 128.3, hostid 2.3

11000000 00000000 00000001 11111111 = 192.0.1.255
= class C, all hosts broadcast on
netid 192.0.1

Example 6.1

Assuming the IP address formats shown in Figure 6.5, derive the range of host addresses for classes A, B, and C. Give your answer in dotted decimal notation and also straight decimal.

Answer:

Class A:
Netid = 1 to 127   Hostid = 0.0.0 to 255.255.255
   = 126 networks   = 16 777 214 hosts

Class B:
Netid = 128.0 to 191.255   Hostid = 0.0 to 255.255
   = 16 382 networks   = 65 534 hosts

Class C:
Netid = 192.0.0 to 223.255.255   Hostid = 0 to 255
   = 2 097 152 networks   = 254 hosts

Note that we have not used hostids of all 0s or all 1s.

Class D addresses are reserved for multicasting. As we explained in Section 3.2, in a LAN a frame can be sent to an individual, broadcast, or group address. The group address is used by a station to send a copy of the frame to all stations that are members of the same multicast group (and hence have the same multicast address). In the case of LANs, the group address is a MAC address and the class D IP address format is provided to enable this mode of working to be extended over the complete Internet.

As we can see, unlike the three unicast address classes, the 28-bit multicast group address has no further structure. As we shall expand upon in Section 6.6.9, multicast group addresses are assigned by ICANN. Although most of these are assigned dynamically (for conferences and so on), some are reserved to identify specific groups of hosts and/or routers. These are known as **permanent multicast group addresses**. Examples are 224.0.0.1, which means all hosts (and routers) on the same broadcast network, and 224.0.0.2, which means all routers on the same site network.

6.4.2 Subnetting

As we described in Section 3.3.2, MAC bridges are used to interconnect LAN segments of the same type. This solution is attractive for routing purposes since the combined LAN then behaves like a single network. When interconnecting dissimilar LAN types, as we explained earlier, the differences in frame format and, more importantly, frame length mean that routers are normally used since the fragmentation and reassembly of packets/frames is a function of the network layer rather than the MAC sublayer. However, the use of routers means that, with the basic address formats, each LAN must have its own netid. In the case of large sites, there may be a significant number of such LANs.

This means that with the basic class-based addressing scheme, all the routers relating to a site need to take part in the overall Internet routing function. As we shall expand upon in Section 6.5, the efficiency of any routing scheme is strongly influenced by the number of routing nodes that make up the Internet. The concept of **subnets** has been introduced to decouple the routers – and hence routing – associated with a single site from the overall routing function in the global internetwork. Essentially, instead of each LAN associated with a site having its own netid, only the site is allocated a netid. Each LAN is then known as a **subnet** and the identity of each (LAN) subnet then forms part of the hostid field. This refined address format is shown in Figure 6.6(a). It is defined in RFC 950.

The same address classes and associated structure are used, but the netid now relates to a complete site rather than to a single subnet. Hence, since only a single gateway/router attached to a site performs Internet-wide routing, the netid is considered as the **Internet part.** For a single netid with a number of associated subnets, the hostid part consists of two subfields: a **subnetid part** and a **local hostid part**. Because these have only local significance,

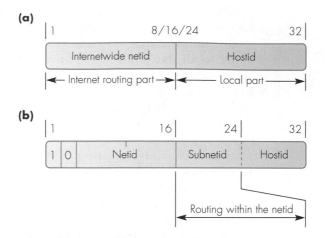

Figure 6.6 Subnet addressing: (a) address structure; (b) example.

they are known collectively as the **local part**. Also, to discriminate between the routers in the global internetwork and those in a local site network, the latter are known as **subnet routers.**

Because of the possibly wide range of subnets associated with different site networks, no attempt has been made to define rigid subaddress boundaries for the local address part. Instead, an **address mask** is used to define the subaddress boundary for a particular network (and hence netid). The address mask is kept by the site gateway and all the subnet routers at the site. It consists of binary 1s in those bit positions that contain a network address – including the netid and subnetid – and binary 0s in positions that contain the hostid. Hence an address mask of

$$11111111 \ 11111111 \ 11111111 \ 00000000$$

means that the first three bytes (octets) contain a network/subnet identifier and the fourth byte contains the host identifier.

For example, if the mask relates to a class B address – a zero bit in the second bit position – this is readily interpreted as: the first two bytes are the Internet-wide netid, the next byte the subnetid, and the last byte the hostid on the subnet. Such an address is shown in Figure 6.6(b).

Normally, dotted decimal is used to define address masks and hence the above mask is written:

$$255.255.255.0$$

Byte boundaries are normally chosen to simplify address decoding. So with this mask, and assuming the netid was, say, 128.10, then all the hosts attached to this network would have this same netid. In this way, the presence of a possibly large number of subnets and associated (subnet) routers is transparent to all the other Internet gateways and routers for routing purposes.

Example 6.2

The administrator of a campus LAN is assigned a single class B IP address of 150.10.0.0. Assuming that the LAN comprises 100 subnets, each of which is connected to a Fast Ethernet switch using a subnet router, define a suitable address mask for the site if the maximum number of hosts connected to each subnet is 70.

Answer:

A class B IP address means that both the netid part and the local part are each 16 bits. Hence the simplest way of meeting this requirement is to divide the local part into two: 8 bits for the subnetid and 8 bits for the hostid.

This will allow for up to 254 subnets and 254 hosts per subnet ignoring all 1s and all 0s.

The address mask, therefore, is 255.255.255

6.4.3 Classless addresses

This scheme was introduced in the mid-1990s and is defined in RFC 1519. With classless addresses, the network part of an IP address can be any number of bits rather than being constrained to the fixed class boundaries. A classless address is represented in dotted decimal form as w.x.y.z / n where n indicates the number of bits in the network part of the address.

For example, if an organization requests a network address with a block of, say, 1000 host addresses, then this could be allocated a block of 1024 addresses. The dotted decimal representation of this would then be w.x.y.z / 22, which indicates that the leading 22 bits of the address w.x.y.z represent the netid and the last 10 bits the hostid. Note that subnetting can still be used on the hostid part of the address. In addition, although this scheme leads to a more efficient use of the address space, the routing of packets is more complicated. The routing method is called **classless inter-domain routing** (**CIDR**) and is defined in RFC 1519.

The approach adopted with CIDR is similar to that we described in the previous section relating to subnetting. As we saw, with subnetting the hostid field is itself divided into a subnetid part and a hostid part with no fixed boundary between them; instead, the division point is indicated by an address mask. In a similar way, as we show in Example 6.3, an address mask is used to indicate the boundary between the netid and hostid parts of the complete IP address.

Example 6.3

A network within a large network has been allocated a block of 1024 addresses from 200.30.0.0 through to 200.30.3.255. Assuming the CIDR addressing scheme, represent these addresses in binary form and hence derive the address mask to be used in dotted decimal form and the netid of this network.

Answer:

Address 200.30.0.0   = 11001000 00011110 00000000 00000000

Address 200.30.3.255 = 11001000 00011110 00000011 11111111

Hence address mask   = 11111111 11111111 11111100 00000000

                     = 255 . 255 . 252 . 0

and netid = 200.30.0.0

Each router within a large network then contains a copy of the address mask of each of the networks that make up the larger network together with the base address – netid – of the corresponding network. In this way, a router, on receiving a packet, reads the destination IP address from the packet header and then performs a logical AND operation on this and each of the address masks that it is holding. On detecting a match – that is, the resulting netid is the same as that stored with the corresponding mask – the router uses the netid and the related routing protocol to route the packet to the next router along the path to the destination network.

As we can deduce from this, each router must also contain a copy of the address masks of all the networks that make up the larger network. Also, each access gateway has a copy of its own address mask and, by using this, it first extracts the netid from the destination IP address and then uses it to route the packet to that host.

Finally, as we can see in Example 6.4, it is possible for a number of hosts associated with a network that has been allocated a large block of addresses to produce a match with a mask relating to a network with a smaller block of addresses. However, since all masks are tested for a match, this will be in addition to the match relating to the mask with the smaller block of addresses. When this happens, then the mask with the smaller block of addresses – and hence larger number of 1s in its address mask – is chosen as the most probable match.

Example 6.4

Two networks within a larger network have been allocated the following block of addresses:

Network 1: Addresses = 200.64.16.0 through to 200.64.31.255
Mask = 255.192.16.0

Network 2: Addresses = 200.64.17.0 through to 200.64.17.255
Mask = 255.255.255.0

Assuming the CIDR addressing scheme, determine the address of a host attached to network 1 that will produce a match with the mask of network 2.

Answer:

Network 1   Netid = 11001000 01000000 0001/xxxx xxxxxxxx

Network 2   Netid = 11001000 01000000 00010001/ xxxxxxxx

Hence

Network 1   Hostid = 11001000 01000000 0001/0001 xxxxxxxx

6.4.4 Network address translation

In the case of a local ISP with a large number of subscribers using low bit rate modems that are located in homes and in small businesses, normally the ISP is allocated a block of IP addresses that is significantly less than the number of subscribers it serves. Hence to overcome this, each IP address is allocated on-demand for the duration of a session and, on completion, it is then reused. In this way only a relatively small number of IP addresses are required. However, with the arrival of broadband modems, since these are permanently on, a dedicated IP address is required for each subscriber, or worse, for each member of a household/business. The same is true for each campus, company and wireless LAN.

The aim of the network address translation (NAT) scheme is for each access network to be allocated just a single IP address or, for a large site, a small number of addresses. The allocated address is then used by all the hosts for communicating outside their local access network. For communications within the access network, however, every host (interface) is allocated its own (private) IP address. NAT is defined in RFC 3022.

To implement the NAT scheme, three blocks of IP addresses have been declared as private; that is, a household/company, etc., can allocate them to PCs/servers within their own network as they like but they must not be used outside the network and hence within the Internet. The three blocks of addresses are shown in Figure 6.7(a).

(a)

$$10.0.0.0 - \quad 10.255.255.255/8 = 16{,}777{,}216 \;\text{Host interfaces}$$
$$172.16.0.0 - \quad 172.31.255.255/12 = \quad 1{,}048{,}576$$
$$192.168.0.0 - 192.168.255.255/16 = \qquad 65{,}536$$

(b)

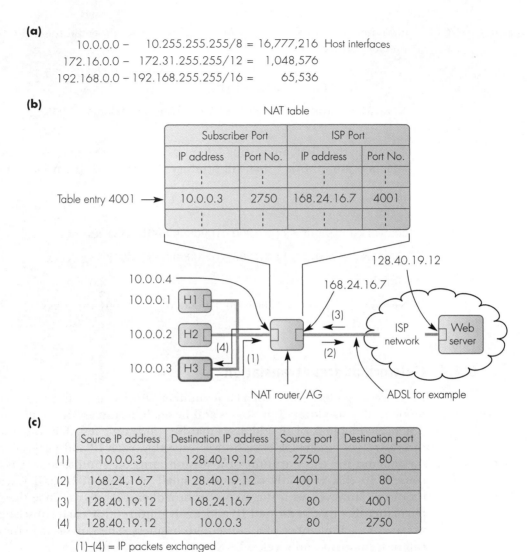

Source IP address	Destination IP address	Source port	Destination port
(1)	10.0.0.3	128.40.19.12	2750	80
(2)	168.24.16.7	128.40.19.12	4001	80
(3)	128.40.19.12	168.24.16.7	80	4001
(4)	128.40.19.12	10.0.0.3	80	2750

(1)–(4) = IP packets exchanged

Figure 6.7 Network address translation: (a) blocks of private addresses; (b) NAT operation schematic; (c) IP/TCP header fields.

To explain how the scheme operates, consider the simple home/small business network shown in Figure 6.7(b). Typically, the three host devices are PCs and each wants to use the services of the Internet such as Web access. As we can see in the figure, the three hosts have been allocated a private IP address of 10.0.0.1/2/3 respectively. As we saw earlier in Section 1.5.2, when an Internet application – a Web browser for example – wants to communicate with, say, a remote Web server, the application uses the services of the TCP layer. As we will expand upon in the next chapter, within the header of each TCP protocol data unit (PDU) is a *source port number* that identifies the application making the request and a *destination port number* that identifies the correspondent application in the remote computer. For a Web server, for example, this is one of the reserved – also called well-known – port numbers and is 80. We assume also that the source port number selected by the PC is 2750 and that the IP address of the Web server on the Internet is 168.24.16.7. We shall explain how an IP address is obtained from a domain name later in Chapter 8 when we study Internet applications in more detail.

Associated with the site NAT router/access gateway is a **NAT table** and, as we can see in the figure, for each session this contains two entries. On the subscriber port side the entry comprises the private IP address of the host interface and the allocated source port number. On the ISP port side the entry is composed of the Internet IP address of the site and a new TCP source port number allocated by the NAT router. This is done to avoid the possibility of the same TCP source port number being selected by a different host. The sequence of datagrams/packets that are exchanged is shown in the figure together with the contents of the source and destination IP addresses and TCP port numbers in the respective header fields in part (c).

First host H3 creates an IP datagram and sends it to the NAT router (1). On receipt of this, the NAT router reads the source IP address and source port number from the datagram – 10.0.0.3 and 2750 respectively. The NAT router then proceeds to replace these two fields with the site IP address and the new source port number. It then makes two entries in the NAT table using the new source port number – 4001 in the example - as an index to the NAT table. Next, since the IP and TCP checksums in the respective headers are now invalid, these are recomputed and their respective fields updated. The IP datagram is then forwarded to the ISP access network (2).

As we show in part (c), when the response from the Web server is created, the two pairs of address fields in the header are simply exchanged. Hence, when the response datagram from the Web server is received (3), the NAT router reads the source port number from the datagram and uses this as an index to the NAT table. It then proceeds to read the original IP address and source port number from the table entry and writes these into the corresponding fields in the packet header. The IP and TCP checksums are then updated as before and the datagram is then relayed out to the interface of host 3.

In conclusion, before leaving this subsection it should be said that NAT is viewed as a temporary fix to avoid running out of IPv4 addresses and that the introduction of IPv6 will accelerate as the new set of IP addresses created by NAT are used up.

6.5 Routing algorithms

All routing within the total global internetwork is carried out by the IP in each router using the netid part of the destination IP address in each datagram header. In practice, as we shall see in the following subsections, there are only a small number of different routing algorithms used and, in order to explain their principle of operation, we shall use the simple internetwork topology shown in Figure 6.8.

As we can see, each of the routers in the interconnection network has a number of access networks attached to it by means of (access) gateways. We assume that each access network is a local ISP or a site/campus LAN with a single netid.

The interconnection network itself comprises four routers (R1–R4) that are interconnected by, say, leased lines. For description purposes, each line has a pair of numbers associated with it. The first we shall use as a line identifier and the second is what is referred to as the **cost** of the line. For example, the cost could be based on the line bit rate and, normally, the higher the line bit rate the lower the cost value. As we shall see, the cost value associated with each line is used during the routing of datagrams/packets and hence is also known as a **routing metric**. The cost of a route/path through the interconnection network is determined by summing together

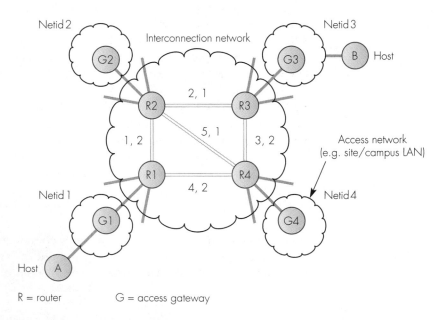

Figure 6.8 Example internetwork topology.

the cost value associated with each line that makes up the path. This is known as the **path cost** and, when different paths between two routers are available, the path with the least path cost value is known as the **shortest path**. Other metrics used in relation to the computation of the shortest paths are based on the physical length – and hence propagation delay – of each line, the number of lines (**hops**) in the route (**hop count**), and the mean queuing delay within each router associated with a line.

Let us assume that host A on netid 1 wants to send a datagram to host B on netid 3. On determining that the destination netid in the datagram header is for a different netid from its own, gateway G1 forwards the datagram to router R1 over the connecting line/link. On receipt of the datagram, R1 proceeds to forward it first to R3 over the interconnection network and then to G3. At this point, the IP in G3 knows how to route the datagram to host B using the hostid part of the destination IP address and the related MAC address of B. What we do not know is how the datagram is routed across the interconnection network.

There are three unanswered questions involved:

(1) How does R1 know from the netid contained within the destination IP address that the destination router is R3?
(2) How does R1 know the shortest path route to be followed through the interconnection network to R3?
(3) How does R3 know how to relay the datagram to G3 instead of one of the other gateways that is attached to it?

In relation to the last point, we can accept that a simple protocol can be used to enable each gateway to inform the router to which it is attached of the netid of the access network. The first two points, however, are both parts of the routing algorithm associated with the interconnection network. There are a number of different algorithms that can be used and we shall describe a selection of them in the following subsections. Note that when discussing routing algorithms, the more general term "packet" is used.

6.5.1 Static routing

With this type of routing, the outgoing line to be used to reach all netids is loaded into the routing table of each router when it is first brought into service. As an example, we show the routing table for each of the four routers in the example internet in Figure 6.9. To avoid unnecessary repetition, we assume only one gateway/netid is attached to each router.

To route a packet from a host attached to, say, netid 1 to another that is attached to netid 3, on receipt of the packet, R1 consults its routing table and determines it should forward the packet on line 1. Similarly, on receipt of the packet, R2 determines it should be forwarded on line 2. Finally, R3 forwards the packet to G3 and from there it is forwarded by G3 to the host specified in the hostid part of the IP address.

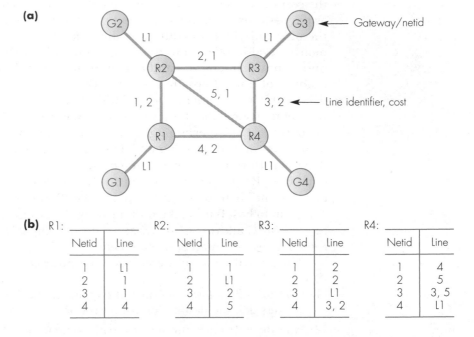

Figure 6.9 Static routing: (a) internet topology; (b) routing table entries.

As we show in the routing tables for routers R3 and R4, two alternative lines are given for routing packets between these two routers. As we can deduce from the cost values, both routes have the same path cost of 2, one using only line 3 and the other going via R2 and lines 2 and 5. Clearly, however, if a second routing metric of, say, distance was used, then the second path would be longer and hence only a single path would be present. For this reason, more than one metric is sometimes used and the choice of path is then based on the information contained within the related set of routing tables.

We can also make a second observation from this set of routing tables; that is, to go from R1 to R3, the shortest path is via R2 using lines 1 and 2. Also, when we look at the routing table for R2, the shortest path from R2 to R3 is also line 2. More generally, if the shortest path between two routers, A and C, is via an intermediate router B, then the shortest path from B to C is along the same path. This is known as the **optimality principle** and it follows from this that each router along the shortest path need only know the identity of its immediate neighbor along the path. The routing operation is known, therefore, as **next-hop routing** or **hop-by-hop routing**.

The disadvantage of static routing is that all the routing table entries may need to be changed whenever a line is upgraded or a new line is added. Also, should a line or router develop a fault, when the fault is reported, the routing tables in all affected routers need to be changed. For these reasons, static routing is inappropriate for a large, continuously changing network like the Internet.

6.5.2 Flooding

To explain the operation of the flooding algorithm, we return to Figure 6.8 and again assume we are sending a datagram from host A to host B. The steps followed are summarized in Figure 6.10.

On receipt of the packet from G1, R1 sends a copy of it over both lines 1 and 4. Similarly, on receipt of their copy of the packet, routers R2 and R4 determine from the netid within it that the packet is not for one of their own networks and hence proceed to forward a copy of the packet onto lines 2 and 5 (R2) and lines 5 and 3 (R4). However, since line 2 has a higher bit rate – lower cost value – than line 3, the copy of the packet from R2 will arrive at R3 first and, on determining that it is addressed to one of its own netids, R3 forwards the packet to G3. Additional copies of the packet will then be received

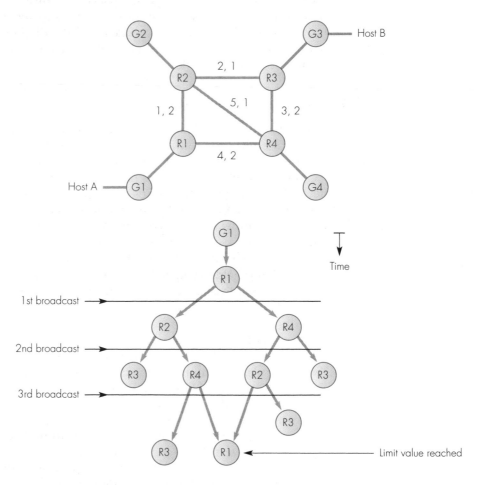

Figure 6.10 Flooding example.

by R3 but, remembering that each copy will have the same value in the *identifier* field, these can be detected as duplicates and discarded by R3.

In order to limit the number of copies of the packet that are produced, a limit is set on the number of times each copy of the packet is forwarded. In the example, it is assumed that a limit value of 3 has been placed in the *time-to-live* field of the packet header by R1. Prior to forwarding copies of the packet, the limit value is decremented by 1 by the recipient router and only if this is above zero are further copies forwarded.

As we can deduce from the figure, the flooding algorithm ensures that the first copy of the packet flows along the shortest path and hence is received in the shortest time. Also, should a line or router fail, providing an alternative path is available, a copy of each packet should always be received. Flooding, therefore, is an example of an **adaptive** – also known as **dynamic** – routing algorithm. Nevertheless, as we can see from this simple example, even with a limit of three hops, the packet is transmitted 10 times. This compares with just two transmissions using the shortest path. Hence the very heavy bandwidth overheads associated with flooding mean that it is used primarily during the initialization phase that enables each router to determine the topology of a network.

6.5.3 Distance vector routing

The distance vector algorithm is a distributed algorithm that enables each router to build up a routing table (the vector) that contains the path cost (the distance) to reach all the netids in the internetwork.

Initially, each router knows only the identity of, firstly, the netids of the networks that are attached to it – through gateways – and their related local line numbers, and secondly, the identity of the lines – and their cost – that form direct links to other routers. Normally, this information is entered either by network management or by the exchange of configuration messages with the other routers when each router is first brought into service. The information is held in a table known as a *connectivity* or *adjacency* table and the contents of the four tables for our example internetwork, together with the contents of the initial routing table for each router, are shown in Figure 6.11(a).

In order for each router to build up its complete routing table – containing the minimum distance (shortest path) to reach all netids – at predefined time intervals, each router first adds the known cost of the lines that connect the router to its neighbors to the current distance values in its own routing table and forwards a copy of the related updated table to each of its neighbors. Then, based on the information received, if a reported distance is less than a current entry, each router proceeds to update its own routing table with the reported distance. The same procedure then repeats with the updated table contents. This procedure repeats for a defined number of iterations, after which each router has determined the path with the minimum distance to be followed to reach all netids.

(a)

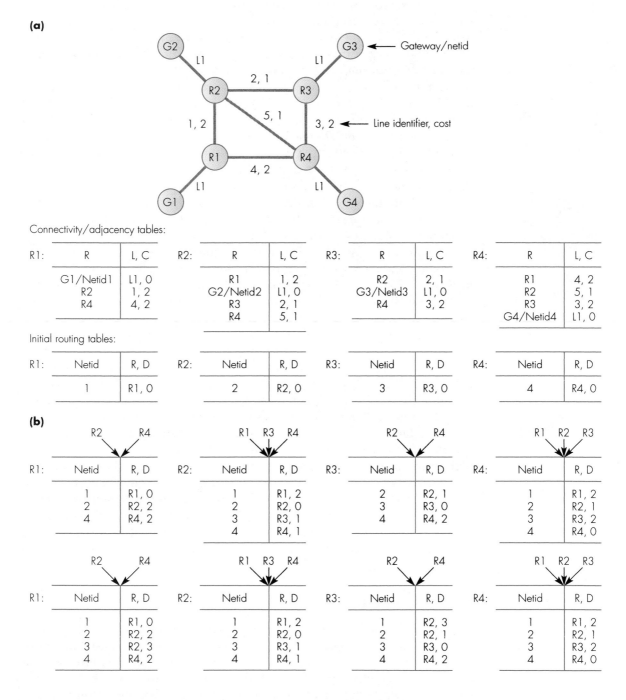

Connectivity/adjacency tables:

R1:	R	L, C
	G1/Netid1	L1, 0
	R2	1, 2
	R4	4, 2

R2:	R	L, C
	R1	1, 2
	G2/Netid2	L1, 0
	R3	2, 1
	R4	5, 1

R3:	R	L, C
	R2	2, 1
	G3/Netid3	L1, 0
	R4	3, 2

R4:	R	L, C
	R1	4, 2
	R2	5, 1
	R3	3, 2
	G4/Netid4	L1, 0

Initial routing tables:

R1:	Netid	R, D
	1	R1, 0

R2:	Netid	R, D
	2	R2, 0

R3:	Netid	R, D
	3	R3, 0

R4:	Netid	R, D
	4	R4, 0

(b)

R2   R4

R1:	Netid	R, D
	1	R1, 0
	2	R2, 2
	4	R4, 2

R1 R3 R4

R2:	Netid	R, D
	1	R1, 2
	2	R2, 0
	3	R3, 1
	4	R4, 1

R2   R4

R3:	Netid	R, D
	2	R2, 1
	3	R3, 0
	4	R4, 2

R1 R2 R3

R4:	Netid	R, D
	1	R1, 2
	2	R2, 1
	3	R3, 2
	4	R4, 0

R2   R4

R1:	Netid	R, D
	1	R1, 0
	2	R2, 2
	3	R2, 3
	4	R4, 2

R1 R3 R4

R2:	Netid	R, D
	1	R1, 2
	2	R2, 0
	3	R3, 1
	4	R4, 1

R2   R4

R3:	Netid	R, D
	1	R2, 3
	2	R2, 1
	3	R3, 0
	4	R4, 2

R1 R2 R3

R4:	Netid	R, D
	1	R1, 2
	2	R2, 1
	3	R3, 2
	4	R4, 0

Figure 6.11 Distance vector algorithm: (a) internet topology and initial tables; (b) derivation of final routing tables.

As an example, the build-up of the final routing table for each of the four routers in our example internetwork is shown in Figure 6.11(b). To avoid repetition, we assume that only a single gateway/netid is attached to each router and, as we can see, for this simple internet the contents of each routing table are complete after just two routing table updates.

In the case of R1, this receives the updated contents of the routing tables held by R2 and R4. Hence after R1 receives the first set of updated tables from them, it determines that the shortest path to reach netid 2 has a distance of 2 via R2 and, to reach netid 4, the distance is 2 via R4. At the same time, R2 and R4 have themselves received update information from their own neighbors and, as a result, on receipt of the second set of updated tables from them, R1 determines that the shortest path to reach netid 3 has a distance of 3 via R2. Note that with the distance vector algorithm an entry is updated only if a new distance value is less than the current value, and that routes with equal path cost values are discarded.

The final routing table of each router contains the next-hop router and the corresponding distance (path cost) value to reach all of the netids in the internetwork. Hence to route a packet, the netid is first obtained from the destination IP address in the packet header and the identity of the next-hop router read from the routing table. The corresponding line number on which the packet is forwarded is then obtained from the connectivity table.

To ensure that each table entry reflects the current active topology of the internet, each entry has an associated timer and, if an entry is not confirmed within a defined time, then it is timed-out. This means that each router transmits the contents of its complete routing table at regular intervals which, typically, is every 30 seconds. Again, for a small internet this is not a problem but for a large internet like the Internet, the bandwidth and processing overheads associated with the distance vector algorithm can become very high. Also, since entries are updated in the order in which they are received and paths of equal distance/cost are discarded, routers may have dissimilar routes to the same destination. As a result, packets addressed to certain destinations may loop rather than going directly to the desired router/gateway. Nevertheless, the **routing information protocol (RIP)** which uses the distance vector routing algorithm is still widely used in many of the individual networks that make up the Internet.

6.5.4 Link-state shortest-path-first routing

As the name implies, this type of routing is based on two algorithms: link-state (LS) and shortest-path-first (SPF). The link-state algorithm is used to enable each router to determine the current (active) topology of the internet and the cost associated with each line/link. Then, once the topology is known, each router runs (independently) the shortest-path-first algorithm to determine the shortest path from itself to all the other routers in the internet.

Link-state algorithm

As with the distance vector algorithm, initially, each router knows only its own connectivity/adjacency information and, as an example, the table entries for our example internet are repeated in Figure 6.12(a). The link-state algorithm is then run and the build-up of the internet topology by R1 is shown in Figure 6.12(b).

Initially, based on the information R1 has in its own connectivity table, the (incomplete) topology is as shown in (i). At regular intervals, each router broadcasts a **link-state message**, containing the router's identity and its associated connectivity information, to each of its immediate neighbors. Hence in the example, we assume that R2 is the first to send its own connectivity information to R1 and this enables R1 to expand its knowledge of the topology to that shown in (ii). This is followed by the connectivity information of R4, which enables R1 to expand its knowledge of the topology to that shown in (iii). Concurrently with this happening, the same procedure will have been carried out by all of the other routers. Hence in our example internet, R2 and R4, will have received the connectivity information of R3. After this has been received, therefore, R2 and R4 relay this information on to R1 in a second set of link-state messages and this enables R1 to complete the picture of the active topology (iv). Also, since each router has carried out the same procedure, each will have derived the current active topology and, in addition, determined the identity of the router to which each netid is attached. At this point, each router runs the shortest-path-first algorithm to determine the shortest path from itself to all the other routers. In practice, there are a number of algorithms that can be used to find the shortest path but we shall restrict our discussion to the Dijkstra algorithm.

Dijkstra shortest-path-first algorithm

We shall explain the Dijkstra algorithm in relation to our example internet topology. This is shown in Figure 6.13(a) together with the cost of the lines that link the routers together. The sequence of steps followed by R1 to derive the shortest paths to reach the other three routers is shown in Figure 6.13(b).

Shown in parentheses alongside each of the other routers is the aggregate cost from that router back to the source via the router indicated. Hence an entry of (4,R4) means that the cost of the path back to R1 is 4 via R4. Initially, only the path cost of those routers that are directly connected to R1 are known (R2 and R4) and those not directly connected (R3) are marked with an infinite path cost value. Also, until a cost value is known to be the minimum cost, it is said to be **tentative**, and only when the cost value is confirmed as the minimum value is it said to be **permanent**. The router is then shown in bold.

Initially, since R1 is the source it is shown in bold and the path costs back to R1 from the two directly connected routers (R2 and R4) are shown equal to the respective line costs (i). Hence R2, for example, has an entry of (2,R1) indicating the cost is 2 to get back to R1 via the direct line linking it to R1. Also, since R3 is not connected directly to R1, it is shown with a path cost of infinity.

(a)

Connectivity/adjacency tables:

R1:

R	L, C
G1/Netid1	L1, 0
R2	1, 2
R4	4, 2

R2:

R	L, C
R1	1, 2
G2/Netid2	L1, 0
R3	2, 1
R4	5, 1

R3:

R	L, C
R2	2, 1
G3/Netid3	L1, 0
R4	3, 2

R4:

R	L, C
R1	4, 2
R2	5, 1
R3	3, 2
G4/Netid4	L1, 0

(b)

Topology build-up by R1:
(i) Initial:

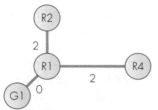

(ii) After connectivity information from R2:

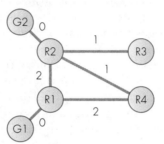

(iii) After connectivity information from R4:

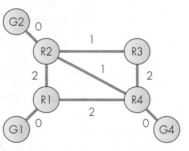

(iv) After connectivity information from R3 via R2:

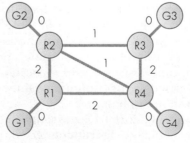

G/Netid	R
G1/1	R1
G2/2	R2
G3/3	R3
G4/4	R4

Figure 6.12 Link state algorithm: (a) initial connectivity/adjacency tables; (b) derivation of active topology and netid location.

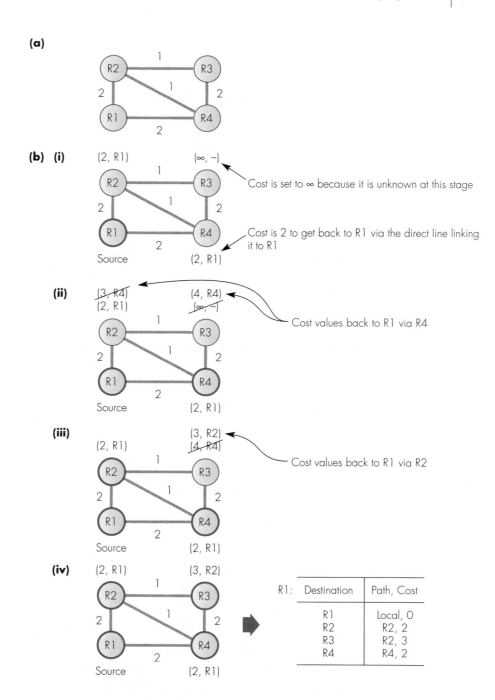

Figure 6.13 Dijkstra algorithm: (a) initial topology; (b) derivation of shortest paths from R1 to each other router.

Once this has been done, the next step (ii) is to choose the router with the minimum path cost value from all the remaining routers that are still tentative. Hence in our example, the choice is between R2 and R4 – since both are tentative and have a path cost value of 2 – and, arbitrarily, we have chosen R4. This is now marked permanent and the new set of aggregate path cost values via R4 are computed. For example, the cost of the path from R2 to R1 via R4 is 3 (1 from R2 to R4 plus 2 from R4 to R1) but, since this is greater than the current cost of 2, this is ignored. In the case of R3, however, the cost of 4 via R4 is less than the current value of infinity and hence (4,R4) replaces the current entry.

The router with the minimum path cost value is again chosen from those that remain tentative and, since R2 has a path cost of 2, this is marked permanent and the new path costs to R1 via R2 are computed (iii). As we can see, the path cost from R3 to R1 via R2 is only 3 and hence an entry of (3,R2) replaces the current entry of (4,R4). Finally (iv), R3 is made permanent as it is the only remaining router that is still tentative and, now that the minimum path costs from each of the other routers back to R1 are known, the routing table for R1 is complete.

In Figure 6.14 we show the same procedure applied first with R2 as the source – part (a) – then with R3 – part (b) – and finally with R4 – part (c). From these derivations we can make some observations about the algorithm:

- The derived shortest path routes adhere to the optimality principle.
- If the computed path costs associated with two or more tentative routers are the same, then an arbitrary selection can be made as to which is made permanent.
- If the computed aggregate path cost from a (tentative) router to the source via a different router is the same as that via another router, then both can be retained. The choice of route is then arbitrary and load sharing becomes possible.

Datagram routing procedures

The routing of a datagram involves a combination of both link-state tables – one containing the location of all netids and the other the connectivity information – and the derived set of shortest-path routing tables. These are used in slightly different ways depending on the choice of routing method, hop-by-hop routing or source routing. We shall explain the procedure followed with each method using the example of a host attached to netid 1 sending a datagram/packet to a host attached to netid 3.

The procedure followed with hop-by-hop routing is summarized in Figure 6.15(a). Using this method, each router computes only its own routing table contents and uses this together with the contents of its own connectivity table. On receipt of the packet from gateway G1, router R1 obtains the netid from the destination IP address in the packet header – netid 3 – and uses its copy of the link-state table to determine that this is reached via router R3. It

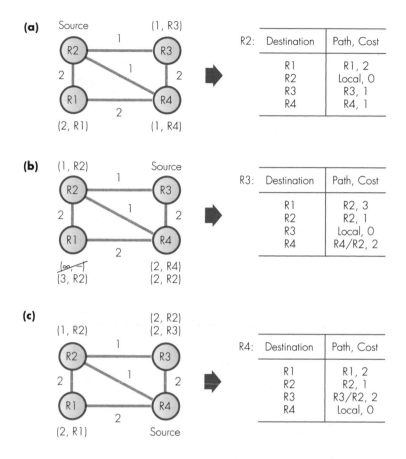

(a)

R2:

Destination	Path, Cost
R1	R1, 2
R2	Local, 0
R3	R3, 1
R4	R4, 1

(b)

R3:

Destination	Path, Cost
R1	R2, 3
R2	R2, 1
R3	Local, 0
R4	R4/R2, 2

(c)

R4:

Destination	Path, Cost
R1	R1, 2
R2	R2, 1
R3	R3/R2, 2
R4	Local, 0

Figure 6.14 Shortest path derivations: (a) by R2; (b) by R3; (c) by R4.

then determines from the contents of its routing table that the next-hop router on the shortest path to R3 is R2 and hence proceeds to forward the packet to R2 over the line indicated in its connectivity table, line 1.

The same procedure is repeated by router R2 – using its own link-state, routing, and connectivity tables – to forward the packet to R3 over line 2. Finally, on receipt of the packet, R3 determines from its own tables that the packet is addressed to netid 3 and that this is attached to one of its local lines, L1. The packet is then forwarded to the attached gateway and from there to the destination host.

The procedure followed with source routing is summarized in Figure 6.15(b). Using this method, once all the routers have built up a picture of the current active topology using the link-state algorithm, they each compute the complete set of four routing tables. Then, on receipt of a packet from one of its attached gateways – G1 in the example – the source router – R1 – uses the set of tables to determine the list of routers that form the shortest path to the

(a)

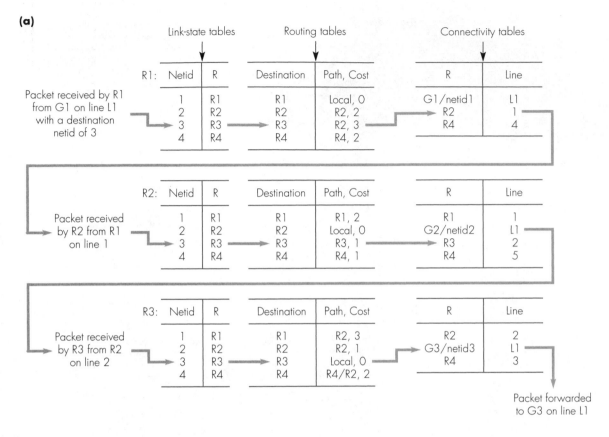

Figure 6.15 LS-SPF routing examples: (a) hop-by-hop routing; (b) source routing.

(b)

1. Datagram received by R1 from G1 on line L1
2. R1 uses its set of routing tables to determine the least path cost is via routers R2, R3, and writes this list into an options field in the datagram header.
3. R1 uses its own connectivity table to forward the packet to the first router in the list, R2, using line 1.

4. On receipt of the packet, R2 reads the second router from the list, R3, and uses its own connectivity table to forward the packet on line 2.

5. On receipt of the packet, R3 determines it is for one of its local gateways and uses its own connectivity table to forward the packet to G3 on line L1.

intended destination – R2 and R3. The list is then inserted into an *options* field of the datagram header by R1 and the packet forwarded to the first router in the path, R2, using the corresponding line number obtained from R1's own connectivity table, line 1.

On receipt of the packet, R2 reads from the *options* field the identity of the next router along the path, R3, and uses its own connectivity table to determine the line the packet should be forwarded on, line 2. On receipt of the packet, R3 determines that it is intended for one of its local gateways and uses its own connectivity table to determine the packet should be forwarded to gateway G3 on line L1.

Additional comments

Although in the various examples, internet-wide identifiers have been used to identify each of the lines in the example internet topology, this has been done to simplify the related descriptions. In practice, as we can deduce from the description of the LS-SPF algorithm the line identifiers associated with each router have only local significance and, since these are part of the router's configuration information, normally, a different set of line identifiers is used by each router.

In our discussion of the link-state algorithm, we assumed that the transmission of the link-state messages was reliable and that none was lost as a result of transmission errors. Clearly, should a link-state message be corrupted, then the routing tables in each router may be inconsistent and, amongst other things, cause packets to loop. To overcome this, each link-state message, in addition to the identity of the router that created the message and its associated connectivity information, also contains a sequence number and a timeout value. As we have mentioned, link-state information is distributed by each router relaying a copy of the messages it receives from each of its neighbors on to its other neighbors. Hence to avoid messages being relayed unnecessarily, when each new message it created – at defined time intervals – it is assigned a sequence number equal to the previous number plus one. Each router then keeps a record of the sequence number contained within the last message it received from each of the other routers and only if a new message is received – that is, one with a higher sequence number – is a copy forwarded to its other neighbors. In addition, the associated timeout value in each message is decremented by each router and, should this reach zero, the received message is discarded.

Although in the simple example we used to describe the LS-SPF algorithm only a single routing metric (cost value) was used, multiple metrics can be used. In such cases, therefore, there may be a different shortest path between each pair of routers for each metric. Although this leads to additional computation overheads, the choice of path can then be made dependent on the type of information contained within the datagram being routed. For example, for real-time information such as digitized speech, the choice of path may be based on minimum delay rather than bit rate.

As we can deduce from the description of the distance vector algorithm in Section 6.5.3, for large internets, the amount of routing information passed between routers is substantial and, in the limit, involves each router transferring the contents of its complete routing table at regular intervals. In contrast, the link-state shortest-path-first algorithm involves only the transfer of the link-state information of each router. Hence it is far more efficient in terms of the amount of bandwidth that is utilized for routing updates. It is for this reason, that the LS-SPF algorithm is now the preferred algorithm. The protocol based on this is known as the open shortest path first (OSPF) routing protocol and, as we showed earlier in Figure 6.2, this forms an integral part of the IP.

6.5.5 Tunneling

In the previous sections we have assumed that all networks within the global internetwork operate in a connectionless mode using the IP and its associated routing protocols. In practice, however, this is not always the case. As we indicated earlier, the Internet is made up of many separately managed networks and internetworks that, in some instances, use a different operational mode and/or protocol from the IP.

For example, consider a small enterprise consisting of two sites, both of which have LANs that operate using the TCP/IP stack, but for security reasons only one of the sites has an access gateway connected to the Internet. Also, for cost reasons, instead of using a leased line to connect the two site LANs together, a public (or private) data network is used that operates in a connection-oriented mode and with a different protocol from the IP. Clearly, it is not possible to transfer each IP datagram directly over the public data network and instead a technique known as **tunneling** is used. Figure 6.16 illustrates this approach.

As we can see, in order to link the two sites together, a device known as a **multiprotocol router** is connected to each site LAN. As the name implies, a multi-protocol router operates using two different protocol stacks: the IP protocol stack on the site side and the protocol stack associated with the non-IP network on the other. The IP in each host simply treats the multiprotocol router as the site Internet access gateway. To send and receive packets to and from a host – a server for example – that is connected to the Internet, the IP simply sends the packet to the multiprotocol router using, for example, the ARP.

Typically, the IP in the source router is given the (non-IP) network address of the multiprotocol router at the remote site by network management. On receipt of the packet, the IP in the source router, on determining that the netid in the destination IP address is not for this site, looks up the non-IP network address of the remote router and passes this, together with the datagram, to the network layer protocol associated with the non-IP network. The latter treats the datagram as user data and proceeds to transfer the datagram to the peer network layer in the remote router using the protocol stack of the non-IP network with the datagram encapsulated in a data packet relating to the network layer protocol.

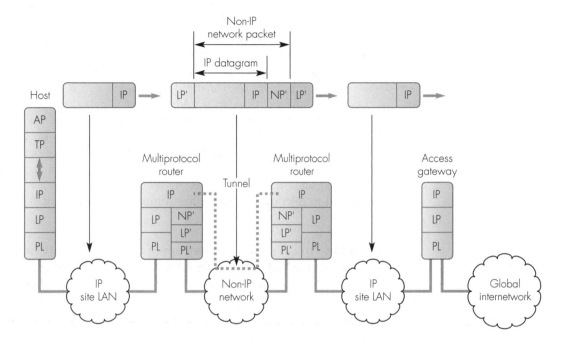

Figure 6.16 Tunneling example.

On receipt of the data packet by the peer network layer protocol in the remote router, the user data – the datagram – contained within it is passed to the IP. The IP first determines from the destination IP address that the required host is not attached to the site LAN and hence proceeds to send the packet to the IP in the Internet access gateway using, for example, the ARP. A similar procedure is followed in the reverse direction to transfer the packets containing the related reply message. Thus, the presence of the non-IP network is transparent to the IP in each host and the access gateway.

In addition to using tunneling to transfer an IP packet over a non-IP network, the same technique is used to send an IP packet over an IP network. As we shall expand upon in Section 6.6.8, tunneling is used by an IP router to relay a packet that contains a multicast destination address to a different router that can handle multicast packets. Normally, the IP address of their nearest multicast router is known by all the other routers and, on receipt of a packet with a multicast address, the source router encapsulates the packet within a new packet with the IP address of the multicast router as the destination IP address.

6.5.6 Broadcast routing

As we explained in Chapter 3, LANs such as Ethernet operate by a station/host broadcasting each frame over the LAN segment to which it is attached. The frame is then received by all the other stations that are attached to the same segment and, by examining the destination (MAC) address in the frame header, the network interface software within each host can decide whether to pass the frame contents on to the IP layer for further processing or to discard the frame. A frame is accepted if the destination MAC address is the same as its own individual address, or is a broadcast address, or is equal to one of the group addresses of which the station is a member. For a bridged LAN, this mode of working is extended to cover the total LAN by each bridge relaying all frames that contain either a broadcast or a multicast address on to all the other LAN segments to which the bridge is attached. In this section we explain how broadcasting is achieved at the IP layer and, in the next section, how multicasting is achieved.

As we identified in Section 6.4, there are a number of different types of IP broadcast address:

- **limited broadcast**: this is used to send a copy of a packet to the IP in all the hosts that are attached to the same LAN segment or bridged LAN. To achieve this, the destination IP address is set to 255.255.255.255.255. Neither subnet routers nor access gateways forward such packets;

- **subnet-directed broadcast**: this is used to send a copy of a packet to the IP in all the hosts that are attached to the subnet specified in the destination IP address. To achieve this, the subnet mask associated with the subnet must be known and this is then used to determine the hostid part and set all these bits to 1. Such packets are forwarded by subnet routers but only if the destination netid is different from the source netid are they forwarded by access gateways and any internet gateways;

- **net-directed broadcast**: this is used to send a copy of a packet to the IP in all the hosts that are attached to the network specified in the netid part of the destination IP address. Such packets are forwarded by subnet routers but only if the destination netid is different from the source netid are they forwarded by access gateways and any internet gateways.

Thus, a packet with a net-directed broadcast address whose destination netid is different from the source netid may need to be forwarded across the global internetwork. Since the destination netid is known, however, then the datagram can be routed by interior – and if necessary exterior – gateways in the same way as a packet with a unicast address. This also applies to a packet with a subnet-directed broadcast address whose destination netid is different from the source netid. Also, since with a subnet-directed broadcast address all the subnet routers in both the source and destination networks have a copy of the subnet mask, then they too can use the unicast routing algorithm associated with the network to route the packet to the subnet router specified in the IP address. The latter then broadcasts the packet over this subnet. With a net-directed broadcast, however, this is not possible and the unanswered question is how the packet is broadcast to all the subnets belonging to the network specified in the netid part of the address.

One solution is to use flooding but, as we concluded at the end of Section 6.5.2, this has very high bandwidth overheads associated with it. Two alternative approaches are employed, the choice being determined by the routing algorithm that is used to route unicast packets over the network. For description purposes we shall use the example of a large site/campus network that comprises a large number of subnets all interconnected by subnet routers. The aim of both algorithms is then for the arriving packet with a net-directed broadcast address to be broadcast over all the subnets using a minimum amount of bandwidth.

Reverse path forwarding

This algorithm is used primarily with networks that use the distance vector (DV) algorithm to route unicast packets. To explain the operation of the algorithm we use the network topology shown in Figure 6.17(a). We assume that subnet router 1 (SR1) also acts as the (single) access gateway for the network and that all subnets (SNs) are broadcast LANs.

Using the DV algorithm we explained in Section 6.5.3, in addition to each subnet router deriving the shortest paths to each subnet, they can also derive the shortest paths to reach each of the other subnet routers. To see how this is done, the initial and final routing tables built up by each subnet router (based on a routing metric of hop count) are shown in Figure 6.17(b).

Once the routing tables have been created, the reverse path forwarding algorithm used to route (broadcast) packets works as follows. On receipt of a packet/datagram, the IP in each subnet router (SR) consults its routing table and only forwards a copy of it – onto each of the ports of the SR except the port the packet arrived on – if the packet arrived from an SR that is on the shortest path from SR1 to the SR that is processing the packet. If it is not, then the packet is discarded. Based on this simple rule, the path followed by each copy of an incoming packet is shown in Figure 6.17(c).

As we can see, on receipt of a packet, SR1 broadcasts a copy of it out onto subnets SN1 and SN3. Hence a copy of the packet is received by the IP in SR2 and SR4 respectively. On receiving the packet, the IP in SR2 first consults its routing table and determines from the (first) entry in the table that SN1 (from which the packet was received) is on the shortest path back to SR1. Similarly, when the IP in SR4 consults its routing table it also determines that SN3 (from which the packet was received) is also on the shortest path back to SR1. Hence both SR2 and SR4 are shown in bold in the figure and each proceeds to broadcast a copy of the packet, SR2 onto SN2 and SN4, and SR4 onto SN7.

After the second set of broadcasts, on receipt of its copy of the packet, the IP in SR3 determines from its routing table that SN2 is on the shortest path back to SR1, and similarly for the copy SR5 receives from SR2 via SN4. Hence both SR3 and SR5 are shown in bold and proceed to broadcast a copy of the packet, SR3 onto SN5 and SN6, and SR5 onto SN5, SN7 and SN8.

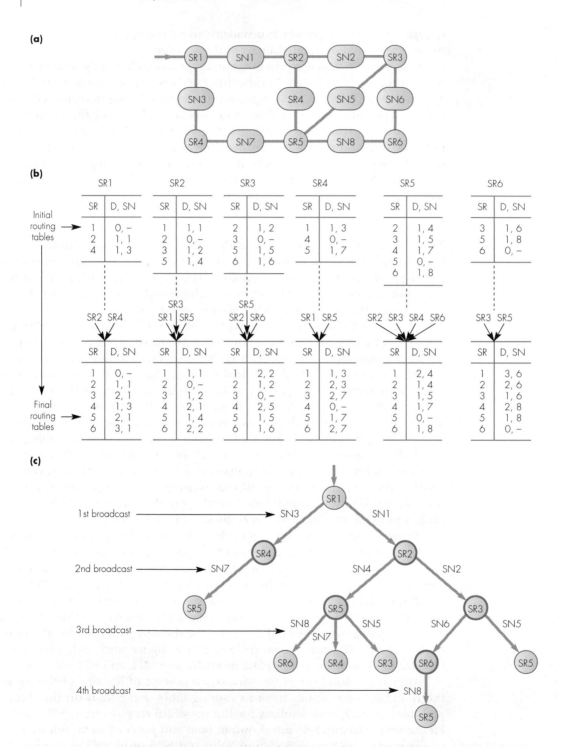

Figure 6.17 Reverse path forwarding: (a) network topology; (b) distance vector routing tables using a hop-count metric; (c) broadcast sequence.

However, in the case of the packet received by SR5 from SR4 via SN7, SR5 determines that SN7 is not on the shortest path back to SR1. Hence SR5 along this path is not shown in bold and the arriving packet is discarded.

The same procedure is repeated by SR5 and SR6 after the third set of broadcasts have been received but this time only SR6 determines from its routing table that SN6 is on the shortest path back to SR1 and proceeds to broadcast a copy of the packet onto SN8. The copies of the packet received from SR5 by SR3, SR4 and SR6 are all discarded as the related subnets – SN5, SN7 and SN8 – are not on the shortest paths back to SR1. Likewise, the packet received by SR5 from SR6 after the fourth broadcast is also discarded.

As we can deduce from this example, a copy of the packet is broadcast over all the eight subnets that make up the network and only SN7 and SN8 receive two copies. However, since both copies of the packet have the same value in the identifier field of the packet header, the second copy can be detected by each of the hosts on these subnets as a duplicate and is discarded. Note also that the same set of routing tables can be used to perform the same algorithm if a second (or different) SR acts as an additional (or alternative) access gateway, and also if the broadcast is over the source network.

Spanning tree broadcast

With networks that use a routing algorithm based on the link-state algorithm, an alternative way of routing broadcast packets/datagrams is for each router to use the link-state information to establish a spanning tree active topology with the access gateway/router as the root node.

As we saw in Section 6.5.4, the information gathered as part of the link-state algorithm is used by each router to derive the current active topology of the internetwork. In a similar way, therefore, with networks that consist of multiple subnets interconnected by subnet routers, each subnet router builds up knowledge of the current active topology of the network and then uses this to compute the shortest path to reach all the subnetids in the network.

Hence with the spanning tree broadcast algorithm, in addition to each subnet router computing the shortest paths, they all derive the (same) spanning tree topology from the current active topology. A spanning tree topology is established in order to avoid frames looping within the total network. This is done by defining the ports associated with each subnet router as either **root ports** or **designated ports**. All ports that are either root or designated ports are then set into the forwarding state and all the other ports are set into the non- forwarding (blocked) state.

Using the same approach, we can derive a spanning tree by setting selected subnet router ports into the forwarding and blocked state. For example, using the network topology we showed in Figure 6.17(a) and, assuming each subnet router knows the root SR, each will derive the spanning tree shown in Figure 6.18(b). The resulting broadcast sequence is therefore as shown in Figure 6.18(c).

We can make a number of observations from this example:

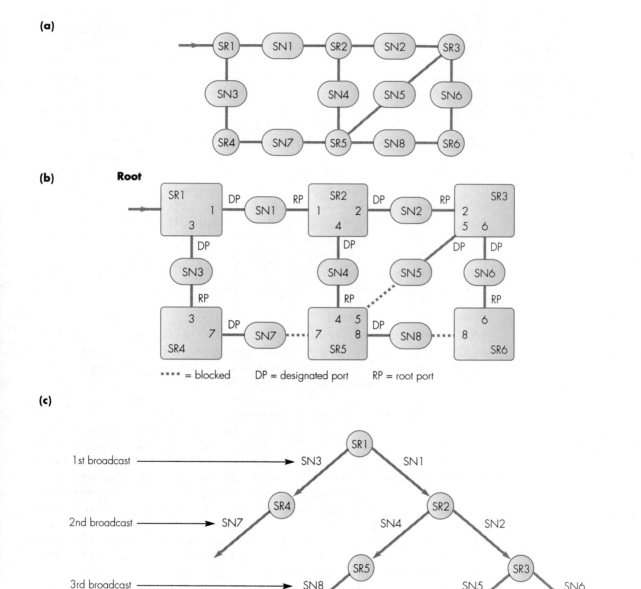

Figure 6.18 Spanning tree broadcast: (a) network topology; (b) spanning tree derived by each subnet router; (c) broadcast sequence.

- For consistency, the port numbers associated with each subnet router are determined by the (known) identifier of the attached subnet.

- Each SR has a root port (RP) associated with it which is the port with the shortest path back to the root. The path costs in the example are based on hop count and, in the event of a tie, the port with the smallest port number is chosen.

- For each subnet, there is a designated port (DP) which is the router port on the shortest path from the root to the subnet. In the event of a tie, the SR with the smallest identifier is chosen.

- All router ports that are not root or designated ports (DP) are set into the blocked state.

- Only a single copy of each received packet/datagram is broadcast over each subnet.

- The same spanning tree can be used to broadcast packets if a second (or different) SR acts as an additional (or alternative) access gateway and if the broadcast is over the source network.

6.6 Routing in the Internet

In the previous two sections we have built up an understanding of IP addresses and the different types of routing algorithms that are available. We can now build on this knowledge to explain how routing is carried out in the Internet. We shall start with a description of the current structure of the Internet and then proceed to use this to describe the specific routing algorithms that are used.

6.6.1 Internet structure and terminology

As we explained earlier in Section 2.6.5, the Internet is composed of many thousands of access networks that are geographically distributed around the world. As a result, the global internetwork that is used to interconnect the access gateways associated with these networks is not a single network but a collection of different types of regional, national and international networks that have evolved over the lifetime of the Internet. The general structure of the Internet is shown in Figure 6.19 and, as we can deduce from this, the Internet is often described as a **network-of-networks**.

At the lowest level in the hierarchy – known as **Tier 3** – are the various types of access networks – site/campus LANs, local ISP networks, cable networks, wireless LANs, etc. Associated with each access network is an access gateway and this is connected to the nearest gateway of a regional ISP network or, in some instances, a legacy regional network/internetwork, for a small country, a national network – **Tier 2**.

At the highest level in the hierarchy, each country has its own ISP/legacy backbone networks – **Tier 1**. These are composed of a geographically distributed

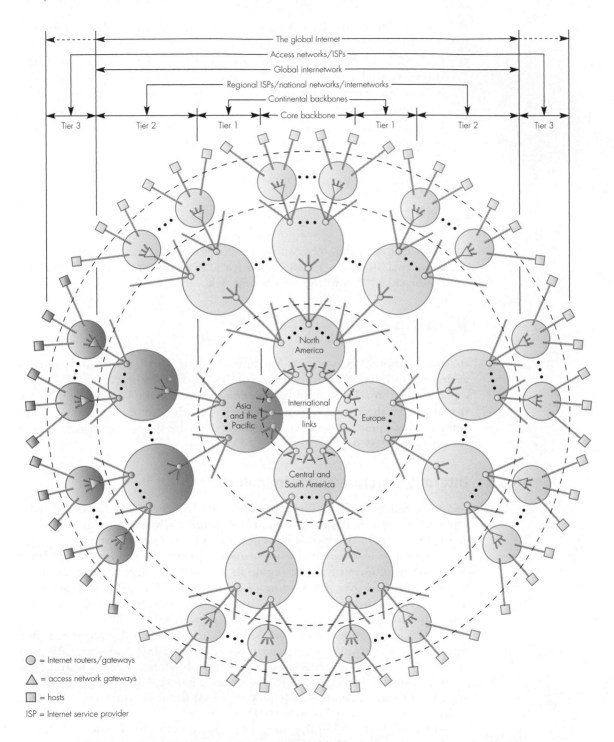

Figure 6.19 General architecture of the global Internet.

set of very high throughput routers that are interconnected using very high bit rate optical fiber lines leased from one or more telecommunication providers. The country backbones are then interconnected together by means of a smaller number of either very high throughput leased lines or devices known as **network access points** (**NAPs**).

In addition, as we indicated earlier in Section 2.6.5, because the networks at the different layers are operated by a number of different companies, private agreements are reached between them – normally on cost grounds – to provide direct links between selected routers in the same peer networks. This practice is called **private peering**.

Clearly, it is not possible for every router in the hierarchy to maintain routing information relating to every other router. Hence in order to make the routing of datagrams/packets around the global Internet manageable, the overall structure is broken down into a hierarchical structure involving a large number of what are called **autonomous systems** (**ASs**). The ASs are then interconnected by an intercontinental backbone network. As we can deduce from this, there are a large number of ASs in the Internet. Each Tier 3 and Tier 2 network within an AS is called an **area** and one of these networks is selected to be the backbone area of this AS. Every AS is then connected to a higher-level backbone area.

The routing algorithm used within an AS is called an **interior gateway protocol** – or sometimes an **intra-AS routing protocol** – and, in principle, each AS can use its own routing protocol. In practice, there are just two protocols used. The first is based on the distance vector algorithm and is called the **routing information protocol** (**RIP**). The second is based on the link-state shortest path first algorithm and is called the **open shortest path first** (**OSPF**) protocol. The original interior gateway protocol was RIP and there are still many ASs in the Internet that use this. However, the preferred protocol is now OSPF as this has been found to be more robust than RIP when erroneous routing updates occur. As a result, OSPF is now supported by all the major router manufacturers. The latest version is version 2 and this is defined in RFC 2328.

The routing protocol used for communications between ASs is called the **border gateway protocol** (**BGP**). The latest version of this is version 4 – BGP-4 – and is specified in RFCs 1771/2/3/4. It is called a **path vector protocol** in the standard since neighbor BGP routers that have a direct link between them – also known as **BGP peers** – exchange path information rather than link cost values. Typically, the path information is a list of the ASs that lie on a path to a particular destination AS. The total routing table for an AS is then built up by each AS exchanging routing updates with its directly connected neighbors.

In this section we shall describe the operation of both the OSPF and BGP routing protocols. Before we do this, however, we shall first describe the operation of two of the protocols that are used widely in access networks. These are ARP/RARP and DHCP.

6.6.2 ARP and RARP

As we outlined in Section 6.1 and illustrated in Figure 6.2, the address resolution protocol (ARP) and the reverse ARP (RARP) are used by the IP in hosts that are attached to a broadcast LAN. The ARP is used to determine the MAC address of another host or gateway that is attached to the same LAN given the IP address of the host gateway. It is defined in **RFC 826**. The RARP performs the reverse function and is defined in **RFC 903**. We explain the operation of each separately.

ARP

Associated with each host are two addresses: its IP address and its MAC address, which, since it is assigned to the MAC integrated circuit when it is manufactured, is known also as the host's hardware (or physical) address. Normally, both addresses are stored in the configuration file of the host on the hard disk. In order to describe the operation of the ARP, we shall use the LAN topology shown in Figure 6.20.

As we can see, this comprises three Ethernet hubs (H1, H2 and H3) that are interconnected by means of a fourth hub (H4). There is also a connection between H4 and the site access gateway (AG). We assume that all the hubs are simple repeater hubs and that all hosts have just been switched on

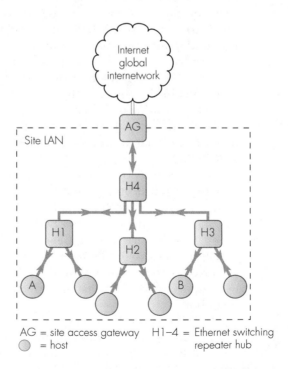

AG = site access gateway   H1–4 = Ethernet switching
○ = host   repeater hub

Figure 6.20 Example topology for describing the operation of the ARP.

and hence have sent no frames. Associated with each ARP is a routing table known as the **ARP cache**. This contains a list of the IP/MAC address-pairs of those hosts with which host A has recently communicated and, when the host is first switched on, it contains no entries. First we shall explain the steps taken by the ARP in host A to send a datagram to another host on the same LAN – host B – and then to a host on a different LAN via the gateway.

On receipt of the first datagram from the IP in host A, the ARP in A reads the destination IP address of B contained in the datagram header and determines it is not in its cache. Hence it broadcasts an **ARP request message** in a broadcast frame over the LAN and waits for a reply. The request message contains both its own IP/MAC address-pair and the (target) IP address of the destination, host B. Being a broadcast frame this is received by the ARP in all hosts attached to the LAN.

The ARP in host B recognizes its own IP address in the request message and proceeds to process it. It first checks to see whether the address-pair of the source is within its own cache and, if not, enters them. This is done since it is highly probable that the destination host will require the MAC address of the source when the higher-layer protocol responds to the message contained within the datagram payload. The ARP in host B then responds by returning an **ARP reply** message (containing its own MAC address) to the ARP in host A using the latter's MAC address contained in the request message. On receipt of the reply message, the ARP in host A first makes an entry of the requested IP/MAC address-pair in its own cache and then passes the waiting datagram to either the LLC sublayer (if one is present) or (if not) to the MAC sublayer together with the MAC address of host B that indicates where it should be sent. At B the datagram is passed directly to the IP for processing.

Being on the same broadcast network as all the site hosts, the LAN port of the gateway receives a copy of all broadcast frames containing ARP request and reply messages. On receipt of each message, the ARP first checks to see if it has the IP/MAC address-pair(s) contained in the message in its cache and, if not, adds them to the cache. In this way, the site gateway learns the address-pair of all the hosts that are attached to the site LAN.

To send a datagram from, say, host A to a host on a different LAN – and hence netid – the ARP in A broadcasts the request message as before. In this case, however, on receipt of the message, the gateway determines that the netid part of the destination IP address relates to a different network and responds by returning a reply message containing its own address-pair. Hence A makes an entry of this in its cache and proceeds to forward the datagram to the gateway as if it was the destination host. The gateway then forwards the datagram/packet over the Internet using one of the global internetwork routing protocols we shall describe later. The ARP in the gateway is known as a **proxy ARP** since it is acting as an agent for the ARP in the destination host.

When the gateway receives the response packet from the destination host, it reads the destination IP address from the header – host A – and obtains from its cache the MAC address of A. It then transfers the packet to the IP in A using the services provided by the MAC sublayer. A similar procedure is followed for bridged LANs and for router-based LANs except that with the latter, the ARP in the subnet router that is connected to the same subnet as the source host acts as the proxy ARP. Also, in order to allow for hosts to change their network point of attachments, entries in the ARP cache timeout after a predefined time interval.

RARP

As we indicated at the start of the last section, normally the IP/MAC address-pair of a host is stored in the configuration file of the host on its hard disk. With diskless hosts, clearly this is not possible and hence the only address that is known is the MAC address of the MAC chipset. In such cases, therefore, the alternative reverse address resolution protocol (RARP) is used.

The server associated with a set of diskless hosts has a copy of the IP/MAC address-pair of all the hosts it serves in a configuration file. When a diskless host first comes into service, it broadcasts a **RARP request** message containing the MAC address of the host onto its local LAN segment. Being a broadcast, the server receives this and, on determining it is a RARP message, the MAC/LLC sublayer passes the message to the RARP. The latter first uses the MAC address within it to obtain the related IP address from the configuration file and then proceeds to create a **RARP reply** message containing the IP address of the host and also its own address-pair. The server then sends the reply message back to the host and, once its own address-pair is known, the ARP in the diskless host can proceed as before.

ARP/RARP message formats and transmission

As we show in Figure 6.21(a), the formats, of the ARP and RARP request and reply messages are the same, both having a fixed length of 28 bytes. Note that the term "hardware address" is used to refer to a MAC address and "target" to the recipient of a request.

The *hardware type* field specifies the type of hardware (MAC) address contained within the message, for example 0001 (hex) in the case of an Ethernet. The ARP and RARP can be used with other network protocols (as well as the IP) and the *protocol type* indicates the type of network address being resolved; for example, 0800 (hex) is used for IP addresses. The *HLEN* and *PLEN* fields specify the size in bytes of the hardware (MAC) and protocol (IP) address lengths respectively, for example 06 (hex) for an Ethernet and 04 (hex) for the IP. The *operation* field indicates whether the message (resolution operation) is an ARP request (0001) or reply (0002) or a RARP request (0003) or reply (0004).

The next four fields specify the hardware (MAC)/IP address-pair of the sender (source) and the target (destination). For example, in an ARP request message just the address-pair of the sender is used while in the reply message all four addresses are used.

As we indicated in the introduction, both the ARP and RARP are integral parts of IP inasmuch as, once the MAC address relating to an IP address is present in the ARP cache, the IP can use this to initiate the transmission of a datagram to its intended recipient directly. Hence, as we can deduce from Figure 6.2, on receipt of a frame, the receiving MAC/LLC sublayer must be able to determine to which protocol the frame contents should be sent: IP, ARP, or RARP. To achieve this, when each of the protocols passes a message/datagram to the LLC/MAC sublayer for transmission, in addition to the MAC address of the intended recipient, it specifies the name of the (peer) protocol in the destination (IP/ARP/RARP) to which the message/datagram should be passed.

As we show in Figure 6.21(b), this is specified in a two-byte *type* field that immediately precedes the message/datagram in the user data field of the

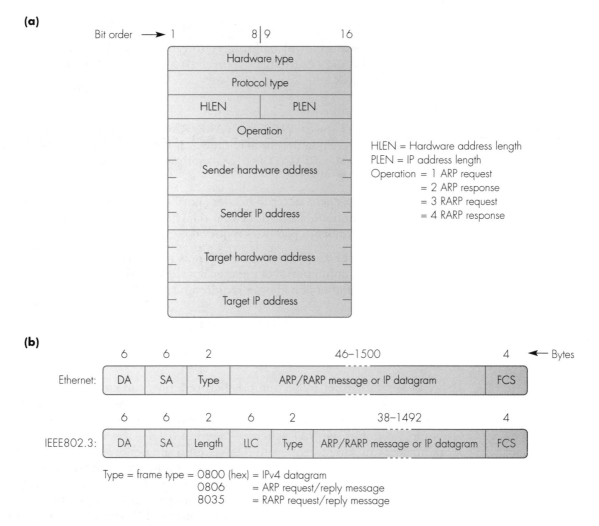

Figure 6.21 ARP and RARP message formats and transmission: (a) ARP and RARP message formats; (b) MAC frame format with Ethernet and IEEE802.3.

MAC frame. As we explained in Section 3.6.3, normally, the LLC sublayer is not used with the original Ethernet MAC standard and hence the *type* field immediately follows the MAC *source address* (*SA*). With the more recent IEEE802.3 MAC standard, however, the LLC sublayer is present and hence the *type* field immediately follows the six bytes required for the LLC protocol. However, the maximum frame length associated with the 802.3 standard (1500 bytes) means that the length indicator value in the header is always different from the three *type* field values. Hence the receiving MAC sublayer can readily determine which of the two standards is being used and, therefore, where the *type* field is located. With a token ring LAN, since there is only one standard, this problem does not arise.

Example 6.5

Determine the amount of padding required in a MAC frame when transmitting an ARP/RARP message over (i) an Ethernet LAN and (ii) an IEEE802.3 LAN.

Answer:

As we showed in Figure 6.21(a), each ARP/RARP message comprises 28 bytes. Also, as we explained in Section 3.2.3, the minimum frame size associated with the CSMA/CD MAC method is 512 bits (64 bytes) including the FCS.

(i) With an Ethernet LAN, the header plus FCS requires 18 bytes and hence the minimum size of the user data field is $(64 - 18) = 46$ bytes. Thus the number of pad bytes required $= (46 - 28) = 18$ bytes.

(ii) With an IEEE802.3 LAN, the header plus FCS requires 26 bytes and hence the minimum size of the user data field is $(64 - 26) = 38$ bytes. Thus the number of pad bytes required $= (38 - 28) = 10$ bytes.

6.6.3 DHCP

As we described earlier in Section 6.1, before a host can communicate over the Internet it must have an IP address. The role of the **dynamic host configuration protocol** (**DHCP**) is to obtain an IP address on behalf of the host. For example, assuming the NAT scheme – Section 6.4.4 – this involves the network manager making a request to ICANN for a site netid with an indication of the number of hostids that are required. The network manager is then responsible for allocating IP addresses for hosts as they are attached to the network and reallocating them as hosts are removed. As we can deduce from this, the allocation, installation and administration of IP addresses can entail considerable effort. To alleviate this, an autoconfiguration facility is available that enables a host to obtain an IP address over the network and, in the case of mobile hosts, use it for the duration of a single session.

The DHCP scheme is defined in RFCs 2131 and 2132. It involves the host communicating with a site – or enterprise – IP address server using an application protocol called the DHCP. To explain how it works, we shall use the simple example network shown in Figure 6.22(a). In this, we assume that a person arrives with a laptop and wants to communicate over the Internet to obtain e-mail from his/her home network. We assume the network supports autoconfiguration by way of a server that has DHCP as one of its applications. If this was not supported – for example the site LAN is part of a larger enterprise network – then the server runs a related application called a **DHCP relay agent**. This, as its name implies, relays requests and responses to/from the DHCP address server that is located in a different part of the enterprise network. The sequence of messages relating to the DHCP that are exchanged is shown in diagrammatic form in Figure 6.22(b).

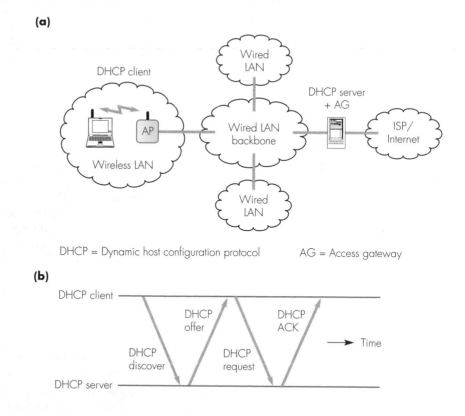

Figure 6.22 The DHCP protocol: (a) example network topology; (b) DHCP message exchange sequence.

As we can see, the DHCP is a simple client-server protocol and a brief description of each message follows.

- **DHCP discover**: this is sent by the DHCP client – that runs in the host – to all hosts/stations using the broadcast destination IP address of 255.255.255.255 and a source address of 0.0.0.0. The message then contains a **transaction ID** so that the client can relate the response from the server to this request.
- **DHCP offer**: this is returned by the DHCP server running in the site server and contains the same transaction ID that was in the discover message, the proposed IP address for the client, the IP address mask, and a duration value indicating the duration of time the IP address is valid.
- **DHCP request**: this is the response to the DHCP offer message and contains the same parameters as were present in the DHCP offer message.
- **DHCP ACK**: this is returned by the server and contains the same set of parameters so acknowledging their receipt by the client.

Normally, the value in the duration field is for a fixed period of time and the IP address is said to be **leased** for this length of time. Then, should the time expire, the client can no longer use the address. To avoid this occurring, prior to the time expiring, the client can make a request to have the time period renewed.

6.6.4 OSPF

The open shortest path first (OSPF) routing protocol is now the preferred interior gateway protocol; that is, for routing within an autonomous system (AS). The latest version is defined in RFC 2328. This is a public document, of course, and explains the use of the word *open* in the name. It can be used with many different types of network including simple point-to-point lines, enterprise LANs, and both regional and national networks. In order to explain how OSPF works and the terminology associated with it, we shall use the (much simplified) Internet structure shown in Figure 6.23.

As we can see in the figure, to route a datagram/packet over the Internet requires four types of router. These are shown as 1, 2, 3 and 4 in the figure and their roles are as follows:

- **Internal routers (1)**: these are found only in non-backbone areas and carry out the routing of packets within an area.
- **Backbone routers (2)**: these are found only in an AS backbone area and carry out the routing of packets within the AS backbone.
- **Area border routers (3)**: these are used to connect an area within an AS to the AS backbone. They are considered to be part of both the area and the backbone area.

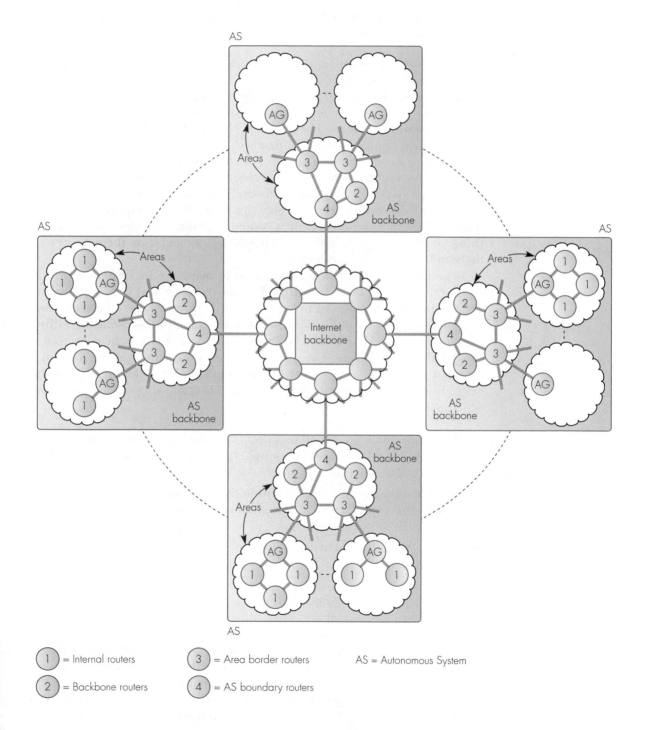

Figure 6.23 Simplified Internet structure for routing purposes.

- **AS boundary routers** (**4**): these have a connection to the Internet backbone and use BGP to carry out the routing of packets between ASs.

To route a packet within an AS, the packet is first routed to the area border using the routing protocol of that area. Then, since all area border routers are also part of the AS backbone area, the packet is routed over the AS backbone area – using OSPF – to the area border router that is connected to the required destination area. The packet is then forwarded to the destination host using the routing protocol of that area.

To route a packet from a host that is attached to an area network in one AS – AS(1) – to a host attached to an area network within a different AS – AS(2) – the packet is first routed to the boundary router of AS(1) using OSPF. The BGP is then used to relay the packet to the required boundary router of AS(2). The packet is then routed over the AS(2) backbone – again using OSPF – to the destination area border router and from there to the destination host using the area protocol.

The operation of OSPF is the same in principle to the LS-SPF algorithm we described earlier in Section 6.5.4. To explain how it works, we shall use the (much simplified) AS shown in Figure 6.24(a). As we can see, it is composed of two areas plus a single backbone area. First, using the link state algorithm, the topology of each area network within the AS is built up by each router using link state messages. The network is then represented in the form of a **directed graph** and, as an example, the graph of the backbone area in the simplified AS is shown in Figure 6.24(b). The following should be noted when interpreting the graph:

- Two routers that are joined by a point-to-point line – for example the link between R6 and R7 – are represented in the graph by a pair of arcs with the cost value alongside.

- When multiple routers are present in the same network, each router has a pair of arcs and their related cost values. In the example these are equal but may be different.

- When a router is attached to a single network, just a single arc is used called a **stub**.

Each router uses the shortest path first algorithm to compute the shortest path between itself and all the other routers using the cost values associated with each link. The cost values are user-configurable and can be based on delay/distance, bit rate and other parameters. A feature of OSPF is that it equalizes the load over paths that have equal path costs. This has been found to improve the network throughput. As an example, the SPF tree computed by R10 is shown in Figure 6.24(c) and, as we can see, the path cost from R9–R6–R7 is the same as that from R9–R7 and hence both paths can be used by R9 to share the load.

(a)

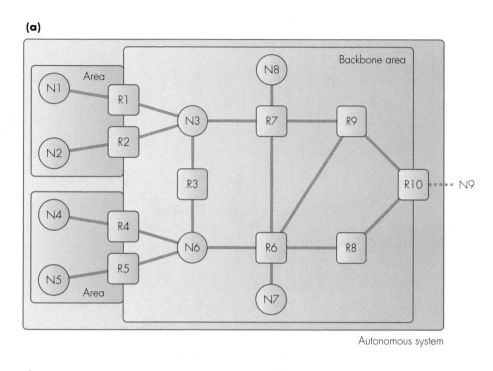

(b)

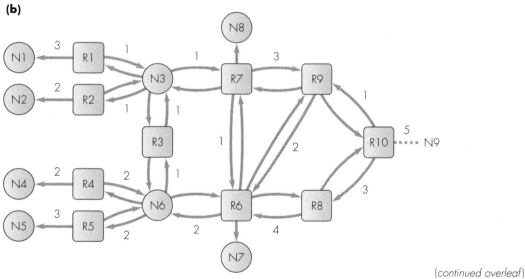

(continued overleaf)

Figure 6.24 OSPF: (a) example AS; (b) directed graph of AS; (c) SPF tree computed by R10.

(c)

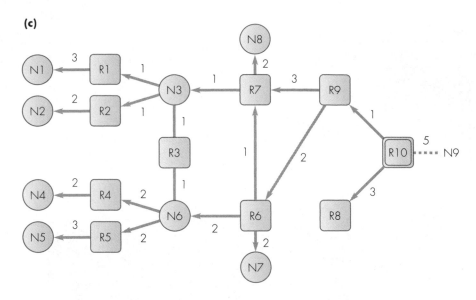

Figure 6.24 Continued.

Once the SPF tree has been computed, each router then creates its own routing table. This contains an entry for each destination netid, the next-hop router to use, and the total path cost to this destination. As an example, the routing table for router R10 is shown in Table 6.1.

Table 6.1 Routing table held by R10.

Destination netid	Next-hop router	Distance
N1	R9	9
N2	R9	8
N3	R9	5
N4	R9	9
N5	R9	10
N6	R9	5
N7	R9	5
N8	R9	6
N9	Backbone	5

Although the LS-SPF algorithm works for relatively small networks, in practice, many AS backbone networks in the Internet contain a very large number of routers/networks and, as a result, the overheads associated with every router within an AS backbone exchanging routing information with every other router in the backbone would be too large. To overcome this, one router is assigned to be the **designated router** for the AS backbone and all the other routers are then said to be **adjacent** to it. The exchange of routing information then only takes place between the designated router and each adjacent router so reducing considerably the amount of information that is exchanged. The downside of this, however, is that should the designated router crash, then the whole AS backbone is affected. Hence to overcome this possibility, a backup is always available and the routing information it contains mirrors that of the current active designated router.

The message types used in OSPF to enable a router to perform the various routing functions are:

- **Hello**: this is used by a router to discover the networks/routers to which it is directly connected together with the cost value associated with each link.

- **Link state update**: these are sent at periodic intervals by the designated router to all its adjacent routers using flooding, the principles of which we described in Section 6.5.2. These are used to inform each router of the cost and state of each link in the current topological database held by the designated router. Each new update message has a sequence number in it that is used by the receiver to determine whether the message is a new update or an old copy. These messages are also sent by a router if the state or cost of a line changes.

- **Link state ACK**: this acknowledges the correct receipt of the link state update and is returned by each adjacent router.

- **Database description**: this is used to inform the receiver of the message the list of updates that it possesses. Each receiver can then determine whether it has the most up-to-date information.

- **Link state request**: this is used to request link state update information from each adjacent router to it.

Each of the above messages is sent in a separate IP packet.

6.6.5 BGP

The border gateway protocol (BGP) runs in each AS boundary router. Its role is to communicate routing information to the border routers associated with each of the other ASs that make up the Internet backbone network. The protocol involves the exchange of messages which, in practice, are sent over TCP connections. As we can deduce from this, therefore, BGP is an application protocol rather than a network protocol.

Unlike OSPF, BGP does not communicate cost values to each of its neighbor boundary routers (BR) but instead details of the path followed between itself and the other BRs. Hence when communicating routing information a BR informs its neighbors of the path that it is currently using to reach each other BR. For example, consider the backbone network shown in Figure 6.25.

Assume that the path taken by BR2 to BR5 is 2–3–4–5 and that the paths taken by its two neighbors – BR3 and BR1 – are as shown in the figure. On receipt of the paths from BR1 and BR3 it is easy for BR2 to determine that, based on the number of hops, the path via BR1 is shorter. Each BGP router runs an algorithm that computes the *distance* for each path. Keeping in mind that the AS boundary routers may be located in different countries, the *distance* is determined not just on physical parameters like bit rate and hop count but also by political issues. For example, if two countries fall out with each other then the cost of using that BR is set to infinity and hence it is omitted from all paths.

There are just four message types associated with BGP:

- **Open**: this is used to open a relationship with another AS boundary router to which it is connected.

- **Update**: this is used both to transmit routing information relating to a single route and to list multiple routes to be withdrawn.

- **Keepalive**: this is used both to acknowledge receipt of an *open* message and to periodically confirm the relationship with the other AS boundary router.

- **Notification**: this is used to inform the receiver that an error condition has been detected.

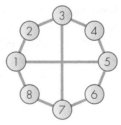

Assume the path used by: BR1 to BR5 is B1–B5
BR2 to BR5 is B2–B3–B4–B5
BR3 to BR5 is B3–B4–B5
and BR2 receives an update message from BR1.
BR2 then determines that the better route to BR5 is BR2–BR1–BR5

Figure 6.25 Routing over the Internet backbone.

To reflect the different types of routing protocol that are involved in routing a packet over the Internet the total routing information is organized hierarchically:

- Hosts maintain sufficient routing information to enable them to forward packets directly to other hosts on the same network, to a subnet router (if subnetting is being used), and to an access gateway.
- Subnet routers maintain sufficient routing information to enable them to forward packets to other subnet routers belonging to the same network and to the network access gateway.
- Access gateways maintain sufficient routing information to enable them to route a packet within its own (access) network either directly to a host or, if subnet routing is used, to the subnet router that is on the shortest path to the destination host.
- Area border routers maintain sufficient routing information to enable them to route a packet to another area border router within the same autonomous system and to the AS boundary router if the destination address of the packet is to a different AS.
- AS boundary routers maintain sufficient routing information to route a packet that is destined for a different AS over the Internet backbone network.

This is summarized in Figure 6.26.

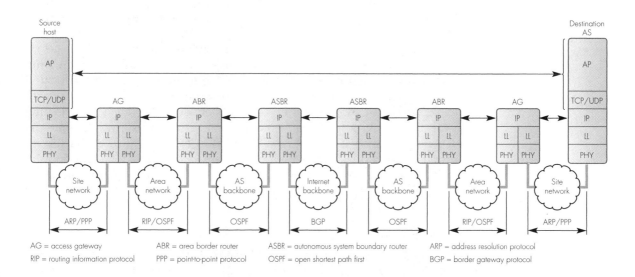

Figure 6.26 A summary of the routers and routing protocols used in the Internet.

6.6.6 Multicast routing

As we explained in Chapter 1, applications such as audio- and videoconferencing require a copy of the information generated by each host participating in a conference to be sent to all the other hosts that belong to the same conference. The term **multicasting** is used to describe the diffusion of a copy of the packets/datagrams generated by each host to all the other hosts and the term **multicast group** is used to identify the hosts that are members of the same conference. Clearly, there can be many conferences in progress concurrently, each involving a different group of hosts. It is to support applications of this type that class D multicast addresses were defined. As we showed in Figure 6.5 and explained in the accompanying text, a single class D address is used to identify all the hosts that are members of the same multicast group. Also, since 28 bits are available, many different multicast groups can be in place concurrently.

A number of multicast addresses are reserved to identify specific groups. For example, all the hosts (and subnet routers) that are attached to a site broadcast network are members of the group with the reserved multicast address of 224.0.0.1. Hence the IP in all hosts that can support multicasting will have this address permanently in their **multicast address table** (**MAT**) and, should a packet be received with this address, the datagram contents will be passed to (and acted upon) by a related application process. Similarly, all the subnet routers belonging to the same network are members of the multicast address 224.0.0.2.

For applications such as a conference or meeting that is being transmitted over a LAN or the Internet, a relatively large number of participants – and hence hosts – may be involved. Moreover, hosts may wish to join and/or leave the conference/meeting whilst it is in progress. It is to meet this type of application that multicasting using IP multicast addresses is used.

With this mode of working, the organizer of the conference/meeting first obtains an IP multicast address for it from the ICANN. The allocated address is then made known to all the registered participants together with the conference/meeting start time and its likely duration. Each participating host can then request to join the conference at any time during the time the conference/meeting is in progress. To do this, two operating scenarios are used that depend on whether the participating hosts are all attached to the same LAN/subnet or, as is more usual, are attached to many different networks that are geographically distributed around the Internet. We shall discuss each separately.

Multicasting over a LAN

The ICANN has been allocated a block of Ethernet MAC addresses for applications that involve multicasting. As we described in Section 3.2.3, Ethernet MAC addresses are 48 bits in length and the reserved block of addresses in dotted decimal are from

0.0.94.0.0.0 through to 0.0.94.255.255.255

Half of these addresses are used for multicasting. Hence, remembering that all centrally administered Ethernet group (multicast) addresses must start with 10 binary, the block of Ethernet addresses used for centrally administered multicasting applications are from

128.0.94.0.0.0 through to 128.0.94.127.255.255

Thus for a particular conference/meeting, a 3-byte address in the range

0.0.0 through to 127.255.255

is allocated by the ICANN. In the case of an Ethernet LAN, this forms the least significant 24 bits of the 48-bit destination MAC address – starting with the three bytes 128.0.94 – and, in the case of the Internet, the least significant 24 bits of the destination IP multicast address. As we explained earlier, class D IP addresses are 28 bits in length – the first four bits being 1110 – and hence, as we show in Figure 6.27(a), the four remaining bits are all set to 0.

So to join a conference/meeting that is being broadcast over the same LAN, once the multicast address is known, the application process running in the host that is managing the information associated with the conference/meeting simply loads the allocated IP multicast address into its MAT and the related 48-bit Ethernet group address derived from this into its **group address table** (**GAT**). Each datagram relating to the conference/meeting then has the allocated multicast address in the destination IP address field of the datagram header. Each packet is then broadcast over the LAN in an Ethernet frame containing the derived 48-bit group address in the destination MAC address field of the frame header.

On receipt of a frame, the MAC sublayer in each host that is a member of the same multicast group first checks to see whether the destination MAC address in the frame header is present in its group address table and, if it is, it passes the frame contents – the datagram – on to the IP layer. The latter first determines that the destination IP address is a multicast address and also that it is present in its multicast address table. It therefore passes the information contained within the datagram on to the related application process via the TCP or UDP. This procedure is shown in Figure 6.27(b).

Multicasting over an internet

When the hosts that are part of a multicast group are attached to different networks/subnetworks geographically distributed around an internet, then intermediate subnet routers and gateways may be involved. Thus, since an IP multicast address has no structure – and hence no netid – associated with it, a different type of routing from that used to route unicast packets must be used.

The sequence of steps followed to route a packet with a multicast address is as follows:

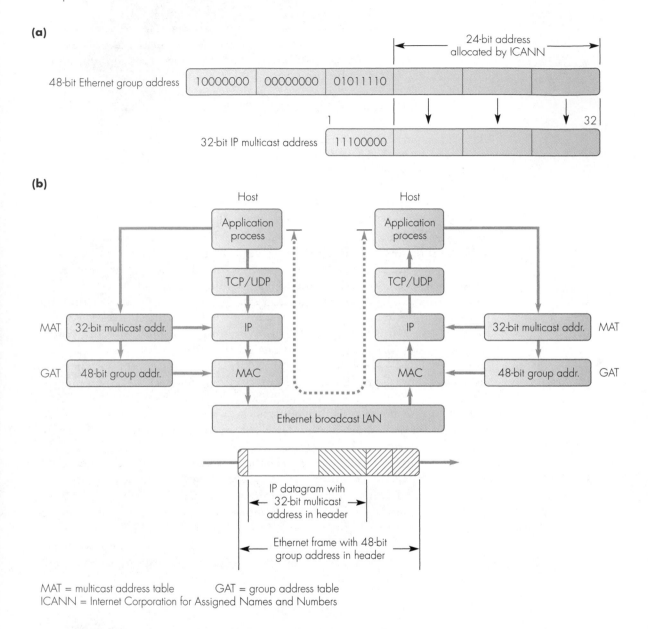

(a)

24-bit address allocated by ICANN

48-bit Ethernet group address | 10000000 | 00000000 | 01011110 | | |

1   32

32-bit IP multicast address | 11100000 | | |

(b)

Figure 6.27 Multicasting over a LAN: (a) address allocation principle; (b) address usage.

- A router that can route packets containing a (destination) IP multicast address is known as a **multicast router** (**mrouter**).
- Normally, in the case of a network that comprises multiple subnets interconnected by subnet routers, a single subnet router also acts as the mrouter for that network.

■ Each mrouter learns the set of multicast group addresses of which all the hosts attached to the networks that the mrouter serves are currently members.

■ The information gathered by each mrouter is passed on to each of the other mrouters so that each knows the complete list of group addresses that each mrouter has an interest in.

■ On receipt of a packet with a destination IP multicast address, each mrouter uses an appropriate routing algorithm to pass the packet only to those mrouters that are attached to a network which has an attached host that is a member of the multicast group indicated in the destination IP address field.

As with broadcast routing, two different algorithms are used, the choice being determined by the routing algorithm used to route unicast packets. The aim of both algorithms is to minimize the amount of transmission bandwidth required to deliver each multicast packet to those multicast routers that have an interest in the packet. To explain the two algorithms, we shall use the internetwork topology shown in Figure 6.28(a). The letters by each multicast router (MR) – A, B and C – indicate the multicast address(es) that each has an interest in and, since all MRs exchange this information, they each have a copy of the multicast address table shown in Figure 6.28(a).

DVMRP

When distance vector routing is being used, an additional set of routing tables (to those used to route unicast packets) based on MR-to-MR distances are derived and, for the six MRs, these are given in Figure 6.28(b). They are based on a routing metric of hop count and have been derived using the same procedure we described earlier in Section 6.5.3. Together with the contents of the MAT in each MR, they are used to route all packets that have a destination multicast address.

The protocol is known as the **distance vector multicast routing protocol** (**DVMRP**). To explain how it works, assume a packet with a multicast address of A is received by the IP in MR1 from one of its attached networks. The sequence is as follows:

■ The IP first consults its MAT and finds that a copy of the packet should be sent to MR2 and MR6. It then proceeds to consult its routing table (RT) and finds that the shortest path to MR6 is also via MR2 and hence sends just a single copy of the packet to MR2.

■ On receipt of the packet, MR2 consults its MAT and sees that a copy of the packet should be sent out onto its own network and also to MR1 and MR6. On consulting its RT, however, it finds that the shortest path to MR1 is on the line/port the packet was received and hence it only sends a copy of the packet to MR6. The RT indicates that the shortest path to MR6 is via MR3 and hence it forwards a copy of the packet to MR3.

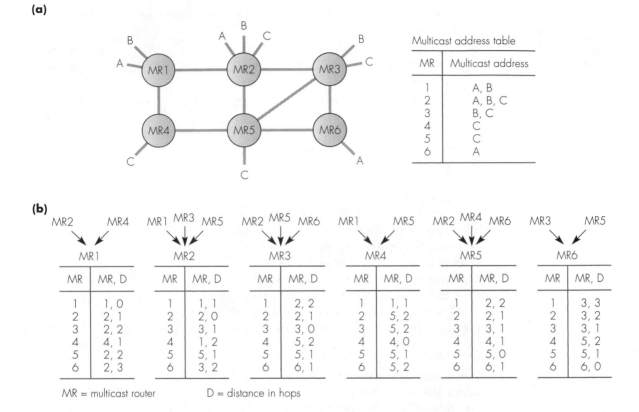

Figure 6.28 Distance vector multicast routing: (a) example topology and multicast address table; (b) unicast routing tables of MR1–6.

- On receipt of the packet, MR3 determines from its MAT that MR1, MR2, and MR6 should be sent a copy of the packet. On consulting its RT it finds that the shortest path to both MR1 and MR2 is via MR2. Hence, since this is the line/port the packet arrived on, it only sends a copy of the packet to MR6.

- On receipt of the packet, MR6 determines from its MAT that a copy of the packet should be sent out on its own network and also to MR1 and MR2. However, since the shortest path to both MR1 and MR2 is via the line/port the packet arrived on, it only sends a copy out on its local network.

MOSPF

When link-state routing is being used, since each MR knows the current active topology of the internetwork, as we explained in Section 6.5.6, each computes a spanning tree for the internetwork using the algorithm we showed in Figure 6.18 and described in the accompanying text. For example, for the internetwork shown in Figure 6.29(a), the spanning tree computed by each MR is shown in Figure 6.29(b). The numbers shown by each line are used as global line identifiers and as port numbers in the derivation of the spanning tree.

At any point in time, each MR knows from its MAT the multicast addresses that each has an interest in. For each address – A, B and C in the example – each MR proceeds to produce a pruned spanning tree by removing selected links. For the internetwork shown in Figure 6.29(a), the pruned spanning trees produced by each MR for each of the three multicast addresses are as shown in Figure 6.29(b).

For each address, these are produced by starting at the tip of each branch of the basic spanning tree and pruning each line that does not form a path back to the root for this address. Packets are then only forwarded on those lines that make up the resulting pruned spanning tree. The protocol is known as the **multicast open shortest path first** (**MOSPF**) routing protocol and, to explain how it works, assume that a packet with a (multicast) address

(a)

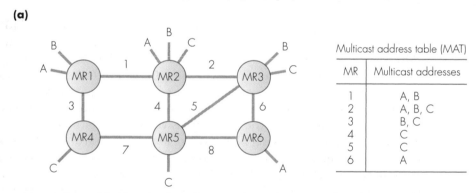

Multicast address table (MAT)

MR	Multicast addresses
1	A, B
2	A, B, C
3	B, C
4	C
5	C
6	A

Note: 1–8 are global line identifiers. These are also used as port numbers in the derivation of the spanning tree

(b)

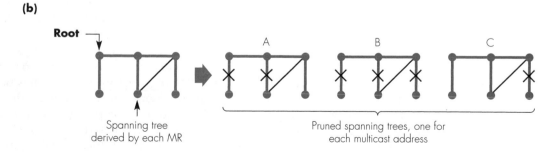

Figure 6.29 Spanning-tree multicast routing: (a) example topology and multicast address table; (b) set of spanning trees for each multicast address.

of A is received from a network attached to MR1. The steps followed by each MR are as follows:

■ On detecting the (multicast) address in the packet header is A, MR1 uses the pruned spanning tree for A to determine that a copy of the packet should be sent to MR2.

■ On receipt of the packet, MR2 first determines from its MAT that a copy of the packet should be sent out onto its own network. It then uses its own copy of the pruned spanning tree for A to determine that a copy of the packet should also be sent to MR3.

■ On receipt of the packet, MR3 first determines from its MAT that it has no interest in the packet. It then uses its own copy of the pruned spanning tree for A to determine that a copy of the packet should be sent to MR6.

■ On receipt of the packet, MR6 first determines from its MAT that a copy of the packet should be sent out onto its own network. It then uses its own copy of the pruned spanning tree for A to determine that it is at the end of a branch of the tree and hence discards the packet.

6.6.7 IGMP

The two routing algorithms we described in the last section – the DVMRP and MOSPF – both assumed that each multicast router has stored in its multicast address table the complete list of multicast addresses that are currently in use and also the multicast addresses that each multicast router has an interest in. As we explained, the contents of the MAT are obtained by, first, each multicast router learning the set of multicast addresses of which all the hosts attached to the networks/subnets that the mrouter serves are currently members, and second, this information being passed on to all the other mrouters. Clearly, the second step can be carried out using a broadcast procedure similar to that used in the distance vector algorithm to distribute network-wide routing information. Hence the unanswered question is how an mrouter learns the multicast addresses associated with its own attached networks/subnets. In practice, this is the role of the Internet group management protocol (IGMP) that we identified earlier in Figure 6.2. The IGMP is an integral part of the IP layer in all hosts and routers that support multicasting. It is defined in RFC 1112.

As we explained at the start of the last section, an application process (AP) within a host can join and leave a currently active multicast group at any time. To do this, the AP must know the 24-bit group address that has been allocated to this group by the ICANN. As we showed in Figure 6.27, the AP uses this to derive both the IP multicast address of the group and the corresponding Ethernet group address. It then writes these into the MAT and the corresponding GAT respectively. In the case of a multicast session involving a group of APs in hosts that are all attached to the same LAN, this is all that is needed. In the case of a multicast session over the Internet, however, it is necessary for the host to inform its local mrouter of the multicast address of the session that it wishes to join. The sequence of steps followed to do this is shown in Figure 6.30.

In this example, an AP running in a host that is attached to net/subnet 1 wishes to take part in a multicast session that has a derived multicast address of A. We assume that three other APs/hosts attached to the same multicast router are already members of two existing multicast groups, two with a multicast address of B and one with an address of C. In the case of B, one is attached to net/subnet 1 and the other to net/subnet 2 and, in the case of C, this is attached to net/subnet 2. Hence the contents of the initial tables are as shown in Figure 6.30(b).

First the IGMP in host (A) sends out a message – known as a *report* – to the IGMP in the attached mrouter (MR) containing the multicast address (MA) of the group it wishes to join (A). In addition to the MAT that is used for routing over the backbone network, a separate MAT and GAT are maintained by the MR for both net/subnet 1 and net/subnet 2. Hence on receipt of the report message, the IGMP first writes the MA into the MAT and the related Ethernet group address into the GAT of net/subnet 1. Also, since A is not already present in the backbone routing MAT, this is added to it and the new contents forwarded to each of the attached MRs.

Hosts do not need to inform an MR when it leaves a multicast group. At regular intervals, the IGMP in each MR broadcasts a *query* message to all hosts on each net/subnet requesting a report of which MAs they are currently members. On receipt of a query, the IGMP in each host responds by returning a separate report message for each MA of which the host is currently a member. In the example shown in Figure 6.30, we assume the host that was a member of MA C has now left the group and hence a report message for C is not returned. Hence the IGMP in the MR removes the entries for C from its tables and proceeds to forward the updated table contents to each of the attached MRs.

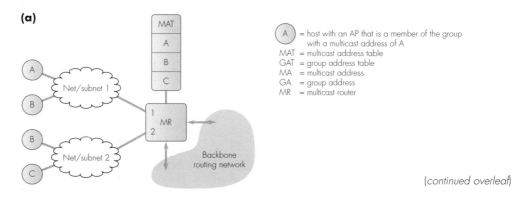

(continued overleaf)

Figure 6.30 IGMP summary: (a) example network topology; (b) IGMP message transfer sequence to join and leave a multicast session; (c) IGMP message format.

(b)

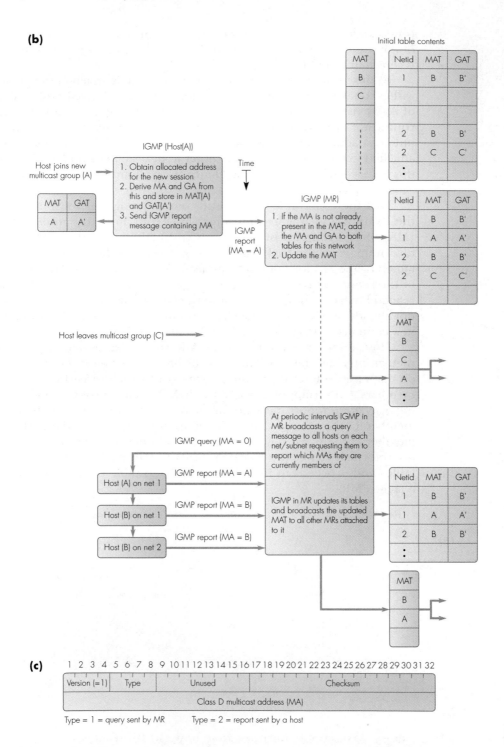

(c)

Type = 1 = query sent by MR   Type = 2 = report sent by a host

Figure 6.30 Continued.

The format of the two types of IGMP message – query and report – is the same and is shown in Figure 6.30(c). The *version* field is equal to 1 and the *type* field is either 0 for a report message (sent by a host) or 1 for a query message (sent by a MR). The *checksum* applies to the complete message and is computed using the same 1s complement procedure used with the header of an IP datagram. The *group address* is a 32-bit class D multicast address. In a query message it is set to all 0s and in a report it is set to the multicast group address being reported. Both are transmitted over the attached net/subnet in an IP packet with a *protocol* value of 2 and a *time-to-live* value of 1. In the case of a query, the *destination IP address* is the all-hosts broadcast address of 224.0.0.1 and the *source IP address* is the IP address of the MR. In the case of a report, the two addresses are the group MA being reported and the host IP address respectively.

6.6.8 M-bone

As we explained in Section 6.6.6 when we discussed the two multicast routing algorithms, currently, only a subset of the routers that make up the Internet global internetwork are capable of routing IP packets that have a multicast destination address. These are known as multicast routers (mrouters) and the network formed by the interconnected set of mrouters is known as the **multicast backbone** (**M-bone**) **network**. The two routing algorithms we described in Section 6.6.6 are then used to route multicast packets between the mrouters that make up the M-bone.

In practice, therefore, because only a subset of the routers in the global internetwork can route multicast packets, there may be other routers that do not support multicasting present in the physical path that links two mrouters together. Hence many of the transmission paths that link the mrouters that form the M-bone are logical links that are implemented using IP tunneling. As we explained in Section 6.5.5, with tunneling, in order to send an IP datagram containing a multicast group address over the logical link that links two mrouters together, the datagram is carried in the user data field of a second IP datagram. This has the (known) IP unicast address of the intended destination mrouter in the destination IP address field of the second datagram. In this way, the packet is routed over the global internetwork in the same way as a unicast packet using either the distance vector or the link-state shortest-path-first algorithm. Then, on arrival at the destination mrouter, the latter extracts the multicast datagram contained within the packet and proceeds to route it using one of the two related multicast routing algorithms we described in Section 6.6.6.

As we can deduce from this, in order to implement the M-bone, each mrouter has the IP (unicast) address of the adjacent mrouters that are (logically) connected to it stored in their connectivity/adjacency table. Normally, this information is entered by the management authority responsible for the network in which the mrouter is located. In this way, the possible presence of other (unicast) routers between two mrouters is transparent to the two mrouters which simply route (multicast) packets as if there is a physical transmission line linking them together.

6.6.9 ICMP

The Internet control message protocol (ICMP) forms an integral part of all IP implementations. It is defined in RFC 1256 and is used by hosts, routers and gateways for a variety of functions, and especially by network management. The main functions associated with the ICMP are as follows:

- error reporting,
- reachability testing,
- congestion control,
- route-change notification,
- performance measuring,
- subnet addressing.

The message types associated with each of these functions are shown in Table 6.2. Each is transmitted in a standard IP datagram.

Since the IP is a best-effort (unacknowledged) protocol, packets may be discarded while they are in transit across the Internet. Of course, transmission errors are one cause, but packets can be discarded by a host, router, or gateway for a variety of reasons. In the absence of any error reporting functions, a host does not know whether the repeated failure to send a packet to a given destination is the result of a poor transmission line (or other fault within a network) or simply the destination host being switched off. The various messages associated with the **error reporting** function are used for this purpose.

If a packet is corrupted by transmission errors, it is simply discarded. If a packet is discarded for any other reason, the ICMP in the host, router, or gateway that discards the packet generates a *destination unreachable* error report message and returns it to the ICMP in the source host with a reason code. Reasons include the following:

- destination network unreachable,
- destination host unreachable,
- parameter problem,
- specified protocol not present at destination,
- fragmentation needed but don't fragment (DF) flag set in datagram header,
- communication with the destination network not allowed for administrative reasons,
- communication with the destination host not allowed for administrative reasons.

Table 6.2 ICMP message types and their use

Function	ICMP message	Use
Error reporting	Destination unreachable	A datagram has been discarded for the reason specified in the message
	Time exceeded	Time-to-live parameter in a datagram expired and hence datagram discarded
	Parameter error	A parameter in the header of a datagram is unrecognizable
Reachability testing	Echo request/reply	Checks the reachability of a specified host or gateway
Congestion control	Source quench	Requests a host to reduce the rate at which datagrams are sent
Route exchange	Redirect	Used by a gateway to inform a host attached to one of its networks to use an alternative gateway on the same network for forwarding datagrams to a specific destination
Performance measuring	Time-stamp request/reply	Determines the transit delay between two hosts
Subnet addressing	Address mask request/reply	Used by a host to determine the address mask associated with a subnet

ICMP = Internet control message protocol

Although in most cases error reports are received as a result of some type of failure condition arising, in some instances an error report is used to gain some knowledge of the operational characteristics of the path/route followed by a packet. In general, the transfer of a message over the global internetwork is much quicker if no fragmentation is involved. Most networks (and subnetworks) support a maximum transmission unit (MTU) equal to or greater than 576 bytes. Hence one way of ensuring no fragmentation takes place is for the source IP to adopt this as the maximum size of all datagrams (including the IP header). In most cases, however, the actual MTU of the path will be greater than this and hence this would result in more packets being used to send each message than is necessary.

An alternative is for the source IP to use a procedure known as **path MTU discovery** to determine the MTU of a path/route prior to sending any datagrams relating to a session/call. Essentially, the first message received from the transport layer protocol relating to a new call/session is sent in a single datagram with the *don't fragment* bit set. Normally, if a router along the path followed by the packet cannot forward the packet over an attached link without fragmenting it, the router will return an ICMP error report with *fragmentation needed* as a reason code and an indication of the size of MTU that is possible. The source IP then adopts the latter as its own MTU to send all the remaining messages relating to the call/session.

Other error report messages include *time exceeded*, which indicates that the time-to-live parameter in a discarded packet has expired, and *parameter error*, which indicates that a parameter in the header of the discarded packet was not recognized.

If a network manager receives reports from a user that a specified destination is not responding, the reason must be determined using the *reachability testing* function, which is implemented in a program called **ping**. Typically, on receipt of such a report, the network manager initiates the sending of an *echo request* message to the suspect host to determine whether it is switched on and responding to requests. On receipt of an echo request message, the ICMP in the destination simply changes this to an *echo reply* message that it returns to the source. A similar test can be performed on selected routers and gateways if necessary.

If a packet is discarded because no free memory buffers are available as a result of a temporary overload condition, a *source quench* message is returned to the ICMP in the source host. Such messages can be generated either by a host or by a router or gateway. They request the source host to reduce the rate at which it sends packets. When a host receives such a message, it reduces the sending rate by an agreed amount. A new source quench message is generated each time a packet is discarded so that the source host incrementally reduces the sending rate. Such messages help to alleviate congestion within the global internetwork. Congestion is discussed further in Section 6.7.

When a network has multiple gateways attached to it, a gateway may receive datagrams from a host even though it determines from its routing table that they would be better sent via a different gateway attached to the same network. To inform the source host of this, the ICMP in the gateway returns a *redirect* message to the ICMP in the source indicating which is the better gateway to the specified destination. The ICMP in the source then makes an entry in its routing table for this destination.

An important operational parameter for an internet is the mean transit delay of packets/datagrams. This is a measure of the time a datagram takes to traverse the internet from a specified source to a specified destination. To ascertain this time, a host or a network manager can send a *time-stamp request* message to a specific destination. Each message contains the following three time-related parameters (known as *time-stamps*):

- the time the datagram was sent by the source,
- the time the datagram was received by the destination,
- the time the datagram was returned by the destination.

On receipt of a time-stamp request message, the ICMP in the destination simply fills in the appropriate time-stamp fields and returns the message to the source. On receipt of the reply, the source can quantify the current round-trip delay to that destination and from this determine the packet transit delay.

Finally, when subnet addressing is being used, the *address mask request* and corresponding reply messages are used by a host to ascertain the address mask associated with a local subnet. This is needed by a host to determine, for example, whether a specified destination is attached to the same subnet. The address mask is held by the local router associated with the subnet. The ICMP in a host can obtain the address mask by sending a request message and reading the mask from the reply.

ICMP message formats and transmission

The format of an ICMP message is shown in Figure 6.31. The first three fields are the same for all messages. The *type* field indicates the ICMP message type and these are related to the functions we listed earlier. For example, a *type* field of 0 relates to the error reporting function, 3 to reachability testing, 4 to congestion control, and so on. The *code* field then gives additional information such as the reason why a destination is unreachable. For example, 6 indicates that the destination network is unknown and 7 that the destination host is unknown. The *checksum* covers the entire ICMP message and uses the same algorithm as that used for the checksum present in the IP header. The

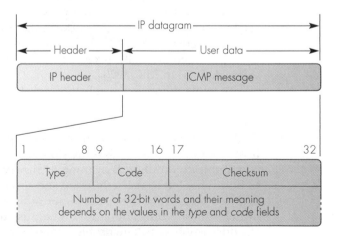

Figure 6.31 ICMP message format and transmission.

number and meaning of the following 32-bit words then depend on the *type* and *code* fields in the header.

As we showed in Figure 6.3 and explained in the accompanying text, the *protocol* field in each datagram header is used to route the payload in a datagram to the appropriate protocol – ICMP, IGMP, OSPF, TCP or UDP. In the case of reply messages, normally, these are for use by the local IP. When unsolicited error reports are received, in most cases, they are passed to an application-level process and result in an appropriate error message being output on the host screen.

6.6.10 Mobile IP

We studied the various types of wireless access networks in Chapter 4 and, as we summarized in Figure 4.22, a user with a mobile device – laptop, mobile phone, notebook, etc. – can now gain access to the Internet from virtually anywhere in the world. As we showed in the figure, this can be through a public/private wireless LAN or, with a Bluetooth-enabled mobile phone, a mobile phone network. In this subsection we study how a user with, say, a laptop is able to temporarily relocate to a different network and still be able to be contacted by a correspondent host that is located in a different place/network.

A host that is permanently attached to a fixed network such as a home/campus/office LAN is said to be **stationary** and the IP address associated with it is the home location **permanent address**. As we learned from the earlier sections of the chapter, the netid part of the permanent IP address relates to a fixed network which, in this case, is the home/campus/office LAN. Also, all the routing tables within the Internet are built up to route the IP packets relating to a session to/from any other stationary device that is located anywhere in the world back to the home location of the host. Clearly, therefore, it is not possible for the owner of a laptop to simply take it away and attach it to a different network since the netid part of the IP address relates only to the home network. In this subsection, we shall study how this problem is overcome. The Internet architecture and the terminology and protocols used are collectively called **mobile IP** and the standard relating to this is defined in RFC 3220.

To explain how this is achieved, we shall use the simplified network architecture shown in Figure 6.32. In this, host A is located in a different network – called the correspondent network – from the home location network of host B. Whilst in its own network host B has a permanent IP address. The user of host A knows this address – the domain name in practice – and hence can communicate with host B by using it. However, we now assume that the owner of host B has left to visit a different site and has taken his/her laptop to the visited network. Whilst there, the owner of host A wants to communicate with the owner of host B but cannot do this because he/she knows only the permanent IP address of host B. The problem, therefore, is how does host A communicate with host B now that it has been relocated to the visited network.

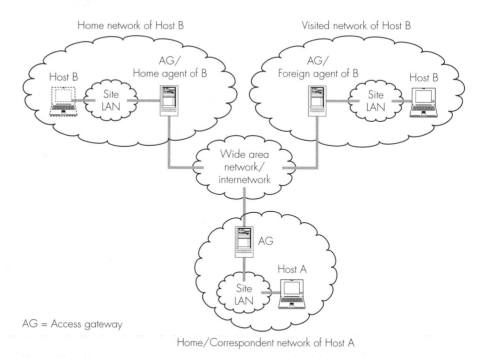

AG = Access gateway

Home/Correspondent network of Host A

The problem: Host A wants to communicate with Host B but B has left his/her home network and has taken his/her laptop to a different network – the visited network. Host A knows only the IP address of B at the home network. How does Host A communicate with Host B when it is in the vistied network?

Figure 6.32 Mobile IP – the simplified network architecture and terminology.

As we show in the figure, associated with the home network of host B is a **home agent** (**HA**). This is a process and in the figure it is running in the access gateway of the home network. The role of the home agent is to keep a record of any hosts that have a permanent IP address at the home network and are currently visiting a different network. Similarly, the network host B is visiting has a **foreign agent** (**FA**). This also is a process that, in the figure, is shown running in the access gateway of the visited network. The role of the foreign agent is to keep a record of all mobile hosts that are currently visiting this network. Each time a mobile host becomes attached to the visited network the host must register itself with both the foreign agent and also its home agent. The procedure followed is summarized in Figure 6.33.

To start the procedure, the host must first obtain the IP address of the foreign agent. This can be done in one of two ways. In the first method – called **agent advertisement** – at periodic intervals the foreign agent broadcasts an ICMP message that contains the IP address of the foreign agent. As we can see, the *Type* field has a value of 9, which indicates it is a **router advertisement**

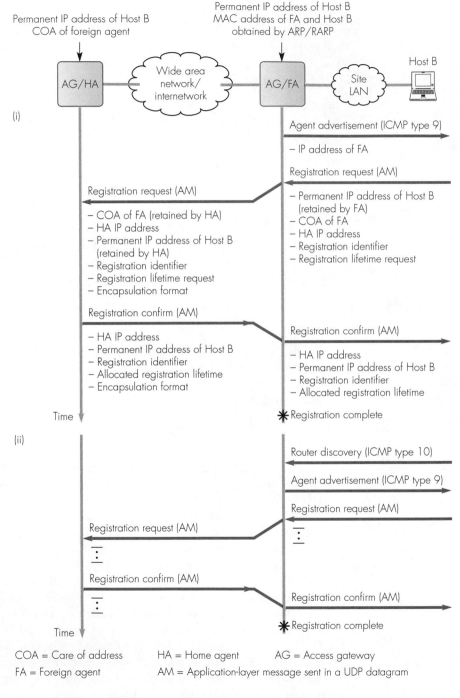

Figure 6.33 Mobile IP – registration of a mobile host (Host B) with the FA and HA.

message. The IP address of the foreign agent is then found in the *Router address* field of the ICMP message. The information in the extension message includes a *Registration identifier* field, a *Registration lifetime* field and one or more **care-of-address** (**COA**) fields. *The Registration* identifier is a 64-bit field and is present in each ICMP message that relates to a single registration operation. There is a fixed time duration for which the registration is valid and this is indicated in the *Registration lifetime* field.

In this example, the COA is that of the foreign agent. Host B then registers with the foreign agent by returning a *Registration request message* that contains the parameters shown in the figure and some security information that includes a time-stamp indicating the time the visiting host was registered. On receipt of this, the FA enters the permanent IP address of host B and the COA of the FA into its routing table and forwards the message to the HA. On receipt of this, the HA enters the permanent IP address of host B and the COA of the FA into its routing table. It then returns a *Registration confirm message* back to the FA with the contents as shown in the figure. At this point the registration is complete.

In the second method – called **agent solicitation** – the mobile host does not wait for an *agent advertisement message* and instead broadcasts an ICMP message with a *Type* value of 10. This indicates that it is an ICMP **router discovery** message. On receiving this, the foreign agent returns an agent advertisement ICMP message to the visiting host directly and the host then proceeds as in the first method. Once the registration of the mobile host with the home and foreign agents has been carried out, the exchange of packets between host A and host B can start. The route followed by each packet is shown in Figure 6.34.

Each IP packet relating to the session contains in its header the IP address of the correspondent host – host A – and the permanent IP address of the mobile host – host B. Hence when the packet is to be sent to the home agent this can be done directly – shown as (1) in the figure. However, when the packet is sent from the home agent to the foreign agent – (2) – it is necessary to encapsulate the packet inside another packet that has the IP address of the foreign agent in the destination address field and the IP address of the home agent in the source address field. On receipt of the packet, the foreign agent simply extracts the original packet from the received packet and then sends it over the visited network using the MAC address of host B obtained using ARP – (3). Similarly, when host B replies, the foreign agent receives a copy of the packet using the MAC address of the FA and detects that the destination IP address in the packet header is that of host A and the source address is the permanent IP address of host B. It therefore sends the packet directly to host A unchanged – (4).

As we can see in the figure, the above procedure is relatively inefficient since the route followed by each pair of packets that are exchanged involves four hops. There are a number of ways of improving this but, in general, these involve the home agent of the correspondent network and hence involve additional procedures.

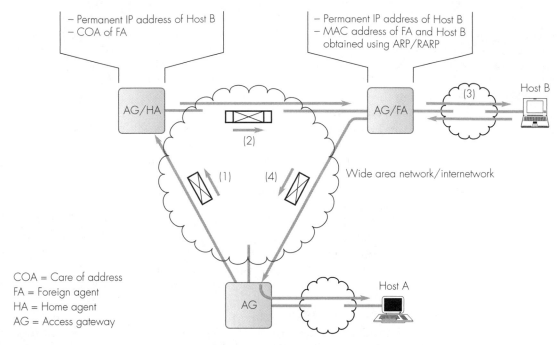

- IP packet sent from Host A to Host B using the permanent IP address of Host B in the destination address and the IP address of Host A in the source address. (1)
- HA reads the permanent IP address of Host B and, from its routing table, determines the packet must be rerouted to the COA of FA.
- HA encapsulates the packet inside a new packet with COA of FA in the destination address field. (2)
- FA receives the encapsulated packet and extracts the original packet. It then determines from its routing table and the destination address field in the packet header that the packet is for the visiting Host B.
- The FA then proceeds to broadcast the packet over the LAN in a frame with the destination MAC address of Host B. (3)
- Host B receives the packet and generates a response packet with the permanent IP address of Host B in the source address field and the IP address of Host A in the destination address field. It then sends the response packet to the FA using the MAC address of the FA.
- The FA relays the packet unchanged to the AG of Host A and from there to Host A. (4)

Figure 6.34 Mobile IP – indirect routing of packets after Host B has registered with the FA and HA.

6.7 QoS support

Congestion arises within a network when the demand for a network resource exceeds the level that is provided. For example, if a burst of packets arrive at a router (within the global internetwork) on a number of different input lines that all require the same output line, then the output line will become congested if the rate of arrival of packets is greater than the rate they can be output. To allow for this possibility, each output line has a first-in first-out

(FIFO) queue associated with it which is used to hold a defined number of packets that are awaiting output on that line. Hence, providing the burst is of a relatively short duration and the number of packets to be queued is less than the number of packet buffers available, the congestion will be transient and the only effect should be a small increase in the end-to-end transfer delay experienced by each packet using that line. In the event of a longer burst, however, then all the packet buffers may become full and, as a result, some packets will have to be discarded.

Similarly, at a network-wide level, since the Internet is a best-effort connectionless network, the global internetwork will become congested if, over a sustained period, the aggregate rate at which packets are entering the internetwork exceeds its total capacity in terms of transmission bandwidth and packet buffers. As we saw in Section 1.2.4, associated with each call is a defined set of parameters that form what is called the minimum quality of service (QoS) requirements for the call. For example, with a packet-switched network like the Internet, these include a defined minimum mean packet throughput rate and a maximum end-to-end packet transfer delay. Hence, if as a result of congestion these requirements are not met, then the quality of the call may no longer be acceptable to the user. This is the case with applications involving real-time media streams, for example, such as Internet telephony.

As we can conclude from the above, two levels of congestion control are required, one that operates at the global internetwork level and the other that operates at the router level. The aim of the first is to limit the aggregate rate at which packets are entering the global internetwork to below its maximum rate, and the aim of the second is to maximize the flow of packets through each router. In the following subsections we discuss aspects of two of the schemes that are used to perform these functions. In addition, we describe the essential features of a technique called MultiProtocol Label Switching (MPLS). This is a scheme that is used to improve IP routing performance in high-throughput core IP networks.

6.7.1 Integrated services

Most early applications of the Internet were text based and hence relatively insensitive to delay and jitter. Examples include FTP and e-mail, both of which can tolerate the added delays incurred by the use of a host-to-host retransmission control mechanism to overcome the effect of lost packets resulting from the best-effort service provided by IP. Other text-based applications, however, cannot tolerate the delay caused by retransmissions but nevertheless require minimal packet losses. Examples of this type of application are those relating to network control.

More recently, a number of interpersonal applications involving packetized speech and video were introduced. These require the packets that are generated at the source to be transferred over the Internet and played out at the destination in real time. This means that the retransmission of lost packets is not possible and that the packet flow is particularly sensitive to lost packets and jitter. Such applications also require a guaranteed minimum bandwidth. To meet this more varied set of QoS requirements, two schemes have been researched and standardized, one called integrated services (IntServ) and the other differentiated services (DiffServ). In this section we describe aspects of the IntServ scheme while aspects of DiffServ are described in Section 6.7.2.

In both schemes, the packets relating to the different types of call/ session are each allocated a different value in the precedence bits of the *type of service* field of the IP packet header. This is used by the routers within the Internet to differentiate between the packet flows relating to the different types of call. The IntServ solution defines three different classes of service:

- **guaranteed**: in this class, a specified maximum delay and jitter and an assured level of bandwidth are guaranteed. It is intended for applications involving the playout of real-time streams;

- **controlled load** (also known as predictive): in this class, no firm guarantees are provided but the flow obtains a constant level of service equivalent to that obtained with the best-effort service at light loads. Examples of applications in this class are those involving real-time streams that have the capability of adjusting the amount of real-time data that is generated to the level that is offered;

- **best-effort**: this is intended for text-based applications.

To cater for the three different types of packet flows, within each router, three separate output queues are used for each line, one for each class. In addition, appropriate control mechanisms are used to ensure the QoS requirements of each class are met. We shall first discuss a number of these as these are used in both the IntServ and the DiffServ schemes.

Token bucket filter

This is used with each of the packet flows in both the guaranteed and predictive service classes. A portion of the bandwidth of the outgoing line and an amount of buffer/queue space is reserved for the packet flow relating to each call. A control mechanism called the token bucket filter is used to enforce these allocations so that the guaranteed QoS requirements in terms of bandwidth, delay, and jitter are met.

Associated with each flow is a container called a *bucket* into which tokens are entered at a rate determined by the bandwidth requirement of the flow. The size of the bucket is the same as the maximum amount of buffer/queue space the flow may consume. A packet relating to a flow can only be transferred to the output queue if there are sufficient tokens currently in the bucket. The number of tokens required is determined by the packet length and, if sufficient tokens are currently in the bucket, the packet is queued and the corresponding number of tokens taken from the bucket. As we can deduce from this, therefore, providing the arrival rate of packets is less than or equal to the rate of entry of tokens into the bucket, then both the agreed bandwidth and delay/jitter will be met. If the arrival rate of packets exceeds the allocated bandwidth, normally these are relegated to the best-effort queue.

Weighted fair queuing

Since the packet rate – and hence bandwidth – associated with each flow may be different, when the packets relating to each flow are queued for transmission, in order to ensure the guaranteed delay bounds are met, it is necessary to ensure that the packets relating to each flow are not delayed by the packets of other flows. Hence a queue management scheme is also required to schedule the order that queued packets are transmitted. The **weighted fair queuing (WFQ)** scheme performs this function.

In order to ensure the delay bounds for each flow are met, the order of transmission of packets from the queue is changed each time a new packet arrives for queuing. When a packet arrives at an incoming line of the router it is given a time-stamp. This is determined from the arrival time of the packet and its scheduled departure time, the latter computed from the bandwidth associated with the flow and the packet length. The time-stamp of the packet is then compared with the time-stamps of the packets that are currently queued and the packet with the smallest time-stamp is transmitted first. In this way the delay bounds of each flow are met.

Random early detection

The requirements of the queue management scheme used with the best-effort queue are different from those of the other two queues. As we indicated earlier, normally, a router simply discards/drops a packet if the required output queue is already full. However, as we shall describe later in Section 7.3.2, with TCP, each time a packet relating to a call/session is lost, the TCP in the source host detects this and halves its current rate of entry of new packets for the call. Since this is done by all the hosts that lose a packet, the utilization of the link bandwidth falls dramatically. This is also detected by the affected TCPs which then quickly ramp-up the rate of entry of new packets. This, in turn, often results in full queues and dropped packets occurring, again with the effect that the utilization of the available transmission bandwidth is poor. To stop this occurring, the **random early detection (RED)** queue management scheme is often used.

With RED, when a packet arrives for an output queue and the queue is full, instead of discarding the packet, a packet that is already in the queue is randomly selected for discarding. This has the affect that a reduced number of different applications are affected and hence the bandwidth utilization of the link is much improved.

To implement the scheme, two thresholds relating to the queue are defined: a minimum threshold (MinTH) and a maximum threshold

(MaxTH). Also, the average length (AvrLEN) of the queue is continuously monitored and used as a measure of the current level of traffic using the line. The action taken by the scheduler is determined by the current AvrLEN relative to the two thresholds as follows:

AvrLEN < MinTH:	the new packet is entered into the queue;
AvrLEN < MaxTH:	the new packet is dropped;
MaxTH < AvrLEN < MinTH:	a randomly-selected packet from the queue is dropped and the new packet is queued.

As we can deduce from the last condition, the probability of packets that are already in the queue being dropped increases as the AvrLEN increases. This has been found to give high levels of bandwidth utilization during periods of congestion.

Resource reservation protocol

With the IntServ scheme, in order to ensure the aggregate bandwidth of real-time traffic flows does not exceed that which is allocated for both the guaranteed and controlled-load traffic, the resources required for each flow (in terms of transmission bandwidth and buffer capacity) are reserved in advance of each packet flow starting. The protocol used to do this is called the **resource reservation protocol** (**RSVP**).

Because many of the new real-time applications involve multiple participants, RSVP is used to reserve resources in each router along either a unicast or a multicast path. The actual routing of the packets associated with both types of call, however, are not part of RSVP and these are carried out in the normal way using one of the routing algorithms we described earlier in Section 6.6. A selection of the messages associated with RSVP are shown in Figure 6.35(a).

Each traffic flow is identified uniquely by the combined source and destination addresses in the IP header and the port number in the UDP header. To perform a reservation, the AP in the host that wishes to set up the call/session sends a *path* message in a UDP datagram with either the unicast or multicast address of the other host(s) in the destination address field of the IP header and the port number in the UDP datagram header. The purpose of the *path* message is, firstly, to enable each router along the path/route followed by the packet to create an entry in a table known as the **path-state table** and, secondly, to gather information about the resources that are currently available in each router along the path. The entry in the path-state table includes the flow identifier, a specification of the required parameters associated with the call/session – known as the traffic specification or Tspec – and the (IP) address of the router from which it received the *path* message.

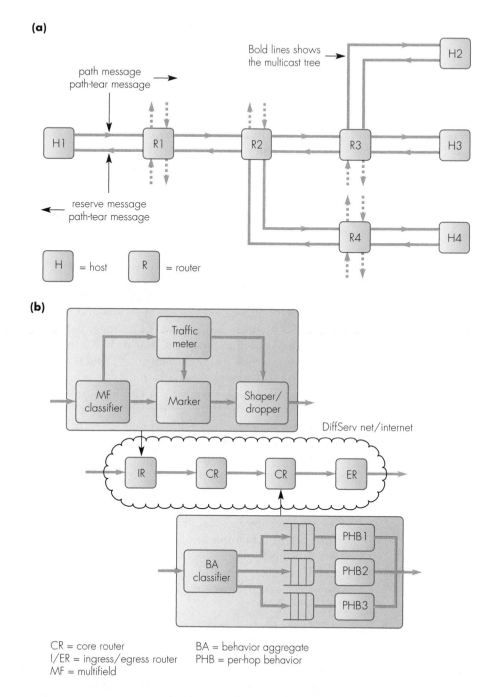

Figure 6.35 QoS support mechanisms: (a) RSVP principles; (b) DiffServ architecture.

On receipt of the *path* message, the AP (identified by the port number) in the destination host(s) uses the resource levels reported by each router to determine which type of call – guaranteed, controlled-load, or neither – the path can support. Assuming the call can be accepted, the AP in each destination host then returns a *reserve* message (containing the Tspec for the call) to the router from which it received the *path* message. If the router still has the necessary resources, it reserves these for the flow (the resources may be different in each direction), makes an entry in the path-state table of the address of the router which sent it the message, and then sends the (*reserve*) message to the next router along the path. If the resources are not available, then a *path-tear* message is returned along the forward and return paths in order to release any resources that have been reserved and delete the entry in the path-state table. This procedure is repeated by each router along the path back to the source which, on receipt of the *reserve* message, proceeds with the call.

The path associated with each call/session may change during the lifetime of a call, for example due to a router going down. To allow for this occurring, associated with each entry in the path-state table kept by each router is a timer called the *cleanup timer* and, should this expire, the entry is deleted. The timer is restarted each time a *path* message relating to the call is received. At periodic intervals – less than the cleanup timeout period – the source host sends a new *path* message, which is acted upon by each router in the same way as the first *path* message. Hence should the new path not include a particular router, its cleanup timer will expire and the related path-state information be deleted. This mode of operation is known therefore as *soft-state* since it may change during a call.

Finally, on completion of the call/session, the AP that set up the call sends out a *path-tear* message which results in the entry in the path-table held by each router along the path(s) being deleted. The RFCs associated with RSVP and the other IntServ procedures are in RFC 2205–2216.

The major disadvantage of RSVP is that state information is retained by each router for each call/flow. Although this may be acceptable in a company intranet, for example, in a backbone router of the Internet the tables used for this purpose can be very large. Hence with the very high bit rates that are used, the heavy overheads per call can be unacceptably high. It is for this reason that the alternative DiffServ scheme was developed.

6.7.2 Differentiated services

Using the DiffServ approach, individual flows are not identified and instead the individual flows in each service class are aggregated together. Flows are then treated on a per-class basis rather than a per-flow basis. The general architecture used with a DiffServ network is shown in Figure 6.35(b).

The incoming packet flows relating to individual calls – referred to as microflows – are classified by the router/gateway at the edge of the DiffServ-compliant net/internet into one of the defined service/traffic classes by examining selected fields in the various headers in the packet. Within the DiffServ network the *type of service* (*TOS*) field in the IP packet header is replaced by a new field called the *differentiated services* (*DS*) *field*. As we saw earlier in Section 6.2, this is an 8-bit field, although currently only six bits are used for the DS field. The six bits form what is called the (**DS**) **packet codepoint** (**DSCP**), which is used to enable each router to determine the traffic class to which the packet data relates and the output queue into which the packet should be put. The queue management/scheduling procedure relating to each queue is called a **per-hop behavior** (**PHB**) and, since this applies to an aggregated set of packet flows, a PHB is said to be applied to a **behavior aggregate** (**BA**).

Within the DiffServ network, a defined level of resources in terms of the buffer space within each router and the bandwidth of each output line is allocated to each traffic class using, for example, a token bucket filter. As each packet arrives at the ingress router it is first classified as belonging to a particular traffic class. In some instances, however, as we shall see later, the actual classification is also a function of how well the microflow (to which the packet relates) is conforming to the agreed traffic profile for the flow. This is determined by the **traffic meter module** and, based on the level of conformance, the traffic meter informs the **marker module** whether the packet should be marked with a low, medium, or high drop precedence. In addition, the traffic meter also informs the **shaper/dropper** module of this and the latter decides whether the packet should be dropped or allowed into the network.

Normally, real-time microflows with hard QoS guarantees are placed in the highest-priority traffic class. Typically, the traffic meter for this type of stream is a token bucket filter with a defined rate and bucket depth. Hence if an arriving packet relating to a flow in this class is deemed to be out-of-profile, the traffic meter informs the shaper/dropper module of this. The latter then either drops the packet or relegates it to the best-effort class by setting all six DSCP bits to zero.

Once within the network, as each packet arrives at a core router, the **BA classifier** first determines to which traffic class the packet belongs and hence to which output queue the packet should be transferred. Each queue is then serviced using an appropriate PHB. Currently, two PHBs have been defined: **expedited forwarding** (**EF**) and **assured forwarding** (**AF**). The EF PHB is similar to the guaranteed service class associated with IntServ and hence has the highest priority. The PHB used with this is based on a queue scheduling procedure such as weighted fair queuing.

The AF PHB has four ordered traffic classes associated with it, each of which has three drop procedure levels: low, medium and high. Should congestion arise, this is used together with the traffic class to determine which packet(s) should be dropped. The PHB used in this case, therefore, is based on a queue scheduling procedure such as random early discard. The RFCs associated with DiffServ are in RFC 2474–5.

6.7.3 MPLS

Before describing how a packet is forwarded in an MPLS network it is helpful to first review how a packet is forwarded in a standard IP-based network. A schematic diagram illustrating the forwarding of packets by a router in a conventional IP-based network is shown in Figure 6.36.

On receipt of a packet from one of the input queue interfaces, the router first reads the IP destination address in the packet header and proceeds to determine the netid by using the related address mask. It then uses the netid to determine from its forwarding table the outgoing port/line that is on the shortest path route to this netid. In addition, the ToS field in the packet header is passed to the **packet classifier**, which uses this to determine the queuing and scheduling rules to be applied to the packet. This information is then passed to the output queue interface unit and this determines the output queue relating to the output port/line that should be used to forward the packet to the next-hop router.

As we have just seen, with the introduction of integrated services three different classes of service are supported, each of which has a separate output queue associated with it. A queuing and scheduling rule is then used for each class and this is then passed to the output interface unit to ensure the QoS requirements of each class are met.

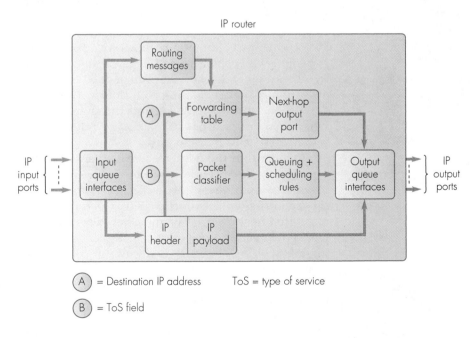

Figure 6.36 Packet forwarding in a conventional IP router.

Using differentiated services – DiffServ – individual flows are not identified and instead the individual flows in each service class are aggregated together. Flows are then treated on a per-class basis rather than a per-flow basis.

As we can conclude from this summary, the efficiency of the forwarding mechanism used within each router becomes all important and especially so in the routers that make up the high-throughput core networks within the Internet. Hence, as we indicated in Section 6.7, **MultiProtocol Label Switching** (**MPLS**) is a technique that is now widely used in the routers within these core networks to obtain higher forwarding rates of packets. MPLS is defined in RFC 3031.

As we saw earlier in Section 6.6.1, the Internet is composed of a large number of autonomous systems (ASs). Associated with each AS is a backbone area network and it is within these that MPLS is most widely deployed. In order to see where the various QoS mechanisms are used, we shall use the example network architecture shown in Figure 6.37. Typically, DiffServ is used for traffic aggregation and the differentiation of the packet flows with different classes of service. MPLS is then used for traffic aggregation and load balancing which, collectively, are referred to as **traffic engineering** (**TE**).

The access gateway/router classifies all packet flows entering the backbone area network. This is based on the IP source and destination addresses and the TCP/UDP source and destination port numbers. Normally, the

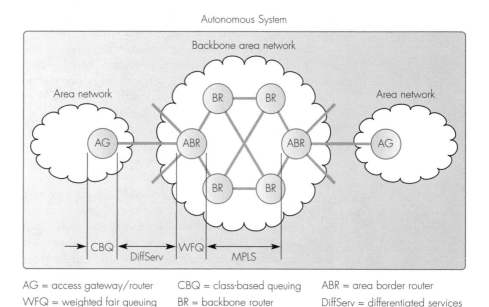

Figure 6.37 MPLS example network architecture with related QoS mechanisms.

access gateway (AG) uses **class-based queuing** (**CBQ**) for this function since it must distinguish between a large number of applications and users. Typically, these are implemented as a set of software queues.

Once the traffic flows have been classified and queued, the AG schedules and separates – known as **shaping** – each flow. Shaping is necessary because there may be many different classes of flows but, once they are within the backbone area network, the area border router segregates the flows – known as **grooming** – into a relatively small number of queues, for example, real time, non-real time and best effort. The AG also controls the allocation of DiffServ values for the different packet flows. The main aim of DiffServ is to achieve the differentiation of packet flows using a short classification key. This, in turn, simplifies the design of very high throughput routers. Normally, the DiffServ values are marked by hosts – in the DS/ToS field in the IP packet header and then used by the AG. In addition, the AG may assign DiffServ values as a means of classifying network management and signaling messages which, as we shall see, are used by all the routers in the AS backbone.

Area border routers

Each area border router (ABR) receives packet flows from a set of access gateways. The ABR also serves as a **label edge router** (**LER**) since they append and remove MPLS headers to/from the head of IP packets. In contrast to an IP destination address that is used to forward a packet over the entire shortest-path-route through the network, an MPLS label has only per-hop significance. This is done so that an MPLS packet can be forced to follow a specific path through the network by using a sequence of labels – and hence keys into the related forwarding tables – to the intended destination ABR/LER.

This is an important aspect of traffic engineering since, when all shortest-path routes are being used, some routers can become overloaded and form what are called hotspots. Hence to overcome this, specific routes can be selected that bypass potential **hotspots**. This is called **load balancing**. The backbone routers within the AS then simply read the MPLS label and forward the packet on the new output port/line with a new label at very high throughput rates. This mode of operation is known as **label switching** and a simple example illustrating this is shown in Figure 6.38.

Normally, all the router functions in backbone routers are implemented in hardware. For example, the set of queues associated with each output port/line are implemented in hardware and, typically, use a weighted fair queuing (WFQ) scheduling procedure. The queues are based on a relatively small number of different network classes of service. These include real time packet flows, non-real time, best effort, signaling, and network management. As a result, the packet flows relating to the different user applications are combined and assigned to a particular network class of service.

As we indicated earlier, the primary role of MPLS is for traffic engineering and, more generally, optimizing the use of network resources. To achieve

(a)

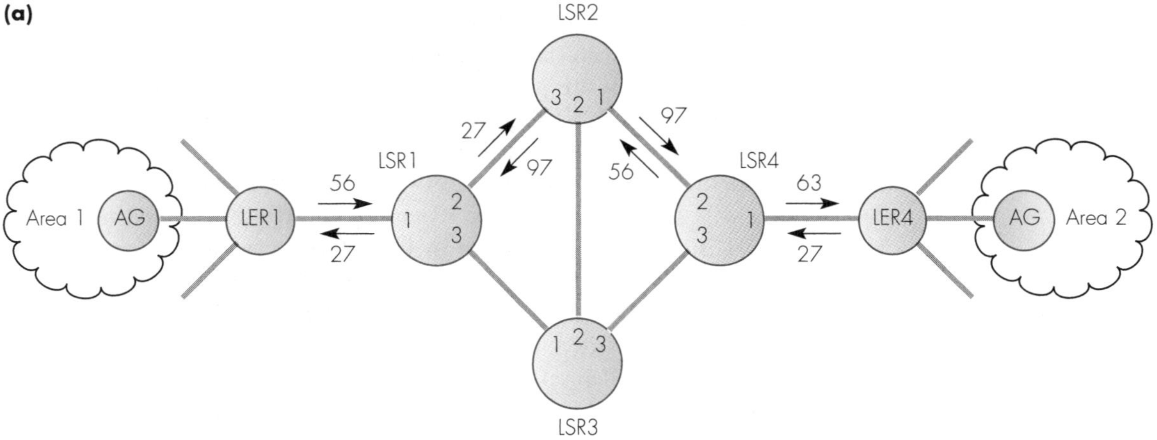

(b)

LSR1
Port 1

Output port	Label	Q + S rule
2	27	3

1,56 →

Port2

Output port	Label	Q + S rule
1	27	5

2,97 →

Port3

Output port	Label	Q + S rule

LSR2
Port 1

Output port	Label	Q + S rule
3	97	5

1,56 →

Port2

Output port	Label	Q + S rule

Port3

Output port	Label	Q + S rule
1	97	3

3,27 →

LSR4
Port 1

Output port	Label	Q + S rule
2	56	5

1,27 →

Port2

Output port	Label	Q + S rule
1	63	3

2,97 →

Port3

Output port	Label	Q + S rule

Note: two different flows (i) from Area 1 to Area 2 and (ii) from Area 2 to Area 1

Figure 6.38 Label switching schematic.

this, all packet flows are constrained to follow a specific **label switched path** (**LSP**) through the backbone network. All the flows that are grouped together with the same label are said to belong to the same **forward equivalent class** (**FEC**) since all the packets are then forwarded in the same way. At the destination the ABR/LER terminates the LSP by removing the MPLS label. The destination IP address is then used to forward the packet to the addressed access gateway/network. Once in the access gateway, the original classification is restored based on the IP source and destination addresses and the TCP/UDP source and destination port numbers. The IP destination address is then used to forward the packet to the intended recipient host in the normal way. A schematic diagram illustrating the functionality of an ABR/LER is shown in Figure 6.39(a).

On receipt of an IP packet, the IP destination address in the packet header is used first to obtain the output port/line from the forwarding table. This is then passed, together with the DiffServ value in the DS field, to the LSP table module. This then uses these to select a new next-hop label for this flow and the queuing and scheduling rules to be used with it. The MPLS header is then created and appended to the IP packet. This is then passed to the output queue interface module ready for forwarding using the selected output port and its associated queuing and scheduling rules.

As we can see in Figure 6.39(b), the length of the *label* field in the MPLS header is 20 bits which is sufficient to identify a significant number of unique next-hop labels and output port/line identifiers. The 3-bit *CoS* field is then used to select a specific queuing and scheduling rule for this flow. The 8-bit *time to live* field is used to detect and discard packets that are looping. It is set to an initial value by the ingress ABR/LER and decremented by each BR/LSR it visits and, should it become zero, the packet is discarded.

The *S bit* is used primarily to support multiple virtual private networks. A service provider can separate out the packet flows relating to each virtual private network by stacking a number of 32-bit MPLS labels at the head each original IP packet and setting the S bit to 0. Each BR/LSR along a path then pops the top entry from the stack and uses the 32-bit value to forward the packet. Then, when there is only a single entry in the stack left, the S bit is set to 1. Hence when only a single MPLS network is present, the S bit is set to 1.

Normally, the lines linking the BRs/LSRs within the backbone network are derived from SDH/SONET lines which we described in Section 2.2.5. Each MPLS packet is then transmitted using the PPP protocol we described in Section 2.6.4. Also, since all routing within the core backbone network is carried out using the MPLS label, the payload of the MPLS packet can relate to any protocol – IP, IPX, etc. This is the origin of the term MultiProtocol in the title.

Signaling

As we indicated in Section 6.6.4, within the area backbone network of an AS the routing protocol is OSPF. This is used to determine both the topology of

(a)

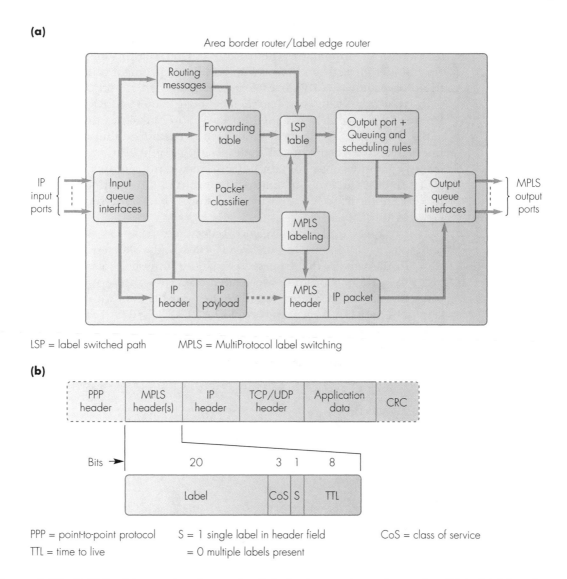

LSP = label switched path   MPLS = MultiProtocol label switching

(b)

PPP = point-to-point protocol   S = 1 single label in header field   CoS = class of service

TTL = time to live   = 0 multiple labels present

Figure 6.39 MPLS: (a) area border router/label edge router schematic; (b) MPLS header details.

the network and the shortest-path route assignments for each router. As we indicated earlier, however, with MPLS the route assignments are simply per-hop identifiers. Hence with MPLS it is necessary to have what is called a signaling protocol to determine a set of label-switched paths through the network and to assign a set of MPLS labels that identify uniquely each path. In practice, there are a number of ways of doing this so we shall study just one approach as an example.

In what is called basic MPLS, every label switched router (LSR) within the backbone network is assigned an IP address and runs the OSPF protocol to establish the topology of the backbone. However, the shortest-path routes are not used directly and instead an additional protocol called the **label distribution protocol** (**LDP**) is used to create a complete set of label-switched paths (LSPs) between each ingress label edge router (LER) and egress LER. Unique labels are then assigned for each hop in each of the label-switched paths. The use of OSPF in this way has the advantage that routing changes can be readily incorporated. The disadvantage is that the set of shortest path routes computed may contain hotspots as we indicated earlier. Hence the actual routes used are sometimes different from the computed shortest-path routes. To illustrate this, consider the simple backbone topology shown in Figure 6.40.

As we can see, this involves two access networks – areas A and B – that both want to communicate with area C. Clearly, the shortest path route from A to C is the same as that from B to C. Hence if these are used, the link from LSR3 to LER5 may become overloaded even though there is an alternative route through LSR4. Hence to utilize the available bandwidth in a more efficient way, the path from B to C could be LER2 – LSR3 – LSR4 – LER5 since although this route is longer, the transmission bandwidth is more distributed. This approach is called **constraint routed LSPs** (**CR-LSPs**) and the modified protocol is called the **constraint routed label distribution protocol** (**CR-LDP**).

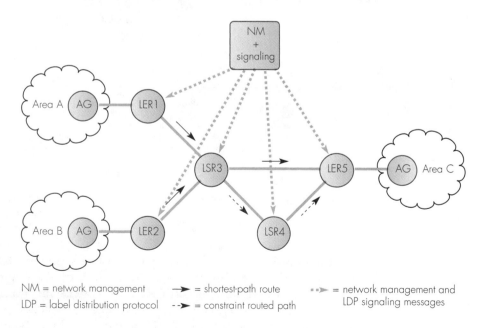

NM = network management   ⟶ = shortest-path route   ⋯▶ = network management and
LDP = label distribution protocol   --▶ = constraint routed path   LDP signaling messages

Figure 6.40 Constraint routed LSPs as used with CR-LDP.

Finally, as we show in the figure, the signaling component of the network management station computes the label switched paths between each pair of LERs using CR analysis. Each router within the backbone runs LDP and the network management station then uses LDP to download the contents of the LSP table held within each router. All the signaling and network management messages are downloaded using the same set of lines/links that are used to carry MPLS packets. As we can deduce from this, all the paths allocated are under the control of the network operator.

6.8 IPv6

Until the mid-1990s the Internet was used primarily by universities, government agencies, research establishments and some sectors of industry. Since that time, however, it has gone through unprecedented growth owing to a large extent to the rapid rise in interest in the use of the World Wide Web. As a result, most schools, colleges, and many homes now have PCs with connections to the Internet. These are now being used, in addition to Web access, to exploit the range of other applications that are supported by the Internet. Moreover, this growth is predicted to increase even faster as new applications emerge: for example, the widespread use of hybrid mobile phones/computers with Internet interfaces, television set-top boxes with integral Web browsers, plus a potentially vast number of consumer products – such as meters, household appliances, office equipment, and so on – many of which may have an Internet interface.

Although the introduction of CIDR has extended considerably the usable address space of IPv4, the IETF has already defined and is using a new version of IP which has a number of features that have been introduced to meet the predicted growth levels. This is known as **IP version 6** (**IPv6**) or sometimes **IP next generation** (**IPng**). It is defined in RFCs 1883–7 and a number of supporting RFCs. In addition to providing a large increase in the number of IP addresses, the IETF has taken the opportunity to correct some of the deficiencies associated with IPv4 and to provide a number of other features. The main new features of IPv6 are:

■ a much increased address space from 32 bits to 128 bits;

■ hierarchical addresses to reduce the size of the routing tables associated with the routers in the core backbone network;

■ a simplified header to enable routers and gateways to process and route packets faster;

■ the introduction of improved security and data integrity features including authentication and encryption;

■ an autoconfiguration facility that enables a host to obtain an IP address via the network without human intervention;

- harder quality-of-service guarantees by means of the preferential treatment by routers of the packets associated with interactive and multimedia applications relative to those relating to traditional applications such as e-mail and file transfers;

- support for mobile computing by the use of autoconfiguration to obtain an IP address dynamically via the network for the duration of a call/session.

Although many of the above features require some radical changes to IPv4 – for example a different address structure and datagram/packet format – in terms of the protocols that are used within the expanded global internet-work, these operate in much the same way as the current IPv4 protocols. For example, the LS-SPF (OSPF) routing algorithm we described in Section 6.5.4 is used as the standard interior gateway protocol (IGP) for IPv6 except, of course, that 128-bit addresses are used in the link-state and routing tables. There is also an updated version of the RIP – based on the distance vector routing algorithm we described in Section 6.5.3 – called **RIPng**. Similarly, at the backbone level, the border gateway protocol (BGP) we described in Section 6.6.5 (including the CIDR we described in Section 6.4.3) is used but with extensions to allow reachability information based on IPv6 hierarchical addresses to be exchanged. Hence in the remainder of this section we limit our discussion to a selection of the new features that are used.

6.8.1 Datagram format

In relation to the IPv4 datagram/packet header, a number of fields have been dropped and others have been made optional. The result is a basic/main header of 40 bytes, the contents and format of which are shown in Figure 6.41(a). The use of each field is as follows:

Version

This is set to 6 to enable routers to discriminate IPv6 packets from IPv4 packets. It is envisaged that both will need to coexist for many years.

Traffic class

This field plays a similar role to the *ToS* byte in the IPv4 header. It allows the source IP to allocate a different priority to packets relating to, say, multimedia applications involving real-time streams from those relating to traditional applications. It contains a 4-bit priority field and hence 16 priorities are possible; the higher the priority value, the higher the packet priority. Values in the range 0–7 are for packets relating to applications for which best-effort delivery is acceptable; for example network news (1) and FTP(4). Both these applications are less sensitive to delay and delay variation (jitter) than applications involving real-time media but FTP is more sensitive to packet loss than network news. Values in the range 8–15 are for packets containing real-time streams such as audio and video. Typically, such streams/packets are more sensitive to delay and jitter than the packets in the first category and hence should be transmitted before them during periods of congestion. Also, within the second category, packets containing compressed video are more sensitive to packet loss than packets containing just audio and hence are given a higher priority.

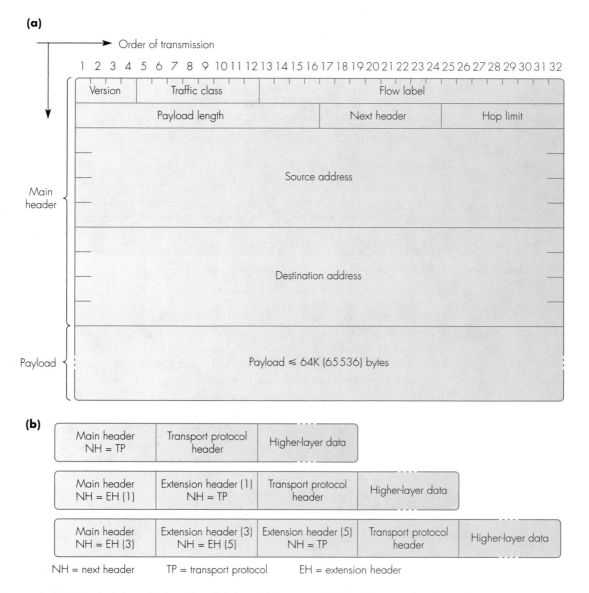

Figure 6.41 IPv6: (a) main header fields and format; (b) position and order of extension headers.

Flow label

This is a new field and is closely linked to the *traffic class* field. It is set to zero in best-effort packets and, in packets in the second category, it is used to enable a router to identify the individual packets relating to the same call/session. As we saw earlier in Section 6.7.1, one approach to handling packets containing real-time streams is to reserve resources – for example transmission bandwidth – for such calls in advance of sending the packets relating to the call. During the reservation procedure, the call is allocated a *flow label* by the source. Also, each router along the reserved path keeps a record of this, together with the source and destination IP addresses, in a table. Routers then use the combined *flow label* and source IP address present in each packet header to relate the packet to a specific call/flow. The related routing information is then retrieved from the routing table and this is used, together with the *traffic class* value, to ensure the QoS requirements of the call/flow are met during the forwarding procedure.

Payload length

This indicates the number of bytes that follow the basic 40-byte header in the datagram. The minimum length of a basic datagram is 536 bytes and the maximum length is 64K bytes. The *payload length* is slightly different from the *total length* field used in the header of an IPv4 datagram since, as we explained in Section 6.2, the *total length* includes the number of bytes in the datagram header.

Next header

As we show in Figure 6.41(b), a basic IPv6 datagram comprises a main header followed by the header of the peer transport layer protocol (TCP/UDP) and, where appropriate, the data relating to the higher layers. With a basic datagram, therefore, the *next header* field indicates the type of transport layer protocol (header) that follows the basic header. If required, however, a number of what are called **extension headers** can be inserted between the main header and the transport protocol header. Currently, there are six types of extension header defined and, when present, each extension header starts with a new *next header* field which indicates the type of header that follows. The *next header* field in the last extension header always indicates the type of transport protocol header that follows. Thus, the *next header* field in either the main header or the last extension header plays the same role as the *protocol* field in an IPv4 datagram header.

Hop limit

This is similar to the *time-to-live* parameter in an IPv4 header except the value is a hop count instead of a time. In practice, as we explained in Section 6.2, most IPv4 routers also use this field as a hop count so the change in the field's name simply reflects this. The initial value in the *hop limit* field is set by the source and is decremented by 1 each time the packet/datagram is forwarded. The packet is discarded if the value is decremented to zero.

Source address and destination address

As we indicated earlier, these are 128-bit addresses that are used to identify the source of the datagram and the intended recipient. In most cases this will be the destination host but, as we shall explain later, it might be the next router along a path if source routing is being used. Unlike IPv4 addresses, an IPv6 address is assigned to the (physical) interface, not to the host or router. Hence in the case of routers (which have multiple interfaces) these are identified using any of the assigned interface addresses.

6.8.2 Address structure

As we showed in Figure 6.19, the various networks and internetworks that make up the global Internet are interconnected in a hierarchical way with the access networks at the lowest level in the hierarchy and the global backbone network at the highest level. However, the lack of structure in the netid part of IPv4 addresses means that the number of entries in the routing tables held by each gateway/router increases with increasing height in the hierarchy. At the lowest level, most access gateways associated with a single site LAN have a single netid, while at the highest level, most backbone routers/gateways have a routing table containing many thousands of netids.

In contrast, the addresses associated with telephone networks are hierarchical with, for example, a country, region, and exchange code preceding the local number. This has a significant impact on the size of the routing tables held by the switches since, at a particular level, all calls with the same preceding code are routed in the same way. This is known as **address aggregation**.

As we explained earlier in Section 6.4.3, classless inter-domain routing is a way of introducing a similar structure with IPv4 addresses and reduces considerably the size of the routing tables held by the routers/gateways in the global backbone. From the outset, therefore, IPv6 addresses are hierarchical. Unlike telephone numbers, however, the hierarchy is not constrained just to a geographical breakdown. The large address space available means that a number of alternative formats can be used. For example, to help interworking with existing IPv4 hosts and routers, there is a format that allows IPv4 addresses to be embedded into an IPv6 address. Also, since the majority of access networks are now Internet service provider (ISP) networks, there is a format that allows large blocks of addresses to be allocated to individual providers. The particular format being used is determined by the first set of bits in the address. This is known as the **prefix format** (**PF**) and a list of the prefixes that have been assigned – together with their usage – is given in Figure 6.42(a).

Unicast addresses

As we can see, addresses starting with a prefix of 0000 0000 are used to carry existing IPv4 addresses. There are two types, the formats of which are shown

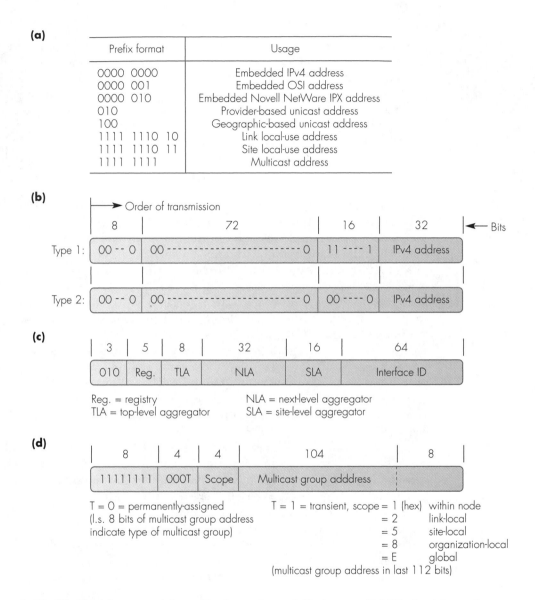

Figure 6.42 IPv6 addresses: (a) prefix formats and their use; (b) IPv4 address types; (c) provider-based unicast address format; (d) multicast address format.

in Figure 6.42(b). As we shall expand upon in Section 6.9, a common requirement during the transition from IPv4 to IPv6 is to tunnel the IPv6 packets being generated by the two communicating IPv6 hosts – often written **V6 hosts** – over an existing IPv4 network/internetwork. Hence to simplify the routing of the IPv4 packet – containing the IPv6 packet within it – the IPv6 address contains the IPv4 address of the destination gateway embedded within it. The second type is to enable a V4 host to communicate with a V6 host. The IPv4 address of the V4 host is then preceded by 96 zeros. In addition, two addresses in this category are reserved for other uses. An address comprising all zeros indicates there is no address present. As we shall expand upon in Section 6.8.4, an example of its use is for the source address in a packet relating to the autoconfiguration procedure. An address with a single binary 1 in the least significant bit position is reserved for the loopback address used during the test procedure of a host protocol stack.

The OSI and NetWare address prefixes have been defined to enable a host connected to one of these networks to communicate directly with a V6 host. The most widely used is the provider-based prefix as this format reflects the current structure of the Internet. A typical format of this type of address is shown in Figure 6.42(c). As we saw in Figure 6.19, the core backbone of the Internet consists of a number of very high bandwidth lines that interconnect the various continental backbones together. The routers that perform this function are owned by companies known as **top-level aggregators** (**TLAs**). Each TLA is allocated a large block of addresses by what is called a **registry**, the identity of which is in the field immediately following the 010 prefix. Examples include the North American registry, the European registry, the Asia and Pacific registry, and so on.

From their allocation, the TLAs allocate blocks of addresses to large Internet service providers and global enterprises. These are known as **next-level aggregators** (**NLAs**) and, in the context of Figure 6.19, operate at the continental backbone and national and regional levels. The various NLAs allocate both single addresses to individual subscribers and blocks of addresses to large business customers. The latter are known as **site-level aggregators** (**SLAs**) and include ISPs that operate at the regional and national levels. The 64-bit **interface ID** is divided locally into a fixed subnetid part and a hostid part. Typically, the latter is the 48-bit MAC address of the host and hence 16 bits are available for subnetting.

As we can deduce from Figure 6.42(c), the use of hierarchical addresses means that each router in the hierarchy can quickly determine whether a packet should be routed to a higher-level router or to another router at the same level simply by examining the appropriate prefix. Also, the routers at each level can route packets directly using the related prefix. The same overall description applies to the processing of geographic-based addresses.

As their names imply, the two types of **local-use addresses** are for local use only and have no meaning in the context of the global Internet. As we shall expand upon in Section 6.8.4, *link local-use addresses* are used in the autoconfiguration procedure followed by hosts to obtain an IPv6 address from a local router. The router only replies to the host on the same link the request was received and hence this type of packet is not forwarded beyond the router.

The *site local-use addresses* are used, for example, by organizations that are not currently connected to the Internet but wish to utilize the technology associated with it. Normally, the 64-bit interface ID part is subdivided and used for routing purposes within the organization. In this way, should the organization wish to be connected to the Internet at a later date, it is only necessary to change the site local-use prefix with the allocated subscriber prefix.

Multicast addresses

The format of an IPv6 multicast address is shown in Figure 6.42(d). As we can see, following the multicast prefix are two additional fields that have been introduced to limit the geographic scope of the related multicast operation. The first is known as the *flags* field and is used to indicate whether the multicast is a permanently-assigned (reserved) address (0000) or a temporary (transient) address (0001). In the case of a permanently-assigned address, the least significant 8 bits of the *multicast group address* field identify the type of the multicast operation, while for a transient address, the full 112 bits identify the multicast group address.

In both cases, the 4-bit *scope* field defines the geographic scope of the multicast packet. The various alternatives are identified in the figure and mrouters use this field to determine whether the (multicast) packet should be forwarded further or discarded.

Anycast addresses

In addition to unicast and multicast addresses, a new address type known as an **anycast group address** has been defined. These are allocated from the unicast address space and are indistinguishable from a unicast address. With an anycast address, however, a group of hosts or routers can all have the same (anycast) address. A common requirement in a number of applications is for a host or router to send a packet to any one of a group of hosts or routers, all of which provide the same service. For example, a group of servers distributed around a network may all contain the same database. Hence in order to avoid all clients needing to know the unique address of its nearest server, all the servers can be members of the same anycast group and hence have the same address. In this way, when a client makes a request, it uses the assigned anycast address of the group and the request will automatically be received by its nearest server. Similarly, if a single network/internetwork has a number of gateway routers associated with it, they can all be allocated the same anycast address. As a result, the shortest-path routes from all other networks/internetworks will automatically use the gateway nearest to them.

In order to perform the routing function, although an anycast address has the same format as a unicast address, when an anycast address is assigned to a group of hosts or routers, it is necessary for each host/router to be explicitly informed – by network management for example – that it is a member of an anycast group. In addition, each is informed of the common part of the address prefixes which collectively identify the topological region in which all the hosts/routers reside. Within this region, all the routers then maintain a separate entry for each member of the group in its routing table.

Address representation

A different form of representation of IPv6 addresses has been defined. Instead of each 8-bit group being represented as a decimal number (with a dot/period between them), groups of 16 bits are used. Each 16-bit group is then represented in its hexadecimal form with a colon between each group. An example of an IPv6 address is:

FEDC:BA98:7654:3210:0000:0000:0000:0089

In addition, a number of abbreviations have been defined:

- One or more consecutive groups of all zeros can be replaced by a pair of colons.
- Leading zeros in a group can be omitted.

Hence the preceding address can also be written as:

FEDC:BA98:7654:3210::89

Also, for the two IPv4 embedded address types, the actual IPv4 address can remain in its dotted decimal form. Hence assuming a dotted decimal address of 15.10.0.6, the two embedded forms are:

:: 150.10.0.6   (IPv4 host address)
:: FFFF:150.10.0.6   (IPv4 tunnel address)

Example 6.6

Derive the hexadecimal form of representation of the following link-local multicast addresses:

(i) a permanently-assigned multicast group address of 67,

(ii) a transient multicast group address of 317.

Answer:

The formats of the two types of multicast addresses were shown in Figure 6.42(d). Hence:

The most significant 16 bits are FF02 = permanently-assigned, link-local
and FF12 = transient, link-local

(i) A permanently-assigned multicast group address of 67 = 0043 (hex)
     Hence IPv6 address = FF02 :: 67

(ii) A transient multicast group address of 317 = 013D (hex)
     Hence IPv6 address = FF12 :: 13D

6.8.3 Extension headers

As we have just indicated, if required, a number of extension headers can be added to the main header to convey additional information, either to the routers visited along the path followed or to the destination host. The six types of extension header currently defined are:

- **hop-by-hop options**: information for the routers visited along a path;
- **routing**: list of routers relating to source routing information;
- **fragment**: information to enable the destination to reassemble a fragmented message;
- **authentication**: information to enable the destination to verify the identity of the source;
- **encapsulating security payload**: information to enable the destination to decrypt the payload contents;
- **destination options**: optional information for use by the destination.

The two options headers can contain a variable number of option fields, each possibly of a variable length. For these, each option field is encoded using a **type-length-value** (**TLV**) format. The *type* and *length* are both single bytes and indicate the option type and its length (in bytes) respectively. The *value* is then found in the following number of bytes indicated by the *length*. The option type identifiers have been chosen so that the most significant two bits specify the action that must be taken if the type is not recognized. These are:

00   ignore this option and continue processing the other option fields in the header;

01   discard the complete packet;

10   discard the packet and return an ICMP error report to the source indicating a parameter problem and the option type not recognized;

11   same as for 10 except the ICMP report is only returned if the destination address is not a multicast address.

Note also that since the type of extension header is indicated in the preceding *next header* field, the related decoder that has been written to decode the contents of the header is invoked automatically as each header is processed. Some examples of each header type now follow.

Hop-by-hop options

This type of header contains information that must be examined by all the gateways and routers the packet visits along its route. The *next header* value for this is 0 and, if this header is present, it must follow the main header. Hence the *next header* field in the main header is set to 0. An example of its use is for a host to send a datagram that contains a payload of more than 64K bytes. This is particularly useful, for example, when a host is transferring many very large files over a path that supports a maximum transmission unit (MTU) significantly greater than 64 kbytes. Datagrams that contain this header are known as **jumbograms** and the format of the header is shown in Figure 6.43(a).

As we can see, this type of header is of fixed length and comprises two 32-bit words (8 bytes). The *header extension length* field indicates the length of the header in multiples of 8 bytes, excluding the first 8 bytes. Hence in this case the field is 0. This option contains only one option field, the *jumbo payload length*. As we indicated earlier, this is encoded in the TLV format. The *type* for this option is 194 (11000010) and the *length* is 4 (bytes). The *value* in the *jumbo payload length* is the length of the packet in bytes, excluding the main header but including the 8 bytes in the extension header. This makes the *payload length* in the main header redundant and hence this is set to zero.

Routing

This plays a similar role to the (strict) *source routing* and *loose source routing* optional headers used in IPv4 datagrams. The *next header* value for this type of

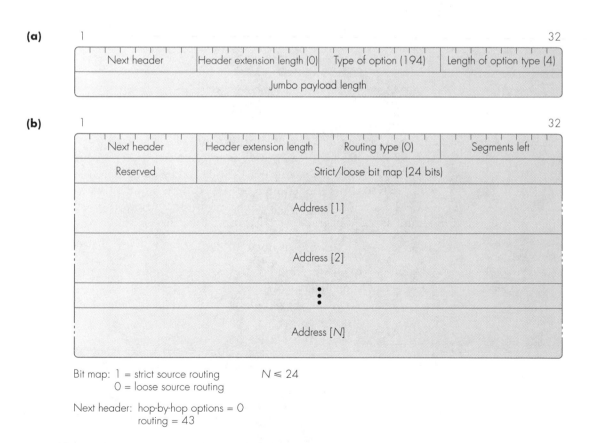

Bit map: 1 = strict source routing   N ⩽ 24
         0 = loose source routing

Next header: hop-by-hop options = 0
             routing = 43

Figure 6.43 Extension header formats: (a) hop-by-hop options; (b) routing.

header is 43. Currently only one type of routing header has been defined, the format of which is shown in Figure 6.43(b).

The *header extension length* is the length of the header in multiples of 8 bytes, excluding the first 8 bytes. Hence, as we can deduce from the figure, this is equal to two times the number of (16-byte) addresses present in the header. This must be an even number less than or equal to 46. The *segments left* field is an index to the list of addresses that are present. It is initialized to 0 and is then incremented by the next router in the list as it is visited. The maximum therefore is 23.

The second 4-byte word contains a *reserved* byte followed by a 24-bit field called the *strict/loose bit map*. This contains one bit for each potential address present starting at the leftmost bit. If the related bit is a 1, then the address must be that of a directly attached (neighbor) router – that is, strict source routing. If the bit is a 0, then the address is that of a router with possibly several other routers in between – loose source routing. The latter is used, for example, when tunneling is required to forward the datagram. In the case of strict source routing, at each router the destination address in the main header is changed to that obtained from the list of addresses before the index is incremented. In the case of loose source routing, the destination address will be that of an attached neighbor which is on the shortest-path route to the specified address.

Example 6.7

A datagram is to be sent from a source host with an IPv6 address of A to a destination host with an IPv6 address of B via a path comprising three IPv6 routers. Assuming the addresses of the three routers are R1, R2, and R3 and strict source routing is to be used, (i) state what the contents of the initial values in the various fields in the extension header will be and (ii) list the contents of the source and destination address fields in the main header and the *segments left* field in the extension header as the datagram travels along the defined path.

Answer:

(i) Extension header initial contents:
        Next header = Transport layer protocol
        Header extension length = $2 \times 3 = 6$
        Routing type = 0
        Segments left = 0
        Strict/loose bit map = 11100000 00000000 00000000
        List of addresses = R1, R2, R3 (each of 16 bytes)

(ii) Contents of main header fields:
        At source SA = A DA = R1 Segments left = 0
        At R1   SA = A DA = R2 Segments left = 1
        At R2   SA = A DA = R3 Segments left = 2

Fragment

This header is present if the original message submitted by the transport layer protocol exceeds the MTU of the path/route to be used. The *next header* value for a *fragment* extension header is 44. The fragmentation and reassembly procedures are similar to those used with IPv4 but, in the case of IPv6, the fragmentation procedure is carried out only in the source host and not by the routers/gateways along the path followed by the packet(s). As we saw in Figure 6.41(a), there is no don't fragment (D) bit in the IPv6 main header since, in order to speed up the processing/routing of packets, IPv6 routers do not support fragmentation. Hence, as we explained in Section 6.6.9, either the minimum MTU size of 576 bytes must be used or the *path MTU discovery* procedure is used to determine if the actual MTU size is greater than this. In either case, if the submitted message (including the transport protocol header) exceeds the chosen MTU (minus the 40 bytes for the IPv6 main header), then the message must be sent in multiple packets, each with a main header and a *fragment* extension header. The various fields and the format of each *fragment* extension header are shown in Figure 6.44(a). An example is shown in Figure 6.44(b).

Each packet contains a main header – plus, if required, a *hop-by-hop options* header and a *routing* header – followed by a *fragment* extension header and the fragment of the message being transmitted. Thus the maximum size of the payload (and hence message fragment) in each packet will be the MTU size being used minus the number of 8-byte fields required for the main header and any extension headers that are present. The *payload length* field in the main header of the first packet indicates the total number of bytes in the message being transmitted – including the IP header – plus the number of bytes that are required for the other extension headers that are being used. The *payload length* in the main header of the remaining packets indicates the number of bytes in the packet following the main header.

The various fields in each *fragment* header have similar functions to those used with IPv4. The *fragment offset* indicates the position of the first byte of the fragment contained within the packet relative to the start of the complete message being transmitted. Its value is in units of 8-bytes. The *M-bit* is the *more fragments bit*; it is a 1 if more fragments follow and a 0 if the packet contains the last fragment. Similarly, the value in the *identification* field is used by the destination host, together with the source address, to relate the data fragments contained within each packet to the same original message. Normally, the source uses a 32-bit counter (that is incremented by 1 for each new message transmitted) to keep track of the next value to use.

Authentication and encapsulating security payload

As we shall expand upon in Section 10.7.1, authentication and the related subject of encryption are both mechanisms that are used to enhance the security of a message during its transfer across a network. In the case of authentication, this enables the recipient of a message to validate that the

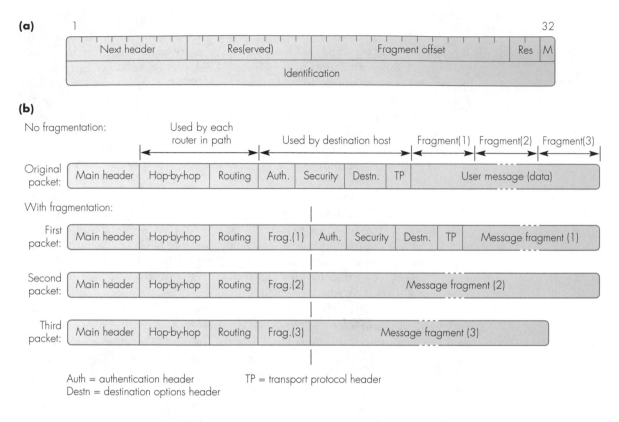

Figure 6.44 IPv6 fragmentation: (a) fragment header fields and format; (b) example.

message was indeed sent by the source address present in the packet/ datagram header and not by an impostor. Encryption is concerned with ensuring that the contents of a message can only be read by – and hence have meaning to – the intended recipient. The *authentication* and *encapsulating security payload* (ESP) extension headers are present when both these features are being used at the network layer.

When using IPv6 authentication, prior to any information (packets) being exchanged, the two communicating hosts first use a secure algorithm to exchange secret keys. An example is the MD5 algorithm we describe later in Section 10.3. Then, for each direction of flow, the appropriate key is used to compute a checksum on the contents of the entire datagram/packet. The computed checksum is then carried in the authentication header of the packet. The same computation is repeated at the destination host, and only if the computed checksum is the same as that carried in the authentication header is it acknowledged that the packet originated from the source host address indicated in the main header and also that the packet contents have

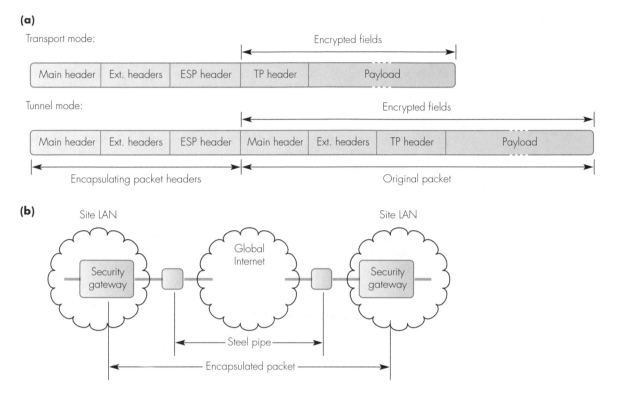

Figure 6.45 Encapsulating security payload: (a) transport and tunnel modes; (b) example application of tunnel mode.

not been modified during its transfer over the network. We discuss the subject of authentication further in Section 10.4.

The encryption algorithm used with the ESP is also based on the use of an agreed secret key. An example is the DES algorithm we describe later in Section 10.2.3. The agreed key is used to encrypt either the transport protocol header and payload parts of each packet or, in some instances, the entire packet including the main header and any extension headers present. In the case of the latter, the encrypted packet is then carried in a second packet containing a completely different main and, if necessary, extension headers. The first is known as **transport mode encryption** and the second **tunnel mode encryption**. Figure 6.45(a) illustrates the principle of operation of both modes.

As we can deduce from the figure, the overheads associated with the tunnel mode are significantly higher than those of the transport mode. The extra security obtained with the tunnel mode is that the information in the main and extension headers of the original packet cannot be interpreted by a person passively monitoring the transmissions on a line. An example use of this mode is in multisite enterprise networks that use the (public) Internet to transfer packets from one site to another. The general scheme is shown in Figure 6.45(b).

As we will show in Figure 9.4(a) and explain in the accompanying text, associated with each site is a security gateway through which all packet transfers to and from the site take place. Hence to ensure the header information (especially the routing header) of packets is not visible during the transfer of the packet across the Internet, the total packet is encrypted and inserted into a second packet by the IP in the security gateway with the IPv6 address of the two communicating gateways in the source and destination address fields of the main header. The path through the Internet connecting the two gateways is referred to as a **steel pipe**.

Destination options

These are used to convey information that is examined only by the destination host. As we indicated earlier, one of the ways of encoding options is to use the type-length-value format. Hence in order to ensure a header that uses this format comprises a multiple of 8 bytes, two *destination options* have been defined. These are known as Pad1 and Pad$N$, the first to insert one byte of padding and the second two or more bytes of padding. Currently these are the only two options defined.

6.8.4 Autoconfiguration

As we described earlier in Section 6.1, the allocation of the IP addresses for a new network involves a central authority to allocate a new netid – the ICANN – and a local network administrator to manage the allocation of hostids to each attached host/end system. Thus, the allocation, installation and administration of IPv4 addresses can entail considerable effort and expenditure. To alleviate this, IPv6 supports an autoconfiguration facility that enables a host to obtain an IP address dynamically via the network and, in the case of mobile hosts, use it just for the duration of the call/session.

Two types of autoconfiguration are supported. The first involves the host communicating with a local (site) router using a simple (stateless) request-response protocol. The second involves the host communicating with a site (or enterprise) address server using an application protocol known as the **dynamic host configuration protocol** (**DHCP**). The first is suitable for small networks that operate in the broadcast mode (such as an Ethernet LAN) and the second for larger networks in which the allocation of IP addresses needs to be managed.

With the first method, a simple protocol known as **neighbor discovery** (**ND**) is used. As we show in Figure 6.46, this involves the host broadcasting a *router solicitation* packet/message on the subnet/network and the router responding with a *router advertisement* message. Both messages are ICMPv6 messages and hence are carried in an IPv6 packet. The latter is then broadcast over the LAN in a standard frame.

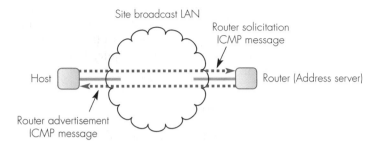

Figure 6.46 Neighbor discovery protocol messages.

The main header of the IPv6 packet containing the router solicitation message has an IPv6 source address created by the host. This is made up of the (standard) link-local address prefix and the 48-bit MAC address of the host's LAN interface. As we indicated earlier, with IPv6 a number of permanent multicast group addresses have been defined including an all-routers group address. Hence the destination address in the packet main header is set to this and, since the packet is broadcast over the LAN, it is received by the ICMP in all the routers that are attached to the LAN.

A single router is selected to process this type of ICMP message and this responds to a router solicitation message with a route advertisement message containing the Internet-wide address prefix for the subnet/network. On receipt of this, the ICMP in the host proceeds to create its own IPv6 address by adding its 48-bit MAC address to the prefix. As we can deduce from this, in relation to IPv4, this is equivalent to the router providing the netid of the site and the host using its own MAC address as the hostid. Also, the same procedure can be used by mobile hosts.

With the second method, the host requests an IPv6 address from the site address server using the DHCP. The **DHCP address server** first validates the request and then allocates an address from the managed list of addresses the server contains. Alternatively if a site does not have its own address server – for example if the site LAN is part of a larger enterprise network — then a designated router acts as a **DHCP relay agent** to forward the request to the DHCP address server.

6.9 IPv6/IPv4 interoperability

The widespread deployment of IPv4 equipment means that the introduction of IPv6 is being carried out in an incremental way. Hence a substantial amount of the ongoing standardization effort associated with IPv6 is concerned with the interoperability of the newer IPv6 equipment with existing IPv4 equipment. Normally, when a new network/internetwork is created, it is based on the IPv6 protocol and, in the context of the existing

(IPv4) Internet, it is referred to as an **IPv6 island**. It is necessary to provide a means of interworking between the two types of network at both the address level and the protocol level. In this section, we identify a number of situations where interoperability is required and describe a selection of the techniques that are used to achieve this.

6.9.1 Dual protocols

Dual stacks are already widely used in networks that use dissimilar protocol stacks, for example a site server that supports IPX on one port and IP on a second port. In a similar way, dual protocols can be used to support both IPv4 and IPv6 concurrently. An example is shown in Figure 6.47.

In this example, the site has a mix of hosts, some that use IPv4 and others IPv6. In order to be able to respond to requests originating from both types of host, the server machine has both an IPv4 and an IPv6 protocol at the network layer. The value in the version field of the datagram header is then used by the link layer protocol to pass a datagram to the appropriate IP. In this way the upper layer protocols are unaware of the type of IP being used at the network layer.

6.9.2 Dual stacks and tunneling

A common requirement is to interconnect two IPv6 islands (networks/inter-networks) through an intermediate IPv4 network/internetwork. To achieve this, the gateway/router that connects each IPv6 island to the IPv4 network

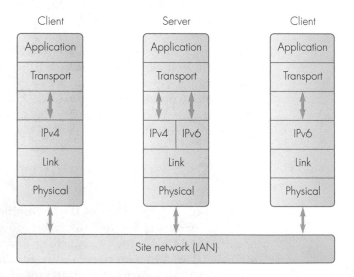

Figure 6.47 IPv6/IPv4 interoperability using dual (IPv6/IPv4) protocols.

must have dual stacks, one that supports IPv6 and the other IPv4. The IPv6 packets are then transferred over the IPv4 network using tunneling. The general approach is illustrated in Figure 6.48(a) and the protocols involved in Figure 6.48(b).

As we showed earlier in Figure 6.16 and explained in the accompanying text, tunneling is used to transfer a packet relating to one type of network layer protocol across a network that uses a different type of network layer protocol. Hence in the example shown in Figure 6.48, each IPv6 packet is transferred from one (IPv6/IPv4) edge gateway to the other edge gateway within an IPv4 packet. As we show in the figure, in order to do this, the two

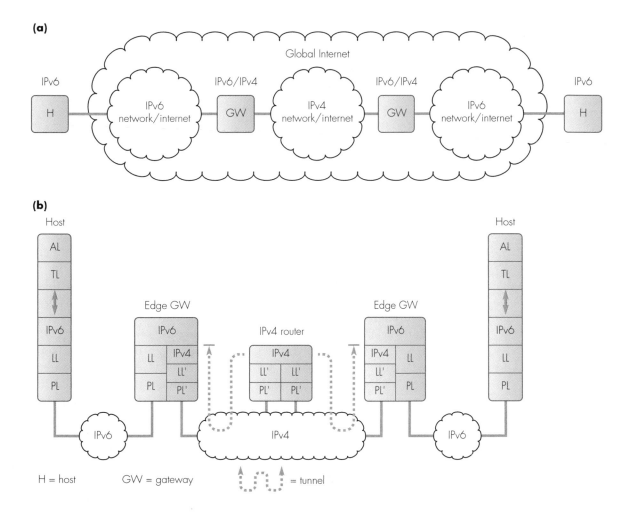

Figure 6.48 IPv6/IPv4 interoperability using dual stacks and tunneling: (a) schematic; (b) protocols.

edge gateways contain dual stacks each of which has a related IPv6/IPv4 address associated with it. Normally, entered by network management, the routing table entry for the remote destination IPv6 host is the IPv4 address of the remote edge gateway.

The IPv6 in each gateway, on determining from its routing table that an (IPv6) packet should be forwarded to a remote IPv6 network via an IPv4 tunnel, passes the packet to the IPv4 protocol together with the IPv4 address of the remote gateway. The IPv4 protocol first encapsulates the IPv6 packet in an IPv4 datagram/packet with the IPv4 address of the remote gateway in the destination address field. It then uses this address to obtain the (IPv4) address of the next-hop router from its own (IPv4) routing table and proceeds to forward the packet over the IPv4 network/internetwork. On receipt of the packet, the IPv4 in the remote gateway, on detecting from its own routing table that it is a tunneled packet, strips off the IPv4 header and passes the payload – containing the original IPv6 packet – to the IPv6 layer. The latter then forwards the packet to the destination host identified in the packet header in the normal way.

6.9.3 Translators

A third type of interoperability requirement is for a host attached to an IPv6 network – and hence having an IPv6 address and using the IPv6 protocol – to communicate with a host that is attached to an IPv4 network – hence having an IPv4 address and using the IPv4 protocol. In this case, both the addresses and the packet formats are different and so a translation operation must be carried out by any intermediate routers/gateways. As we show in Figure 6.49, the translations can be performed at either the network layer – part (a) – or the application layer – part (b).

Using the first approach, on receipt of an IPv6/IPv4 packet, this is converted into a semantically equivalent IPv4 /IPv6 packet. This involves a **network address translator** (**NAT**) and a **protocol translator** (**PT**). The intermediate gateway is then known as a **NAT-PT gateway**. As we explained earlier in Section 6.8.2, an IPv4 address can be embedded in an IPv6 address. Hence to send a datagram/packet from a host with an IPv6 address to a host with an IPv4 address, the NAT in the gateway can readily obtain the destination IPv4 address from the destination address in the main header of the IPv6 packet. The issue is what the source address in the IPv4 packet header should be.

A proposed solution is for the NAT to be allocated a block of hostids for the destination IPv4 network. These, together with the netid of the destination network, then form a block of unique IPv4 addresses. For each new call/session, the NAT allocates an unused IPv4 address from this block for the duration of the call/session. It then makes an entry in a table containing the IPv6 address of the V6 host and its equivalent (temporary) IPv4 address. The NAT translates between one address and the other as the packet is relayed. A timeout is applied to the use of such addresses and, if no packets are received within the timeout interval, the address is transferred back to the free address pool.

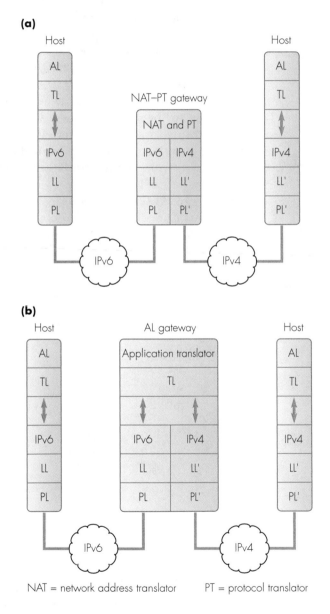

Figure 6.49 IPv6/IPv4 interoperability using translators: (a) network level; (b) application level.

The protocol translation operation is concerned with translating the remaining fields in the packet header and, in the case of ICMP messages, converting ICMPv4 messages into and from ICMPv6 messages. As we indicated in Section 6.8.1, most of the fields in the IPv6 main header have the same meaning as those in the IPv4 header and hence their translation is relatively straightforward. In general, however, there is no attempt to translate the fields in the options part. Similarly, since ICMPv6 messages have different *type* fields, the main translation performed is limited to changing this field. For example, the two ICMPv4 query messages have *type* values of 8 and 0 and the corresponding ICMPv6 messages are 128 and 129.

The use of a NAT-PT gateway works providing the packet payload does not contain any network addresses. Although this is the case for most application protocols, a small number do. The FTP application protocol, for example, often has IP addresses embedded within its protocol messages. In such cases, therefore, the translation operation must be carried out at the application layer. The associated gateway is then known as an **application level gateway** (**ALG**). This requires a separate translation program for each application protocol. Normally, therefore, most translations are performed at the network layer – using a NAT and a PT – and only the translations relating to application protocols such as FTP are carried out in the application layer.

Summary

A summary of the topics discussed in this chapter is given in Figure 6.50.

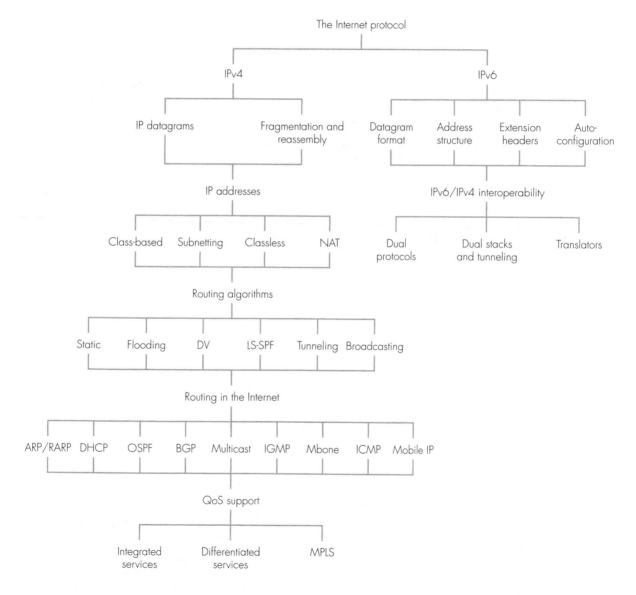

Figure 6.50 Internet protocol summary.

Exercises

Section 6.1

6.1 With the aid of the network schematic shown in Figure 6.1, explain briefly the role of the following network components and protocols:
(i) access network gateway,
(ii) routing gateway,
(iii) internet protocol (IP),
(iv) datagram/packet.

6.2 With the aid of the protocol stack shown in Figure 6.2, explain briefly the meaning of the term "adjunct protocol" and how the IP in the destination host determines to which protocol the contents/payload of a received IP datagram should be passed.

Section 6.2

6.3 In relation to the IP datagram/packet format shown in Figure 6.3, explain the role of the following header fields:
(i) IHL,
(ii) TOS,
(iii) Total length and Identification,
(iv) flag bits,
(v) Fragment offset,
(vi) Time-to-live,
(vii) Protocol,
(viii) Header checksum,
(ix) Options.

Section 6.3

6.4 Assume a message block of 7000 bytes is to be transferred from one host to another as shown in the example in Figure 6.4. In this instance, however, assume the token ring LAN has an MTU of 3000 bytes. Compute the header fields in each IP packet shown in the figure as it flows
(i) over the token ring LAN,
(ii) over the Ethernet LAN.

6.5 State why fragmentation is avoided whenever possible and the steps followed within each host IP to achieve this.

Section 6.4

6.6 List the four types of IP address schemes that are in use and give a brief summary of the use of each scheme.

6.7 Explain the meaning of the term "IP address class" and why these classes were created. Hence, with the aid of the three (unicast) address classes identified in Figure 6.5, identify a particular application for each class.

6.8 State the meaning of the following addresses:
(i) an address with a netid of all 0s,
(ii) an address with a netid of all 1s,
(iii) an address with a hostid of all 0s,
(iv) an address of all 1s.

6.9 Explain the meaning of the term "dotted decimal". Hence derive the netid and hostid for the following IP addresses expressed in dotted decimal notation:
(i) 13.0.0.15,
(ii) 132.128.0.148,
(iii) 220.0.0.0,
(iv) 128.0.0.0,
(v) 224.0.0.1.

6.10 With the aid of the example in Figure 6.6, explain why subnetting was introduced. Hence state the meaning of a subnet router and an address mask.

6.11 A site with a netid of 127.0 uses 20 subnet routers. Suggest a suitable address mask for the site which allows for a degree of expansion in the future. Give an example of a host IP address at this site.

6.12 With the aid of Example 6.3, explain the classless inter-domain routing (CIDR) scheme.

6.13 With the aid of Example 6.4, explain how, with CIDR, multiple address matches are possible with a network that has been allocated a large block of addresses. State which of these matches is chosen and why.

6.14 Explain why the network address translation (NAT) scheme is now used with most new access networks.

6.15 In relation to the NAT scheme shown in Figure 6.7(a), determine the number of host addresses/interfaces that have been declared for private use.

6.16 In relation to the outline operation of NAT shown in Figure 6.7(b), explain:
   (i)   how the four IP addresses are used and the role of the NAT table,
   (ii) how the source and destination addresses in the related IP and TCP fields are derived.

Section 6.5

6.17 State the meaning of the following terms relating to the routing of packets over an internet:
   (i)   line cost,
   (ii) path cost,
   (iii) hopcount,
   (iv) routing metric,
   (v)   shortest path.

6.18 With the aid of the routing table entries shown in Figure 6.9, explain the meaning of the terms:
   (i)   static routing tables,
   (ii) next-hop routing,
   (iii) optionality principle,
   (iv) alternative paths.

6.19 With the aid of the broadcast diagram shown in Figure 6.10, explain:
   (i)   why the broadcast following the route via R2 is assumed to arrive first
   (ii) how duplicate copies of a packet are determined by R3
   (iii) how the number of copies of the packet produced is limited
   (iv) why flooding is an example of an adaptive/dynamic routing algorithm.

6.20 In relation to the distance vector algorithm, with the aid of the example shown in Figure 6.11, explain:

   (i)   the meaning of the term "connectivity/adjacency table" and how the table's contents are obtained,
   (ii) how the final routing table entries for R3 are built up,
   (iii) how a packet from a host attached to netid3 is routed to a host attached to netid1,
   (iv) the limitations of the algorithm including how looping may arise.

6.21 Assuming the connectivity/adjacency tables given in Figure 6.12(a), show how the overall network topology is built up by router R3 using the link state algorithm. Hence derive the contents of the netid location table for R3.

6.22 Assuming the initial network topology shown in Figure 6.13(a), use the Dijkstra algorithm to derive the shortest paths from R3 to each other router. State the meaning of the terms "tentative" and "permanent" relating to the algorithm and the implications of alternative paths/routers.

6.23 Using the set of link state, routing, and connectivity tables for R1, R2 and R3 in Figure 6.15, explain how a packet received by R3 from G3 with a destination netid of 1 is routed using hop-by-hop routing.

6.24 Explain how a packet received by R3 from G3 with a destination netid of 1 is routed using source routing. Include how the routing tables you use are derived.

6.25 In relation to the link-state algorithm, explain why each link-state message contains a sequence number and a timeout value. How are these used?

6.26 Explain the term "tunneling" and when it is used. Hence with the aid of the schematic diagram shown in Figure 6.16, explain how the host on the left of the diagram sends an IP datagram/packet to a host attached to the Internet. Include in your explanation the role of the two multiprotocol routers.

State an application of tunneling IP packets over an IP network.

6.27 What are the aims of both the reverse path forwarding algorithm and the spanning tree broadcast algorithm?

6.28 Use the final routing tables and broadcast sequence relating to the reverse path forwarding algorithm shown in Figure 6.17 to explain why only the (broadcast) packet received by SR6 from SR3 is broadcast at the fourth stage. What is the number of duplicate broadcasts that occur?

6.29 Assuming the network topology shown in Figure 6.18(a) and that SR3 is an access gateway, determine the spanning tree derived by each subnet router. Use this to derive the broadcast sequence.

Section 6.6

6.30 With the aid of the generalized Internet architecture shown in Figure 6.19, give an example of the type of network that is used at each tier in the hierarchy and the routing method that is used with it.

6.31 Define the terms "IP address", "MAC address", and "hardware/physical address". Also explain the terms "address-pair" and "ARP cache".

6.32 In relation to the simple network topology shown in Figure 6.20, explain why:
   (i)   on receipt of an ARP request message, each host retains a copy of the IP/MAC address-pair of the source host in its ARP cache,
   (ii) on receipt of an ARP reply message, the ARP in the source host makes an entry of the IP/MAC address-pair in its own cache,
   (iii) the Lan port of the gateway keeps a copy of the IP/MAC address-pair from each ARP request and reply message that it receives.

6.33 Explain the role of a proxy ARP. Hence explain how an IP packet sent by a host at one site is routed to a host at a different site. Also explain how the reply packet is returned to the host that sent the first packet.

6.34 Explain how the reverse ARP is used to enable a diskless host to determine its own IP address from its local server.

6.35 With the aid of the two frame formats shown in Figure 6.21, explain:
   (i)   how the MAC sublayer in the receiver determines whether a received frame is in the Ethernet format or IEEE802.3,
   (ii) the number of pad bytes required with each frame type.

6.36 State the role of the dynamic host configuration protocol (DHCP).

6.37 Use the example network topology shown in Figure 6.22(a) to describe the DHCP message exchange sequence to obtain an IP address.

6.38 In relation to the simplified Internet structure shown in Figure 6.23, explain the function of the four types of router.

6.39 With the aid of the simplified autonomous system (AS) topology shown in Figure 6.24(a), describe the operation of the OSPF algorithm. First describe how the directed graph is derived and then the derivation of the SPF tree for R7.

6.40 List the message types used with OSPF and explain their function when routing within an AS.

6.41 List the four message types that are used in the border gateway protocol (BGP) and explain their function.

6.42 Given the example backbone topology shown in Figure 6.25, give an example of an update message that changes the route followed between a pair of boundary routers.

6.43 In relation to multicasting over a LAN, describe how ICANN controls the allocation of multicast addresses. Also explain how the 48-bit MAC address and 28-bit IP address of a host are derived from the allocated address. Hence with the aid of the schematic diagram shown in Figure 6.27(b), describe how a host joins a multicast session that is taking place over the LAN. Include the role of the multicast address table and group address table held by each member of the group.

6.44 What is the meaning of the term "multicast router"? Outline the sequence of steps that are followed to route an IP packet with a multicast address over the Internet.

6.45 Assume the same topology, multicast address table contents, routing table contents, and routing table entries as shown in Figure 6.28. Assuming the DVMRP, explain how a packet arriving from one of its local networks with a multicast address of C is routed by MR3 to all the other MRs that have an interest in this packet.

6.46 Repeat Exercise 6.45 but this time using the MOSPF routing protocol and the spanning tree shown in Figure 6.29(b).

6.47 What is the role of the IGMP protocol?
    With the aid of the example shown in Figure 6.30, explain how a host that is attached to a local network/subnet of an MR joins a multicast session. Include in your explanation the table entries retained by both the host and the MR and how multicast packets relating to the session are then routed to the host.

6.48 With the aid of the example shown in Figure 6.30, explain the procedure followed when a host that is attached to a local network/subnet of an MR leaves a multicast session.

6.49 The multicast backbone (M-bone) network shown in Figures 6.28 and 6.29 comprised a set of multicast routers interconnected by single links. In practice, these are logical links since each may comprise multiple interconnected routers that do not take part in multicast routing. Explain how a multicast packet is sent from one mrouter to another using IP tunneling.

6.50 Explain briefly the role of the ICMP protocol and the different procedures associated with it. Hence explain how the path MTU discovery procedure is used to determine the MTU of a path/route prior to sending any datagrams.

6.51 In the simplified network architecture shown in Figure 6.32, explain the use of the following terms:
    (i)   home agent,
    (ii) foreign agent.

    Discuss the issues to be resolved when Host A wants to communicate with Host B.

6.52 In relation to the example shown in Figure 6.33, use a sequence diagram to illustrate the exchange of mobile IP messages in order to register a mobile host (Host B) with its HA and FA. List the main addresses held by both the HA and the FA after the registration procedure is complete.

6.53 Using the example shown in Figure 6.34, describe the indirect routing method used to route packets between Host A and Host B once Host B has been registered with the HA and FA.

Section 6.7

6.54 Discuss the reasons why improved levels of QoS support are now being used within the Internet.

6.55 Describe the role and principle of operation of the following control mechanisms used within Internet routers:
    (i)   token bucket filter,
    (ii) weighted fair queuing,
    (iii) random early detection.

6.56 Define the three different classes of service used with the IntServ scheme. With the aid of the network topology shown in Figure 6.35(a) describe the operation of the resource reservation protocol (RSVP). Include in your

description the meaning/role of the following:
(i)   path, reserve, and path-tear messages,
(ii)   path-state table,
(iii) cleanup timer,
(iv) soft-state.

6.57 Define the usage of the type of service (ToS) field in each packet header with the DiffServ scheme including the meaning of the term "DS packet codepoint".

6.58 With the aid of the general architecture shown in Figure 6.35(b), describe the operation of the DiffServ scheme. Include in your description the meaning/role of the following components of an ingress router:
(i)   behavior aggregate,
(ii)   traffic meter module,
(iii) MF classifier,
(iv) marker module,
(v)   shaper/dropper.

6.59 Use the schematic diagram of a router in Figure 6.36 to explain the packet forwarding procedure in a conventional router.

6.60 Explain the terms traffic engineering, class-based queuing, shaping and grooming in an MPLS network.

6.61 In relation to the MPLS network architecture shown in Figure 6.37, explain where and why the various QoS mechanisms are located.

6.62 Using the example topology shown in Figure 6.38, insert two further sets of table entries to illustrate the label switching procedure.

6.63 Use the schematic diagram of the area border router/label edge router shown in Figure 6.39 to explain the MPLS forwarding procedure. Include in your explanation the role of the packet classifier, the LSP table, the output queue interfaces and the associated scheduling rules.

6.64 Explain how alternative routes to those computed using OSPF are used with the

constraint-routed label distribution protocol (CR-LDP). Describe how the alternative routing tables are downloaded after the CR analysis.

Also explain the meaning/role of the following components of a core router:
(i)   BA classifier,
(ii)   per-hop behavior,
(iii) expedited forwarding,
(iv) assured forwarding.

Section 6.8

6.65 Discuss the reasons behind the definition of IP version 6, IPv6/IPng, including the main new features associated with it.

6.66 With the aid of the frame format shown in Figure 6.41(a), explain the role of the following fields in the IPv6 packet header:
(i)   traffic class,
(ii)   flow label,
(iii) payload length (and how this differs from the total length in an IPv4 packet header),
(iv) next header,
(v)   hop limit,
(vi) source and destination addresses.

6.67 In relation to IPv6 addresses, with the aid of the prefix formats shown in Figures 6.42(a) and (b), explain the meaning/use of:
(i)   address aggregation,
(ii)   prefix formats,
(iii) embedded IPv4 addresses.

6.68 With the aid of the frame format shown in Figure 6.42(c), explain the meaning/use of the following IPv6 fields:
(i)   registry,
(ii)   top-level aggregators,
(iii) next-level agrregators,
(iv) site-level aggregators,
(v)   interface ID.
Comment on the implications of adopting a hierarchical address structure.

6.69 With the aid of examples, explain the use of a link local-use address and a site local-use address.

6.70 Explain the format and use of
(i) a multicast address,
(ii) an anycast address.

6.71 With the aid of examples, show how an IPv6 address can be represented:
(i) in hexadecimal form,
(ii) with leading zeros removed,
(iii) when it contains an IPv4 embedded address.

6.72 Explain the role of the extension headers that may be present in an IPv6 packet. List the six types of extension header and state their use. Also, with the aid of examples, state the position and order of the extension headers in relation to the main header.

6.73 The fields in an options extension header are encoded using a type-length-value format. Use the hop-by-hop options header as an example to explain this format.

6.74 In relation to the routing extension header, explain:
(i) the difference between strict and loose source routing, and the associated bit map,
(ii) the use of the segments left field.

6.75 In relation to the packet formats shown in Figure 6.44, explain:
(i) the meaning and use of the identification field and the M-bits in each extension header,
(ii) why the hop-by-hop and routing headers are present in each fragment packet.

6.76 In relation to the encapsulating security payload header, with the aid of diagrams, explain:
(i) the difference between transport mode and tunnel mode encryption,
(ii) the meaning and use of the term "steel pipe".

6.77 State the aim of the autoconfiguration procedure used with IPv6 and the application domain of:
(i) the neighbor discovery (ND) protocol,
(ii) the dynamic host configuration protocol (DHCP).

6.78 With the aid of Figure 6.46, explain the operation of the ND protocol. Include the role of the router solicitation and router advertisement messages and how a host creates its own IP address.

6.79 Explain how an IPv6 address is obtained:
(i) using a DHCP address server,
(ii) using a DHCP relay agent.

Section 6.9

6.80 With the aid of Figure 6.47, explain how a LAN server can respond to requests from both an IPv4 and an IPv6 client using dual protocols.

6.81 With the aid of Figure 6.48, explain how two hosts, each of which is attached to a different IPv6 network, communicate with each other if the two IPv6 networks are interconnected using an IPv4 network. Include the addresses that are used in each message transfer.

6.82 State the meaning of the terms "network address translation" (NAT) and "protocol translation" (PT). Hence, with the aid of the schematic diagram shown in Figure 6.49(a), explain the role and operation of a NAT-PT gateway. Include what the source address in each IPv6 packet should be.

6.83 Identify when the use of a NAT-PT gateway is not practical. Hence, with the aid of the schematic diagram shown in Figure 6.49(b), explain the role of an application level gateway.

transport protocols

7.1 Introduction

As we saw earlier in Section 1.2, although the range of Internet applications (and the different types of access network used to support them) are many and varied, the protocol suites associated with the different application/network combinations have a common structure. As we saw in Section 1.2.2, the different types of network operate in a variety of modes – circuit-switched or packet-switched, connection-oriented or connectionless – and hence each type of network has a different set of protocols for interfacing to it. Above the network-layer protocol, however, all protocol suites comprise one or more application protocols and a number of what are called application-support protocols.

For example, in order to mask the application protocols from the services provided by the different types of network protocols, all protocol suites have one or more transport protocols. These provide the application protocols with a network-independent information interchange service and, in the case of the TCP/IP suite, they are the **transmission control protocol** (**TCP**) and the **user datagram protocol** (**UDP**). TCP provides a connection-oriented (reliable) service and UDP a connectionless (best-effort) service. Normally, both protocols are present in the suite and the choice of protocol used is determined by the requirements of the application. In addition, when the application involves the transfer of streams of audio and/or video in real time, the timing information required by the receiver to synchronize the incoming streams is provided by the **real-time transport protocol** (**RTP**) and its associated **real-time transport control protocol** (**RTCP**). There is also a version of TCP for use with wireless networks. We describe the operation of these five protocols and the services they provide to application protocols.

7.2 TCP/IP protocol suite

Before describing the various protocols, it will be helpful to illustrate the position of each protocol relative to the others in the TCP/IP suite. This is shown in Figure 7.1. Normally, the IP protocols and network-dependent protocols below them are all part of the operating system kernel with the various application protocols implemented as separate programs/processes. The two transport protocols, TCP and UDP, are then implemented to run either within the operating system kernel, as separate programs/processes, or in a library package linked to the application program.

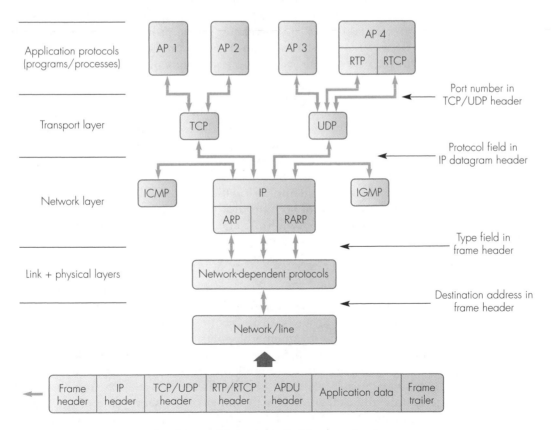

Figure 7.1 TCP/IP protocol suite and interlayer address selectors.

With most networked applications, the client–server paradigm is used. The client application protocol/program runs in one computer – typically a PC or workstation – and this communicates with a similar (peer) application program that runs (normally continuously) in a remote server computer. Examples of applications of this type are file transfers and the messages associated with electronic mail, both of which require a reliable service; that is, the transferred information should be free of transmission errors and the messages delivered in the same sequence that they were submitted. Hence applications of this type use the reliable service provided by TCP.

Thus the role of TCP is to convert the best-effort service provided by IP into a reliable service. For other applications, a simple best-effort service is acceptable and hence they use UDP as the transport protocol. Examples of applications of this type are interpersonal applications that involve the transfer of streams of (compressed) audio and/or video in real time. Clearly, since new information is being received and output continuously, it is inappropriate to request blocks that are received with errors to be retransmitted. Also, it is for applications of this type that RTP and RTCP are used. Other applications that use UDP are application protocols such as HTTP and SNMP, both of which involve a single request-response message exchange.

As we saw in Figure 6.1 and its accompanying text, all message blocks – protocol data units (PDUs) – relating to the protocols that use the services of the IP layer are transferred in an IP datagram. Hence, as we can deduce from Figure 7.1, since there are a number of protocols that use the services of IP – TCP, UDP, ICMP and IGMP – it is necessary for IP to have some means of identifying the protocol to which the contents of the datagram relate. As we saw in Section 6.2, this is the role of the *protocol* field in each IP datagram header. Similarly, since a number of different application protocols may use the services of both TCP and UDP, it is also necessary for both these protocols to have a field in their respective PDU header that identifies the application protocol to which the PDU contents relate. As we shall see, this is the role of the source and destination *port numbers* that are present in the header of the PDUs of both protocols. In addition, since a server application receives requests from multiple clients, in order for the server to send the responses to the correct clients, both the source port number and the source IP address from the IP datagram header are sent to the application protocol with the TCP/UDP contents.

In general, within the client host, the port number of the source application protocol has only local significance and a new port number is allocated for each new transfer request. Normally, therefore, client port numbers are called **ephemeral ports** as they are short-lived. The port numbers of the peer application protocol in the server application protocols are fixed and are known as **well-known port numbers**. Their allocation is managed by ICANN and they are in the range 1 through to 1023. For example, the well-known port number of the server-side of the file transfer (application) protocol (FTP) is 21. Normally, ephemeral port numbers are allocated in the range 1024 through to 5000.

As we can see in Figure 7.2, all the protocols in both the application and transport layers communicate directly with a similar peer protocol in the remote host computer (end system). The protocols in both these layers are said, therefore, to communicate on an end-to-end basis. In contrast, the IP protocols present in each of the two communicating hosts are network-interface protocols. These, together with the IP in each intermediate gateway/router involved, carry out the transfer of the datagram across the internetwork. The IP protocol in each host is said to have local significance and the routing of each datagram is carried out on a hop-by-hop basis.

7.3 **TCP**

The transmission control protocol (TCP) provides two communicating peer application protocols – normally one in a client computer and the other in a server computer – with a two-way, reliable data interchange service. Although the APDUs associated with an application protocol have a defined structure, this is transparent to the two communicating peer TCP protocol entities which treat all the data submitted by each local application entity as a stream of bytes. The stream of bytes flowing in each direction is then transferred (over the underlying network/internet) from one TCP entity to the other in a reliable way; that is, to a high probability, each byte in the stream flowing in

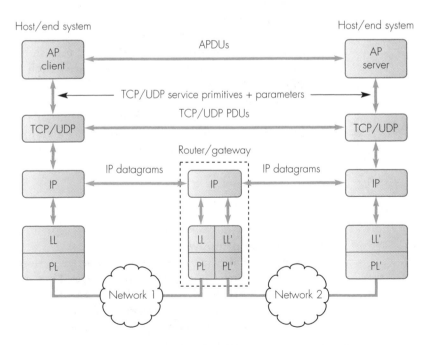

Figure 7.2 TCP/IP protocol suite interlayer communications.

each direction is free of transmission errors, with no lost or duplicate bytes, and the bytes are delivered in the same sequence as they were submitted. The service provided by TCP is known, therefore, as a **reliable stream service**.

As we explained in Section 6.2, the service provided by IP is an unreliable best-effort service. Hence in order to provide a reliable service, before any data is transferred between the two TCP entities, a logical connection is first established between them in order for the sequence numbers in each TCP entity – which are required for error correction and flow control purposes – to be initialized. Also, once all data has been transferred in both directions, the logical connection is closed.

During the actual data transfer phase, in order for the receiving TCP to detect the presence of transmission errors, each TCP entity divides the submitted stream of bytes into blocks known as **segments**. For interactive applications involving a user at a terminal, a segment may contain just a single byte, while for large file transfers a segment may contain many bytes. There is an agreed **maximum segment size** (**MSS**) used with a connection that is established by the two peer TCP entities during the setting up of the connection. This is such that an acceptable proportion of segments are received by the destination free of transmission errors. The default MSS is 536 bytes although larger sizes can be agreed. Normally, the size chosen is such that no fragmentation is necessary during the transfer of a segment over the network/internet and hence is determined by the path MTU. The TCP protocol then includes a retransmission procedure in order to obtain error-free copies of those segments that are received with transmission errors.

In addition, the TCP protocol includes a flow control procedure to ensure no data is lost when the TCP entity in a fast host – a large server for example – is sending data to the TCP in a slower host such as a PC. It also includes a congestion control procedure which endeavors to control the rate of entry of segments into the network/internet to the rate at which segments are leaving.

In the following subsections we discuss firstly the user services provided by TCP, then selected aspects of the operation of the TCP protocol, and finally the formal specification of the protocol. Collectively these are defined in RFCs 793, 1122 and 1323.

7.3.1 User services

The most widely used set of user service primitives associated with TCP are the **socket primitives** used with Berkeley Unix. Hence, although there are a number of alternative primitives, in order to describe the principles involved, we shall restrict our discussion to these. They are operating system calls and collectively form what is called an **application program interface** (**API**) to the underlying TCP/IP protocol stack. A typical list of primitives is given in Table 7.1 and their use is shown in diagrammatic form in Figure 7.3.

Table 7.1 List of socket primitives associated with TCP and their parameters.

Primitive	Parameters
socket ( )	service type, protocol, address format, return value = socket descriptor or error code
bind ( )	socket descriptor, socket address (= host IP address + port number), return value = success or error code
listen ( )	socket descriptor, maximum queue length, return value = success or error code
accept ( )	socket descriptor, socket address, return value = success or error code
connect ( )	socket descriptor, local port number, destination port number, destination IP address, precedence, optional data (for example a user name and a password), return value = success or error code
send ( )	socket descriptor, pointer to message buffer containing the data to send, data length (in bytes), push flag, urgent flag, return value = success or error code
receive ( )	socket descriptor, pointer to a message buffer into which the data should be put, length of the buffer, return value = success or end of file (EOF) or error code
close ( )	socket descriptor, return value = success or error code
shutdown ( )	socket descriptor, return value = success or error code

Each of the two peer user application protocols/processes (APs) first creates a communications channel between itself and its local TCP entity. This is called a **socket** or **endpoint** and, in the case of the server AP, involves the AP issuing a sequence of primitive (also known as system of function) calls each with a defined set of parameters associated with it: *socket( )*, *bind( )*, *listen( )*, *accept( )*. Each call has a return value(s) or an error code associated with it.

The parameters associated with the *socket( )* primitive include the service required (reliable stream service), the protocol (TCP), and the address format (Internet). Once a socket has been created – and send/receive memory buffers allocated – a **socket descriptor** is returned to the AP which it then uses with each of the subsequent primitive calls. The AP then issues a

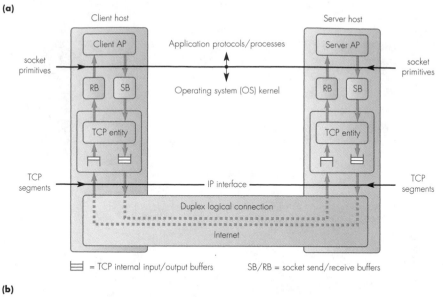

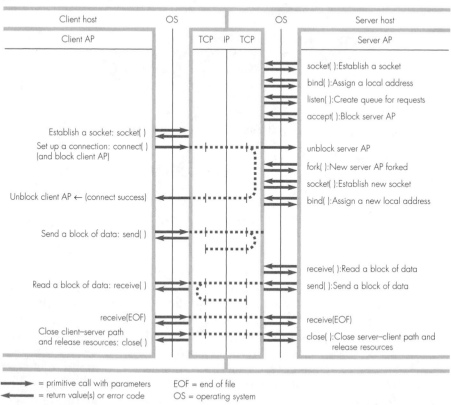

Figure 7.3 TCP socket primitives: (a) socket interface; (b) primitives and their use.

bind( ) primitive, which, in addition to the socket descriptor, has an address parameter associated with it. This is the address the AP wishes to be assigned to the newly created socket and is called the **socket address**. This comprises the Internet-wide IP address of the host and, in the case of the server AP, the 16-bit well-known port number associated with this type of application protocol (FTP and so on).

The *listen( )* primitive call results in the local TCP entity creating a queue (whose maximum length is given as a parameter) to hold incoming connection requests for the server AP. The *accept( )* primitive is then used to put the AP in the blocked state waiting for an incoming connection request to be received from a client TCP entity. Collectively, this sequence of four primitives forms what is called a **passive-open**.

In the case of a client AP, since it can only set up a single TCP connection at a time and the socket address has only local significance, it simply issues a *socket( )* primitive to create a new socket with the same parameters as those used by the server (AP). This is then followed by a *connect( )* primitive, which, in addition to the locally allocated socket descriptor, has parameters that contain the IP address of the remote (server) host, the well-known port number of the required server AP, the local port number that has been assigned to this socket by the client AP, a precedence value, and an optional item of data such as a user name and a password.

The local port number, together with the host IP address, forms the address to be assigned to this socket. The precedence parameter is a collection of parameters that enable the IP protocol to specify the contents of the *type of service* field in the header of the IP datagram that is used to transfer the segments associated with the connection over the Internet. We identified the contents of this field in Figure 6.2 when we discussed the operation of the IP protocol. Note that the IP address of the remote (server) host and the precedence parameters are used by the IP protocol and not TCP. They are examples of what are called **pass-through parameters**, that is, a parameter that is passed down from one protocol layer to another without modification.

Once the *connect( )* call has been made, this results in the calling AP being put into the blocked state while the local TCP entity initiates the setting up of a logical connection between itself and the TCP entity in the server. Collectively, these two primitives form what is called an **active-open**.

The TCP entity in a client host may support multiple concurrent connections involving different user APs. Similarly, the TCP entity in a server may support multiple connections involving different clients. Hence in order for the two TCP entities to relate each received segment to the correct connection, when each new connection is established, both TCP entities create a **connection record** for it. This is a data structure that contains a *connection identifier* (comprising the pair of socket addresses associated with the connection), the agreed *MSS* for the connection, the *initial sequence number* (associated with the acknowledgment procedure) to be used in each direction, the *precedence value*, the *size of the window* associated with the TCP flow control procedure, and a number of fields associated with the operation of the protocol entity including *state variables* and the current state of the protocol entity.

At the server side, when a new connection request (PDU) is received, the server AP is unblocked and proceeds to create a new instance of the server AP to service this connection. Typically, this is carried out using the Unix *fork primitive*. A new socket between the new AP and the local TCP entity is then created and this is used to process the remaining primitives associated with this connection. The parent server AP then either returns to the blocked state waiting for a new connection request to arrive or, if one is already waiting in the server queue, proceeds to process the new request. Once a new instance of the server AP has been created and linked to its local TCP entity by a socket, both the client and server APs can then initiate the transfer of blocks of data in each direction using the *send( )* and *receive( )* primitives.

Associated with each socket is a *send buffer* and a *receive buffer*. The send buffer is used by the AP to transfer a block of data to its local TCP entity for sending over the connection. Similarly, the receive buffer is used by the TCP entity to assemble data received from the connection ready for reading by its local AP. The *send( )* primitive is used by an AP to transfer a block of data of a defined size to the send buffer associated with the socket ready for reading by its local TCP entity. The parameters include the local socket descriptor, a pointer to the memory buffer containing the block of data, and also the length (in bytes) of the block of data. With TCP there is no correlation between the size of the data block(s) submitted (by an AP to its local TCP entity for sending) and the size of the TCP segments that are used to transfer the data over the logical connection. As we saw in Section 7.2, normally the latter is determined by the path MTU and, in many instances, this is much smaller than the size of the data blocks submitted by an AP.

With some applications, however, each submitted data block may be less than the path MTU. For example, in an interactive application involving a user at a keyboard interacting with a remote AP, the input data may comprise just a few bytes/characters. So in order to avoid the local TCP entity waiting for more data to fill an MTU, the user AP can request that a submitted block of data is sent immediately. This is done by setting a parameter associated with the *send( )* primitive called the *push flag*. A second parameter called the *urgent flag* can also be set by a user AP. This again is used with interactive applications to enable, for example, a user AP to abort a remote computation that it has previously started. The (urgent) data – string of characters – associated with the abort command are submitted by the source AP with the urgent flag set. The local TCP entity then ceases waiting for any further data to be submitted and sends what is outstanding, together with the urgent data, immediately. On receipt of this, the remote TCP entity proceeds to interrupt the peer user AP, which then reads the urgent data and acts upon it.

Finally, when a client AP has completed the transfer of all data blocks associated with the connection, it initiates the release of its side of the connection by issuing a *close( )* – or sometimes a *shutdown( )* – primitive. When the server AP is informed of this (by the local TCP entity), assuming it also has finished sending data, it responds by issuing a *close( )* primitive to release the other side of the connection. Both TCP entities then delete their connection records and also the server AP that was forked to service the connection. As we shall expand upon later, the *shutdown( )* primitive is used when only half of the connection is to be closed.

7.3.2 Protocol operation

As we can see from the above, the TCP protocol involves three distinct operations: setting up a logical connection between two previously created sockets, transferring blocks of data reliably over this connection, and closing down the logical connection. In practice, each phase involves the exchange of one or more TCP segments (PDUs) and, since all segments have a common structure, before describing the three phases we first describe the usage of the fields present in each segment header.

Segment format

All segments start with a common 20-byte header. In the case of acknowledgment and flow control segments, this is all that is present. In the case of connection-related segments, an options field may be present and a data field is present when data is being transferred over a connection. The fields making up the header are shown in Figure 7.4(a).

The 16-bit *source port* and *destination port* fields are used to identify the source and destination APs at each end of a connection. Also, together with the 32-bit source and destination IP addresses of the related hosts, they form the 48-bit socket address and the 96-bit connection identifier. Normally, the port number in a client host is assigned by the client AP while the port number in a server is a well-known port.

The *sequence number* performs the same function as the send sequence number in the HDLC protocol and the *acknowledgment number* the same function as the receive sequence number. Also, as with HDLC, a logical connection involves two separate flows, one in each direction. Hence the *sequence number* in a segment relates to the flow of bytes being transmitted by a TCP entity and the *acknowledgment number* relates to the flow of bytes in the reverse direction. However, with the TCP, although data is submitted for transfer in blocks, the flow of data in each direction is treated simply as a stream of bytes for error and flow control purposes. Hence the *sequence* and *acknowledgment numbers* are both 32-bits in length and relate to the position of a byte in the total session stream rather than to the position of a message block in the sequence. The *sequence number* indicates the position of the first byte in the *data* field of the segment relative to the start of the byte stream, while the *acknowledgment number* indicates the byte in the stream flowing in the reverse direction that the TCP entity expects to receive next.

The presence of an *options* field in the segment header means that the header can be of variable length. The *header length* field indicates the number of 32-bit words in the header. The 6-bit *reserved* field, as its name implies, is reserved for possible future use.

All segments have the same header format and the validity of selected fields in the segment header is indicated by the setting of individual bits in

(a)

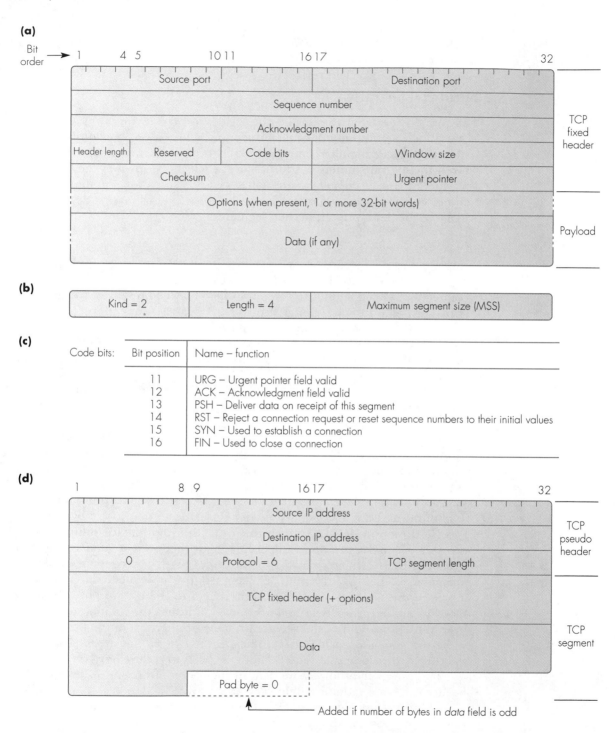

(b)

(c)

(d)

Figure 7.4 TCP segment format: (a) header fields; (b) MSS option format; (c) code bit definitions; (d) pseudo header fields.

the 6-bit *code* field; if a bit is set (a binary 1), the corresponding field is valid. Note that multiple bits can be set in a single segment. The bits have the meaning shown in Figure 7.4(c).

The *window size* field relates to a sliding window flow control scheme the principles of which we considered in Section 1.4.4. The number in the window size indicates the number of data bytes (relative to the byte being acknowledged in the *acknowledgment* field) that the receiver is prepared to accept. It is determined by the amount of unused space in the receive buffer the remote TCP entity is using for this connection. The maximum size of the receive buffer – and hence the maximum size of the window – can be different in each direction and has a default value which, typically, is 4096, 8192 or 16 384 bytes.

As we saw in Section 6.2, the checksum field in the header of each IP datagram applies only to the fields in the IP header and not the datagram contents. Hence the *checksum* field in the TCP segment header covers the complete segment; that is, header plus contents. In addition, since only a simple checksum is used to derive the checksum value in the IP header, in order to add an additional level of checking, some selected fields from the IP header are also included in the computation of the TCP checksum. The fields used form what is called the (TCP) **pseudo header** and these are identified in Figure 7.4(d).

As we can see, these are the source and destination IP addresses and the protocol value (= 6 for TCP) from the IP header, plus the total byte count of the TCP segment (header plus contents). The computation of the checksum uses the same algorithm as that used by IP. As we saw in Section 6.2, this is computed by treating the complete datagram as being made up of a string of 16-bit words that are then added together using 1s complement arithmetic. Since the number of bytes in the original TCP segment *data* field may be odd, in order to ensure the same checksum is computed by both TCP entities, a **pad byte** of zero is added to the data field whenever the number of bytes in the original *data* field is odd. As we can deduce from this, the byte count of the TCP segment must always be an even integer.

When the URG (urgent) flag is set in the *code* field, the *urgent pointer* field is valid. This indicates the number of bytes in the *data* field that follow the current *sequence number*. This is known as **urgent data** – or sometimes **expedited data** – and, as we mentioned earlier, it should be delivered by the receiving TCP entity immediately it is received.

The *options* field provides the means of adding extra functionality to that covered by the various fields in the segment header. For example, it is used during the connection establishment phase to agree the maximum amount of data in a segment each TCP entity is prepared to accept. During this phase, each indicates its own preferred maximum size and hence can be different for each direction of flow. As we indicated earlier, this is called the maximum segment size (MSS) and excludes the fixed 20-byte segment header. If one of the TCP entities does not specify a preferred maximum size then a default value of 536 bytes is chosen. The TCP entity in all hosts connected to the Internet must accept a segment of up to 556 bytes – 536 plus a 20-byte header – and all IPs must accept a datagram of 576 bytes – 556 bytes plus a further

20-byte (IP) header. Hence the default MSS of 536 bytes ensures the datagram (with the TCP segment in its payload) will be transferred over the Internet without fragmentation. The format of the MSS option is shown in Figure 7.4(b). Also, although not shown, if this is the last or only option present in the header, then a single byte of zero is added to indicate this is the end of the option list.

Connection establishment

On receipt of a *connect( )* primitive (system call) from a client AP, the local TCP entity attempts to set up a logical connection with the TCP entity in the server whose IP address (and port number) are specified in the parameters associated with the primitive. This is achieved using a three-way exchange of segments. Collectively, this is known as a **three-way handshake** procedure and the segments exchanged for a successful *connect( )* call are shown in Figure 7.5(a).

As we indicated in the previous section, the flow of data bytes in each direction of a connection is controlled independently. The TCP entity at each end of a connection starts in the CLOSED state and chooses its own *initial sequence number* (*ISN*). These are both non-zero and change from one connection to another. This ensures that any segments relating to a connection that get delayed during their transfer over the internet – and hence arrive at the client/server after the connection has been closed – do not interfere with the segments relating to the next connection. Normally, each TCP entity maintains a separate 32-bit counter that is incremented at intervals of either 4 or $8 \mu s$. Then, when a new ISN is required, the current contents of the counter are used.

- To establish a connection, the TCP at the client first reads the ISN to be used (from the counter) and makes an entry of this in the *ISN* and *send sequence variable* fields of the connection record used for this connection. It then sends a segment to the TCP in the server with the SYN code bit on, the ACK bit off, and the chosen ISN (X) in the sequence (number) field. Note that since no window or MSS option fields are present, then the receiving TCP assumes the default values. The TCP entity then transfers to the SYN_SENT state.

- On receipt of the SYN, if the required server AP – as determined by the destination port and IP address – is not already in the LISTEN state, the server TCP declines the connection request by returning a segment with the RST code bit on. The client TCP entity then aborts the connection establishment procedure and returns an error message with a reason code to the client AP. Alternatively, if the server AP is in the LISTEN state, the server TCP makes an entry of the ISN (to be used in the client–server direction and contained within the received segment) in its own connection record – in both the *ISN* and *receive sequence variable* fields – together with the ISN it proposes to use in the return direction. It then proceeds to create a new segment with the SYN bit on and the chosen ISN(Y) in the sequence field. In addition, it sets the ACK bit on

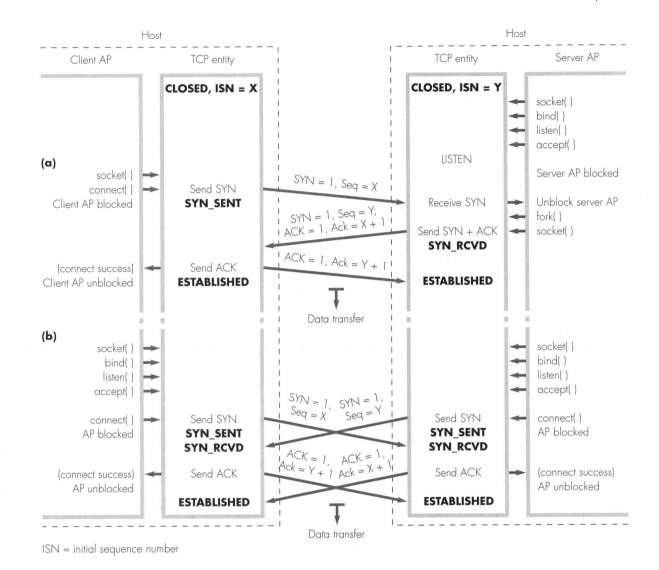

ISN = initial sequence number

Figure 7.5 TCP connection establishment examples: (a) client–server; (b) connection collision.

and returns a value of X+1 in the acknowledgment field to acknowledge receipt of the client's SYN. It then sends the segment to the client and enters the SYN_RCVD state.

■ On receipt of the segment, the client TCP makes an entry of the ISN to be used in the server–client direction in its connection record – in both the *ISN* and *receive sequence variable* fields – and increments the send sequence variable in the record by 1 to indicate the SYN has been acknowledged. It then acknowledges receipt of the SYN by returning a segment with the ACK bit on and a value of Y+1 in the acknowledgment field. The TCP entity then enters the (connection) ESTABLISHED state.

■ On receipt of the ACK, the server TCP increments the send sequence variable in its own connection record by 1 and enters the ESTABLISHED state. As we can deduce from this, the acknowledgment of each SYN segment is equivalent to a single data byte being transferred in each direction. At this point, both sides are in the ESTABLISHED state and ready to exchange data segments.

Although in a client–server application the client always initiates the setting up of a connection, in applications not based on the client–server model the two APs may try to establish a connection at the same time. This is called a **simultaneous open** and the sequence of segments exchanged in this case is as shown in Figure 7.5(b).

As we can see, the segments exchanged are similar to those in the client–server case and, since both ISNs are different, each side simply returns a segment acknowledging the appropriate sequence number. However, since the connection identifier is the same in both cases, only a single connection is established.

Data transfer

The error control procedure associated with the TCP protocol is similar to that used with the HDLC protocol. The main difference is that the sequence and acknowledgment numbers used with TCP relate to individual bytes in the total byte stream whereas with HDLC the corresponding send and receive sequence numbers relate to individual blocks of data. Also, because of the much larger round-trip time of an internet (compared with a single link), with TCP the window size associated with the flow control procedure is not derived from the sequence numbers. Instead, a new window size value is included in each segment a TCP entity sends to inform the other TCP entity of the maximum number of bytes it is willing to receive from it. This is known also as a **window size advertisement**.

In addition, because the TCP protocol may be operating (on an end-to-end basis) over a number of interconnected networks rather than a single line, it includes a congestion control procedure. This endeavors to regulate the rate at which the sending TCP entity sends data segments into the internet to the rate segments are leaving the internet. We shall discuss the main features of the different procedures that are used by means of examples.

Small segments

In order to explain the features of the protocol that relate to the exchange of small segments – that is, all the segments contain less than the MSS – we shall consider a typical data exchange relating to a networked interactive application. An example application protocol of this type is Telnet. Typically, this involves a user at the client side typing a command and the server AP in a remote host responding to it. An example set of segments is shown in Figure 7.6(a).

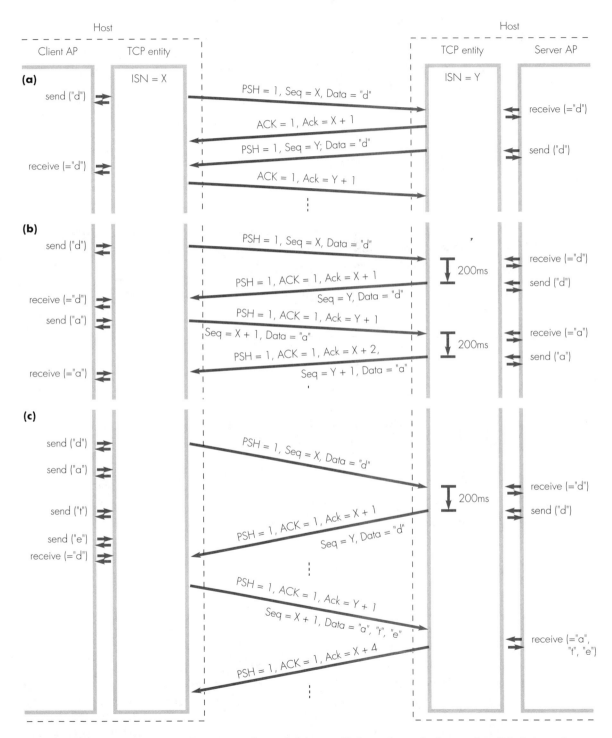

Figure 7.6 Small segment data transfers: (a) immediate acknowledgments; (b) delayed acknowledgments; (c) Nagle algorithm.

With interactive applications involving a user at a keyboard, each character typed is sent directly by the client AP to the server side. The server AP then reads the character from the receive buffer and immediately echoes the character back to the client side by writing it into the send buffer. On receipt of the character, the client AP displays it on the host screen. Hence each typed character is sent directly in a separate segment with the PSH flag on. Similarly, the echoed character is also sent in a separate segment with the PSH flag on. In addition to these two segments, however, each TCP entity returns a segment with the ACK bit on to acknowledge receipt of the segment containing the typed/echoed character. This means that for each character that is typed, four segments are sent, each with a 20-byte header and a further 20-byte IP header.

In practice, in order to reduce the number of segments that are sent, a receiving TCP entity does not return an ACK segment immediately it receives an (error-free) data segment. Instead, it waits for up to 200 ms to see if any data is placed in the send buffer by the local AP. If it is, then the acknowledgment is piggybacked in the segment that is used to send the data. This procedure is called **delayed acknowledgments** and, as we can see in Figure 7.6(b), with interactive applications it can reduce significantly the number of segments that are required.

Although this mode of working is acceptable when communicating over a single network such as a LAN, when communicating over an internet which has a long round-trip time (RTT), the delays involved in waiting for each echoed character can be annoying to the user. Hence a variation of the basic delayed acknowledgment procedure is often used. This is called the **Nagle algorithm** and is defined in RFC 896. When the algorithm is enabled, each TCP entity can have only a single small segment waiting to be acknowledged at a time. As a result, in interactive applications, when the client TCP entity is waiting for the ACK for this segment to be received, a number of characters may have been typed by the user. Hence when the ACK arrives, all the waiting characters in the send buffer are transmitted in a single segment. A sequence diagram showing this is given in Figure 7.6(c).

In these examples, the window size has not been shown since, in general, when small segments are being exchanged it has no effect on the flow of the segments. Also, the Nagle algorithm is not always enabled. For example, when the interactions involve a mouse, each segment may contain a collection of mouse movement data and, when echoed, the movement of the cursor can appear erratic. An example application of this type is X-Windows.

Error control

As we saw in Figure 7.4(a), each TCP segment contains only a single acknowledgment number. Hence should a segment not arrive at the destination host, the receiving TCP can only return an acknowledgment indicating the next in-sequence byte that it expects. Also, since the packets relating to a message are being transmitted over an internet, when the path followed has alternative routes, packets may arrive at the destination host out of sequence. Hence the receiving TCP simply holds each out-of-sequence segment that it receives in temporary storage and returns an ACK indicating the next in-sequence byte – and hence segment – that it expects. Normally, the out-of-sequence segment arrives within a short time interval at which point the receiving TCP returns an ACK that acknowledges all the segments now received including those held in temporary storage.

At the sending side, the TCP receives an ACK indicating a segment has been lost but, within a short time interval, it receives an ACK for a segment that it transmitted later (so acknowledging receipt of all bytes up to and including the last byte in the later segment). Hence, since this is a relatively frequent occurrence, the sending TCP does not initiate a retransmission immediately it receives an out-of-sequence ACK. Instead, it only retransmits a segment if it receives three duplicate ACKs for the same segment – that is, three consecutive segments with the same acknowledgment number in their header – since it is then confident that the segment has been lost rather than simply received out of sequence.

In addition, to allow for the possibility that the sending TCP has no further segments ready for transmission, when a loss is detected it starts a *retransmission timer* for each new segment it transmits. A segment is then retransmitted if the TCP does not receive an acknowledgment for it before the timeout interval expires. An example illustrating the two possibilities is shown in Figure 7.7. In the example we assume:

- there is only a unidirectional flow of data segments;
- the sending AP writes a block of data – a message – comprising 3072 bytes into the send buffer using a *send( )* primitive;
- the MSS being used for the connection is 512 bytes and hence six segments are required to send the block of data;
- the size of the receive buffer is 8192 bytes and hence the sending TCP can send the complete set of segments without waiting for an acknowledgment;
- an ACK segment is returned on receipt of each error-free data segment;
- segments 2 and 6 are both lost – owing to transmission errors for example – as is the final ACK segment.

To follow the transmission sequence shown in the figure we should note the following:

- The sending TCP has a send sequence variable, V(S), in its connection record, which is the value it places in the sequence number field of the next new segment it sends. Also it has a *retransmission list* to hold segments waiting to be acknowledged. Similarly, the receiving TCP has a receive sequence variable, V(R), in its connection record (which is the sequence number it expects to receive next) and a *receive list* to hold segments that are received out of sequence.

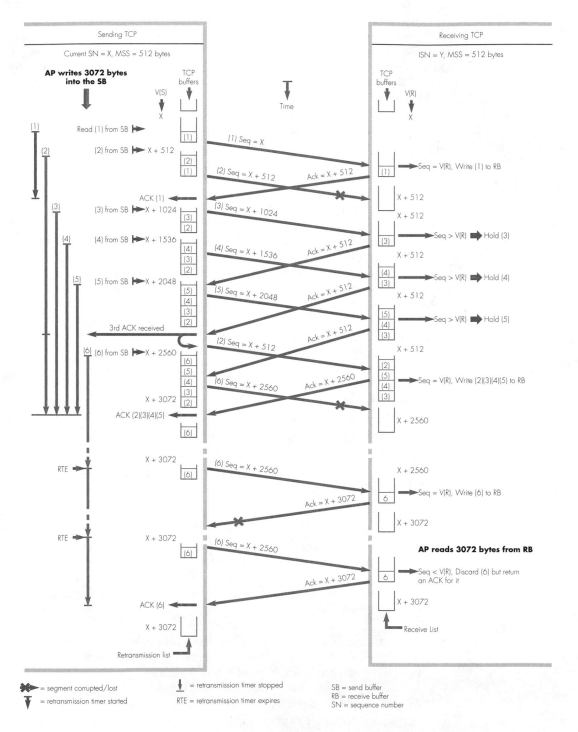

Figure 7.7 Example segment sequence showing TCP error control procedure.

- Segment (1) is received error-free and, since its sequence number (Seq=X) is equal to V(R), the 512 bytes of data it contains are transferred directly into the receive buffer (ready for reading by the destination AP), V(R) is incremented to X+512, and an ACK (with Ack=X+512) is returned to the sending side.

- On receipt of the ACK, the sending TCP stops the retransmission timer for (1) and, in the meantime, segment (2) has been sent.

- Since segment (2) is corrupted, no ACK for it is returned and hence its timer continues running.

- The sending TCP continues to send segments (3), (4) and (5), all of which are received error-free. However, since they are out of sequence – segment (2) is missing – the receiving TCP retains them in its receive list and returns an ACK with Ack=X+512 in each segment for each of them to indicate to the sending TCP that segment (2) is missing.

- On receipt of the third ACK with an ACK=X+512, the sending TCP retransmits segment (2) without waiting for the retransmission timer to expire. As we indicated earlier, this is done since if three or more ACKs with the same acknowledgment number are received one after the other, it is assumed that the segment indicated has been lost rather than received out of sequence. Because the retransmission occurs before the timer expires, this procedure is called **fast retransmit**.

- This time segment (2) is received error-free and, as a result, the receiving TCP is able to transfer the contents of segments (2), (3), (4) and (5) to the receive buffer – ready for reading by the AP – and returns an ACK with Ack=X+2560 to indicate to the sending TCP that all bytes up to and including byte 2560 have been received and their timers can be stopped.

- In the meantime, segment (6) has been transmitted but is corrupted. Hence, since no other segments are waiting to be sent, its timer continues running until it expires when the segment is retransmitted.

- This time the segment is received error-free and so its contents are passed to the receive buffer directly and an ACK for it is returned. Also, it is assumed that at this point the receiving AP reads the accumulated 3072 bytes from the receive buffer using a *receive( )* primitive.

- The ACK for segment (6) is corrupted and hence the timer for the segment expires again and the segment is retransmitted. However, since the sequence number is less than the current V(R), the receiving TCP assumes it is a duplicate. Hence it discards it but returns an ACK to stop the sending TCP from sending another copy.

As we can see from this example, a key parameter in the efficiency of the error control procedure is the choice of the **retransmission timeout (RTO) interval**. With a single data link the choice of an RTO is straightforward since the worst-case round-trip time – the time interval between sending a packet/frame and receiving an ACK for it – can be readily determined. The

RTO is then set at a value slightly greater than this. With an internet, however, the RTT of a TCP connection can vary considerably over relatively short intervals as the traffic levels within routers build up and subside. Hence choosing an RTO when the internet is lightly loaded can lead to a significant number of unnecessary retransmissions, while choosing it during heavy load conditions can lead to unnecessary long delays each time a segment is corrupted/lost. The choice of RTO, therefore, must be dynamic and vary not only from one connection to another but also during a connection.

The initial approach used to derive the RTO for a connection was based on an **exponential backoff** algorithm. With this an initial RTO of 1.5 seconds is used. Should this prove to be too short – that is, each segment requires multiple retransmission attempts – the RTO is doubled to 3 seconds. This doubling process then continues until no retransmissions occur. To allow for network problems, a maximum RTO of 2 minutes is used at which point a segment with the RST flag bit on is sent to abort the connection/session.

Although very simple to implement, a problem with this method is that when an ACK is received, it is not clear whether this is for the last retransmission attempt or an earlier attempt. This is known as the **retransmission ambiguity problem** and was identified by Karn. Because of this, a second approach was proposed by Jacobson and is defined in RFC 793. With this method, the RTO is computed from actual RTT measurements. The RTO is then updated as each new RTT measurement is made. In this way, the RTO for each connection is continuously being updated as each new estimate of the RTT is determined.

As we indicated earlier, when each data segment is sent, a separate retransmission timer is started. A connection starts with a relatively large RTO. Then, each time an ACK segment is received before the timer expires, the actual RTT is determined by subtracting the initial start time of the timer from the time when the ACK was received. The current estimate of the RTT is then updated using the formula

$$RTT = \alpha\,RTT + (1-\alpha)\,M$$

where M is the measured RTT and α is a smoothing factor that determines by how much each new M influences the computation of the new RTT relative to the current value. The recommended value for α is 0.9. The new RTO is then set at twice the updated RTT to allow for a degree of variance in the RTT.

Although this method performed better than the original method, a refinement of it was later introduced. This was done because by using a fixed multiple of each updated RTT ($\times 2$) to compute the new RTO, it was found that it did not handle well the wide variations that occurred in the RTT. Hence in order to obtain a better estimate, Jacobson proposed that each new RTO should be based not just on the mean of the measured RTT but also on the variance. In the proposed algorithm, the mean deviation of the RTT measurements, D, is used as an estimate of the variance. It is computed using the formula:

$$D = \alpha\,D + (1-\alpha)|RTT - M|$$

where α is a smoothing factor and $|RTT - M|$ is the modulus of the difference between the current estimate of the RTT and the new measured RTT (M). This is also computed for each new RTT measurement and the new estimate of the RTO is then derived using the formula:

$$RTO = RTT + 4D$$

As we indicated earlier, to overcome the retransmission ambiguity problem, the RTT is not measured/updated for the ACKs relating to retransmitted segments.

Note also that although in the above example an ACK is returned on receipt of each data segment, this is not always the case. Indeed, in most implementations, providing there is a steady flow of data segments, the receiving TCP only returns an ACK for every other segment it receives correctly. On sending each ACK, a timer – called the **delayed ACK timer** – is started and, should a second segment not be received before it expires, then an ACK for the first segment is sent. Note, however, that when a single ACK is sent for every other segment, since the V(R) is incremented on receipt of each segment, then the acknowledgment number within the (ACK) segment acknowledges the receipt of all the bytes in both segments.

Flow control

As we indicated earlier, the value in the *window size* field of each segment relates to a sliding window flow control scheme and indicates the number of bytes (relative to the byte being acknowledged in the *acknowledgment* field) that the receiving TCP is able to accept. This is determined by the amount of free space that is present in the receive buffer being used by the receiving TCP for the connection. Recall also that the maximum size of the window is determined by the size of the receive buffer. Hence when the sending TCP is running in a fast host – a large server for example – and the receiving TCP in a slow host, the sending TCP can send segments faster than, firstly, the receiving TCP can process them and, secondly, the receiving AP can read them from the receive buffer after they have been processed. The window flow control scheme, therefore, is present to ensure that there is always the required amount of free space in the receive buffer at the destination before the source sends the data. An example showing the sequence of segments that are exchanged to implement the scheme is given in Figure 7.8. In the example, we assume:

- there is only a unidirectional flow of data segments;
- the sizes of both the send and the receive buffers at the sending side are 4096 bytes and those at the receiving side 2048 bytes. Hence the maximum size of the window for the direction of flow shown is 2048 bytes;
- associated with each direction of flow the sending side maintains a *send window variable*, W_S, and the receiving side a *receive window variable*, W_R;

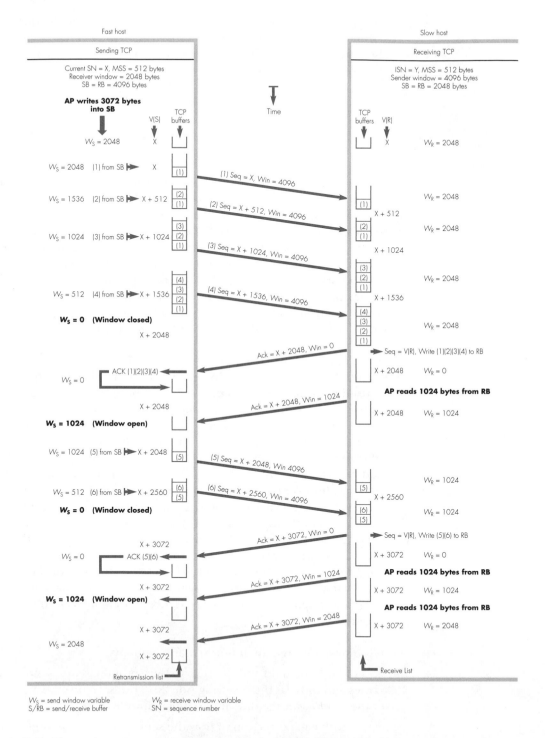

Figure 7.8 Example segment sequence showing TCP flow control procedure.

- the source AP can write bytes into the send buffer up to the current value of W_S and, providing W_S is greater than zero, the sending TCP can read data bytes from its send buffer up to the current value of W_S and initiate their transmission. Flow is stopped when $W_S = 0$ and the window is then said to be closed;

- at the destination, the receiving TCP, on receipt of error-free data segments, transfers the data they contain to the receive buffer and increments W_R by the number of bytes transferred. W_R is then decremented when the destination AP reads bytes from the receive buffer and, after each read operation, the receiving TCP returns a segment with the number of bytes of free space now available in the window size field of the segment.

The following should be noted when interpreting the sequence:

- The flow of segments starts with the AP at the sending side writing 3072 bytes into the send buffer using a *send( )* primitive.

- Since the sending host is much faster than the receiving host, the sending TCP is able to send a full window of 2048 bytes (in four 512-byte segments) before the receiving TCP is able to start processing them. The sending TCP must then stop as W_S is now zero.

- When the receiving TCP is scheduled to run, it finds four segments in its receive list and, since the first segment – segment (1) – has a sequence number equal to V(R), it transfers its contents to the receive buffer. It then proceeds to process and transfer the contents of segments (2), (3) and (4) in the same way and, after it has done this, it returns a single ACK segment to acknowledge receipt of these four segments but with a window size field of zero.

- On receipt of the ACK, the sending TCP deletes segments (1), (2), (3) and (4) from its retransmission list but leaves $W_S = 0$.

- When the receiving AP is next scheduled to run, we assume it reads just 1024 bytes from the receive buffer. On detecting this, the TCP returns a second ACK with the same acknowledgment number but with a window size of 1024. The second ACK is known, therefore, as a **window update**.

- At this point, since its sending window is now open, the sending TCP proceeds to send segments (5) and (6) at which point W_S again becomes zero.

- At the receiving side, when the TCP is next scheduled to run it finds segments (5) and (6) in the receive list and, since their sequence numbers are in sequence, it transfers their contents to the receive buffer. It then returns a single ACK for them but with a window size of zero.

- On receipt of the ACK, the sending TCP deletes segments (5) and (6) from its retransmission list but leaves $W_S = 0$.

- At some point later, the receiving AP is scheduled to run and we assume it again reads 1024 bytes from the receive buffer. Hence when the TCP next runs it returns a window update of 1024.

- Finally, after the receiving AP reads the last 1024 bytes from the RB, the TCP – some time later – returns a window update of 2048. After this has been received, both sides are back to their initial state.

We should note that there are a number of different implementations of TCP and hence the sequence shown in Figure 7.8 is only an example. For example, the receiving TCP may return two ACKs – one for segments (1) and (2) and the other for segments (3) and (4) – rather than a single ACK. In this case there would be a different distribution of segments between the TCP buffers and the receive buffer. Nevertheless, providing the size of the TCP buffers in the receiver is the same as the receive buffer, then the window procedure ensures there is sufficient buffer storage to hold all received segments. A schematic diagram summarizing the operation of the sliding window procedure is given in Figure 7.9.

Congestion control

A segment may be discarded during its transfer across an internet either because transmission errors are detected in the packet containing the

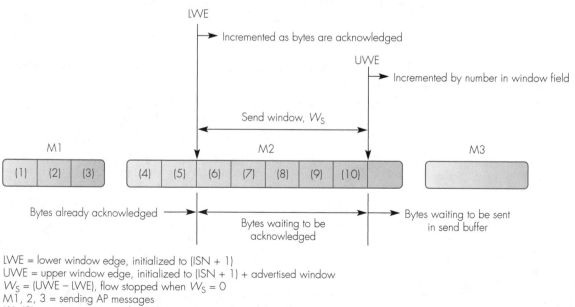

LWE = lower window edge, initialized to (ISN + 1)
UWE = upper window edge, initialized to (ISN + 1) + advertised window
W_S = (UWE − LWE), flow stopped when W_S = 0
M1, 2, 3 = sending AP messages
(1), (2) etc. = segments sent by TCP entity
Note: TCP chooses the size of segments it sends

Figure 7.9 TCP sliding window.

segment or because a router or gateway along the path being followed becomes congested; that is, during periods of heavy traffic it temporarily runs out of buffer storage for packets in the output queue associated with a line. However, the extensive use of optical fiber in the transmission network means that the number of lost packets due to transmission errors is relatively small. Hence the main reason for lost packets is congestion within the internet.

To understand the reason for congestion, it should be remembered that the path followed through an internet may involve a variety of different transmission lines some of which are faster – have a higher bit rate – than others. In general, therefore, the overall speed of transmission of segments over the path being followed is determined by the bit rate of the slowest line. Also, congestion can arise at the sending side of this line as the segments relating to multiple concurrent connections arrive at a faster rate than the line can transmit them. Clearly, if this situation continues for even a relatively short time interval, the number of packets in the affected router output queue builds up until the queue becomes full and packets have to be dropped. This also affects the ACKs within the lost segments and, as we have just seen, this can have a significant effect on the overall time that is taken to transmit a message.

In order to reduce the likelihood of lost packets occurring, the TCP in each host has a congestion control/avoidance procedure that, for each connection, uses the rate of arrival of the ACKs relating to a connection to regulate the rate of entry of data segments – and hence IP packets – into the internet. This is in addition to the window flow control procedure, which, as we have just seen, is concerned with controlling the rate of transmission of segments to the current capacity of the receive buffer in the destination host. Hence in addition to a send window variable, W_S, associated with the flow control procedure, each TCP also has a **congestion window** variable, W_C, associated with the congestion control/avoidance procedure. Both are maintained for each connection and the transmission of a segment relating to a connection can only take place if both windows are in the open state.

As we can see from the above, under lightly loaded network conditions the flow of segments is controlled primarily by W_S and, under heavily loaded conditions, it is controlled primarily by W_C. However, when the flow of segments relating to a connection first starts, because no ACKs have been received, the sending TCP does not know the current loading of the internet. So to stop it from sending a large block of segments – up to the agreed window size – the initial size of the congestion window, W_C, is set to a single segment which, because W_C has a dimension of bytes, is equal to the agreed MSS for the connection.

As we show in Figure 7.10, the sending TCP starts the data transfer phase of a connection by sending a single segment of up to the MSS. It then starts the retransmission timer for the segment and waits for the ACK to be received. If the timer expires, the segment is simply retransmitted. If the ACK is received before the timer expires, W_C is increased to two segments, each equal to the MSS. The sending TCP is then able to send two segments and,

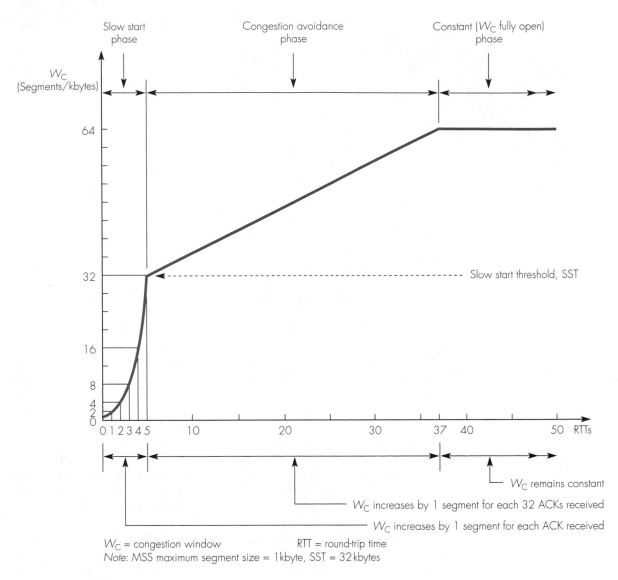

Figure 7.10 TCP congestion control window procedure.

for each of the ACKs it receives for these segments, W_C is increased by one segment (MSS). Hence, the sending TCP can now send four segments and, as we can see, W_C increases exponentially. Even though W_C increases rapidly, this phase is called **slow start** since it builds up from a single segment. It continues until a timeout for a lost segment occurs, or a duplicate ACK is received, or an upper threshold is reached. This is called the **slow start threshold** (**SST**) and, for each new connection, it is set to 64 kbytes. In the example, however, it is assumed to be initialized to 32 kbytes, which, because the MSS is 1 kbyte, is equal to 32 segments. Assuming the SST is reached, this is taken as an indication that the path is not congested. Hence the connection enters a second phase during which, instead of W_C increasing by 1 segment (MSS) for each ACK it receives, it increases by $1/W_C$ segments for each ACK received. Hence, as we can see, W_C now increases by 1 segment for each set of W_C ACKs that are received. This is called the **congestion avoidance** phase and, during this phase, the increase in W_C is additive. It continues until a second threshold is reached and, in the example, this is set at 64 kbytes. On reaching this, W_C remains constant at this value.

The profile shown in Figure 7.10 is typical of a lightly loaded internet in which none of the lines making up the path through the internet is congested. Providing W_C remains greater than the maximum flow control window, the flow of segments relating to the connection is controlled primarily by W_S. During these conditions all segments are transferred with a relatively constant transfer delay and delay variation. As the number of connections using the internet increases, however, so the traffic level increases up to the point at which packet (and hence segment) losses start to occur and, when this happens, the TCP controlling each connection starts to adjust its congestion window in a way that reflects the level of congestion.

The steps taken depend on whether a lost packet is followed by duplicate ACKs being received or the retransmission timer for the segment expiring. In the case of the former, as we saw earlier in Figure 7.7, the receipt of duplicate ACKs is indicative that segments are still being received by the destination host. Hence the level of congestion is assumed to be light and, on receipt of the third duplicate ACK relating to the missing segment – fast retransmit – the current W_C value is halved and the congestion avoidance procedure is invoked starting at this value. This is called **fast recovery** and an example is shown in Figure 7.11(a).

In this example it is assumed that the first packet loss occurs when W_C is at its maximum value of 64 segments, which, with an MSS of 1 kbyte, is equal to 64 kbytes. Hence on receipt of the third duplicate ACK, the lost segment is retransmitted and W_C is immediately reset to 32 segments/kbytes. The W_C is then incremented back up using the congestion avoidance procedure. However, when it reaches 34 segments, a second segment is lost. It is assumed that this also is detected by the receipt of duplicate ACKs and hence W_C is reset to 17 segments before the congestion avoidance procedure is restarted.

In the case of a lost segment being detected by the retransmission timer expiring, it is assumed that the congestion has reached a level at which no packets/segments relating to the connection are now getting through. As we show in the example in Figure 7.11(b), when a retransmission timeout (RTO) occurs, irrespective of the current W_C, it is immediately reset to 1 segment and the slow start procedure is restarted. Thus, when the level of congestion reaches the point at which RTOs start to occur, the flow of segments is controlled primarily by W_C.

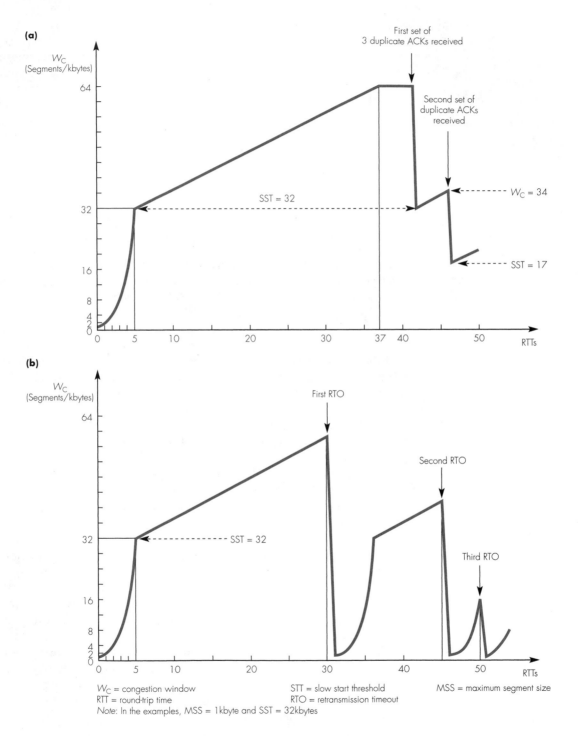

(a)

First set of
3 duplicate ACKs received

Second set of
duplicate ACKs
received

SST = 32

$W_C = 34$

SST = 17

W_C
(Segments/kbytes)

RTTs

(b)

First RTO

Second RTO

Third RTO

SST = 32

W_C
(Segments/kbytes)

RTTs

W_C = congestion window
RTT = round-trip time
Note: In the examples, MSS = 1kbyte and SST = 32kbytes

STT = slow start threshold
RTO = retransmission timeout

MSS = maximum segment size

Figure 7.11 TCP congestion window adjustments: (a) on receipt of duplicate ACKs; (b) on expiry of a retransmission timer.

Connection termination

As we indicated earlier, each TCP connection is duplex and hence data can be transferred in both directions simultaneously. To support this, each TCP entity maintains separate send and receive sequence and window variables and a separate state variable for each direction of flow. When a connection is terminated, each direction of flow is closed separately. In practice, there are a number of ways this is carried out and four examples are given in Figure 7.12.

In most cases, the TCP entity at each end of a connection goes through a different sequence of states. In order to discriminate between the two ends, the AP that issues the first *close( )* – and hence the TCP which sends the first FIN segment – performs what is called an **active close** procedure and the other side, a **passive close**. As we can see in the first example – part (a) – each procedure involves a slightly different sequence:

- In all the examples, both the forward and return paths of the TCP connection are currently in the ESTABLISHED (EST) – data transfer – state.

- The connection termination is started by one of the APs – normally the client – issuing a *close( )* primitive. The TCP entity at this side then goes through the active close procedure and the TCP at the other side the passive close.

- On receipt of the *close( )* primitive, the active TCP entity sends a FIN segment – that is, a segment with the FIN bit on – with a sequence number equal to the current $V(S)$, X. It then enters the FIN_WAIT1 state to indicate it is waiting for an ACK for the first FIN.

- On receipt of the FIN, the passive TCP first returns an ACK indicating correct receipt of the FIN and, when its local AP does the next *receive( )*, an end-of-file (EOF) is returned to indicate that no more data will be coming from the other side for this connection. It then enters the CLOSE_WAIT state to indicate it is waiting for a *close( )* from its local AP. Note that the ack number in the ACK is equal to X + 1 since a FIN consumes a byte of the byte stream.

- On receipt of the ACK, the TCP performing the active close simply enters the FIN_WAIT2 state to indicate it is now waiting for a FIN from the passive side.

- At some time later the AP in the passive side issues a *close( )* primitive and, as a result, the local TCP sends a FIN to indicate the closure of the connection in the reverse direction. It then enters the LAST_ACK state to indicate it is now waiting for the last ACK.

- On receipt of the FIN at the active side, the TCP first returns an ACK for the segment. It then starts a timer called the **2MSL timer** and enters the TIMED_WAIT state. When configuring each TCP entity a parameter called the **maximum segment lifetime** (**MSL**) is entered. This is the maximum time duration a segment can exist in the internet before being

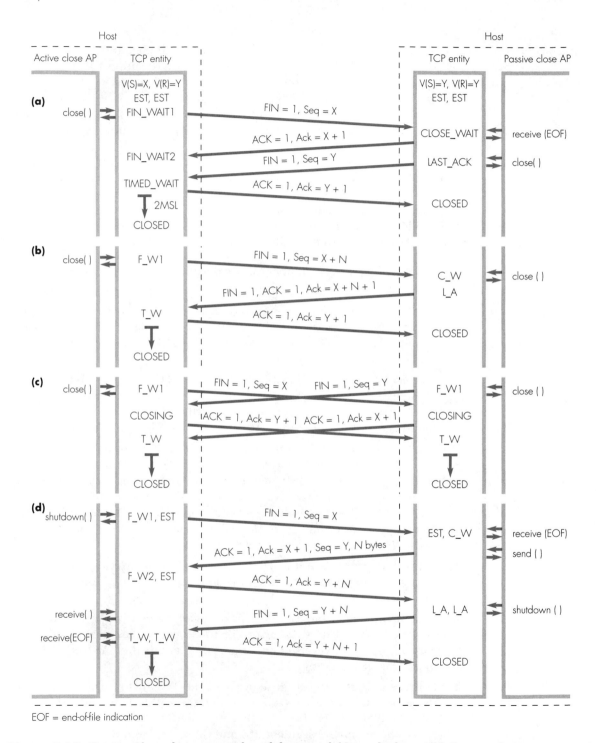

EOF = end-of-file indication

Figure 7.12 Connection close examples: (a) normal (4-way) close; (b) 3-way close; (c) simultaneous close; (d) half-close.

discarded. In practice, therefore, it is related to the time-to-live value used in each IP packet header. Typical values for the MSL are between 30 seconds and 2 minutes. This means that should the ACK for the second FIN be lost, the active TCP is still able to receive the retransmitted FIN.

■ Finally, on receipt of the ACK, the TCP at the passive side deletes the connection record relating to this connection and, when the 2MSL timer expires, the TCP at the active side does the same.

The segment sequence shown in Figure 7.12(b) is similar to that in the first example except that at the passive side data is still waiting to be acknowledged when the *close( )* is received. Hence the passive TCP piggybacks the ACK for the data in the same segment that carries the FIN in the reverse direction. This occurs when the *close( )* is received before the FIN arrives and, as we can see, this reduces the standard closure to a three-way segment exchange rather than a four-way exchange. Note that with this, however, data may be lost at the passive side if both sides of the connection are closed on receipt of the *close( )* primitive.

The segment sequence shown in Figure 7.12(c) illustrates what happens when the AP in both hosts issue a *close( )* simultaneously. As we can see, in this case the TCP at both sides carries out the active close sequence. Here, however, the intermediate state CLOSING is entered on receipt of the FIN from the opposite side. Then, as before, on receipt of the related ACK segment, both sides enter the TIMED_WAIT state to wait for the 2MSL timer to expire before closing down.

When an AP initiates the termination of a connection with a *close( )* primitive, this indicates to its local TCP that it has now completed sending the data/messages relating to the session and expects the remote AP to do the same. As a result, both TCPs proceed to close the (duplex) connection using one of the segment exchanges shown in the first three examples. With some applications, however, although the AP in the active side has completed sending data, it still expects to receive further data from the correspondent AP. Clearly, since both directions of a TCP connection are managed separately, this is possible. Hence to enable its local TCP to discriminate between this and a normal close, the AP issues a *shutdown( )* call. The local TCP initiates the closure of its side of the connection but leaves the other side in the ESTABLISHED state. This is known as a **half-close** and an example showing a typical segment sequence is shown in Figure 7.12(d). The following points should be noted:

■ In the figure, we show the state of both the forward and return paths of the connection at both sides and, as before, initially these are both in the ESTABLISHED (EST) state.

■ On receipt of the *shutdown( )* call, the local TCP leaves the return path in the EST state but proceeds to close the forward path. Hence it sends a FIN segment and enters the FIN_WAIT1 state.

- On receipt of this, an EOF is returned to the correspondent AP in response to the next *receive( )* to indicate that it will not receive any further data. It then changes the state of this side of the connection to the CLOSE_WAIT state. The AP then receives some data to send in the return direction and, since this path is still open, it sends the data and, in the same segment, piggybacks the acknowledgment of the FIN segment.

- On receipt of this, the other TCP returns an ACK for the data and, in response to the ACK for the FIN it sent, changes the state of this side of the connection to the FIN_WAIT2 state. Also, at some time later the AP reads the data using a *receive( )* call.

- After the ACK for the data is received, a *shutdown( )* is received from the AP. This results in a FIN segment being sent for the return path and the state of both paths being set into the LAST_ACK state.

- On receipt of the FIN, an EOF is returned to the local AP in response to the next *receive( )* to inform it that no further data will be coming. An ACK for the FIN is then returned and the state of both sides of the connection changed to the TIMED_WAIT state.

- On receipt of the ACK, the TCP deletes the connection record relating to this connection and, when the 2MSL timer expires, the TCP at the other side does the same.

The sequences shown in all four examples relate to what is called an **orderly release** since both FINs are sent either with or after all outstanding data relating to the session has been sent. In some instances, however, a connection is closed abruptly by the TCP at one side sending a segment with the RST bit on. This results in both sides of the connection being closed immediately and hence any data currently being held by either TCP will be lost. This is called an **abortive release** and an example of its use is when the sequence numbers relating to the connection become unsynchronized.

7.3.3 Additional features

The various examples we used in the data transfer section were chosen to explain the main procedures relating to this part of the TCP protocol. In addition, however, there are a number of details relating to these procedures that the examples did not show. In this section we identify a number of these.

Persist timer

In the example shown in Figure 7.8, it was assumed that the duplicate ACK containing the window update – Ack = X + 2048, Win = 1024 – was received by the sending TCP error free. In practice, of course, the packet containing this segment may have been corrupted or lost. If this had occurred, since the TCP entity at the receiving side has initiated the reopening of the window, it is now waiting to receive further segments. However, because the ACK is not received, the send window of the sending TCP is still zero and so it continues to assume that it cannot send any more segments. Although the data within segments is acknowledged, acknowledgments are not. Hence if the window update was not received, deadlock would occur with each side waiting for the other. Figure 7.13 shows how this can be avoided.

As we can see, the example relates directly to the sequence we showed earlier in Figure 7.8. Whenever the sending TCP sets its send window, W_S, to

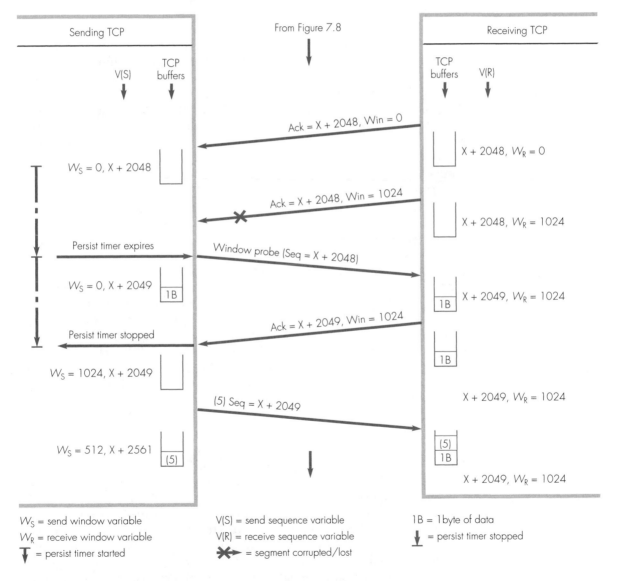

Figure 7.13 Persist timer: application and operation.

zero, it starts a timer. This is known as the **persist timer**, and if a segment containing a window update is not received before the timer expires, the sending TCP sends what is called a **window probe** segment. Even though the send window is zero, a TCP can always send a single byte of data. Hence the probe segment contains the first byte of the remaining data and, as we can see, if the ACK for this has a nonzero window value, then the flow of data segments can be resumed. Alternatively, should the value still be zero, then the timer is restarted and the procedure repeats. This is repeated at 60 s intervals until either a nonzero window value is received or the connection is terminated.

Keepalive timer

Once a connection between two TCP entities has been set up, it remains in place until the connection is terminated by the two communicating APs. As we saw in the previous section, this involves the two APs initiating the closure of their side of the connection. In most client–server applications, however, if the client host is simply switched off (instead of going through the normal log off procedure) then the connection from the server to the client will remain in place even though the client host is no longer responding. To overcome this, although not part of the TCP specification, many TCP implementations in servers include a timer known as the **keepalive timer**. The way this is used is shown in the example in Figure 7.14.

A separate timer is kept by the server TCP for all the connections – of which there can be many – that are currently in place. The default value of the keepalive timer is 2 hours and, should no data segments be exchanged over a connection during this time interval, the TCP in the server sends a probe segment to the client and sets the timer this time to 75 s. The probe segment has no data and has a *sequence number* of one less than the current V(S) of the server–client side of the connection. If the client host is still switched on – and the TCP connection is still in place – the client TCP simply returns an ACK for this with its current V(R) within it and, on receipt of this, the server TCP restarts the keepalive timer at 2 hours. If the client TCP does not respond, then the timer expires and the TCP in the server sends a second probe with the timer again set to 75 s. This procedure is repeated and, if no reply is received after 10 consecutive probes, the client is assumed to be switched off (or unreachable) and the server terminates the connection.

Silly window syndrome

The combined IP and TCP packet/segment headers are at least 40 bytes. Hence the larger the number of bytes in the data field of each segment, the smaller are the overheads associated with each transfer and the higher is the mean end-to-end data transfer rate. In the flow control example shown earlier in Figure 7.8, it was assumed that the AP at the receiving side read large (1024-byte) blocks of data from the receive buffer which, in turn, enabled the sending TCP to operate efficiently by always sending segments containing large amounts of data. In some interactive applications, however, a condition can arise that results in a very small number of bytes being sent in

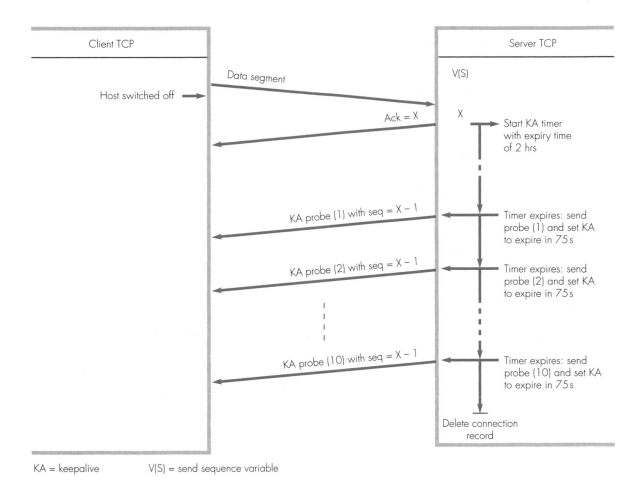

Figure 7.14 Keepalive timer: application and operation.

each segment. It is known as the **silly window syndrome** (**SWS**) and can arise either at the receiving side or the sending side.

To avoid this occurring, an added feature defined by Clark is incorporated into the basic flow control procedure we discussed earlier. At the receiving side this forbids a receiving TCP entity from advertising a small window and, at the sending side, it forbids a sending TCP entity from sending segments containing small amounts of data. Note that both features are complementary to the Nagle algorithm we discussed earlier and, in many instances, both operate together.

To illustrate how the problem can arise at the receiver, assume that in an interactive application a server AP initiates the transfer of a large character file to a client AP but the latter proceeds to read it (from the receive buffer of the receiving TCP) a single character at a time. On receipt of the first block of characters/bytes sent by the TCP in the server – up to the current maximum window size – the receiving TCP in the client would first return an ACK for the complete block but with a window value of zero. Then, assuming the procedure we showed in the earlier example in Figure 7.8, each time the client AP reads a character from the TCP receive buffer, the client TCP will return a window update to inform the TCP at the server side that it can now send a further character/byte. This it duly does and, on its receipt, the client TCP returns an ACK for it but again with a window value of zero. Similarly, when the next character is read by the AP, the client TCP returns a second window update of one byte/character and the procedure repeats until the complete file has been transferred in this way.

To avoid this happening, a receiving TCP is prevented from sending a window update until there is sufficient space in its buffer either for a segment equal to the maximum segment size in use or for one half of the maximum buffer capacity – and hence window capacity – whichever is the smaller. An example showing this is given in Figure 7.15. Part (a) illustrates the problem and part (b) shows how the solution attributed to Clark avoids the problem occurring.

In the example it is assumed that the window size in use is 1024 bytes and the MSS is also 1024 bytes. Hence, as we can deduce from part (a), after the first 1024-byte block has been transferred, without the Clark extension, each of the remaining 1024 bytes is transferred in a separate segment. Moreover, each of these may require an ACK and a window update segment. With the Clark extension, however, as we can see from part (b), after the first 1024 bytes have been transferred the remaining bytes are transferred in just two 512-byte segments, the choice of 512 being half of the buffer capacity.

As we indicated earlier, the same problem can arise at the sending side. For example, in an interactive application in which a user enters a string of characters at a keyboard, the sending AP may write each character into the send buffer as it is entered. In the absence of the Clark extension, the sending TCP may then proceed to send each character in a single segment. With the Clark extension, however, the sending TCP is made to wait until it has accumulated enough bytes/characters to fill a segment equal to either the MSS in use with the connection or to, one half of the buffer capacity of the receiving TCP. The latter is determined from the maximum window update value the sending TCP has received from the receiving TCP.

Window scale option

During our discussion of the HDLC protocol in Section 1.4.9, we saw that for transmission links that have a large bandwidth/delay product, the sizes of the send and receive sequence number fields in the frame header are extended in order to allow a larger window size to be used. As we saw in Example 1.6, this improves the utilization of the available link bandwidth. This can also be a requirement with TCP when the transmission path followed through the Internet covers a large distance – and hence has a large signal propagation delay – and a high mean bit rate.

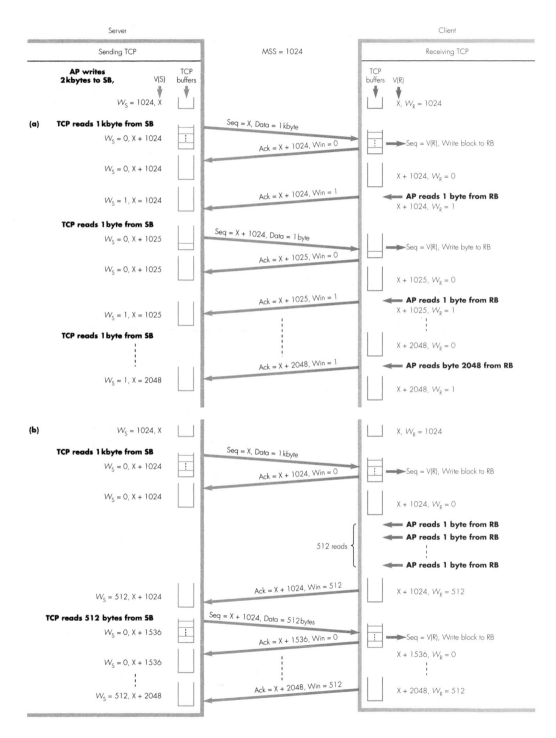

Figure 7.15 Silly window syndrome example: (a) the problem; (b) Clark's solution.

As we saw in Figure 7.4, the *window size* field in the segment header is 16 bits which allows a maximum window size of 65 535 bytes. However, when the path involves intercontinental lines, for example, a typical propagation delay is 40 ms. Also, since optical fiber is now widely used, mean bit rates in excess of 155 Mbps are common. This means that, in order to fully utilize the available transmission capacity, a window size in excess of 775 000 bytes is required. Hence, even though a single connection may only use a portion of the available bit rate, it can be seen that, for connections that span large distances, a larger maximum window size is required.

In order to achieve this without changing the format of the segment header, an option has been defined that enables a scaling factor to be applied to the value specified in the *window size* field. This is called the **window scale option** and is defined in **RFC 1323**. The format of this option is shown in Figure 7.16.

Normally, the option is included in the SYN segment when a connection is being established and, since the actual window size is determined by the size of the receive buffer, a different scaling factor can be agreed for use in each direction. Also, since the option is only three bytes in length, it is always preceded by a single byte containing a value of 1. This is known as a **no operation** (**NOP**) **option** and they are used as pad bytes so that all options are multiples of four bytes.

The scaling factor is defined in the *shift count* field of the option. As we can see, this is a one-byte field and the count value can be between 0 – no scaling in use – and 14. Although the *window size* field in each segment header is only 16 bits, the send and receive window variables kept by each TCP entity are both 32-bit values. The actual window value is then computed by first writing the 16-bit value from the *window size* field into the corresponding window variable and then shifting this left – and hence multiplying it by 2 – by the number in the *shift count* field. A shift count of 1, therefore, means that the maximum window size can be up to $65\,535 \times 2^1 = 131\,070$ bytes, and a shift count of 14 means that the maximum size can be $65\,535 \times 2^{14} = 1\,073\,725\,440$ bytes. As we indicated earlier, however, the maximum window size that can be used in each direction is determined by the size of the corresponding receive

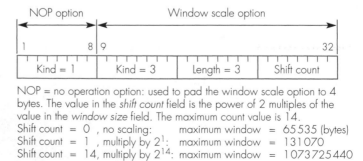

NOP = no operation option: used to pad the window scale option to 4 bytes. The value in the *shift count* field is the power of 2 multiples of the value in the *window size* field. The maximum count value is 14.
Shift count = 0 , no scaling: maximum window   = 65 535 (bytes)
Shift count = 1 , multiply by 2^1: maximum window   = 131 070
Shift count = 14, multiply by 2^{14}: maximum window   = 1 073 725 440

Figure 7.16 Window scale option format.

buffer. Normally, therefore, the shift count to be used for each direction is chosen by the TCP entity since it knows the amount of memory that has been allocated for the receive buffer.

Time-stamp option

During our discussion of the error control procedure, it was assumed that the measurement procedure used to estimate the worst-case round-trip time (RTT) – used by a TCP to compute the retransmission timeout (RTO) interval – is carried out for every data segment that is sent. Although this is the case in some implementations, in others a measurement update occurs only for one segment per window. In general, this is sufficient for transfers involving a small window size – and hence small number of segments per window – but, with a large window, the use of a single segment per window can lead to a poor estimate of the RTT. As we indicated, this can result in many unnecessary retransmissions. Hence to obtain a more accurate estimate of the RTT, the **time-stamp option** is used with these implementations when a large window size is detected. The option is defined in **RFC 1323** and allows the sending TCP to obtain an estimate of the RTT with each ACK it receives.

The option is requested by the TCP that performs an active open, by including the time-stamp option in the SYN segment. The request is then accepted if the receiving TCP includes a time-stamp option in the SYN segment that it returns. Once accepted, both TCPs can then include a time-stamp option in every data segment that they send. The format of the option is shown in Figure 7.17(a) and, as we can see, since it is 10 bytes long, the option is preceded by two NOP option bytes.

The TCP at each side of a connection keeps a 32-bit *timeout timer* that it uses to estimate the RTT for its own direction of transmission. The timer at each side is independent – not synchronized – and is incremented at intervals of between 1 ms and 1 s, a typical interval being 500 ms. For every data segment it sends, the sending TCP reads the current time from the timer and writes this into the *time-stamp value* field. Then, when the TCP returns an ACK for a segment, it writes the same time-stamp value in the *time-stamp echo reply* field. Hence on receipt of each ACK segment, the sending TCP can estimate the RTT for its direction of the connection by computing the difference between the current time in its timer and the time-stamp value contained in the option field of the ACK.

This procedure will work providing the receiving TCP returns an ACK for each data segment it receives. In many implementations, however, as we showed earlier in Figure 7.8, an ACK may be returned only after multiple data segments have been received. Indeed, following the widespread introduction of optical fiber, most TCP implementations now return an ACK for every other data segment received. In such cases, the question arises as to which of the time-stamps – one from each of the data segments that it has received – does the receiving TCP return in the *echo reply* field of the ACK. The answer is the time-stamp from the first in-sequence segment that the receiving TCP received after it returned the last ACK.

(a)

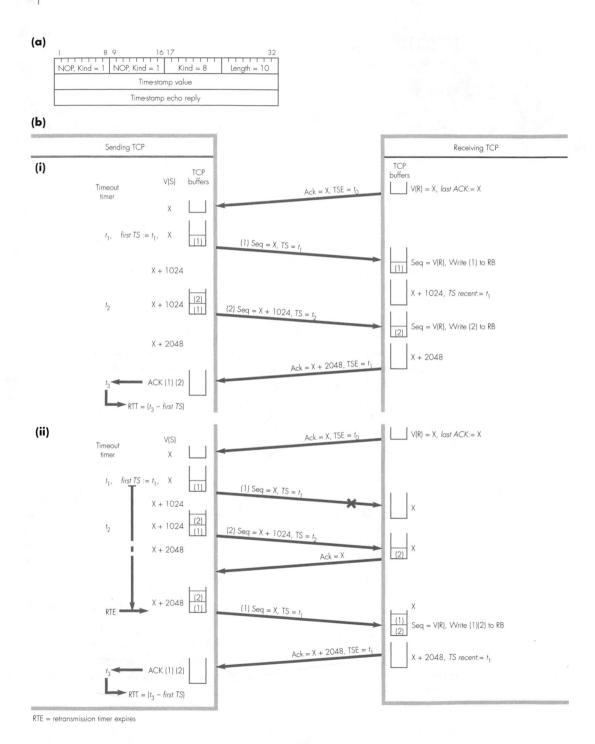

Figure 7.17 Time-stamp option: (a) option format; (b) two examples.

To implement this, the receiving TCP maintains two variables in its connection record: *lastACK* and *TSrecent*. Each time the receiving TCP returns an ACK, it keeps a record of the V(R) that it sent in the ACK in *lastACK*. Then, when the first data segment arrives after it has returned the ACK, if the sequence number in the segment header equals that stored in *lastACK*, it keeps a record of the time-stamp value it contains in *TSrecent*. As each subsequent data segment arrives, the TCP simply processes it in the normal way and, when it returns an ACK, includes the current value in *TSrecent* in the *echo reply* field of the option. Thus, the RTT computed by the sending TCP will reflect that the receiving TCP is only returning an ACK on receipt of multiple data segments.

If the sequence number in a segment is not that expected – that is, the sequence number is greater than V(R) – this indicates that a segment has been lost. In this case, the receiving TCP simply returns an ACK and proceeds to wait for the missing segment to be received. Then when it arrives, the time-stamp from this is echoed, not the time-stamp from the out-of-sequence segment. To allow for the possibility of the first segment in a new sequence being corrupted or lost, the sending TCP keeps a record of the time it first sent the segment in a variable called *firstTS*. Should the segment need retransmitting, the value in *firstTS* is used as the *time-stamp value*. In this way, the corrupted RTT also includes the time to retransmit the segment. Although this is an overestimate of the RTT, it is considered to be better than an underestimate, as would have been the case if the later time had been used. Two examples of sequences that show the two alternatives are shown in Figure 7.17(b).

In the first example, it is assumed that no lost segments occur and an ACK is returned on receipt of every other data segment. The time the first segment is sent, t_1, is stored in *firstTS* and, at the receiving side, since it is the segment expected, *TSrecent* becomes equal to the time-stamp value from the segment, t_1. Then, when the ACK is returned after the second segment is received, the value in the *time-stamp echo* field is set to t_1. The RTT is then computed as the difference between the time when the ACK was received and the value in *firstTS*, t_1.

In the second example, it is assumed that the first data segment in the new sequence is corrupted/lost but the second is received error free. In this case, *TSrecent* is not updated until the second copy of the retransmitted first segment is received. However, since this has the same *time-stamp value* as the corrupted first segment, the *time-stamp echo* is the same as before. Hence, as we can see, the computed RTT includes the time taken to retransmit the first segment.

SACK-permitted option

As we indicated earlier, for connections that involve paths through the Internet that span large distances, the propagation delay – also referred to as latency – of the path can be several tens of milliseconds. Hence in addition to influencing the choice of window size, it also has an impact on the efficiency of the error control scheme. As we showed in the example in Figure 7.7, to allow for segments being received out of sequence, a segment is retransmitted only after three duplicate ACKs have been received. Clearly, with connections that have a large RTT associated with them, the delays involved each time a packet/segment is lost or corrupted can be large. In order to reduce this delay, the alternative selective repeat/acknowledgment error control scheme can be used. This is defined in **RFC 2018** and is requested by including the **SACK-permitted option** in the SYN segment header. It is then accepted if the receiving TCP includes the same option in the SYN segment that it returns.

We explained the principle of operation of the selective repeat error control scheme in Section 1.4.3 and gave two example frame sequences showing how the protocol overcomes both a corrupted I-frame and a corrupted ACK-frame. A similar protocol is used with TCP SACK except in this, the SACK segment returned by a receiving TCP contains a list of the data segments that are missing in a specified window of data. In this way, all the missing segments are retransmitted in a single RTT.

Protection against wrapped sequence numbers

When very large amounts of data are being transferred between two hosts using a high bit rate LAN, for example, to speed up the transfer, the window scale option is often used with the maximum shift count of 14. An example is performing a backup of the contents of a disk over a LAN where, since this may involve many gigabytes, it is possible for the sequence numbers to wrap around during the backup. This means that a segment that is lost during one pass through the sequence numbers may be retransmitted and received during a later pass through the numbers so ruining the integrity of the transfer.

To overcome this possibility, the **PAWS** – protection against wrapped sequence numbers – algorithm is often used. This involves the time-stamp option being selected and both sides using the current 32-bit time-stamp as an extension to the 32-bit sequence number. Effectively, this produces 64-bit sequence numbers, which overcomes the problem.

7.3.4 Protocol specification

To finish our discussion of TCP we shall illustrate how the segment sequences shown in the various examples, coupled with the socket primitives shown in Table 7.1, relate directly to the formal specification of the TCP protocol entity. Recall from Section 1.4.7 that protocol specifications are carried out in a number of ways. One of the most widely used methods is to use a combination of a state transition diagram and an extended event–state table. A state transition diagram illustrates the various sequences in a pictorial form and hence the various examples relate directly to this. The extended event–state table method, however, is better for implementing a protocol since, as we saw in the example in Section 1.4.7, program code can be derived directly from this. To avoid too much detail, we shall consider only the specification of the connection establishment and termination phases of a basic client TCP and the related server TCP since, as we saw in Figure 1.33, the data transfer phase contains many state variables and predicates.

Using the methodology we established in Section 1.4.7, the various incoming events, protocol states, outgoing events, and specific (internal) actions for both the client and server are shown in parts (a) and (b) of Table 7.2 respectively. As we can see, these relate directly to the segment sequence shown in Figure 7.5(a) – connection establishment – and Figure 7.12(a) – connection termination. The specifications of both the client TCP and the server TCP protocols in both state transition diagram and extended event–state diagram forms are then shown in parts (a) and (b) of Figure 7.18 respectively.

Table 7.2 Abbreviated names used in the specification of the TCP protocol: (a) client TCP; (b) server TCP.

(a) Incoming events

Name	Interface	Meaning
connect ( )	AP_user	Initiate the setting up of a connection
SYN+ACK	IP_provider	SYN+ACK received from server (TCP)
DATA	IP_provider	Block of data received from server
close( )	AP_user	Initiate the closure of a connection
ACK	IP_provider	ACK received from server
2MSL	Timer	2MSL timer expires
FIN	IP_provider	FIN received from server
RST	IP_provider	Abort connection

States

Name	Meaning
CLOSED	No connection in place
SYN_SENT	SYN sent to server (TCP)
ESTABLISHED	SYN received from server, connection now in place
FIN_WAIT1	FIN sent to server
FIN_WAIT2	ACK to FIN received from server
TIMED_WAIT	FIN received from server

Outgoing events

Name	Interface	Meaning
SendSYN	IP provider	Send SYN to server (TCP)
SendACK	IP provider	Send ACK to server
SendDATA	IP provider	Send block of data to server
SendFIN	IP provider	Send FIN to server

Table 7.2 Continued.

Specific actions

[1] Block client AP   [3] Write EOF to receive buffer (RB)
[2] Unblock client AP   [4] Start 2MSL timer

(b) Incoming events

Name	Interface	Meaning
listen ( )	AP_user	Create queue for connection requests
accept ( )	AP_user	Block server AP
SYN	IP_provider	SYN received from client
RST	IP_provider	RST received from client
ACK	IP_provider	ACK received from client
DATA	IP_provider	DATA received from client
FIN	IP_provider	FIN received from client
RST	IP_provider	Abort connection

States

Name	Meaning
CLOSED	No connection in place
LISTEN	Server AP blocked, TCP waiting for a SYN
SYN_RCVD	SYN received from a client AP
ESTABLISHED	ACK for own SYN received, connection now in place
CLOSE_WAIT	FIN received from client TCP
LAST_ACK	FIN sent and waiting for an ACK

Outgoing events

Name	Interface	Meaning
SendSYN+ACK	IP_provider	Send SYN+ACK to client (TCP)
SendDATA	IP_provider	Send block of data to client
SendFIN	IP_provider	Send FIN to client
SendACK	IP_provider	Send ACK to client

Specific actions

[1] Create queue for connection requests   [3] Unblock server AP
[2] Block server AP   [4] Write EOF to receive buffer (RB)

(a)

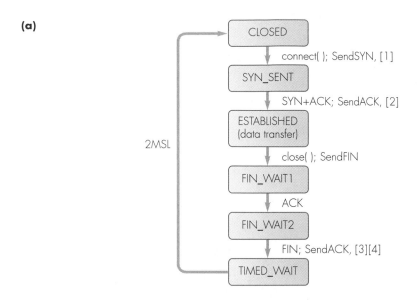

Present state \ Incoming event	connect( )	SYN+ACK	close( )	ACK	FIN	2MSL
CLOSED	1	0	0	0	0	0
SYN_SENT	0	2	0	0	0	0
ESTABLISHED	0	0	3	0	0	0
FIN_WAIT1	0	0	0	4	0	0
FIN_WAIT2	0	0	0	0	5	0
TIMED_WAIT	0	0	0	0	0	6

0 = SendRST, CLOSED   1 = SendSYN, [1], SYN_SENT
2 = SendACK, [2], ESTABLISHED   3 = SendFIN, FIN_WAIT1
4 = FIN_WAIT2   5 = SendACK, [3][4], TIMED_WAIT
6 = CLOSED

(continued overleaf)

Figure 7.18 TCP protocol specifications: (a) client; (b) server.

It should be stressed that the specifications are only simplified versions of the real specifications. For instance, they do not include the actions taken in the event of simultaneous connection requests or simultaneous closes occurring. Also, when in the ESTABLISHED state, many predicates – for example to check whether sequence numbers are valid and within the current window – and state variables are used when determining the required action and new state. Again, a good insight into the latter can be obtained from the example sequences associated with the data transfer phase.

(b)

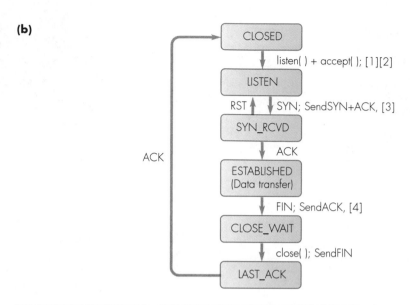

Present state \ Incoming event	listen( ) + accept( )	SYN	RST	ACK	FIN	close( )
CLOSED	1	0	0	0	0	0
LISTEN	0	2	0	0	0	0
SYN_RCVD	0	0	3	4	0	0
ESTABLISHED	0	0	0	0	5	0
CLOSE_WAIT	0	0	0	0	0	6
LAST_ACK	0	0	0	7	0	0

0 = SendRST, CLOSED
2 = SendSYN+ACK, [3], SYN_RCVD
4 = ESTABLISHED
6 = SendFIN, LAST_ACK

1 = [1][2], LISTEN
3 = LISTEN
5 = SendACK, [4], CLOSE_WAIT
7 = CLOSED

Figure 7.18 Continued.

7.4 UDP

Recall that with TCP there is no correlation between the size of the messages/blocks of data submitted by a user AP and the amount of data in each TCP segment that is used to transfer the messages. Typically, as we saw in Section 7.2, the latter is determined by the path MTU to avoid fragmentation of each segment occurring.

In contrast, with UDP each message/block of data that is submitted by a user AP is transferred directly in a single IP datagram. On receipt of the message, the source UDP simply adds a short header to it to form what is called a **UDP datagram**. This is then submitted to the IP layer for transfer over the internet using, if necessary, fragmentation. At the destination, the IP first determines from the *protocol* field in the datagram header that the destination protocol is UDP, and then passes the contents of the (IP) datagram to the UDP.

The latter first determines the intended user AP from a field in the UDP datagram header and then passes the contents of the (UDP) datagram to the peer user AP for processing. There are no error or flow control procedures involved and hence no connection setup is required. The service offered by UDP to a user AP, therefore, is simply an extension of the service provided by IP. Hence in addition to two-party calls, multicast group calls can be supported. Nevertheless, the set of service primitives and the protocol are both simpler than those of TCP. As with TCP, we shall discuss the services and the protocol separately.

7.4.1 User services

As with TCP, the most widely used set of user service primitives associated with UDP are the Berkeley Unix socket primitives. With most applications that use UDP, the two user APs either exchange messages on a request-response basis or simply initiate the transfer of blocks of data as these are generated. A typical list of service primitives – system/function calls – is given in Table 7.3 and their use is shown in diagrammatic form in Figure 7.19.

Table 7.3 List of socket primitives associated with UDP and their parameters.

Primitive	Parameters
socket( )	service type, protocol, address format, return value = socket descriptor or error code
bind( )	socket descriptor, socket address (= host IP address + port number) return value = success or error code
sendto( )	socket descriptor, local port number, destination port number, destination IP address, precedence, pointer to message buffer containing the data to send, data length (in bytes), return value = success or error code
receive( )	socket descriptor, pointer to message buffer into which the data should be put, length of the buffer, return value = success/error code or end-of-file (EOF)
shutdown( )	socket descriptor, return value = success or error code

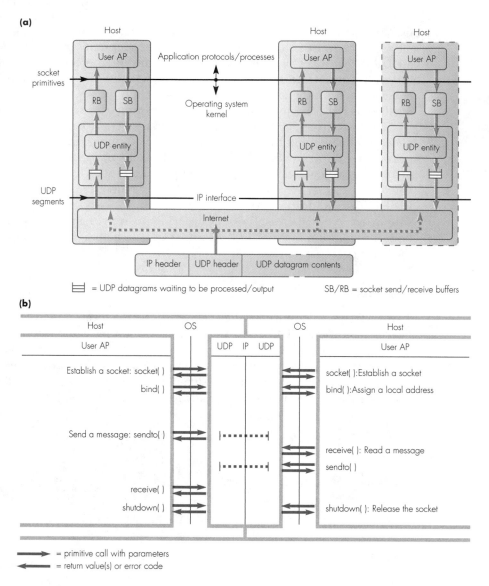

Figure 7.19 UDP socket primitives: (a) socket interface; (b) primitives and their use.

As we can see in Figure 7.19(b), prior to exchanging any messages, each of the user APs involved in the call must first establish a socket between itself and its local UDP. The parameters associated with the *socket( )* primitive include the service required (datagram service), the protocol (UDP), and the address format (Internet). Once a socket has been created – and send/receive memory buffers allocated – a socket descriptor is returned to the AP which it then uses with each of the subsequent primitive calls. If this is the only AP that is running in the host, the AP can now start to send and receive messages. If not – for example a server is involved – the AP then issues a *bind( )* primitive which, in addition to the socket descriptor, has an address parameter. This comprises the IP address of the host plus the 16-bit port number the AP wishes to be assigned to the socket. In the case of a server AP, for example, this will be the related well-known port number. When a *bind( )* is not used, the port number will be an ephemeral port number and assigned locally.

Once a socket has been created, the user AP can start to send and receive messages. However, since no connection is involved – and hence no connection record has been created – in addition to the message, the AP must specify the IP address of the destination host – or the IP multicast address in the case of multiple destinations – and the port number of the destination socket/AP. Also, if required, it must specify a precedence value to be sent in the *type of service* field of the IP datagram header. Hence, as we can see in Table 7.3, the *sendto( )* primitive includes each of these fields in its set of parameters. Finally, when all the data transfers associated with the call/session have been carried out, the socket is released by issuing a *shutdown( )* call.

7.4.2 Protocol operation

The format of each UDP datagram is shown in Figure 7.20(a). The *source port* is the port number of the sending application protocol/socket and the *destination port* is that of the peer (receiving) application protocol(s). Both are 16-bit integers. The value in the *length* field is the number of bytes in the complete (UDP) datagram and includes the 8-byte header and the contents of the *data* field. The *checksum* covers the complete datagram, header plus contents. In addition, as with TCP, since only a simple checksum is used to compute the checksum value in the IP header, in order to add an additional level of checking, some selected fields from the IP header are also included in the computation of the UDP checksum. The fields used form what is called the **UDP pseudo header**. These are identified in Figure 7.20(b) and, as we can see, they are the source and destination IP addresses and the protocol value (= 17 for UDP) from the IP header, plus the value from the length field in the UDP header.

The computation of the UDP checksum uses the same algorithm as that used by IP. As we saw in Section 6.2, this is computed by treating the complete datagram as being made up of a string of 16-bit words that are added together using 1s complement arithmetic. Using 1s complement number representation, a value of zero is represented as either all 1s or all 0s. With UDP, however, if the computed 1s complement sum is all 0s, then the checksum is sent as all 1s. This is done because the use of a checksum with UDP is optional and, if the value in the checksum field is all 0s, this indicates the sender has not sent a checksum.

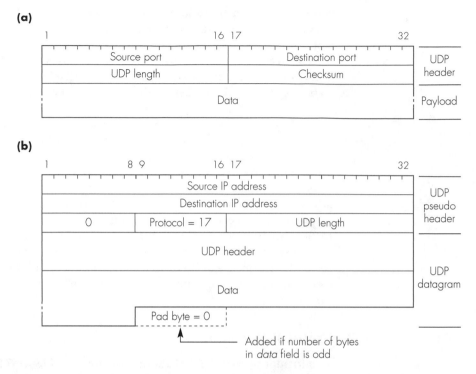

Figure 7.20 UDP datagram format: (a) UDP header fields; (b) fields used in pseudo header for computation of checksum.

Since the number of bytes in the original UDP data field – and hence submitted application protocol data unit – may be odd, in order to ensure the same checksum is computed by both UDPs, a pad byte of zero is added to the data field whenever the number of bytes in the original data field is odd. Thus the value in the length field must always be an even integer. Also, since the UDP datagram is carried in a single IP datagram, as we saw in Section 6.3, in order to avoid fragmentation, the size of each submitted application protocol data unit must be limited to that dictated by the MTU of the path followed through the Internet by the IP datagram. For example, assuming a path MTU of 1500 bytes, allowing for the 8 bytes in the UDP header and 20 bytes in the IP header, the maximum submitted application PDU should be limited to 1472 bytes if fragmentation is to be avoided.

Finally, although the maximum theoretical size of a UDP datagram – as determined by the maximum size of an IP datagram, which is 65 535 (64K − 1) bytes – is 65 507 (65 535 − 20 − 8) bytes, the maximum value supported by most implementations is 8192 bytes or less.

7.5 **RTP and RTCP**

As we showed in Figure 7.1 and explained in the accompanying text, when an application involves the transfer of a real-time stream of audio and/or video over a packet network – for example the speech relating to an Internet phone call – the timing information that is required by the receiver to output the received packet stream at the required rate is provided by the **real-time transport protocol** (**RTP**). In addition, for applications that involve both audio and video streams – for example the audio and video associated with a videophone call – the **real-time transport control protocol** (**RTCP**) is used to synchronize the two media streams prior to carrying out the decoding operation. In this section we describe the main features of both protocols.

7.5.1 **RTP**

Normally, the audio and/or video associated with an application are digitized separately using a particular codec. In addition, when the bitstreams are to be transported over a packet network like the Internet, each of the bitstreams must be sent in the form of a stream of packets using, for example, the UDP protocol. Similarly, at the receiver, the bitstream must be reconstructed from the stream of received packets. During their transfer over the Internet, however, some packets may be lost and/or delayed by varying amounts. Also, since the packets may follow different paths through the Internet, they may arrive at the destination in a different order. Hence before the reconstructed bitstream can be passed to the decoder, any missing packets must be detected and compensated for. Similarly, any delay variations in the packet arrival times must be allowed for. These are the functions performed by RTP and a schematic diagram illustrating its use is shown in Figure 7.21(a).

The packet format used with RTP is shown in Figure 7.21(b). The *version* (*V*) field indicates the version of RTP that is being used, *P* is a pad bit and *X* an extension flag to allow extensions to the basic header to be defined and added in the future.

In a multicast call/session, each of the participants that contributes to the session – rather than passively listening – is called a **contributing source** (**CSRC**) and is uniquely identified by means of a 32-bit identifier that, typically, is the IP address of the source. During a multicast session the packet stream from multiple sources may be multiplexed together for transmission purposes by a device known as a **mixer**. Hence the resulting RTP packet may contain blocks/frames of digitized information from multiple sources and, to enable the receiver to relate each block/frame to the appropriate participant, the CSRC identifier for each block/frame is included in the header of the new packet. The number of CSRC identifiers present in the packet is given in the *CSRC count* (*CC*) field. Since this is a 4-bit field, up to 15 contributing sources – and hence CSRC identifiers – can be present in the RTP packet header.

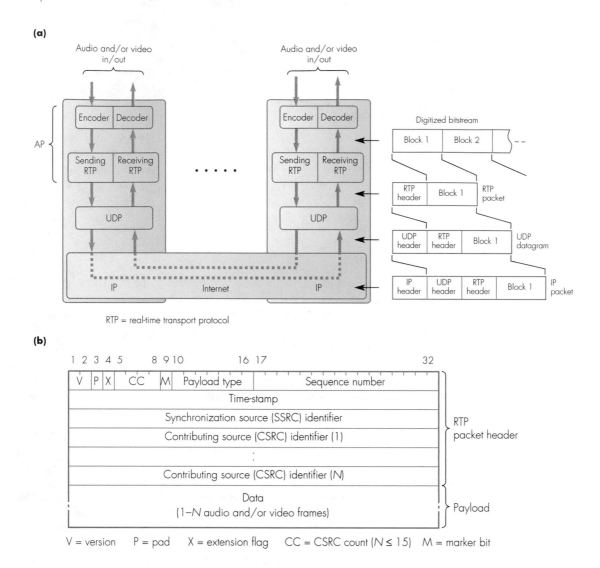

Figure 7.21 Real-time transport protocol: (a) usage; (b) packet format.

Normally, the bitstream produced by the different types of audio and video codecs is made up of a sequence of blocks or frames each with a unique start and end delimiter. Associated with the *marker* (*M*) bit is a profile that enables the receiver to interpret the packet data on the correct block/frame boundaries. Also, since there is a range of different audio and video codecs, the *payload type* field indicates the type of encoder that has been used to encode the data in the packet. Moreover, since each packet contains this field, the type of encoder being used can be changed during a call should the QoS of the network being used change.

Each packet contains a *sequence number* that is used to detect lost or out-of-sequence packets. In the case of a lost packet being detected, normally, the contents of the last correctly received packet are used in its place. The effect of out-of-sequence packets being received is overcome by buffering a number of packets before playout of the data they contain starts.

The value in the *time-stamp* field indicates the time reference when the packet was created. It is used to determine the current mean transmission delay time and the level of jitter that is being experienced. This information, together with the number of lost packets, forms the current QoS of the path through the Internet. As we shall see, periodically this information is returned to the sending RTP by the related real-time transport control protocol. Then, should the QoS change, the sending RTP may modify the resolution of the compression algorithm that is being used. Also, as we saw in Figure 1.7, the level of jitter is used to determine the size of the playout buffer that is required.

The *synchronization source (SSRC) identifier* identifies the source device that has produced the packet contents. In a videoconferencing call, for example, the data generated by each contributing source may be from multiple different devices – a number of microphones, cameras, computers, and so on – and the SSRC indicates from which device the source information has come. The receiving RTP then uses the SSRC to relay the reconstructed bitstream to the related output device interface.

As we can deduce from Figure 7.21(a), on receipt of each IP packet, the various fields in the UDP datagram header are used within the destination host to deliver the RTP packet to the receiving RTP entity. The various fields in the RTP packet header then enable the receiving RTP to reconstruct the bitstream for each device decoder associated with the session.

7.5.2 RTCP

As we can conclude from the previous section, RTP is concerned with the transfer of the individual streams of digitized data associated with a multimedia call/session. The real-time transport control protocol (RTCP) then adds additional system-level functionality to its related RTP such as the means for a receiving RTP to integrate and synchronize the individual packet streams together and for a sending RTP to be informed of the currently prevailing network QoS. Hence, the RTCP operates alongside RTP and shares information with it. However, each RTCP has a different (UDP) port number associated with it so that it can operate independently of RTP.

The RTCP in all of the systems involved in a call/session periodically exchange messages with one another. Each message is sent in a RTCP packet to the same network address – but with the RTCP port number – as the RTP to which the message relates. The general scheme is shown in Figure 7.22 and the messages that are exchanged relate to:

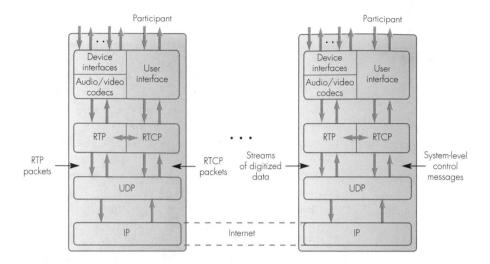

Figure 7.22 Real-time transport control protocol (RTCP) usage.

■ **integrated media synchronization**: in applications that involve separate audio and video streams that need to be integrated together, a common system time clock is used for synchronization purposes. Normally, the system that initiates the call/conference provides this function – or sometimes a separate reference time server – and the RTCPs in all of the other systems then exchange messages with the RTCP in this system so that they are utilizing the same system time clock;

■ **QoS reports**: as we indicated earlier, the number of lost packets, the level of jitter, and the mean transmission delay are continuously computed by each RTP for the packet streams they receive from all of the other contributing sources. The adjoining RTCP then sends a message containing the related information to the RTCP in each of these systems at periodic intervals. The RTCP in each of these systems then performs any system-level functions that may need to be performed, for example changing the resolution of the compression algorithm or the size of the playout buffer;

■ **participation reports**: these are used during a conference call, for example, to enable a participant to indicate to the other participants that it is leaving the call. Again, this is done by means of the RTCP in the participant's system. The participant enters an appropriate message and this is then sent via RTCP to the RTCP in each of the other systems. Typically, a related message is then output on the screen of each of the other systems;

■ **participation details**: information such as the name, e-mail address, phone number, and so on of each participant is sent to all of the other participants in a RTCP message. In this way, each of the participants knows the identity and contact information of all of the other participants.

7.6 Wireless TCP

As we saw in Figure 7.10 and explained in the accompanying text, within a fixed-wire network the loss of an acknowledgment associated with the slow start procedure is assumed to be caused by congestion. However, as we explained in Section 4.2.5, the bit error rate probability of wireless links is several orders of magnitude higher than that of fixed-wire links. As a result, within a wireless network the loss of an acknowledgment is more likely to be caused by a corrupted packet than by congestion. This means, therefore, that if the same slow start procedure is used with a wireless network, the slowing down of acknowledgments will lead to a considerably worse performance than that obtained with a fixed-wire network.

To overcome this, a number of alternative modes of operation of TCP have been developed for use with wireless networks. In this section we shall study two schemes that are intended for use with wireless LANs and a third scheme that involves the use of a number of TCP options that are intended for use with cellular radio networks.

7.6.1 Indirect TCP

A condition in the first two schemes is that the standard TCP scheme should not be changed in the fixed-wire part of any connections. With **Indirect TCP** (**I-TCP**), therefore, the TCP connection is divided into a fixed-wire part and a wireless part as we show in Figure 7.23.

As we can see, in this scheme wireless TCP is used over the wireless link between the mobile host and the access point (AP) of the wireless LAN, and standard TCP is used over the connection between the AP and the correspondent host/server in the fixed-wire part. With this arrangement the wireless

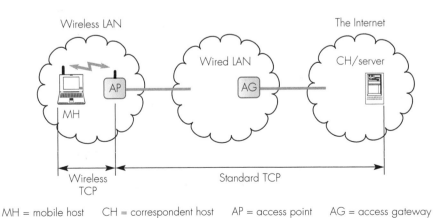

MH = mobile host   CH = correspondent host   AP = access point   AG = access gateway

Figure 7.23 Indirect TCP schematic.

TCP can be the same as standard TCP since the much shorter round-trip time associated with the wireless LAN means faster retransmissions. The disadvantage of this scheme is the loss of the end-to-end semantics of standard TCP. For example, the AP acknowledges receipt of each TCP segment sent by the mobile host in the normal way but this does not mean that the correspondent host/server received the segment.

7.6.2 Snooping TCP

This is an enhancement to the previous scheme in that it utilizes just a single TCP end-to-end connection. It involves using what is called a **snooping agent** (**SA**) in the AP. The main features of the scheme are illustrated in Figure 7.24.

The SA relays the TCP segments that are sent by the correspondent host/server on to the mobile host and, while it does this, it retains a copy of each segment in a memory cache. Similarly, the SA caches the acknowledgments that it receives from the mobile host before relaying them on to the server. Then, when the SA does not receive an acknowledgment for a TCP segment within the very short round-trip time of the wireless LAN, it simply retransmits the segment. The SA then continues to do this until it receives an acknowledgment for the segment. In addition, if duplicate acknowledgments are received by the SA (from the mobile host) this indicates the loss of a segment by the mobile host. Hence the SA retransmits the segment and again, this is a much faster retransmission compared with that involving the server. When this occurs, however, the SA does not relay the duplicate ACKs and instead discards them since they would be interpreted as the onset of congestion by the server if they were forwarded.

In the reverse direction, the SA monitors the stream of segments that it receives from the mobile host as it relays them on to the server in order to detect any missing sequence numbers. Then, when a missing segment is detected, the SA returns a SACK segment to the mobile host. The mobile host then retransmits the missing segment immediately. We described the use of SACKs in Section 7.3.3.

7.6.3 TCP over cellular radio networks

We gave an overview of the operation of cellular radio networks and how these provide access to the Internet in Section 4.4. Clearly, the transfer of Internet data over cellular – mobile radio – networks is now widely used and hence must be made as efficient as possible whilst still retaining the basic operational mode of TCP.

In terms of the data transferred, most TCP connections are asymmetric since most mobile applications involve a subscriber making a short request – for a Web page or some music/audio/video for example – and the requested data being downloaded to the mobile device. Typical data rates are 64 kbps in the uplink direction and 115–384 kbps in the downlink direction. In addition,

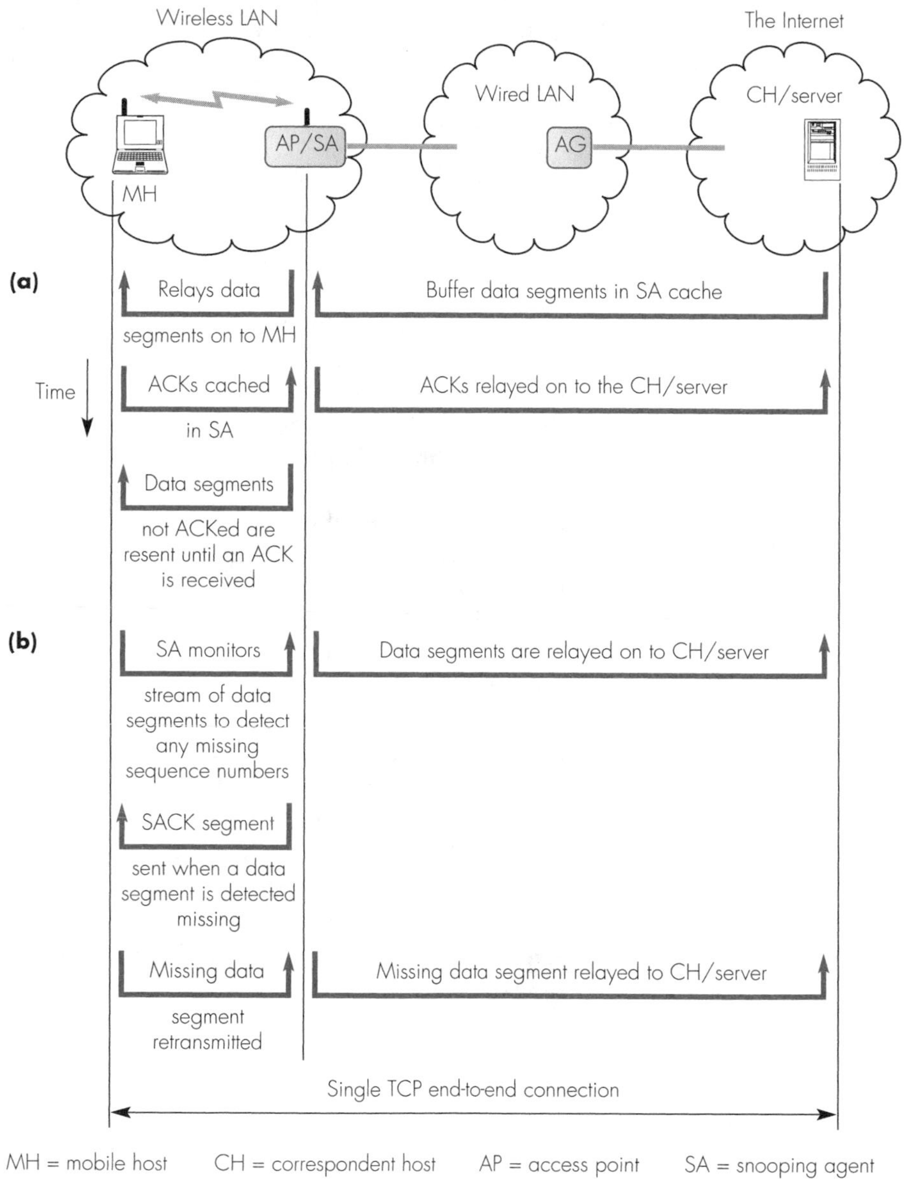

Figure 7.24 Snooping TCP schematic: (a) flow of segments from CH/server to MH; (b) flow of segments from MH to CH/server.

the use of forward error correction and short message segments means that the round trip delay of the link can vary widely between tens of milleseconds to several seconds so introducing jitter. The number of lost packets is also much higher than with a fixed network. In order to reduce the impact of these characteristics, a number of operational parameters have been proposed to adapt TCP to these different environments. A description of a selection of these follows:

- **Large window size**: the high bandwidth/delay product of cellular networks means a larger buffer size must be used. This is accomplished using the window scale option we described in Section 7.3.3.

- **Large maximum transfer unit** (**MTU**): as we explained in Section 7.3.1, the default TCP maximum segment size (MSS) in the Internet is 536 bytes since this ensures an IP packet – with a TCP segment in its payload – will be transferred over the Internet without fragmentation. In cellular networks, however, the link layers fragment packets for transmission over wireless links into smaller segments to improve performance. Hence a large TCP segment size – and hence maximum transfer unit (MTU) – should be adopted instead of the default size. This can be done using the *path MTU discovery* procedure we explained in Section 6.6.9 (IPv4) and Section 6.8.3 (IPv6).

- **Use of selective acknowledgments** (**SACKs**): as we explained in Section 7.3.3, SACK is used when the latency of a path through the Internet is high. With a cellular radio network, however, this is always the case and hence SACK should be a standard feature rather than an option as it is with the wired Internet.

- **Explicit congestion notification** (**ECN**): some routers within the Internet now support this feature. It is defined in RFC 3168 and, when used, a receiver informs a sender of congestion in the Internet by setting the ECN-Echo flag (bit) in the IP packet header. This then helps the sender to distinguish between the loss of a packet caused by transmission errors and that caused by congestion.

- **Time-stamp**: as we explained in Section 7.3.3, the time-stamp option is employed when a large window size is being used. It allows the sending TCP to obtain an estimate of the round-trip time (RTT) with each ACK it receives. Research has shown that frequent time-stamps help TCP to tolerate transit delay spikes without experiencing spurious timeouts.

When these operational parameters are used, the protocol is called **TCP with a wireless profile**.

Summary

A summary of the topics discussed in this chapter is given in Figure 7.25.

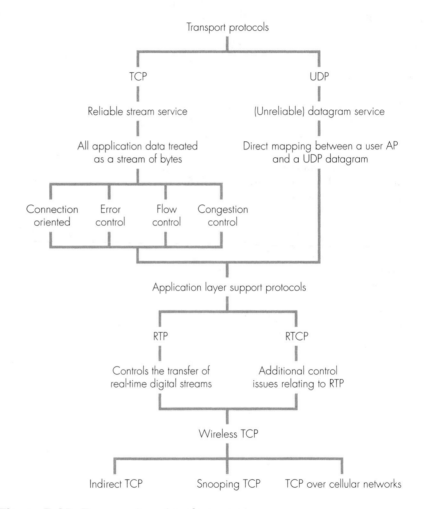

Figure 7.25 Transport protocols summary.

Exercises

Section 7.2

7.1 By means of a diagram, show the position of the TCP, UDP, RTP, and RTCP protocols in relation to the various network layer and application protocols in the TCP/IP protocol suite. Include in your diagram a received message that contains the headers relating to the various protocols and indicate the interlayer address selectors that are used to route the application data in the received message to the intended application protocol/process.

7.2 In relation to the port numbers that are present in the TCP and UDP protocol headers, explain the meaning of the terms "ephemeral" and "well-known port numbers".

7.3 With the aid of a diagram showing how two application protocols/processes communicate with each other using the TCP/IP protocol suite, explain the meaning of the terms:
    (i)   end-to-end communication,
    (ii) TCP/UDP service primitives,
    (iii) network-interface protocol,
    (iv) hop-by-hop transfer.

Section 7.3

7.4 Explain the meaning of the term "reliable stream service" in relation to the operation of TCP and why a logical connection between the two communicating TCP entities must be established to provide this service.

7.5 In relation to the data transfer phase of TCP, explain the meaning of the terms:
    (i)   segment,
    (ii) maximum segment size (MSS),
    (iii) path MTU.

7.6 State why both flow control and congestion control procedures are required with TCP.

Section 7.3.1

7.7 With the aid of a diagram, explain the meaning of the following terms relating to TCP:
    (i)   socket interface,
    (ii) socket primitives,
    (iii) application program interface (API),
    (iv) TCP (protocol) entity.

7.8 List the set of four socket primitives that are issued by a server AP to carry out a passive open, that is, to establish a socket between itself and its local TCP entity. Explain the use of each primitive and the meaning of the terms "socket descriptor" and "socket address".

7.9 By means of a diagram, show the set of socket primitives that are issued by a client AP to carry out an active open and those that are issued by the server in response to these. Describe the effect of each primitive at both the client and server sides and, in relation to the *connect( )* primitive, the parameters that are associated with it.

7.10 Explain the meaning and use of the following relating to a socket:
    (i)   socket descriptor,
    (ii) socket address,
    (iii) pass-through parameter.

7.11 State why the TCP entity in both a client and a server needs to create and maintain a connection record for each new (TCP) connection. List the main fields that are present in a connection record and describe their use.

7.12 Associated with a socket is a send buffer and a receive buffer. Explain the use of each and how they relate to the segments that are sent/received by the two TCP entities. Include in your explanation how an AP can force the transmission of a small block of data.

Section 7.3.2

7.13 Use the TCP segment format given in Figure 7.4(a) to explain the use of the following:
    (i)   source and destination port numbers,

(ii) sequence and acknowledgment numbers,
(iii) code bits,
(iv) window size,
(v)   urgent pointer,
(vi) options and the header length.

7.14 Describe the role of the checksum field in a TCP segment header. Include in your description why additional header fields are added to those in the TCP header and why pad bytes are used.

7.15 With the aid of a time sequence diagram, explain how a logical connection between two TCP entities is established using a three-way handshake procedure. Include in your diagram the socket primitives at both the client and server sides that trigger the sending of each segment. Also, explain how the initial sequence number in each direction is selected.

7.16 Identify and explain briefly the essential procedures that are followed by two correspondent TCP entities during the data transfer phase.

7.17 With the aid of a time sequence diagram, show how the individual characters entered by a user at a keyboard are transferred over a TCP connection using immediate acknowledgments. Hence quantify the overheads associated with this mode of operation.

7.18 Use a time sequence diagram to show how the overheads identified in Exercise 7.17 are reduced using
(i)   delayed acknowledgments, and
(ii) the Nagle algorithm.

Explain the reason why the Nagle algorithm is the preferred mode of working with interactive applications over the Internet.

7.19 Explain why additional buffers to the send and receive buffers associated with the socket are required within the TCP entity at each side of a connection.

7.20 Explain why the sending TCP entity only retransmits a segment if it receives three duplicate acknowledgments for the segment. Include in your explanation the role of the retransmission timer used by the sending TCP entity and the meaning of the term "fast retransmit".

7.21 The following questions relate to the time sequence diagram shown in Figure 7.7.
(i)   Assuming no segments had been corrupted/lost, deduce how many data and ACK segments would have been sent.
(ii) Assuming segment (2) had not been corrupted/lost, deduce the segments that would have been sent by both TCP entities.
(iii) Explain why the second copy of segment (2) is discarded but an ACK is returned.
(iv) Assuming the MSS for the (TCP) connection was 1024 bytes and one (data) segment was corrupted, deduce how many data and ACK segments would be sent.

7.22 State the meaning of the term "retransmission timeout (RTO) interval" in relation to a TCP connection and why it is necessary to determine this dynamically for each new connection.

7.23 Explain the operation of the exponential backoff algorithm that is used to derive the RTO for a TCP connection. Also explain the retransmission ambiguity problem that can arise with this.

7.24 Explain the early Jacobson algorithm that was used to derive the RTO for a TCP connection. Describe the refinement that was later made to it.

7.25 Explain the meaning of the term "delayed ACK timer" in relation to TCP and why this is required.

7.26 State the relationship between the value in the *window size* field and the value in the *acknowledgment* field in the header of a TCP segment. How is the value in the *window size* field determined?

7.27 The following relate to the time sequence diagram shown in Figure 7.8.
  (i) Why does the Win(dow) field in segments sent by the sending TCP remain the same?
  (ii) Why does the V(R) in the receiving TCP stay at X until after the first four segments have been received?
  (iii) Why does the second ACK returned by the receiving TCP contain a Win = 1024 instead of Win = 2048?
  (iv) Why is the second ACK called a window update?

7.28 With the aid of a diagram, explain the meaning of the following terms relating to the TCP window flow control procedure. Include in your diagram a sequence of messages being sent each of which requires multiple segments to send:
  (i) lower window edge,
  (ii) upper window edge,
  (iii) sliding window.

7.29 What is the main reason for lost packets in the Internet? Hence explain how each host endeavors to minimize this effect. Include in your explanation the meaning of the term "congestion window".

7.30 Explain in a qualitative way the relationship between the send window, W_S, and the congestion window, W_C, that are maintained by the TCP entity in a host for each (TCP) connection. Include in your explanation why W_C is initialized to 1 segment.

7.31 In relation to the graph shown in Figure 7.10, explain the meaning of the following terms:
  (i) slow start phase, including why this is shown to increase exponentially,

  (ii) slow start threshold and the congestion avoidance phase, including why this is shown to increase linearly,
  (iii) constant phase.

7.32 The graph shown in Figure 7.10 relates to a lightly loaded internet. During these conditions, what effect does the congestion window, W_C, have on the send window, W_S?

7.33 Explain in a qualitative way why the adjustments to the W_C for a connection depend on whether a lost packet is detected as a result of duplicate ACKs being received or the retransmission timer expiring.

7.34 With the aid of a graph showing the variation of W_C as a function of the connection RTT, show and explain how W_C is affected by:
  (i) a set of three duplicate ACKs being received for a segment,
  (ii) the retransmission timer for a segment expiring.

7.35 Use the time sequence diagrams shown in Figure 7.12(a) and (d) to explain the sequence of segments that are exchanged with:
  (i) a normal connection close,
  (ii) a half close.

  Include in your explanations why two FIN_WAIT states and a final TIMED_WAIT state are required.

7.36 Explain the role of the persist timer. Hence with the aid of the time sequence diagram shown in Figure 7.13, explain how the effect of a corrupted ACK containing a window update is overcome.

7.37 Explain the role of the keepalive timer. Hence with the aid of the time sequence diagram shown in Figure 7.14, explain how the effect of a client host being switched off is overcome.

7.38 Explain how the phenomenon called the silly window syndrome can arise and the steps that are taken at the client and server sides to avoid this happening. Using the two time sequence diagrams shown in Figure 7.15, explain how the Clark extension prevents this from occurring.

7.39 By means of an example, show how for transmission paths that have a large bandwidth/delay product a window size field of 16 bits may be insufficient. Hence by means of an example, describe how the window scale option used in the TCP segment header can overcome this problem.

7.40 The computation of the RTO for a connection using the method in Exercise 7.24 required the RTT to be computed for every data segment. Explain how, with a large window size, this can lead to a poor estimate of the RTT.

Hence, with the aid of the time sequence diagram shown in Figure 7.17, explain how the number of updates can be reduced by using a time-stamp option field. Include in your explanation the use of the *time-stamp value* and *time-stop echo reply* fields and how the receiving TCP overcomes the fact that not all segments are acknowledged.

7.41 Explain the principles behind:
(i) the SACK-permitted option,
(ii) how protection against wrapped sequence numbers can be overcome by using the time-stamp option.

7.42 Use the time sequence diagrams associated with the connection established (Figure 7.5) and connection close (Figure 7.12) procedures to follow the state transitions that occur at the client and server sides shown in Figure 7.18(a) and (b) respectively.

Section 7.4

7.43 What are the main differences between UDP and TCP?

7.44 By means of a diagram, show the socket interface associated with UDP in relation to a user AP. Include in your diagram the send and receive buffers associated with the socket and the input and output buffers associated with the UDP entity.

7.45 Show on a diagram a typical sequence of socket primitives that are issued at both the sending and the receiving sides to:
(i) establish a socket connection,
(ii) exchange a single UDP datagram,
(iii) release the socket connection.

Identify the main parameters associated with each primitive.

7.46 In relation to the UDP datagram format shown in Figure 7.20(b), explain how the checksum is corrupted.

State why the maximum size of UDP datagram is often less than the theoretical maximum.

Section 7.5

7.47 Describe the use of the RTP protocol and, by means of a diagram, show its position in relation to the TCP/IP protocol stack.

7.48 In relation to the RTP packet format shown in Figure 7.21(b), explain the meaning and use of the following fields:
(i) CC and CSRC,
(ii) M and payload type,
(iii) sequence number,
(iv) time-stamp,
(v) SSRC.

7.49 Describe the use of the RTCP protocol and, by means of a diagram, show its position in relation to the TCP/IP protocol stack.

7.50 Identify and give a brief explanation of the four main functions performed by RTCP.

Section 7.6

7.51 With the aid of a diagram, explain the operation of Indirect TCP (I-TCP).

Identify a disadvantage of this scheme.

7.52 With the aid of a diagram, explain the operation of Snooping TCP. Include in your explanation the role of the snooping agent (SA) and the flow of segments from the server to the mobile host and in the reverse direction.

7.53 Identify and explain the operational parameters associated with TCP with a wireless profile.

Internet applications

8.1 Introduction

As we showed in Figure 7.1 and explained in the accompanying text, in the TCP/IP protocol suite, given the IP address and port number of a destination application protocol/process (AP), the services provided by TCP or UDP enable two (or more) peer APs to communicate with each other in a transparent way. That is, it does not matter whether the correspondent AP(s) is(are) running in the same computer, another computer on the same network, or another computer attached to a network on the other side of the world. Also, since neither TCP nor UDP examines the content of the information being transferred, this can be a control message (PDU) associated with the application protocol, a file of characters from a selected character set, or a string of bytes output by a particular audio or video codec. Hence application protocols are concerned only with, firstly, ensuring the PDUs associated with the protocol are in the defined format and are exchanged in the specified sequence and secondly, the information/data being transferred is in an agreed transfer syntax so that it has the same meaning to each of the applications.

In this chapter, we discuss both the role and operation of a selection of the application protocols associated with the Internet. These are the simple (electronic) mail transfer protocol (SMTP) and the related multipurpose Internet mail extensions (MIME) protocol, the file transfer protocol (FTP) and a simpler version of this (Trivial FTP), and Internet telephony. In addition, we describe two protocols that, in many instances, a user of the Internet is unaware of. The first is invoked every time we use the Internet and is called the Domain Name System (DNS). The second is concerned with the management of the various networking devices that make up the Internet and is called the **simple network management protocol** (**SNMP**). Because of its role, we shall describe the DNS protocol first.

8.2 Domain name system

As we saw in Figure 7.1 and its accompanying text, an application protocol/process (AP) communicates with a correspondent AP using the latter's IP address and port number. The IP address of the destination AP is first used to route a message – contained within one or more datagrams – across the Internet to the required host and the port number is then used within the host protocol stack to route the received message to the required destination AP. As we saw, however, in the TCP/IP protocol suite the port number of a server AP is allocated a well-known port number which is known by all the client APs that communicate with it. Hence in order to communicate with a remote AP, the source AP need only know the IP address of the host in which the AP is running. Nevertheless, even if this is represented in dotted decimal, it can require up to 12 decimal digits to be remembered, with many more for an IPv6 address. To avoid users from having to cope with such numbers, a directory service similar to that used with a PSTN is used. This is called the **Domain Name System** (**DNS**) and it enables each host computer attached to the Internet to be allocated a **symbolic name** in addition to an IP address.

There are many millions of hosts attached to the Internet each of which has a unique IP address assigned to it. Each host, therefore, must also have a unique name assigned to it and hence an efficient naming scheme is a major part of the DNS. In addition, given a symbolic name, this must be mapped into the related IP address before any communication can take place. This procedure is called name-to-address mapping and is part of the DNS. As we indicated in the introduction, this must be done every time a network application is run and hence it is essential that the procedure is carried out in an efficient way. We shall limit our discussion of the DNS to these two components. They are defined in RFCs 1034 and 1035.

8.2.1 Name structure and administration

All the data in the DNS constitutes what is called the **domain name space** and its contents are indexed by a name. The structure of the name space is important since it strongly influences the efficiency of both the administration of the name space and the subsequent address resolution operation. Basically there are two approaches. One is to adopt a **flat structure** and the other a **hierarchical structure**. Although a flat structure uses the overall name space more efficiently, the resulting DNS must be administered centrally. Also, since in a large network like the Internet multiple copies of the DNS are required to speed up the name-to-address mapping operation, using a flat structure would mean that all copies of the DNS would need to be updated each time a change occurred. For these reasons, the domain name space uses a hierarchical naming structure.

In terms of the administration of the name space, the advantages of using a hierarchical structure can best be seen by considering the structure and assignment of subscriber numbers in the telephone system. At the highest level there is a country code, followed by an area code within that country, and so on. The assignment of numbers can be administered in a distributed rather than a centralized way. The assignment of country codes is administered at an international level, the assignment of area codes within each country at a national level, and so on, down to the point where the assignment of numbers within a local area can be administered within that area. This can be done knowing that as long as each higher-level number is unique within the corresponding level in the address hierarchy, the combined number will be unique within the total address space.

The adoption of a hierarchical structure also means that it is possible to partition the DNS in such a way that most name-to-address mapping operations – and other services – can be carried out locally. For example, if names are assigned according to the geographical location of hosts, then the name space can be partitioned in a similar way. Since most network transactions, and hence requests, are between hosts situated in the same local area – for example, between a community of workstations and a local server or e-mail system – then the majority of service requests can be resolved locally and relatively few referred to another site.

As we show in Figure 8.1, the overall structure of the domain name space is represented in the form of an inverted tree with the single root at the top. The root is called the **root domain** and the top-level branch nodes in the tree, domain nodes or simply **domains**. Each domain has further branches associated with it until, at the lowest level of the tree, is a single host that is attached to the Internet. The names of the top-level domains reflect the historical development of the Internet. Initially, when the Internet spanned just the United States with a small number of international organizations linked to it, at the top level was a set of what are called **generic domains** each of which identified a particular organization to which the owner of the host belonged. These are:

> *com*: this identifies hosts that belong to a commercial organization,
>
> *edu*: an educational establishment,
>
> *gov*: the US federal government,

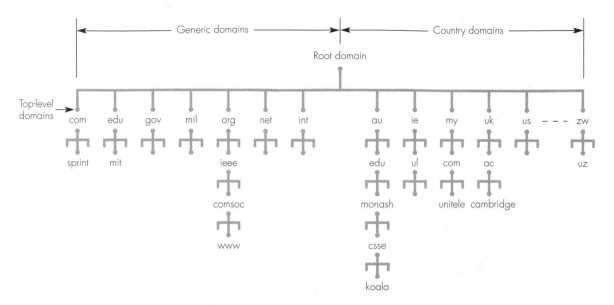

Figure 8.1 The structure of the domain name system together with some examples.

mil: the US armed forces,

org: a non-profit organization,

net: a network provider,

int: an international organization.

Later, as the Internet expanded its area of coverage, so a set of **country domains** were introduced. There is now a separate country domain for each country and these are defined in **ISO 3166**. For this reason, most hosts in the United States are identified by means of a generic domain and those outside the US by their country domain. However, this is not always the case. Most large multinational companies, for example, often use the *com* generic domain. Also, since each domain is responsible for allocating the names of the (sub)domains that are linked to it, then some countries use different names from those used in the generic domain. For example, in the UK and a number of other countries, the domain name for *edu* is *ac* – academic community – and that for *com*, *co*. Note also that all names are case-insensitive and hence can be written in either upper-case or lower-case and still have the same meaning.

As we indicated earlier, the allocation of names is managed by the authority responsible for the domain where the name is to appear. For example, if a host located within the electrical engineering department of a new university is to be attached to the Internet, then, assuming the country is outside the US, first the university is assigned a name within the edu/ac domain of the country by the appropriate national authority, then the name of the department by an authority acting at a university level, and finally the name of the host by an authority within the department. The name of the host is then derived by listing the various domain names – each called a *label* – starting with the host name back to the root. These are listed from left to right with each label separated by a period (.), which is pronounced "dot". In this way, providing each label is unique within its own domain, then the resulting name is unique within the context of the total domain name space of the Internet. Note that the root has a null label and hence some examples are:

> *sprint.com.*
>
> *cambridge.ac.uk.*
>
> *unitele.com.my.*

Note that since each name ends in a period, they are all examples of **absolute domain names**, which are also called **fully qualified domain names** (**FQDN**). If the name does not end in a period, it is said to be incomplete or relative.

8.2.2 DNS resource records

Each domain name in the DNS name space may have information associated with it. This is stored in one or more **resource records**, each of which is indexed by the related domain name. A host name, for example, has a resource record that contains the IP address of the host. In practice there are a number of different types of record each of which has the standard format shown in Figure 8.2(a).

The *domain name* is the name of the domain to which the record relates. It consists of the string of labels that make up the domain name and is in the format shown in Figure 8.2(b). Each label is preceded by a one-byte count that indicates the number of characters/bytes in the label. A label can be up to 63 characters long and the full domain name must be less than 256 characters. The final byte is always 0, which indicates the root.

The *type* field indicates the record type and a selection of these are listed in Figure 8.2(c). A type-A record, for example contains an IPv4 address which is stored in its 32-bit binary form. A type-NS record contains the name of the name server for this domain and is stored in the same format as the domain name. A type-PTR record contains an IP address stored in its dotted decimal form. A type-HINFO record contains the type of host and its operating system both of which are stored as an ASCII string. An MX-record contains the name of a host – an e-mail gateway, for example – that is prepared to accept e-mail for forwarding on a non-Internet (IP) site. There is also a type-AAAA record, which contains an IPv6 address stored in its hexadecimal form. We shall discuss the use of some of these records in the next section.

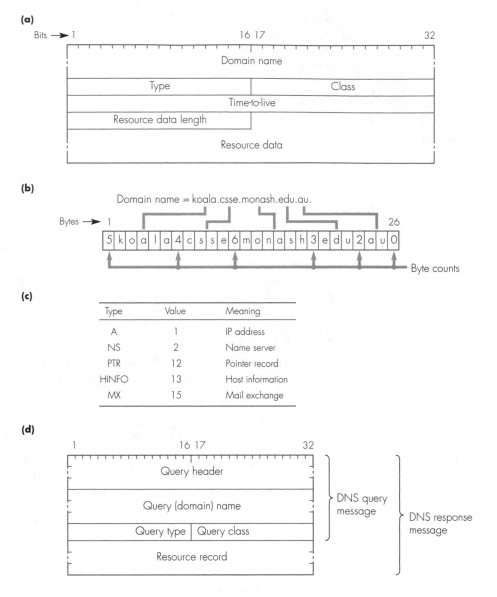

Figure 8.2 DNS resource records and queries: (a) resource record format; (b) domain name format; (c) a selection of resource record types; (d) query and response message formats.

For Internet records the *class* field is always 1 and has the mnemonic IN. The *time-to-live* field indicates the time in seconds the information contained within the record is valid. As we shall see, this is required when the IP address contained in the record has been cached. A typical value is 172 800, which is the number of seconds in 2 days.

The *resource data length* field specifies the length of the *resource data* field. As we have just indicated, the format of the latter differs for different record types and hence the number in the length field relates to the type of data present. For example, if it is an IPv4 address then the length field is 4 to indicate 4 bytes.

8.2.3 DNS query messages

The DNS database is queried using a similar list of (query) types to those used to describe the list of different resource record types. Hence there is a name-to-address resolution query – type A – and so on. A standard format is used to represent each query and this is shown in Figure 8.2(d).

The *query name field* holds the domain name – and hence resource record – to which the query relates. So for a name-to-address resolution query, for example, this contains the domain name of the host and this has the same format that we showed in Figure 8.2(b).

To initiate a query of the DNS – also called a *question* – a **DNS query message** is formed by adding a standard 12-byte header to the particular query. The **DNS response message** is then made up of the query message with one or more resource records – also called *answers* – appended to it. The 12-byte header contains a 16-bit *identification* field and a 16-bit *flags* field. The value in the identification field is assigned by the client that sent the query. It is then returned unchanged by the server in the response message and is used by the client to relate the response to a given query.

The flags field consists of a number of subfields. For example, a 1-bit field is used to indicate whether the message is a query (= 0) or a response (= 1). There is also a 4-bit field to indicate the type of search involved. As we shall see, this can be standard, recursive, iterative or inverse.

8.2.4 Name servers

As we indicated earlier, the adoption of a hierarchical structure also facilitates the partitioning of the total DNS database so that most service requests – name-to-address mappings for example – can be carried out locally. To do this, the total domain name space is partitioned into a number of **zones** each of which embraces a unique portion of the total name space. Each zone is then administered by a separate authority which is also responsible for providing one or more **name servers** for the zone. Depending on its position in the hierarchy, a name server may have authority over a single zone or, if it is higher up in the hierarchy, multiple zones.

Associated with each zone is a *primary (name) server* and possibly one or more *secondary (name) servers*. The allocation of names and addresses within the zone is carried out through the primary server and it keeps this information – and hence its portion of the total database – in a block of resource records on hard disk. The resource records within its database are said therefore to be **authoritative records**. The records held in a secondary server are held in volatile storage and are cached versions of those held in a primary server. As we shall see, caching occurs when a primary or secondary server, on finding it does not have the resource record relating to a request, refers the request to a higher-level server. Then, on receipt of the requested IP address, the server that initiated the request retains a copy of this in its cache for a limited time period. The time is stored in the time-to-live field of the accessed resource record and, as we indicated earlier, typically, it is set to 2 days.

Some examples of (fictitious) zones are shown in Figure 8.3. As we can see, the top-level zones in the hierarchy have authority over multiple zones. The zone boundaries in the lower levels are intended to reflect the level of administrative overheads – and hence query requests – associated with the zone.

8.2.5 Service requests

All the information that is stored in each primary name server is accessible to both its secondary servers and also to any other primary server. Because of the excessive overheads that would be involved, however, each primary name server does not know how to contact – that is, does not have the IP address of – every other primary name server. Instead, each primary server knows only how to contact a set of top-level *root name servers*. There are only a small number of these and their IP addresses are stored in the configuration file of each primary server. In turn, each root server holds the name and IP address of each of the second-level servers in the hierarchy and, on receipt of a request from a primary server, the root server returns the name and IP address of the second-level server that should be used. The primary then proceeds to query this server and so on down the hierarchy until a resource record containing the required IP address is obtained. This procedure is

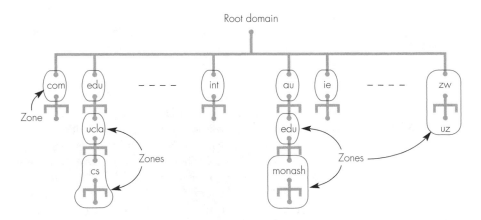

Figure 8.3 Some examples of DNS zones.

called a **recursive name resolution**. Alternatively, in order to reduce the amount of processing done by each name server, an iterative approach can be used. Before we describe each of these approaches, however, we shall describe first how a simple name resolution is carried out using a name server that is local to the host making the request.

Local name resolution

As we show in Figure 8.4, an AP running in a host that is attached to the Internet obtains the IP address of a named host through a piece of software called a **resolver**. Normally, this is a library procedure that is linked to the AP when the AP is first written. The resolver is given the IP address of the local name server – either a primary or a secondary server – that it should use to carry out name-to-address resolutions. Note that the (well-known) port number of a name server is 53.

As we shall see later, as part of all applications – file transfers, e-mail transfers, and so on – the source (client) AP is given the name of the host in which the required destination (server) AP is running. Then, prior to initiating the networked application/transaction, the source AP invokes the resolver to obtain the IP address of the given destination host name (1). In the figure it is assumed that the resolver first sends a type-A query to its local name server requesting the IP address of the (destination) host specified in the query name field (2).

In this example it is assumed that the local name server has the resource record containing the IP address and hence this is returned in a type-A

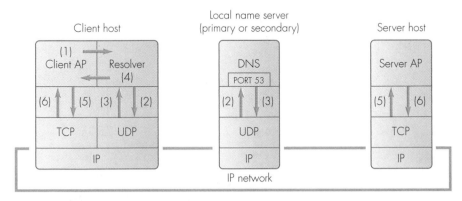

(1) = resolver invoked by client AP with the name of the server host
(2) = resolver sends a type-A query containing the name of the server host to its local DNS
(3) = local DNS returns a type-A resource record containing the IP addresss of the server
(4) = resolver returns IP address of the server to the client AP
(5)/(6) = client and server APs carry out networked application/transaction

Figure 8.4 Example showing the sequence of messages exchanged for a local name resolution.

resource record (3). This is passed first to the resolver in the source – using UDP – and the resolver then returns the IP address contained within the record to the linked source AP (4). Once the source (client) AP has the IP address of the destination (server) AP, the two can start to carry out the networked application using TCP (5)/(6).

Recursive name resolution

When a local name server does not have a resource record relating to a given destination host name, it carries out a search for it. A schematic diagram showing the procedure followed using the recursive search method is given in Figure 8.5.

As we indicated earlier, all primary name servers have the IP addresses of the set of top-level root name servers. Hence as we can see, the local name server first sends a *recursive query* message containing the name of the required host – for example the *sprint.com.* gateway – to one of the *root* name servers (1). From the name in the query message, the root server determines that the *com* name server should be queried and hence it returns the IP address of this in the reply – called an answer – message (2). On receipt of this, the local server sends a second query message to the *com* name

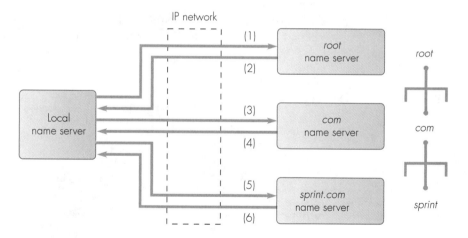

(1) = local name server sends a recursive query message containing name of the destination host – for example, the *sprint.com.* gateway – to the *root* name server
(2) = the *root* server returns the IP address of the *com* server
(3) = local server sends a recursive query to *com* name server
(4) = the *com* server returns the IP address of the *sprint.com* server
(5) = local server sends a recursive query to *sprint.com* server
(6) = the *sprint.com* server sends IP address of *sprint.com.* gateway (host)

Figure 8.5 Example showing the sequence of messages exchanged for a recursive name resolution.

server using the returned IP address (3). In response, the *com* name server determines from the name in the query that the *sprint.com* name server should be queried and hence it returns the IP address of this in the reply (4).

On receipt of this, the local server sends a third query message to the *sprint.com* server (5) and, in the example, it is assumed that this has the requested resource record. Hence it returns this – containing the IP address of the destination host – to the local name server (6). The latter then relays the answer to the resolver in the source host and this, in turn, returns the IP address in the answer message to the source AP. The related client–server application can then start.

Note that in this example it was assumed that the local server was a primary server. If it was a secondary server, however, then this would send the first query to its (known) primary server and it is this that would initiate the sequence shown. Also, in order to reduce the number of queries that take place, each name server retains all resource records it receives – each containing an IP address – in a cache. In many instances, therefore, the answer to a query from a resolver is available in the cache so avoiding any external queries being sent out.

Iterative name resolution

In order to avoid always going to a root server – and hence to the top of the name tree – to initiate the search for an unknown resource record, with the iterative search method the local server starts its search for the requested record from the server that is nearest to it. Figure 8.6 illustrates the procedure.

To support the iterative method, instead of each primary name server having the IP addresses of the set of top-level root servers, it has the name and IP address of the next higher-level server to it in the naming hierarchy. Then, when a resolver sends a query – this time called an *iterative query* message – to its local server, if the local server does not have the requested resource record, instead of sending a query to a root server, it sends an (iterative) query to the next higher-level name server in the hierarchy – the *com* server in the example. If this has the record, it responds directly. If it hasn't, then it parses the name and returns a response containing the IP address of the server that it thinks might have (or is nearest to) the requested record. The local server then sends an (iterative) query to this server and so on until it receives a response message containing the requested record/IP address. As we can deduce from the figure, the search only proceeds up the tree to the level that is necessary to obtain the requested record thereby reducing the load on the top-level root servers.

Pointer queries

Although most queries of the DNS database relate to name-to-address translations, there are also queries that require an address-to-name translation. These are called *pointer queries* and, normally, they are from a system program that carries out a diagnostic operation, for example. They are also used by e-mail servers and file servers to validate users.

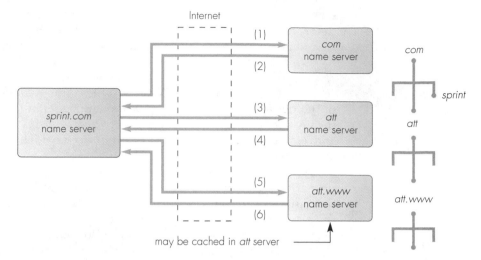

(1) = local name server sends an iterative query message containing the name of the
      destination host − *att.www* − to the next higher-level server − *com*
(2) = the *com* server replies with the IP address of the *att* server
(3) = local server sends an iterative query to the *att* server
(4) = the *att* server returns the IP address of the *att.www* server
(5) = local server sends an iterative query to the *att.www* server
(6) = the *att.www* server returns the IP address of the requested Web host

**Figure 8.6 Example showing the sequence of messages exchanged for
an iterative name resolution.**

To support this type of query, the resolver, given the IP address of a host,
must initiate a search of the DNS and return the host name. As we indicated
earlier, however, the search key of the DNS is a domain name. This means
that with the database structure we showed in Figure 8.3, this type of query
would require a complete search of the database starting with the set of
top-level domain names. Clearly this is impractical and hence to support
pointer queries an additional branch in the DNS name space to those shown
in Figure 8.1 is present. This is shown in Figure 8.7.

As we can see, it starts with the top-level domain name *arpa*, followed by
the second-level name *in-addr*. This is then followed by the four bytes
(in dotted-decimal) that make up the IP address of each host whose name is
in the DNS name space starting with the address-type byte. This order is
used since the netid part of the address is assigned by *arpa.in-addr* and the
hostid part by the authority that has been allocated the netid. Hence to be
consistent with the other types of query message, the domain name in the
pointer-type query message for the IP address 132.113.56.25 is:

25.56.113.132.in-addr.arpa

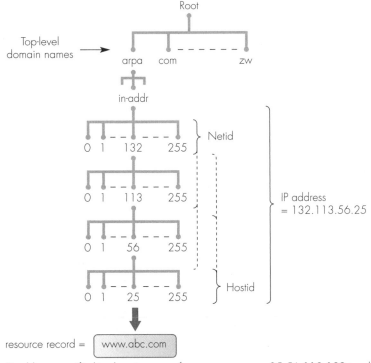

resource record = www.abc.com

IP address specified in domain name of query message as 25.56.113.132.in-addr.arpa.
Host name in reply message assumed to be www.abc.com.

Figure 8.7 Pointer query principles.

that is, it starts with the last byte of the IP address first. The search of this portion of the database then yields a resource record as before but this time it contains the domain name of the host that has the given IP address. Hence in the example shown in the figure, this is assumed to be *www.abc.com*. Because of the reverse order of the labels in the domain name, a pointer query is also known as an **inverse query**.

8.3 Electronic mail

From a user perspective, electronic mail (e-mail) – apart from Web browsing which we describe in the next chapter – is probably the most popular application on the Internet. As we show in Figure 8.8, an e-mail system comprises two main components: an e-mail client and an e-mail server. Normally, an e-mail client is a desktop PC or workstation running a program called the **user agent** (**UA**). This provides the user interface to the e-mail system and provides facilities to create, send, and receive (e-mail) messages.

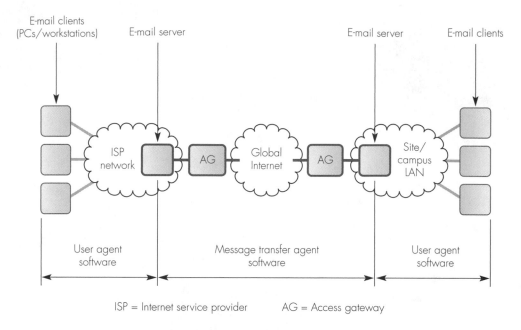

Figure 8.8 E-mail over the Internet.

To do this, the UA maintains an IN and an OUT mailbox and a list of selections to enable the user to create, send, read and reply to a message, as well as selections to manipulate the individual messages in the two mailboxes, such as forward and delete.

The e-mail server is a server computer that maintains an IN mailbox for all the users/clients that are registered with it. The set of mailboxes in the e-mail server are contained in a database known as the **message store**. In addition, the server has software called the UA server to interact with the UA software in each client and also software to manage the transfer of mail messages over the Internet. The software associated with the latter function is called the **message transfer agent** (**MTA**) and is concerned with the sending and receiving of mail messages to/from other e-mail servers that are also connected directly to the Internet.

The protocol stack that is used to support e-mail over the Internet is shown in Figure 8.9. Normally, the protocol stack associated with the access network – the Internet service provider (ISP) network and the site/campus LAN shown in the figure – is either the PPP protocol we described in Section 2.6.4 – used with an ISP network – or, with a PC network, a protocol stack such as Novell NetWare. A number of different vendors then provide proprietary software to carry out the various interaction functions between the user and the UA client. In addition, there are a number of protocols that can be used to control the transfer of messages over the access network. For example, the **POP3 protocol** – post office protocol 3 – is often used to fetch

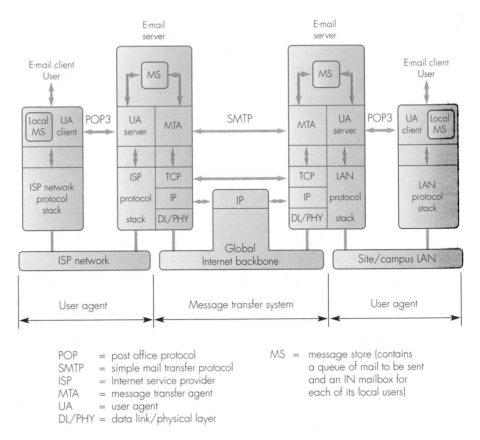

POP   = post office protocol
SMTP = simple mail transfer protocol
ISP   = Internet service provider
MTA   = message transfer agent
UA   = user agent
DL/PHY = data link/physical layer

MS = message store (contains
a queue of mail to be sent
and an IN mailbox for
each of its local users)

Figure 8.9 Protocol stack to support e-mail over the Internet.

messages from the user's IN mailbox in the server to the IN mailbox maintained by the UA. Essentially, POP3 defines the format of the various control messages that are exchanged between the UA client and UA server to carry out a transfer and also the sequence of the messages that are exchanged. POP3 is specified in RFC 1939.

The application protocol that is used to control the transfer of messages between two MTAs over the Internet is called the **simple mail transfer protocol (SMTP)**. It is specified in RFC 821. In this section we first describe the structure of mail messages and the use of the various fields in each message header. We then present an overview of how a typical message transfer is carried out and, finally, the operation of SMTP.

8.3.1 Structure of e-mail messages

When we send a letter using a postal service, we first write our own name and address at the head of the letter followed by the message we wish to send. Typically, this comprises the name and address of the intended recipient followed by the actual letter/message content. We then insert the letter into an envelope and write the name and address of the intended recipient on the front of the envelope. Also, to allow for the possibility of the recipient having changed address, we often write our own name and address on, say, the back of the envelope. We then deposit the envelope into a mailbox provided by the postal service. The latter then uses the name and address on the front of the envelope to forward and deliver it to the address of the intended recipient. Alternatively, if this is not possible, it uses the address on the back of the envelope to return it to the sender. The recipient knows who sent the letter by the name and address at the head of the letter.

Thus there are two distinct procedures involved in sending a letter: the first involving the sender of the letter and concerned with the preparation of the letter itself and the second with the transfer of the addressed envelope to the intended recipient by the postal service. We note also that the structure and content of the letter itself has only meaning to the sender and recipient of the letter.

In a similar way, the sending of electronic mail involves two separate procedures. The first is concerned with the entry of various fields – including the sender's and recipient's name/address at the head of the message – and the actual message content via the UA; the second with the encapsulation of the message into an (electronic) envelope containing the sender's and recipient's address and with the transfer of the envelope over the network by the message transfer system. In the case of electronic mail, however, since the writing of the addresses on the envelope is performed by the mail system itself, it is necessary for the addresses at the head of the message to have a standard structure so that they can be extracted and used directly by the message transfer system. The terminology associated with the structure of an e-mail message showing these two parts is shown in Figure 8.10(a).

As we can see, during its transfer across the network an e-mail message is composed of an *envelope* and the *message*. The envelope contains the e-mail address of the sender of the message (*MAIL FROM*) and its intended recipient (*RCPT TO*). In the case of the Internet, all e-mail addresses are of the form *user-name@mailserver-name* where *mailserver-name* is the DNS name of the mail server and *user-name* is selected by the user and confirmed by the local mail manager at subscription/registration time. The manager also creates an IN mailbox for the user on the mail server at the same time.

The format of an e-mail address is defined in RFC 821 and, as we shall see, the recipient mailserver-name is used by the message transfer system to route the message over the Internet to the intended recipient mail server and the user-name is then used by the MTA to determine the IN mailbox into which the mail should be deposited. Like a DNS name, the user-name is case insensitive and the two names are separated by the @ symbol.

The message itself is composed of a *header* and a *body*, the latter containing the actual message that has been entered by the user via the UA. As we show in Figure 8.10(b), the header comprises a number of fields some of which are optional. Also, since there are many different vendors of UA

(a)

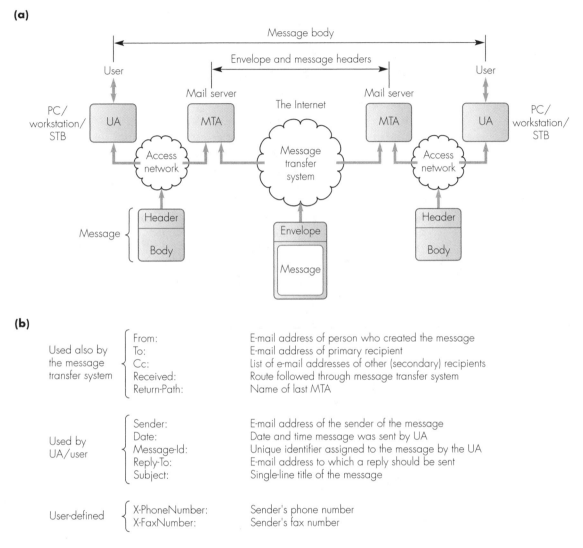

(b)

Used also by the message transfer system	From:	E-mail address of person who created the message
	To:	E-mail address of primary recipient
	Cc:	List of e-mail addresses of other (secondary) recipients
	Received:	Route followed through message transfer system
	Return-Path:	Name of last MTA
Used by UA/user	Sender:	E-mail address of the sender of the message
	Date:	Date and time message was sent by UA
	Message-Id:	Unique identifier assigned to the message by the UA
	Reply-To:	E-mail address to which a reply should be sent
	Subject:	Single-line title of the message
User-defined	X-PhoneNumber:	Sender's phone number
	X-FaxNumber:	Sender's fax number

Figure 8.10 E-mail message structure: (a) terminology and usage; (b) selection of the fields in the message header and their use.

software, the optional fields that are used by the UA in the sender and those used by the recipient UA may differ. However, all of the header fields have a standard format that is defined in RFC 822. Each field comprises a single line of ASCII text starting with the (standardized) field name. This is terminated by a colon and is followed by the field value. A single blank line is then used to separate the header from the message body.

As we can see, some fields are also used by the message transfer system and others by the UA/user. It is also possible for a user to add one or more private header fields. Some examples of fields in each category are shown in the figure together with their usage. Most are self explanatory. Note, however, that *From:* and *Sender:* may be different. For example, the person who created – and is sending – the message (*From:*) may be the secretary of the person who is identified in the *Sender:* field. Also, if the reply to the message should be sent to a third party, then the e-mail address of the person who is to receive the reply is in the *Reply-To:* field.

Note also that even though the *Received:* and *Return-Path:* fields are in the header of the message – rather than the envelope – they are used primarily by a network manager during fault diagnosis to determine the path that is followed by a message through the message transfer system. To initiate this procedure, the source MTA enters its own name together with the message identifier and the date and time the message was sent in a *Received:* field. A new *Received:* field containing the same information is then added to this by each MTA along the path that the message takes. In the case of the *Return-Path:* field, this contains only the name of the last MTA. In practice, however, this field is often not used and, if present, contains only the e-mail address of the sender. Note that user-defined fields must always start with the character sequence *X-*.

In RFC 822, the transfer syntax used for all the header fields is the US version of the ASCII code we showed earlier in Figure 1.14 with the addition that each 7-bit character is first converted into an 8-bit byte by adding a 0 bit in the most-significant bit position. Also, the codeword used to represent an *end-of-line* is the 2-byte combination of a carriage return (CR) and a line feed (LF) and, because of this, the codeword for a CR is the 2-byte combination of a CR and a NUL. This modified version of the ASCII codeword set is called **network virtual terminal (NVT) ASCII**.

8.3.2 Message content

With the RFC 822 standard the content part of a message – the body – can only be lines of ASCII text with the maximum length of each line set at 1000 characters. The sending UA then converts each character into NVT ASCII as the transfer syntax with each character converted into its 8-bit form. This ensures that there can be no combinations of codewords in the content field that can be misinterpreted by an MTA as a protocol message.

The RCF 822 standard was first introduced in 1983 and is still used widely for sending text messages. As the use and coverage of the Internet widened, however, so the demand for alternative message types increased, for example, to allow messages to contain binary data and other media types such as audio and video. Also messages containing different languages and alphabets. As a result, an extension to the RFC 822 standard was introduced. This is known as **Multipurpose Internet Mail Extensions (MIME)**. It was first specified in **RFC 1341** and later updated in **RFCs 2045/8**.

The aim of MIME was to enable users to send alternative media types in messages but still use the same message transfer system. The solution was to add a number of extra header fields to the existing fields that collectively enable the user to define alternative media types in the message body. It also provided a way of converting the alternative media types that are supported into strings of ASCII characters that can then be transferred using NVT ASCII.

MIME headers

The additional MIME header fields and their meaning are listed in part (a) of Table 8.1. The first field following the standard header fields is the *MIME-Version:* which, when present, informs the recipient UA that an alternative

Table 8.1 MIME: (a) additional header fields; (b) alternative content types.

(a)	Header		Meaning
	MIME-Version:		Defines the version of MIME that is being used
	Content-Description:		Short textual description of the message content
	Content-Id:		Unique identifier assigned by the UA
	Content-Type:		Defines the type of information in the body
	Content-Transfer-Encoding:		The transfer syntax being used
	Content-Length		The number of bytes in the message body

(b)	Type	Subtype	Content description
	Text	Plain	Unformatted ASCII
		Richtext	Formatted text based on HTML
	Image	GIF	Digitized image in GIF
		JPEG	Digitized image in JPEG
	Audio	Basic	Digitized audio
	Video	MPEG	Digitized video clip or movie
	Application	Octet-stream	A string of bytes
		Postscript	A printable document in PostScript
	Message	Rfc822	Another MIME message
		Partial	Part of a longer message
		External-body	Pointer to where message body can be accessed
	Multipart	Mixed	Each part contains a different content and/or type
		Alternative	Each part contains the same content but with subtype of a different type
		Parallel	The parts should be output simultaneously
		Digest	Multiple messages

message content to ASCII text is present in the message body. It also includes the version number of MIME that is being used. If the field is not present, the recipient UA assumes the content is NVT ASCII. When it is present, the following four fields then expand upon the type of content that is there and the transfer syntax that is being used.

The *Content-Description:* field is present to allow a user to enter a short textual string in ASCII to describe to the recipient user what the contents are all about. It is similar, therefore, to the *subject:* field in the standard header. One or other is often used to decide whether the message/mail is worth reading. Similarly, the *Content-Id:* field performs a similar function to the *Message-Id:* field in the standard header.

The *Content-Type:* field defines the type of information in the message body. The different types are defined in RFC 1521 and a selection of them are listed in part (b) of the table. As we can see, each type comprises two parts: a specification of the type of information – text, image, and so on – followed by a subtype. The type of information in the message body is then defined by a combination of the type and its subtype, each separated by a slash. Some examples are:

> *Content-Type:Text/Richtext*
>
> *Content-Type:Image/JPEG*

Some contain one or more additional parameters. The format used is as follows:

> *Content-Type:Text/Plaintext; charset=US-ASCII*
>
> *Content-Type:Multipart/Alternative;boundary="NextType"*

Clearly, for each type/subtype combination a standard format must be used so that the recipient UA can interpret (and output) the information in a compatible way with how it has been encoded by the sending UA. Hence associated with each combination is a defined (abstract) syntax. For example, the Text/Plaintext combination implies the contents are ASCII text while for the Text/Richtext combination a markup language similar to HTML is used, an example of which we show in Figure 9.10. Similarly, digitized images, audio, and video are all represented in their compressed form. As we explain in Appendix A, there is a range of standard compression algorithms available with each of these media types. In the case of images, for example, the two alternative subtypes supported are GIF and JPEG. The subtype selected for audio is a form of PCM and that for video a version of MPEG. In the case of a movie (video with sound), the MPEG subtype is used with the audio and video integrated together.

The *Application:* type is used when the body contents require processing by the recipient UA before they have meaning on the user's display. For example, an *Octet-stream* subtype is simply a string of bytes representing, say, a compiled program. Typically, therefore, on receipt of this type of information the UA would prompt the user for a file name into which the data should be written, and similarly for the *Postscript* subtype unless the UA contains a PostScript interpreter to display the contents on the screen.

The *Message:* type is used when the contents relate to another MIME message. For example, if the contents contain another RFC 822 message, then the Rfc822 subtype is used, possibly to forward a message. Similarly, the *Partial* subtype is used when the contents contain a fragment of a (larger) message. Typically, additional parameters are then added by the sending UA to enable the recipient UA to reassemble the complete message. This feature is used, for example, to send a long document or audio/video sequence. The *External-body* subtype is used when the message content is not present in the message and instead an address pointer to where the actual message can be accessed from, for example the DNS name of a file server and the file name. This feature is often used to send an unsolicited message such as a long document. Typically, the UA is programmed to ask the user whether he or she wishes to access the document or not. Some examples of parameters with the different message subtypes are:

Content-Type:Message/Partial;id="file-name@host-name";number=1;total=20

Content-Type:Message/External-Body;access-type="mail-server";server="server-name"

The *Multipart:* type is used to indicate that the message body consists of multiple parts/attachments. Each part is clearly separated using a defined delimiter in a parameter. With the *Mixed* subtype each part can contain a different content and/or type. With the *Alternative* subtype each part contains the same content but with a different subtype associated with it; for example, the same message in text or audio or in a number of different languages/ alphabets. Normally, the alternative parts are listed in the preferred order the user/sending UA would like them to be output. The *Parallel* subtype indicates to the recipient UA that the different parts should be output together; for example a piece of audio with a digitized image. Finally the *Digest* subtype is used to indicate that the message body contains multiple other messages; for example to send out a set of draft documents that the sender may have received from a number of different members of a working group.

An example of a simple multimedia mail showing a number of the features we have just considered is shown in Figure 8.11. The message is simply ***Happy birthday Irene*** and this is sent in three different formats. The first is in the form of an audio message, which would necessitate the recipient's PC/workstation having a sound card with associated software. Also, the recipient UA must have software to interpret the contents of the accessed audio file and output this to the sound card. If this is not available, normally the UA is programmed to move to the next option and, if the UA cannot interpret richtext, then the message will be output in plaintext. As we can see from this, what we have described in this section relates only to the (abstract) syntax of the messages that are used by a UA to send a multimedia mail to another UA. What the user sees/hears depends on how the UA has been programmed.

Transfer encoding

The next-to-last field in the MIME header we showed earlier in Table 8.1 is the *Content-Transfer-Encoding:* field and an example of its use was shown in Figure 8.11. As the name implies, it is concerned with the format of the

From: xyz@abc.com
To: abc@xyz.com
Subject: Happy birthday Irene
MIME-Version: 1.0
Content-Type: Multipart/Alternative; boundary = "TryAgain";

– – TryAgain

Content-Type: Message/External-body;
   name = "Irene.audio";
   directory = "Irene";
   access-type = "anon-ftp";
   site = "myserver.abc.com";
Content-Type: Audio/Basic;   *(Message in audio accessed remotely)*
Content-Transfer-Encoding: Base64

– – TryAgain

Content-Type: Text/Richtext;
<B> ∗∗∗Happy birthday Irene∗∗∗ </B> *(Message in richtext)*

– – TryAgain

Content-Type: Text/Plain;
   ∗∗∗Happy birthday Irene∗∗∗ *(Message in plaintext)*

– – TryAgain

Figure 8.11 MIME: example type and subtype declarations.

message content during its transfer over the Internet. Since all the extension fields in the extension header are in 7-bit ASCII, they are encoded in 8-bit NVT ASCII. Recall also that with an RFC 822 message, the UA uses the same transfer syntax to send lines of 7-bit ASCII over the Internet in order to ensure there can be no combinations of codewords in the content field that can be misinterpreted by an MTA as an SMTP protocol message. With the additional media types associated with MIME, however, the message content may be in an 8-bit form with a binary 1 in the eighth bit – a string of 8-bit speech samples for example. As we indicated earlier, the aim of MIME is to use the same message transfer system, which means that the message body should be encoded in NVT ASCII. Hence once the message contents have been input, the UA first converts all non-ASCII data first into lines of (7-bit) ASCII characters and then into lines of NVT ASCII. Collectively this is referred to as transfer encoding.

Two alternative transfer encodings are defined in RFC 1521 for use with an RFC 821-conformant message transfer system (MTA):

■ **quoted-printable**: this is used to send messages that are composed of characters from an alternative character set that is mostly ASCII but has a small number of special characters which have their eighth bit set to 1. Examples are all the Latin character sets;

■ **base64**: this is used to send blocks of binary data and also messages composed of strings of characters from a character set that uses 8-bit codewords such as EBCDIC.

When the MIME header field contains *Content-Transfer-Encoding: Quoted-printable*, the UA converts the codewords of those characters that have their eighth bit set into a string of three characters. The first is the = character and this is followed by the two characters that represent the (8-bit) character in hexadecimal. For example, if the codeword for a special character was 1110 1001, then the hexadecimal representation of the character is E9 (hex). Hence this would be converted into the three-character sequence =E9.

When the MIME header field contains *Content-Transfer-Encoding:Base64*, the message content, instead of being treated as a string of 8-bit bytes, is treated as a string of 24-bit values. Each value is then divided into four 6-bit subvalues, each of which is then represented by an ASCII character. The 64 ASCII characters used to represent each of the possible 6-bit values are listed in Table 8.2. In the event that the contents of a message do not contain a multiple of three bytes, then one or two = characters are used as padding.

Table 8.2 Base64 encoding table.

6-bit value (Hex)	ASCII char	6-bit value (Hex)	ASCII char	6-bit value (Hex)	ASCII char	6-bit value (Hex)	ASCII char
00	A	10	Q	20	g	30	w
01	B	11	R	21	h	31	x
02	C	12	S	22	i	32	y
03	D	13	T	23	j	33	z
04	E	14	U	24	k	34	0
05	F	15	V	25	l	35	1
06	G	16	W	26	m	36	2
07	H	17	X	27	n	37	3
08	I	18	Y	28	o	38	4
09	J	19	Z	29	p	39	5
0A	K	1A	a	2A	q	3A	6
0B	L	1B	b	2B	r	3B	7
0C	M	1C	c	2C	s	3C	8
0D	N	1D	d	2D	t	3D	9
0E	O	1E	e	2E	u	3E	+
0F	P	1F	f	2F	v	3F	/

Example 8.1

A binary file containing audio data contains the following string of four 8-bit samples:

> 10010101   11011100   00111011   01011000

Assuming Base64 encoding,

(i)   using the codewords for ASCII characters given earlier in Figure 1.14, derive the contents of the file in NVT ASCII;

(ii) show how the original contents are derived from the received NVT ASCII string.

Answer:

(i)   Input first converted into two 24-bit values using two = characters as padding:

Value 1 = 10010101	11011100	00111011
Value 2 = 01011000	00111101 (=)	00111101 (=)

Each 24-bit value is converted into four 6-bit values:

Value 1 = 10 0101	01 1101	11 0000	11 1011
2 5	1 D	3 0	3 B
Value 2 = 01 0110	00 0011	11 0100	11 1101
1 6	0 3	3 4	3 D

Using Table 8.2:

> Value 1 represented as the four ASCII characters: *ldw*7
> Value 2 represented as the four ASCII characters: *WD*09

Hence from codewords in Figure 1.14, contents in NVT ASCII are:

Value 1 = 0 110 1100	0 110 0100	0 111 0111	0 011 0111
Value 2 = 0 101 0111	0 100 0100	0 011 0000	0 011 1001

(ii) Received bytestream first converted back into the equivalent ASCII string using codewords in Figure 1.14:

> Value 1 = *ldw*7
> Value 2 = *WD*09

The equivalent four 6-bit subvalues then obtained from Table 8.2:

Value 1 = 2 5	1 D	3 0	3 B
= 10 0101	01 1101	11 0000	11 1011
Value 2 = 1 6	0 3	3 4	3 D
= 01 0110	00 0011	11 0100	11 1101

These are then combined and converted into two 24-bit values:

Value 1 = 10010101   11011100   00111011
Value 2 = 01011000   00111101   00111101

Last two 8-bit values of the last (second) 24-bit value are the NVT ASCII of the = character and hence are discarded.

File contents restored as:

10010101   11011100   00111011   01011000

8.3.3 Message transfer

The main components that make up the message transfer system are shown in Figure 8.12(a). Once a user has created a mail message and clicked on the SEND button, the UA first formats the message into NVT ASCII and then sends it to the UA server in its local mail server using the protocol stack of the access network. On receipt of the message, the UA server deposits the message into the message queue ready for sending by the MTA over the Internet.

The client MTA checks the contents of the message queue at regular intervals and, when it detects a message has been placed in the queue, it proceeds to format and send the message. The MTA first reads the e-mail addresses from the *From:* and *To:* fields of the message header and writes them into the *MAIL FROM:* and *RCPT TO:* fields in the envelope header. It then examines the *Cc:* field in the message header and, if other recipients are listed, it proceeds to create further copies of the message each with a different *RCPT TO:* value in the envelope header.

As we saw earlier, all e-mail addresses are in the form *user-name@mailserver-name* where *mailserver-name* is the DNS name of the mail server. Hence before the client MTA can send any of the formatted messages over the Internet, it must first obtain the IP address of each of the recipient mail servers. As we saw in Section 8.2.5, this is done using the resolver procedure that is linked to all Internet APs. Once the set of IP addresses have been obtained, the client MTA is ready to initiate the transfer of each message. The protocol that is used to control the transfer of a message from one MTA to another is the simple mail transfer protocol (SMTP). The various control messages that are used by SMTP and the sequence in which they are exchanged are defined in RFC 821. All the control messages are encoded in NVT ASCII.

Each message is transferred over a previously established TCP connection. Hence to send each message, the client MTA first initiates the establishment of a logical connection between itself and the MTA server in the recipient mail server using the latter's IP address and port 25 – which is the well-known port number for SMTP. The server MTA accepts the incoming (TCP)

(a)

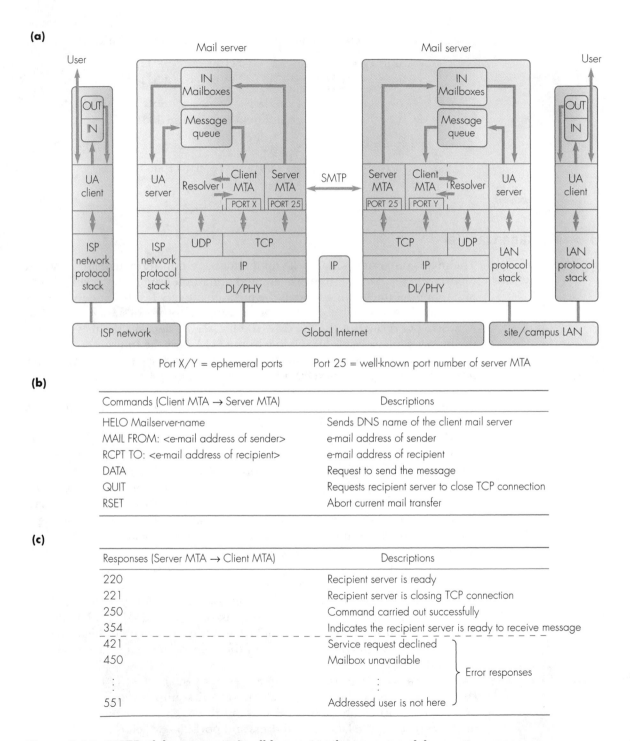

Port X/Y = ephemeral ports   Port 25 = well-known port number of server MTA

(b)

Commands (Client MTA → Server MTA)	Descriptions
HELO Mailserver-name	Sends DNS name of the client mail server
MAIL FROM: <e-mail address of sender>	e-mail address of sender
RCPT TO: <e-mail address of recipient>	e-mail address of recipient
DATA	Request to send the message
QUIT	Requests recipient server to close TCP connection
RSET	Abort current mail transfer

(c)

Responses (Server MTA → Client MTA)	Descriptions
220	Recipient server is ready
221	Recipient server is closing TCP connection
250	Command carried out successfully
354	Indicates the recipient server is ready to receive message
421	Service request declined ⎫
450	Mailbox unavailable
⋮	⋮ ⎬ Error responses
551	Addressed user is not here ⎭

Figure 8.12 SMTP: (a) components; (b) command messages; (c) response messages.

connection request and, once this is in place, proceeds to exchange SMTP control messages (PDUs) with the client MTA to transfer the message. The control messages that are sent by the MTA client are called *commands* and a selection of these are shown in Figure 8.12(b). As we can see, most are composed of four uppercase characters. The MTA server responds to each command with a three-digit numeric reply code with (optionally) a readable string. A selection of the reply codes are given in Figure 8.12(c).

A typical exchange sequence of SMTP control messages to send a mail message is shown in Figure 8.13. To avoid confusion, the TCP segments that are used to transfer the messages are not shown. As we can see, once the server has received the acknowledgment indicating a TCP connection is now in place, the server MTA returns a 220 response indicating it is ready to start the message transfer sequence. This starts with the MTA client sending a HELO command and the MTA server returning a 250 response indicating it is prepared to accept mail from the sending server. The client MTA then sends the sender's e-mail address and, if this is accepted, it sends the intended recipient's e-mail address. In the example, this is accepted by a 250 response. If this was not acceptable, typically the MTA server would return either a 450 (mailbox unavailable) or a 551 (addressed user is not here).

Assuming both addresses are valid, the client proceeds to send a DATA command to determine if the server MTA is now ready to receive the message itself. If it is, the server returns a 350 response and, on receipt of this, the transfer of the message takes place. The message consists of multiple lines, each of up to 1000 characters, with a single "." character on the last line. All characters are encoded in NVT ASCII. Note also that the number of TCP segments used to transfer the message is determined entirely by the two TCP entities. On receipt of the (reassembled) message, the server MTA transfers the message to the IN mailbox of the recipient user and returns a 250 response to the client MTA. The latter then sends a QUIT command to request the MTA server closes the TCP connection.

The UA client in each user terminal periodically sends an enquiry to its local UA server to determine whether any new mail has arrived. Hence when the UA server next receives an enquiry from the UA client in the recipient's terminal, it transfers the received message to the UA client. The latter then places the message in the user's IN mailbox and, typically, outputs a message indicating a new (mail) message has arrived.

At the sending side, once the MTA client receives the final 250 response indicating the message has been transferred successfully, it informs the UA server. The letter then informs the UA client in the sending terminal and this, in turn, informs the user that the message has been sent.

8.3.4 E-mail gateways

The structure we showed earlier in Figure 8.9 assumed that both e-mail servers were connected to the Internet and hence could communicate directly using the SMTP/TCP/IP protocol stack. With many companies and

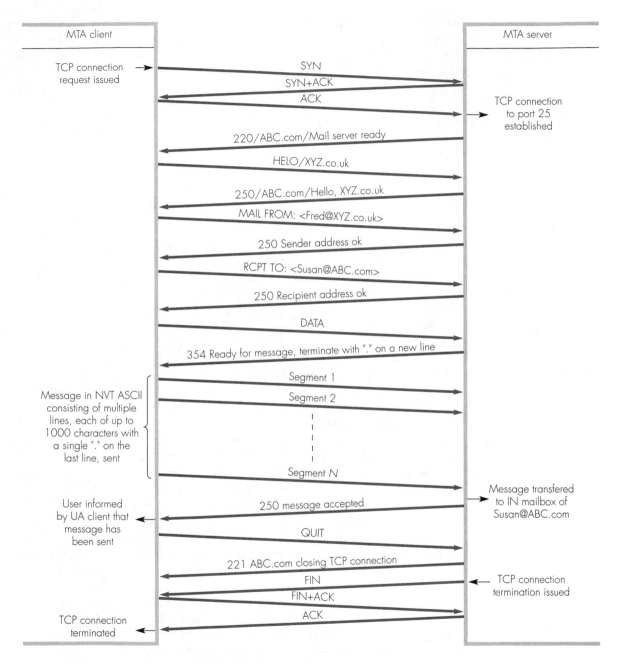

Figure 8.13 Example e-mail message transfer from Fred@XYZ.co.uk to Susan@ABC.com using SMTP.

large enterprises, however, often this is not the case and instead a different e-mail system is used. Nevertheless, in addition to sending and receiving mail to/from other employees within the company/enterprise, many of these employees may also require to send and receive mail to/from people whose computers/PCs are connected either to a different company/enterprise network or to the Internet. In practice, there are two problems associated with doing this: first the format of the mail messages is often different and second the application protocols are also different. To overcome these problems, a device known as an **e-mail gateway** is used, the general arrangement being as shown in Figure 8.14.

As we show in the figure, the gateway has a number of interfaces, one for connecting to the local e-mail server at the site and the others for connecting to those networks (including the Internet) with which the employees at the site wish to communicate. To transfer a message that is addressed to an outside network, the e-mail server first transfers the message to a message buffer in the e-mail gateway using the protocol stack associated with the company/enterprise network. The e-mail address in the header of the message is then read by an application-level program to determine the network over which the mail should be forwarded. Assuming the external network is the Internet, the program proceeds to reformat the message into the RFC 822 format and then forwards this using the TCP/IP protocol stack as described previously. A similar procedure is followed in the reverse direction except the message format has to be changed from RFC 822 to the format used by the company network.

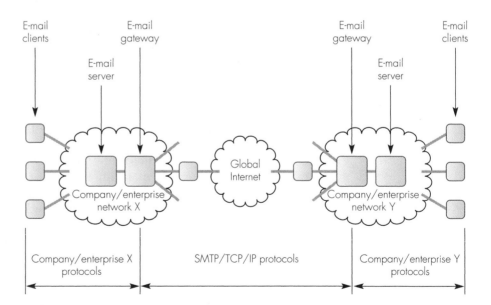

Figure 8.14 E-mail across dissimilar networks using an e-mail gateway.

As we can see from the above, the translation procedure can be a time consuming process, especially when a number of different networks are involved and the message contents comprise more than just text. It is for this reason that, increasingly, companies are converting their networks to work using the SMTP/TCP/IP protocols. In the case of a large multisite company, the complete enterprise network is then known as an intranet. This has the advantage of not only removing the need for e-mail gateways, but also enabling employees of the company to access and browse the World Wide Web directly and for selected servers – containing product literature for example – to be accessed by people outside the company.

8.4 FTP

The transfer of the contents of a file held on the file system of one computer to a file on another computer is a common requirement in many distributed/networked applications. In some applications the two computers involved may both be large servers each running a different operating system with a different file system and character set. In another application, one of the computers may be a server and the other an item of equipment such as a cable modem or a set-top box which does not have a hard disk. Hence in this case all the data that is transferred must have been formatted specifically for running in the cable modem or set-top box. Clearly, therefore, the file transfer protocol associated with the second type of application can be much simpler than the first. Hence to meet the different requirements of these two types of application, there are two Internet application protocols associated with file transfer. The first is called the **file transfer protocol** (**FTP**) and the second the **trivial file transfer protocol** (**TFTP**). In this section we give an overview of the operation of FTP and we describe the operation of TFTP in the next section.

8.4.1 Overview

FTP is a widely used Internet application protocol that has been designed to enable a user at a terminal to initiate the transfer of the contents of a named file from one computer to another using the TCP/IP protocol suite. The two computers may use different operating systems with different file systems and, possibly, different character sets. It also supports the transfer of a number of different file types such as character and binary. It is specified in RFC 959. We describe first how the file contents are represented and then the operation of the protocol itself. We conclude with some examples.

8.4.2 File content representation

Although FTP has been designed to enable files stored in many different types of computer to be transferred, to gain an understanding of FTP's operation without including too much detail, we shall limit our description to file transfers involving just two different file types, ASCII and binary, and files containing a stream of bytes with no internal structure. As with the contents of e-mail messages, for a file containing 7-bit ASCII characters the file contents are first converted into NVT ASCII by the sending side before they are transferred. They are then converted back again into 7-bit ASCII at the recipient side for storage. With a binary file, the end of the file is signaled by the sending side initiating the closure of the TCP connection.

8.4.3 FTP operation

A schematic diagram showing the essential components involved in a file transfer using FTP is shown in Figure 8.15. The computer initiating the transfer request is called the client and the computer responding to the request the server.

As we can see, each FTP entity consists of two parts: a control part and a data transfer part. The control part is concerned with the exchange of control messages – commands and their replies – relating to the file to be transferred, and the data transfer part with the actual transfer of the file contents.

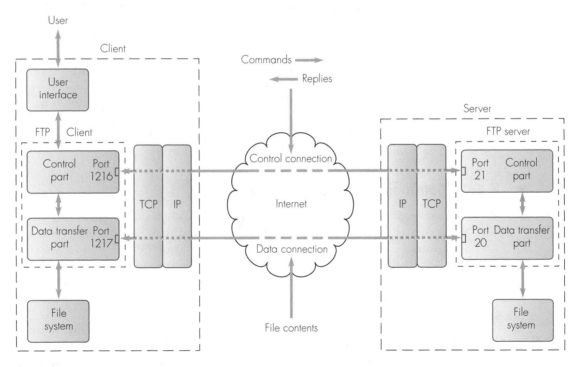

Ports 1216/1217 = ephemeral ports

Port 21 = well-known port of control connection
Port 20 = well-known port of data connection

Figure 8.15 FTP components and terminology.

The user interacts with his or her local FTP through an appropriate (user) interface. The user interface software then converts each command that is selected/entered by the user into a standard format that is understood by the FTP control part. There is also a standard format used for each FTP command and response message exchanged by the control part in the two computers.

On receipt of the first command from the user, the (FTP) control part in the client initiates the establishment of a TCP connection between itself and the control part in the server. This is called the **control connection** and it remains in place until the related file transfer has been carried out. The port number at the client side is an ephemeral port – shown as 1216 in Figure 8.15 – and that at the server side is port 21, which is the well-known port number for the FTP control connection. The reply message to a command is returned by the control part in the server over the control connection.

A second TCP connection called the **data connection** is used for the transfer of the contents of a specified file. Once the control part in the client has sent and received the replies to all the command messages it has sent relating to the file transfer, it sends a further command informing the server side of the ephemeral port number that should be used for its side of the data connection. The control part in the client then issues a passive open and waits for a TCP connection request (SYN) segment from the server side. On receipt of the port number, the control part in the server proceeds to establish the TCP data connection using port 20 – the well-known port number for the FTP data connection – as the source port and the received ephemeral port as the destination port. Once this is in place, the contents of the specified file are transferred over this connection. Note that this can be in either direction depending on the command and after the transfer has taken place, the data connection is then closed by the side that sends the data. Finally, the control connection is closed by the client.

8.4.4 Command and reply message format

A selection of some of the more common command messages that are sent across the control connection (from the control part in the client to the control part in the server) are listed in part (a) of Table 8.3 and the structure of the reply messages that are returned in the opposite direction in part (b). All the command and reply messages are made up of ASCII characters. They are encoded for transmission into 8-bit NVT ASCII with each command/reply terminated by a CR/LF pair of characters.

As we can see, all the commands are in upper-case and many have parameters – referred to as arguments – associated with them. Most of the commands are self explanatory. In the case of the *PORT* command, however, the six parameters associated with it (n1–n6) are all decimal numbers. The four decimal numbers n1–n4 form the IP address of the client host in dotted decimal. The two numbers n5–n6 then specify the ephemeral port number for the data connection on the client side. Each port number is 16 bits long

Table 8.3 FTP client–server communication: (a) example commands; (b) structure of the replies.

(a) Command	Description
USER username	User name on the (FTP) server
PASS password	User's password on the server
SYST	Type of operating system requested
TYPE type	File type to be transferred: A (ASCII), I (Image/Binary)
PORT n1, n2, n3, n4, n5, n6	Client IP address (n1–n4) and port number (n5, n6)
RETR filename.type	Retrieve (get) a file
STOR filename.type	Store (put) a file
LIST filelist	List files or directories
QUIT	Log off from server

(b) Reply	Description
1yz	Positive reply, wait for another reply before sending a new command
2yz	Positive reply, a new command can be sent
3yz	Positive reply, another command is awaited
4yz	Negative reply, try again
5yz	Negative reply, do not retry
x0z	Syntax
x1z	Information
x2z	Control or data connection
x3z	Authentication
x4z	Unspecified
x5z	File status

and n5 is the decimal equivalent of the most significant 8 bits and n6 the least significant 8 bits. Hence the two parameters n5 and n6 for port 1217 would be 4, 193; that is, $4 \times 256 + 193$.

Each of the reply messages comprises a 3-digit code followed by an optional text message. The first digit indicates the type of reply, positive (successful) or negative. The second digit expands on this by indicating to what the reply relates (control or data connection, data, and so on) and the third digit gives additional information relating to error messages. A selection of some of the more common reply messages, together with a typical text message, are as follows:

220   FTP server ready

331   Password required for \<username>

230   User \<username> logged in

215   Server OS Name Type: Version

200   File type acknowledged

200   PORT command successful

150   Opening ASCII/Binary mode data connection for \<file name>

226   File transfer complete

221   Goodbye

425   Data connection cannot be opened

500   Unrecognized command

501   Invalid arguments

530   User access denied

8.4.5 Example

In order to illustrate the use of some of the listed commands and their replies we shall show some example message exchanges.

There are three types of file transfer supported over the data connection:

■ the transfer of the contents of a named file from the client file system to the server system;

■ a similar transfer in the server–client direction;

■ the transfer of the listings of the files (or the directories in a file) held by the server and saved in a named file on the client.

A typical exchange of commands and replies to carry out (successfully) the transfer of a named file and file type from the server file system to the client system is shown in Figure 8.16. The following additional comments should be noted when interpreting the exchange sequence:

■ The client FTP control part has a resolver procedure linked to it and, when the DNS name of the server is passed to it by the user interface, it uses the resolver to obtain the IP address of the server.

■ If the user had issued a put\<filename.type>, then the client (control part) would send a STOR\<filename.type> command. Also, since the file transfer is in the client–server direction, if the TYPE is I, then the client would initiate the closure of the data connection.

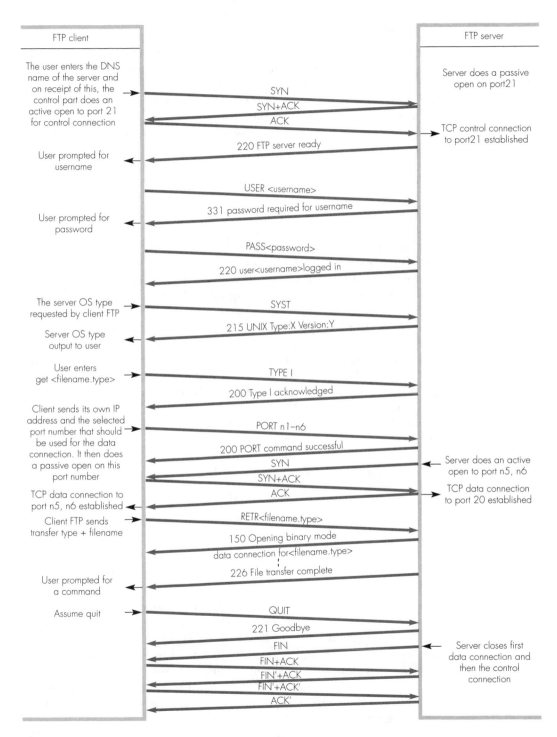

Figure 8.16 Example of command–reply message exchange sequence to get a file from the FTP server.

8.4.6 Anonymous FTP

The example shown in Figure 8.16 assumed that the (client) user had a user-name/password on the named server. This is not always the case since FTP is also used to access information from a server that allows unknown users to log in to it. To access information from this type of server, the user must know the DNS name of the server but, when prompted for a username, he or she enters *anonymous* and, for the password, his or her e-mail address. Normally, in response, the server replies with something like

> 230 Visitor login ok, access granted

at which point the same procedure shown in the example in Figure 8.16 follows.

In some instances, however, before granting the user access, the server carries out a rudimentary check that the client host has a valid domain name. Although the IP address of the client host has not been formally sent at this point – this does not occur until the PORT command is sent – it is present in the (IP) source address field of each of the IP datagrams that have been used to set up the (TCP) control connection and to send the username and password. Hence before granting access, the control part in the server uses its own resolver to check that the IP address of the host is in the DNS database. As we saw earlier in the latter part of Section 8.2.5, this involves the control part issuing a pointer query to the resolver with the host IP address in the query name. If a valid domain name is returned, then access is granted as before. If a negative response is received then access to the server is blocked and, typically, the server sends a reply of

> 530 User access denied, unknown IP address

8.5 TFTP

As we mentioned at the start of Section 8.4, TFTP is used mainly in applications in which one of the two communicating hosts does not have a hard disk. Typically, TFTP is then used to download – normally referred to as bootstrapping – the application code that is to be run on the diskless host. We showed an application of TFTP earlier in Figure 4.5 and, as we explained in the accompanying text, it is used to download the application code for cable modems from the cable modem termination system (CMTS). As we showed in the figure, TFTP uses UDP as the transport protocol since this is less complicated than TCP and hence requires less memory. The specification of TFTP is given in **RFC 1350**.

8.5.1 Protocol

There are just five message types (PDUs) associated with the TFTP protocol and their format is shown in Figure 8.17. The first field in each message is called the *opcode* and indicates the message type. The different types are shown in the figure.

As with FTP the host/item of equipment that initiates a transfer is called the client and the host that responds to the request the server. Each transfer starts with the client making a request to the server either for a named file – read request – or to receive a named file – write request. Hence in an application such as downloading code, the diskless host is the client and the first message that is sent is a *read request* (*RRQ*). The *filename* field in the message is used to specify the name of the file on the server to be transferred/ downloaded. The filename is an NVT ASCII string that is terminated by a byte of zero. This is followed by the *mode* field which is also an NVT ASCII string indicating whether the file contents are lines of ASCII text – *netascii* – or a string of 8-bit bytes – *octet*. In both cases the string is terminated by a byte of zero.

The contents of the requested file are transferred by the server in one or more *DATA* messages. Since UDP is a best-effort protocol, normally an error control protocol is used to transfer the complete file contents. The protocol supported is based on the stop-and-wait (idle RQ) error control scheme. It is a variant of the protocol we showed earlier in Figure 1.23, the difference being that there are no NAK messages and hence the retransmission of a lost DATA message is triggered by the timer for the message expiring. An example message exchange illustrating the main features of the protocol is shown in Figure 8.18.

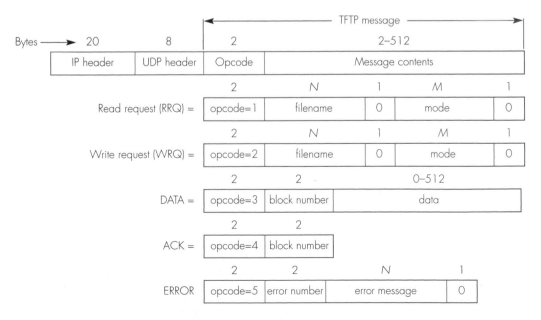

Figure 8.17 TFTP PDU message formats.

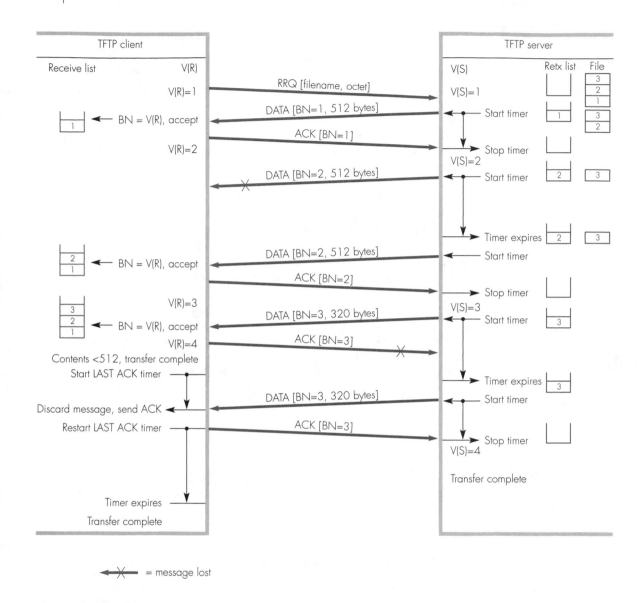

Figure 8.18 TFTP example PDU message exchange.

Recall that with the idle RQ protocol, the total message – the file contents – are first divided into multiple blocks, the size of each block being determined by the characteristics of the underlying data link/transport service. With the TFTP protocol the maximum size of each block – the *data* field in each DATA message – is 512 bytes. The end of a message/file transfer is then indicated when a DATA message is received containing less than 512 bytes in it, that is, a data field containing 0–511 bytes.

As with idle RQ, to detect duplicates, each DATA message contains a sequence number – called the *block number* (*BN*) in TFTP – in the message header and, on receipt of each error-free DATA message, an *ACK* message is returned containing the same BN within it as that contained in the DATA message. To implement the scheme, the server side maintains a send sequence variable, V(S), which contains the BN that is to be allocated to the next DATA message to be transmitted, and the client side maintains a receive sequence variable, V(R), which indicates the BN in the next in-sequence DATA message it expects to receive. Both are initialized to 1.

The transfer starts with the client sending a RRQ message containing the filename and file type. In response, the server proceeds to send the contents of the filename. In the example file transfer shown in Figure 8.18 the file contents are assumed to require three DATA messages shown as 1, 2, and 3. The following should be noted when interpreting the sequence shown:

- The first DATA message (BN = 1) is assumed to be received and acknowledged correctly and hence both V(S) and V(R) are now incremented to 2.
- The second DATA message (BN = 2) is corrupted and hence is not received. This can be due, for example, to the IP datagram containing the DATA message being discarded during its transfer or the checksum in the UDP header failing in the client.
- At the server side, the absence of an ACK for BN2 means that the retransmission timer expires and another attempt is made to send it.
- This time it is assumed to be received correctly and both V(S) and V(R) are now incremented to 3.
- When the last DATA message is sent (BN = 3), this is received free of errors and hence V(R) is incremented to 4 and an ACK is returned with BN = 3.
- During its transfer, the ACK is corrupted/lost and hence the retransmission timer in the server expires. The server retransmits another copy of BN3 which is assumed to be received error free.
- The client determines from the BN that the message is a duplicate – BN = 3 instead of 4 – and hence discards it but returns an ACK to stop the server from sending another copy.
- The client determines that the file has now been received by the fact that the contents of BN3 are less than 512 bytes.
- The LAST ACK timer is used to allow for the possibility of the last ACK being lost.
- Should the number of attempts to send a block exceed a defined limit, then an error message is sent and the transfer aborted.

In the case of a write request, the client sends a WRQ message with the filename and mode in it and, if the server is prepared to accept the file, it returns an ACK message with a BN = 0. The client side then proceeds to send the file contents using the same procedure as for a read request.

A number of error messages are also provided. The particular error message is indicated by the value in the *error number* field. The contents in the *error message* field then contain an additional text message in NVT ASCII that is terminated by a byte of zero. In addition, even though there is no authentication procedure associated with TFTP, in most implementations the server only allows the client to read or write from/to a specific file name or names.

8.6 Internet telephony

Unlike e-mail, which uses the services provided by the message transfer system as an intermediary between the two (or more) communicating participants, Internet telephony requires a communications path that supports real-time communications between the two or more participants involved in the call/session. Also, although the early IETF standards relating to Internet telephony were concerned with providing a basic two-party telephony service between two IP hosts, the more recent standards provide a more versatile facility supporting multiparty calls/sessions involving audio, video and data integrated together in a dynamic way. The number of participants involved can vary as the session proceeds. Also, the location of each participant is not necessarily at a fixed IP address. For example, at one point in time a participant may be using a workstation attached to an enterprise network while at another time using a PC at home or, possibly, a fixed or mobile phone.

Thus the main requirement associated with Internet telephony is a set of signaling protocols that support, in addition to call/session establishment, features for dynamic user location and the negotiation of a suitable set of capabilities that are supported by all the user devices involved. In this section we describe the main features of three of the protocols that have been defined by the IETF to provide these services. These are the **session initiation protocol** (**SIP**), the **session description protocol** (**SDP**), and the **gateway location protocol** (**GLP**). In addition, we describe the main features of an alternative set of protocols defined by the ITU in Recommendation H.323.

8.6.1 SIP

SIP provides services for user location, call/session establishment, and call participation management. It is a simple request-response – also known as transaction – protocol and is defined in RFC 2543. The user of a host device that wants to set up a call sends a request message – also known as a command or method – to the user of the called host device, which responds by returning a suitable response message. Both the request and response are made through an application program/process called the **user agent** (**UA**), which maps the request and its response into the standard message format used by SIP.

Each UA comprises two parts, a **UA client** (**UAC**), which enables the user to send request messages – to initiate the setting up of a call/session for example –

and a **UA server** (**UAS**), which generates the response message determined by the user's response. A schematic diagram showing a typical stack associated with Internet telephony is shown in Figure 8.19(a) and a list of the request and response messages used by SIP – together with their usage – is shown in part (b).

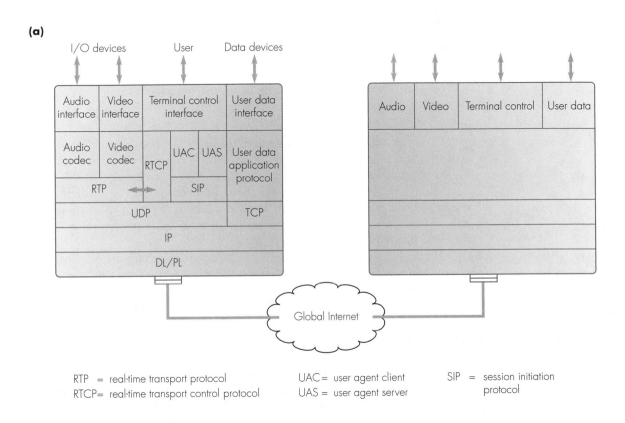

(a)

RTP = real-time transport protocol
RTCP = real-time transport control protocol

UAC = user agent client
UAS = user agent server

SIP = session initiation protocol

(b)

SIP message	Usage
INVITE	Invites a user to join a call/session
ACK	Used to acknowledge receipt of an INVITE response messge
REGISTER	Used to inform a SIP redirect server of the current location of a user
OPTIONS	Used to request the capabilities of a host device
CANCEL	Terminates a search for a user
BYE	Inform the other user(s) that the user is learning a call/session

Figure 8.19 Internet telephony: (a) example host device protocol stack; (b) SIP request/response signaling message types.

Each request and response message comprises a header and a body. The header contains a set of fields a number of which are similar to those used with e-mail. For example, a selection of the header fields associated with the INVITE request/response message include:

To:	The SIP address of the called participant
From:	The SIP address of the caller
Subject:	A brief title of the call
Call-ID:	Unique call identifier assigned by the caller
Require:	List of capabilities the host device can support
Content-Type:	Type of information in the message body
Content-Length:	Length of body contents

Each SIP name/address is similar to an e-mail name/address with the addition that it has a prefix of *sip.* Hence two example SIP name/addresses might be *sip:tom.C@university.edu* and *sip:karen.S@company.com.*

The type of call/session being set up is determined by the contents of the message body, which describes the individual media streams to be used in the call. These are defined using the companion SDP protocol, which we describe in the next section.

As we have just seen, a SIP name/address is similar to an e-mail name/address. Hence before a SIP message can be sent over the Internet it is necessary first to obtain the IP address of the intended recipient host. As we indicated earlier, a user may be contactable at a number of alternative locations. Hence when a user registers to use the Internet telephony service, the user provides a number of alternative SIP addresses where it can be located. For example, karen.S may be contactable at either *sip:karen.S@company.com* or *sip:karen.S@organization.org.* This list of names is then sent to a server called the *redirect server* at each of the sites involved – for example, *company.com* and *organization.org* – using a REGISTER message with the list of alternative addresses in the *Contact:* header field.

To explain how a call/session is set up we shall use two examples. In the first, we assume the called user is currently at the given SIP address. Figure 8.20(a) shows the protocols and network components that are used to set up the call. To simplify the description, assume that the SIP name/address of the calling user is *sip:tom.C@university.edu* and that of the called user is *sip:karen.S@company.com.*

Associated with each access network – enterprise network, campus, and so on – is a second server called a *proxy server* to which all SIP INVITE messages are sent. In the figure we show these as PS-A and PS-B. Each host knows the IP address of its local proxy server. Also, the proxy server knows the SIP name and address of each user that is currently logged in at the site and the IP address of the user's host device. Typically, the latter is determined using ARP.

(a)

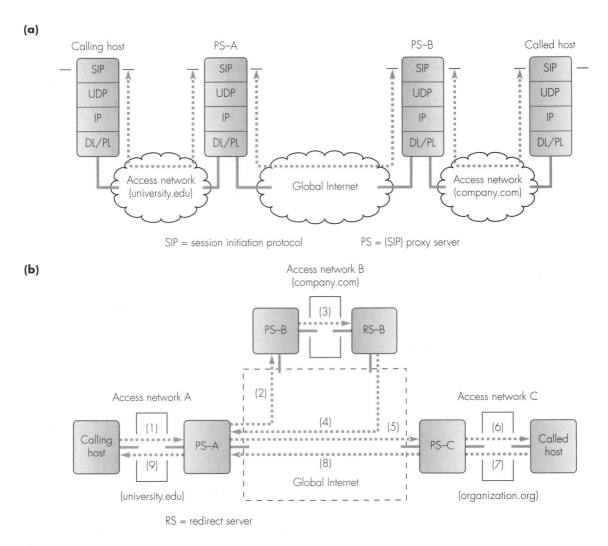

(b)

Figure 8.20 SIP message routing examples: (a) direct using proxy servers; (b) indirect using a redirect server.

On receipt of an INVITE request message from the calling host, PS-A first reads the SIP name/address from the *To:* field in the message header and proceeds to obtain the IP address of the proxy server for *company.com* (PS-B) using the domain name service (DNS). On receipt of this, the SIP in PS-A sends the INVITE request message to PS-B. The latter first reads the SIP name/address from the *To:* field in the message header and determines from this, firstly, that *karen.S* is currently logged in at this location and, secondly, the local IP address of the called host. It then uses the IP address to send the INVITE request to the called host. Assuming the latter is able to accept the call, an INVITE response message is returned over the same path. On receipt of this, the

SIP in the calling host returns an ACK message and it is at this point that the two users/hosts can start to exchange the information relating to the call.

In the second example we assume that the called user *sip:karen.S* is currently located at *organization.org*, not *company.com*. Hence this time, on receipt of the INVITE request from PS-A, PS-B determines that *karen.S* is not currently logged in at this location and hence forwards the request to the redirect server for the site, RS-B. As we indicated earlier, the latter has the list of alternative SIP addresses for this user and determines from this that *karen.S* can also be located at *organization.org*. The SIP in RS-B returns this information in a *Contact:* header field in the INVITE response message. On receipt of this, PS-A proceeds as before but this time by first obtaining the IP address of the SIP proxy server at *organization.org* using the DNS. A summary of the message sequence involved is shown in Figure 8.20(b).

8.6.2 SDP

As we indicated earlier, the role of the session description protocol (SDP) is to describe the different media streams that are to be involved in a call/session and also additional information relating to the call. This is described in each SIP message body in a textual format and includes:

- **media streams**: a multimedia call/session may involve a number of different media streams, including speech, audio, video and more general data. The proposed list of media types and their format are contained in the message body. Each SIP INVITE request message contains a list of the media types and the compression formats that are acceptable to the calling user (host device) and the INVITE response message contains a possibly modified version of this that collectively indicates what is acceptable to the called user;

- **stream addresses**: for each media stream, the destination address and UDP port number for sending and/or receiving each stream is indicated;

- **start and stop times**: these are used with broadcast sessions and enable a user to join a session during the time the broadcast is being carried out.

8.6.3 GLP

The two examples we considered in Section 8.6.1 assumed that the two host devices – or more if multicast addresses are used – were both attached directly to the Internet. In some instances, however, one of the host devices may be attached to a different network such as a PSTN or ISDN. Such cases require a device called a gateway to convert the different signaling messages – a **signaling gateway** (**SGW**) – and the different media formats – a **media gateway** (**MGW**).

In practice, both the PSTN/ISDN and the Internet are global networks/internetworks. Hence when the called user is attached to a PSTN/ISDN, because of the potentially higher bandwidth associated with the Internet, it is preferable to utilize the Internet for as much of the connection path as possible. To do this requires, firstly, a gateway associated with each PSTN/ISDN access network and, secondly, when a call is made, to utilize the gateway that is closest to the called – or calling – user. As we saw earlier in Figure 6.19, the Internet is composed of an interconnected set of networks/internetworks. Typically, therefore, each Internet regional/national network has a number of gateways associated with it. Also, each of these networks has one or more **location servers** (**LS**). This general architecture is shown in Figure 8.21.

As we can deduce from the figure, when the called user device is attached to a segment/subnet of a PSTN/ISDN, the SIP INVITE message must be sent to the (signaling) gateway that is nearest to the segment/subnet to which the called terminal equipment is attached. The main issue, therefore, is, given a conventional telephone number, how is the INVITE message routed to the gateway that is nearest to the subscriber with this number? This is the role of the location servers and their operation is as follows.

Each gateway knows the regional/national code of the segment of the PSTN/ISDN to which it is attached. Typically this is entered by network

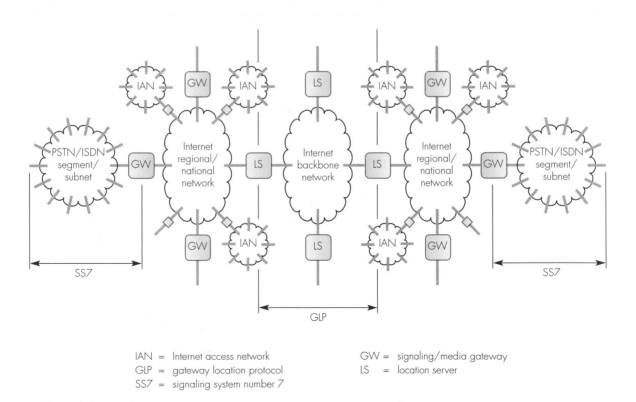

IAN = Internet access network
GLP = gateway location protocol
SS7 = signaling system number 7

GW = signaling/media gateway
LS = location server

Figure 8.21 Interworking between Internet hosts and PSTN/ISDN terminal equipment.

management. In addition, on the Internet side, each gateway has an IP address and it also knows the IP address of the LS(s) that is (are) attached to the same (Internet) regional/national network. Each gateway then uses the IP address of each of its local LSs to inform them of the regional/national code of the segment of the PSTN/ISDN to which it is attached. In this way, each LS learns the regional/national codes of the segments of the PSTN/ISDN to which all of its gateways are attached and, from this, the IP address of the gateway that should be used for each of these codes.

Each LS then exchanges this information with each of the other LSs using the gateway location protocol (GLP). In this way each LS builds up a database of the IP address of the LS that should be used to reach all of the gateways in other regional/national networks and also the PSTN/ISDN codes associated with each of these gateways. Thus the gateway local protocol that carries out this function is very similar to the interdomain routing protocol BGP – the border gateway protocol – which we described earlier in Section 6.6.5. Indeed, GLP is based on BGP and hence we shall not expand upon it here.

8.6.4 H.323

As we described earlier in Section 1.1, normally, the access network used with both an intranet and the Internet is a campus/site LAN. Hence the H.323 standard pertaining to packet-switched networks relates primarily to how interpersonal communications are achieved between stations – called end systems in this standard – that are attached either to the same LAN or to different LANs that are interconnected together in some way. The H.323 standard is intended for use with LANs that provide a non-guaranteed QoS which, in practice, as we saw in Chapter 3, applies to the majority of LANs.

As we show in Figure 8.22, the standard comprises components for the packetization and synchronization of the audio and video streams, an administration control procedure for end systems to join a conference, multipoint conference control, and interworking with terminals that are connected to different types of circuit-switched networks. The standard is independent of the underlying transport and network interface protocols and hence can be used with any type of LAN. It is assumed, however, that the network layer is IP and the transport layer provides both an unreliable (best-effort) service (UDP) and a reliable service (TCP) which, in practice, is the case for most LANs.

Audio and video coding

In order to simplify interworking with terminals/computers attached to the different types of circuit-mode networks, the H.323 standard allows a variety of coding options to be used for the audio and video streams. Prior to a call commencing, however, an agreed coding standard must be negotiated to avoid the necessity of transcoding the audio and video streams.

The output streams of both the audio and video codecs are formatted into packets for transfer over the network using the real-time transport protocol (RTP). This is used for the transfer of real-time information and at

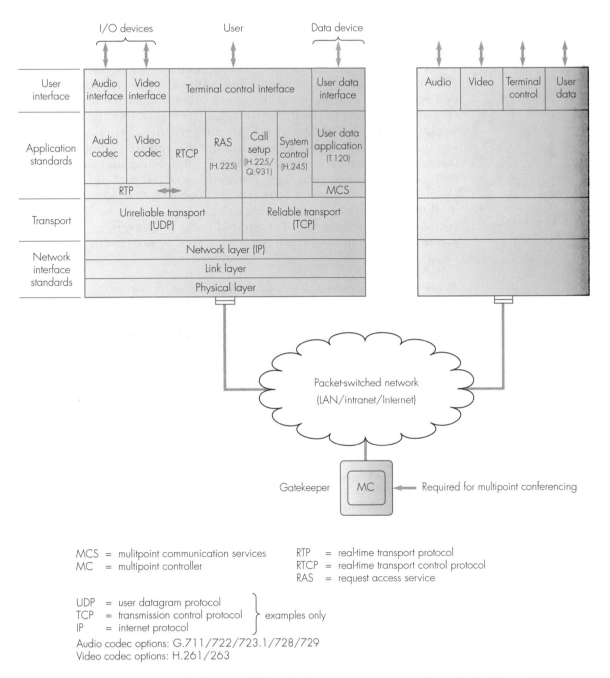

Figure 8.22 Structure of the H.323 interpersonal communication standards for packet-switched networks.

the head of each RTP packet is a format specification that defines how the packet contents/payload are structured. There are standardized formats for the information streams produced by all the different audio and video codecs. In addition, as part of the real-time transport control protocol (RTCP), the sending end system sends information to enable the receiving end system to synchronize the audio and video streams. Other information transferred as part of the RTCP includes the transmitted packet rate, the packet transmission delay (sender to receiver), the percentage of packets lost/corrupted, and the interarrival jitter (receiver to sender). This information can then be used to optimize the number and size of receiver buffers and to determine if the retransmission of lost packets is feasible. For example, if the transmission delay is below a defined threshold – for example if all the end systems are attached to the same LAN – it may be feasible to request the retransmission of corrupted packets. Conversely, if the delay is greater than the threshold then retransmissions are not possible.

Call setup

As we saw in Chapter 3, LANs that do not provide a guaranteed QoS have no procedures to limit the number of calls/sessions that are using the LAN concurrently. Although this is acceptable with applications such as text-based file transfers that require only short bursts of bandwidth, with applications that involve audio and video this approach is often not acceptable, since the potentially large bandwidth that would be required to support many concurrent calls/sessions could exceed the total bandwidth available with the LAN. In order to limit the number of concurrent calls that involve multimedia, a device called an **H.323 gatekeeper** can (optionally) be used.

Essentially, during the setting up of a multimedia conferencing call, each end system involved in the conference must first obtain permission from the gatekeeper. Then, depending on the current level of usage of the LAN, the gatekeeper decides whether the call can take place. If an increase in the allocated bandwidth is required during a call, then again prior permission must be obtained from the gatekeeper. The messages that are exchanged to set up a call are shown in Figure 8.23.

As we show in the figure, the setting up of a call is carried out in two stages. First, the end system initiating the call obtains permission from the gatekeeper to set up a call by sending an *access request (ARQ)* message to the gatekeeper (1) and the gatekeeper responds with either an *access confirm (ACF)* or an *access reject (ARJ)* message (2). Assuming permission is received, for a two-party call the initiating terminal then sends a *setup* request message directly to the called end system (3). The latter first acknowledges receipt of the setup request by returning a *call proceeding* message directly to the initiating end system (4) and then proceeds to obtain permission from the gatekeeper to take part in the call by means of the exchange of *ARQ* (5) and *ACF* (6) messages. Assuming permission is granted, the called end system sends an *alerting* message directly to the initiating end system (7), which is equivalent to the ringing tone heard when setting up a telephone call over a PSTN. Finally, if the user accepts the call, then the called end system returns a *connect* message directly to the initiating end system (8).

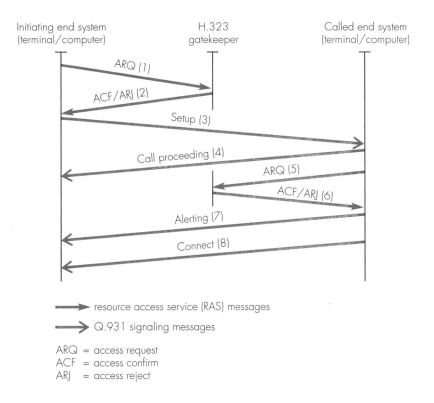

Figure 8.23 Two-party call setup procedure using an H.323 gatekeeper.

The messages exchanged with the gatekeeper concerned with the two end systems obtaining permission to set up a call are part of the **resource access service (RAS) protocol** and the example messages concerned with call setup that are exchanged directly by the two end systems are part of the Q.931 signaling protocol. In practice, both the RAS and Q.931 protocols are part of recommendation H.225. A similar procedure is followed for a multiparty conference call except all the messages are exchanged via the gatekeeper.

Once a call has been set up, the exchange of system control messages using the H.245 control protocol can then start. These include the negotiation of capabilities and the opening of logical channels for the audio, video, and user data streams. As we saw in Section 7.2, associated with both the UDP and the TCP protocols is a port number. This is carried in the header of the protocol data unit (PDU) associated with each protocol and is used to identify the application protocol to which the PDU contents relate. Also, as we explained in Section 6.2, in the IP header is the identity of the protocol (UDP or TCP) that created the packet to be transferred. Hence, as we show in Figure 8.24, on receipt of each packet from the network, the IP uses the protocol identifier to route the packet contents to either the UDP or the TCP. The latter then uses the port number at the head of the packet to relay the packet

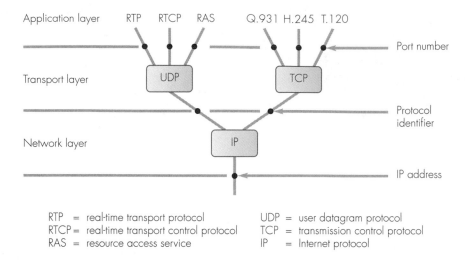

RTP = real-time transport protocol	UDP = user datagram protocol
RTCP = real-time transport control protocol	TCP = transmission control protocol
RAS = resource access service	IP = Internet protocol

Figure 8.24 H.323 multiplexing/demultiplexing.

contents – the application protocol data unit – to the appropriate application protocol. Thus the multiplexing and demultiplexing operations associated with H.323 are carried out by the IP/UDP/TCP combination.

Interworking

In addition to the operation of the end systems, the H.323 standard also defines how interworking with end systems that are attached to a circuit-mode network is achieved. This is through a device known as an **H.323 gateway** and the general scheme is shown in Figure 8.25.

The role of a gateway is to provide translations between the different procedures (and related control messages) associated with each network type. Hence translations are necessary for the procedures and messages associated with call setup and clearing (signaling), system control, and the two different multiplexing techniques. Also, if the two (or more) communicating end systems are using different audio and video codec standards, then transcoding between the two different coding techniques must be carried out. In order to minimize the amount of transcoding required in the gateway, the same audio and video codec standards are used whenever possible. Hence, to make interworking easier, selected audio and video codec standards are made mandatory, which means that the end system must always be able to operate with these codecs. If a common standard is not supported – determined during the capability exchange procedure – then the gateway must perform the appropriate transcoding procedures. However, as we show in Figure 8.25, a gateway can have multiple interfaces and, in practice, can support multiple calls simultaneously. Hence if transcoding is necessary, this restricts the number of simultaneous calls.

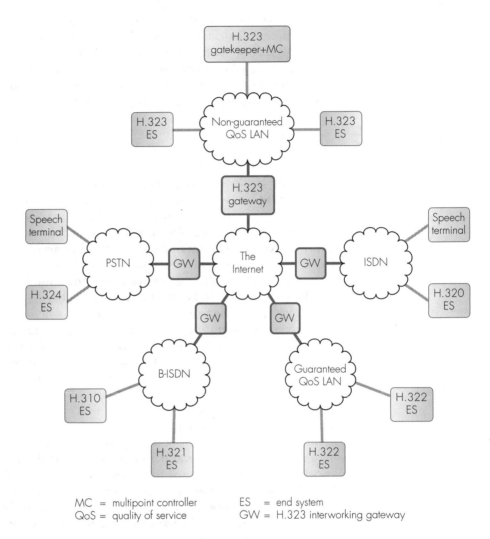

Figure 8.25 Interworking using an H.323 gateway.

Also, as with a gatekeeper, in some instances the gateway minimizes the amount of traffic on the LAN itself.

A second function associated with a gateway relates to address translation. This is necessary when interworking between end systems that are attached to different networks because each uses a different addressing scheme. For example, in the case of a LAN that uses the TCP/IP protocol set, the address of an end system is an IP address while with a PSTN or an ISDN the address is a conventional telephone number, all of which have a different format. Also, in the case of a LAN, end systems (computers in practice) are often referred to by a symbolic name rather than by their IP address. So to simplify interworking, all the end systems on a LAN are given an alias PSTN and/or ISDN number that can be used by a caller from outside that is connected to either a PSTN or an ISDN. Similarly, all the end systems that are external to the LAN can be allocated an alias IP address or symbolic name. The gatekeeper then performs the necessary translations between the different address types during the call setup procedure.

8.7 SNMP

The simple network management protocol (SNMP) is concerned not with providing Internet-wide application services to users – SMTP, FTP, and so on – but rather with the management of all the networking equipment and protocols that make up the Internet. As we saw in earlier chapters, the Internet is composed of a range of different items of networking equipment. These include LAN bridges, subnet routers, access gateways, interior gateways/routers, exterior gateways, communication links/subsystems, and so on, all of which need to be functioning correctly.

Clearly, in any networking environment, if a fault develops and service is interrupted, users will expect the fault to be corrected and normal service to be resumed with a minimum of delay. This is often referred to as **fault management**. Similarly, if the performance of the network – for example, its response time or throughput – starts to deteriorate as a result of, say, increased levels of traffic in selected parts of the network, users will expect these to be identified and additional equipment/transmission capacity to be introduced to alleviate the problem. This is an example of **performance management**. In addition, most of the protocols associated with the TCP/IP suite have associated operational parameters, such as the time-to-live parameter associated with the IP protocol and the retransmission timer associated with TCP. As a network expands, such parameters may need to be changed while the network is still operational. This type of operation is known as **layer management**. Others include **name management**, **security management** and **accounting management**.

Associated with each managed element – a protocol, bridge, gateway, and so on – is a defined set of management-related information. This includes variables – also known as **managed objects** – that can be either read or written to by the network manager via the network. It also includes, when appropriate, a set of **fault reports** that are sent by a managed element when a related fault occurs. In the case of IP, for example, a read variable may relate to, say, the number of IP datagrams/packets discarded when the time-to-live parameter expires, while a write variable may be the actual time-to-live timeout value. Similarly, in the case of an exterior gateway, if a neighbor gateway ceases to respond to HELLO messages, in addition to modifying its routing table to reflect the loss of the link, the gateway may create and send a fault report – via the network – to alert the management system of the problem. If the management system receives a number of such reports from other neighbors, it can conclude that the gateway is probably faulty and not just a communications line failure.

SNMP is an application protocol so a standard communication platform must be used to enable associated messages – PDUs – to be transferred concurrently with the messages relating to user services. To achieve this, normally SNMP uses the same TCP/IP protocols as the user application protocols. The general scheme is shown in Figure 8.26.

The role of the SNMP is to allow the **manager process** in the manager station to exchange management-related messages with the management processes – each referred to as a **management agent** – running in the various managed elements: hosts, gateways, and so on. The management process in these elements is written to perform the defined management functions

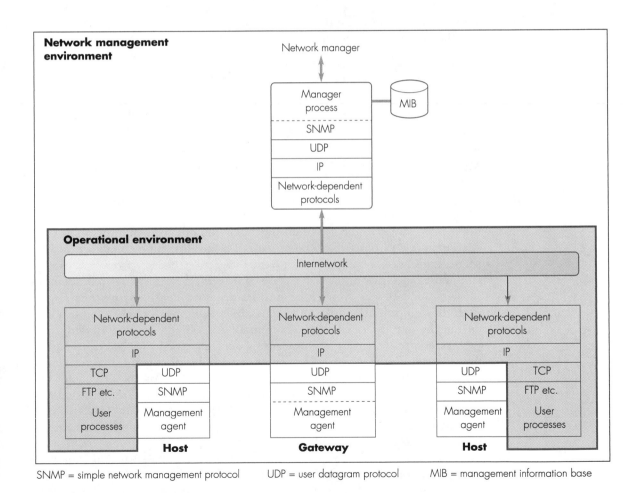

SNMP = simple network management protocol   UDP = user datagram protocol   MIB = management information base

Figure 8.26 Network management schematic and terminology.

associated with that element. Examples include responding to requests for specified variables (counts), receiving updated operational variables, and generating and sending fault reports.

Management information associated with a network/internet is kept at the network manager station (host) associated with that network/internet in a **management information base** (**MIB**). A network manager is provided with a range of services to interrogate the information in the MIB, to initiate the entry and collection of additional information, and to initiate network configuration changes. Clearly, the manager station is the nerve center of the complete network, so strict security and authentication mechanisms are implemented. Normally, there are various levels of authority depending on the operation to be performed. In large internetworks like the Internet, multiple manager stations are used, each responsible for a particular part of the Internet. Examples include each campus/enterprise access network, each regional/national network, the global backbone network and its gateways, and so on. We shall describe first the structure of the management information associated with the Internet and then the operation of the SNMP protocol.

8.7.1 Structure of management information

The management agent software in each networking element maintains a defined set of variables – managed objects – which are accessible by the network manager process using SNMP. In some instances, a variable can only be read (read-only) and in others it can also be written to (read-write). The MIB contains a similar set of variables/objects each of which reflects the current value/state of the same variable in the managed element.

Clearly, in a large network/internet, the managed equipment may come from a variety of different vendors, each with its own preferred processor/ microprocessor. Hence, since all the management information relating to each item of equipment is to be processed by a single management process – often running on a computer that has a different processor from that used in the managed equipment – it is essential to ensure that the management information relating to each item of equipment has the same meaning in both the equipment and the manager station. One way of achieving this is to define the data types of each of the managed objects associated with each item of equipment using an abstract syntax such as **ASN.1**. Then, to ensure that the value(s) associated with each managed object is interpreted in the same way in both the equipment and the manager station, before each value is transferred over the network it is first converted into the related standard transfer syntax using the basic encoding rules associated with ASN.1. This is now the standard approach used with most network management systems including that associated with the Internet.

The current version of the MIB for the Internet is **MIB-II** and is defined in RFC 1213. The data types of all the variables (managed objects) in the MIB are a subset of the ASN.1 types. These are listed in Figure 8.27(a). In addition, a number of subtypes are used and a selection of these, together with a description of their use, is given in Figure 8.27(b).

(a)

Simple types:	INTEGER	Constructed types:	SEQUENCE
	BITSTRING		SEQUENCEOF
	OCTETSTRING		CHOICE
	Display String		
	NULL		
	OBJECT IDENTIFIER		

(b)

Subtypes:	IpAddress	–	OCTETSTRING of length 4 (IP address in dotted decimal)
	PhyAddress	–	OCTETSTRING of length 6 (MAC address)
	Counter32	–	a 32-bit counter, that increments modulo 2^{32}
	Gauge32	–	an unsigned integer in the range 0 to $2^{32}-1$
	Integer32	–	a 32-bit INTEGER
	TimeTicks	–	a 32-bit counter that increments at $1/100$s intervals

(c)

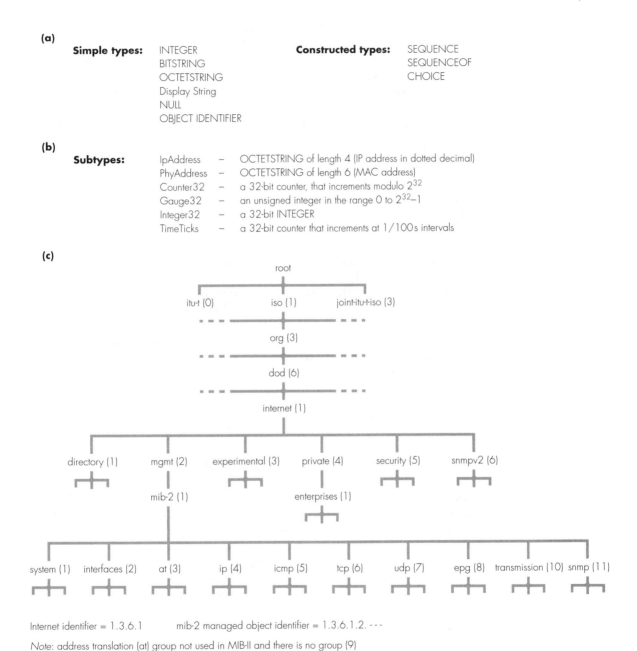

Internet identifier = 1.3.6.1   mib-2 managed object identifier = 1.3.6.1.2. - - -

Note: address translation (at) group not used in MIB-II and there is no group (9)

Figure 8.27 Structure of management information: (a) ASN.1 types used; (b) subtypes; (c) portion of ASN.1 object naming tree relating to the Internet.

The OBJECT IDENTIFIER data type is used to identify a managed object within the context of an internationally defined object naming tree. The portion of this tree that relates to the Internet MIB is shown in Figure 8.27(c).

As we can see, each branch node in the tree is identified by means of a label and a number. A specific node is then identified by listing either the label – together with its number – or simply the number of each branch node starting at the root. In this way, all the managed objects within the total Internet MIB can be uniquely identified and all start with

iso(1) org(3) dod(6) internet(1) mgmt(2) mib-2(1) ...

or, more usually,

1.3.6.1.2.1 ...

Note that the address translation (*at*) group – arp and rarp – is not present in MIB-II as this is now part of the *ip* group. Note also that there is no group (9) and that path 1.3.6.1.4.1 is defined for vendor-specific MIBs. This is necessary to ensure that there is no ambiguity when equipment from a number of different vendors is being used.

Each item of equipment that is to be managed, and the various managed objects associated with it, are defined using the object name tree shown in Figure 8.27(c) as a template. The system (1) group contains a number of variables that include the name (textual description) of the equipment, the vendor's identity, the hardware and software it contains, the domain name of the equipment, and its location on the Internet. All the management information that is subsequently obtained from this location relates to the given named item of equipment in the object name tree.

Each managed object can be defined either as an individual entity or, more usually, as a member of a larger group of related objects. Also related groups of objects can be defined in the form of a module. For example, a group may contain all the managed objects (variables) associated with a particular protocol such as IP, while a module may contain the complete set of managed object groups associated with a particular item of equipment.

Each managed object definition is in the form of a macro with a minimum of four defined parameters associated with it. An example of an object/variable definition relating to the eighteenth variable in the IP group is as follows:

IpFragFails OBJECT TYPE
SYNTAX Gauge32   -- a count value up to $2^{32}-1$
MAX-ACCESS read-only   -- the manager station can only read this object
STATUS current   -- the object is currently supported
DESCRIPTION "Number of IP datagrams discarded because don't fragment flag set"
::={ip18}

As we can see, the object/variable name precedes the reserved word OBJECT TYPE. The meanings of the four required parameters associated with each object definition are:

- SYNTAX: defines the data type of the object;
- MAX-ACCESS: defines whether the variable is read-only or read-write (as viewed from the manager station);
- STATUS: indicates whether the variable is current or obsolete;
- DESCRIPTION: an ASCII string describing what the object is used for. When the macro is invoked, the final ::= sign places the variable into the object name tree of the device.

When a number of groups are collectively defined in a module, the module is defined using a macro that starts with MODULE-IDENTITY. Its parameters include the name and address of the implementer of the module and its revision history. This is followed by an OBJECT-IDENTITY macro, which identifies where the module is located in the object name tree, and a list of OBJECT TYPE macros.

Each managed object in the MIB is uniquely identified and some examples relating to the *ip* group are shown in Figure 8.28. As we can see, an object can be either a simple variable with a single value – for example *ipForwarding(1)* – or a table containing a set of variables – for example *ipAddrTable(21)*. The object identifier of a simple variable in the MIB is the name/identifier of the variable/object with .0 appended to it. For example, the simple variable *ipForwarding* – which indicates whether the system is forwarding IP datagrams (= 1) or not (= 2) – is accessed using either *ipForwarding.0* or, more specifically, as 1.3.6.1.2.1.4.1.0 since this is the form

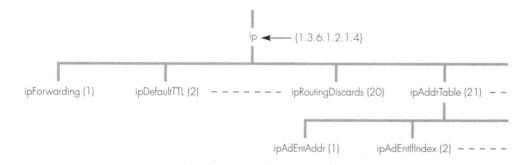

ipDefaultTTL identifier = 1.3.6.1.2.1.4.2.0
ipAdEntAddr identifier = 1.3.6.1.2.1.4.21.1

Figure 8.28 Example MIB objects in the *ip* group.

used by the SNMP protocol to transfer the value over the Internet. In the case of a table of values, normally the index used is the name/identifier of the table and this is then followed by a string of get-next value commands until the complete table of values has been obtained. For example, assuming the table *ipAddrTable(21)* – which contains the list of addresses (IP address, subnet mask) and other information – this would first be accessed using *ipAddrTable* – 1.3.6.1.2.1.4.21.

8.7.2 Protocol

As we can deduce from the previous section, the management of an item of equipment – host, router, and so on – involves the manager process reading the current value of a defined set of variables (managed objects) that are being maintained by the agent process in the equipment and also with transferring a value to the agent for writing into a given variable. It also involves receiving fault reports from the agent in the equipment should these occur. To perform these functions, there is a set of request-response messages supported by the SNMP and also a separate command – known as a trap – message for fault reporting. The list of message/PDU types used in SNMPv1 are defined in RFC 1157. They are summarized in Figure 8.29(a).

Each SNMP message is transferred over the Internet as a separate entity using UDP. The UDP well-known port number of the SNMP in the agent for the three request messages is port 161 and that in the manager station for trap messages port 162. As we can deduce from this, the use of UDP as the transport protocol means that there is no guarantee that a message is delivered. Hence when this is deemed to be necessary, a timer is often used and, if a response is not received within a defined time interval, the request is resent.

The role of each of the five messages that are used is as follows:

■ *Get-request*: this is used by the manager to get the current value(s) of one or more named variables from an agent. The agent then returns the value(s) using a *Get-response* message. The name/identity of each variable is in its numeric form and each value in the response message is encoded using the basic encoding rules of **ASN.1**. Each returned value is in the form of a variable-length byte/octet string comprising a type, length, and value field. In the case of the *Get-request* message, the type of each value field is set to Null;

■ *Get-next-request*: this is used by the manager to get the next variable that is located in the MIB name tree immediately following each variable in the list of names in the message. These are then returned in a *Get-response* message. This type of message is used primarily to obtain the consecutive values relating to a table variable;

■ *Set-request*: this is used by the manager to write a given set of values into the corresponding named variables;

(a)

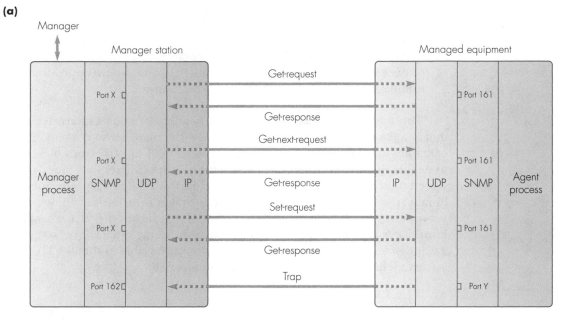

Port X/Y = ephemeral ports

(b)

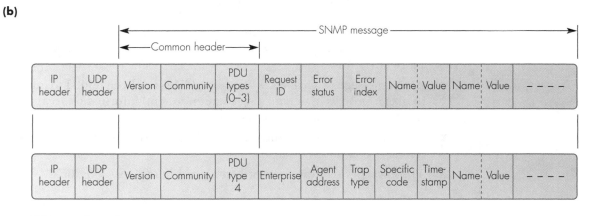

PDU type 0 = Get-request
          1 = Get-next-request
          2 = Set-request
          3 = Get-response
          4 = Trap

Figure 8.29 SNMPv1 messages/PDUs: (a) types and their sequence; (b) formats.

- *Trap*: this is used by the agent in the equipment identified in the *enterprise* field to notify the manager of the occurrence of a previously defined event. The event type is specified by the value in the *trap type* field together with the value in the specific code field. The time of occurrence of the event is specified in the *time-stamp* field and, where appropriate, a number of related variable values may be returned.

The *community* field in the common header contains a character string that is a password in cleartext exchanged by the manager and agent. Typical examples are public and secret. The *request ID* field in PDU types 0–3 is used to enable the manager to relate a response to a specific request message. It is selected by the manager and is returned in the related response message. Finally, the *error status* is an integer value that is returned by an agent in a *Get-response* message. For example, a value of 0 indicates no errors, a value of 1 indicates the response is too big to fit into a single SNMP message, and a value of 2 indicates that there is a nonexistent variable in the list. The latter is then identified by the value in the *error index* field.

SNMPv2

SNMP is continuously evolving and there is now a second version defined in RFC 1441. This is directed primarily at internets in which multiple manager stations are involved. The main additions in SNMPv2 are:

- A new message type called *Get-bulk-request*. This has been added to enable the retrieval process of the contents of large tables to be carried out more efficiently.
- A new message type called *Inform-request*. This has been added to enable a manager process in one manager station to send information to a manager process in another manager station.
- An additional MIB for handling the variables associated with manager-to-manager communication.
- The encryption of the password contained in the *community* field.

Summary

A summary of the topics discussed in this chapter is given in Figure 8.30.

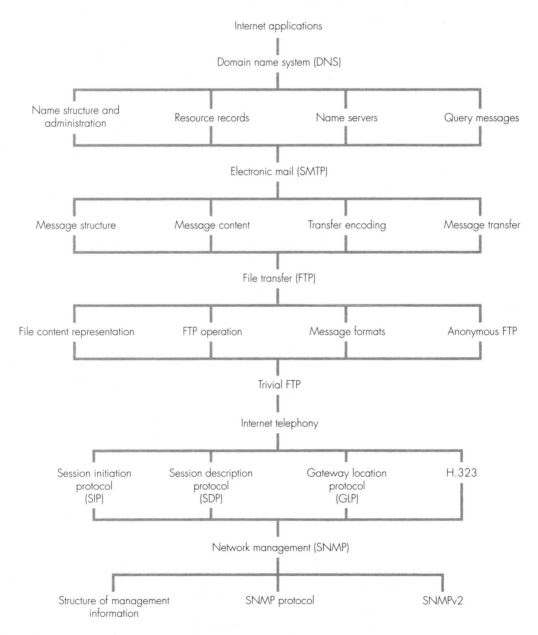

Figure 8.30 Internet applications summary.

Exercises

Section 8.2

8.1 Explain why a domain name system (DNS) is required with the Internet and describe its main functional parts.

8.2 In relation to the DNS, explain why a hierarchical naming structure is used instead of a flat structure.

8.3 Show the structure adopted for the DNS in the form of a diagram. Include in your diagram:
   (i)   the root domain,
   (ii) a selection of generic domains,
   (iii) a selection of country domains,
   (iv) some examples of fully qualified domain names.

8.4 Each domain name in the DNS name space/database has a resource record associated with it. With the aid of diagrams, explain:
   (i)   the format of a resource record,
   (ii) the format used for a domain name,
   (iii) a selection of the resource record types,
   (iv) the use of the time-to-live field.

8.5 Show in outline the format of a DNS query and response message.
   Hence give an example of a query relating to a type-A name-to-address resolution query. State the use of the identification and flag fields used in the query header.

8.6 Explain the meaning of the following terms relating to the administration of DNS name servers:
   (i)   zones,
   (ii) primary name server,
   (iii) secondary name server,
   (iv) authoritative (resource) records.

8.7 With the aid of a diagram, show the sequence of query/response messages that are exchanged to carry out a local name-to-address resolution. Include in your diagram a client host, a local name server, and a server host. Also include the resolver and the set of higher-level protocols that are used in each.

8.8 With the aid of a diagram, show the sequence of query/response messages that are exchanged to carry out a recursive name-to-address resolution. Include in your diagram a root name server, a top-level name server, and a lower-level name server.

8.9 With the aid of a diagram, show the sequence of query/response messages that are exchanged to carry out an iterative name-to-address resolution. Include in your diagram a top-level name server and a lower-level name server.

8.10 Explain the meaning of the term "pointer query" and why pointer queries cannot be resolved using the database structure shown in Figure 8.1. Hence with the aid of a diagram, show the extension to this structure that is used with pointer queries. Give an example showing how an IP address in a query message is resolved into a host name.

Section 8.3

8.11 With the aid of a diagram, explain the function/meaning of the following terms relating to e-mail over the Internet. Include in your diagram two communicating hosts and two related mail servers. Also include the structure of the messages during their transfer over the access networks and the Internet:
   (i)   user agent,
   (ii) message transfer agent,
   (iii) POP3,
   (iv) message transfer system,
   (v)   SMTP.

8.12 List a selection of the fields that are present in a message header and the envelope header of an e-mail message. Identify the use of each field in relation to the diagram you used in Exercise 8.11.
   Show how user-defined fields are added to the header and give an example of their use.

8.13 Explain the transfer syntax that is used for both the contents of a text-only e-mail message and all the header fields. Include in your description how each field is delimited and how the end of the message header is indicated.

8.14 List a selection of the additional header fields that are used with MIME. Explain the use of each field and how the recipient UA determines the type of contents that are present in the message body and their transfer syntax.

8.15 By means of an example, show how a short message can be sent in both richtext and plaintext. Include the MIME headers that are required and how each form of the message is separated. Is the order of the two message types important?

8.16 Explain the transfer encoding scheme that is used to transfer messages comprising strings of 8-bit bytes. Include in your explanation the use of Base64 and how this relates to NVT ASCII.

8.17 A binary file containing a string of 8-bit audio samples is to be sent in an external file attached to an e-mail message. Assuming the first three bytes in the file are:

    10010101   11011100   00111011

use the Base64 table in Table 8.2 and the list of ASCII codewords in Figure 1.14 to show how these three bytes are converted and sent in NVT ASCII. Show also how the recipient UA determines the original three bytes from the received NVT ASCII string.

8.18 With the aid of a diagram, explain the function of the various components that make up the application process in a mail server to transfer an e-mail message over the Internet. Include in your diagram the protocol stack that is used in two peer mail servers and also how the UA in each server interacts with the UA in each of the client hosts.

8.19 Using the list of SNMP command and response messages given in Figure 8.12, show a typical message interchange between an MTA client and an MTA server to transfer an e-mail message over the Internet.

8.20 With the aid of a diagram, explain how e-mail messages are transferred across dissimilar networks using an e-mail gateway.

Section 8.4

8.21 With the aid of a diagram, describe the role of the control and data transfer parts of the AP in both a client and a server to transfer the contents of a file over a TCP/IP network using the file transfer protocol (FTP). Include in your description how the FTP in the client and the server are involved in the establishment and closing down of a TCP connection.

8.22 With the aid of a time sequence diagram, use the list of FTP command and reply messages given in Table 8.3 to show a typical exchange of messages to carry out the transfer of a named file from the file system on a server to the file system on a client. Explain how the port numbers in both the client and server sides are determined.

8.23 Outline the steps that are taken by a user to log in to a remote server using anonymous FTP. Explain how the server side performs a check on the user before granting the user access.

Section 8.5

8.24 Explain how trivial FTP (TFTP) is different from FTP. Give an example of the use of each protocol.

8.25 List the five message types associated with TFTP. Hence show an example message exchange that illustrates the main features of the protocol. Include in your example how the sending side detects a lost/corrupted data message and a lost/corrupted acknowledgment message. Also include the use of a LAST ACK timer.

Section 8.6

8.26 Outline the different types of call/session associated with Internet telephony. Hence identify the main requirements of the set of signaling protocols that are associated with it, namely, the session initiation protocol (SIP), the session description protocol (SDP), and the gateway location protocol (GLP).

8.27 By means of a diagram, identify the protocol stack that is present in each host device that wishes to take part in an Internet telephony call/session. Describe briefly the role of each protocol.

8.28 In relation to the SIP, explain briefly the usage of the following (SIP) message types: INVITE, ACK, REGISTER, OPTIONS, CANCEL and BYE.

8.29 List a selection of the header fields associated with a SIP INVITE message and state their use. Give an example of a SIP address.

8.30 Outline how a user informs the system that he or she can be contacted at a number of different locations using a SIP REGISTER message.

8.31 With the aid of a diagram, explain how a call/session is set up using SIP between a user and a called user who is currently located at their primary SIP address. Include in your diagram the proxy server at each of the sites involved and the protocol stack that is used in both hosts and proxy servers. Explain clearly the role that is carried out by the proxy servers.

8.32 With the aid of a diagram, explain how the sequence followed in Exercise 8.31 is different when the called user is currently located at a secondary address. Explain clearly the role carried out by the redirect server in setting up the call/session.

8.33 Assuming the session description protocol is being used, explain the use of the following fields that may be present in the body part of a SIP INVITE message:
(i) media streams,
(ii) stream address,
(iii) start and stop times.

8.34 With the aid of a diagram, explain how interworking between a host that is attached to an IP network and a terminal equipment – a telephone for example – that is attached to a PSTN/ISDN is carried out. Include in your diagram a signaling/media gateway and a location server. Hence explain the role of the gateway location protocol (GLP) in relation to the interworking procedure.

Section 8.7

8.35 Describe the role of the simple network management protocol (SNMP) in relation to the Internet. Include in your description the role of fault, performance, and layer management and the meaning of the term "managed object".

8.36 By means of a diagram, show the protocol stack associated with a host and a router that enables them to be managed from a remote management station attached to the Internet. Include in your diagram a management agent and a manager process and explain how the two interact.

8.37 Explain the role of the management information base (MIB). Also explain why ASN.1 is used to define the structure of all the management information that it contains.

8.38 All managed objects within the Internet are identified within the context of an internationally defined object naming tree. By means of a diagram, show the structure of this tree down to a level that includes the various managed objects in a particular item of equipment. Give an example of the identifier of one of the managed objects in the tree.

8.39 Using the object naming tree you derived as part of Exercise 8.37 as a template, explain how a specific managed object within a particular item of equipment is (uniquely) identified.

8.40 By means of an example, show how a managed object/variable relating to the IP protocol is defined. Include in your definition an OBJECT TYPE, SYNTAX, STATUS and DESCRIPTION parameter. State the role of each parameter and how the variable is placed in the object name tree of the device in the MIB.

8.41 By means of examples, show how each managed object/variable in the MIB is identified uniquely. Use for example purposes a variable with a single value and also one comprising a table of values.

8.42 With the aid of a diagram, list the five message/PDU types associated with SNMPv1. Include in your diagram the protocol stack and the well-known port numbers that are used.

Explain briefly the role of each of the five message types and how a lost message can be detected.

8.43 With the aid of the SNMP message/PDU formats defined in Figure 8.29(b), explain how a manager process obtains the current value of a named variable – managed object – from the agent process in a specified item of (managed) equipment. Include in your explanation the use of the Community, RequestID, Error Status and Error Index fields in the SNMP messages/PDUs.

8.44 Outline the extensions to SNMPv1 that are present in SNMPv2. Hence explain how the security features of SNMPv1 have been enhanced.

chapter 9

the World Wide Web

9.1 Introduction

The World Wide Web – normally abbreviated to "the Web" or sometimes "the Net" – is a vast collection of electronic documents each composed of a linked set of pages written in HTML. The documents are stored in files on many thousands of computers that are distributed around the global Internet. The concepts behind the Web were conceived in 1989 by Tim Berners-Lee when he was working at the European Particle Physics Laboratory, CERN. An agreement was signed in 1994 between CERN and the Massachusetts Institute of Technology, MIT, to set up a consortium whose aim was to further develop the Web and to standardize the protocols associated with it. The National Center for Supercomputing Applications (NCSA) also made a major contribution to the current widespread use of the Web with the development of MOSAIC, which was the first interactive Web browser based on a graphical user interface. Since that time, many related developments have taken place and, in terms of volume, the Web is now the largest source of data transferred over the Internet.

In this chapter we first present an overview of the operation of the Web and the essential protocols and standards associated with it. We then expand upon these descriptions as we discuss the following:

- **URLs and HTTP**: a URL comprises the name of the file and the location of the server on the Internet where the file is stored while HTTP is the protocol used by a browser program to communicate with a server program over the Internet;

- **HTML**: this is used to define how the contents of each Web page are displayed on the screen of the user's machine – a PC, workstation or set-top box – and to set up the hyperlinks with other pages;

- **forms and CGI script**: these are used in e-commerce applications. Fill-in forms are integrated into a Web page and displayed on the screen of the browser machine to get input from the user and a CGI script is then used at the server to process this information;

- **helper applications and plug-ins**: these are used to process and output multimedia information such as audio and/or video that is incorporated into an HTML page;

- **Java applets**: these are separate programs that are called from an HTML page and downloaded from a Web server. They are then run on the browser machine. Typically, they are used for code that may change or to introduce interactivity to a Web page such as for games playing;

- **JavaScript**: this is also used to add interactivity to a Web page but in this case the code is not a separate program but is included in the page"s HTML code;

- **security** in e-commerce applications;

- **the operation of the Web** including the role of search engines and portals.

In relation to HTML and Java/JavaScript, since there are now many books on each of these topics, the aim here is to give sufficient detail for you to build up a working knowledge of them. Further details can then be found in the bibliography for this chapter.

9.2 Overview

As we have just indicated, in the context of multimedia communications, most interactive applications over the Internet are concerned with interactions with a World Wide Web server. Hence in this section we shall identify a selection of the standards that have been defined for use with this type of interactive application. We shall identify and explain the role of these standards by considering various application scenarios.

9.2.1 Information browsing

The most basic type of interaction using the Web is for information browsing since with this, the Web user wishes only to browse through information that has been made available on a particular Web server at a site. Typically, the information comprises an integrated set of one or more Web pages. Each page in the set contains linkages to other pages, which can be located either on the same server or on any other server that is connected to the Internet. Typically, the Web pages are written in the HyperText Markup Language (HTML) and contain all the information necessary both to display the contents of a page – text, images, and so on – on the screen of the user/client machine and also to locate the other pages that have linkages with the page. The general arrangement used for information browsing is as shown in Figure 9.1.

A page is accessed and its contents displayed by means of a program known as a **browser** that runs on the user/client machine. The browser locates and fetches each requested page and, by interpreting the formatting commands that the page contains, the page contents are displayed. In addition, by the user clicking the mouse on a linkage point within the displayed page, the page that is linked to that point is accessed by the browser and displayed in the same way. There are a number of browser programs available, some popular examples being Netscape Navigator, NSCA Mosaic and Microsoft Internet Explorer.

A page can contain two types of text – plaintext and underlined text (hypertext) – tables, images, and sometimes other media such as a sound track or a video clip. In the case of underlined text, in addition to the text, this contains all the information that is necessary for the browser to access the contents of the linked page. This is known as a **hyperlink** and the linkage comprises the name of the application protocol (also known as the **scheme**)

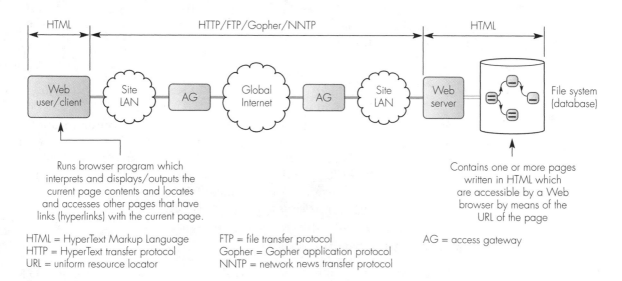

Figure 9.1 Information browsing.

that is to be used – normally the **hypertext transfer protocol** (**HTTP**) – and the symbolic Internet name of the server machine (also known as the **domain**) in which the page is stored. Normally, this contains the top-level page for the site, which in turn contains hyperlinks to all the next-level pages. Alternatively, if a specific page is required, it is also possible to specify the (local) directory and name of the file that contains the required page. Collectively, these fields form what is called the **uniform resource locator** (**URL**) for the page. Two examples are:

http://www.microsoft.com
http://www.mpeg.org/index.html

Note that all the characters can be either upper or lower case.

In the case of images (and other media types), the media type is in the form of a **tag** (**IMG**) with a parameter that indicates the name of the field where the image is stored. These are written in the page text at the point where the image is to be displayed and, when the browser interprets the tag, it reads the (compressed) image from the file. The file name also includes the image format and, by using a corresponding decompression algorithm, the browser displays the (decompressed) image at the appropriate point on the screen. In the case of audio and video, these are output either in a similar way (if the browser contains the appropriate decompression code) or the contents of the file containing the audio/video are passed by the browser to a separate program for output known as a **helper application** or **external viewer**.

Each page is accessed and transferred over a TCP connection using the HTTP application-level protocol. Each HTTP interaction comprises a request from the browser written in the form of an ASCII string and a response from the server written in the RFC 822 format with MIME extensions, both of which we described earlier in Section 8.3.2. In order to allow for the possibility that the linked set of pages may be distributed over a number of different servers, a separate TCP connection is established between the client and server for each interaction and, once the response has been received, the TCP connection is cleared. HTTP is known, therefore, as a **stateless protocol** and we shall describe it in more detail in Section 9.3.2.

In addition to using HTTP to access pages written in HTML, a browser can also access other information using a number of the older application protocols. These allow access to the contents of:

- a file on the client machine on which the browser is running,
- a remote file using the **file transfer protocol** (**FTP**),
- a Gopher (text-only) file using the **gopher protocol**,
- a news article from a UseNet server using the **network news transfer protocol** (**NNTP**).

A summary of the protocols that we have identified is presented in Figure 9.2. In the figure it is assumed that all pages are written in HTML and that

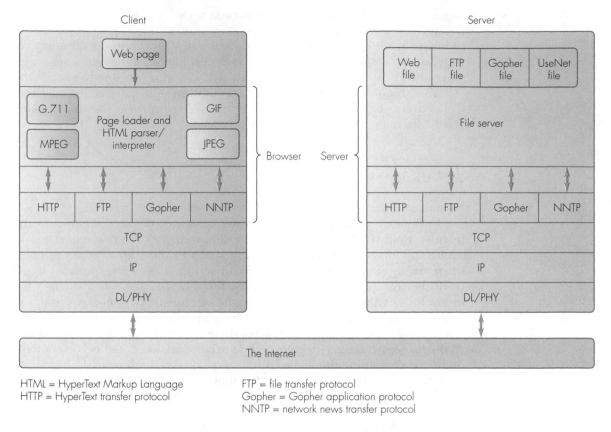

HTML = HyperText Markup Language
HTTP = HyperText transfer protocol

FTP = file transfer protocol
Gopher = Gopher application protocol
NNTP = network news transfer protocol

Figure 9.2 Protocol stack to support information browsing.

the browser, in addition to HTTP, supports all the other application protocols we have just listed. Also, that it has various support facilities to decompress the contents of image, audio and video files that may be included in a page.

9.2.2 Electronic commerce

When browsing the Web for information, the flow of information is unidirectional from the server to the client machine. However, some applications also involve the transfer of information in the reverse direction from the client to a server; for example, after browsing the information at a site, to send details of your credit card in order to purchase, say, a book or theater ticket. This is just one example of what is known more generally as **electronic commerce** or **e-commerce** and there is a range of standards associated with this type of application.

In order to meet this requirement, it is possible to include what is known as a **form** into an HTML page. In the same way that a printed order form contains blank spaces for you to enter your name and other information and to make selections, so a typical HTML form is written to have a similar appearance. The user then uses the mouse and keyboard to enter the requested information and, when all the information has been entered and the appropriate selections made, typically, the user clicks on a symbolic **submit** button to initiate the sending of the entered information back to the server machine.

In addition to having a standardized way for a user of a client machine to enter and initiate the sending of information (forms/submit), there is also a standard for use at the server for processing the received information. This is known as the **common gateway interface** (**CGI**) and, in addition to accepting and processing the input from forms, the CGI may also initiate the output of other (unsolicited) pages that contain related information. The general arrangement that is used to support e-commerce is shown in Figure 9.3 and we shall present further details of forms and CGI in Section 9.4.6.

As we shall see, a second function associated with CGI is that of **network security**. Clearly, when information such as credit card details is sent over a network, it is essential that it is received only by the intended recipient. Hence there are standards for achieving this and, as we shall expand upon in Section 10.8, they are based on either a **private** or **public key encryption** scheme. At the application level, it is also necessary to authenticate that a particular transaction was initiated by the owner of the credit card and not an impostor. Again there are associated standards that we shall also discuss in Section 10.8.

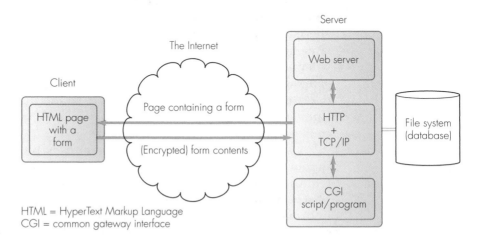

Figure 9.3 Electronic commerce.

9.2.3 Intermediate systems

The discussion in the previous two sections assumed that both the client and server machines were connected directly to the Internet. In some instances, however, this is not the case and communication between the client and server is achieved through a networking device known as an **intermediate system**.

For example, as we explained in Section 3.7, many enterprise networks now use the same set of protocols as are used with the Internet, the enterprise network then being known as an intranet. This is done both to simplify access to the Web from the various sites that make up the enterprise network and also to enable (external) Web users to access information that is stored on a server connected to the enterprise network. Normally, however, for security reasons access to a server that is connected to an intranet is not provided directly but rather through an intermediate system known as a **firewall** or **security gateway**.

As we show in Figure 9.4(a), the gateway controls the flow of information both to and from the intranet. To do this, the gateway intercepts all incoming requests from the Internet for access to the enterprise server and also all responses from the server that need to be forwarded over the Internet. Each Internet packet contains the IP address of both the source of the packet and the intended recipient/destination. Hence in the most basic type of gateway, the gateway simply maintains a separate list of all source and destination IP addresses that are allowed to pass both into and out from the intranet and any packets that have addresses different from these are discarded. This approach is known as **packet filtering** and is often used when the intranet itself comprises a large number of interconnected sites. In practice, however, it is not too difficult for a hacker to break this system and hence an alternative approach that performs the filtering operation at the application layer rather than the IP layer is also used. With this approach, the gateway behaves like the enterprise server to all incoming requests and only if the gateway is satisfied that a request is from a legitimate user is it relayed to the real server. Similarly, all responses from the real server are sent via the gateway. The same controls are applied to internal requests from a client connected to the intranet for an external server.

A second type of intermediate system is required when a browser supports only the HTTP application protocol. To access information that requires a different application protocol from HTTP it is necessary to use what is known as a **proxy server**. As we show in Figure 9.4(b), all requests for information are passed to the proxy server using the HTTP, but a proxy server can also communicate with other servers using application protocols such as FTP, NNTP and Gopher. Hence if the information requested requires a different application protocol from HTTP, the proxy server makes the request on behalf of the client using the appropriate protocol. Similarly, on receipt of the requested information, this is passed to the client using HTTP. As we show in the figure, a proxy server can support a number of clients and,

(a)

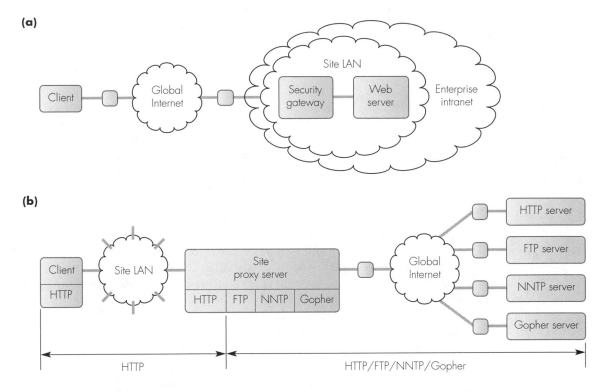

(b)

Figure 9.4 **Intermediate systems: (a) security gateway; (b) proxy server.**

in some instances, performs other functions such as those associated with a security gateway.

9.2.4 Java and JavaScript

A disadvantage of using only HTML to write Web pages is that it is then relatively difficult to incorporate new features into pages – such as a new decoder – since this would necessitate modifications to the browser code. To overcome this constraint, it is possible to implement portions of the code for a page as self-contained subprograms – known as **applets** – which are independent of the HTML interpreter. Then, in the same way that an image is accessed and displayed when its tag is interpreted (by the HTML interpreter), so an applet is identified by a tag and, when this is interpreted, the applet code is loaded and run.

The advantage of using applets is that since each applet is a self-contained program, by implementing those parts of a page that contain code that is likely to change in the form of applets (for example media decoders), then any changes that do occur can be incorporated into the server rather than the browser. For example, if the browser contained only a particular type of image decoder and pages became available that contained images that were encoded using a different coder, then without applets the browser code would need to be modified. By using applets, however, the new decoder could be written as an applet – located either on the same server as the current page or on a different server – and, by simply specifying the applet with an applet tag within the page, so the applet for the new decoder would be loaded and run without any modifications to the browser itself. It is also possible to include applets for sound and video. The sound/video can then be output either when the applet is loaded or under control of the user at the click of the mouse.

An example of a programming language that is used to produce applets that are downloaded from a server is **Java**. This is based on C++ but, in order to obtain portability, there are no input/output statements associated with Java. A program written in Java is compiled to run on any machine. The compiled program is known as an applet and, in order for the applet to be run on a variety of different types of (client) machine, the applet code produced by the compiler is for what is called a **virtual machine**. The compiled/applet code is known as **bytecode** and, to run the applet, the browser, in addition to an HTML interpreter, must also contain an interpreter of the Java bytecode. The general scheme is shown in Figure 9.5.

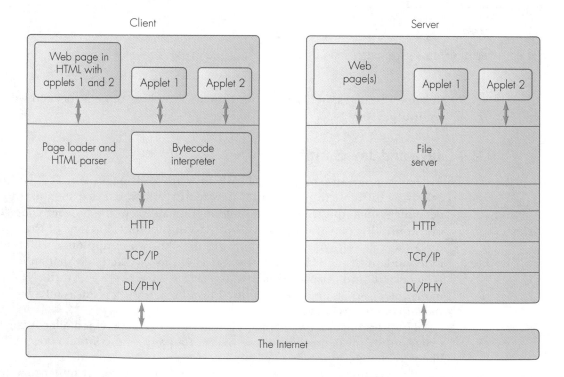

Figure 9.5 Protocol stack to support the browsing of pages containing Java applets.

In addition to downloading applets into pages written in HTML, it is also possible to implement a browser simply as a collection of applets. In this case, at startup, the browser comprises just a Java loader/interpreter and everything else is then implemented in the form of applets that are loaded on demand. Hence to access a page written in HTML, the HTML loader/interpreter would be loaded first and, if the accessed page contains an image, then the corresponding image decoder would be loaded and so on. Again, the advantage of this approach is that new versions of the various software components can be introduced more readily.

It is also possible to embed Java code into an HTML page directly. The language used to do this is called **JavaScript**. We shall return to the subject of Java and JavaScript in Section 9.5.

9.3 URLs and HTTP

The Web is made up of a vast collection of documents/pages that are stored in files located on many thousands of (server) computers distributed around the global Internet. As we saw in Section 9.2.1, using HTML it is possible to create on a server an electronic document in the form of a number of pages with defined linkages between them. A user then gains access to a specific page using a client program called a browser which runs on a multimedia PC/workstation/set-top box that has access to the Internet.

Associated with each access request is the uniform resource locator (URL) of the requested file/page. This comprises the domain name of the server computer on which the file/page is stored and the file name. To obtain a page the browser communicates with a peer application process in the named Web server computer using the HyperText transfer protocol (HTTP). The contents of the named file are then transferred to the browser and displayed on the screen according to the HTML markup descriptions the page contains. A schematic diagram showing this overall mode of operation is given in Figure 9.6. In this section we describe first the structure of URLs and then the operation of HTTP. We defer how a URL is embedded into an HTML page until section 9.4 when we describe HTML in more detail.

9.3.1 URLs

The standard format of the URL of an HTML page consists of:

- the application protocol to be used to obtain the page,
- the domain name of the server computer,
- the pathname of the file,
- the file name.

Thus an example URL referring to an HTML page on the Web is:

http://www.mpeg.org/mpeg-4/index.html

where *http* is the protocol used to obtain the Web page, *www.mpeg.org* is the domain name of the server, */mpeg-4* is the path name, and *index.html* is the file name.

Normally, a browsing session starts by a user entering the URL of the home page associated with a particular document in the *location* field provided by the browser. If the URL of the page is not known then it can be obtained either from the user's own local Web/Net directory – which is built up from previously given or previously used URLs – or by using the search facility supported by the browser. We shall expand upon this feature later in Section 9.7. Once a URL has been entered, the browser proceeds to access the (home) page from the server named in the URL using the specified protocol and the given file name.

Note that when we access most home pages it is not necessary to specify the full URL since the server will look for the file named *index.html* if one is not specified. For example, the home page associated with the above URL could be specified as:

> *http://www.mpeg.org*

Note also that a final forward slash is used to indicate the URL relates to a directory rather than a file name. For example:

> *http://www.mpeg.org/mpeg-4/*

In addition to obtaining a page/file using HTTP, most browsers allow a user to obtain a file using a range of other application protocols. In general,

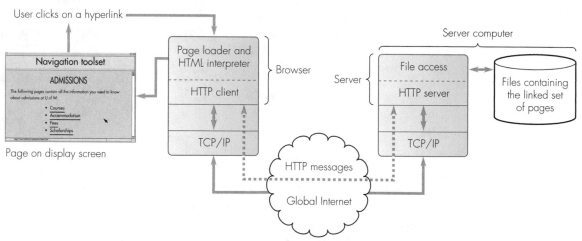

Note: Hyperlinks contain a URL which includes the domain name of the server computer and the name of the file containing the HTML code of the selected page

Figure 9.6 Basic principles and terminology associated with the World Wide Web.

these are standard Internet application protocols that predate the Web. For example, as we saw in Section 8.4, FTP is the standard Internet application protocol used to transfer a file. As a result, many servers still use FTP for all file transfers. Hence to obtain the contents of a file from such a server it is possible to specify *ftp:* as the protocol in a URL instead of *http:*. An example of a typical URL is then of the form:

ftp://yourcompany.com/pub/

Typically, this file will contain the list of publications/files – note that *pub/* indicates a directory – that are available from the file server *yourcompany.com*. Normally, as we saw in Section 8.4.6, a user logs on to most public domain FTP servers using *anonymous* for the user name and his or her e-mail address for the password. Hence these are entered when requested by the browser. The browser then obtains the file using the FTP protocol and displays the contents on the browser screen.

A protocol name of *file:* is used to indicate the file is located on the same computer as the browser; that is, your own computer. This is a useful facility when developing a Web page since it allows you to view the contents of the page before you make it available on the Web. An example URL is:

file://hypertext/html/mypage.htm

Note that since some older versions of DOS allow only three characters in a file name extension, the final *l* of *html* is sometimes missing.

The *news:* protocol relates to an Internet application protocol defined in RFC 977 called the **network news transfer protocol** (**NNTP**). It is used to transfer the text-only messages associated with **UseNet** which is also called **NetNews**. This consists of a world-wide collection of **newsgroups** each of which is a discussion forum on a specific topic. Two examples are COMP, which has topics relating to computers, computer science and the computer industry, and SCI, which has topics relating to the physical sciences and engineering. A person interested in a particular topic can subscribe to be a member of the related newsgroup. A subscriber can then post (send) an article to all the other members of the same newsgroup and receive the articles that are written by all the other members of the same group.

To do this, a user agent similar to that used with SMTP is used. This is called a **news reader** and the protocol that is used to transfer the messages associated with UseNet is NNTP. Some examples of the request/command messages associated with NNTP are:

- LIST: this is used to obtain a list of all the current newsgroups and their articles;
- GROUP *grp*: this is used to obtain a list of the articles associated with the newsgroup *grp*;
- ARTICLE *id*: this is used to obtain article *id*;

■ POST *id*: this is used to send article *id* to the members of a specified newsgroup.

The *news*: protocol enables a member to both read a news article and to post an article from within a Web page. An example of a URL relating to a newsgroup involved in the preparation of HTML documents is:

news:comp.infosystems.www.authoring.html

Note that in this case the two forward slashes following the colon are not required. When this URL is entered, typically, the news reader part of the browser responds by first obtaining the list of articles on this topic using the GROUP command and the NNTP protocol. It then displays the articles on the screen in the form of a scrollable list. The user can then click on a specific article in the list and the browser/news reader will obtain the article contents using the ARTICLE command and display this on the screen. Normally, each article has the e-mail address of the author, his or her affiliation, and the date the article was posted. A similar procedure is followed to post an article using the POST command. Normally, the user is prompted by the news reader for, say, the name of the (local) file containing the article. The file contents are then sent using NNTP.

The *gopher*: protocol relates to an Internet application protocol called Gopher. The Gopher system is similar in principle to the Web inasmuch as it is a global delivery and retrieval system of documents. In Gopher, however, all items of information are text only. When a user logs on to a Gopher server a hierarchical menu of files and directories is presented each of which may have links to the menus on other servers. A user can then access the contents of a file or directory by clicking on it. The *gopher*: protocol enables the user of the browser to do this within a Web page.

The *mailto*: protocol is provided to enable a user to send an e-mail from within a Web page. Typically, this facility is initiated by the user entering a URL with *mailto*: in the protocol part. This is followed by the e-mail address of the intended recipient. Normally, the (e-mail) user agent part of the browser responds by displaying a **form** containing the other (e-mail) header fields at the top (to be filled in) and space for the actual message. A facility is then provided to initiate the sending of the mail, which, typically, is sent using either SMTP or, if the e-mail server supports it, HTTP. An example URL is:

mailto:yourname@youruniversity.edu

Note that the two forward slashes following the colon are not required with this protocol.

Universal resource identifiers (URIs)

A limitation of a URL is that it specifies a single host name. In many instances, however, a Web site may have so many access requests/hits for a particular document/page that copies of the document must be placed on multiple hosts. Also, to reduce the level of Internet traffic, each of these hosts may be geographically distributed around the Internet. To enable this to be implemented, an alternative page identifier called a URI can be specified with some browsers. Essentially, this is a generic URL since, typically, it contains only the file name. The remaining parts of the URL are determined by the context in which the URI is given and these are filled in by the browser itself. We shall give an example of this in the next section when we discuss cache servers.

9.3.2 HTTP

HTTP is the standard application protocol – also known as a method – that is used to obtain a Web page and also other items of information relating to a page such as an image or a segment of audio or video. The earlier version of HTTP is defined in RFC 1945 and a later version (1.1) in RFC 2068. It is a simple request-response protocol: the browser side sends a request message and the server side returns a response message. Figure 9.7(a) shows the protocol stack associated with Web browsing, and a selection of the *commands/methods* associated with request messages, together with their use, are shown in part (b) of the figure.

In general, these are self explanatory. Note, however, that the GET method is used also to, say, obtain an image or segment of audio – shown as a block of data – from a named file. We shall expand upon this in later sections. Also, as we shall see in Section 9.4.6, the POST method is used to send the information entered by a user in e-commerce applications.

The well-known port number of HTTP is port 80. The Web server application process (AP) at each Web site continuously listens to this port for an incoming TCP connection request (SYN) from a Web browser. Note that in a Unix machine the AP is referred to as a **daemon** and the HTTP in these machines is sometimes called **HTTPD**. When a browser has an HTTP request message to send, it initiates the establishment of a new TCP connection to port 80 on the named server in the URL. It then initiates the sending of the request message over the established connection and, with earlier versions of HTTP, after the related response message has been received correctly by the browser, the server initiates the release of the connection. The TCP connection associated with this mode of operation is called **nonpersistent**.

As we can deduce from our earlier discussion of TCP in Section 7.3.2, the use of a new TCP connection for each request/response message transfer has a number of disadvantages. Firstly, when accessing a Web page that contains multiple entities within it – an image for example – a time delay is incurred for each entity that is transferred while a new TCP connection is established. This is a function of the network round-trip time (RTT), which can be significant. Secondly, each new transfer starts with the slow start procedure and hence for a large entity, this can lead to additional delays.

(a)

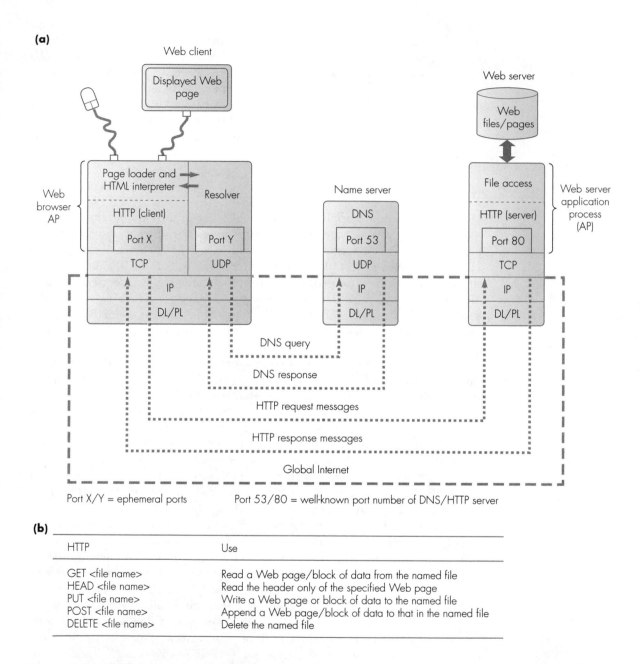

Port X/Y = ephemeral ports   Port 53/80 = well-known port number of DNS/HTTP server

(b)

HTTP	Use
GET <file name>	Read a Web page/block of data from the named file
HEAD <file name>	Read the header only of the specified Web page
PUT <file name>	Write a Web page or block of data to the named file
POST <file name>	Append a Web page/block of data to that in the named file
DELETE <file name>	Delete the named file

Figure 9.7 HTTP principles: (a) protocol stack; (b) a selection of the requests/methods supported.

To reduce the effect of these delays, when multiple entities are specified within a page – and hence to be transferred – many browsers set up a number of TCP connections so that each entity can be transferred concurrently. Typically, a browser may establish up to five or even ten concurrent connections. However, although this can reduce the overall time delay associated with a Web access, the use of multiple connections leads to added overheads at both the client and server sides since both must maintain state information for each of the connections. This can be particularly significant for a popular/busy server, which may get many hundreds of concurrent requests.

Hence with later versions of HTTP – version 1.1 onwards – unless informed differently, the server side leaves the initial TCP connection in place for the duration of the Web session. The TCP connection is then called **persistent** and, once in place, the browser may send multiple requests without waiting for a response to be received. Typically, the end of a session is determined by a timer expiring when no further transfers over the connection take place. Note, however, that the different versions of HTTP can interwork with each other.

Message formats

All HTTP request and response messages are NVT ASCII strings similar to those used with SMTP. With the earlier versions of HTTP – up to HTTP version 0.9 – what are called *simple request/response messages* are used. This means there is no type information associated with the request message, which comprises only the method – GET, HEAD, and so on – followed by the related file name in the form of an ASCII string. The response message is in the form of a block of ASCII characters with no headers and no MIME extensions. An example of a simple HTTP request message is:

GET/mpeg-4/index.html

which is sent over the previously established TCP connection to the related server AP.

With the later versions of HTTP – version 1.0 onwards – MIME extensions are supported using what are called *full request/response messages*. To discriminate a full request from a simple request, a field containing the HTTP version number is added to the request line. This is followed by the text associated with a number of other RFC 822 headers, each of which is on a separate line. These were given earlier in Table 8.1 and include:

- **general headers**: these do not relate to the entity to be transferred and an example is the MIME version number;
- **request headers**: these are used to specify such things as the sender"s name/e-mail address and the media types and encodings that the browser supports;

- **entity headers**: these relate to the entity to be transferred and include the content type and, when sending an entity, the content length.

The end of the header is indicated by a blank line. Then, if the request contains a message body, this is followed by the entity being transferred such as a block of HTML text – a script – relating to a page.

The header fields associated with a full response message start with the HTTP version number followed by the response status code. Some examples are:

200   accepted

304   not modified: the requested page has not been modified

400   bad request

404   not found: requested page does not exist on this server.

This is followed by the name and location of the server and, if the response contains an entity in the message body, a *Content-Type:* and a *Content-Length:* field. Also, if the contents relate to a binary file, they are followed by a *Content-Transfer-Encoding: Base64* header field.

An example showing a selection of the header fields associated with a full request/response message interchange is shown in Figure 9.8. The example relates to the transfer of the HTML page with the URL of:

http://www.mpeg.org/mpeg-4/index.html

Hence prior to sending the GET message, a TCP connection to the server *www.mpeg.org* will have been established.

The meanings of the various fields in the request message shown in part (a) of the figure are as follows. The *Connection: close* header line indicates to the server that the browser does not need a persistent connection. The *User-agent:* line contains the name of the browser and its version number. Often the server contains a number of versions of a page and this enables the server to send the version that is best suited to the browser. The *Accept:* line indicates the entity types that the browser is able to accept, which, as we can see, is determined by the compression software/hardware it supports.

The meanings of the various header fields in the response message shown in part (b) are mainly self explanatory. In the example, the body contains an entity comprising a string of NVT ASCII characters representing the HTML text of a Web page. Alternatively, if the *Content-Type:* was, say, *image/jpeg* then a *Content-Type-Encoding: Base64* header field would be present. For a more complete list of the MIME headers you should refer back to Table 8.1 and Figure 8.9 and their accompanying text.

Conditional GET

As we saw earlier in Figure 9.4(b), in many instances a browser does not communicate directly with the required server but rather through an

(a) Example request message relating to a URL of

http://www.mpeg.org/mpeg-4/index.html

```
GET/mpeg-4/index.HTML HTTP/1.1
Connection:close
User-agent: Browser name/version number
Accept: text/html, image/gif, image/jpeg
```

(b) Example response message relating to this request:

```
HTTP/1.1 200 Accepted
Server: Aname
Location: www.mpeg.org
Subject: MPEG home page
Last-Modified: Day/month/year/time
Content-Type: text/html
Content-Length: 7684
```

```
Entity body comprising a string
of 7684 NVT ASCII characters
```

Figure 9.8 An example of a full request/response message relating to HTTP: (a) request message; (b) response message.

intermediate system called a proxy server. In the figure it was assumed that the browsers at a site supported only the HTTP protocol and that the proxy server was used to access the contents of files using different protocols such as FTP and NNTP. As we can deduce from our discussion of URLs, this will avoid each of the browsers having the code of each of these protocols. In addition, however, a proxy server normally caches the Web pages and other entities that it obtains – on behalf of the browsers that it serves – on hard disk. Then, when a browser makes a request for a page/entity that the proxy server has cached, the proxy server can return this directly without going back to the server holding the original source. The latter is called the **origin server** and, when it performs this function, the proxy server is also known as a (Web) **cache server**.

Although caching reduces the response time for subsequent requests for a cached page/entity, there is a possibility that the cached entity may be out of date as a result of the original being modified/updated subsequent to the cache server receiving it. Hence because caching is widely used, an additional request message called a **conditional GET** is used by the cache server to ensure the response messages that are returned to the browsers contain up-to-date information.

A conditional GET request message is one that includes a header line of *If-Modified-Since:* and its use is illustrated in Figure 9.9. To avoid duplication, the header fields that have already been discussed are left out of the messages shown. The following should be noted when interpreting the message sequence.

- It is assumed that the browsers in all the client machines attached to the access network – site/campus LAN, ISP network, and so on – have been configured to send all request messages to the proxy/cache server.

- The sequence starts with a browser requesting an HTML page from the proxy server using a GET request message (1).

- The proxy server has a cached copy of the page and, associated with it, the day/date/time when the page was cached. This is obtained from the *Last-Modified:* header field in the response message returned by the origin server to an earlier request.

- Before returning the cached page to the browser, the proxy server sends a conditional GET request message to the origin server – defined in the page URL – with the date and time the current copy of the page it holds was last modified in the *If-Modified-Since:* header field (2).

- On receipt of this, the origin server checks to see if the requested page has been modified since the date in the *If-Modified-Since:* field.

- In the figure it is assumed that the contents have not been changed and hence the origin server returns a simple response message with a status code of *304 Not modified* in the header and an empty entity body (3).

- On receipt of this, the proxy server returns a copy of the cached page to the browser (4).

In the event that the requested page/entity had been changed, then a copy of the new page/entity would be returned by the origin server. A copy of

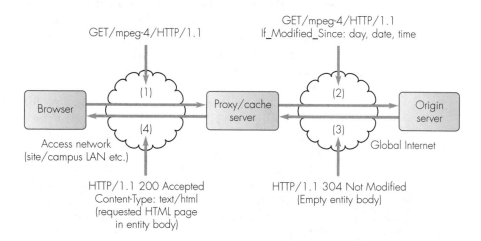

Figure 9.9 Proxy/cache server operation with conditional GET.

the new page would then be cached by the proxy server – together with the date and time from the *Last-Modified:* field – before it is forwarded to the browser. Thus the savings obtained with a cache server come from the absence of an entity body in the response message from the origin server. Clearly for large pages/entities this can be considerable. In addition, further savings can be obtained by also having a higher-level cache server associated with, for example, each regional/national network. The proxy server associated with each access network is then configured to send all request messages to a specified higher-level cache server. In general, the higher the level this is in the Internet hierarchy the more requests it will receive and, as a result, the more cached pages/entities it holds.

9.4 HTML

The HyperText Markup Language, HTML, is the standard language used to write Web pages. As we saw in Section 9.2.1, HTML is the markup language that is used to describe how the contents of a document/page are to be displayed on the screen of the computer by the browser. Moreover, since the markup commands relate to a complete page, the browser automatically displays the page contents within the bounds allocated for the page; that is, irrespective of whether this is a small window on a low resolution screen or a large window on a high-resolution screen.

The markup/format commands are known as directives in HTML and the majority are specified using a pair of **tags**. In addition to the various types of directive associated with a string of text – which specify how the string is to be presented on the display – there are tags to enable a hyperlink to be specified as well as tags to specify an image or a segment of audio or video within a page and how these are to be displayed/output. There are also fill-in forms and other features. In this section we describe how each of these features is specified in HTML. It should be stressed, however, that HTML is continuously being revised and what follows should be considered only as an introduction to the subject.

9.4.1 Text format directives

The HTML text associated with a Web page is written in the ISO 8859-1 Latin-1 character set, which, for the English alphabet, is the same as the ASCII character set. However, for someone creating Web pages in a Latin alphabet, when using an ASCII keyboard, escape sequences must be used. For example, the Latin character *è* is represented by the ASCII string *&egrave* and *é* by *&eacute*.

The HTML text can be entered using either a word processor with facilities for creating and editing an HTML document/page or directly using the facilities provided by a Web browser. Typically, the complete string of characters consists of a number of substrings each of which may be displayed in a different format when the substring is output on the display by the HTML parser/interpreter part of the browser. In order for the interpreter to do this, each substring is sandwiched between a pair of tags that specify the format directive to be used. For example, if the substring

this is easy

is to be displayed in boldface, then this is written as

<B>this is easy</B>

As we can see, the opening tag comprises the format directive (B) between the pair of characters < and > and the closing tag is the same directive between </ and >. Note that the directive itself is case insensitive but normally upper-case is used to make the directives easier to identify. This format is used for a majority of the tags and a selection are listed in Table 9.1.

An example of an HTML script that includes some of these tags is shown in Figure 9.10(b). Typically, since this is the home page of the UoW, its URL would be:

http:www.UoW.edu

The start of a page is indicated in the script by a <HTML> tag and the end of the page by a </HTML> tag. The <HTML> tag is followed by the page header, which is entered between the <HEAD> and </HEAD> tags. Primarily, the header contains the title of the page, which is written between the <TITLE> and </TITLE> tags. Note that the title is not output as part of the displayed page. In some instances, however, it is output by the browser in a field at the top or bottom of the display. The displayed page contents are then entered between the <BODY> and </BODY> tags.

In the example, there is only one heading and this is written between the <H1> and </H1> tags. If there were some subheadings, they would each be defined in the place they are to be displayed using the format:

<H2>Subheading name</H2>

Note, however, that it is the browser that decides the relative size of each heading/subheading on the display screen. Normally, they are in decreasing size with the first-level heading <H1> displayed in the largest font size and, typically, in boldface with one or more blank lines above and below it. Each level of subheading is then displayed in a decreasing size.

Table 9.1 A selection of the HTML text format directive/tags.

Opening tag	Closing tag	Use
<HTML>	</HTML>	Specify the start and end of the complete document/page
<HEAD>	</HEAD>	Specify the start and end of the page header
<TITLE>	</TITLE>	Specify the title of the page. It is not displayed as part of the page
<BODY>	</BODY>	Specify the start and end of the contents of the displayed page
<Hn>	</Hn>	Specify the start and end of a level n heading
<B>	</B>	Display the related text in boldface
<I>	</I>	Display the related text in italics
<UL>	</UL>	Specify the start and end of an unordered/bulleted list
<OL>	</OL>	Specify the start and end of an ordered/numbered list
<LI>		Specifies the start of a listed item
 		Specifies the start of a new line
<P>		Specifies the start of a new paragraph
<A HREF="URL">	</A>	Specify an anchor/link to another page
<A HREF="#NAME">	</A>	Specify an anchor/link to another point in the same page
<!- ->	- ->	Start and end of comments

The <BR> is used to ensure that the welcome message starts on a new line. This is followed by an unordered (bulleted) list of items. These are listed between the <UL> and </UL> tags with each item starting with a single <LI> tag. The default for the start of the items in a first-level list is a solid bullet. In the example, each bulleted item is a hyperlink to a different page and hence starts with the <A HREF = "URL"> tag where A stands for **anchor**. This is followed by the textual name of the hyperlink – for example, The University – that is to appear on the display screen. Also, since this is a hyperlink name, the HTML interpreter displays it highlighted using, for example, an underline – as shown – or, if colored text is being used, a different color. Then, when this is clicked on, the interpreter uses the URL to fetch the related file. The end of a hyperlink is indicated by the </A> tag.

Note that since the prospectus consists of a linked set of pages, all of which are stored at the same site/server, once the full URL of the home page

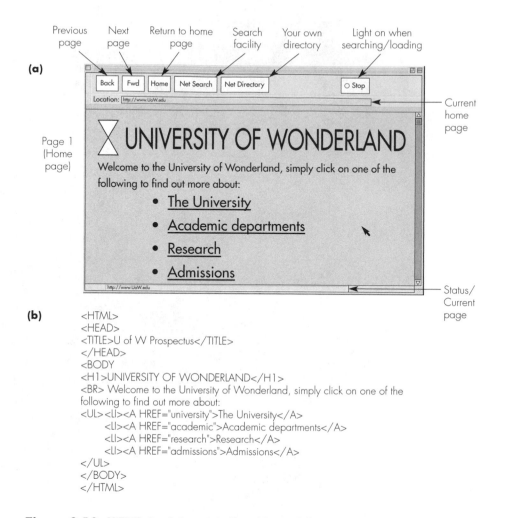

Figure 9.10 HTML text format directives: (a) example Web page; (b) the HTML script for the page.

has been given, any links in the remaining linked set of pages can each use a **relative URL**. This means that the file names used in these URLs are assumed to have the same protocol/method and site/server domain name as that of the home page; that is, in the example, the browser assumes that each is preceded by:

http:www.UoW.edu/

For this reason, therefore, the URL of the home page is said to be an **absolute URL**. Hence as we can deduce from this example, by using relative

URLs in all the remaining linked set of pages, it is then straightforward to relocate them by changing only the (absolute) URL of the home page.

In this example, the page containing the top-level index is relatively short and so fits into the display window. Also, it was assumed that further details relating to each of the listed headings were on a different page and accessed by an external link. However, if the index were larger and could not be displayed in a single window, then the user would have to scroll the page to find the remainder of the index. Alternatively, if the page/index is particularly long, it is sometimes preferable to have internal links within the page.

For example, if the second-level subheadings relating to each first-level heading were all on the same page, then the link associated with each first-level heading would be an internal link. These are specified using the format:

<A HREF "#University">The University</A>

The words *The University* would then be displayed highlighted and, if the user clicks on this, the parser would jump to the point in the current page where the words *The University* next occur and start to display from this point in the page. The related subheadings could then be either internal links if further subheadings are defined or, if not, external links to the pages where the actual descriptions are located.

9.4.2 Lists

The example shown in Figure 9.10(b) contained a single unordered list. In addition, an ordered (numbered) list can be used as well as nested lists of different types. An example of an HTML script that illustrates these features is shown in Figure 9.11(b) and the resulting displayed page is shown in part (a).

As we can see, the listed items appear in the HTML script in the order they are to be displayed. The format directives associated with each item then enable the HTML interpreter in the browser to determine the position of each item in relation to the others. Note that the default for an ordered list is a numeric value but it is also possible to define a number of alternatives. This is done by adding the required type to the opening tag:

<OL TYPE=X>

where X is the type of numbering. For example, X = i selects lowercase roman numerals (i, ii, and so on). It is also possible for a user to define the number he or she wants by using

<OL><LI VALUE=Y>

where Y indicates the number. Note that the default for the start of the items in a second-level unordered list is a hollow bullet and that it is the browser that determines the level of indentation.

(a)

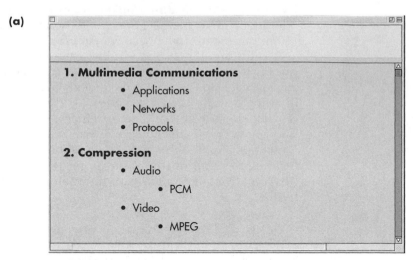

(b)

```
<HTML>
<HEAD><TITLE>Lists</TITLE></HEAD>
<BODY>
<OL><LI>Multimedia Communications
      <UL><LI>Applications
            <LI>Networks
            <LI>Protocols
      </UL>
      <LI>Compression
      <UL><LI>Audio
            <UL><LI>PCM</UL>
            <LI>Video
            <UL><LI>MPEG</UL>
</OL>
</BODY></HTML>
```

Figure 9.11 Lists in HTML: (a) example of displayed page; (b) HTML script for this page.

9.4.3 Color

Color is used in a number of ways by browsers to enhance a displayed page. For example, hyperlinks are often highlighted in the color blue and, when a hyperlink has been selected, normally the color changes from blue to purple. In addition to these colors, however, most browsers allow the user to specify their own color for the background color (BGCOLOR), the text (TEXT), a hyperlink (LINK) and a visited link (VLINK) as part of the <BODY> tag at the head of the HTML script.

The way a color is defined in HTML is determined by the number of bits used to represent each color on the display of the machine the browser is running. This can range from 8 bits through to 24 bits. Normally, each 8 bits is represented by two hexadecimal digits and hence each alternative color to be used is specified using either two (8 bits), four (16 bits) or six (24 bits) hexadecimal digits. For example, if 24 bits are used for each color, normally, the three sets of 8 bits represent the strength of each of the three primary colors (red, green and blue) the color contains. The format used to represent the color is then:

#RRGGBB

where RR are the two hexadecimal digits that represent the strength of the color red, GG the color green and BB the color blue. Hence the three primary colors are represented as:

#FF0000 = red, #00FF00 = green, #0000FF = blue

Some other examples are:

#FFFFFF = white, #FCE503 = yellow, #F1A60A = orange, #000000 = black

Hence if, for example, the background color is to be blue, the text is to be yellow, a hyperlink orange, and a visited hyperlink green, these would be specified as:

<BODY BGCOLOR="#0000FF" TEXT="#FCE503" LINK="#F1A60A" VLINK="#00FF00">

Note, however, that most browsers use a color look-up table (CLUT), which displays only a defined set of 256 colors. Also, a number of these are reserved for the browser's own use. Hence although in theory a vast range of colors can be defined, in practice most browsers will simply approximate most of them to the nearest color-match in the usable colors in their CLUT. Typically, the usable colors that are available consist of any combination of the hexadecimal pairs:

00 33 66 99 CC FF

Hence when defining colors, if these hexadecimal pairs are used then the colors will be displayed in their unmodified form.

9.4.4 Images and lines

Images can be used both as an alternative to a white background for a page and for displaying a specific object within the page itself. Although the image can be in any format, most browsers support only GIF and JPEG images; that is, they only have the software to decompress an image held in either a *gif* or *jpeg* file. Horizontal lines in various forms can also be displayed on a page. We shall outline each feature separately.

Background images

In order to specify an alternative background image for a page, the file containing the image – for example *bgimage.gif* – is specified as part of the <BODY> tag using the format:

<BODY BACKGROUND = "bgimage.gif " >

For example, most Web browsers have a file called *clouds.gif* that is often accessed and used as an alternative background. When the parser encounters this, the interpreter first obtains the contents of the file and, after this has been decompressed, displays this on the screen as the background. The page contents are then superimposed on it.

Images

An image that is displayed from within a page is specified at the point in the HTML script – that is, relative to the other markup directives in the script – where the image is to be displayed using the tag

<IMG SRC="*file name*">

where *file name* is the name of the file containing the image on the current page server. For example, assuming the file name containing the logo/crest of the UoW is *crest.jpeg*, this could be displayed on the page by replacing the first line in the body of the HTML script shown earlier in Figure 9.10(b) with

<IMG SRC="crest.jpeg"><H1>UNIVERSITY OF WONDERLAND</H1>

Note, however, that some later versions of HTML may use the tag <OBJECT> to include an image, where <OBJECT> applies not only to images but also to a number of other data items/objects. We shall expand on this later in Section 9.6.1.

Using the above method it is the browser that ultimately decides on the size and the position of the image. Hence it is possible that the heading will be displayed below the logo/crest with the above script. In addition, however, a number of optional attributes – also called parameters – can be defined with the IMG tag to inform the browser of the required position and other attributes. These include the ALT and the ALIGN attributes. The ALT attribute is used to specify a text string that should be displayed if the browser is not able to display an image. For example,

<IMG SRC="crest.jpeg" ALT"UoW crest">

could be used to display the words *UoW crest* instead of the actual crest/logo if, for example, the user has disabled images or the related decompression software is not supported.

The ALIGN attribute is used to align an image with respect to either the display window or some displayed text. In the first case, the related image can be displayed aligned to the LEFT window edge, which is the default, in the CENTER of the page, or aligned with the RIGHT edge. An example showing a segment of an HTML script to align an image in the center of the page is shown in Figure 9.12(a).

An image can also be aligned with respect to some given text. In this case the text following an IMG tag can start at various specified points relative to the image. For example, the text can start on the first line at the TOP of the image, the MIDDLE, or the BOTTOM. A segment of HTML script showing how the text starts at the middle of the image is shown in Figure 9.12(b).

Normally, before displaying any text that comes after a specified image, the browser waits until it receives the complete image to determine the amount of display space the image needs. For a large image this can delay the display of the complete page. To overcome this (and speed up the display process) the size of the image can be included with the image specification. Also, the size of the margin that should be left around the image. With this information the browser is able to reserve the requisite amount of display space and, while the image is being transferred and displayed, output any remaining text. The format used to do this is:

```
<IMG WIDTH="x" HEIGHT="y" HSPACE="a" VSPACE="b"
SRC="image.gif" >
```

where x, y, a and b are all specified in screen pixels. Note, however, that by specifying the dimensions in pixels the size of the displayed image will depend on the pixel resolution of the display. An image can also be used as a hyperlink by including the image specification within the hyperlink tags:

```
<A HREF="http://www.UoW.edu/images"><IMG
SRC="image.gif" ></A>
```

The displayed image *image.gif* will then be displayed highlighted and the user can click on any part of this to activate the hyperlink.

Lines

A horizontal line – referred to as a rule – can be displayed from within a page using the <HR> tag. The thickness, length, and position of the line/rule can be varied by using attributes. These include:

- SIZE=s: defines the thickness of the line as a multiple of the default thickness;

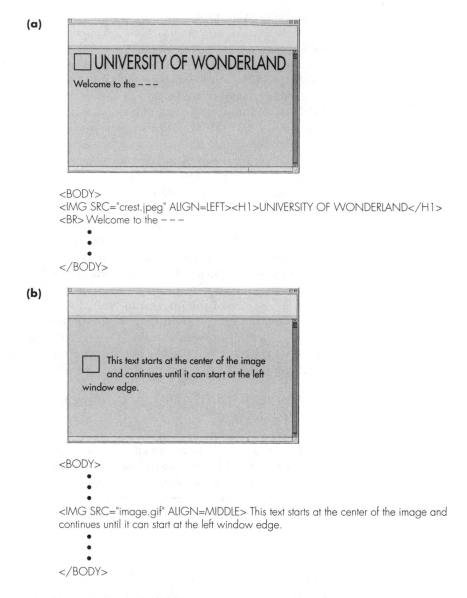

(a)

```
<BODY>
<IMG SRC="crest.jpeg" ALIGN=LEFT><H1>UNIVERSITY OF WONDERLAND</H1>
<BR> Welcome to the – – –
    •
    •
    •
</BODY>
```

(b)

```
<BODY>
    •
    •
    •
<IMG SRC="image.gif" ALIGN=MIDDLE> This text starts at the center of the image and
continues until it can start at the left window edge.
    •
    •
    •
</BODY>
```

Figure 9.12 Aligning in-line images: (a) with respect to the display screen; (b) with respect to subsequent text.

- WIDTH=w: defines the length of the line as a percentage of the width of the display window;
- ALIGN=y: defines whether the line is aligned to the left, center or right of the display window.

An example showing a selection of displayed lines and the related fragment of HTML script is given in Figure 9.13.

9.4.5 Tables

Tables can be used in Web pages not only to display a particular set of data in tabular form but also to control the overall layout of a page. A table consists of one or more rows and one or more columns. The intersection of each row and column is called a **cell** and a cell can contain a string of text, a number, an image, a hyperlink or, if required, another table. Each column can have a heading and, if required, a heading can span multiple columns. A selection of the tags that can be used to create a table are shown in Figure 9.14(a), an example of a displayed table in part (b) of the figure, and the HTML script relating to this in part (c).

As we can see, both the headings and the contents of each cell are defined a row at a time starting at the left column using the <TH> and <TD> tags respectively. Note that, normally, the column headings are displayed in boldface

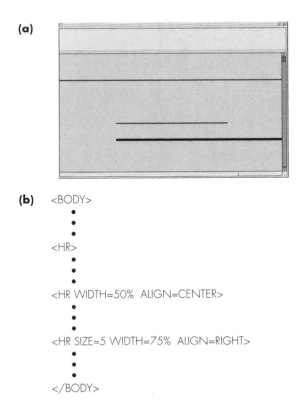

(a)

(b) <BODY>
   •
   •
   •
<HR>
   •
   •
   •
<HR WIDTH=50% ALIGN=CENTER>
   •
   •
   •
<HR SIZE=5 WIDTH=75% ALIGN=RIGHT>
   •
   •
   •
</BODY>

Figure 9.13 Horizontal lines: (a) a selection of displayed lines; (b) associated fragments of HTML.

by the browser and that the <CAPTION> tag is defined within the pair of <TABLE> tags. Also, as we can deduce from this example, an unboxed table can be used to control the layout of a page by dividing the page into regions/cells.

The position of the table on the display and the size of each cell are determined by the browser based on the maximum length of either the heading or the contents of each cell in a column and the number of rows. The contents of each heading and cell are then centered within the cell. Alternatively, the ALIGN attribute can be used with the <TABLE>, <TH> and <TD> tags to align the table/heading/cell contents to either the left edge of the display/cell, the right edge, or the center. Two examples showing the format used are:

<TABLE BORDER ALIGN=CENTER>
<TH ALIGN=LEFT>

(a)

Opening tag	Closing tag	Use
<TABLE>	</TABLE>	Start and end of an unboxed table
<TABLE BORDER>	</TABLE>	Start and end of a boxed table
<TR>	</TR>	Start and end of a row
<TH>	</TH>	Start and end of a heading
<TD>	</TD>	Start and end of a cell content
<CAPTION>	</CAPTION>	Start and end of a table caption

(b)

NETWORK	CO/CLS	CBR/VBR
PSTN/ISDN	co	cbr
LAN	cls	vbr
ATM	co	vbr
Internet	cls	vbr

Network operating modes

(c)

```
<HTML><HEAD><TITLE>Example table</TITLE></HEAD>
<BODY>
<TABLE BORDER  ALIGN=CENTER>
<TR><TH>NETWORK</TH><TH>CO/CLS</TH><TH>CBR/VBR</TH></TR>
<TR><TD>PSTN/ISDN</TD><TD>co</TD><TD>cbr</TD></TR>
<TR><TD>LAN</TD><TD>cls</TD><TD>vbr</TD></TR>
<TR><TD>ATM</TD><TD>co</TD><TD>vbr</TD></TR>
<TR><TD>Internet</TD><TD>cls</TD><TD>vbr</TD></TR>
<CAPTION>Network operating modes</CAPTION>
</TABLE>
</BODY></HTML>
```

Figure 9.14 HTML tables: (a) selection of tags; (b) an example of a displayed table; (c) HTML script for the table.

In addition, a user can define the size of the table themselves by specifying either the number of pixels to be used or as a percentage of the actual table size relative to the size of the display window. The format used is:

<TABLE BORDER WIDTH=50% LENGTH=50%>

Also, the size of individual cells can be defined by adding attributes to the <TH> and <TD> tags. Some examples are:

<TH ROWSPAN=2> <!- -> the depth of the heading should be 2 rows - ->
<TD COLSPAN=3> <!- -> the cell should span 3 columns - ->

9.4.6 Forms and CGI scripts

The previous subsections have been concerned with how a selection of the HTML directives/tags associated with text, images, and tables can be used to specify the contents of a Web page, and how the page is displayed on the screen of a client machine by the browser. However, as we saw in Section 9.2.2, in applications relating to e-commerce, for example, in addition to the server returning the contents of a file/page that have been requested by a browser, it is also a requirement for the server to receive and process information that has been input by the user. For example, payment card details and other information relating to the purchase of a ticket or product. As we saw, this is entered by means of a fill-in form and, typically, the entered information is then sent back to the server where it is processed by a piece of software called a common gateway interface (CGI) script. In this section we expand upon both these topics.

Forms

A form provides the means for the browser to get input from a user. A form is declared within an HTML page between the <FORM> and </FORM> tags. In addition, the <FORM> tag has two mandatory attributes, ACTION and METHOD. The ACTION attribute specifies the URL of the server where the data entered by the user should be sent and includes the path name and the name of the file containing the CGI script that will process the data. The METHOD attribute specifies how the entered data should be sent. When using HTTP it is always set to POST, which means that the data will be sent using a POST request message over a previously established TCP connection between the browser and the named server. An example showing the format used is:

<FORM ACTION="http://company.com/cgi-bin/orderform1"
METHOD=POST>

A form can contain a number of alternative ways for obtaining input from a user. These include fill-in boxes for textual input and check-boxes or pull-down menus for making selections. Then, when the user has completed filling in the form, the user can either initiate the sending of the entered information to the named server (if all is well) or, if not, reset the form to its initial state and start again.

When creating a form – normally within a page – to obtain input from a user, the <INPUT> tag is used. There is a range of attributes associated with the tag which determine how the information is to be obtained. A selection of these are as follows:

■ <INPUT TYPE=TEXT NAME="aname" Size="n" >: this is used to create a fill-in box of length n characters. The entered text is given an identifier of the value in NAME, that is, *aname*;

■ <TEXTAREA NAME="aname" ROWS="m" COLS="n"> </TEXTAREA>: this is similar to the previous type except that the fill-in box comprises m rows each of length n characters. Normally, the box has a scroll bar for more than two rows;

■ <INPUT TYPE=PASSWORD NAME="aname" SIZE="n">: this is similar to TEXT except that the entered password is displayed on the screen of the browser as a string of * characters, one per entered character;

■ <INPUT TYPE=CHECKBOX NAME="aname" VALUE="avalue">: this is used to select a single option from a list of options of which the user can select more than one. All the options in the list have the same NAME ("aname") but each option has a unique VALUE;

■ <INPUT TYPE=RADIO NAME="aname" VALUE="avalue">: this is the same as CHECKBOX except that the user can select only one from the list;

■ <INPUT TYPE=SUBMIT VALUE="aname">: this is used to create a submit button with the name given in the VALUE attribute displayed on the face of the button. When selected, this causes the browser to send the set of data entered by the user to the server;

■ <INPUT TYPE=RESET VALUE="aname">: this is used to create a reset button with the name given in the VALUE attribute displayed on the face of the button. When selected, this causes the browser to reset the form to its initial state;

■ <INPUT TYPE=BUTTON VALUE="aname">: this is used to create additional buttons each of which can have a script associated with it that is invoked when the button is activated.

An example of a displayed form that has been created using a selection of the above is shown in Figure 9.15(a) and the HTML script associated with this is given in part (b). Note that if no TYPE is specified it is assumed that the INPUT is plain text.

Once the user activates the SUBMIT button – given the label *Submit request* in the example – this causes the browser to send the set of data entered by the user to the CGI script/program in the server named in the URL of the

(a)

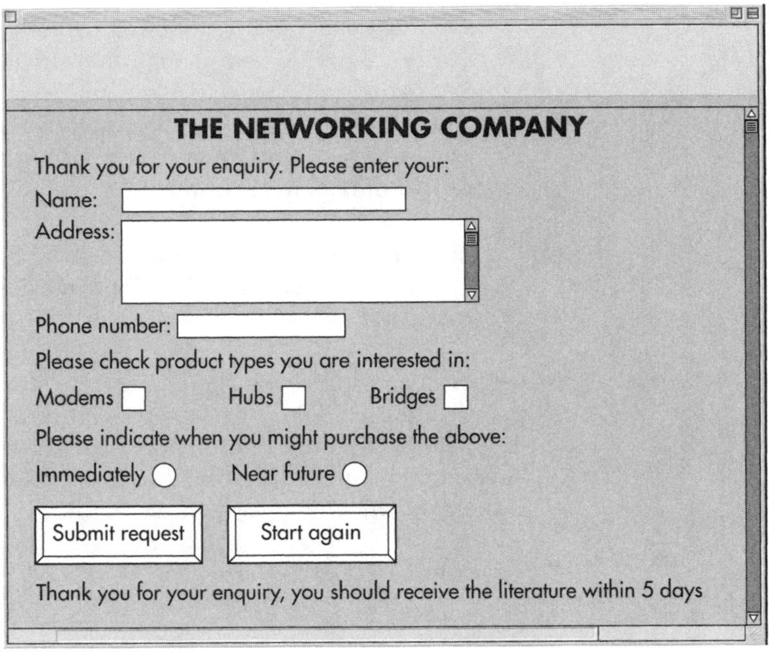

(b)

```
<HTML><HEAD><TITLE>Literature Request</TITLE></HEAD>
<BODY>
<H1>THE NETWORKING COMPANY</H1>
<FORM ACTION="http://www.NetCo.com/cgi-bin/literature" METHOD=POST>
Thank you for your enquiry. Please enter your:<P>
Name: <INPUT NAME="name" SIZE=30> <P>
Address: <TEXTAREA NAME="address" ROWS=3 COLS=40></TEXTAREA>
Phone number: <INPUT NAME="phoneno" SIZE=20><P>
Please check product types you are interested in:<P>
Modems <INPUT TYPE=CHECKBOX NAME="ProdType" VALUE="modems">
Hubs <INPUT TYPE=CHECKBOX NAME="ProdType" VALUE="hubs">
Bridges <INPUT TYPE=CHECKBOX NAME="ProdType" VALUE="bridges"><P>
Please indicate when you might purchase the above:<P>
Immediately <INPUT TYPE=RADIO NAME="PurchDate" VALUE="now">
Near future <INPUT TYPE=RADIO NAME="PurchDate" VALUE="later"><P>
<INPUT TYPE=SUBMIT VALUE="Submit Request">
<INPUT TYPE=RESET VALUE="Start Again"><P>
</FORM></BODY></HTML>
```

**Figure 9.15 HTML forms: (a) an example of a displayed form;
(b) HTML script for the form.**

ACTION attribute. The data is sent in a POST request message containing the name of each variable followed by an = character and the value entered by the user. Note, however, that only those variables that have an entered value are sent. Each variable name and its associated value is separated by an **&** character and any spaces in the entered value are replaced by a + character. For example, assuming the displayed form shown in Figure 9.15(a), an entered set of data might comprise the block of characters:

> name=FirstName+Surname&address=AStreet+ATown+ACountry &phoneno=888-99999&ProdType=modems&ProdType=hubs& PurchDate=now

with no spaces between the characters. Hence assuming the URL shown in part (b), the HTTP in the browser first establishes a TCP connection to port 80 – the HTTP well-known port – in server *www.NetCo.com*. The block of characters is then sent over this connection using a POST request message with a file name of */cgi-bin/literature* and

> Content-Type: *text/html*
>
> Content-Length: *115*

in the message header. This is followed by a blank line and the block of 115 characters in the message body.

Normally, on receipt of a POST request message with a directory name of *cgi-bin* the HTTP in the server invokes the CGI script/program in the named file and passes the contents of the request message to it for processing. The CGI script, after processing the contents of the POST message, may then return in the POST response message that it returns to the HTTP in the browser, a message such as that shown at the bottom of the display in the figure or, if some information is missing, a request to fill in the form again. Alternatively, it might return a Web page containing descriptions of the selected products.

An alternative way of selecting an item from a list of options is in the form of a pull-down menu. A menu is created by defining each option between the <SELECT> and </SELECT> tags. Associated with the opening <SELECT> tag is a NAME attribute which is assigned the name of the list of options. Also, if more than one option can be selected, a MULTIPLE attribute. An example showing how the two list of options in the example in Figure 9.15 could be displayed in the form of pull-down menus is shown in Figure 9.16(a) and the HTML script for this is given in part (b).

As we can see, since more than one option can be selected from the first menu, the MULTIPLE attribute is included. We can also see that the SELECTED attribute is used with one of the <OPTION> tags to show a default selection at start-up. The option selected with *PurchDate* is then sent in the form (say):

> &PurchDate=Immediately

(a)

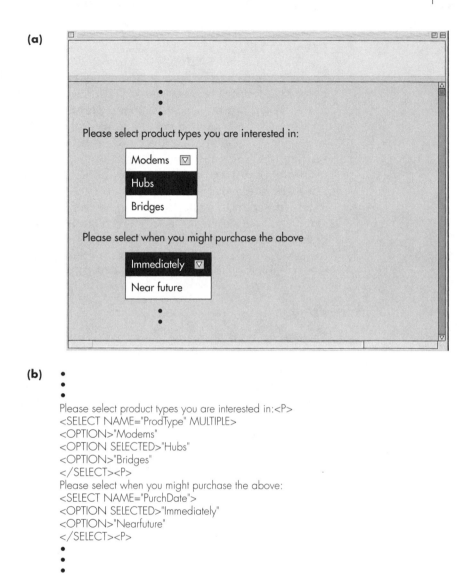

(b)

Please select product types you are interested in:<P>
<SELECT NAME="ProdType" MULTIPLE>
<OPTION>"Modems"
<OPTION SELECTED>"Hubs"
<OPTION>"Bridges"
</SELECT><P>
Please select when you might purchase the above:
<SELECT NAME="PurchDate">
<OPTION SELECTED>"Immediately"
<OPTION>"Nearfuture"
</SELECT><P>

Figure 9.16 HTML pull-down menus: (a) two examples; (b) HTML script.

9.4.7 Web mail

In addition to a user communicating with an e-mail server – to send and receive mail messages – using an (e-mail) user agent and, say, the POP3 protocol, it is also possible for a user to communicate with an (HTTP-enabled) e-mail server using a Web browser and HTTP. In this case, the browser performs the user agent functions and all message transfers between the browser machine and the user's e-mail server are carried out using HTTP rather than POP3.

As we saw in Section 8.3, a protocol like POP3 is used to transfer messages to/from the user agent and the user's e-mail server over a point-to-point link. Using a browser and HTTP, however, has the advantage that, since any browser can be used to access a (registered) user's e-mail server, the browser can be located anywhere around the world. The disadvantage is that accessing and sending mail in this way can be relatively slow. As we saw in the last section, since information – an entered e-mail message in HTML for example – must be returned by the browser to the server, then all interactions with the e-mail server must be through the intermediary of a form and an associated CGI script. In general, therefore, if a conventional e-mail user agent can be used, this is the preferred choice when the user is working at his or her home or place of work. A Web browser is used when the user is away from home. In both cases, however, all message transfers between the e-mail servers involved are carried out using SMTP.

9.4.8 Frames

Frames are used to enable the user to display and interact with more than one page on the display window of the browser at the same time. This is achieved by dividing the display window into multiple self-contained areas. Each area is called a **frame** and a separate page can be displayed in each frame. The user is able to interact with the page displayed in one frame while the pages in each of the other frames remain unchanged on the screen.

To divide the display window into multiple frames the start and end tags <FRAMESET> and </FRAMESET> are used. Associated with the <FRAMESET> tag are two attributes: COLS, which is used to divide the display vertically, and ROWS which is used to divide the display horizontally. For example, to divide the display vertically into two frames of equal size the following definition is used:

<FRAMESET COLS="50%,50%">

It is then possible to subdivide one or both of these frames using the ROWS attribute. For example, the left frame can be divided by following the previous definition with:

<FRAMESET ROWS="70%,30%">

Once the display has been divided into the required number of frames (each of a defined size), the URL (or local file name) of the page to be displayed in each frame is defined using the SRC attribute in a <FRAME> tag. The HTML script of the page to be displayed in each frame is defined independently in the standard format (using all of the previously described

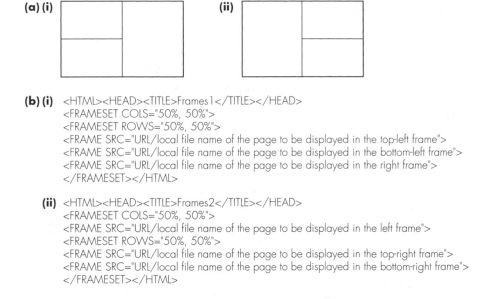

Figure 9.17 HTML frames: (a) two example frame divisions; (b) order of the related HTML scripts.

features) and is stored in the related URL or local file name. Two example structures are shown in Figure 9.17(a) and the HTML script associated with each structure in part (b). Note that the <FRAMESET> tag effectively replaces the <BODY> tag when frames are being used.

In these two examples, any images and/or hyperlinks in the displayed pages are accessed by the browser in the standard way and displayed in the frame displaying the related page. In addition, it is possible for a hyperlink in a page displayed in one frame to be used to access and display a page in one of the other frames. To do this it is necessary to give a name to the frame that is to be used to display the page when the frame is defined, for example left, right, and so on. This is done using the NAME attribute with the <FRAME> tag. The same name is then added to the URL (or local file name) of the page that is to be displayed in this frame using the TARGET attribute. An example illustrating this feature is shown in Figure 9.18(a) with the HTML script in part (b) of the figure.

The example relates to that shown earlier in Figure 9.10 and the modifications that are necessary to the HTML script shown in Figure 9.10(b) to display the home page in the left frame and the selected pages from this in the right frame are given in Figure 9.18(c). As we can see, for the frame on the right we have given it an initial URL of *The University* and a NAME="*right*". Also, in order for the browser to know to display all the subsequently accessed pages in the right frame, each URL has an added attribute of TARGET="*right*".

(a)

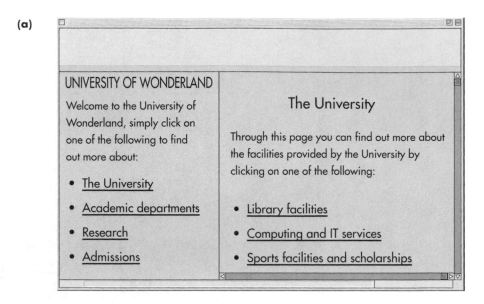

(b)
```
<HTML><HEAD><TITLE>Frames2</TITLE></HEAD>
<FRAMESET COLS="35%, 65%">
<FRAME SRC="http://www.UoW.edu">
<FRAME SRC="university" NAME="right">
</FRAMESET></HTML>
```

(c)
```
        •
        •
        •
<UL><LI><A HREF="university" TARGET="right">The University</A>
        •
        •
        •
    <LI><A HREF="admissions" TARGET="right">Admissions</A>
        •
        •
        •
```

Figure 9.18 Nested frames: (a) example display composed of two vertical frames; (b) HTML script for the display; (c) modifications to the HTML script shown earlier in Figure 9.10(b).

In addition to dividing the display window into multiple fixed-sized frames, it is also possible to display a second page in another frame that is defined in the HTML script of the currently displayed page. The second frame is called an **in-line frame** as it is created by inserting an <IFRAME> tag in the place in the current page where the frame is to be created. The <IFRAME> tag has a number of attributes which include SRC to specify the URL (or local file name) of the page to be displayed in the second frame, WIDTH and

(a)

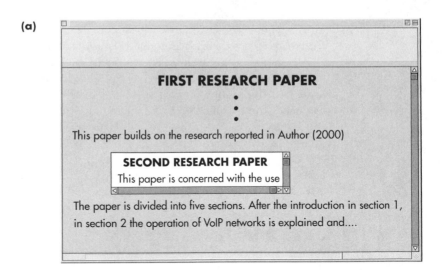

(b)
```
<HTML><HEAD><TITLE>In-line frames</TITLE></HEAD>
<BODY>
<H1>FIRST RESEARCH PAPER</H1><P>
        •
        •
        •
This paper builds on the research reported in Author (2000)<P>
<IFRAME SRC=" URL of page Author (2000)" WIDTH="600" HEIGHT="200"
        FRAMEBORDER="1"></IFRAME><P>
The paper is divided into five sections. After the introduction in section 1, in section 2 the
operation of VoIP networks is explained and....
        •
        •
        •
```

Figure 9.19 In-line frames: (a) a segment of a displayed page containing an in-line frame; (b) a segment of the HTML script to produce this.

HEIGHT to define the size of the second frame, and FRAMEBORDER to indicate whether the frame should have a border (=1) or not (=0). An example is shown in Figure 9.19(a) and the HTML script for this in part (b).

As we can see, in this example the in-line frame is used to display the contents of a second paper that is referenced in the first paper. In this way, if the reader of the first paper is not familiar with the referenced paper then he or she can read it through the in-line frame.

9.4.9 Extended HTML

As we can deduce from the previous subsections, HTML does not provide any structure to a Web page since it mixes the contents of the page with its formatting, much of which is determined by the browser that is being used. Hence the aim of the latest version of HTML is to separate out these two functions to create what are called **dynamic Web pages**; that is, the content of a page can be generated on demand rather than (statically) stored on a disk.

The latest version of HTML is called **extended HTML (XHTML)**. To separate out the contents of a page from its display format, two new languages are used: the **extensible Markup Language (XML)**, which is used to describe the contents of a Web page in a structured way, and the **extensible style language (XSL)** which describes the display format of the page. Essentially, XHTML is HTMLv4 that has been reformulated using XML to remove formatting tags. An XSL file is then used to define the formatting of the associated page. XHTML is now the new standard for creating Web pages.

9.5 Java and JavaScript

Both Java and JavaScript are used primarily to add some form of action and interactivity to a Web page in a more flexible way than helper applications and plug-ins. Essentially, with Java, a program written in the Java programming language is first compiled into what is called an *applet*. Each applet is held in a file on a Web server and can be called from within an HTML page. When called, the applet is downloaded from the file (in the server named in the URL) in a similar way to downloading the contents of an image file. When the browser receives the applet code, however, it passes it directly to an integral piece of software called a *Java interpreter* that proceeds to execute the applet code. A simple example that shows how action can be added to a Web page is an applet that obtains an audio file and plays this out as background music while the page is displayed. Alternatively, a moving object/image could be displayed in a small window. A more complex example that shows how interactivity can be introduced is an applet that obtains and displays a digitized map on the browser screen and, given a pair of coordinates – for example entered by the user in a frame in a separate window – calculates and displays the best route between the two coordinates. Games playing within a Web page is implemented in a similar way.

Similar functionality can be obtained using JavaScript except, like HTML, this is a scripting language and the action/interactivity is obtained by embedding individual scripts written in JavaScript into an HTML page when it is written. Each script is entered into the HTML script of a page between a pair of tags and, when the start tag is encountered, the HTML interpreter invokes the JavaScript interpreter to execute the script.

Both Java and JavaScript have many similar features to those provided by the C and C++ programming languages. Hence a complete description of them is outside of the scope of this book. In this section, therefore, we restrict our discussion to how an applet/script written in these languages is incorporated into an HTML page.

9.5.1 Java

Java applets provide a browser with similar functionality to helper applications and plug-ins. In the case of the latter, however, they are an integral part of the browser whereas a Java applet is downloaded from a Web server when it is required. The advantage of this is that the applet code can be changed at any time without modifying the browser code. Then, when the old version of the applet is replaced with the new version, this is downloaded automatically the next time the applet is called. For example, if the applet implements a compression algorithm and a new one is developed, the existing applet can be replaced by a new applet without changing the page contents or the browser.

In order for the downloaded code of an applet – the file of which has the type **class** – to run on a range of different computers/machines, when an applet is written it is compiled into a machine-independent code called **bytecode** and it is this version of the applet that is stored in the file on the Web server. Essentially, the bytecode of an applet is an intermediate code between the high-level Java programming language code and the machine-code version of the applet produced for running directly on a specific target machine. To run the bytecode version of an applet, a browser that supports applets has an integral piece of software – or sometimes a helper application – called a **bytecode interpreter**. This parses the bytecode to identify the individual commands – called **methods** – that it contains and then executes each of these using a related procedure/ function written in the machine code of the target machine. Hence when an applet is called from within a Web page, the downloaded bytecode is simply passed by the browser to the bytecode interpreter for execution.

Applet tags

In versions of HTML before HTML 4.0, the inclusion of a Java applet in an HTML page is carried out using the <APPLET> tag. For example, assuming the URL of the current Web page is:

http://www.UoW.edu/java-apps/"

to include the applet stored in the file *bgsound.class* on the same server as the current Web page, the script

<APPLET CODE="bgsound.class"></APPLET>

is used. When the HTML interpreter in the browser encounters the <APPLET> tag in the HTML code, it proceeds to obtain the contents of the file – the bytecode – from *bgsound.class* and passes it to the bytecode interpreter. The latter proceeds to interpret the bytecode of the applet, which, typically, accesses a specific file of compressed audio, decompresses it and then outputs the resulting byte stream to the sound card to play the background music.

As we can deduce from this, there is no separation between the applet bytecode and the data on which it operates. Also, there is no type definition associated with the data. So to obtain more flexibility, in HTML 4.0 and later versions, the <APPLET> tag is replaced with the more general <OBJECT> tag. Using this, in addition to Java applets, a number of other types of object can be included within an HTML page. These include an image (file), an audio and/or video (file) or, if required, another Web page (file). To achieve this added flexibility, the <OBJECT> tag has a number of attributes associated with it. These include:

- CODEBASE: this is the URL of the file server and the pathname of where the objects – for example the applet and any data it operates on – are located;
- CLASSID: this specifies the name of the file containing the agent – for example the applet bytecode – that will render the data. Normally, the file name of an applet is prefaced by the new URL type *java*;
- DATA: this specifies the name of the file containing the object/data on which the agent specified in CLASSID operates;
- CODETYPE: this specifies the type of the object/data defined in DATA in MIME format;
- ALIGN, HEIGHT, WIDTH, ALT: these have the same meaning as those we defined earlier in Section 9.4.4 relating to images.

An example declaration showing the use of some of these attributes – using the same URL as before – is as follows:

```
<OBJECT CODEBASE="http://www.UoW.edu/java-apps/"
    CLASSID="java:bgaudio.class"
    DATA="bgaudio.data"
    CODETYPE="audio/MP3"></OBJECT>
```

In this example when the HTML interpreter in the browser encounters the <OBJECT> tag, it requests the Java applet stored in the file specified in CLASSID to be downloaded by the server specified in CODEBASE (which also includes the pathname of the file). The name of the file specified in DATA and the datatype – audio/MP3 – specified in CODETYPE are then passed to the bytecode interpreter together with the bytecode of the applet. In the case of an image or video object, the HEIGHT and WIDTH attributes would be used to specify the size of the window that should be used to display the image/video.

Java basics

Java is an object-oriented language, which means that almost everything is defined in the form of an **object**. Normally, like a procedure or function in a programming language like Pascal or C, an object contains one or more variables encapsulated within it. Also, associated with each object are one or more operations called **methods** and it is these that are invoked to manipulate the variables within the object. This concept is referred to as **encapsulation**.

Multiple instances of an object can be created – either statically or dynamically during the execution of a program/applet – each of which is said to be an instance of the same object *class*. A typical Java applet comprises many objects – and hence methods – each of which is an instance of a particular object class. Also, in addition to writing your own object class definitions from scratch, like all programming languages, there is a large library of standard object classes that can be included with your own. These are grouped into what are called **packages** and two examples are:

- **Java.io**: all input and output such as reading a file, outputting a byte stream, and so on is done using the methods associated with the object classes in this package;

- **Java.applet**: this contains object classes and methods for getting a Web page from a given URL, displaying a Web page, decompressing and playing out the contents of an audio and/or video file, and so on.

There is also a range of Java development kits available that can be used to create applets. A good source of information for this is at

http://www.javasoft.com/

9.5.2 JavaScript

As we indicated earlier, despite its name, JavaScript is a completely different language from Java. It is a scripting language and the script is embedded within an HTML Web page between the <SCRIPT> and </SCRIPT> tags. Providing the browser is able to interpret JavaScript code, when it detects the <SCRIPT> tag it proceeds to interpret the code up to the </SCRIPT> tag as JavaScript rather than HTML.

Unlike HTML, JavaScript has many high-level programming language features similar to those available with C and C++. For example, a variable can be of type boolean, numeric or string. Also, arithmetic, logical, and bitwise operators are supported as are for( ) and while( ) control loops. Functions are also supported.

Objects

JavaScript is object-oriented. Each object has one or more methods associated with it that allow the object to be manipulated in some way. For example, the current displayed Web page – referred to as a document in JavaScript – is an example of a library/predefined object class and one or more expressions (such as a text string) can be displayed in the page window using

document.write (text string/expression(s))

(a)

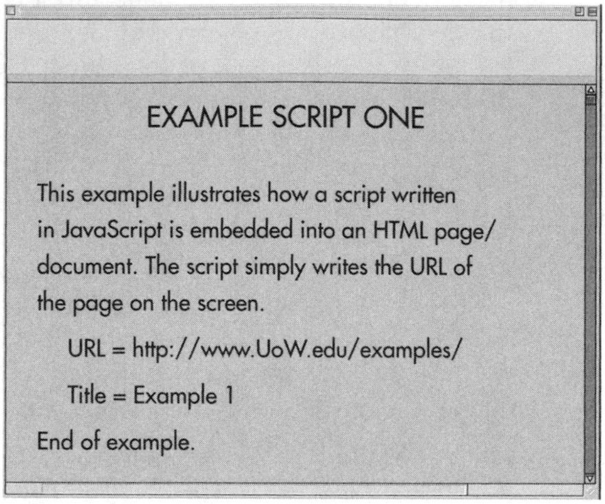

EXAMPLE SCRIPT ONE

This example illustrates how a script written
in JavaScript is embedded into an HTML page/
document. The script simply writes the URL of
the page on the screen.

URL = http://www.UoW.edu/examples/

Title = Example 1

End of example.

(b)

```
<HTML><TITLE>Example 1</TITLE>
<BODY>
<H1>EXAMPLE SCRIPT ONE</H1>
This example illustrates how a script written in JavaScript is embedded
into an HTML page/document. The script simply writes the URL of the page
on the screen:<P>
<SCRIPT LANGUAGE="JavaScript">
document.write ("URL=", document.URL)<P>
document.write ("Title=", document.title)</SCRIPT>
<P>End of example.
</BODY></HTML>
```

**Figure 9.20 JavaScript principles: (a) an example of a displayed
page/document containing a JavaScript embedded into it; (b) the
script for the page.**

Here the object name is *document* and the method is *write* – *writeln* can also be
used. Additional methods are also provided to determine such things as:

■ the URL of the document: *document.URL*,

■ the title of the document: *document.title*.

A simple example that shows how a JavaScript is embedded into an HTML
page and how the above two methods can be used is shown in Figure 9.20.

Another widely used predefined object class that is used to obtain
interactivity is *window* and again several methods are provided with this. For
example, to create a new window – as a dialog box for example – the *open*
method is used. An example statement is:

"MyWindow"=window.open (width="200", height="200", scrollbars="Yes")

This would open a new window called *MyWindow* of a defined size (in pixels) and with scrollbars. Some text could then be included in the script and this would be displayed within the window. The same window can later be closed using the *close* method. The statement in this case would be:

Mywindow.close

Other widely used methods associated with the window object class are:

■ *window.confirm ("message")*: this is used to display a confirmatory dialog box with the specified message within it and an OK and Cancel button;

■ *window.prompt ("message")*: this is used to display a prompt dialog box with the specified message within it and an input field;

■ *window.alert ("message")*: this is used to display a box with the specified message within it.

Some other predefined object classes are array, boolean, date, and math. For example, the math object class includes methods to return a value for pi and to carry out the sin and cos functions. An example segment of script showing their use is:

avariable=math.PI*math.cos (math.PI/6)

Alternatively, when the script contains several occurrences of methods from the same object class the *with* statement can be used:

with (math)
{avariable=PI*cos (PI/6)}   //comment: note the use of curly braces

A new instance of an object class can be created within a script using the *new* operator and the keyword *this* is used to refer to the current object in which the keyword appears.

Forms and event handling

We introduced the <FORM> and <INPUT> tags earlier in Section 9.4.6. As we saw, these provide the means for the browser to get input from a user which, typically, is sent to a CGI script in a remote server for processing. In addition, a form can be declared without the ACTION and METHOD attributes and the input processed locally by the browser using a JavaScript script. Also, in order to enhance this capability, JavaScript allows a number of what are called **event handlers** to be specified. Then, when a specific event occurs – for example the user clicks on an entry in a displayed table of values – a related block of JavaScript code is invoked, which, for example, might be to perform a computation on the value that has been clicked on. Two examples of event handlers that are supported are:

- **onBlur**: a Blur event occurs when an option from a list on a form is selected or some text is entered in a text field;

- **onClick**: the Click event occurs when an option on a form is clicked. The option can be selected using either a button, check-box, radio, reset, submit or link.

An example showing a segment of script that illustrates the use of an event handler is given in Figure 9.21. In this example the user is prompted for his or her user name and password and, when each is entered, the related onBlur event handler is invoked to check its validity. As we can see, each is checked using a different function and, if either fails, an appropriate message is output in an alert window.

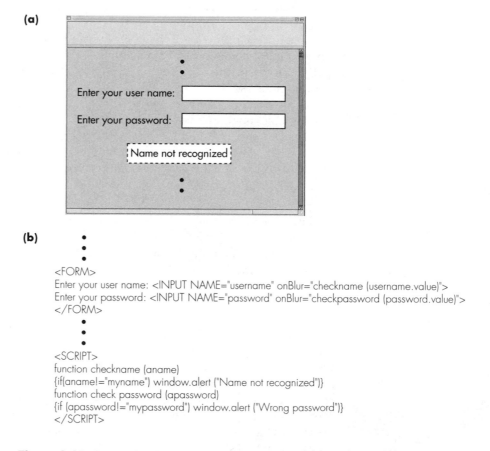

Figure 9.21 Example showing event handling within a form: (a) a portion of the display; (b) the script associated with it.

9.6 Audio and video

With Web pages comprising text and/or images, the contents of the file containing the page are downloaded from the server to the client machine. The browser then displays the page contents on the screen and, in the case of a large file/page, the user can use the scrolling facilities to view the whole page.

In the case of audio and video, however, the volume of information to be transferred increases linearly with time and hence is determined by the duration of the audio/video clip. As we indicate in Appendix A, typical bit rates for compressed audio – for example MPEG layer 3 (**MP3**) – are 128 kbps for two-channel stereo and 1.5 Mbps for MPEG-1 video with sound. Hence even a short audio/video clip can require a significant time to download. For example, a five-minute audio clip/track compressed using MP3 produces $5 \times 60 \times 128 \times 10^3$ bits or 38.4 Mbits. Even with a relatively high access rate of, say, 1 Mbps this requires 38.4 s to download, which, for this type of application, may not be acceptable. For video, of course, the delay would be an order of magnitude larger.

Hence when a user requests a file containing (compressed) audio and/or video, except for relatively short files containing spoken messages and short audio and/or video clips, the contents of the file must be played out as they are being received. This mode of working is called **streaming**. Also, as we saw in Section 1.2.5, to overcome variations in the time between each received packet in the stream – jitter – normally a **playout buffer** is used. This operates using a first-in first-out (FIFO) discipline and typically, holds several seconds of audio and/or video. The received compressed bitstream is then passed through the buffer and output from the buffer does not start until the buffer is, say, half full.

Each of these functions is in addition, of course, to the decompression of the audio and/or video bitstream. To perform these various functions the browser uses a range of helper applications. Normally, these are referred to as **media players** as they form the interface between the incoming compressed media bitstream and the related sound and/or video output card(s). In the case of audio, the appropriate audio media player – MP3 for example – decompresses the audio bitstream taken from the playout buffer and passes it to the sound card. The latter first converts the decompressed bitstream(s) back into an analog signal(s) and, after amplification, the signal(s) is/are output to the speakers. For video, the browser first creates a window in the Web page from where the request was initiated and then passes the coordinates of the window to the selected video media player. The latter first initializes the video card with the assigned coordinates and, as it decompresses the video bitstream taken from the playout buffer, it passes it to the video card for rendering on the browser screen.

In addition, with entertainment applications such as audio/video-on-demand, the user requires control of the playout process using features such as pause and rewind. Hence with this type of application it is necessary for the media player to pass the control commands to the server. To do this, the media player is divided into two parts: the first that performs the preceding playout functions – playout buffering and decompression – and the second that manages the portion of the browser display window that has been assigned for the various control buttons. This displays and monitors the buttons on the screen and, when a button is selected, it first adapts the playout process – for example stops output if the pause button is activated – and then passes an appropriate command to a remote server. A protocol has been defined to perform this function called the **real-time streaming protocol** (**RTSP**). The server then implements the command by, for example, stopping further output from the file.

Although it has been implied that the server is a conventional Web server, in most entertainment applications involving streaming, in order to meet the very high playout rates that are required when a large number of browsers are accessing the server simultaneously, special servers called **streaming servers** have to be used. In this section we shall expand upon several of these issues.

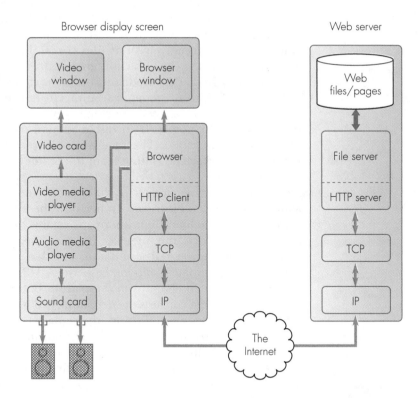

Figure 9.22 Schematic of audio/video streaming with a conventional server.

9.6.1 Streaming using a Web server

Before describing how an audio and/or video file is accessed using a streaming server, it will be helpful first to review how such files are accessed using a conventional Web server. Figure 9.22 shows the protocols that are used.

Using this structure, when the user clicks on a hyperlink in a page for an audio or video file, the browser follows the same procedure as for a text/image file. Hence the HTTP in the browser first establishes a TCP connection with the HTTP in the server named in the hyperlink. It then sends a request for the contents of the file named in the hyperlink using a GET request message. The server responds by returning the contents of the file in a GET response message. On receipt of this, the browser determines from the *Content-Type* field at the head of the message – for example *Content-Type = Audio/MP3 –* that the accessed file contains audio that has been compressed using MP3. Hence the browser proceeds to invoke the MP3 media player and, at the same time, passes the contents of the compressed file to it. The media player then proceeds to decompress the contents of the file and outputs the resulting byte stream to the sound card.

As we can deduce from this, the disadvantage of this approach is that since the browser must first receive the contents of the file in its entirety, an unacceptably long delay is introduced if the contents are of any significant size. Hence for larger files, an alternative approach is used which enables the file to be sent directly to the media player rather than through the browser. A schematic diagram showing how this is achieved is shown in Figure 9.23.

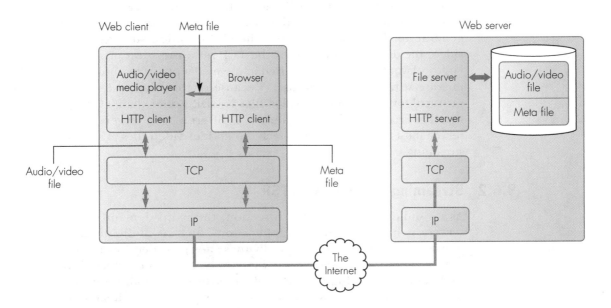

Figure 9.23 Audio/video streaming with a conventional server and a meta file.

Using this approach, when an audio and/or video file is created, a second file is also created. The second file contains the URL of the first/original file – containing the compressed audio/video – and also a specification of the content type that is in the file. The second file is called the **meta file** of the original file or, because of its function, a **presentation description file**. This also has a URL associated with it and, when the creator of a page wishes to include a hyperlink to an audio/video file in the page, he or she uses the URL of the meta file rather than that of the original file.

Thus when a user clicks on the hyperlink, the GET response message contains the contents of the meta file. The browser first accesses the *Content-Type:* field from it and then uses this to invoke the related media player as before but this time it simply passes the presentation description in the meta file to the media player. The media player, on determining that this is a meta file, reads the URL of the original file and then proceeds to obtain the contents of the original file in the normal way using HTTP/TCP. On receipt of the file contents, the media player simply streams the received compressed contents into the playout buffer. After a predefined delay to allow the playout buffer to partially fill – tens of seconds with audio – it starts to read the stream from the buffer and, after decompression, outputs the resulting byte stream to the sound/video card as we showed in Figure 1.7.

As we can see from the above, this approach removes the delays that are introduced when the file contents are accessed through the browser and hence it is widely used when the audio/video is stored on a conventional Web server. The limiting factor with this approach is that since the audio/video file is accessed in the same way as a text or image file using HTTP and TCP, as we saw in Section 7.3, TCP will transfer the file contents in segments and, if it detects a segment is missing, the TCP at the server side will retransmit it. In general, for files containing real-time information such as audio and/or video, the delays introduced by the TCP retransmission process mean that large playout buffers are required in the media player to mask the effect of a missing segment from the user. Because of this, the preferred transport protocol for audio and/or video files is UDP rather than TCP. This means that HTTP cannot be used and so a different file server from the Web server must be used to hold the audio and/or video files. This is called the streaming server.

9.6.2 Streaming servers and RTSP

As we indicated earlier in this section, the main demand for streaming servers is in entertainment applications such as audio-on-demand and movie/video-on-demand. Typically these are provided by either a TV or a multimedia PC/workstation via a set-top box that is connected to either a cable modem or a high-speed modem. With such applications, in order to meet the very high playout rates that are required when a large number of concurrent users are involved, special-purpose streaming servers are used.

Also, as we indicated at the end of the last section, in order to overcome the delays introduced by the retransmission procedure associated with TCP, the preferred transport protocol is UDP. Hence when accessing an audio/video file from a streaming server, normally UDP is used with the real time transport protocol (RTP) to transfer the integrated audio and video. A typical set-up for movie/video-on-demand is shown in Figure 9.24. A similar set-up is used for audio-on-demand – Internet radio, for example – except no video is involved.

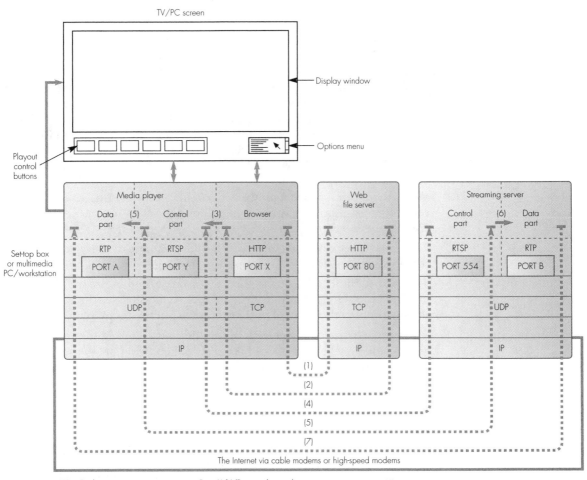

Figure 9.24 Protocols associated with audio/video streaming.

As we can see, the set-up is similar to that shown in Figure 9.23 except the streaming server is separate from the Web server. Also, at the browser side, the media player is divided into two parts: a data part and a control part both of which interact with peer parts in the streaming server. The data part is concerned with the transfer of the integrated audio and video packet streams from the server to the client, the buffering of the incoming packet stream in the playout buffer, the demultiplexing and decompression of the audio and video components, and the output of synchronized audio and video to the respective media cards. The control part manages the playout process according to the commands entered by the user via the set of on-screen control buttons.

Typically, the screen of the TV/PC is divided by the browser into three windows. The first is for use by the browser itself to display a menu of audios (CDs) and movies/videos, the second for use by the control part of the media player to display the set of control buttons, and the third for use by the data part of the media player to display the video output. Also, as with streaming using a conventional Web server, associated with each file containing the integrated audio/video packet stream is a meta file containing the URL of the file and a description of such things as the compression algorithms used and the presentation format.

The sequence of steps that occur when the user selects a movie/video from the menu are identified as (1) through (7) in Figure 9.24. These are:

1 When the user clicks on a movie/video, the browser sends an HTTP GET request message for the related meta file to the Web server named in the URL of the selected hyperlink.

2 The Web server responds by returning the contents of the meta file to the browser in a (HTTP) GET response message.

3 The browser determines from the *Content-Type:* field in the meta file the media player – helper application – to invoke and passes the contents of the meta file to the control part of the selected media player.

4 The control part reads the URL of the file(s) containing the integrated audio/video packet stream and requests the control part in the streaming server (named in the URL) for permission to start a new session by sending an *RTSP SETUP* request message. Associated with this are a number of parameters including the name of the file containing the movie/video, the RTSP session number, the required operational mode (PLAY, although RECORD is supported also), the RTP port number to use, and authorization information. In response, if these are acceptable, the control part in the server returns an RTSP accept response message, which includes a unique session identifier allocated by the server for use with subsequent messages relating to the session.

5 When the user clicks on the *play* button, the control part of the media player sends a *RTSP PLAY* request message – which includes the allocated session identifier – to the control part in the streaming server. The latter knows from the identifier that access permission has been granted and

returns an acknowledgment to this effect to the control part in the media player. On receipt of this, the latter prepares the data part to receive the incoming integrated audio/video packet stream.

6 At the streaming side, after a short delay to allow the client side to prepare to receive the packet stream, the control part initiates the access and transmission of the packet stream using the allocated port number of RTP – port A – in the header of each UDP datagram.

7 The stream of packets containing the integrated audio and video are first passed into the playout buffer of the data part of the media player and, after a preset time delay, the packets are read from the buffer. Each packet in the stream is first identified – audio or video – and then decompressed using the previously agreed algorithm.

Once the play button has been selected and the movie/video started, the user may wish to activate further control buttons such as pause, visual fast forward, rewind, stop and quit. In order to relay the appropriate command to the streaming server, RTSP has a corresponding set of control messages. A selection of these are shown in the example in Figure 9.25(a) and the format of some of the messages in part (b).

Note that in order for the streaming server to send the integrated stream of audio/video packets to the data part of the media player, the port number that has been allocated by the control part to RTP – port A – is included in the SETUP request message. The data part of the streaming server inserts this in the destination port field of each UDP datagram header. Note also that the session identifier – allocated by the control part in the streaming server – is returned in the response message to the SETUP request and that this is used subsequently in all further request messages relating to this session. Normally, the RTSP TEARDOWN request message is sent by the control part of the media server when the user activates the quit/end button.

9.7 Wireless Web

As we explained in Chapter 4, a subscriber with a mobile device – phone, laptop, etc. – can gain access to the Web using either a private/public wireless LAN or a mobile phone network. In practice, in order for the mobile device to interact with a Web server, this requires a protocol stack above the link and physical layers we described in Chapter 4. Unfortunately, in the first generation of mobile phone networks two different protocol stacks were defined: one that originated in Japan called **information-mode** (**i-mode**) and the other that is an international standard and is called the **Wireless Application Protocol** (**WAP**).

The most widely used protocol stack is that of the i-mode and this is supported by over a thousand Web sites in Japan alone. The sites are categorized into e-mail, news, weather, games, and so on. Unfortunately, the original

(a)

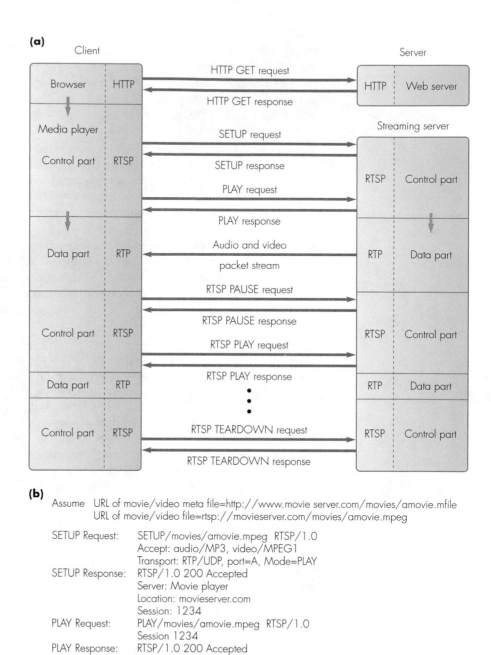

(b)

Assume   URL of movie/video meta file=http://www.movie server.com/movies/amovie.mfile
URL of movie/video file=rtsp://movieserver.com/movies/amovie.mpeg

SETUP Request: SETUP/movies/amovie.mpeg RTSP/1.0
Accept: audio/MP3, video/MPEG1
Transport: RTP/UDP, port=A, Mode=PLAY
SETUP Response: RTSP/1.0 200 Accepted
Server: Movie player
Location: movieserver.com
Session: 1234
PLAY Request: PLAY/movies/amovie.mpeg RTSP/1.0
Session 1234
PLAY Response: RTSP/1.0 200 Accepted

**Figure 9.25 Real-time streaming protocol (RTSP): (a) example
message exchange sequence; (b) a selection of message formats.**

i-mode was a proprietary system since it used many non-standard protocols and features. As a result, a second generation of WAP – **WAP 2.0** – was standardized by what is called the WAP Forum. This is an international body and the standard incorporates many of the features of i-mode but in a standardized form. In this section, therefore, we shall describe the protocol stack and basic operational mode of WAP 2.0.

9.7.1 WAP 2.0

As we explained in Section 7.6.3, when using existing TCP/IP protocols, because of the different characteristics of wireless links, selected operational parameters must be used in order to obtain a satisfactory performance. The protocol is then said to have a **wireless profile**. A schematic diagram showing the basic structure of an example WAP 2.0 configuration and its associated protocol stacks is shown in Figure 9.26.

As we show in the figure, the browser associated with the wireless device supports XHTML Basic, which is intended for use with handheld devices that have small displays with limited input facilities. All the tags are defined in

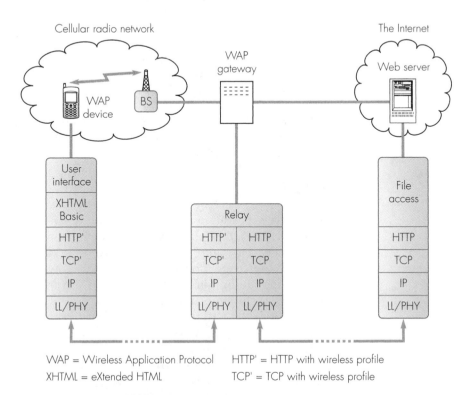

Figure 9.26 WAP 2.0 protocol stack for Web access.

XML and include structure tags for defining title/head and body, itemized lists, fill-in forms, tables, images/pictures, and many others. More details of XHTML can be found at *www.w3.org*.

As we can see in the figure, the connection between a mobile device and an Internet server is split into two parts: a wireless part and a fixed-wire part with what is called a **WAP gateway** performing the relaying functions between the two parts. Over the wireless part of a connection, HTTP with a wireless profile and TCP with a wireless profile are used while over the fixed-wire part of a connection standard HTTP and TCP are used.

9.8 Web operation

So far in this chapter we have described a range of topics relating to how a Web page is created and transferred over the Internet. In this section we describe a number of issues relating to how the Web is organized and its key operational parts.

The first issue is how the presence of a server with a new set of pages/documents becomes known to users of the Web. There are a number of ways this can be done. For example, as we saw earlier in Section 9.3.1, the URL of the home page (together with a description of what the page is offering) can be posted to a related newsgroup within UseNet using the *news:* protocol/method. Alternatively, a more popular method is to use what is called a **search engine** together with a special browser called a **spider** (or **robot**).

The volume of information on the Web is already vast and is increasing continuously. In practice, however, only a small subset of this information is of interest to a particular user. The second issue, therefore, is how a user gains access to this subset of information without having to search the entire Web. This is done using an intermediary called a **portal**. We shall describe each of these issues separately.

9.8.1 Search engines

Before we can describe how a new Web page is made available over the Web we must first build up an understanding of how the search process is carried out by a search engine to find and retrieve a Web page. As we saw in Section 9.3, each Web page/document is accessed using the page's URL, which, since it contains the unique domain name of the server computer on which the page/file is stored, is unique within the entire Web/Internet. Hence providing we know the URL of a page, a browser can readily obtain and display the page contents. To help with this, all browsers allow the user to keep a list of URLs in a table and provide facilities for the user to select, add and delete entries. Nevertheless, in many instances, when searching for information on the Web, the user does not have a URL but rather he or she is interested in, say, any pages relating to a specific topic/subject. As a result, a directory is required. This is analogous to a telephone directory since, for each entry, a Web directory contains some information that describes the contents of the page plus its URL. A key issue is what this information should be and how it is used to find a specific URL.

A second issue relates to the size of the directory. As we have said, the number of Web pages is already vast and is increasing continuously. It would be totally infeasible to have a single large directory since the time required to carry out each search operation would be endless. This also applies to the telephone directory system of course and, to make searching the latter faster, the directory is fragmented into many separate sections. Typically, this is based on geographic location and, at a local level, the directory is divided into business and residential subscribers. When the telephone number of a customer is required, in addition to the customer's name, the location of the customer and whether it is a business or private residence is requested. In this way the search for the given name is restricted to a small subsection of the total directory.

The same approach is followed for the Web directory except the partitioning of the directory is not as straightforward. As we indicated earlier, with the Web the search information/index is based on a given topic/subject which is much less precise than a given name and location. For example, since each page has a title field, in principle, this could be used as the search index for the page. In practice, this cannot be done since in many instances a title is not given and, when one is given, it often bears no relation to the actual page contents. Instead, therefore, for each page, an additional block of information – normally in the form of a string of **keywords** – that describes the contents of the page is defined and it is these that are used as search indexes.

In practice, the choice of keywords to go with each URL varies widely and, as a result, there are a large number of different search engines in existence. In general, however, most allow a user to add the URL of the home page of a new set of pages to their current set of directories. Normally, this is done by first accessing the home page of the company that manages the search engine and, through this, a fill-in form is obtained. This is then filled in by the user and, when it is submitted, the page is added to the related directory. Alternatively, there are commercial organizations which, when a new URL is submitted, will add this to a number of search engines for you.

Spiders and robots

There are two different ways to obtain the search indexes for each page. One involves the person who submits the page providing a set of keywords in the same fill-in form that is submitted/posted to the owner of the search engine. These are then used to determine into which directory the URL should be inserted. In the second method, only the URL is submitted and it is the company which manages the search engine that obtains the keywords. It does this by using a special browser called a spider – also called a robot or simply **bot** – which, when given the submitted URL, accesses and then searches the contents of the page for specific keywords. It then uses these to enter the

URL into the most appropriate directory(ies). The spider then follows all the links from the submitted home page and derives a set of keywords for each of these pages too. In addition, to make people aware that a new set of pages is now available, most search engine companies allow the URL of the home page (together with an associated set of keywords) to be posted to their **What's New** site. Normally, the page is then kept in the What's New directory for a set period of time.

Since in the second method it is the spider/robot that determines the set of keywords to be used, these may not be an optimum set as seen by the writer of the page. Hence when a spider is used, it is possible to direct the spider by including in the page header a list of the keywords that the writer feels should be used. The given list of keywords is called the **meta information** for the page and is included in the page header between the <HEAD> and </HEAD> tags. The list of keywords is given within the <META> tag using the following arguments:

- NAME="keywords": to allow for other types of meta information, this informs the HTML interpreter that what follows is a list of keywords;
- LANG="language": the language used for the keywords, for example en-US, es (Spanish), fr (French);
- CONTENT="list of keywords": the list of keywords with a space between each.

An example format is:

```
<META NAME="keywords"
        LANG="en-US"
        CONTENT="vacations holidays walking beach activity hotels
                        scubadiving - - -">
```

9.8.2 Portals

As we indicated earlier, there are many different search engine companies/ sites available which, given a set of keywords, will carry out a search through their directories and return details of a list of up to, say, 10 Web sites that give the best matches with a given set of keywords. Typically, the returned details for each site are in the form:

Match:	"80%"
Title:	"The name of the Web site"
URL:	"The URL of the home page"
Summary:	"A summary of what this site has to offer"
More:	"Click on this link to initiate a search for more pages like this one"

and are listed according to their match field.

To help you find the best search engine sites, most browsers have a button on the display that, when clicked, returns a list of a number of sites together with some information about what each has to offer. In addition, many Internet service providers (ISPs) provide a facility to help a user find the best search engine site(s) for a given set of keywords. This is referred to as the ISP's portal since it acts as a gateway to the vast collection of Web sites/pages that are now available.

Essentially, the portal has knowledge of a large collection of search engine sites and their directories. Given a set of keywords, the portal will select the site that it thinks has the best directory relating to the query. In addition, some portals will interact with the user through a form to obtain a more focussed set of requirements before returning the URL of what it thinks is the best site. Some ISPs also allow a user to create his or her own personalized portal. Then, by simply clicking on the portal page, the user is able to access his or her own preferred sources of information relating to, say, news, sport, weather, entertainment, and so on.

Summary

A summary of the topics discussed in this chapter is given in Figure 9.27.

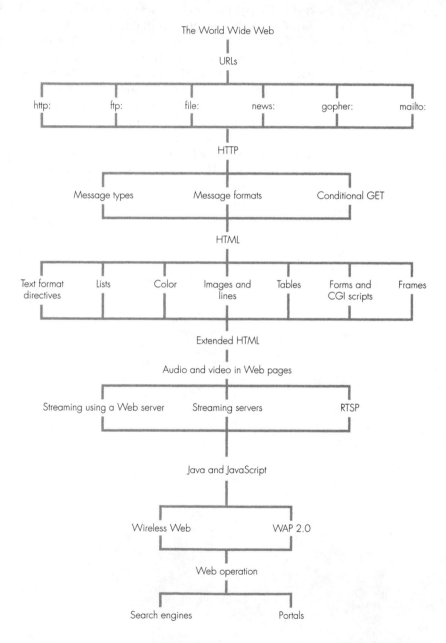

Figure 9.27 World Wide Web summary.

Exercises

Section 9.3

9.1 With the aid of a diagram, in a few sentences, explain each of the following terms relating to the Web: a browser, a server, HTTP, HTML, hyperlinks, URLs.

9.2 Assuming the URL of a Web page is:

   http://www.UoW.edu/prospectus/index.html

   identify the application protocol/method that is used to access the page, the domain name of the server, the pathname of the file, and the file name.

9.3 Assuming the URL

   ftp://www.mpeg.org/mpeg-4/

   determine the directory and file name of the page.

9.4 Assuming a user clicks on the URL

   ftp://www.mpeg.org/mpeg-4

   explain what type of information is returned.

9.5 Give an example of a URL that uses the *file:* method and explain one of its uses.

9.6 Outline the operation of UseNet including the role of newsgroups, a news reader, and NNTP. Hence explain how the home page of a new set of linked pages could be announced from within a Web page to a related newsgroup over UseNet.

9.7 Outline the steps that are followed by the browser to enable a user to send an e-mail message from within a Web page.

9.8 Explain the meaning of the term "URI" and how it differs from a URL.

9.9 With the aid of a diagram, show the protocol stack that is used in a Web client and Web server to obtain a page/block of data using the HTTP application protocol/method.

Include in your diagram a DNS name server and explain its role in relation to obtaining the page.

9.10 Describe how it is possible to obtain satisfactory performance with a simple request/response application protocol for transferring a page over the Web.

9.11 List the advantages and disadvantages of using the following types of TCP connections for a Web session:
   (i) nonpersistent connections,
   (ii) multiple concurrent nonpersistent connections,
   (iii) persistent connections.

9.12 In relation to HTTP, state the difference between a simple request message and a full request message. How does HTTP discriminate between the two message types?

9.13 Using the example HTTP request/response messages shown in Figure 9.8:
   (i) state the implications of the presence of the *HTTP/1.1* and *Connect:close* fields in the request message,
   (ii) if the response message related to, say, a JPEG image rather than an HTML page, give a typical set of content-related fields.

9.14 Explain the role of a cache server and how its use can speed up the time to obtain a Web page. Clearly indicate where the savings arise and how they can be reduced further by using a hierarchy of cache servers.

9.15 State how a conditional GET request message differs from a GET request. Hence, with the aid of a diagram, illustrate the message sequence that is followed when a browser obtains the contents of a named file from a named (origin) server via a proxy/cache server. Assume the contents of the file have been modified since the date given in the conditional GET request message.

Section 9.4

9.16 With the aid of an example, explain the terms "absolute URL" and "relative URL" including the relationship between the two.

9.17 In relation to the HTML script shown in Figure 9.10, assume the contents of the page accessed through the link *The University* are as shown in the right frame of Figure 9.18(a). Assuming frames are not being used, write the HTML script for the portion of the page that is displayed.

9.18 In relation to the HTML script shown in Figure 9.10, show the changes to the script if the complete prospectus was on a single page rather than a linked set of pages. State the advantages and disadvantages of doing this.

9.19 Assuming the index for this book is to be on a single Web page, write the fragment of HTML script for the first five entries in the list of contents for this chapter using the <OL> tag.

9.20 In order to enhance your Web page, you decide to introduce color into it. Show how you could direct the HTML interpreter in a browser to make the background color yellow, the text in the page orange, each link red, and a visited link blue.

9.21 In relation to the two displayed images shown in Figure 9.12, produce a segment of HTML script:
  (i) to display the UoW crest/logo in the center of the page with the first-level heading starting below it – part (a),
  (ii) to start the text at the top edge of the text – part (b)
  (iii) to make the image shown in part (b) a hyperlink.

9.22 Give the additions to the HTML script shown in Figure 9.10 to produce a bold line that divides the heading from the remaining text.

9.23 Assume the table shown in Figure 9.14(b) is to be changed so that there are four columns CO, CLS, CBR and VBR with a + character in those column positions where the related feature is true. For example, for the LAN row, the CLS and VBR columns would each have a + character and the other two columns would be left blank. Produce the HTML script for the table.

9.24 Give the changes to the HTML script shown in Figure 9.14(c) to align the contents of the cells in the NETWORK column to the left edge of the cell.

9.25 Give the outline of an HTML script to produce a table that comprises three columns and three rows with the second and third cells of the first column combined and the second and third cells of the second row combined. Assume the three cells in the first row are for headings and the contents of all cells are to be left blank.

9.26 (i) State the purpose of a fill-in form and an associated CGI script.
  (ii) Use an example FORM declaration to explain the use of the ACTION and METHOD attributes.
  (iii) List some of the alternative ways input can be obtained from a user.

9.27 Use the <INPUT> tag with appropriate attributes to create the following form. Include in your HTML script an example URL for the ACTION attribute.

ICE CREAM ORDER FORM
Name:
Address:

Phone number:
Please check flavors:
Vanilla ☐ Chocolate ☐ Strawberry ☐
Please indicate how many boxes you require:
One ☐ Two ☐ Three ☐
Payment card Type: MC ☐ Visa ☐
Number: Expiry date:
Submit order   Reset order

9.28 List a typical set of responses for the various fields in the form shown in Exercise 9.27. Explain how these are sent to a CGI script/program in the server given in your example URL.

9.29 Show how the choice of flavors in your HTML script for Exercise 9.27 could be presented using a pull-down menu.

9.30 Assume you want to create an album for your digitized photographs on your own computer which can be viewed through the browser. Write a segment of an HTML script for a page template that divides the display window into four quarters using frames. Include in your script the URL of the image/photograph you want to display in each frame.

9.31 Explain the meaning and use of an in-line frame. Write a segment of an HTML script that shows how a second frame can be used to display the contents of a page that is referenced in the current page.

Section 9.5

9.32 Both Java and JavaScript can be used to add action and interactivity to a Web page. Explain briefly how this is done in each case.

9.33 In relation to the Java programming language, explain the meaning of the following terms:
(i)   an applet,
(ii) bytecode,
(iii) bytecode interpreter.

9.34 Give an example segment of HTML script that uses the <APPLET> tag. Explain the actions that are followed by the HTML parser and bytecode interpreter when the tag is encountered in the script. Include in your description an example URL for the page and the name of the file associated with the <APPLET> tag.

9.35 In HTML 4.0 and later versions, the <OBJECT> tag is used in preference to the <APPLET> tag. Explain why this change has come about. Give an example declaration of a Java applet using the <OBJECT> tag and an associated set of attributes. Clearly identify the role performed by each attribute.

9.36 Explain the meaning of the following terms relating to the Java programming language:
(i)   an object,
(ii) a method,
(iii) encapsulation,
(iv) object class,
(v)   package.
Give two examples of a Java library package and explain their function.

9.37 Like Java, JavaScript is object-oriented. Show how the *document* object class and the associated *.write*, *.URL* and *.title* methods can be used in a JavaScript that is embedded in an HTML page.

9.38 By means of examples, explain the meaning of the term "event handler" in the context of the JavaScript programming language. Hence explain how an event handler can be used in conjunction with a form to perform a specific action when the event occurs. Use as an example a form that takes as input the name and password entered by a user and performs checks on these.

Section 9.6

9.39 When downloading a Web page comprising audio and/or video, by means of examples, explain why streaming and a playout buffer are used. Hence list and explain the functions performed by a media player.

9.40 With the aid of a diagram, explain how a file containing a short video clip – comprising audio and video – is streamed from a Web server and played out by a browser that has both an audio and a video media player. Include in your diagram the protocols that are used to transfer the media.

9.41 With the aid of a diagram, explain how the playout process used in the last exercise can be improved by using a meta file. Include in your diagram the protocols that are used to transfer the meta file and the media streams.

Identify the limitations associated with this approach.

9.42   With the aid of a diagram, explain how a movie/video is accessed from a streaming server and played out by a browser. Include in your diagram the protocols that are used at both the server side and the client side including, in the case of the various application protocols, their port numbers and use. Include in your explanation the sequence of steps that occur when the user first selects a movie/video.

9.43   List a typical set of control buttons associated with the playout of a movie/video on the screen of a TV/PC. Hence use a diagram to illustrate the application protocol and control/data parts of the media player that is involved when the user carries out the following sequence:
   (i)   initiates the showing of a movie/video
   (ii)   activates the play button
   (iii)   activates the pause button
   (iv)   activates the quit button.

Section 9.7

9.44   Explain the meaning of the terms "i-mode" and "WAP" in the context of the wireless Web.

9.45   Explain the meaning of the term "wireless profile" and where and why it is used.

9.46   With the aid of a diagram, describe how access to the Web is achieved in WAP 2.0. Include in your diagram a WAP gateway and the two sets of protocols that are used.

Section 9.8

9.47   Outline the role of a search engine. Identify the two main issues that influence its design and explain why keywords are used.

9.48   Explain the role of a spider/robot in relation to a search engine and how this can be influenced by the writer of a page by providing meta information. By means of an example, show how the latter is included in a Web page using the <META> tag and the NAME, LANG, and CONTENT attributes.

9.49   By means of an example, explain the structure of the information that is returned from a search operation. Also explain the role of a portal in carrying out a search.

security

10.1 Introduction

Increasingly people are using networks such as the Internet for on-line banking, shopping, and many other applications. The generic term used is **electronic commerce** or **e-commerce** and this often involves the transfer of sensitive information such as credit card details over the network. Hence to support this type of networked transaction, a number of security techniques have been developed which, when combined together, provide a high level of confidence that any information relating to the transaction that is received from the network:

- has not been altered in any way – **integrity**;
- has not been intercepted and read by anyone – **privacy/secrecy**;
- has come from an authorized sender – **authentication**;
- has proof that the stated sender initiated the transaction – **nonrepudiation**.

In this chapter we shall describe a number of the techniques that are used to carry out these four functions. As we shall see, secrecy and integrity are achieved by means of **data encryption** while authentication and nonrepudiation require the exchange of a set of (encrypted) messages between the two communicating parties. In addition, we give some examples of applications that use these techniques.

10.2 Data encryption

As the knowledge of computer networking and protocols has become more widespread, so the threat of intercepting and decoding message data during its transfer across a network has increased. For example, the end systems (stations/hosts) associated with most applications are now attached to a LAN. The application may involve a single LAN or, in an internetworking environment, the Internet. However, with most LANs, transmissions on the shared transmission medium can readily be intercepted by any system if an intruder sets the appropriate MAC chipset into the promiscuous mode and records all transmissions on the medium. Then, with a knowledge of the LAN protocols being used, the intruder can identify and remove the protocol control information at the head of each message, leaving the message contents. The message contents, including passwords and other sensitive information, can then be interpreted.

This is known as **listening** or **eavesdropping** and its effects are all too obvious. In addition and perhaps more sinister, an intruder can use a recorded message sequence to generate a new sequence. This is known as **masquerading** and again the effects are all too apparent. Therefore, encryption should be applied to all data transfers that involve a network. In the context of the TCP/IP reference model, the most appropriate layer to perform such operations is the application layer. This section provides an introduction to the subject of data encryption.

10.2.1 Terminology

Data encryption (or **data encipherment**) involves the sending party – for example, the application protocol entity – in processing all data prior to transmission so that if it is accidentally or deliberately intercepted while it is being transferred it will be incomprehensible to the intercepting party. Of course, the data must be readily interpreted – **deycrypted** or **deciphered** – by the intended recipient. Consequently, most encryption methods involve the use of an **encryption key**, which is hopefully known only by the two correspondents. The key features in both the encryption and the decryption processing. Prior to encryption, message data is normally referred to as **plaintext** and after encryption as **ciphertext**. The general scheme is illustrated in Figure 10.1.

When deciding on a particular encryption algorithm we must always assume that a transmitted message can be intercepted and recorded, and that

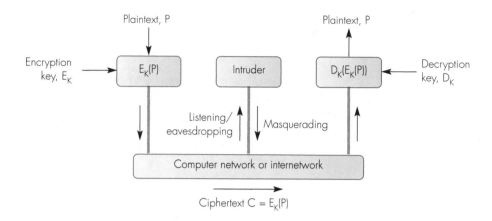

Figure 10.1 Data encryption terminology.

the intruder knows the context in which the messages are being used, that is, the type of information being exchanged. The aim is to choose an encryption method such that an intruder, even with access to a powerful computer, cannot decipher the recorded ciphertext in a realistic time period. There are two widely used algorithms but before we discuss them, let us consider some of the more fundamental techniques on which they are based.

10.2.2 Basic techniques

The simplest encryption technique involves **substituting** the plaintext alphabet (codeword) with a new alphabet known as the **ciphertext alphabet**. For example, a ciphertext alphabet can be defined with the plaintext alphabet simply shifted by n places where n is the key. Hence, if the key is 3, the resulting alphabet is as follows:

  Plaintext alphabet: a b c d e f g . . .
  Ciphertext alphabet: d e f g h i j . . .

The ciphertext is obtained by substituting each character in the plaintext message by the equivalent letter in the ciphertext alphabet.

  A more powerful variation is to define a ciphertext alphabet that is a random mix of the plaintext alphabet. For example:

  Plaintext alphabet   a b c d e f g . . .
  Ciphertext alphabet: n z q a i y m . . .

The key is determined by the number of letters in the alphabet, for example, 26 if just lower-case alphabetic characters are to be transmitted or 128 if, say, the ASCII alphabet is being used. There are therefore $26! \simeq 4 \times 10^{26}$ possible keys with the first alphabet or many times this with the larger alphabet. Notice that in general, the larger the key the more time it takes to break the code.

Although this may seem to be a powerful technique, there are a number of shortcuts that can be used to break such codes. The intruder is likely to know the context in which the message data is being used and hence the type of data involved. For example, if the messages involve textual information, then the statistical properties of text can be exploited: the frequencies of occurrence of individual letters (e, t, o, a, and so on) are all well documented. By performing statistical analyses on the letters in the ciphertext such codes can be broken relatively quickly.

Substitution involves replacing each character with a different character, so the order of the characters in the plaintext is preserved in the ciphertext. An alternative approach is to reorder (**transpose**) the characters in the plaintext. For example, if a key of 4 is used, the complete message can first be divided into a set of 4-character groups. The message is then transmitted starting with all the first characters in each group, then the second, and so on. As an example, assuming a plaintext message of "this is a lovely day", the ciphertext is derived as follows:

1	2	3	4	←	key
t	h	i	s		
–	i	s	–		
a	–	l	o		
v	e	l	y		
–	d	a	y		

Ciphertext = t–av–hi–edisllas–oyy

Clearly, more sophisticated transpositions can be performed but, in general, when used alone transposition ciphers suffer from the same shortcomings as substitution ciphers. Most practical encryption algorithms tend to use a combination of the two techniques and are known as **product ciphers**.

Product ciphers

These use a combination of substitutions and transpositions. Also, instead of substituting/transposing the characters in a message, the order of individual bits in each character (codeword) is substituted/transposed. The three alternative transposition (also known as **permutation**) operations are shown in Figure 10.2(a). Each is normally referred to as a **P-box**.

The first involves transposing each 8-bit input into an 8-bit output by cross-coupling each input line to a different output line as defined by the key.

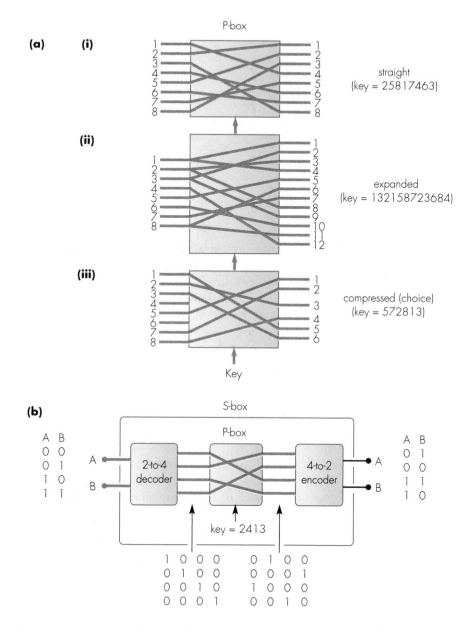

Figure 10.2 Product cipher components: (a) P-box examples; (b) S-box example.

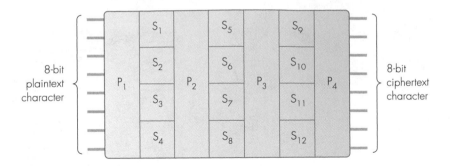

Figure 10.3 Example of a product cipher.

This is known as a **straight permutation**. The second has a larger number of output bits than input bits; they are derived by reordering the input bits and passing selected input bits to more than one output. This is known as an **expanded permutation**.

The third has fewer output bits than inputs; it is formed by transposing only selected input bits. This is known as a **compressed** or **choice permutation**.

To perform a straight substitution of 8 bits requires a new set (and hence key) of 2^8 (= 256) 8-bit bytes to be defined. This means the key for a single substitution is 2048 bits. To reduce this, a substitution is formed by encapsulating a P-box between a decoder and a corresponding encoder, as shown in Figure 10.2(b). The resulting unit is known as an **S-box**. The example performs a 2-bit substitution operation using the key associated with the P-box. An 8-bit substitution will require four such units.

Product ciphers are formed from multiple combinations of these two basic units, as shown in Figure 10.3. In general, the larger the number of stages the more powerful the cipher. A practical example of product ciphers is the **data encryption standard** (**DES**) defined by the US National Bureau of Standards. This is now widely used. Consequently, various integrated circuits are available to perform the encryption operation in hardware thereby speeding up the encryption and decryption operations.

10.2.3 The data encryption standard

The DES algorithm is a **block cipher**, which means that it works on fixed-sized blocks of data. Thus, a complete message is first split (segmented) into blocks of plaintext, each comprising 64 bits. A (hopefully) unique 56-bit key is used to encrypt each block of plaintext into a 64-bit block of ciphertext, which is subsequently transmitted through the network. The receiver uses the same key to perform the inverse (decrpytion) operation on each 64-bit data block it receives, thereby reassembling the blocks into complete messages.

The larger the number of bits used for the key, the more likely it is that the key will be unique. Also, the larger the key, the more difficult it is for someone to decipher it. The use of a 56-bit key in the DES means that there are in the order of 1017 possible keys from which to choose. Consequently, DES is regarded as providing sufficient security for most commercial applications.

A diagram of the DES algorithm is shown in Figure 10.4(a). The 56-bit key selected by the two correspondents is first used to derive 16 different subkeys, each of 48 bits, which are used in the subsequent substitution operations. The algorithm comprises 19 distinct steps. The first step is a simple transposition of the 64-bit block of plaintext using a fixed transposition rule. The resulting 64 bits of transposed text then go through 16 identical iterations of substitution processing, except that at each iteration a different subkey is used in the substitution operation. The most significant 32 bits of the 64-bit output of the last iteration are then exchanged with the least significant 32 bits. Finally, the inverse of the transposition that was performed in step 1 is carried out to produce the 64-bit block of ciphertext to be transmitted. The DES algorithm is designed so that the received block is deciphered by the receiver using the same steps as for encryption, but in the reverse order.

The 16 subkeys used at each substitution step are produced as follows. Firstly, a fixed transposition is performed on the 56-bit key. The resulting transposed key is then split into two separate 28-bit halves. Next, these two halves are rotated left independently and the combined 56 bits are then transposed once again using a compression operation to produce a subkey of 48 bits. The other subkeys are produced in a similar way except that the number of rotations performed is determined by the number of the subkey.

The processing performed at each of the 16 intermediate substitution steps in the encryption process is relatively complex as it is this that ensures the effectiveness of the DES algorithm. This processing is outlined in Figure 10.4(b). The 64-bit output from the previous iteration is first split into two 32-bit halves. The left 32-bit output is simply the right 32-bit input. However, the right 32-bit output is a function of both the left and right inputs and the subkey for this stage. The principle is shown in Figure 10.4(c).

As we can deduce from the figure, in the forward (encryption) direction:

$$L_x = R_{x-1}$$

and

$$R_x = L_{x-1} \oplus f_n (R_{x-1}, K_x)$$

where f_n is a bitwise function called the **Feistel cipher**. First, since the subkey for the stage, K_x, is 48 bits, R_{x-1} is expanded into a 48-bit value using a P-box – similar to that shown in part (ii) of Figure 10.2(a) – with a fixed key. This is then exclusive-ORed with K_x and the 48-bit output is then converted back again into a 32-bit value. This is done by first dividing the 48-bit value into eight 6-bit groups and then passing each group through an S-box – similar to

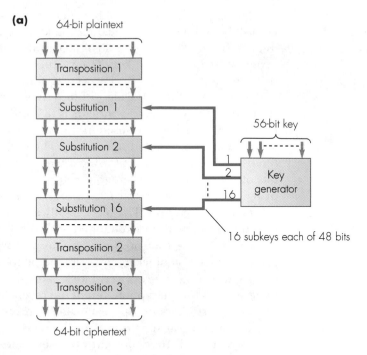

(a)

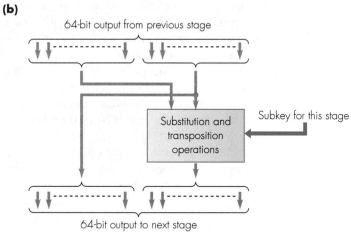

(b)

Figure 10.4 DES algorithm principles: (a) overall schematic; (b) substitution schematic; (c) substitution operation.

that shown in Figure 10.2(b) – each with a different key. In this case, however, the internal P-box performs a compression operation by transposing the 64-bit output from the 6-to-64 decoder into 16 bits. The resulting 16 bits are then passed to a 16-to-4 bit encoder to produce a 4-bit value. The 4-bit output

(c)

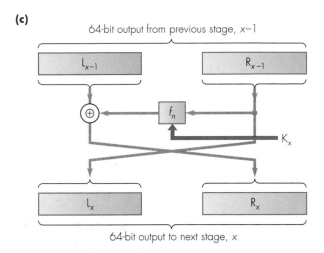

Figure 10.4 Continued.

from each of the eight S-boxes is then combined to form a 32-bit value which is passed through a second (straight) P-box to produce the output of the function block (f_n).

As we indicated earlier, the DES algorithm is designed so that the received block is deciphered by the receiver using the same steps as for encryption, but in the reverse order. As we can deduce from Figure 10.4(a), since transposition 1 is the inverse of transposition 3 and transposition 2 is a simple swap operation, by passing the received input through the stack in the reverse direction the output at the top will be the original plaintext. This is only true of course, if passing the 64-bit block through each substitution operation in the reverse direction also produces the inverse of that produced in the forward direction.

To illustrate that the Feisel cipher has this property, as we can deduce from Figure 10.4(c), in the reverse (decryption) direction:

$$R_{x-1} = L_x$$

and

$$L_{x-1} = R_x \oplus f_n(L_x, K_x)$$

Hence, since $L_x = R_{x-1}$, the output of the Feisel cipher – and hence each substitution operation – is invertible.

For example, if we work with two 4-bit groups and assume f_n is a simple exclusive OR operation with a key, K_x, of 1011, then if:

$$L_{x-1} = 1001 \text{ and } R_{x-1} = 0110$$

in the forward (encryption) direction:

$$L_x = 0110 \ \text{ and } \ R_x = 0100$$

and in the reverse (decryption) direction:

$$R_{x-1} = 0110 \ \text{ and } \ L_{x-1} = 1001$$

which, as we can see, are the same as the two original inputs.

Triple DES

Although DES is still widely used, the use of a 56-bit key means that, with increasingly powerful computers, the time taken to exhaustively try each of the possible keys is reducing steadily. To counter this, a variant called **triple DES** has been developed. The principle of the scheme is shown in Figure 10.5.

As we can see, the scheme involves the use of two keys and three executions of the DES algorithm. Key K_1 is used with the first (DES) block, K_2 with the second block, and K_1 again with the third block. The use of two keys gives an effective key length of 112 bits and, because of this, the scheme is now widely used in many financial applications.

Chaining

The basic mode of working of DES is known as **electronic code book (ECB)** since each block of ciphertext is independent of any other block. Thus each 64-bit block of ciphertext has a unique matching block of plaintext, which is analogous to entries in a code book. The ECB mode of working is shown in Figure 10.6(a).

As we can deduce from the figure, the ECB mode of operation of DES has good secrecy properties and gives good protection against errors or changes that may occur in a single block of enciphered text. It does not, however, protect against errors arising in a stream of blocks. Since each block

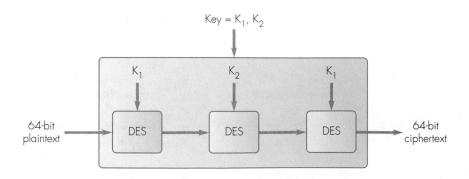

Figure 10.5 Triple DES schematic.

is treated separately in the ECB mode, the insertion of a correctly enciphered block into a transmitted stream of blocks is not detected by the receiver; it simply deciphers the inserted block and treats it as a valid block. Consequently, the stream of enciphered blocks may be intercepted and altered by someone who knows the key without the recipient being aware that any modifications have occurred. Also, if the order of the blocks is changed in some way then this will not be detected. The ECB mode, therefore, has poor integrity properties. Hence to obtain integrity as well as secrecy, an alternative mode of operation of DES based on a technique called **chaining** is often used. It is called the **chain block cipher** (**CBC**) mode and is shown in Figure 10.6(b).

As we can see, although the chaining mode uses the same block encryption method as previously described, each 64-bit block of plaintext is first exclusive-ORed with the enciphered output of the previous block before it is enciphered. The first 64-bit block of plaintext is exclusive-ORed with a 64-bit random number called the **initial vector**, which is sent prior to the cipher text. Then, after the first block has been encoded/decoded using this, subsequent blocks are encoded/decoded in the chained sequence shown in the figure. Thus, since the output of each block is a function both of the block contents and the output of the previous block, any alternations to the transmitted sequence can be detected by the receiver so giving a high level of integrity. Also, identical blocks of plaintext yield different blocks of ciphertext, which makes the breaking of the code much more difficult. For these reasons, this is the mode of operation normally used for digital communication applications.

Since the basic CBC mode operates with 64-bit blocks, all messages must be multiples of 64 bits. Otherwise padding bits must be added. However, as we have seen in earlier chapters, the contents of all messages consist of strings of octets, so the basic unit of all messages is 8 bits rather than 64. An alternative mode of DES known as the **cipher feedback mode** (**CFM**) has also been defined which operates on 8-bit boundaries. A schematic of the scheme is shown in Figure 10.6(c).

With this mode, a new DES encryption operation is performed after every 8 bits of input rather than 64 with the CBC mode. A new 8-bit output is also produced which is the least significant 8 bits of the DES output, exclusive-ORed with the 8 input bits. Then, after each 8-bit output has been loaded into the output buffer, the 64-bit contents of the input shift register are shifted by 8 places. The 8 most significant bits are thus lost and the new 8-bit input is loaded into the least significant 8 bits of the input shift register. The DES operation is performed on these new 64 bits and the resulting 64-bit output is loaded into the output register. The least significant 8 bits of the latter are then exclusive-ORed with the 8 input bits and the process repeats.

CFM is particularly useful when the encryption operation is being performed at the interface with the serial transmission line. This mode of operation is used with the DES integrated circuits; each new 8-bit output is loaded directly into the serial interface circuit.

(a)

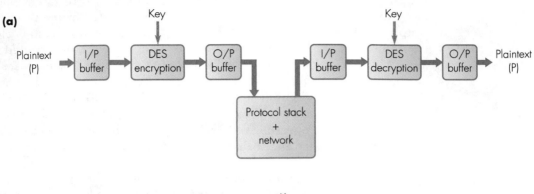

(b)

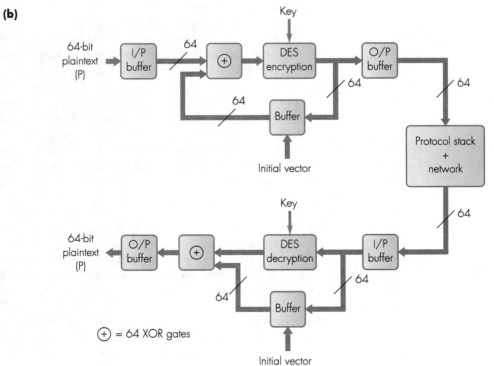

Figure 10.6 DES operational modes: (a) electronic code book (ECB); (b) chain block cipher (CBC); (c) cipher feedback mode (CFM).

(c)

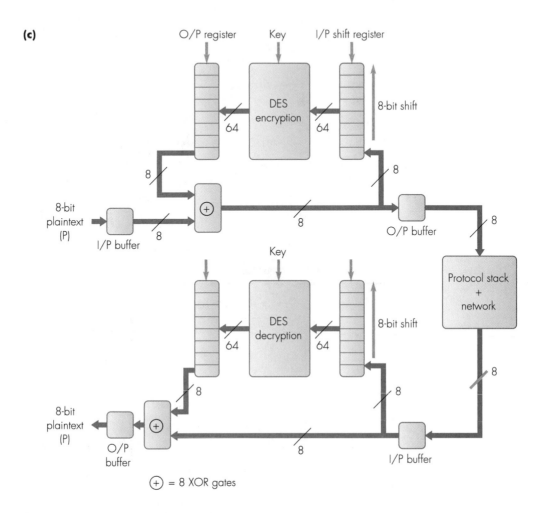

Figure 10.6 Continued.

10.2.4 IDEA

The **international data encryption algorithm (IDEA)** is another block cipher method that is similar in principle to DES since it also operates on 64-bit blocks of plaintext. It can also be used, therefore, in the various chaining modes we described in the last section. To obtain added resilience, however, it uses a 128-bit key and more sophisticated processing during each phase of the encryption operation. Also, it has been designed so that it can be implemented equally well in both hardware and software. A schematic diagram of the encryption operation is shown in Figure 10.7(a).

As we can see, each 64-bit block of plaintext passes through a series of eight bit-manipulation iterations followed by a final transposition. At each of

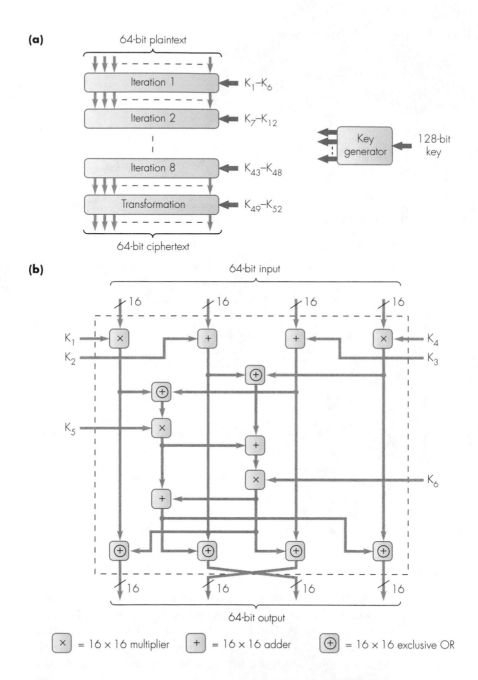

Figure 10.7 IDEA: (a) encryption schematic; (b) single iteration detail.

the eight iterations, each of the 64 output bits is a function of all 64 input bits. The various processing operations that are carried out to achieve this are shown in Figure 10.7(b).

The 128-bit key is first used to generate 52 subkeys each of 16 bits. As we can see in the figure, six subkeys are used at each iteration and the remaining four subkeys are used in the final transposition stage. Decryption uses the same algorithm but with a modified set of keys.

Each 64-bit input is first divided into four 16-bit words each of which goes through a series of multiplication, addition, and exclusive-OR operations. All the lines shown in the figure are 16 bits and all the multiplication operations involve first the 32-bit product of the two 16-bit inputs being computed and then dividing this by $2^{16} + 1$. The output is then the 16-bit remainder. In the case of the addition operations, the two 16-bit inputs are added together and any carry that is generated is ignored.

10.2.5 The RSA algorithm

Both DES and IDEA rely, of course, on the same key being used for both encryption and decryption. An obvious disadvantage is that some form of key notification must be used before any encrypted data is transferred between two correspondents. This is perfectly acceptable as long as the key does not change very often, but in fact it is common practice to change the key on a daily, if not more frequent, basis. Clearly, the new key cannot reliably be sent via the network, so an alternative means, such as a courier, must be used. The distribution of keys is a major problem with private key encryption systems. An alternative method, based on a public rather than a private key, is sometimes used to overcome this problem. The best known public key method is the **RSA algorithm**, named after its three inventors: Rivest, Shamir and Adelman.

The fundamental difference between a private key system and a public key system is that the latter uses a different key to decrypt the ciphertext from the key that was used to encrypt it. A public key system uses a pair of keys: one for the sender and the other for the recipient.

Although this may not seem to help, the inventors of the RSA algorithm used number theory to develop a method of generating a pair of numbers – the keys – in such a way that a message encrypted using the first number of the pair can be decrypted only by the second number. Furthermore, the second number cannot be derived from the first. This second property means that the first number of the pair can be made available to anyone who wishes to send an encrypted message to the holder of the second number since only that person can decrypt the resulting ciphertext message. The first number of the pair is known as the **public key** and the second the private or **secret key**. The principle of the method is shown in Figure 10.8.

As indicated, the derivation of the two keys is based on number theory and is therefore outside the scope of this book. However, the basic algorithm used to compute the two keys is simple and is summarized here together with a much simplified example.

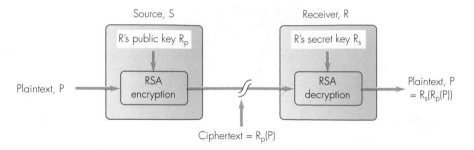

Figure 10.8 RSA schematic.

To create the public key K_p: *Example:*

■ select two large positive prime numbers P and Q $P = 7$, $Q = 17$

■ compute $X = (P - 1) \times (Q - 1)$ $X = 96$

■ choose an integer E which is prime relative
  to X, i.e., not a prime factor of X or a multiple
  of it, and which satisfies the condition
  indicated below for the computation of K_s $E = 5$

■ compute $N = P \times Q$ $N = 119$

■ K_p is then N concatenated with E $K_p = 119, 5$

To create the secret key K_s:

■ compute D such that MOD $(D \times E, X) = 1$ $D \times 5/96 = 1$, $D = 77$
■ K_s is then N concatenated with D $K_s = 119, 77$

To compute the ciphertext C of plaintext P:

■ treat P as a numerical value $P = 19$
■ $C = \text{MOD} (P^E, N)$ $C = \text{MOD} (19^5, 119)$ $C = 66$

To compute the plaintext P of ciphertext C:

■ $P = \text{MOD} (C^D, N)$ $P = \text{MOD} (66^{77}, 119)$
                                                                                  $P = 19$

The choice of E and D in this example is best seen by considering the factors of 96. These are 1, 2, 3, 4, 6, 8, 12, 16, 24, 32, 48. The list of numbers that are prime relative to 96 are thus 5, 7, 9, 10, 11, and so on. If we try the first of these, $E = 5$, then there is also a number $D = 77$ that satisfies the condition MOD $(D \times E, X) = 1$ and hence these are chosen.

We can deduce from this example that the crucial numbers associated with the algorithm are the two prime numbers P and Q, which must always be kept secret. The aim is to choose a sufficiently large N so that it is impossible to factorize it in a realistic time. Some example (computer) factorizing times are:

$N = 100$ digits ≈ 1 week

$N = 150$ digits ≈ 1000 years

$N > 200$ digits ≈ 1 million years

The RSA algorithm requires considerable computation time to compute the exponentiation for both the encryption and decryption operations. However, there is a simple way of avoiding the exponentiation operation by performing instead the following algorithm which uses only repeated multiplication and division operations:

$C := 1$

begin for i $= 1$ to E *do*

$C := \text{MOD}\ (C \times P, N)$

end

Decryption is performed in the same way by replacing E with D and P with C in the above expression; this yields the plaintext P. For example, to compute $C = \text{MOD}\ (19^5, 119)$:

Step 1: $C = \text{MOD}\ (1 \times 19, 119) = 19$

2: $C = \text{MOD}\ (19 \times 19, 119) = 4$

3: $C = \text{MOD}\ (4 \times 19, 119) = 76$

4: $C = \text{MOD}\ (76 \times 19, 119) = 16$

5: $C = \text{MOD}\ (16 \times 19, 119) = 66$

Note also that the value of N determines the maximum message that can be encoded. In the example this is 119 and is numerically equivalent to a single ASCII-encoded character. Therefore, a message comprising a string of ASCII characters would have to be encoded one character at a time.

Although a public key system offers an alternative to a private key system to overcome the threat of eavesdropping, if the public key is readily available it can be used by a masquerader to send a forged message. The question then arises as to how the recipient of a correctly ciphered message can be sure that it was sent by a legitimate source. As we indicated earlier, this relates to authentication and nonrepudiation and there are a number of solutions to this problem.

10.3 Nonrepudiation

Public key systems like RSA are particularly useful for nonrepudiation; that is, proving that a person sent an electronic document. With a paper document,

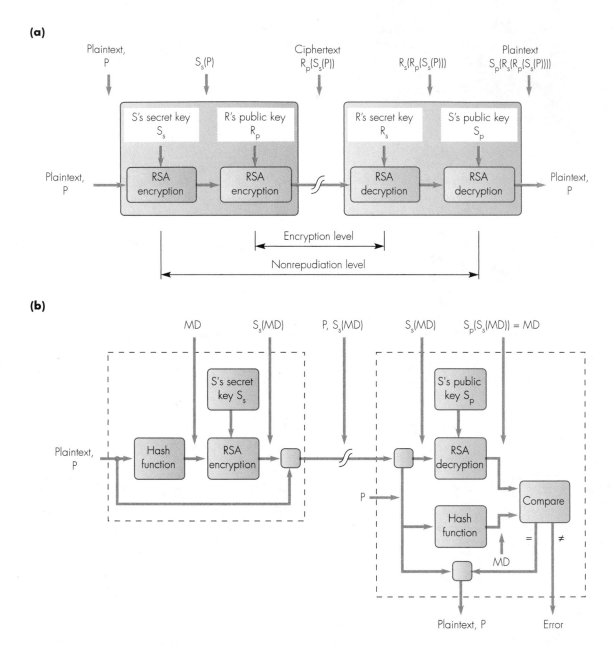

Figure 10.9 Nonrepudiation using RSA: (a) on complete message; (b) on message digest.

normally a person adds his or her signature at the end of the document – sometimes with the name and signature of a witness – and, should it be necessary, this is then used to verify that the person whose signature is on the document sent it.

One solution is to exploit the dual property of public key systems, namely that not only is a receiver able to decipher all messages it receives (which have been encrypted with its own public key) using its own private key, but any receiver can also decipher a message encrypted with the sender's private key, using the sender's public key.

Figure 10.9(a) shows how this property may be exploited to achieve non-repudiation. Encryption and decryption operations are performed at two levels. The inner level of encryption and decryption is as already described. However, at the outer level, the sender uses its own private key to encrypt the original (plaintext) message. If the receiver can decrypt this message using that sender's public key, this is proof that the sender did in fact initiate the sending of the message. The scheme is said therefore to produce a **digital signature**.

Although this is an elegant solution, it has a number of limitations. Firstly, the processing overheads associated with the RSA algorithm are high. As we saw with the earlier (much simplified) example, even with a small message (value), the numbers involved can be very large. Therefore a complete message must be divided into a number of smaller units, the size of which is a function of the computer being used. Hence, even though integrated circuits are available to help with these computations, the total message throughput with RSA is still relatively low. Secondly, the method requires two levels of encryption even though it may not be necessary to encrypt the actual message, that is, although only nonrepudiation is required, the actual message contents must still be encrypted.

One solution is to compute a much shorter version of the message based on the message contents, similar in principle to the computation of a CRC. The shorter version is called the **message digest** (**MD**) and the computation function that is used to compute it the hash function. The principle of the scheme is shown in Figure 10.9(b).

The MD is first computed using the chosen hash function. This is then encrypted using the sender's private key. The encrypted MD is then sent together with the plaintext message. At the receiver, the encrypted MD is decrypted using the sender's public key. The MD of the received plaintext message is also computed and, if this is the same as the decrypted MD, this is taken as proof that no one has tampered with the message and the sender whose public key was used to decrypt the MD did in fact send the message.

There are two widely used schemes that use this approach. One is called **MD5**, which was designed by Rivest, and the other the **secure hash algorithm** (**SHA**), which is a US government scheme. Both schemes operate on 512-bit blocks of plaintext. In the case of MD5 the computed MD is 128 bits long and for SHA, 160 bits long. As we shall see in the following sections, MD5 is widely used with Internet applications and, because of its origin, SHA is used in government applications.

10.4 Authentication

In general, authentication is required when a client wishes to access some information or service from a networked server. Before the client is allowed access to the server, he or she must first prove to the server that they are a registered user. Once authenticated the user is then allowed access. The authentication process can be carried out using either a public key or a private key scheme. We shall give an example of each approach.

10.4.1 Using a public key system

The general principle of a scheme that is based on a public key system is shown in Figure 10.10. The scheme assumes that all potential users know the public key of the server, S_p. The client first creates a message containing the client's user name, U, the client's public key, C_p, and a time-stamp, t_c. The latter indicates when the message was created and a record of this is kept by the client. The message is then encrypted using S_p and sent to the server (1).

The server first decrypts the message using its own secret key, S_s, and then proceeds to validate that there is such a registered user from the user name, U. Assuming this is the case, it then proceeds to create a response message comprising the client's user name, U, and time-stamp, t_c, plus a second time-stamp indicating when the response was created by the server, t_s. The server keeps a record of this and encrypts the message using the client's public key, C_p. It then sends the encrypted message to the client (2).

On receipt of the response, the client first decrypts the message using its own secret key, C_s, and, on determining that the t_c within it is the same as it sent, assumes that it has been authenticated by the server. It then proceeds to acknowledge this by creating a second message containing the client's user name, U, and the server's time-stamp, t_s. This again is encrypted using the

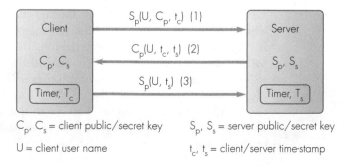

Figure 10.10 User authentication using a public key scheme.

server's public key, S_p, and sent to the server (3). The server decrypts this using its own secret key, S_s, and, on determining the t_s within it is the same as it sent, prepares to accept service requests from the client.

Note that in both cases, if the time the message was received exceeds the time-stamp value in the related response message by more than a defined time interval, then the message is discarded and access remains blocked. Also, should the transaction require the subsequent messages to be encrypted, then the key to be used would be returned by the server in message (2).

10.4.2 Using a private key system

An example of a method that is based on a private key system is **Kerberos**. This is widely used in many practical systems and, as we shall see, the method requires a trusted third party to act as a **key distribution server**.

The basic security control mechanism employed in Kerberos is a set of encrypted **tickets** – also known as control or permission tokens – which are used to control access to the various servers that make up the system. These include a range of application servers – file servers, electronic mail servers, and so on – and the system server that issues the tickets is known as the **ticket granting server**. All messages that are exchanged between a user and the ticket granting server, and between a user and an application server, are encrypted using private keys that form part of the corresponding ticket. In addition, each message/ticket has a **nonce** associated with it. This comprises two date-and-time values the first of which specifies when the nonce was first generated. A nonce is used both to verify the origin of a message and to limit the validity of a ticket to a defined lifetime. This is determined by the second date-and-time value in the nonce. This feature means an eavesdropper has only a limited time to decrypt an intercepted ticket.

The key distribution server is a networked system with which all users and application servers must be registered. It comprises two servers: an **authentication server** and a ticket granting server. The authentication server provides, firstly, management services to allow all users, together with their related passwords, to be registered. It also provides the names and secret keys of all Kerberos servers, including the ticket granting server and all application servers. This information is retained in an **authentication database**. It then provides additional runtime services to enable a user to be authenticated as a registered user of the system before being allowed to access any of the Kerberos servers. A schematic diagram summarizing the various interactions between a user and the two types of server is given in Figure 10.11(a).

Running within each client workstation is a process called the **user agent** and it is through this that all interactions between a user and the various Kerberos servers take place. Before a user (agent) can access an application server, it must first obtain from the ticket granting server an **authentication ticket** and a **session key**; the first verifies that the user has been authenticated

(a)

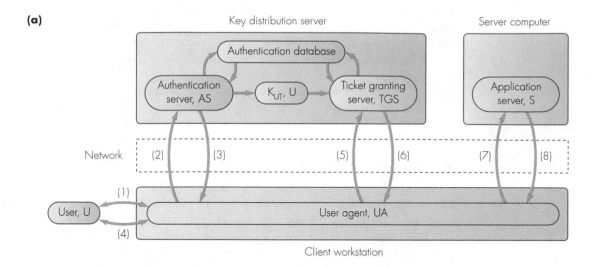

(b) K_U = The private key of the user – the user password
K_T = The private key of the TGS
K_S = The private key of the application server
K_{UT} = A session key to encrypt UA $\leftrightarrow$ TGS dialog units
K_{US} = A session key to encrypt UA $\rightarrow$ S dialog units

TGS ticket, $T_{UT} = K_T (U, T, t_1, t_2, K_{UT})$
Application server ticket, $T_{US} = K_S (U, S, t_1, t_2, K_{US})$
t_1, t_2 = start, end of ticket lifetime

(c)

	Direction	Message
(1)	U $\leftrightarrow$ UA	User name, U
(2)	UA $\rightarrow$ AS	(U, T, n_1)
(3)	AS $\rightarrow$ UA	$K_U (K_{UT}, n_1)$; T_{UT}
(4)	U $\leftrightarrow$ UA	User password, K_U
(5)	UA $\rightarrow$ TGS	$K_{UT} (U, t)$; T_{UT}, S, n_2
(6)	TGS $\rightarrow$ UA	$K_{UT} (K_{US}, n_2)$; T_{US}
(7)	UA $\rightarrow$ S	$K_{US} (U, t)$; T_{US}, n_3
(8)	S $\rightarrow$ UA	$K_{US} (n_3)$

$K_{UT}/K_{US} (U, t)$ are both authenticators and t is a time-stamp

Figure 10.11 User authentication using Kerberos: (a) terminology and message exchange; (b) key and ticket definitions; (c) message contents.

as a registered user and the second is used to encrypt all the subsequent dialog units that are exchanged in this session between the user agent and the application server. Note that in practice more than one application server can be involved in a single session. Also, both keys have a limited lifetime associated with them to guard against a user, whose registration has expired for example, from reusing a ticket.

At the start of a session, the user is prompted by the user agent (UA) for his/her user name (1). Before the UA can communicate with the ticket granting server (TGS), the user must first be authenticated as a registered user and a (permission) ticket obtained to access the TGS. Both these functions are performed by the authentication server (AS). On receipt of the user name, the UA creates a message containing the names of the user and the TGS and a nonce. The UA keeps a record of the nonce used and sends the message to the AS (2).

All subsequent messages associated with the session are encrypted using various keys. These are defined in Figure 10.11(b) together with the components that make up the two tickets, the first granting permission for the UA to communicate with the TGS and the second for the UA to communicate with the application server. The contents of the messages exchanged during a successful session are listed in Figure 10.11(c).

On receipt of the initial UA request message, the AS first validates the user is registered and, if positive, proceeds to create a response message. The latter comprises two parts. The first part consists of a newly generated session key, K_{UT} – to be used to encrypt the subsequent UA/TGS dialog units – together with the nonce, n_1, contained in the initial UA request message. A record is kept of K_{UT} and this part of the response message is then encrypted using the user's password, K_U – obtained from the authentication database – as a key. The second part comprises the permission ticket for the UA to access the TGS, T_{UT} – encrypted using the private key of the TGS, K_T. The two-part message is then returned to the UA (3).

At this point the UA prompts the user to enter his/her password, K_U (4). The latter is then used to obtain, firstly, the nonce, n_1 – which verifies the message relates to its earlier request – and secondly, the key K_{UT}. Clearly, a user impersonating as the registered user would not be able to decrypt this message and hence would be foiled at this stage. The UA then proceeds to use the retrieved key, K_{UT}, to create what is referred to as an **authenticator**. This is a token that verifies the user has been authenticated and comprises the user name, U, and a time-stamp, t, both encrypted using K_{UT}. To this is added the encrypted permission ticket, T_{UT}, the name of the required application server, S, and a second nonce, n_2. The complete message is then sent to the TGS (5).

The authenticator is decrypted by the TGS using the retained key K_{UT} and, since this was granted for the same user, U, it is accepted by the TGS as proof that the user has permission to be granted a session key to communicate with an application server. In response, the TGS generates a new session key, K_{US}, to be used by UA to encrypt the dialog units exchanged with the named server, S. Note that if multiple servers were to be accessed during the session, then multiple keys are issued at this stage, one for use with each server. The TGS then creates a message, the first part comprising K_{US} and the nonce n_2 – encrypted using K_{UT} – and the second comprising an encrypted permission ticket for the UA to access B, T_{US}. The complete message is then sent to the UA (6).

On receipt of this, the UA uses K_{UT} to decrypt the first part of the message to obtain K_{US} and the nonce n_2. The latter is used to confirm the message relates to its own earlier request message to the TGS, and K_{US} is used to create an authenticator, which verifies the user has been granted permission to access the named server. The authenticator is then combined with the permission ticket granted by the TGS, T_{US}, and a third nonce n_3. The resulting message is then sent by the UA to server S (7).

As Figure 10.11(b) shows, the permission ticket, T_{US}, is encrypted using the private key of S, K_S. Hence, on receipt of the message, S proceeds to use its own private key to decrypt T_{US} and obtain the name of the user, U, and the allocated session key, K_{US}. It uses the latter to decrypt the authenticator and confirm that U has been authenticated as a registered user and granted permission to access S. The server responds by returning the nonce, n_3, encrypted using K_{US} (8). This concludes the authentication procedure and the exchange of data messages between UA and S can now commence. If required, the data messages are encrypted using K_{US}.

10.5 Public key certification authorities

In the examples in previous sections that used the RSA public key scheme it was assumed that the public key was obtained in some way, for example by sending it in an e-mail message prior to the transfer or making it available in a Web page. However, sending a public key in this way without any supporting proof of identify has potential drawbacks. The example shown in Figure 10.12 illustrates one of these.

In this example it is assumed that the person sending the message wants to discredit the person whose name is on the message. To do this, he or she sends a message that will achieve this in such a way that the recipient thinks the message has been sent by the person whose name is on it. To avoid this type of misuse of public key systems, in most applications the public key is obtained from a recognized **certification authority** (**CA**).

When a person registers with a recognized CA, after careful checks, an electronic **certificate** is created by the CA. This contains, in addition to the public key of the owner of the certificate, other information about the owner. The IETF have defined the complete list of contents of a certificate in RFC 1422 and this is now used widely by a number of CAs. The fields present include:

- **issuer name**: the identify (called the **distinguished name**) of the CA in a syntax defined in RFC 1779;
- **serial number**: the unique identifier of the certificate;
- **subject name**: the identity of the owner of the certificate, for example, an e-mail address, a URL of a Web server, or an IP address of, say, a router;
- **public key**: the owner's public key and the key algorithm, for example RSA;

$$P, S_s(MD)$$

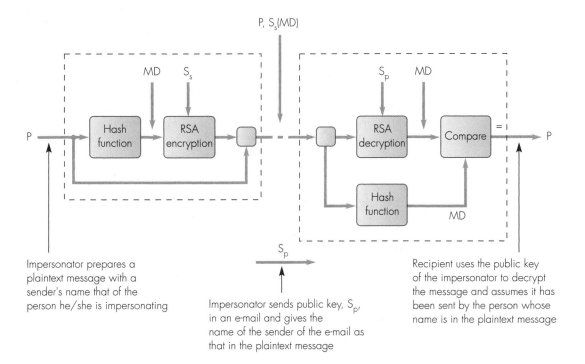

Impersonator prepares a plaintext message with a sender's name that of the person he/she is impersonating

Impersonator sends public key, S_p, in an e-mail and gives the name of the sender of the e-mail as that in the plaintext message

Recipient uses the public key of the impersonator to decrypt the message and assumes it has been sent by the person whose name is in the plaintext message

Figure 10.12 A possible threat when using a public key system.

- **validity period**: start and end date of the validity of the certificate;
- **signature**: the algorithm used by the CA to encrypt the certificate contents, for example RSA.

Once a certificate has been created, the public key it contains can only be accessed through the CA. Typically, the CA is on a list of recognized CAs. The list is located at a well-known Web site and, for each CA on the list, its location and its public key are given. Then, when a public key is required from the CA, the subject's name is submitted and, in response, the CA returns the related certificate. The recipient proceeds to decrypt the contents of the certificate using the public key of the CA. It then reads the public key from the certificate and, before using it, validates that the name of the person on the certificate is that whose key is required.

10.6 E-mail privacy

As with all Internet applications, it is relatively straightforward to read messages during their transmission over the access networks and the

Internet itself. It is now becoming common practice with many companies, for example, to monitor the e-mail that is being sent and received by their employees. Increasingly, therefore, people and organizations are applying encryption methods to the mail messages that they send.

When two people are communicating using ASCII text and wish to foil a casual eavesdropper from reading their mail, a simple approach to obtaining privacy is to encode the message body using Base64 – see Table 8.2 – before it is entered. This can be done very easily by interpreting the stream of ASCII characters that make up the message as a bitstream. Then, by applying Base64 to the bitstream, the resulting transmitted (NVT) ASCII character string is meaningless to the casual eavesdropper.

For example, using the table of ASCII codewords in Figure 1.14, the character string *I LOVE* in 7-bit ASCII is:

1001001(I) 0100000(SP) 1001100(L) 1001111(O) 1010110(V) 1000101(E)

Hence, when this bitstream is interpreted as a string of 6-bit groups, it yields:
100100 101000 001001 100100 111110 101101 000101

In hexadecimal these are equivalent to:

24   28   09   24   3E   2D   05

or, using the Base64 encoding in Table 8.2, the ASCII character string:

k   o   J   k   +   t   F

which, of course, is less interesting should it be observed.

Clearly it is a trivial task to break this code and for applications that demand a high level of security, a number of more sophisticated encryption schemes are now used. Since it uses a number of the encryption methods we discussed in the last chapter, we shall limit our discussion to a widely used scheme devised by Zimmermann called **pretty good privacy** (**PGP**). As we shall see, PGP provides not only a high level of privacy, but also authentication, integrity and nonrepudiation. The various steps followed to encrypt a message are shown in Figure 10.13. Normally the header fields are repeated in the message body, which is then encrypted.

As we can see, the overall process involves a combination of MD5 (Section 10.3), RSA (Section 10.2.5), IDEA (Section 10.2.4) and Base64. It also uses the Lempel–Ziv (LZ) compression algorithm. With the Lempel–Ziv (LZ) compression algorithm, instead of using single characters as the basis of the coding operation, strings of characters are used. For example, for the compression of text, a table containing all the possible character strings – for example words – that occur in the text to be transferred is held by both the encoder and decoder. As each word occurs in the text, instead of sending the word as a set of individual – say, ASCII – codewords, the encoder sends only the index of where the word is stored in the table and, on receipt of each

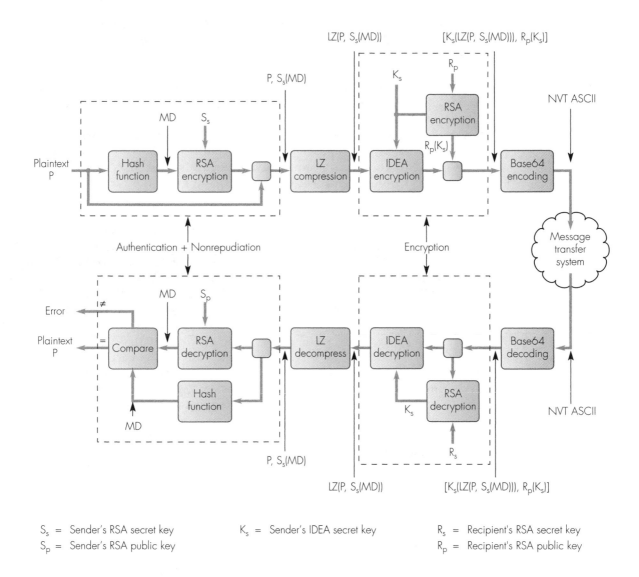

Figure 10.13 E-mail privacy: PGP encryption and decryption.

index, the decoder uses this to access the corresponding word/string of characters from the table and proceeds to reconstruct the text into its original form. Thus the table is used as a dictionary and the LZ algorithm is known as a **dictionary-based** compression algorithm.

Most word-processing packages have a dictionary associated with them that is used for both spell checking and for the compression of text. Typically, they contain in the region of 25 000 words and hence 15 bits – which has 32 768 combinations – are required to encode the index. To send the word "multimedia" with such a dictionary would require just 15 bits instead of 70 bits with 7-bit ASCII codewords. This results in a compression ratio of 4.7:1. Clearly, shorter words will have a lower compression ratio and longer words a higher ratio.

The first block is concerned with authentication and nonrepudiation. It uses the same scheme that we showed in Figure 10.9. This produces the plaintext, P, and a 128-bit message digest (MD). The MD is then encrypted using the sender's RSA secret key, S_s. At the recipient side, the MD is again computed using the same hash function and, if this is the same as the decrypted MD that was sent with the message, this is taken as proof that the message was indeed sent by the sender in the *From:* field of the message header. This is then taken as authenticating the sender and, should it be necessary, nonrepudiation.

The output of the authentication and nonrepudiation block – P, S_s (MD) – is compressed using the LZ algorithm and the output of this is passed to the encryption block. This is based on IDEA and uses a 128-bit secret key, K_s, to encrypt the LZ compressed block. K_s is also encrypted using the recipient's RSA public key, R_p, to produce $R_p(K_s)$. This, together with the output of the IDEA compression block, forms the binary output. Finally, this is Base64 encoded to yield an ASCII string that is then transmitted in the form of an NVT ASCII string, which we described at the end of Section 8.3.1.

The processing at the receiver is the inverse of that carried out at the sending side. First the sender's IDEA secret key, K_s, is obtained by using the recipient's RSA secret key, R_s, to decrypt $R_p(K_s)$. K_s is then used to decrypt the LZ compressed block. After being decompressed, the resulting output is passed to the authentication and nonrepudiation block.

It should be noted that, because of the high processing overheads associated with RSA, the two RSA stages operate only on small block sizes, the first the 128-bit MD and the second the 128-bit secret key used by IDEA. Also the message contents are encrypted using IDEA which, as we saw in Section 10.2.4, is very fast.

10.7 Network security

Security features are located in various parts of a protocol stack. Typically, in fixed-wire networks these start at the network layer where an IETF protocol called **IP security** (**IPsec**) is used. There is then a transport layer protocol called **Transport Layer Security** (**TLS**) that is a derivative of a protocol called the **Secure Socket Layer** (**SSL**). As we have just seen, at the application layer, a security feature is provided for e-mail by a protocol called Pretty Good Privacy (PGP). There are also security features associated with the Web.

In general, because of their mode of operation, even tighter levels of security are provided in wireless networks. These include **Wired Equivalent Privacy** (**WEP**) that is used in IEEE802.11 wireless LANs. In addition, Bluetooth has a number of security features while WAP 2.0 has a full set of security protocols. All are based on the basic security procedures we have discussed in the earlier sections of the chapter. In the following sections we shall describe the essential features of these various protocols.

10.7.1 IP security

There are two main protocols associated with IP security (IPsec): the **Authentication Header (AH) protocol** and the **Encryption Security Payload (ESP) protocol**. The AH protocol supports source authentication and data integrity and the ESP protocol supports both these features plus encryption/confidentiality. Hence either protocol can be used, the choice being determined by the level of security that is required.

With both protocols, before any packets relating to a new session are exchanged between the source and destination hosts, two independent secure logical channels are established: one for packet transfers in, say, the forward direction and the other for packet transfers in the reverse direction. Each logical channel is called a **security association (SA)** and is identified uniquely by:

- the security protocol to be used (AH or ESP),
- the sender's IP address of the related SA,
- a connection identifier called the **security parameter index (SPI)**.

There are two alternative ways of implementing a SA, one called the *transport mode* and the other the *tunnel mode*. With the transport mode, the IPsec header is inserted between the original IP and TCP headers of the packet. With the tunnel mode, the entire original IP packet is encapsulated within a new IP packet with a new header as we explained in Section 6.5.5. This mode of operation is used when the SA terminates at, say, the access gateway of a LAN or, in an enterprise network, the security gateway/firewall whose function we described in Section 9.2.3. In this way, the hosts at a site need not be aware that IPsec is being used. Also, in an enterprise network, a number of IP packets going to the same site can be aggregated together and sent over a single SA. A schematic diagram illustrating the main features of the two protocols is given in Figure 10.14.

Authentication Header protocol
The AH protocol is defined in RFC 2402. When used with the transport mode, the position and contents of the AH header are as shown in Figure 10.15. The roles of the various fields are as follows:

- *Protocol*: In order for the IP layer at the receiver side to be aware that IPsec using the AH protocol is being used, the value in the *protocol* field of the new IP header is set to 51. As we described in Section 6.1, this field is used to identify the network or transport layer protocol at the destination that should receive the packet – ARP/ICMP/IPsec/TCP, etc.

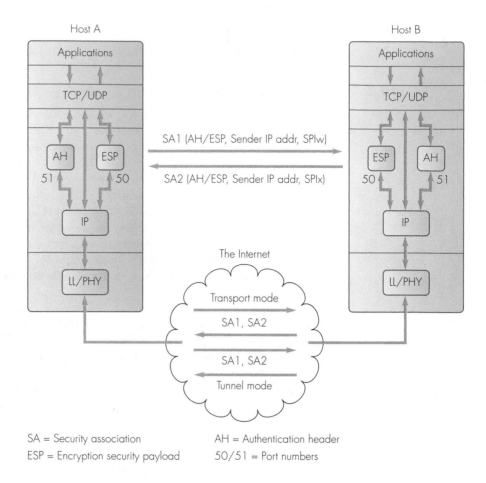

Figure 10.14 **Essential features of AH and ESP security protocols.**

- *Next header:* This is used to hold the value in the protocol field before it was changed to 51. For example, if TCP is being used the value would be 6.
- *Payload length:* This is the number of 32-bit words in the AH minus 2. As we show, the payload may contain padding in order for the authentication algorithm to work on a fixed 32-bit boundary.
- *Security parameters index:* This is the connection identifier of the SPI.
- *Sequence number:* This is used to identify the packet in the sequence of packets that are being sent over the SA. It is present to detect if the packet sequence has been tampered with in any way.
- *Authentication data:* This is a variable-length field and holds the digital signature that has been computed over the original IP packet data plus the value in the IP source address field. Hence it provides host authentication in addition to the integrity of the IP packet data.

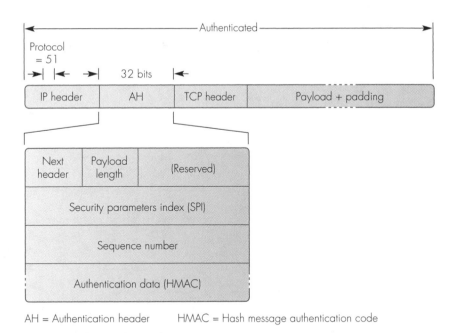

AH = Authentication header   HMAC = Hash message authentication code

Figure 10.15 AH protocol header position and contents in transport mode.

The digital signature – message digest – is computed using the algorithm specified by the SA. Normally, it is either MD5 or SHA, the principles of which we described in Section 10.3. When the SA is first established, the two sides agree on both the signature algorithm that is to be used and the key using the **Internet Key Exchange** (**IKE**) algorithm defined in RFC 2409. In order for packets to be processed quickly, IPsec uses a shared – symmetric – secret key. Then, when the destination receives an IP datagram with an AH header, it first determines the SA and then authenticates the integrity of the packet by processing the contents of the authentication data field using the same secret key as was used to compute this field. This field is called the **Hash Message Authentication Code** (**HMAC**) and is described in RFC 2104.

Encapsulated Security Payload (ESP) protocol

As we indicated earlier, the ESP protocol provides confidentiality/encryption as well as source host authentication and data integrity. A schematic diagram illustrating where the ESP header is located and the fields that are encrypted when using both the transport and tunnel modes is shown in Figure 10.16.

As we can see, the ESP header is composed of the same two 32-bit SPI and sequence number fields as for the AH protocol plus a third field that holds the *Initialization vector* that is to be used for data encryption. The value in the *protocol* field of the new IP header is 50.

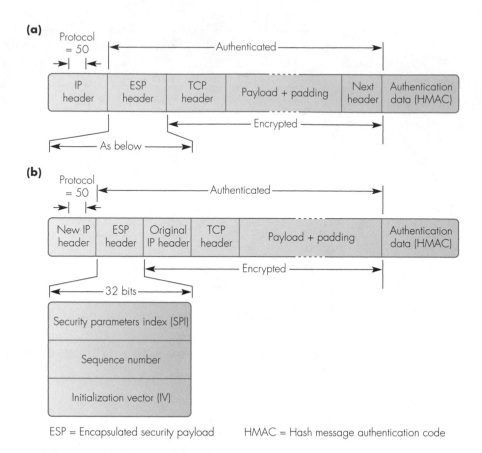

ESP = Encapsulated security payload   HMAC = Hash message authentication code

Figure 10.16 ESP protocol header position and contents: (a) transport mode; (b) tunnel mode.

The ESP uses the same HMAC integrity checks as the AH but with ESP the *Authentication data* field is located at the tail of the packet rather than in the header. Also, in the transport mode, the *Next header* field is located in the ESP trailer since this is then encrypted together with the payload so that the transport layer protocol cannot be determined. The *Authenticated data* field is then computed in the same way as for the AH using the MD5 or SHA algorithm which we described earlier in Section 10.3.

The encryption algorithm used is DES-CBC. We described the operation of this in Section 10.2.3 and it is defined in RFC 2405. As we showed in Figure 10.6(b), this requires a shared key – typically obtained using IKE – and an initialization vector (IV). Normally, as we showed in Figure 10.16, the IV is also included in the ESP header.

10.7.2 Security in wireless networks

Unlike fixed-wire networks in which the conductors within the cable carrying the signal are embedded inside an outer shield to minimize signal attenuation, wireless transmission is achieved by simply broadcasting the signal using a radio transmitter. Hence any device with a suitable radio receiver that is within the field of coverage of a base station/access point can receive the signal and, with the right equipment, the contents of the transmission can be decoded. Clearly, therefore, security within wireless networks is even more necessary than in fixed-wire networks. In this subsection we shall describe the security measures that are used in the three types of wireless network that we described in Chapter 4.

IEEE802.11

Security within an IEEE802.11 wireless LAN is provided at the data link layer. The protocol is called **Wired Equivalent Privacy** (**WEP**) since its aim is to make security within the wireless LAN equivalent to that of a fixed-wire LAN such as Ethernet. Unfortunately, this scheme has already been broken but, since it is still used, we shall use it as an example.

The WEP protocol provides both authentication and data encryption over the wireless/radio link between the access point (AP) and a mobile device using a shared/symmetric key algorithm. Hence when the security feature of the mobile device is enabled, it uses the same key as that used by the AP. However, the WEP specification does not specify a key distribution scheme so we shall assume that the key for both the mobile device and the AP is an embedded feature of both devices.

Authentication is achieved by means of a three-way handshake, the sequence of which is shown in Figure 10.17. First, the mobile device sends an identifier that is recognizable by the AP. The AP then generates a nonce which, in this application, is a number that will be used for only this authentication request, and then sends it to the mobile device. On receipt of the nonce, the mobile device encrypts it using the shared (secret) key and returns the encrypted nonce to the AP. The AP decrypts it using the shared key and, if the decrypted value is the same as the nonce, the mobile device is authenticated.

The WEP encryption algorithm uses a stream cipher called **RC4**, the principle of which is illustrated in Figure 10.18(a). As we can see, a stream of 64-bit keys is generated using the 40-bit secret key and a 24-bit initialization vector (IV), each of which is used to encrypt the corresponding 64-bit block of the frame payload including any padding and the 4-byte CRC/FCS. As we showed in Figure 4.18(a) and explained in the accompanying text, the data field in an IEEE802.11 MAC frame can be up to 2312 bytes and hence is composed of multiple 64-bit blocks. A different IV is then used for each transmitted frame. The principles of the scheme are shown in Figure 10.18(b).

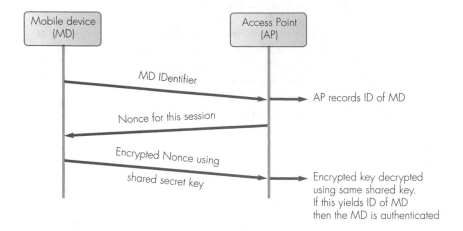

Figure 10.17 Authentication of a mobile device by the AP using a three-way handshake procedure.

Bluetooth

As you may recall from our discussion of Bluetooth in Section 4.2, the Bluetooth standard defines a complete protocol stack for each application profile that it supports. To accompany these, security is provided in a number of the protocol layers. For example, when the link manager protocol in the data link layer of a newly arriving slave device – see Figure 4.10 – communicates with the link manager in the master device to establish a link, a shared/secret key – called the **passkey** – is used. Again it is assumed that both devices know the shared key/passkey. For example, in those applications that involve a pair of devices that are sold together, the passkey is embedded in each device during their manufacture.

First the slave and master check that each has the same passkey and, if this is the case, they then agree on a 128-bit key for this session. Encryption uses a stream cipher called **Eo**, which in practice is the same as that used in 802.11 except that the plaintext is encrypted in 128-bit blocks instead of 64 bits.

WAP 2.0

As we showed in Figure 9.26 and explained in the accompanying text, the WAP 2.0 protocol stack is based on standard Internet protocols at all layers. As a result, all the IETF security protocols can be used in addition to those defined by the WAP Forum. At the application layer, WAP 2.0 defines a set of **cryptographic libraries** for signing data transfers and a set of authentication services to authenticate clients and servers. Alternatively, HTTP client authentication can be carried out using RFC 2617. Similarly, at the transport layer, the WAP 2.0 **wireless transport layer security** (**WTLS**) **protocol** provides secure transport using UDP and the IETF TLS/SSL provides secure transport

(a)

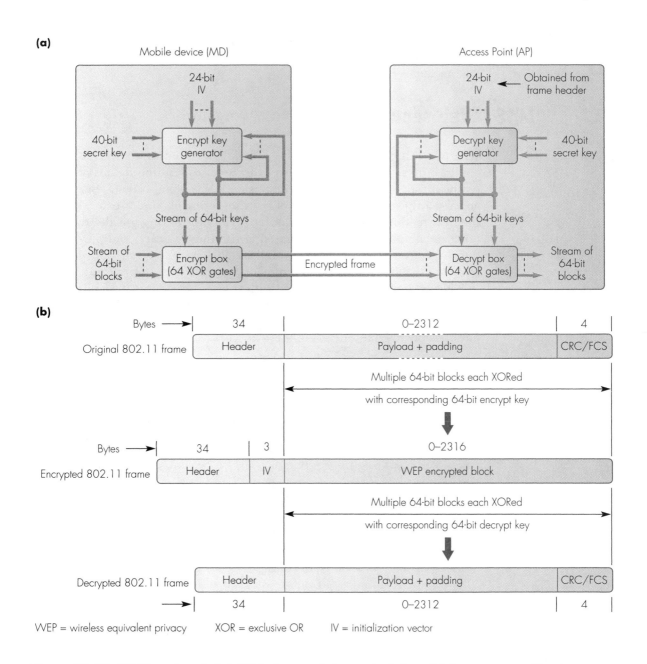

(b)

Figure 10.18 **WEP protocol: (a) RC4 stream cipher principles; (b) frame encryption/ decryption operations.**

over TCP connections. In addition, at the network/IP layer the IPsec proto-col provides a secure datagram service. Collectively, these provide a library of protocols to perform authentication, privacy/secrecy, integrity, and nonrepu-diation services.

10.8 Web security

When carrying out a transaction over the Web relating to an e-commerce application, since in many instances this involves sending details of a user's payment card, the security of such transfers is vitally important. For example, an eavesdropper with knowledge of Internet protocols could readily intercept the information entered on the order form and, having got the name and other details about the card, proceed to use these to carry out purchases of their own. A second potential pitfall is that the Web site from where the purchase is being made may not in reality have anything for sale and, prior to the agreed delivery date, abscond with the money that it has collected. In addition, in electronic banking (e-banking) and other financial applications, a client may masquerade as another person. Any security scheme, therefore, must be able to counter each of these threats.

10.8.1 SSL

An example of a widely used scheme is the Netscape **secure socket layer (SSL)** protocol, later to become the IETF **transport layer security (TLS) protocol**. As the name implies, SSL operates at the socket interface, which, as we saw earlier in Section 7.3.1, is between the transport layer (TCP) and the application layer in the TCP/IP protocol suite. Essentially, SSL carries out the authentication of the server by the client – and the authentication of the client by the server if required – by using a recognized certification authority – see Section 10.4 – and the establishment of a symmetric encryption algorithm and key for the session. It then uses the key – called a **session key** – to encrypt/decrypt all of the messages that are transferred as part of the transaction. The location of the SSL protocol in the stack is shown in Figure 10.19(a) and a summary of the steps that are followed to establish a secure socket connection are listed in part (b) of the figure.

As we can see, the HTML interpreter part of the browser has two pathways/sockets available to it, an insecure socket connection and a secure socket connection. When a user clicks on a link to an SSL-enabled server, the protocol/method part of the URL is *https:* rather than *http:*. On detecting this, the HTML interpreter invokes the SSL protocol code, which proceeds to carry out the steps shown in Figure 10.19(b).

As we can deduce from the list of steps, the establishment of a secure socket connection is carried out by the exchange of an ordered set of HTTP

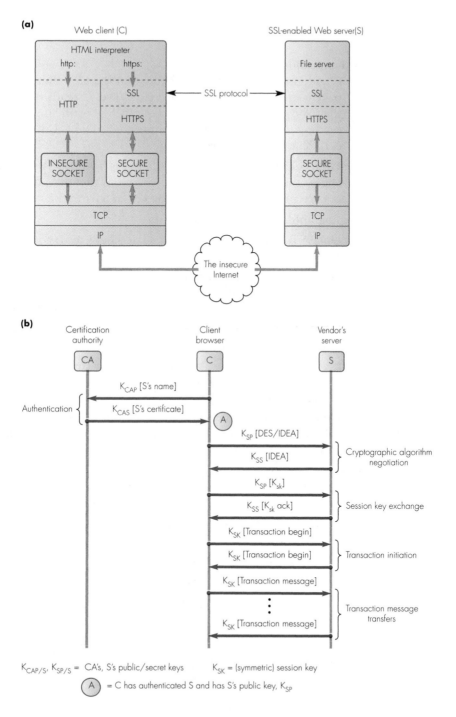

Figure 10.19 The secure socket layer (SSL) protocol: (a) protocol stack; (b) outline of the authentication and transaction initiation phases.

request/response messages, which collectively form the SSL protocol. When interpreting the steps shown in the figure, the following should be noted:

- **Authentication using a CA:**
  - C authenticates S by first checking that the CA named in S's Web page is on the list of recognized CAs. If so, C reads the public key of the CA from the list and then requests S's certificate from the CA by sending it S's name in a request message. The CA then sends the certificate in a response message.
  - On receipt of the certificate, C decrypts it using CA's public key and checks that the name on the certificate is that of S. If so, C assumes S is authentic and reads the public key of S from the certificate.

- **Cryptographic algorithm negotiation:**
  - Once S has been authenticated, C proceeds to negotiate with S a suitable (symmetric) cryptographic algorithm for the transaction.
  - To do this, C sends its preferences – DES or IDEA for example – together with proposed operational parameters in a request message to S. S responds with its choice of one of these in the response message.

- **Session key exchange:**
  - C generates a random (symmetric) key for the transaction and encrypts it using S's public key. C then sends the encrypted key in a message to S.
  - On receipt of the message, S decrypts the message using its own private key and returns a response message to C acknowledging that it, too, now has the session key.

- **Transaction initiation:**
  - C sends an encrypted message to S informing S that it is now ready to start the transaction and that all future messages will be encrypted.
  - On receipt of this, S returns an encrypted response message that it, too, is now ready to start the transaction.

- **Transaction information transfer:**
  - Once a secure socket connection has been established, each message relating to the transaction that is sent/received over the socket is encrypted/decrypted using the agreed symmetric session key.

When using SSL in banking and other financial applications, normally, when a client starts a new session, it is the SSL in the server that authenticates the client before entering into a transaction.

10.8.2 SET

A potential loophole with SSL is that although the scheme allows the client to authenticate that the server is a recognized server, because the server's bank is not involved in the authentication process, the server's certificate does not guarantee that it is authorized to enter into transactions that involve payment cards. Similarly, the client's certificate does not guarantee that the client is using his or her own card. To counter these loopholes, the major card companies have introduced a scheme that has been designed specifically for card transactions over the Web/Internet. The scheme is called **secure electronic transactions (SET)**.

In the SET scheme, in addition to the client (the purchaser) and server (the vendor), the client's and vendor's banks are also involved in carrying out a transaction. The purchaser, vendor, and vendor's bank all have certificates and, in the case of the purchaser and vendor, the certification authority is their respective bank. The purchaser's certificate, in addition to the purchaser's public key, also contains the name of the purchaser's bank. This enables, firstly, the purchaser to verify that the vendor is allowed to enter into payment card transactions and, secondly, the vendor to verify that the purchaser is using a legitimate card.

In practice, the SET scheme is relatively complex. However, an outline of the sequence of steps followed to carry out a card purchase electronically is shown in Figure 10.20. The following should be noted when interpreting the sequence shown:

- Three items of software are involved:
    - the *browser wallet*: this runs in the client and contains details of all the payment cards the vendor currently holds;
    - the *vendor server*: this is the Web server and, in addition to responding to requests for product information, it manages the (electronic) purchase of items from the vendor's catalog;
    - the *acquirer gateway*: this is located in the vendor's bank computer and manages the payment phase of a purchase.
- For each new purchase, the vendor allocates a unique transaction identifier (TI) and this is included in all subsequent messages.
- During the order and purchase phases, the order information sent to the vendor contains only the card name and it is the purchase information that is sent to the vendor's bank that contains the actual card number.
- The payment request is carried out using existing inter-bank fund transfer procedures.

Further information about SET can be found in the bibliography for this chapter.

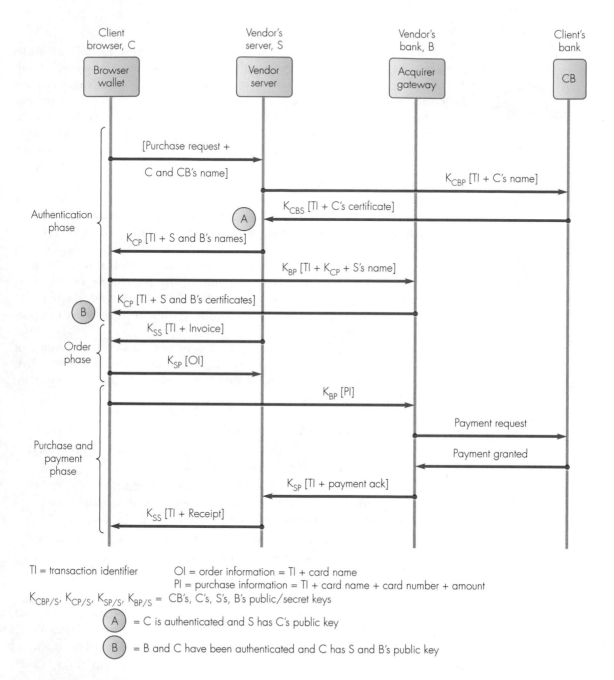

Figure 10.20 Outline of the operation of secure electronic transactions (SET).

Summary

A summary of the topics discussed in this chapter is given in Figure 10.21.

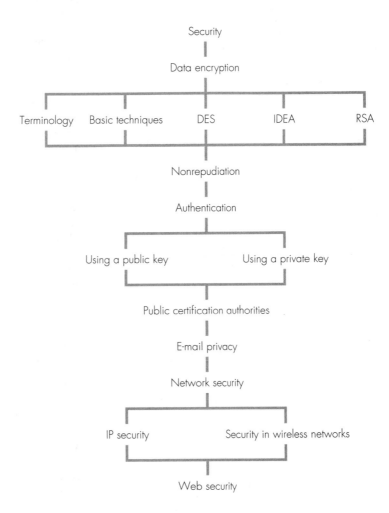

Figure 10.21 Security summary.

Exercises

Section 10.1

10.1 Explain the meaning of the following terms relating to a secure transaction:
  (i) integrity,
  (ii) privacy/secrecy,
  (iii) authentication,
  (iv) nonrepudiation.

Section 10.2

10.2 With the aid of a diagram, explain the meaning of the following terms relating to data encryption:
  (i) plaintext and ciphertext,
  (ii) encryption key and decryption key,
  (iii) eavesdropping and masquerading.

10.3 The following encrypted phrase has been produced using a simple substitution for the ciphertext alphabet. Assuming the phrase relates to communications, derive the ciphertext alphabet and hence the plaintext of the phrase:

ciphertext = frpsxwhu qhwzrunlgj

10.4 The following encrypted phrase has been produced using a simple transposition for the ciphertext alphabet. Derive the key that has been used and hence the plaintext of the phrase:

ciphertext = dcniaoiotmcnnamas ut

10.5 By means of a diagram, show the difference between a straight, expanded, and compressed or choice permutation/transposition. Use for example purposes a P-box with 8 input bits. State the key used in each case.

10.6 Assuming an S-box with 8 input bits, derive the size of the key that is required to perform a straight substitution operation.

  With the aid of a diagram, show how the size of the key can be reduced by encapsulating a P-box between a binary decoder and a corresponding encoder. Use for example purposes an S-box with 2 input bits and 2 output bits.

Define a key for the P-box and hence list the four outputs for the four possible combinations of the two input bits.

10.7 A product cipher uses a combination of transpositions and substitutions. Design an encryption unit based on a product cipher that operates on 8 input bits. The unit is to be composed of a straight P-box followed by a block of four S-boxes of the type used in Exercise 10.6 and a second straight P-box. Define a suitable key for each stage. Hence for a selected 8-bit input, derive the 8-bit encrypted output from the unit.

10.8 With the aid of a diagram, outline the structure of the product cipher used with the DES algorithm. Show the steps that are carried out for each substitution operation within the product cipher assuming the bitwise function used in each substitution is the Feistel cipher.

10.9 State the three transposition operations that are carried out in the DES product cipher algorithm. Hence use a simple example to show that the output of the set of three transpositions is reversible.

  Use a simple example to show how each substitution operation is reversible also. What are the implications of this?

10.10 With the aid of a diagram, describe the operation of the triple DES scheme. Hence explain why it is now being used in place of DES in some applications.

10.11 With the aid of schematic logic diagrams, describe the following operational modes of DES: electronic code book (ECB), chain block cipher (CBC), cipher feedback mode (CFM).

  Quantify the number of encryption operations that are used to encrypt a 2048-byte file using:
  (i) CBC, and
  (ii) CFM.
  Hence identify the main use of CFM.

10.12 With the aid of a schematic diagram, describe the operation of the IDEA scheme. Include in your description the size of the key used and the number and size of the subkeys associated with each encryption stage.

10.13 Each encryption stage in the IDEA scheme involves multiple addition and multiplication operations on pairs of 16-bit operands. Explain how the 16-bit product and 16-bit sum are derived.

10.14 With the aid of an example, explain the principle of operation of the RSA algorithm including how the public and private keys are derived. Use for example purposes the two prime numbers 3 and 11. State the maximum numeric value that can be encrypted with your choice of keys.

10.15 By means of an example, show how the exponentiation operations associated with the encryption and decryption stages of the RSA algorithm can be avoided. Hence assuming only messages composed of the 26 uppercase characters are to be sent, encrypt the string of characters AFKP using the public and private keys you derived in Exercise 10.14. Remember the limitation imposed by the choice of prime numbers.

Section 10.3

10.16 With the aid of a diagram, show how nonrepudiation can be obtained using the RSA algorithm:
(i)   on the complete message,
(ii) on a digest of the message.

Clearly identify on your diagram the keys used and the encrypted/decrypted values at each stage.

Section 10.4

10.17 With the aid of a diagram, explain how user authentication can be carried out using a public key scheme. Include in your diagram the contents of each message and the key used to encrypt the message.

10.18 Explain the meaning and use of the following terms in relation to the authentication procedure associated with Kerberos:
(i)   tickets,
(ii)   ticket granting server,
(iii) nonce,
(iv)   authentication server,
(v)   authentication database,
(vi)   authenticator.

10.19 With the aid of a diagram, identify a possible security threat that can occur with a public key system when the public key is made readily available. Describe how a certification authority can be used to overcome this threat. Include in your description a list of the fields that are present in the certificate and their use.

Section 10.5

10.20 With the aid of a diagram, explain a possible threat when using a public key system and how this is overcome.

Section 10.6

10.21 A number of companies have been invited to prepare and submit a tender for a contract using e-mail. To provide a high level of privacy and to authenticate each tender and ensure nonrepudiation, each company has been asked to encrypt their tender using PGP. By means of a block schematic diagram, assuming no compression is to be used, show the various steps that are followed to carry out:
(i)   the authentication and nonrepudiation steps, and
(ii) the encryption and decryption of the tender contents.

Section 10.7

10.22 In relation to IP security (IPsec), identify the security features provided by:
(i)   the authentication header (AH) protocol,
(ii) the encryption security payload (ESP) protocol.

10.23 Explain the meaning and application of the term security association (SA) and the three parameters relating to this.

10.24 Describe the two alternative ways of implementing a SA and an application of each.

10.25 With the aid of a diagram, show the position of the AH protocol header and its contents in the transport mode. Clearly identify the fields that are authenticated.

10.26 State the role of:
(i) the Internet Key Exchange (IKE) algorithm,
(ii) the Hash Message Authentication Code (HMAC).

10.27 In relation to the ESP protocol, use diagrams to identify the position and contents of the ESP header in both the transport and tunnel modes. Clearly identify the fields that are authenticated and encrypted in each case and the role of the initialization vector.

10.28 State the security features of the wired equivalent privacy (WEP) protocol.

10.29 With the aid of a diagram, explain how authentication in WEP is achieved by means of a three-way handshake procedure.

10.30 With the aid of diagrams, explain the principle of operation of the RC4 stream cipher that is used in the WEP encryption algorithm and the frame encryption/decryption operations.

Section 10.8

10.31 Give three examples of security threats that illustrate the need for additional security measures in e-commerce and e-banking applications.

10.32 In relation to the secure socket layer (SSL) scheme, with the aid of a diagram, explain the function of the various protocols that are used to carry out a secure transaction. Include in your description how the HTML interpreter differentiates between a secure and an insecure transaction.

10.33 To carry out a secure transaction using the SSL scheme, five steps are required:
(i) authentication using a certification authority,
(ii) cryptographic algorithm negotiation,
(iii) session key exchange,
(iv) transaction initiation,
(v) transaction information transfer.

With the aid of a diagram and selected keys, illustrate how each of the above steps is carried out.

10.34 Identify a potential security loophole with the SSL scheme and state how the secure electronic transactions (SET) scheme overcomes this.

10.35 Identify the four main players that are involved in the SET scheme and give a brief description of the role of the software associated with each of them.

10.36 Assuming public key cryptography throughout, use a diagram to show how:
(i) the client authenticates the vendor and vice versa,
(ii) the client sends an order to the vendor,
(iii) the client carries out the purchase and payment operations.

Appendix A Multimedia data representation and compression

A.1 Multimedia data representation

As we explained in Section 1.2.1, there are four basic types of data: text, images, speech/audio and video. The source data relating to text and images is in a digital form and hence can be stored directly in the memory of a computer. In the case of speech, audio and video, however, the source signals are in an analog form whose amplitude varies continuously with time as the amplitude and frequency of the signal vary. Hence before these can be stored in the memory of a computer and integrated with the other media types, the source analog signals must first be converted into digital form. This is carried out using an electronic circuit called an analog-to-digital converter (ADC). This involves sampling the amplitude of the analog signal at regular time intervals; the higher the sampling rate, the better quality is the reproduced signal. The digital signal is reconverted into its analog form using a circuit called an digital-to-analog converter (DAC). In the case of a speech signal – as used in telephony – a typical sampling rate is 8 kHz with 8 bits per sample. This yields a digital signal of 64 kbps, which is the bit rate used in telephone networks. For CD-quality audio, however, a common sampling rate is 44.1 kHz with 16 bits per sample, which produces a bit rate of 705.6 kbps or, for stereo, 1.411 Mbps. In the case of a digitized video signal, the source bit rates are considerably larger than this.

As we can deduce from the above figures – and especially those for audio and video – the raw transmission bit rate required of a communications channel far exceeds the available capacity of most network types. Hence, in almost all Internet applications the source digital data is first compressed using a suitable compression algorithm. As an introduction to the subject, in this appendix we discuss first how the different media types are represented in a digital form and second the various compression algorithms that are used for each media type.

A.1.1 Text

Essentially, there are three types of text that are used to produce pages of documents:

- **unformatted text:** this is also known as **plaintext** and enables pages to be created which comprise strings of fixed-sized characters from a limited character set;

- **formatted text:** this is also known as **richtext** and enables pages and complete documents to be created which comprise of strings of characters of different styles, size, and shape with tables, graphics, and images inserted at appropriate points;

- **hypertext:** this enables an integrated set of documents (each comprising formatted text) to be created which have defined linkages between them.

We shall discuss the three types separately.

A.1.1.1 Unformatted text

An example of a character set that is widely used to create pages consisting of unformatted text strings was shown in Figure 1.14.

The table tabulates the set of characters that are available in the **ASCII character set**, the term "ASCII" being an abbreviation for the **American Standard Code for Information Interchange**. This is one of the most widely used character sets and the table includes the binary codewords used to represent each character. As we can see, each character is represented by a unique 7-bit binary codeword. The use of 7 bits means that there are 128 (2^7) alternative characters and the codeword used to identify each character is obtained by combining the corresponding column (bits 7–5) and row (bits 4–1) bits together. Bit 7 is the most significant bit and hence the codeword for uppercase M, for example, is 1001101.

In addition to all the normal alphabetic, numeric and punctuation characters – collectively referred to as **printable characters** – the total ASCII character set also includes a number of **control characters**. These include:

- **format control characters**: BS (backspace), LF linefeed), CR (carriage return), SP (space), DEL (delete), ESC (escape) and FF (form feed);

- **information separators**: FS (file separator) and RS (record separator);

- **transmission control characters**: SOH (start-of-heading), STX (start-of-text), ETX (end-of-text), ACK (acknowledge), NAK (negative acknowledge), SYN (synchronous idle) and DLE (data link escape).

The latter, as described in Section 1.3.3, are sometimes used to control the transmission of blocks of characters made up of the other characters in the set.

A.1.1.2 Formatted text

An example of formatted text is that produced by most word processing packages. It is also used extensively in the publishing sector for the preparation of papers, books, magazines, journals, and so on. It enables documents to be created that consist of characters of different styles and of variable size and shape, each of which can be plain, bold or italicized. In addition, a variety of document formatting options are supported to enable an author to structure a document into chapters, sections and paragraphs, each with different headings and with tables, graphics and pictures inserted at appropriate points.

To achieve each of these features, the author of the document enters a specific command, which, typically, results in a defined format-control character sequence – normally a reserved format-control character followed by a pair of other alphabetic or numeric characters – being inserted at the beginning of the particular character string, table, graphic or picture. In this way, each page of the document comprises the string of characters that make up the textual part of the page – plus, where appropriate, the associated tables, graphics or pictures – with the corresponding format-control character sequences interspersed at appropriate points. An example formatted text string is as shown in part (a) of Figure A.1 and the printed version of this string is shown in part(b).

As we can deduce from the above, in order to print a document consisting of formatted text, the printer must first be set up – that is, the microprocessor within the printer must be programmed – to detect and interpret the format-control character sequences in the defined way and to convert the following text, table, graphic or picture into a line-by-line form ready for printing. In addition, to help the author visualize the layout of each page prior to printing, commands such as *print preview* are often provided which cause the page to be displayed on the computer screen in a similar way

(a)

```
<B><FONT SIZE=4><P>Formatted Text</P>
</B></FONT>
<P>This is an example of formatted text, it includes:</P>
<FONT SIZE=2>
</FONT><I><P>Italics,</I> <B>Bold</B> and <U>Underlining</P>
</U>
<FONT FACE="French Script MT"><P>Different Fonts</FONT> and <FONT
SIZE=4>Font Sizes</P>
```

(b)

Formatted text
This is an example of formatted text, it includes:
Italics, **Bold** and Underlining
Different fonts and Font Sizes

Figure A.1 Formatted text: (a) an example formatted text string; (b) printed version of the string.

to how it will appear when it is printed. This is the origin of the term **WYSIWYG**, an acronym for what-you-see-is-what-you-get.

A.1.1.3 Hypertext

As we saw earlier in Figure 9.10 (and explained in the accompanying text) hypertext is a type of formatted text that enables the creation of a related set of documents – normally referred to as **pages** – that have defined linkage points – referred to as **hyperlinks** – between each other. For example, most universities describe their structure and the courses and support services they offer in a booklet known as a prospectus. Like most such booklets, this is organized in a hierarchical way and, in order for a reader to find out information about a particular course, and the facilities offered by the university, typically, the reader would start at the index and use this to access details about the various departments, the courses each offers, and so on, by switching between the different sections of the booklet.

In a similar way, hypertext can be used to create an electronic version of such documents with the index, descriptions of departments, courses on offer, library, and other facilities all written in hypertext as pages with various defined hyperlinks between them to enable a person to browse through its contents in a user-friendly way. Two examples of hypertext are HTML – which we described in some detail in Section 9.4 – and *PostScript*, which is known as a printed page description language.

A.1.2 Images

Within the context of this book, images include computer-generated images – more generally referred to as **computer graphics** or simply **graphics** – and digitized images of both documents and pictures.

A.1.2.1 Graphics

There is a range of software packages and programs available for the creation of computer graphics. These provide easy-to-use tools to create graphics that are composed of all kinds of visual objects including lines, arcs, squares, rectangles, circles, ovals, diamonds, stars, and so on, as well as any form of hand-drawn (normally referred to as **freeform**) objects. Typically, these are produced by drawing the desired shape on the screen by means of a combination of a cursor symbol on the screen – a pencil or paint brush for example – and the mouse. Facilities are also provided to edit these objects – for example to change their shape, size or color – and to introduce complete predrawn images, either previously created by the author of the graphic or selected from a gallery of images that come with the package. The latter is often referred to as **clip-art** and the better packages provide many hundreds of such images. Textual information can also be included in a graphic, together with precreated tables and graphs, and digitized pictures and photographs that have been previously obtained. Objects can overlap each other with a selected object nearer to the front than another. In addition, you can add fill or add shadows to objects in order to give the complete image a three-dimensional (3-D) effect.

A computer's display screen can be considered as being made up of a two-dimensional matrix of individual picture elements – pixels – each of which can have a range of colors associated with it. For example, **VGA (video graphics array)** is a common type of display and, as we show in Figure A.2(a), consists of a matrix of 640 horizontal pixels by 480 vertical pixels with, for example, 8 bits per pixel, which allows each pixel to have one of 256 different colors.

All objects – including freeform objects – are made up of a series of lines that are connected to each other and, in practice, what may appear as a

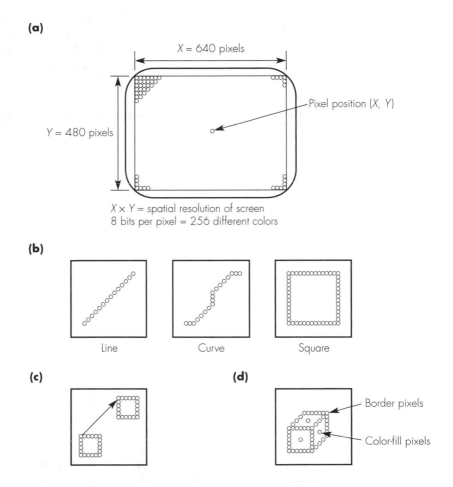

Figure A.2 Graphics principles: (a) example screen format; (b) some simple object examples; (c) effect of changing position attribute; (d) solid objects.

curved line is actually a series of very short lines each made up of a string of pixels that, in the limit, have the resolution of a pair of adjacent pixels on the screen. Some examples are shown in Figure A.2(b).

There are two forms of representation of a computer graphic: a high-level version (similar to the source code of a high-level program) and the actual pixel-image of the graphic (similar to the byte-string corresponding to the low-level machine code of the program and known more generally as the **bit-map format**). A graphic can be transferred over a network in either form. In general, however, the high-level language form is much more compact and requires less memory to store the image and less bandwidth for its transmission. In order to use the high-level language form, however, the destination must of course be able to interpret the various high-level commands. So instead the bit-map form is often used and, to help with this, there are a number of standardized forms of representation such as **GIF** (**graphical interchange format**) and **TIFF** (**tagged image file format**). There are also software packages such as **SRGP** (**simple raster graphics package**) which convert the high-level language form into a pixel-image form.

A.1.2.2 Digitized pictures

In the case of scanners, which are used normally for digitizing continuous-tone monochromatic images – such as a printed picture or scene – more than a single bit is used to digitize each picture element. For example, good quality black-and-white pictures can be obtained by using 8 bits per picture element. This yields 256 different levels of gray per element varying between white and black. In the case of color images, in order to understand the digitization format used, it is necessary first to obtain an understanding of the principles of how color is produced and how the picture tubes used in computer monitors (on which the images are eventually displayed) operate.

Color principles

It has been known for many years that the human eye sees just a single color when a particular set of three primary colors are mixed and displayed simultaneously. In fact, a whole spectrum of colors – known as a **color gamut** – can be produced by using different proportions of the three primary colors red (R), green (G) and blue (B). This principle is shown in Figure A.3 together with some examples of colors that can be produced.

The mixing technique used in part (a) is known as **additive color mixing**, which, since black is produced when all three primary colors are zero, is particularly useful for producing a color image on a black surface as is the case in display applications. It is also possible to perform the complementary **subtractive color mixing** operation to produce a similar range of colors. This is shown in part(b) of the figure and, as we can see, with subtractive mixing white is produced when the three chosen primary colors cyan (C), magenta (M) and yellow (Y) are all zero. Hence this choice of colors is particularly useful for producing a color image on a white surface as is the case in printing applications.

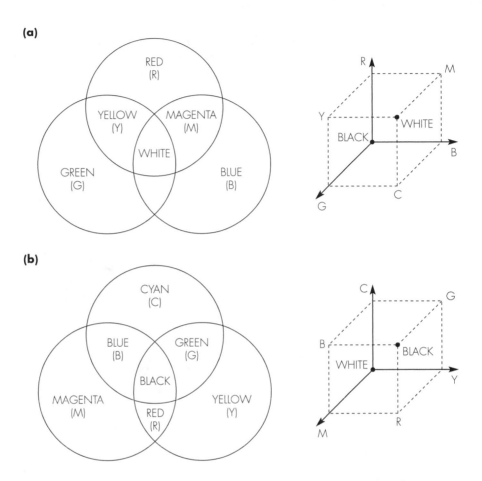

**Figure A.3 Color derivation principles: (a) additive color mixing;
(b) subtractive color mixing.**

The same principle is used in the picture tubes associated with color television sets with the three primary colors R, G and B, and also in most computer monitors since, in general, those used with personal computers use the same picture tubes as are used in television sets. Hence, in order to be compatible with the computer monitors on which digital pictures are normally viewed, the digitization process used yields a color image that can be directly displayed on the screen of either a television set or a computer monitor. The general principles associated with the process are shown in Figure A.4.

Raster-scan principles

The picture tubes used in most television sets operate using what is known as a **raster-scan**. This involves a finely focused electron beam – the raster – being scanned over the complete screen. Each complete scan comprises a number of discrete horizontal lines, the first starting at the top left corner of the screen and the last ending at the bottom right corner. At this point the beam is deflected back again to the top left corner and the scanning operation repeats in the same way. This type of scanning is called **progressive scanning** and is shown in diagrammatic form in Figure A.4(b).

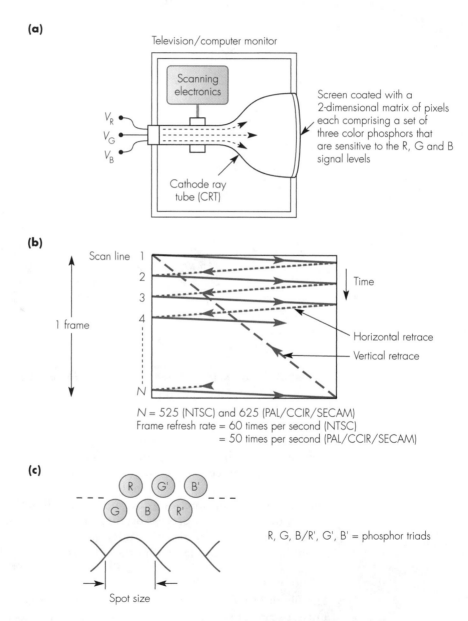

(a)

(b)

$N = 525$ (NTSC) and 625 (PAL/CCIR/SECAM)
Frame refresh rate = 60 times per second (NTSC)
= 50 times per second (PAL/CCIR/SECAM)

(c)

R, G, B/R', G', B' = phosphor triads

Figure A.4 Television/computer monitor principles: (a) schematic; (b) raster-scan principles; (c) pixel format on each scan line.

Each complete set of horizontal scan lines is called a **frame** and, as we can see, each frame is made up of N individual scan lines where N is either 525 (North and South America and most of Asia) or 625 (Europe and a number of other countries). The inside of the display screen of the picture tube is coated with a light-sensitive phosphor that emits light when energized by the electron beam. The amount of light emitted – its brightness – is determined by the power in the electron beam at that instant. During each horizontal (line) and vertical (frame) retrace period the electron beam is turned off and, to create an image on the screen, the level of power in the beam is changed as each line is scanned.

In the case of black-and-white picture tubes just a single electron beam is used with a white-sensitive phosphor. Color tubes use three separate, closely-located beams and a two-dimensional matrix of pixels. Each pixel comprises a set of three related color-sensitive phosphors, one each for the red, green and blue signals. The set of three phosphors associated with each pixel is called a **phosphor triad** and a typical arrangement of the triads on each scan line is as shown in Figure A.4(c). As we can deduce from this, although in theory each pixel represents an idealized rectangular area independent of its neighboring pixels, in practice each pixel has the shape of a **spot** that merges with its neighbors. A typical spot size is 0.025 inches (0.635 mm) and, when viewed from a sufficient distance, a continuous color image is seen.

Television picture tubes were designed, of course, to display moving images. The persistence of the light/color produced by the phosphor, therefore, is designed to decay very quickly and hence it is necessary to continuously **refresh** the screen. In the case of a moving image, the light signals associated with each frame change to reflect the motion that has taken place during the time required to scan the preceding frame, while for a static/still image, the same set of light signals are used for each frame. The **frame refresh rate** must be high enough to ensure the eye is not aware the display is continuously being refreshed. A low refresh rate leads to what is called **flicker**, which is caused by the previous image fading from the eye retina before the following image is displayed. To avoid this, a refresh rate of at least 50 times per second is required. In practice, the frame refresh rate used is determined by the frequency of the mains electricity supply, which is either 60 Hz in North and South America and most of Asia or 50 Hz in Europe and a number of other countries.

Aspect ratio

Both the number of pixels per scanned line and the number of lines per frame vary, the actual numbers used being determined by what is known as the **aspect ratio** of the display screen. This is the ratio of the screen width to the screen height. The aspect ratio of current television tubes is 4/3 with older tubes – on which PC monitors are based – and 16/9 with the widescreen television tubes.

Some example screen resolutions associated with the more common computer monitors based on television picture tubes – together with the amount of memory required to store the corresponding image – are shown in Table A.1.

As we can deduce from the table, the memory requirements to store a single digital image can be high and vary between 307.2 kbytes for an image displayed on a **VGA** (**video graphics array**) screen with 8 bits per pixel through to approximately 2.36 Mbytes for a **SVGA** (**Super VGA**) screen with 24 bits per pixel. It should be noted that the more expensive computer monitors are not based on television picture tubes and hence are not constrained by the 4/3 aspect ratio. An example is $1280 \times 1024 \times 24$, which may have a refresh rate as high as 75 frames per second to produce a sharper image.

Table A.1 Example display resolutions and memory requirements.

Standard	Resolution	Number of colors	Memory required per frame (bytes)
VGA	$640 \times 480 \times 8$	256	307.2 kB
XGA	$640 \times 480 \times 16$	64 K	614.4 kB
	$1024 \times 768 \times 8$	256	786.432 kB
SVGA	$800 \times 600 \times 16$	64 K	960 kB
	$1024 \times 768 \times 8$	256	786.432 kB
	$1024 \times 768 \times 24$	16 M	2359.296 kB

Example A.1

Derive the time to transmit the following digitized images at both 64 kbps and 1.5 Mbps:

■ a $640 \times 480 \times 8$ VGA-compatible image,

■ a $1024 \times 768 \times 24$ SVGA-compatible image.

Answer:

The size of each image in bits is:

$$VGA = 640 \times 480 \times 8 = 2.457600 \text{ Mbits}$$
$$SVGA = 1024 \times 768 \times 24 = 18.874368 \text{ Mbits}$$

Hence the time to transmit each image is:

$$\text{At } 64 \text{ kbps: VGA} = \frac{2.4576 \times 10^6}{64 \times 10^3} = 38.4 \text{ s}$$

$$SVGA = \frac{18.874368 \times 10^6}{64 \times 10^3} = 294.912 \text{ s}$$

$$\text{At } 1.5\,\text{Mbps: VGA} = \frac{2.4576 \times 10^6}{1.5 \times 10^6} = 1.6384\,\text{s}$$

$$\text{SVGA} = \frac{18.874368 \times 10^6}{1.5 \times 10^6} = 12.5829\,\text{s}$$

As we can see, the times to transmit a single image at 64 kbps are such that interactive access would not be feasible, nor at 1.5 Mbps with the higher-resolution SVGA image.

A.1.3 Audio

Essentially, we are concerned with two types of audio signal: speech signals as used in a variety of interpersonal applications including telephony and video telephony, and music-quality audio as used in applications such as CD-on-demand.

A.1.3.1 PCM speech

As we described in Chapter 1, most interpersonal applications involving speech use for communication purposes a public switched telephone network (PSTN). Because this has been in existence for many years the operating parameters associated with it were defined some time ago. Initially, a PSTN operated with analog signals throughout, the source speech signal being transmitted and switched (routed) unchanged in its original analog form. Progressively, however, the older analog transmission circuits were replaced by digital circuits. The digitization procedure is known as **pulse code modulation** or **PCM** and the international standard relating to this is defined in **ITU-T Recommendation G.711**. With PCM, the speech signal is sampled at 8 K samples per second using 8 bits per sample which yields a bit rate of 64 kbps.

A.1.3.2 CD-quality audio

The discs used in CD players and CD-ROMs are digital storage devices for stereophonic music and more general multimedia information streams. There is a standard associated with these devices known as the **CD-digital audio** (**CD-DA**) standard. As indicated earlier, music has an audible bandwidth of 15–20 kHz and hence the minimum sampling rate is 40 ksps. In the standard, however, the actual rate used is higher than this rate so that the resulting bit rate is then compatible with one of the higher transmission channel bit rates available with public networks.

One of the sampling rates used is 44.1 ksps, which means the signal is sampled at 23 μs intervals. Since the bandwidth of a recording channel on a

CD is large, a high number of bits per sample can be used. The standard defines 16 bits per sample which, as indicated earlier, tests have shown to be the minimum required with music. The recording of stereophonic music requires two separate channels and hence the total bit rate required is double that for mono. Hence:

$$\text{Bit rate per channel} = \text{sampling rate} \times \text{bits per sample}$$
$$= 44.1 \times 10^3 \times 16 = 705.6\,\text{kbps}$$

$$\text{Total bit rate} \qquad = 2 \times 705.6 = 1.411\,\text{Mbps}$$

This is also the bit rate used with CD-ROMs, which are widely used for the distribution of multimedia titles. Within a computer, however, in order to reduce the access delay, multiples of this rate are used.

As we can deduce from Example A.2, it is not feasible to interactively access a 30 s portion of a multimedia title over a 64 kbps channel. Even with a 1.5 Mbps channel the time is still too high for interactive purposes.

Example A.2

Assuming the CD-DA standard is being used, derive:

(i) the storage capacity of a **CD-ROM** to store a 60-minute multimedia title,

(ii) the time to transmit a 30-second portion of the title using a transmission channel of bit rate:

- 64 kbps
- 1.5 Mbps.

Answer:

(i) The CD-DA digitization procedure yields a bit rate of 1.411 Mbps. Hence storage capacity for 60 minutes

$$= 1.411 \times 60 \times 60\,\text{Mbits}$$
$$= 5079.6\,\text{Mbits or } 634.95\,\text{Mbytes}$$

(ii) One 30-second portion of the title $= 1.411 \times 30 = 42.33\,\text{Mbits}$
Hence time to transmit this data:

$$\text{At } 64\,\text{kbps} = \frac{42.33 \times 10^6}{64 \times 10^3} = 661.4\,\text{s} \qquad \text{(about 11 minutes)}$$

$$\text{At } 1.5\,\text{Mbps} = \frac{42.33 \times 10^6}{1.5 \times 10^6} = 28.22\,\text{s}$$

A.1.4 Video

Video features in a range of Internet applications:

- **interpersonal**: video telephony and videoconferencing;
- **interactive**: windows containing short video clips.

The quality of the video required, however, varies considerably from one type of application to another. For example, for video telephony, a small window on the screen of a PC is acceptable while for a movie, a large screen format is preferable. In practice, therefore, there is not just a single standard associated with video but rather a set of standards, each targeted at a particular application domain.

A.1.4.1 Digital video

In most Internet applications the video signals need to be in a digital form since it then becomes possible to store them in the memory of a computer and to readily edit and integrate them with other media types. In addition, with digital video it is more usual to digitize the three component signals separately prior to their transmission. Again, this is done to enable editing and other operations to be readily performed.

Since the three component signals are treated separately in digital television, in principle it is possible simply to digitize the three RGB signals that make up the picture. The disadvantage of this approach is that the same resolution – in terms of sampling rate and bits per sample – must be used for all three signals. Studies on the visual perception of the eye have shown that the resolution of the eye is less sensitive for color than it is for luminance. This means that the two chrominance signals can tolerate a reduced resolution relative to that used for the luminance signal. Hence a significant saving in terms of the resulting bit rate – and hence transmission bandwidth – can be achieved by using what are called the luminance (Y) and two chrominance signals (C_b and C_r) instead of the RGB signals directly.

A.1.4.2 PC video

Most Internet applications that involve live video use a window on the screen of a PC monitor for display purposes. Examples include desktop video telephony and videoconferencing, and also **video-in-a-window**.

In order to avoid distortion on a PC screen – for example when displaying a square of $N \times N$ pixels – it is necessary to use a horizontal resolution of 640 (480 $\times 4/3$) pixels per line with a 525-line PC monitor and 768 ($576 \times 4/3$) pixels per line with a 625-line PC monitor. Hence for multimedia applications that involve mixing live video with other information on a PC screen, the line sampling rate is normally modified in order to obtain the required horizontal resolution.

To achieve the necessary resolution with a 525-line monitor, the line sampling rate is reduced from 13.5 MHz to 12.2727 MHz while for a 625-line monitor, the line sampling rate must be increased from 13.5 MHz to

14.75 MHz. In the case of desktop video telephony and videoconferencing, the video signals from the camera are sampled at this rate prior to transmission and hence can be displayed directly on a PC screen. In the case of a digital television broadcast a conversion is necessary before the video is displayed. The various digitization formats for use with PC video are as shown in Table A.2.

Table A.2 PC video digitization formats.

Digitization format	System	Spatial resolution	Temporal resolution	Bit rate
4:2:0	525-line	$Y = 640 \times 480$ $C_b = C_r = 320 \times 240$	60 Hz	162 Mbps
	625-line	$Y = 768 \times 576$ $C_b = C_r = 384 \times 288$	50 Hz	162 Mbps
SIF	525-line	$Y = 320 \times 240$ $C_b = C_r = 160 \times 240$	30 Hz	81 Mbps
	625-line	$Y = 384 \times 288$ $C_b = C_r = 192 \times 144$	25 Hz	81 Mbps
CIF		$Y = 384 \times 288$ $C_b = C_r = 192 \times 144$	30 Hz	81 Mbps
QCIF		$Y = 192 \times 144$ $C_b = C_r = 96 \times 72$	15/7.5 Hz	40.5 Mbps

Y = luminance C_b, C_r = chrominance signals

A.2 Data compression

As we concluded from the examples in the previous section, in most cases the memory and transmission bandwidth requirements for each of the four media types in their raw digital form were such that either the volume of the data to be transmitted – text and images – was very large or the bandwidth required for its transmission – speech, audio and video – was larger than that provided by many access networks. Hence in all Internet applications, compression is applied to the source data prior to its transmission and, on receipt of the compressed data, it is decompressed prior to its display/output. In this subsection we describe the principles of a selection of the compression algorithms that are used with each of the data types.

A.2.1 Compression principles

Before we describe some of the compression algorithms in widespread use, it will be helpful if we first build up an understanding of the principles on which they are based. We shall discuss them under the headings:

- source encoders and destination decoders,
- lossless and lossy compression,
- entropy encoding,
- source encoding.

A.2.1.1 Source encoders and destination decoders

As have just indicated, prior to transmitting the source information relating to a particular multimedia application, a compression algorithm is applied to it. This implies that in order for the destination to reproduce the original source information – or, in some instances, a nearly exact copy of it – a matching decompression algorithm must be applied to it. The application of the compression algorithm is the main function carried out by the **source encoder** and the decompression algorithm is carried out by the **destination decoder**.

A.2.1.2 Lossless and lossy compression

Compression algorithms can be classified as being either lossless or lossy. In the case of a **lossless compression algorithm** the aim is to reduce the amount of source information to be transmitted in such a way that, when the compressed information is decompressed, there is no loss of information. Lossless compression is said, therefore, to be **reversible**. An example application of lossless compression is for the transfer over a network of a text file since, in such applications, it is normally imperative that no part of the source information is lost during either the compression or decompression operations.

In contrast, the aim of **lossy compression algorithms**, is normally not to reproduce an exact copy of the source information after decompression but rather a version of it that is perceived by the recipient as a true copy. In general, with such algorithms the higher the level of compression being applied to the source information the more approximate the received version becomes. Example applications of lossy compression are for the transfer of digitized images and audio and video streams. In such cases, the sensitivity of the human eye or ear is such that any fine details that may be missing from the original source signal after decompression are not detectable.

A.2.1.3 Entropy encoding

Entropy encoding is lossless and independent of the type of information that is being compressed. It is concerned solely with how the information is represented. We shall describe two examples that are in widespread use in compression algorithms in order to illustrate the principles involved. In some applications they are used separately while in others they are used together.

Run-length encoding

Typical applications of this type of encoding are when the source information comprises long substrings of the same character or binary digit. Instead of transmitting the source string in the form of independent codewords or bits, it is transmitted in the form of a different set of codewords which indicate not only the particular character or bit being transmitted but also an indication of the number of characters/bits in the substring. Then, providing the destination knows the set of codewords being used, it simply interprets each codeword received and outputs the appropriate number of characters or bits.

Statistical encoding

Many applications use a set of codewords to transmit the source information. For example, as we described earlier in Section 1.2.1, a set of ASCII codewords are often used for the transmission of strings of characters. Normally, all the codewords in the set comprise a fixed number of binary bits, for example 7 bits in the case of ASCII. In many applications, however, the symbols – and hence codewords – that are present in the source information do not occur with the same frequency of occurrence; that is, with equal probability. For example, in a string of text, the character A may occur more frequently than, say, the character P, which occurs more frequently than the character Z, and so on. Statistical encoding exploits this property by using a set of variable-length codewords with the shortest codewords used to represent the most frequently occurring symbols.

In practice, the use of variable-length codewords is not quite as straightforward as it first appears. Clearly, as with run-length encoding, the destination must know the set of codewords being used by the source. With variable-length codewords, however, in order for the decoding operation to be carried out correctly, it is necessary to ensure that a shorter codeword in the set does not form the start of a longer codeword otherwise the decoder will interpret the string on the wrong codeword boundaries. A codeword set that avoids this happening is said to possess the **prefix property** and an example of an encoding scheme that generates codewords that have this property is the Huffman encoding algorithm, which we shall describe in Section A.2.2.1.

A.2.1.4 Source encoding

Source encoding exploits a particular property of the source information in order to produce an alternative form of representation that is either a compressed version of the original form or is more amenable to the application of compression. Again, we shall describe two examples in widespread use in order to illustrate the principles involved.

Differential encoding

Differential encoding is used extensively in applications where the amplitude of a value or signal covers a large range but the difference in amplitude between successive values/signals is relatively small. To exploit this property of the source information, instead of using a set of relatively large codewords to represent the amplitude of each value/signal, a set of smaller codewords can be used each of which indicates only the difference in amplitude between the current value/signal being encoded and the immediately preceding value/signal. For example, if the digitization of an analog signal requires, say, 12 bits to obtain the required maximum range but the maximum difference in amplitude between successive samples of the signal requires only 3 bits, then by using only the difference values a saving of 75% on transmission bandwidth can be obtained.

Transform encoding

As the name implies, transform encoding involves transforming the source information from one form into another, the other form lending itself more readily to the application of compression. In general, there is no loss of information associated with the transformation operation and this technique is used in a number of applications involving both images and video. For example, as we saw in Section A.1.3.2, the digitization of a continuous-tone monochromatic image produces a two-dimensional matrix of pixel values each of which represents the level of gray in a particular position of the image. As we go from one position in the matrix to the next, the magnitude of each pixel value may vary. Hence, as we scan across a set of pixel locations, the rate of change in magnitude will vary from zero, if all the pixel values remain the same, to a low rate of change if, say, one half is different from the next half, through to a high rate of change if each pixel magnitude changes from one location to the next. Some examples are shown in Figure A.5(a).

The rate of change in magnitude as one traverses the matrix gives rise to a term known as **spatial frequency** and, for any particular image, there will be a mix of different spatial frequencies whose amplitudes are determined by the related changes in magnitude of the pixels. This is true, of course, if we scan the matrix in either the horizontal or the vertical direction and this, in turn, gives rise to the terms **horizontal** and **vertical frequency components** of the image. In practice, the human eye is less sensitive to the higher spatial frequency components associated with an image than the lower frequency components. Moreover, if the amplitude of the higher frequency components falls below a certain amplitude threshold, they will not be detected by the eye. Hence in terms of compression, if we can transform the original spatial form of representation into an equivalent representation involving spatial frequency components, then we can more readily identify and eliminate those higher frequency components that the eye cannot detect

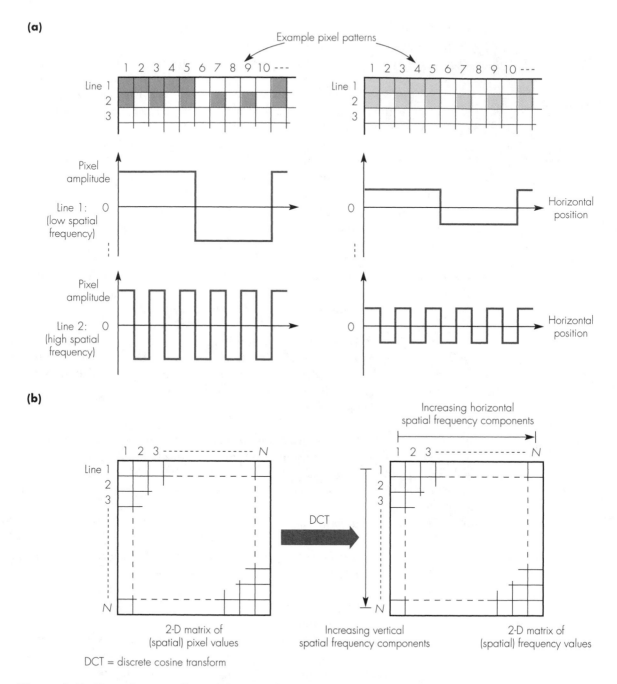

Figure A.5 Transform coding: (a) example pixel patterns; (b) DCT transform principles.

thereby reducing the volume of information to be transmitted without degrading the perceived quality of the original image.

The transformation of a two-dimensional matrix of pixel values into an equivalent matrix of spatial frequency components can be carried out using a mathematical technique known as the **discrete cosine transform (DCT)**. The transformation operation itself is lossless – apart from some small rounding errors in the mathematics – but, once the equivalent matrix of spatial frequency components – known as coefficients – has been derived, then any frequency components in the matrix whose amplitude is less than a defined threshold can be dropped. It is only at this point that the operation becomes lossy. The basic principle behind the DCT is as shown in Figure A.5(b) and we shall describe it in more detail in Section A.2.3.3 when we discuss the topic of image compression.

A.2.2 Text compression

As we saw in Section A.1.2, the three different types of text – unformatted, formatted and hypertext – are all represented as strings of characters selected from a defined set. The strings comprise alphanumeric characters interspersed with additional control characters. The different types of text use and interpret the latter in different ways. As we can deduce from this, any compression algorithm associated with text must be lossless since the loss of just a single character could modify the meaning of a complete string. In general, therefore, we are restricted to the use of entropy encoding and, in practice, statistical encoding methods.

Essentially, there are two types of statistical encoding methods that are used with text: one which uses single characters as the basis of deriving an optimum set of codewords and the other which uses variable-length strings of characters. An example of the former is the Huffman coding algorithm and an example of the latter is the **Lempel–Ziv (LZ) algorithm**. We shall describe the principles of each of these algorithms in this section.

A.2.2.1 Huffman coding

With Huffman coding the character string to be transmitted is first analyzed and the character types and their relative frequency determined. The coding operation involves creating an unbalanced tree with some branches (and hence codewords, in practice) shorter than others. The degree of imbalance is a function of the relative frequency of occurrence of the characters: the larger the spread, the more unbalanced is the tree. The resulting tree is known as the **Huffman code tree**.

A Huffman (code) tree is a **binary tree** with branches assigned the value 0 or 1. The base of the tree, normally the geometric top in practice, is known as the **root node** and the point at which a branch divides, a **branch node**. The termination point of a branch is known as a **leaf node** to which the symbols being encoded are assigned. An example of a Huffman code tree is shown in Figure A.6(a). This corresponds to the string of characters AAAABBCD.

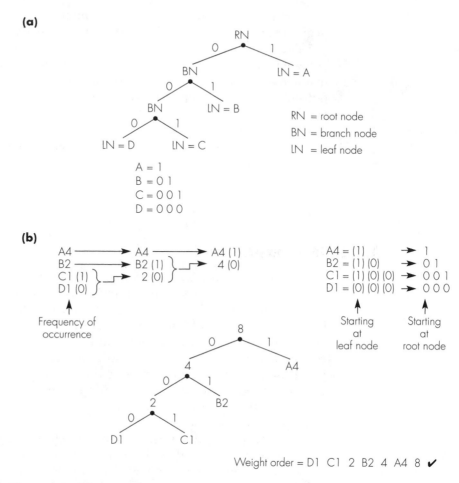

Figure A.6 Huffman code tree construction: (a) final tree with codes; (b) tree derivation.

As each branch divides, a binary value of 0 or 1 is assigned to each new branch: a binary 0 for the left branch and a binary 1 for the right branch. The codewords used for each character (shown in the leaf nodes) are determined by tracing the path *from* the root node out to each leaf and forming a string of the binary values associated with each branch traced. We can deduce from the set of codes associated with this tree that it would take

$$4 \times 1 + 2 \times 2 + 1 \times 3 + 1 \times 3 = 14 \text{ bits}$$

to transmit the complete string AAAABBCD.

To illustrate how the Huffman code tree in Figure A.6(a) is determined, we must add information concerning the frequency of occurrence of each character. Figure A.6(b) shows the characters listed in a column in decreasing (weight) order. We derive the tree as follows.

The first two leaf nodes at the base of the list – C1 and D1 – are assigned to the (1) and (0) branches respectively of a branch node. The two leaf nodes are then replaced by a branch node whose weight is the sum of the weights of the two leaf nodes; that is, two. A new column is then formed containing the new branch node combined with the remaining nodes from the first column, again arranged in their correct weight order. This procedure is repeated until only two nodes remain.

To derive the resulting codewords for each character, we start with the character in the first column and then proceed to list the branch numbers – 0 or 1 – as they are encountered. Thus for character A the first (and only) branch number is (1) in the last column while for C the first is (1) then (0) at branch node 2 and finally (0) at branch node 4. The actual codewords, however, start at the root and not the leaf node hence they are the reverse of these bit sequences. The Huffman tree can then be readily constructed from the set of codewords.

We check that this is the optimum tree – and hence set of codewords – by listing the resulting weights of all the leaf and branch nodes in the tree starting with the smallest weight and proceeding from left to right and from bottom to top. The codewords are optimum if the resulting list increments in weight order.

Example A.3

A series of messages is to be transferred between two computers over a PSTN. The messages comprise just the characters A through H. Analysis has shown that the probability (relative frequency of occurrence) of each character is as follows:

A and B = 0.25,   C and D = 0.14,   E, F, G and H = 0.055

(i)   Use Shannon's formula to derive the minimum average number of bits per character.

(ii) Use Huffman coding to derive a codeword set and prove this is the minimum set by constructing the corresponding Huffman code tree.

(iii) Derive the average number of bits per character for your codeword set and compare this with:

■ the entropy of the messages (Shannon's value),

■ fixed-length binary codewords,

■ 7-bit ASCII codewords.

Example A.3 continued

Answer:

(i) Shannon's formula states:

$$\text{Entropy, } H = -\sum_{i=1}^{8} P_i \log_2 P_i \text{ bits per codeword}$$

Therefore:

$$H = -(2(0.25 \log_2 0.25) + 2(0.14 \log_2 0.14) + 4(0.055 \log_2 0.055))$$
$$= 1 + 0.794 + 0.921 = 2.715 \text{ bits per codeword}$$

(ii) The derivation of the codeword set using Huffman coding is shown in Figure A.7(a). The characters are first listed in weight order and the two characters at the bottom of the list are assigned to the (1) and (0) branches. Note that in this case, however, when the two nodes are combined, the weight of the resulting branch node (0.11) is greater than the weight of the two characters E and F (0.055). Hence the branch node is inserted into the second list higher than both of these. The same procedure then repeats until there are only two entries in the list remaining.

The Huffman code tree corresponding to the derived set of codewords is given in Figure A.7(b) and, as we can see, this is the optimum tree since all leaf and branch nodes increment in numerical order.

(iii) Average number of bits per codeword using Huffman coding is:

$$2 (2 \times 0.25) + 2(3 \times 0.14) + 4(4 \times 0.055) = 2.72 \text{ bits per codeword}$$

which is 99.8% of the Shannon value.

Using fixed-length binary codewords:

There are 8 characters – A through H – and hence 3 bits per codeword is sufficient, which is 90.7% of the Huffman value.

Using 7-bit ASCII codewords:

7 bits per codeword
which is 38.86% of the Huffman value.

Since each character in its encoded form has a variable number of bits, the received bitstream must be interpreted (decoded) in a bit-oriented way rather than on fixed 7/8 bit boundaries. Because of the order in which bits are assigned during the encoding procedure, however, Huffman codewords have the unique property that a shorter codeword will never form the start of a longer codeword. If, say, 011 is a valid codeword, then there

(a)

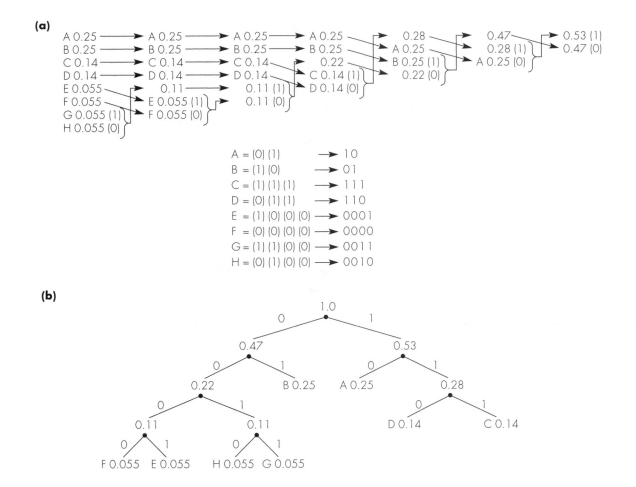

A = (0) (1)   → 10
B = (1) (0)   → 01
C = (1) (1) (1)   → 111
D = (0) (1) (1)   → 110
E = (1) (0) (0) (0) → 0001
F = (0) (0) (0) (0) → 0000
G = (1) (1) (0) (0) → 0011
H = (0) (1) (0) (0) → 0010

(b)

Weight order = 0.055 0.055 0.055 0.055 0.11 0.11 0.14 0.14 0.22 0.25 0.25 0.28 0.47 0.53 ✔

Figure A.7 Huffman encoding example: (a) codeword generation; (b) Huffman code tree.

cannot be any longer codewords starting with this sequence. We can confirm this by considering the codes derived in the earlier examples in Figures A.6 and A.7.

This property, known as the **prefix property**, means that the received bitstream can be decoded simply by carrying out a recursive search bit by bit until each valid codeword is found. A flowchart of a suitable decoding algorithm is given in Figure A.8(a). The algorithm assumes a table of codewords is available at the receiver and this also holds the corresponding ASCII codeword. The received bitstream is held in the variable BITSTREAM and the variable CODEWORD is used to hold the bits in each codeword while it is being constructed. As we can deduce from the flowchart, once a codeword is identified the corresponding ASCII codeword is written into the variable RECEIVE_BUFFER. The procedure repeats until all the bits in the received string have been processed. An example of a decoded string corresponding to the codeword set derived in Figure A.6 is given in Figure A.8(b).

As the Huffman code tree (and hence codewords) varies for different sets of characters being transmitted, for the receiver to perform the decoding operation it must know the codewords relating to the data being transmitted.

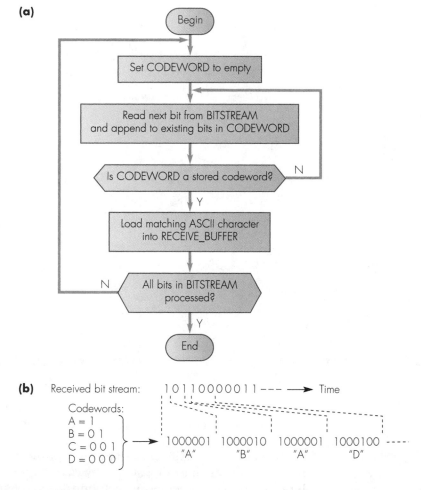

Figure A.8 Decoding of a received bitstream assuming codewords derived in Figure A.6: (a) decoding algorithm; (b) example.

This can be done in two ways. Either the codewords relating to the next set of data are sent before the data is transmitted, or the receiver knows in advance what codewords are being used.

The first approach leads to a form of adaptive compression since the codewords can be changed to suit the type of data being transmitted. The disadvantage is the overhead of having to send the new set of codewords (and corresponding characters) whenever a new type of data is to be sent. An alternative is for the receiver to have one or more different sets of codewords and for the sender to indicate to the receiver (through an agreed message) which codeword set to use for the next set of data.

For example, since a common requirement is to send text files generated by a word processor (and hence containing normal textual information), detailed statistical analyses have been carried out into the frequency of occurrence of the characters in the English alphabet in normal written text. This information has been used to construct the Huffman code tree for the alphabet. If this type of data is being sent, the transmitter and receiver automatically use this set of codewords. Other common data sets have been analyzed in a similar way and, for further examples, you may wish to consult the bibliography at the end of the book.

A.2.2.2 Lempel–Ziv coding

With the Lempel–Ziv (LZ) compression algorithm, instead of using single characters as the basis of the coding operation, uses strings of characters. For example, for the compression of text, a table containing all the possible character strings – for example words – that occur in the text to be transferred is held by both the encoder and decoder. As each word occurs in the text, instead of sending the word as a set of individual – say, ASCII – codewords, the encoder sends only the index of where the word is stored in the table and, on receipt of each index, the decoder uses this to access the corresponding word/string of characters from the table and proceeds to reconstruct the text into its original form. Thus the table is used as a dictionary and the LZ algorithm is known as a **dictionary-based** compression algorithm.

Most word-processing packages have a dictionary associated with them which is used both for spell checking and for the compression of text. Typically, they contain in the region of 25 000 words and hence 15 bits – which has 32 768 combinations – are required to encode the index. To send the word "multimedia" with such a dictionary would require just 15 bits instead of 70 bits with 7-bit ASCII codewords. This results in a compression ratio of 4.7:1. Clearly, shorter words will have a lower compression ratio and longer words a higher ratio.

Example A.4

The LZ algorithm is to be used to compress a text file prior to its transmission. If the average number of characters per word is 6, and the dictionary used contains 4096 words, derive the average compression ratio that is achieved relative to using 7-bit ASCII codewords.

Answer:

In general, a dictionary with an index of n bits can contain up to 2^n entries. Now $4096 = 2^{12}$ and hence an index of 12 bits is required.

Using 7-bit ASCII codewords and an average of 6 characters per word requires 42 bits.

Hence compression ratio = $42/12$ = 3.5:1.

A.2.3 Image compression

Recall from Section A.1.3 how images can be of two basic types: computer-generated (also known as graphical) images and digitized images (of both documents and pictures). Although both types are displayed (and printed) in the form of a two-dimensional matrix of individual picture elements, normally a graphical image is represented differently in the computer file system. Typically, this is in the form of a program (written in a particular graphics programming language) and, since this type of representation requires considerably less memory (and hence transmission bandwidth) than the corresponding matrix of picture elements, whenever possible, graphics are transferred across a network in this form. In the case of digitized documents and pictures, however, once digitized, the only form of representation is as a two-dimensional matrix of picture elements.

In terms of compression, when transferring graphical images that are represented in their program form, a lossless compression algorithm must be used similar, for example, to that in the last section. However, when the created image/graphic is to be transferred across the network in its bit-map form, then this is normally compressed prior to its transfer. There are a number of different compression algorithms and associated file formats in use and we shall describe one of these in the next section.

To transfer digitized images a different type of compression algorithm must normally be employed. It is based on a combination of transform, differential and run-length encoding and has been developed for the compression of both bitonal and color digitized pictures.

A.2.3.1 Graphics interchange format

The **graphics interchange format** (**GIF**) is used extensively with the Internet for the representation and compression of graphical images. Although color images comprising 24-bit pixels are supported – 8 bits each for R, G and B –

GIF reduces the number of possible colors that are present by choosing the 256 colors from the original set of 2^{24} colors that match most closely those used in the original image. The resulting table of colors therefore consists of 256 entries, each of which contains a 24-bit color value. Hence instead of sending each pixel as a 24-bit value, only the 8-bit index to the table entry that contains the closest match color to the original is sent. This results in a compression ratio of 3:1. The table of colors can relate either to the whole image – in which case it is referred to as the **global color table** – or to a portion of the image, when it is referred to as a **local color table**. The contents of the table are sent across the network – together with the compressed image data and other information such as the screen size and aspect ratio – in a standardized format. The principles of the scheme are shown in Figure A.9.

A.2.3.2 Digitized pictures

We described the digitization of both continuous-tone monochromatic pictures and color pictures in Section A.1.3.2. We also calculated the amount of computer memory required to store and display these pictures on a number of popular types of display and tabulated these in Table A.1. The amount of memory ranged from (approximately) 307 kbytes through to 2.4 Mbytes and, as we concluded, all would result in unacceptably long delays in most interactive applications that involve low bit rate networks.

In order to reduce the time to transmit digitized pictures, compression is normally applied to the two-dimensional array of pixel values that represents a digitized picture before it is transmitted over the network. The most widely-adopted standard relating to the compression of digitized pictures has been developed by an international standards body known as the **Joint Photographic Experts Group (JPEG)**. JPEG also forms the basis of most video compression algorithms and hence we shall limit our discussion of the compression of digitized pictures to describing the main principles of the JPEG standard.

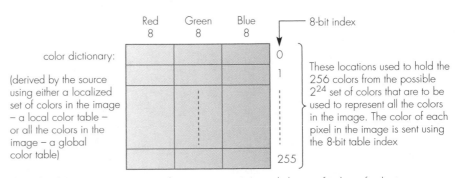

The color dictionary, screen size and aspect ratio are sent with the set of indexes for the image.

Figure A.9 GIF compression principles.

A.2.3.3 JPEG

As we can deduce from the name, the JPEG standard was developed by a team of experts, each of whom had an in-depth knowledge of the compression of digitized pictures. They were working on behalf of the ISO, the ITU, and the IEC and JPEG is defined in the international standard **IS 10918**. In practice, the standard defines a range of different compression modes, each of which is intended for use in a particular application domain. We shall restrict our discussion here to the **lossy sequential mode** – also known as the **baseline mode** – since it is this which is intended for the compression of both monochromatic and color digitized pictures/images as used in Internet applications. There are five main stages associated with this mode: image/block preparation, forward DCT, quantization, entropy encoding and frame building. These are shown in Figure A.10 and we shall discuss the role of each separately.

Image/block preparation

As we described in Section A.1.3.2, in its pixel form, the source image/ picture is made up of one or more 2-D matrices of values. In the case of a continuous-tone monochrome image, just a single 2-D matrix is required to store the set of 8-bit gray-level values that represent the image. Similarly, for a color image, if a CLUT is used just a single matrix of values is required.

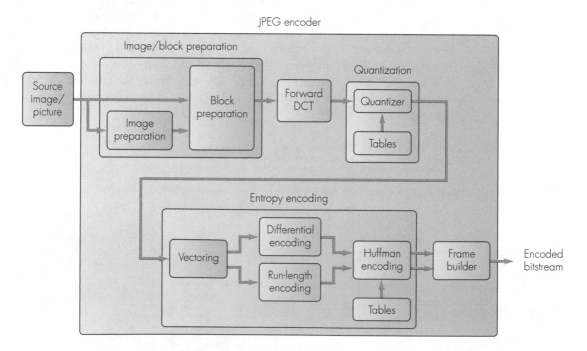

Figure A.10 JPEG encoder schematic.

Alternatively, if the image is represented in an *R, G, B* format three matrices are required, one each for the *R, G* and *B* quantized values. Also, as we saw in Section A.1.5.2 when we discussed the representation of a video signal, for color images the alternative form of representation known as *Y, C_b, C_r* can optionally be used. This is done to exploit the fact that the two chrominance signals, C_b and C_r, require half the bandwidth of the luminance signal, *Y*. This in turn allows the two matrices that contain the digitized chrominance components to be smaller in size than the *Y* matrix so producing a reduced form of representation over the equivalent *R, G, B* form of representation. The four alternative forms of representation are shown in Figure A.11(a).

Once the source image format has been selected and prepared, the set of values in each matrix are compressed separately using the DCT. Before performing the DCT on each matrix, however, a second step known as **block preparation** is carried out. This is necessary since to compute the transformed value for each position in a matrix requires the values in all the locations of the matrix to be processed. It would be too time consuming to compute the DCT of the total matrix in a single step so each matrix is first divided into a set of smaller 8 × 8 submatrices. Each is known as a **block** and, as we can see in part (b) of the figure, these are then fed sequentially to the DCT which transforms each block separately.

Forward DCT

We described the principles of the DCT earlier in Section A.2.1.4. Normally, each pixel value is quantized using 8 bits which produces a value in the range 0 to 255 for the intensity/luminance values – *R, G, B,* or *Y* – and a value in the range –128 to +127 for the two chrominance values – C_b and C_r. In order to compute the (forward) DCT, however, all the values are first centered around zero by subtracting 128 from each intensity/luminance value. Then, if the input 2-D matrix is represented by $P[x, y]$ and the transformed matrix by $F[i, j]$, the DCT of each 8 × 8 block of values is computed using the expression:

$$F[i, j] = \frac{1}{4} C(i) C(j) \sum_{x=0}^{7} \sum_{y=0}^{7} P[x, y] \cos \frac{(2x+1)i\pi}{16} \cos \frac{(2y+1)j\pi}{16}$$

where $C(i)$ and $C(j) = 1/\sqrt{2}$ for $i, j = 0$

$\qquad\qquad\qquad\quad = 1$ for all other values of i and j

and x, y, i and j all vary from 0 through 7.

You can find further details relating to the DCT in the bibliography for Chapter 1 at the end of the book.

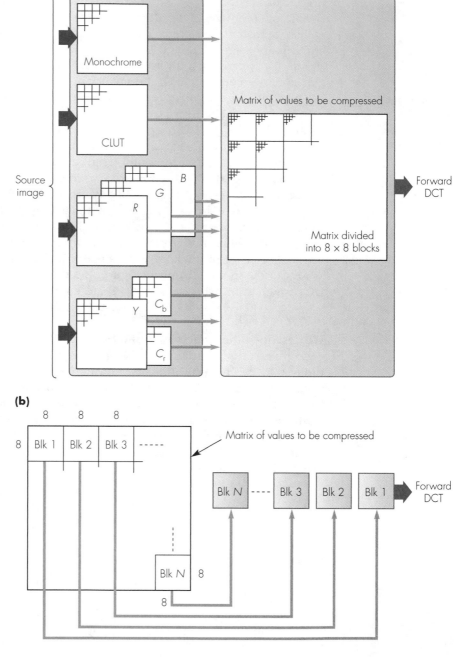

Figure A.11 **Image/block preparation: (a) image preparation; (b) block preparation.**

Quantization

In theory, providing the forward DCT is computed to a high precision using, say, floating point arithmetic, there is very little loss of information during the DCT phase. Although in practice small losses occur owing to the use of fixed point arithmetic, the main source of information loss occurs during the quantization and entropy encoding stages where the compression takes place.

As we identified earlier in Section A.2.1.4 when we first discussed transform encoding, the human eye responds primarily to the DC coefficient and the lower spatial frequency coefficients. Thus if the magnitude of a higher frequency coefficient is below a certain threshold, the eye will not detect it. This property is exploited in the quantization phase by dropping – in practice, setting to zero – those spatial frequency coefficients in the transformed matrix whose amplitudes are less than a defined threshold value.

In practice, the threshold values used vary for each of the 64 DCT coefficients. These are held in a two-dimensional matrix known as the **quantization table** with the threshold value to be used with a particular DCT coefficient in the corresponding position in the matrix.

Entropy encoding

As we saw earlier in Figure A.10, the entropy encoding stage comprises four steps: vectoring, differential encoding, run-length encoding and Huffman encoding. We shall describe the role of each step separately.

Vectoring The various entropy encoding algorithms we described earlier in Section A.2.1.3 operate on a one-dimensional string of values, that is, a vector. As we have just seen, however, the output of the quantization stage is a 2-D matrix of values. Hence before we can apply any entropy encoding to the set of values in the matrix, we must first represent the values in the form of a single-dimension vector. This operation is known as **vectoring**.

Differential encoding The first element in each transformed block is the DC coefficient, which is a measure of the average color/luminance/chrominance associated with the corresponding 8×8 block of pixel values. Hence it is the largest coefficient and, because of its importance, its resolution is kept as high as possible during the quantization phase. Because of the small physical area covered by each block, the DC coefficient varies only slowly from one block to the next.

As we described in Section A.2.1.4, the most efficient type of compression with this form of information structure is differential encoding since this encodes only the difference between each pair of values in a string rather than their absolute values. Hence in this application, only the difference in magnitude of the DC coefficient in a quantized block relative to the value in the preceding block is encoded. In this way, the number of bits required to encode the relatively large magnitudes of the DC coefficients is reduced.

Run-length encoding The remaining 63 values in the vector are the AC coefficients and, in practice, the vector contains long strings of zeros within it. To exploit this feature, the AC coefficients are encoded in the form of a string of pairs of values. Each pair is made up of (*skip, value*) where *skip* is the number of zeros in the run and *value* the next non-zero coefficient.

Huffman encoding Significant levels of compression can be obtained by replacing long strings of binary digits by a string of much shorter codewords, the length of each codeword being a function of its relative frequency of occurrence. Normally, a table of codewords is used with the set of codewords precomputed using the Huffman coding algorithm. The same approach is used to encode the output of both the differential and run-length encoders.

Frame building Typically, the bitstream output by a JPEG encoder – corresponding to, say, the compressed version of a printed picture – is stored in the memory of a computer ready for either integrating with other media if necessary or accessing from a remote computer. As we can see from the above, in order for the decoder in the remote computer to be able to interpret all the different fields and tables that make up the bitstream, it is necessary to delimit each field and set of table values in a defined way. This is the role of the **frame builder**.

JPEG decoding As we can see in Figure A.12, a JPEG decoder is made up of a number of stages that are simply the corresponding decoder sections of those used in the encoder. Hence the time to carry out the decoding function is similar to that used to perform the encoding.

On receipt of the encoded bitstream the **frame decoder** first identifies the control information and tables within the various headers. It then loads the contents of each table into the related table and passes the control information to the **image builder**. It then starts to pass the compressed bitstream to the Huffman decoder, which carries out the corresponding decompression operation using either the default or the preloaded table of codewords. The two decompressed streams containing the DC and AC coefficients of each block are then passed to the differential and run-length decoders respectively. The resulting matrix of values is then dequantized using either the default or the preloaded values in the quantization table.

Each resulting block of 8 × 8 spatial frequency coefficients is passed in turn to the **inverse DCT**, which transforms them back into their spatial form using the expression:

$$P[x, y] = \frac{1}{4} \sum_{i=0}^{7} \sum_{j=0}^{7} C(i)\, C(j)\, F[i, j] \cos\frac{(2x+1)i\pi}{16} \cos\frac{(2y+1)j\pi}{16}$$

where $C(i)$ and $C(j) = 1/\sqrt{2}$ for $i, j = 0$
$= 1$ for all other values of i and j.

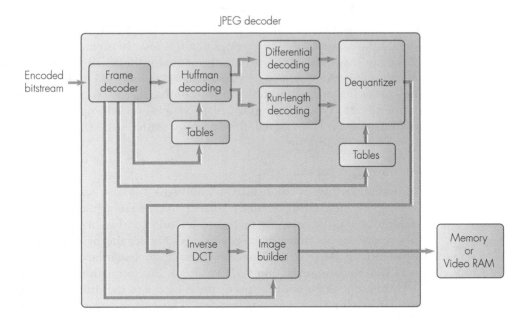

Figure A.12 JPEG decoder schematic.

The image builder then reconstructs the original image from these blocks using the control information passed to it by the frame decoder.

A.2.4 Audio compression

As we described in Section A.1.3 there are two types of audio signals: speech signals as used in Internet telephony and music-quality audio as used when downloading a CD title over the Internet. In this subsection we shall describe each separately.

A.2.4.1 Speech compression

As we described in Section A.1.3.1, the digitization procedure of a basic speech signal is known as pulse code modulation (PCM). With PCM, the (analog) speech signal is sampled at 8k samples per second using 8 bits per sample. This yields a bit rate of 64 kbps and is used in both PSTN and ISDN networks. In practice, however, there is a range of different algorithms each of which yields a lower bit rate. These are then used in private networks where multiple telephone calls can be carried in a single (leased) 64 kbps line/channel and also for Internet telephony. In this subsection we give a summary of the algorithms that are used.

Differential pulse code modulation

This is a derivative of standard PCM and exploits the fact that, for most audio signals, the range of the differences in amplitude between successive samples of the audio waveform is less than the range of the acual sample amplitudes. Hence if only the digitized difference signal is used to encode the waveform then fewer bits are required than for a comparable PCM signal with the same sampling rate. Typical savings with DPCM, are limited to just 1 bit, which, for a standard PCM voice signal, for example, reduces the bit rate requirement from 64 kbps to 56 kbps.

Adaptive differential PCM

Additional savings in bandwidth – or improved quality – can be obtained by varying the number of bits used for the difference signal depending on its amplitude; that is, using fewer bits to encode (and hence transmit) smaller difference values than for larger values. This is the principle of **adaptive differential PCM** (**ADPCM**) and an international standard for this is defined in **ITU-T Recommendation G.721**. This is based on the same principle as DPCM except an eight-order predictor is used and the number of bits used to quantize each difference value is varied. This can be either 6 bits – producing 32 kbps – to obtain a better quality output than with third-order DPCM, or 5 bits – producing 16 kbps – if lower bandwidth is more important.

A second ADPCM standard, which is a derivative of G.721, is defined in **ITU-T Recommendation G.722**. This provides better sound quality than the G.721 standard at the expense of added complexity. To achieve this, it uses an added technique known as **subband coding**. The input speech bandwidth is extended to be from 50 Hz through to 7 kHz – compared with 3.4 kHz for a standard PCM system – and hence the wider bandwidth produces a higher-fidelity speech signal. This is particularly important in conferencing applications, for example, in order to enable the members of the conference to discriminate between the different voices of the members present.

A third standard based on ADPCM is also available. This is defined in **ITU-T Recommendation G.726**. This also uses subband coding but with a speech bandwidth of 3.4 kHz. The operating bit rate can be 40, 32, 24 or 16 kbps.

Linear predictive coding

All the algorithms we have considered so far are based on sampling the time-varying speech waveform and then either sending the quantized samples directly (PCM) or sending the quantized difference signal (DPCM and its derivatives). With the advent of inexpensive digital signal processing circuits, an alternative approach has become possible that involves the source simply analyzing the audio waveform to determine a selection of the perceptual features it contains. These are then quantized and sent and the destination uses them, together with a sound synthesizer, to regenerate a sound that is perceptually comparable with the source audio signal. This is the basis of the **linear predictive coding** (**LPC**) technique and, although with this the generated sound – normally speech – can often sound synthetic, very high levels of compression (and hence low bit rates) can be achieved.

Some LPC encoders use bit rates as low as 2.4 kbps or even 1.2 kbps. As indicated, however, the generated sound at these rates is often very synthetic and hence LPC coders are used primarily in military applications in which bandwidth is all-important.

Code-excited LPC

The synthesizers used in most LPC decoders are based on a very basic model of the vocal tract. A more sophisticated version of this, known as a **code-excited linear prediction (CELP) model**, is also used and, in practice, is just one example of a family of vocal tract models known as **enhanced excitation (LPC) models**. These are also intended primarily for applications in which the amount of bandwidth available is limited but the perceived quality of the speech must be of an acceptable standard for use in various applications.

There are now four international standards available that are based on this principle. These are **ITU-T Recommendations G.728**, **729**, **729(A)** and **723.1** all of which give a good perceived quality at low bit rates. These are summarized in Table A.3.

Table A.3 Summary of CELP-based standards.

Standard	Bit rate	Example application domain
G.728	16 kbps	Low bit rate telephony
G.729	8 kbps	Telephony in cellular (radio) networks
G.729(A)	8 kbps	Digital simultaneous voice and data (DSVD)
G.723.1	5.3/6.3 kbps	Video and Internet telephony

A.2.4.2 Audio compression

Perceptual coding

Both LPC and CELP are used primarily for telephony applications and hence the compression of a speech signal. Perceptual encoders, however, have been designed for the compression of general audio such as that associated with a CD download. They also use a model but, in this case, it is known as a **psychoacoustic model** since its role is to exploit a number of the limitations of the human ear.

Using this approach, sampled segments of the source audio waveform are analyzed – as with CELP-based coders – but only those features that are perceptible to the ear are transmitted. For example, although the human ear is sensitive to signals in the range 15–20 kHz, the level of sensitivity to each signal is non-linear; that is, the ear is more sensitive to some signals than others. Also, when multiple signals are present – as is the case with general audio – a strong signal may reduce the level of sensitivity of the ear to other   signals which are near to it in frequency, an effect known as **frequency masking**. In addition, when the ear hears a loud sound, it takes a short but finite time before it can hear a quieter sound, an effect known as **temporal masking**. A   psychoacoustic model is used to identify those signals that are influenced by both these effects. These are then eliminated from the transmitted signals and, in so doing, this reduces the amount of information to be transmitted.

Sensitivity of the ear The dynamic range of a signal is the ratio of the maximum amplitude of the signal to the minimum amplitude and is measured in decibels (dB). In the case of the ear, its dynamic range is the ratio of the loudest sound it can hear to the quietest sound and is in the region of 96 dB. As we have just seen, however, the sensitivity of the ear varies with the frequency of the signal and, assuming just a single-frequency signal is present at any one time, the perception threshold of the ear – that is, its minimum level of sensitivity – as a function of frequency is shown in Figure A.13(a).

As we can see, the ear is most sensitive to signals in the range 2–5 kHz and hence signals within this band are the quietest the ear is sensitive to. The vertical axis, therefore, indicates the amplitude level of all the other signal frequencies relative to this level – measured in dB – that are required for them to be heard. Hence in the figure, although the two signals A and B have the same relative amplitude, signal A would be heard – that is, it is above the hearing threshold – while signal B would not.

Frequency masking When an audio sound consists of multiple frequency signals is present, the sensitivity of the ear changes and varies with the relative amplitude of the signals. For example, the curve shown in Figure A.13(b) shows how the sensitivity of the ear changes in the vicinity of a loud signal. In this example, signal B is larger in amplitude than signal A and, as we can see, this causes the basic sensitivity curve of the ear to be distorted in the region of signal B. As a result, signal A will no longer be heard even though on its own, it is above the hearing threshold of the ear for a signal of that frequency. This is the origin of the term frequency masking and, in practice, the masking effect also varies with frequency as we show in Figure A.14.

The various curves show the masking effect of a selection of different frequency signals – 1, 4 and 8 kHz – and, as we can see, the width of the masking curves – that is, the range of frequencies that are affected – increase with increasing frequency. The width of each curve at a particular signal level is known as the **critical bandwidth** for that frequency and experiments have shown that, for frequencies less than 500 Hz, the critical bandwidth remains constant at about 100 Hz. For frequencies greater than 500 Hz, however, the critical bandwidth increases (approximately) linearly in multiples of 100 Hz.

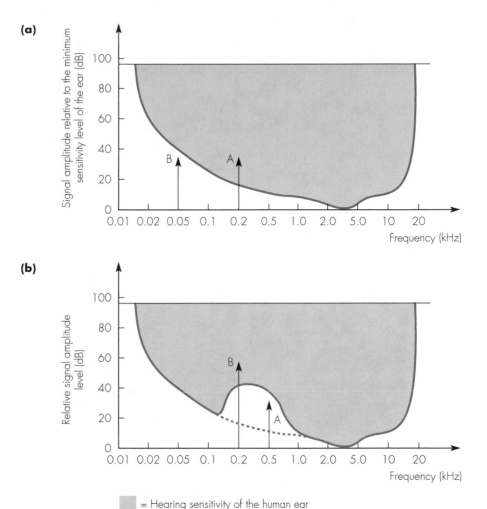

Figure A.13 Perceptual properties of the human ear: (a) sensitivity as a function of frequency; (b) frequency masking.

For example, for a signal of 1 kHz (2 × 500 Hz), the critical bandwidth is about 200 (2 × 100) Hz while at 5 kHz (10 × 500 Hz) it is about 1000 (10 × 100) Hz. Hence if the magnitude of the frequency components that make up an audio sound can be determined, it becomes possible to determine those frequencies that will be masked (and hence inaudible) and do not therefore need to be transmitted.

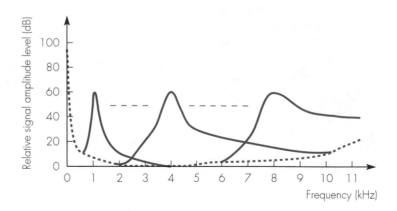

Figure A.14 Variation with frequency of effect of frequency masking.

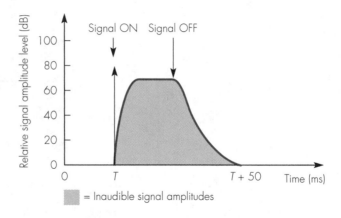

Figure A.15 Temporal masking caused by a loud signal.

Temporal masking As indicated earlier, after the ear hears a loud sound, it takes a further short time before it can hear a quieter sound. This is known as temporal masking and the general effect is shown in Figure A.15. As we can see, after the loud sound ceases it takes a short period of time (in the order of tens of milli-seconds) for the signal amplitude to decay. During this time, signals whose amplitudes are less than the decay envelope will not be heard and hence need not be transmitted. Clearly, however, in order to exploit this phenomenon, it is necessary to process the input audio waveform over a time period that is comparable with that associated with temporal masking.

MPEG audio coders

In practice, perceptual coding is used in a range of different audio compression applications. For example, as we shall describe later, the **Motion**

Pictures Expert Group (**MPEG**) was formed by the ISO to formulate a set of standards relating to a range of multimedia applications that involve the use of video with sound. The coders associated with the audio compression part of these standards are known as **MPEG audio coders** and a number of these use perceptual coding.

All the signal processing operations associated with a perceptual coder are carried out digitally. The time-varying audio input signal is first sampled and quantized using PCM, the sampling rate and number of bits per sample being determined by the specific application. The bandwidth that is available for transmission is divided into a number of **frequency subbands** using a bank of **analysis filters**. Each frequency subband is of equal width and, essentially, the bank of filters maps each set of 32 (time-related) PCM samples into an equivalent set of 32 frequency samples, one per subband. Hence each is known as a **subband sample** and indicates the magnitude of each of the 32 frequency components that are present in a segment of the audio input signal of a time duration equal to 32 PCM samples.

In a basic encoder, the time duration of each sampled segment of the audio input signal is equal to the time to accumulate 12 successive sets of 32 PCM – and hence subband – samples; that is, a time duration equal to 384 (12×32) PCM samples.

In addition to filtering the input samples into separate frequency subbands, the analysis filter bank also determines the maximum amplitude of the 12 subband samples in each subband. Each is known as the **scaling factor** for the subband and these are passed both to a unit called the psychoacoustic model and, together with the set of frequency samples in each subband, to the corresponding quantizer block.

The processing associated with both frequency and temporal masking is carried out by the psychoacoustic model. The 12 sets of 32 PCM samples are first transformed into an equivalent set of frequency components using a mathematical technique known as the **discrete Fourier transform** (**DFT**). Then, using the known hearing thresholds and masking properties of each subband, the model determines the various masking effects of this set of signals. The output of the model is a set of what are known as **signal-to-mask ratios** (**SMRs**) and indicate those frequency components whose amplitude is below the related audible threshold. In a basic encoder, all the frequency components in a sampled segment are encoded and these are carried in a frame.

An international standard based on this approach is defined in **ISO Recommendation 11172-3**. There are three levels of processing associated with this known as layers 1, 2, and 3. Layer 1 is the basic mode and the other two have increasing levels of processing associated with them which, in turn, produce a corresponding increase in the level of compression for the same perceived audio quality. For example, layer 1 does not include temporal masking but this is present in layers 2 and 3.

As we have already indicated, in terms of applications, MPEG audio is used primarily for the compression of general audio and, in particular, for the audio associated with various digital video applications. The performance of the three layers and examples of their corresponding application domains are summarized in Table A.4.

Table A.4 Summary of MPEG layer 1, 2 and 3 perceptual encoders.

Layer	Application	Compressed bit rate	Quality
1	Digital audio cassette	32–448 kbps	Hi-fi quality at 192 kbps per channel
2	Digital audio and digital video broadcasting	32–192 kbps	Near CD-quality at 128 kbps per channel
3	CD-quality audio over low bit rate channels	64 kbps	CD-quality at 64 kbps per channel

Dolby audio coders

The psychoacoustic models associated with the various MPEG coders control the quantization accuracy of each subband sample by computing and allocating the number of bits to be used to quantize each sample. Since the quantization accuracy that is used for each sample in a subband may vary from one set of subband samples to the next, the bit allocation information that is used to quantize the samples in each subband is sent with the actual quantized samples. This information is then used by the decoder to dequantize the set of subband samples in the frame. This mode of operation of a perceptual coder is known, therefore, as the **forward adaptive bit allocation mode** and, for comparison purposes, a simplified schematic diagram showing this operational mode is given in Figure A.16(a). As we indicated at the end of the last section, it has the advantage that the psychoacoustic model is required only in the encoder. It has the disadvantage, however, that a significant portion of each encoded frame contains bit allocation information which, in turn, leads to a relatively inefficient use of the available bit rate.

A variation of this approach is to use a fixed bit allocation strategy for each subband which is then used by both the encoder and the decoder. The principle of operation of this mode is shown in Figure A.16(b). Typically, the bit allocations that are selected for each subband are determined by the known sensitivity characteristics of the ear and the use of fixed allocations means that this information need not be sent in the frame. This approach is used in a standard known as **Dolby AC-1**, the acronym "AC" meaning **acoustic coder**. It uses a low-complexity psychoacoustic model with 40 subbands at a sampling rate of 32 ksps and proportionately more at 44.1 and 48 ksps. A typical compressed bit rate is 512 kbps for two-channel stereo.

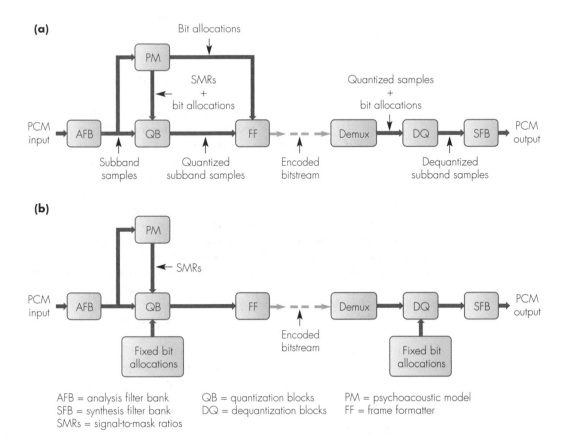

Figure A.16 Perceptual coder schematics: (a) forward adaptive bit allocation (MPEG); (b) fixed bit allocation (Dolby AC-1).

A.2.5 Video compression

Video (with sound) now features in a number of Internet applications:

- **interpersonal**: video telephony and videoconferencing;
- **interactive**: access to stored video in various forms.

However, as we showed in Table A.2, the quality of the video used in these applications varies and is determined by the digitization format and frame refresh rate used. As you may recall, the digitization format defines the sampling rate that is used for the luminance, Y, and two chrominance, C_b and C_r, signals and their relative position in each frame. Hence, there is not just a single standard associated with video but rather a range of standards, each targeted at a particular application domain. In this subsection we shall describe just the principles involved and then list the main features of each standard.

A.2.5.1 Video compression principles

In the context of compression, since video is simply a sequence of digitized pictures, video is also referred to as **moving pictures** and the terms "frame" and "picture" are used interchangeably. In general, we shall use the term frame except where a particular standard uses the term picture.

In principle, one approach to compressing a video source is to apply the JPEG algorithm described earlier in Section A.2.3.3 to each frame independently. This approach is known as **moving JPEG** or **MJPEG**. As we concluded at the end of that section, however, typical compression ratios obtainable with JPEG are between 10:1 and 20:1, neither of which is large enough on its own to produce the compression ratios needed.

In practice, in addition to the spatial redundancy present in each frame, considerable redundancy is often present between a set of frames since, in general, only a small portion of each frame is involved with any motion that is taking place. Examples include the movement of a person's lips or eyes in a video telephony application and a person or vehicle moving across the screen in a movie. In the case of the latter, since a typical scene in a movie has a minimum duration of about 3 seconds, assuming a frame refresh rate of 60 frames per second, each scene is composed of a minimum of 180 frames. Hence by sending only information relating to those segments of each frame that have movement associated with them, considerable additional savings in bandwidth can be made by exploiting the temporal differences that exist between many of the frames.

The technique that is used to exploit the high correlation between successive frames is to predict the content of many of the frames. As we shall describe, this is based on a combination of a preceding – and in some instances a succeeding – frame. Instead of sending the source video as a set of individually-compressed frames, just a selection is sent in this form and, for the remaining frames, only the differences between the actual frame contents and the predicted frame contents are sent. The accuracy of the prediction operation is determined by how well any movement between successive frames is estimated. This operation is known as **motion estimation** and, since the estimation process is not exact, additional information must also be sent to indicate any small differences between the predicted and actual positions of the moving segments involved. The latter is known as **motion compensation** and we shall discuss each issue separately.

Frame types

As we can see from the above, there are two basic types of compressed frame: those that are encoded independently and those that are predicted. The first are known as **intracoded frames** or **I-frames**. In practice, there are two types of predicted frames: **predictive** or **P-frames**, and **bidirectional** or **B-frames**, and because of the way they are derived, the latter are also known as

intercoded or **interpolation frames**. A typical sequence of frames involving just I- and P-frames is shown in Figure A.17(a) and a sequence involving all three frame types is shown in part (b) of the figure.

I-frames are encoded without reference to any other frames. Each frame is treated as a separate (digitized) picture and the Y, C_b and C_r matrices are encoded independently using the JPEG algorithm (DCT, quantization, entropy encoding – described earlier in Section A.2.3.3) except that the quantization threshold values that are used are the same for all DCT coefficients. Hence the level of compression obtained with I-frames is relatively small. In principle, therefore, it would appear to be best if these

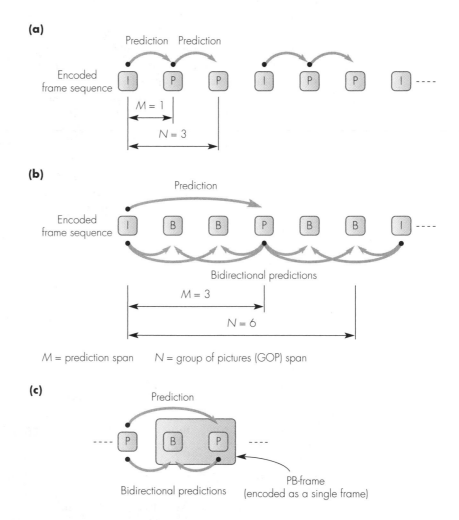

Figure A.17 Example frame sequences with: (a) I- and P-frames only; (b) I-, P- and B-frames; (c) PB-frames.

were limited to, say, the first frame relating to a new scene in a movie. In practice, however, the compression algorithm is independent of the contents of frames and hence has no knowledge of the start and end of scenes. Also, I-frames must be present in the output stream at regular intervals in order to allow for the possibility of the contents of an encoded I-frame being corrupted during transmission. Clearly, if an I-frame was corrupted then, in the case of a movie, since the predicted frames are based on the contents of an I-frame, a complete scene would be lost, which, of course, would be totally unacceptable. Normally, therefore, I-frames are inserted into the output stream relatively frequently. The number of frames/pictures between successive I-frames is known as a **group of pictures** or **GOP**. It is given the symbol N and typical values for N are from 3 through to 12.

As we can deduce from Figure A.17(a), the encoding of a P-frame is relative to the contents of either a preceding I-frame or a preceding P-frame. As indicated, P-frames are encoded using a combination of motion estimation and motion compensation and hence significantly higher levels of compression can be obtained with them. In practice, however, the number of P-frames between each successive pair of I-frames is limited since any errors present in the first P-frame will be propagated to the next. The number of frames between a P-frame and the immediately preceding I- or P-frame is called the **prediction span**. It is given the symbol M and typical values range from 1, as in Figure A.17(a), through to 3, as in Figure A.17(b).

As we shall describe shortly, motion estimation involves comparing small segments of two consecutive frames for differences and, should a difference be detected, a search is carried out to determine to which neighboring segment the original segment has moved. In order to minimize the time for each search, the search region is limited to just a few neighboring segments. In applications such as video telephony, the amount of movement between consecutive frames is relatively small and hence this approach works well. In those applications that may involve very fast-moving objects, however, it is possible for a segment to have moved outside the search region. To allow for this possibility, in applications such as movies, in addition to P-frames, a second type of prediction frame is used. These are the B-frames and, as we can see in Figure A.17(b), their contents are predicted using search regions in both past and future frames. In addition to allowing for occasional fast moving objects, this also provides better motion estimation when, for example, an object moves in front of or behind another object.

As we can deduce from the two example frame sequences shown in Figure A.17, for P-frames their contents are encoded by considering the contents of the current (uncoded) frame relative to the contents of the immediately preceding (uncoded) frame. In the case of B-frames, however, three (uncoded) frame contents are involved: the immediately preceding I- or P-frame, the current frame being encoded, and the immediately succeeding I- or P-frame. This results in an increase in the encoding (and decoding) delay which is equal to the time to wait for the next I- or P-frame in the sequence. In practice, however, B-frames provide the highest level of compression and, because they are not involved in the coding of other frames, they do not propagate errors.

To perform the decoding operation, the received (compressed) information relating to I-frames can be decoded immediately it is received in order to recreate the original frame. With P-frames, the received information is first decoded and the resulting information is then used, together with the decoded contents of the preceding I- or P-frame, to derive the decoded frame contents. In the case of B-frames, the received information is first decoded and the resulting information is then used, together with both the immediately preceding I- or P-frame contents and the immediately succeeding P- or I-frame contents, to derive the decoded frame contents. Hence in order to minimize the time required to decode each B-frame, the order of encoding (and transmission) of the (encoded) frames is changed so that both the preceding and succeeding I- or P-frames are available when the B-frame is received. For example, if the uncoded frame sequence is:

IBBPBBPBBI …

then the reordered sequence would be:

IPBBPBBIBBPBB.

Hence, with B-frames, the decoded contents of both the immediately preceding I- or P-frame and the immediately succeeding P- or I-frame are available when the B-frame is received.

A fourth type of frame known as a PB-frame has also been defined. This does not refer to a new frame type as such but rather the way two neighboring P- and B-frames are encoded as if they were a single frame. The general principle is as shown in Figure A.17(c) and this is done in order to increase the frame rate without significantly increasing the resulting bit rate required.

Finally, although only used in a specific type of application, a fifth type of frame known as a **D-frame** has been defined for use in movie/video-on-demand applications. With this type of application, a user (at home) can select and watch a particular movie/video that is stored in a remote server connected to the Internet. The selection operation is performed by means of a set-top box and, as with a VCR, the user may wish to rewind or fast-forward through the movie. Clearly, this requires the compressed video to be decompressed at much higher speeds. Hence to support this function, the encoded video stream also contains D-frames which are inserted at regular intervals throughout the stream. These are highly compressed frames and are ignored during the decoding of P- and B-frames. As you may recall from our earlier discussion of the DCT compression algorithm in Section A.2.3.3, the DC coefficient associated with each 8×8 block of pixels – for both the luminance and the two chrominance signals – is the mean of all the values in the related block. Hence by using only the encoded DC coefficients of each block of pixels in the periodically inserted D-frames, a low-resolution sequence of frames is provided each of which can be decoded at the higher speeds that are expected with the rewind and fast-forward operations.

Motion estimation and compensation

As we showed earlier in Figure A.17, the encoded contents of both P- and B-frames are predicted by estimating any motion that has taken place between the frame being encoded and the preceding I- or P-frame and, in the case of B-frames, the succeeding P- or I-frame. The various steps that are involved in encoding each P-frame are shown in Figure A.18.

As we show in Figure A.18(a), the digitized contents of the Y matrix associated with each frame are first divided into a two-dimensional matrix of

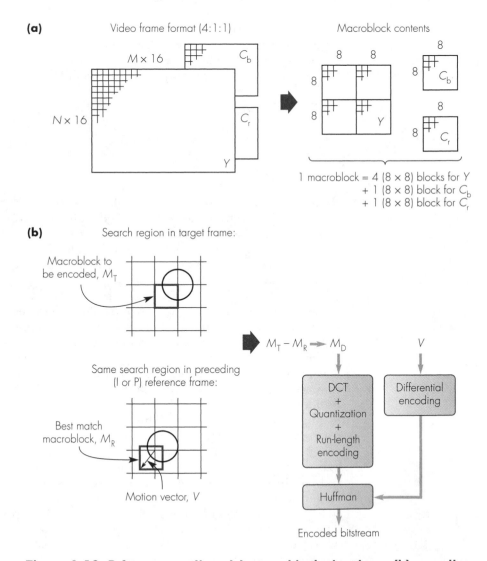

Figure A.18 P-frame encoding: (a) macroblock structure; (b) encoding procedure.

16×16 pixels known as a **macroblock**. In the example, the 4:1:1 digitization format is assumed and hence the related C_b and C_r matrices in the macroblock are both 8×8 pixels. For identification purposes, each macroblock has an **address** associated with it and, since the block size used for the DCT operation is also 8×8 pixels, a macroblock comprises four DCT blocks for luminance and one each for the two chrominance signals.

To encode a P-frame, the contents of each macroblock in the frame – known as the **target frame** – are compared on a pixel-by-pixel basis with the contents of the corresponding macroblock in the preceding I- or P-frame. The latter is known as the **reference frame**. If a close match is found, then only the address of the macroblock is encoded. If a match is not found, the search is extended to cover an area around the macroblock in the reference frame. Typically, this comprises a number of macroblocks as shown in Figure A.18(b).

In practice, the various standards do not specify either the extent of the search area or a specific search strategy and instead specify only how the results of the search are to be encoded. Normally, only the contents of the Y matrix are used in the search and a match is said to be found if the mean of the absolute errors in all the pixel positions in the difference macroblock is less than a given threshold. Hence, using a particular strategy, all the possible macroblocks in the selected search area in the reference frame are searched for a match and, if a close match is found, two parameters are encoded. The first is known as the **motion vector** and indicates the (x, y) offset of the macroblock being encoded and the location of the block of pixels in the reference frame which produces the (close) match. The search – and hence offset – can be either on macroblock boundaries or, as in the figure, on pixel boundaries. The motion vector is then said to be **single-pixel resolution**. The second parameter is known as the **prediction error** and comprises three matrices (one each for Y, C_b and C_r) each of which contains the difference values (in all the pixel locations) between those in the target macroblock and the set of pixels in the search area that produced the close match.

Since the physical area of coverage of a macroblock is small, the motion vectors can be relatively large values. Also, most moving objects are normally much larger than a single macroblock. Hence, when an object moves, multiple macroblocks are affected in a similar way. The motion vectors, therefore, are encoded using differential encoding (DE) and the resulting codewords are then Huffman encoded. The three difference matrices, however, are encoded using the same steps as for I-frames: DCT, quantization, entropy encoding. Finally, if a match cannot be found – for example if the moving object has moved out of the extended search area – the macroblock is encoded independently in the same way as the macroblocks in an I-frame.

To encode a B-frame, any motion is estimated with reference to both the immediately preceding I- or P-frame and the immediately succeeding P- or I-frame. The general scheme is shown in Figure A.19. The motion vector and difference matrices are computed using first the preceding frame as the

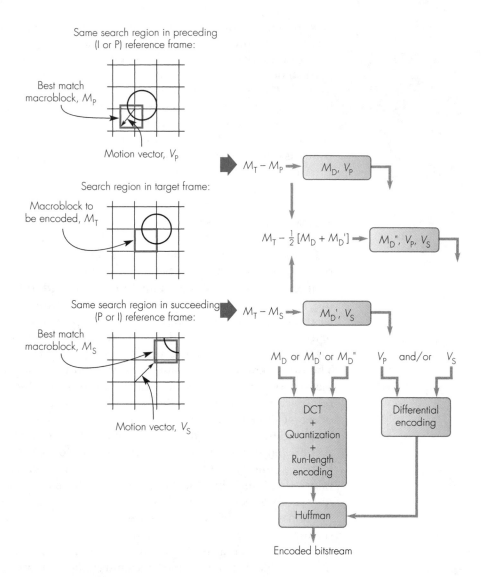

Figure A.19 B-frame encoding procedure.

reference and then the succeeding frame as the reference. A third motion vector and set of difference matrices are then computed using the target and the mean of the two other predicted sets of values. The set with the lowest set of difference matrices is then chosen and these are encoded in the same way as for P-frames. The motion vector is then said to be to a resolution of a fraction of a pixel, for example **half-pixel resolution**.

Performance The compression ratio for I-frames – and hence all intracoded frames – is similar to that obtained with JPEG and, for video frames, typically is in the region of 10:1 through 20:1 depending on the complexity of the frame contents. The compression ratio of both P- and B- frames is higher and depends on the search method used. However, typical figures are in the region of 20:1 through 30:1 for P-frames and 30:1 through 50:1 for B-frames.

H.261

The H.261 video compression standard has been defined by the ITU-T for the provision of video telephony and videoconferencing services over an integrated services digital network (ISDN). Hence, it is assumed that the network offers transmission channels of multiples of 64 kbps. The standard is also known, therefore, as $p \times 64$ where p can be 1 through 30. The digitization format used is either the common intermediate format (CIF) or the quarter CIF (QCIF). Normally, the CIF is used for videoconferencing and the QCIF for video telephony.

$$\text{QCIF: } Y = 176 \times 144, \quad C_b = C_r = 88 \times 72$$

H.263

The H.263 video compression standard has been defined by the ITU-T for use in a range of Internet applications over wireless and public switched telephone networks (PSTNs). The applications include video telephony, videoconferencing, security surveillance, interactive games playing, and so on, all of which require the output of the video encoder to be transmitted across the network connection in real time as it is output by the encoder.

The basic structure of the H.263 video encoder is based on that used in the H.261 standard. At bit rates lower than 64 kbps, however, the H.261 encoder gives a relatively poor picture quality. The use of a low frame rate can also lead to very jerky movements. In order to minimize these effects, the H.263 standard has a number of advanced coding options compared with those used in an H.261 encoder.

MPEG

The **Motion Pictures Expert Group** (**MPEG**) was formed by the ISO to formulate a set of standards relating to a range of applications that involve the use of video with sound. The outcome is a set of three standards that relate to either the recording or the transmission of integrated audio and video streams. Each is targeted at a particular application domain and describes how the audio and video are compressed and integrated together. The three standards, which use different video resolutions, are:

■ **MPEG-1**: this is defined in a series of documents that are all subsets of **ISO Recommendation 11172**. The video resolution is based on the source intermediate digitization format (SIF) with a resolution of up to 352×288 pixels. The standard is intended for the storage of VHS-quality audio and video on CD-ROM at bit rates up to 1.5 Mbps. Normally, however, higher bit rates of multiples of this are more common in order to provide faster access to the stored material.

- **MPEG-2**: this is defined in a series of documents that are all subsets of **ISO Recommendation 13818**. It is intended for the recording and transmission of studio-quality audio and video. The standard covers four levels of video resolution:

  - Low: based on the SIF digitization format with a resolution of up to 352×288 pixels. It is compatible with the MPEG-1 standard and produces VHS-quality video. The audio is of CD quality and the target bit rate is up to 4 Mbps;

  - Main: based on the 4:2:0 digitization format with a resolution of up to 720×576 pixels. This produces studio-quality digital video and the audio allows for multiple CD-quality audio channels. The target bit rate is up to 15 Mbps or 20 Mbps with the 4:2:2 digitization format;

  - High 1440: based on the 4:2:0 digitization format with a resolution of 1440×1152 pixels. It is intended for high-definition television (HDTV) at bit rates up to 60 Mbps or 80 Mbps with the 4:2:2 format.

  - High: based on the 4:2:0 digitization format with a resolution of 1920×1152 pixels. It is intended for wide-screen HDTV at a bit rate of up to 80 Mbps or 100 Mbps with the 4:2:2 format.

- **MPEG-4**: initially, this standard was concerned with a similar range of applications to those of H.263, each running over very low bit rate channels ranging from 4.8 to 64 kbps. Later its scope was expanded to embrace a wide range of interactive multimedia applications over the Internet and the various types of entertainment networks.

MPEG-4

The main application domain of the MPEG-4 standard is in relation to the audio and video associated with interactive applications over the Internet and the various types of entertainment networks. The standard contains features to enable a user not only to passively access a video sequence (or complete video) – using, for example, start/stop/pause commands – but also to access and manipulate the individual elements that make up each scene within the sequence/video. If the accessed video is a computer-generated cartoon, for example, the user may be given the capability – by the creator of the video – to reposition, delete or alter the movement of the individual characters within a scene. In addition, because of its high coding efficiency with scenes such as those associated with video telephony, the standard is also used for this type of application running over low bit rate networks such as wireless and PSTNs. For such applications, therefore, it is an alternative to the H.263 standard.

Scene composition The main difference between MPEG-4 and the other standards we have considered is that MPEG-4 has a number of what are called

content-based functionalities. Before being compressed each scene is defined in the form of a background and one or more foreground **audio-visual objects** (**AVOs**). Each AVO is in turn defined in the form of one or more **video objects** and/or **audio objects**; for example, a stationary car in a scene may be defined using just a single video object while a person who is talking may be defined using both an audio and a video object. In a similar way, each video and audio object may itself be defined as being made up of a number of subobjects. For example, if a person's eyes and mouth are the only things that move, in order to exploit this, the person's face may be defined in the form of three subobjects: one for the head and the other two for the eyes and mouth. Once this has been done, the encoding of the background and each AVO is carried out separately and, in the case of AVOs consisting of both audio and video objects, each has additional timing information relating to it to enable the receiver to synchronize the various objects and subobjects together before they are decoded.

Each audio and video object has a separate **object descriptor** associated with it that allows the object – providing the creator of the audio and/or video has provided the facility – to be manipulated by the viewer prior to it being decoded and played out. The language used to describe and modify objects is called the **binary format for scenes** (**BIFS**). This has commands to delete an object and, in the case of a video object, change its shape, appearance – color for example – and, if appropriate, animate the object in real time. Audio objects have a similar set of commands, to change its volume for example. It is also possible to have multiple versions of an AVO, the first containing the base-level compressed audio and video streams and the others various levels of enhancement detail. This type of compression is called scaling and allows the encoded contents of an AVO to be played out at a rate and resolution that matches those of the interactive terminal being used.

At a higher level, the composition of a scene in terms of the AVOs it contains is defined in a separate **scene descriptor**. This defines the way the various AVOs are related to each other in the context of the complete scene; for example, the position of each AVO on the display screen and the composition of each AVO in terms of the objects and subobjects it comprises.

A simple example illustrating how a frame/scene is defined in the form of a number of AVOs using content-based image coding is shown in Figure A.20. As we can see, each video frame is segmented into a number of **video object planes** (**VOPs**) each of which corresponds to an AVO of interest. Hence in our simple example, the frame is shown as consisting of three VOPs: VOP 0 to represent the person approaching the car, VOP 1 the remainder of the car parked outside the house, and VOP 2 the remainder of the background. Each VOP is encoded separately based on its shape, motion, and texture.

As we show in the figure, each VOP is encapsulated within a rectangle which, in practice, is chosen so that it completely covers the related AVO using the minimum number of macroblocks. The spatial coordinates of the VOP are then relative to the coordinates of the top-left macroblock. The

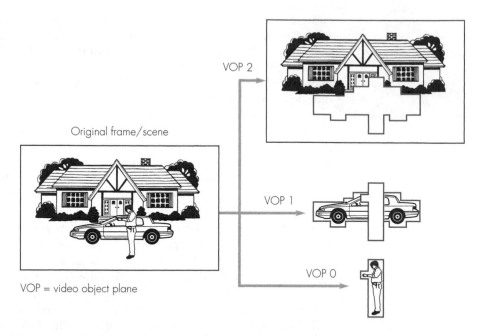

Original frame/scene

VOP = video object plane

Figure A.20 Content-based video coding principles showing how a frame/scene is defined in the form of multiple video object planes.

motion and texture of each VOP are encoded using a procedure similar, for example, to one of those we described earlier in the chapter. The resulting bitstreams are then multiplexed together for transmission together with the related object and scene descriptor information. Similarly, at the receiver, the received bitstream is first demultiplexed and the individual streams decoded. The decompressed information, together with the object and scene descriptions, are then used to create the video frame that is played out on the terminal. Typically, the latter is a multimedia PC or TV set and the audio relating to each scene is played out in time synchronism with the video.

Audio and video compression The audio associated with an AVO is compressed using one of the algorithms we described earlier in the chapter and depends on the available bit rate of the transmission channel and the sound quality required. Examples range from G.723.1 (CELP) for interactive applications over the Internet and video telephony over wireless networks and PSTNs, through to Dolby AC-3 or MPEG Layer 2 for interactive TV applications over entertainment networks.

An overview of the structure of the encoder associated with the audio and video of a frame/scene is shown in part (a) of Figure A.21 and the essential features of each VOP encoder are shown in part (b). As we can see, first each VOP is identified and defined and is then encoded separately.

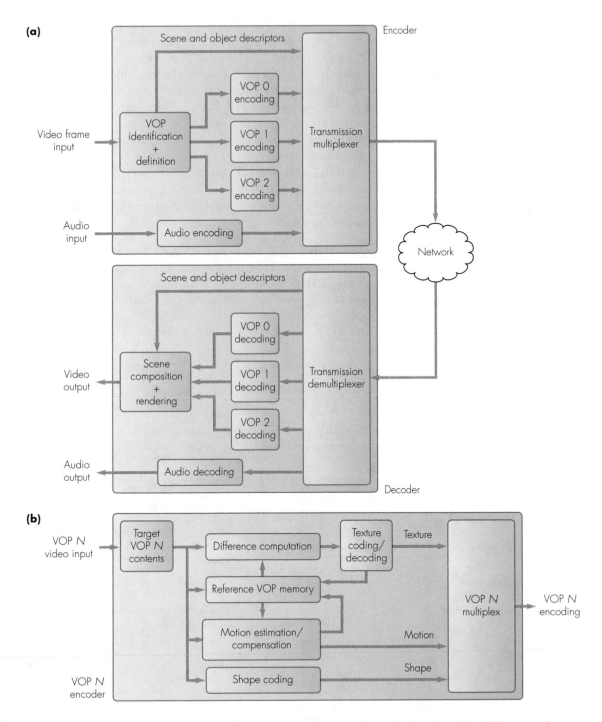

(a)

(b)

Figure A.21 MPEG-4 coding principles: (a) encoder/decoder schematics; (b) VOP encoder schematic.

In practice, the segmentation of a video frame into various objects – from which each VOP is derived – is a difficult image-processing task. In principle, it involves identifying regions of a frame that have similar properties such as color, texture or brightness. Each of the resulting object shapes is then bounded by a rectangle (which contains the minimum number of macroblocks) to form the related VOP. Each is then encoded based on its shape, motion, and texture. Thus any VOP that has no motion associated with it will produce a minimum of compressed information. Also, since the VOP(s) which move often occupy only a small portion of the scene/frame, the bit rate of the multiplexed videostream is much lower than that obtained with the other standards. For applications that support interactions with a particular VOP, a number of advanced coding algorithms are available to perform the shape coding function.

Transmission format As we show in Figure A.22, all the information relating to a frame/scene encoded in MPEG-4 is transmitted over a network in the form of a **transport stream** (**TS**), consisting of a multiplexed stream of **packetized elementary streams** (**PESs**). As indicated earlier, it is intended that MPEG-4

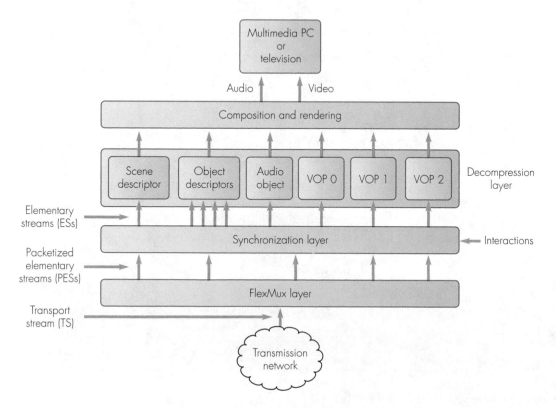

Figure A.22 MPEG-4 decoder schematic.

should be used with applications relating to many different types of network including the Internet, a PSTN, a wireless network, or an entertainment network – cable/satellite/terrestrial. A standard 188-byte packet format has been defined for use in the various types of digital TV broadcast networks. In most cases, the MPEG-4 transport stream uses this same packet format since this helps interworking with the encoded bitstreams associated with the MPEG-1/2 standards.

The compressed audio and video data relating to each AVO in the scene is called an **elementary stream** (**ES**) and this is carried in the payload field of a PES packet. Each PES packet contains a *type* field in the packet header and this is used by the **FlexMux layer** to identify and route the PES to the related synchronization block in the **synchronization layer**. The compressed audio and video associated with each AVO is carried in a separate ES. Associated with each object descriptor is an **elementary stream descriptor** (**ESD**), which is used by the synchronization layer to route each ES to its related decoder. Each PES also contains timing information in the form of time-stamps and these are used to ensure the compressed data relating to each AVO is passed to the decoder at the correct time instants. The stream of object descriptor blocks and the scene descriptor block are both carried in separate elementary streams and these are also passed to their related decoder blocks in time synchronism with the compression data associated with the individual AVOs.

The output from the decoders associated with each AVO making up a frame, together with the related object scene descriptor information, is then passed to the **composition and rendering block**. As the name implies, the latter takes the decompressed data relating to each AVO and, together with the scene descriptor information, uses this to compose each frame ready for output to the display screen. The audio relating to each frame/scene is then played out in time synchronism with the video. See Tables A.5 and A.6 for a summary of compression standards for audio and video.

Table A.5 Summary of compression standards for general audio.

Standard		Compressed bit rate	Quality	Example applications
MPEG Audio	Layer 1	32–448 kbps	Hi-fi quality at 192 kbps	Digital audio cassettes
	Layer 2	32–192 kbps	Near CD at 128 kbps	Digital audio and digital video broadcasting
	Layer 3	64 kbps	CD quality	CD-quality over low bit rate channels
Dolby audio coders	AC-1	512 kbps	Hi-fi quality	Radio and television satellite relays
	AC-2	256 kbps	Hi-fi quality	PC sound cards
	AC-3	192 kbps	Near CD quality	Digital video broadcasting

Table A.6 Summary of video compression standards.

Standard	Digitization format	Compressed bit rate	Example applications
H.261	CIF/QCIF	p × 64 kbps	Video telephony/conferencing over p × 64 kbps channels (p = 1–30) and LANs
H.263	S-QCIF/QCIF	<64 kbps	Video telephony/conferencing and security surveillance over low bit rate channels
MPEG-1/ISO11172	SIF	<1.5 Mbps	Storage of VHS-quality video on CD-ROMs
MPEG-2/ISO13818			
Low	SIF	<4 Mbps	Recording of VHS-quality video
Main	4:2:0	<15 Mbps	Digital video broadcasting
	4:2:2	<20 Mbps	
High 1440	4:2:0	<60 Mbps	High definition television (4/3 aspect ratio)
	4:2:2	<80 Mbps	
High	4:2:0	<80 Mbps	High definition television (16/9 aspect ratio)
	4:2:2	<100 Mbps	
MPEG-4	Various	5 kbps– tens Mbps	Versatile multimedia coding standard
MPEG-7	–	–	Structure and content descriptions of compressed multimedia information

Appendix B Error detection methods

As we indicated in Section 1.3.1, when transmitting a bitstream over a transmission line/channel a scheme is normally incorporated into the transmission control circuit of the NIC to enable the presence of bit/transmission errors in a received block to be detected. In general, this is done by the transmitter computing a set of (additional) bits based on the contents of the block of bits to be transmitted. These are known as error detection bits and are transmitted together with the original bits in the block. The receiver then uses the complete set of received bits to determine (to a high probability) whether the block contains any errors.

The two factors that determine the type of error detection scheme used are the **bit error rate** (**BER**) probability of the line and the type of errors, that is whether the errors occur as random single-bit errors or as groups of contiguous strings of bit errors. The latter are referred to as **burst errors**. The BER is the probability P of a single bit being corrupted in a defined time interval. Thus a BER of 10^{-3} means that, on average, 1 bit in 10^3 will be corrupted during a defined time period.

If we are transmitting single characters using asynchronous transmission (say 8 bits per character plus 1 start and 1 stop bit), the probability of a character being corrupted is $1 - (1 - P)^{10}$ which, if we assume a BER of 10^{-3}, is approximately 10^{-2}. Alternatively, if we are transmitting blocks of say 125 bytes using synchronous transmission, then the probability of a block (frame) containing an error is approximately 1. This means that on average every block will contain an error. Clearly, therefore, this length of frame is too long for this type of line and must be reduced to obtain an acceptable throughput.

The type of errors present is important since, as we shall see, the different types of error detection scheme detect different types of error. Also, the number of bits used in some schemes determines the burst lengths that are detected. The three most widely used schemes are parity, block sum check, and cyclic redundancy check. We shall consider each separately.

B.1 Parity

The most common method used for detecting bit errors with asynchronous and character-oriented synchronous transmission is the **parity bit method**. With this scheme the transmitter adds an additional bit – the parity bit – to each transmitted character prior to transmission. The parity bit used is a function of the bits that make up the character being transmitted. On receipt of each character, the receiver then performs the same function on the received character and compares the result with the received parity bit.

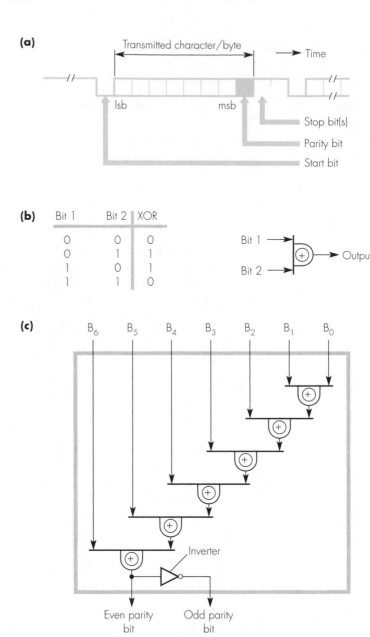

Figure B.1 Parity bit method: (a) position in character; (b) XOR gate truth table and symbol; (c) parity bit generation circuit; (d) two examples.

If they are equal, no error is assumed, but if they are different, then a transmission error is assumed.

To compute the parity bit for a character, the number of 1 bits in the code for the character are added together (modulo 2) and the parity bit is then chosen so that the total number of 1 bits (including the parity bit itself) is either even – **even parity** – or odd – **odd parity**. The principles of the scheme are shown in Figure B.1.

The circuitry used to compute the parity bit for each character comprises a set of **exclusive-OR** (**XOR**) gates connected as shown in Figure B.1(c). The XOR gate is also known as a **modulo-2 adder** since, as shown by the **truth table** in part (b) of the figure, the output of the exclusive-OR operation between two binary digits is the same as the addition of the two digits without a carry bit. The least significant pair of bits are first XORed together and the output of this gate is then XORed with the next (more significant) bit, and so on. The output of the final gate is the required parity bit which is loaded into the transmit PISO register prior to transmission of the character. Similarly, on receipt, the recomputed parity bit is compared with the received parity bit. If it is different, this indicates that a transmission error has been detected.

The term used in coding theory to describe the combined message unit, comprising the useful data bits and the additional error detection bits, is codeword. The minimum number of bit positions in which two valid codewords differ is known as the **Hamming distance** of the code. As an example, consider a coding scheme that has seven data bits and a single parity bit per codeword. If we assume even parity is being used, consecutive codewords in this scheme will be:

$$0000000\ 0$$
$$0000001\ 1$$
$$0000010\ 1$$
$$0000011\ 0$$

We can deduce from this list that such a scheme has a Hamming distance of 2 since each valid codeword differs in at least two bit positions. This means that the scheme does not detect 2-bit errors since the resulting (corrupted) bit pattern will be a different but valid codeword. It does, however, detect all single-bit errors (and all odd numbers of bit errors) since, if a single bit in a codeword is corrupted, an invalid codeword will result.

B.2 Block sum check

When blocks of characters (or bytes) are being transmitted, there is an increased probability that a character (and hence the block) will contain a bit error. The probability of a block containing an error is known as the **block error rate**. When blocks of characters (frames) are being transmitted, we can achieve an extension to the error detecting capabilities obtained from a single parity bit per character (byte) by using an additional set of parity bits computed from the complete block of characters (bytes) in the frame. With this method, each character (byte) in the frame is assigned a parity bit as before (**transverse** or **row parity**). In addition, an extra bit is computed for each bit position (**longitudinal** or **column parity**) in the complete frame. The resulting set of parity bits for each column is referred to as the **block (sum) check character** since each bit making up the character is the modulo-2 sum

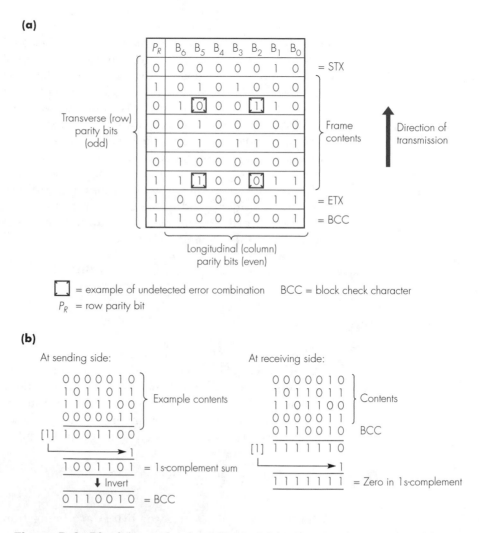

(a)

Transverse (row) parity bits (odd)

Frame contents

Direction of transmission

Longitudinal (column) parity bits (even)

☐ = example of undetected error combination   BCC = block check character

P_R = row parity bit

(b)

At sending side:

At receiving side:

Figure B.2 Block sum check method: (a) row and column parity bits; (b) 1s complement sum.

of all the bits in the corresponding column. The example in Figure B.2(a) uses odd parity for the row parity bits and even parity for the column parity bits, and assumes that the frame contains printable characters only.

We can deduce from this example that although two bit errors in a character will escape the row parity check, they will be detected by the corresponding column parity check. This is true, of course, only if no two bit errors occur in the same column at the same time. Clearly, the probability of this occurring is much less than the probability of two bit errors in a single character occurring. The use of a block sum check significantly improves the error detection properties of the scheme.

A variation of the scheme is to use the 1s-complement sum as the basis of the block sum check instead of the modulo-2 sum. The principle of the scheme is shown in Figure B.2(b).

In this scheme, the characters (or bytes) in the block to be transmitted are treated as unsigned binary numbers. These are first added together using 1s-complement arithmetic. All the bits in the resulting sum are then inverted and this is used as the block check character (BCC). At the receiver, the 1s-complement sum of all the characters in the block – including the block check character – is computed and, if no errors are present, the result should be zero. Remember that with 1s-complement arithmetic, end-around-carry is used, that is, any carry out from the most significant bit position is added to the existing binary sum. Also, zero in 1s-complement arithmetic is represented by either all binary 0s or all binary 1s.

As we shall see in later chapters, since the 1s-complement sum is readily computed, it is used as the error-detection method in a number of applications that require the error detection operation to be performed in software only.

B.3 Cyclic redundancy check

The previous two schemes are best suited to applications in which random single-bit errors are present. When bursts of errors are present, however, we must use a more rigorous method. An error burst begins and ends with an erroneous bit, although the bits in between may or may not be corrupted. Thus, an error burst is defined as the number of bits between two successive erroneous bits including the incorrect two bits. Furthermore, when determining the length of an error burst, the last erroneous bit in a burst and the first erroneous bit in the following burst must be separated by B or more correct bits, where B is the length of the error burst. An example of two different error burst lengths is shown in Figure B.3. Notice that the first and third bit errors could not be used to define a single 11-bit error burst since an error occurs within the next 11 bits.

The most reliable detection scheme against error bursts is based on the use of **polynomial codes**. Polynomial codes are used with frame (or block)

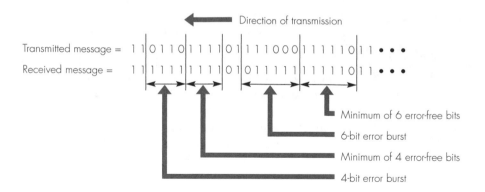

Figure B.3 Error burst examples.

transmission schemes. A single set of check digits is generated (computed) for each frame transmitted, based on the contents of the frame, and is appended by the transmitter to the tail of the frame. The receiver then performs a similar computation on the complete frame plus check digits. If no errors have been induced, a known result should always be obtained; if a different answer is found, this indicates an error.

The number of check digits per frame is selected to suit the type of transmission errors anticipated, although 16 and 32 bits are the most common. The computed check digits are referred to as the **frame check sequence** (**FCS**) or the **cyclic redundancy check** (**CRC**) digits.

The underlying mathematical theory of polynomial codes is beyond the scope of this book but, essentially, the method exploits the following property of binary numbers if modulo-2 arithmetic is used. Let:

$M(x)$ be a k-bit number (the message to be transmitted)

$G(x)$ be an $(n + 1)$-bit number (the divisor or generator)

$R(x)$ be an n-bit number such that $k > n$ (the remainder)

Then if:

$$\frac{M(x) \times 2^n}{G(x)} = Q(x) + \frac{R(x)}{G(x)}, \text{ where } Q(x) \text{ is the quotient,}$$

$$\frac{M(x) \times 2^n + R(x)}{G(x)} = Q(x), \text{ assuming modulo-2 arithmetic.}$$

We can readily confirm this result by substituting the expression for $M(x) \times 2^n / G(x)$ into the second equation, giving:

$$\frac{M(x) \times 2^n + R(x)}{G(x)} = Q(x) + \frac{R(x)}{G(x)} + \frac{R(x)}{G(x)}$$

which is equal to $Q(x)$ since any number added to itself modulo 2 will result in zero, that is, the remainder is zero.

To exploit this, the complete frame contents, $M(x)$, together with an appended set of zeros equal in number to the number of FCS digits to be generated (which is equivalent to multiplying the message by 2^n, where n is the number of FCS digits) are divided modulo 2 by a second binary number, $G(x)$, the **generator polynomial** containing one more digit than the FCS. The division operation is equivalent to performing the exclusive-OR operation bit by bit in parallel as each bit in the frame is processed. The remainder $R(x)$ is then the FCS, which is transmitted at the tail of the information digits.

Example B.1

A series of 8-bit message blocks (frames) is to be transmitted across a data link using a CRC for error detection. A generator polynomial of 11001 is to be used. Use an example to illustrate the following:

(i)   the FCS generation process,

(ii) the FCS checking process.

Answer:

Generation of the FCS for the message 11100110 is shown in Figure B.4(a) overleaf. Firstly, four zeros are appended to the message, which is equivalent to multiplying the message by 2^4, since the FCS will be four bits. This is then divided (modulo 2) by the generator polynomial (binary number). The modulo-2 division operation is equivalent to performing the exclusive-OR operation bit by bit in parallel as each bit in the dividend is processed. Also, with modulo-2 arithmetic, we can perform a division into each partial remainder, providing the two numbers are of the same length, that is, the most significant bits are both 1s. We do not consider the relative magnitude of both numbers. The resulting 4-bit remainder (0110) is the FCS, which is then appended at the tail of the original message when it is transmitted. The quotient is not used.

At the receiver, the complete received bit sequence is divided by the same generator polynomial as used at the transmitter. Two examples are shown in Figure B.4(b). In the first, no errors are assumed to be present, so that the remainder is zero – the quotient is again not used. In the second, however, an error burst of four bits at the tail of the transmitted bit sequence is assumed. Consequently, the resulting remainder is nonzero, indicating that a transmission error has occurred.

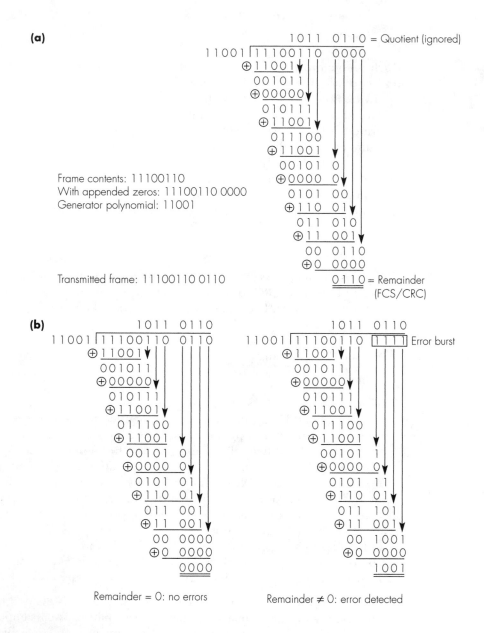

(a)

```
                                    1 0 1 1   0 1 1 0  = Quotient (ignored)
                          1 1 0 0 1 │ 1 1 1 0 0 1 1 0   0 0 0 0
                                  ⊕ 1 1 0 0 1
                                    0 0 1 0 1 1
                                  ⊕ 0 0 0 0 0
                                    0 1 0 1 1 1
                                  ⊕ 1 1 0 0 1
                                    0 1 1 1 0 0
                                  ⊕ 1 1 0 0 1
                                    0 0 1 0 1   0
                                  ⊕ 0 0 0 0   0
                                    0 1 0 1   0 0
                                  ⊕ 1 1 0   0 1
                                    0 1 1   0 1 0
                                  ⊕ 1 1   0 0 1
                                    0 0   0 1 1 0
                                  ⊕ 0   0 0 0 0
                                        0 1 1 0  = Remainder
                                                   (FCS/CRC)
```

Frame contents: 11100110
With appended zeros: 11100110 0000
Generator polynomial: 11001

Transmitted frame: 11100110 0110

(b)

```
              1 0 1 1   0 1 1 0                          1 0 1 1   0 1 1 0
    1 1 0 0 1 │ 1 1 1 0 0 1 1 0   0 1 1 0      1 1 0 0 1 │ 1 1 1 0 0 1 1 0   1 1 1 1   Error burst
            ⊕ 1 1 0 0 1                                ⊕ 1 1 0 0 1
              0 0 1 0 1 1                                0 0 1 0 1 1
            ⊕ 0 0 0 0 0                                ⊕ 0 0 0 0 0
              0 1 0 1 1 1                                0 1 0 1 1 1
            ⊕ 1 1 0 0 1                                ⊕ 1 1 0 0 1
              0 1 1 1 0 0                                0 1 1 1 0 0
            ⊕ 1 1 0 0 1                                ⊕ 1 1 0 0 1
              0 0 1 0 1   0                              0 0 1 0 1   1
            ⊕ 0 0 0 0   0                              ⊕ 0 0 0 0   0
              0 1 0 1   0 1                              0 1 0 1   1 1
            ⊕ 1 1 0   0 1                              ⊕ 1 1 0   0 1
              0 1 1   0 0 1                              0 1 1   1 0 1
            ⊕ 1 1   0 0 1                              ⊕ 1 1   0 0 1
              0 0   0 0 0 0                              0 0   1 0 0 1
            ⊕ 0   0 0 0 0                              ⊕ 0   0 0 0 0
                  0 0 0 0                                    1 0 0 1
```

Remainder = 0: no errors   Remainder ≠ 0: error detected

Figure B.4 CRC error detection example: (a) FCS generation; (b) two error detection examples.

Similarly, on receipt, the received bitstream including the FCS digits is again divided by the same generator polynomial – that is, $(M(x) \times 2^n + R(x))/G(x)$ – and, if no errors are present, the remainder is all zeros. If an error is present, however, the remainder is nonzero.

The choice of generator polynomial is important since it determines the types of error that are detected. Assume the transmitted frame, $T(x)$, is:

$$110101100110$$

and the error pattern, $E(x)$, is:

$$00000000\,1001$$

that is, a 1 in a bit position indicates an error. Hence, with modulo-2 arithmetic:

$$\text{Received frame} = T(x) + E(x)$$

Now:

$$\frac{T(x) + E(x)}{G(x)} = \frac{T(x)}{G(x)} + \frac{E(x)}{G(x)}$$

but $T(x)/G(x)$ produces no remainder. Hence an error is detected only if $E(x)/G(x)$ produces a remainder.

For example, all $G(x)$ have at least three terms (1 bits) and $E(x)/G(x)$ will yield a remainder for all single-bit and all double-bit errors with modulo-2 arithmetic and hence be detected. Conversely, an error burst of the same length as $G(x)$ may be a multiple of $G(x)$ and hence yield no remainder and go undetected.

In summary, a generator polynomial of R bits will detect:

- all single-bit errors,
- all double-bit errors,
- all odd number of bit errors,
- all error bursts < R,
- most error bursts ≥ R.

The standard way of representing a generator polynomial is to show those positions that are binary 1 as powers of X. Examples of CRCs used in practice are thus:

$$\begin{aligned}
\text{CRC-16} \quad &= x^{16} + x^{15} + x^2 + 1 \\
\text{CRC-CCITT} \quad &= x^{16} + x^{12} + x^5 + 1 \\
\text{CRC-32} \quad &= x^{32} + x^{26} + x^{23} + x^{16} + x^{12} + x^{11} + x^{10} + x^8 + x^7 \\
&\quad + x^5 + x^4 + x^2 + x + 1
\end{aligned}$$

Hence CRC-16 is equivalent in binary form to:

$$1\,1000\,0000\,0000\,0101$$

With such a generator polynomial, 16 zeros would be appended to the frame contents before generation of the FCS. The latter would then be the 16-bit remainder. CRC-16 will detect all error bursts of less than 16 bits and most error bursts greater than or equal to 16 bits. CRC-16 and CRC-CCITT are both used extensively with networks such as an ISDN, while CRC-32 is used in most LANs. Also, although the requirement to perform multiple (modulo-2) divisions may appear to be relatively complicated, as we show in Figure B.5 it can be done readily in hardware (and software) and, in practice, this is integrated into the transmission control circuit.

B.4 CRC implementation

Although the requirement to perform multiple (modulo-2) divisions to compute a CRC may appear to be relatively complicated, in practice it can be done quite readily in either hardware or software. To illustrate this, a hardware implementation of the scheme used in Figure B.4 is given in Figure B.5(a).

In this example, since we are to generate four FCS digits, we need only a 4-bit shift register to represent bits x^3, x^2, x^1, and x^0 in the generator polynomial. We often refer to these as the active bits of the generator. With this generator polynomial, digits x^3 and x^0 are binary 1 while digits x^2 and x^1 are binary 0. The new states of shift register elements x^1 and x^2 simply take on the states of x^0 and x^1 directly; the new states of elements x^0 and x^3 are determined by the state of the feedback path exclusive ORed with the preceding digit.

The circuit operates as follows. The FCS shift register is cleared and the first 8-bit byte in the frame is parallel-loaded into the PISO transmit shift register. This is then shifted out to the transmission line, most significant bit first, at a rate determined by the transmitter clock TxC. In time synchronism with this, the same bitstream is exclusive-ORed with x^3 and passed via the feedback path to the selected inputs of the FCS shift register. As each subsequent 8-bit byte is loaded into the transmit shift register and bit-serially transmitted to line, the procedure repeats. Finally, after the last byte in the frame has been output, the transmit shift register is loaded with zeros and the feedback control signal changes from 1 to 0 so that the current contents of the FCS shift register – the computed remainder – follow the frame contents onto the transmission line.

(a)

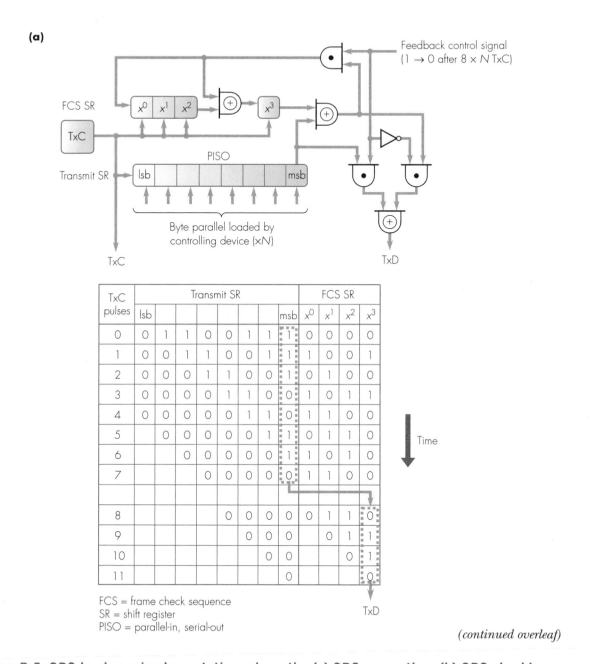

FCS = frame check sequence
SR = shift register
PISO = parallel-in, serial-out

(continued overleaf)

Figure B.5 CRC hardware implementation schematic: (a) CRC generation; (b) CRC checking.

(b)

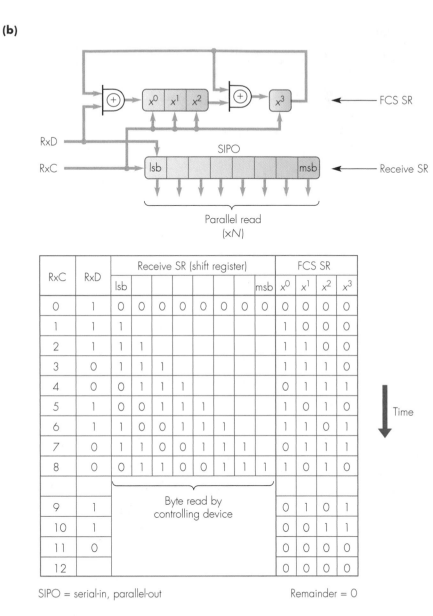

RxC	RxD	Receive SR (shift register)								FCS SR			
		lsb							msb	x^0	x^1	x^2	x^3
0	1	0	0	0	0	0	0	0	0	0	0	0	0
1	1	1								1	0	0	0
2	1	1	1							1	1	0	0
3	0	1	1	1						1	1	1	0
4	0	0	1	1	1					0	1	1	1
5	1	0	0	1	1	1				1	0	1	0
6	1	1	0	0	1	1	1			1	1	0	1
7	0	1	1	0	0	1	1	1		0	1	1	1
8	0	0	1	1	0	0	1	1	1	1	0	1	0
					Byte read by controlling device								
9	1									0	1	0	1
10	1									0	0	1	1
11	0									0	0	0	0
12										0	0	0	0

SIPO = serial-in, parallel-out   Remainder = 0

Figure B.5 Continued.

In Figure B.5(a) the contents of the transmit and FCS shift registers assume just a single-byte frame ($N = 1$), and hence correspond to the earlier example in Figure B.4. In the figure the contents of both the transmit and FCS shift registers are shown after each shift (transmit clock) pulse. The transmitted bitstream is as shown in the hashed boxes.

The corresponding receiver hardware is similar to that used at the transmitter, as shown in Figure B.5(b). The received data (RxD) is sampled (shifted) into the SIPO receive shift register in the centre (or later with Manchester encoding) of the bit cell. Also, as before, in time synchronization with this the bitstream is exclusive-ORed with x^3 and fed into the FCS shift register. As each 8-bit byte is received, it is read by the controlling device. Again, the contents shown are for a frame comprising just a single byte of data.

The hardware in Figure B.5 is normally incorporated into the transmission control circuits associated with bit-oriented transmission. In some instances, however, a CRC is used in preference to a block sum check with character-oriented transmission. In such cases, the CRC must normally be generated in software by the controlling device rather than in hardware. This is relatively straightforward as we can see from the pseudocode in Figure B.6.

The code assumes an 8-bit generator polynomial (divisor) and that the preformatted frame – STX, ETX, and so on – is stored in an array. The same code can be used for CRC generation and checking; for generation the array will contain a byte/character comprising all zeros at its tail.

```
{Assume a preformatted frame to be transmitted (including a zero byte at its tail) or a received frame
is stored in a byte array buff[1.. count]. Also that the 8 active bits of a 9-bit divisor are stored in the
most-significant 8 bits of a 16-bit integer CRCDIV. The following function will compute and return the
8-bit CRC}

function   CRC : byte;
var        i, j : integer;
           data : integer

begin      data := buff[1] shl 8;
           for j := 2 to count do
                begin
                    data := data + buff [j];
                    for i := 1 to 8 do
                        if ((data and $8000) = $8000) then
                        begin data := data shl 1;
                              data := data xor CRCDIV; end
                        else   data := data shl 1;
                end;

           CRC := data shr 8;
end;                                                              (continued overleaf)
```

Figure B.6 Pseudocode for the computation and checking of an 8-bit CRC.

Appendix C Forward error control

C.1 Introduction

With an automatic repeat request (ARQ) error control scheme, additional check digits are appended to each transmitted message (frame) to enable the receiver to detect when an error is present in a received message, assuming certain types of error. If an error is detected, additional control procedures are used to request another copy of the message. With forward error control (FEC), sufficient additional check digits are added to each transmitted message to enable the receiver not only to detect the presence of one or more errors in a received message but also to locate the position of the error(s). Furthermore, since the message is in a binary form, correction is achieved simply by inverting the bit(s) that have been identified as erroneous.

In practice, the number of additional check digits required for error correction is much larger than that needed for just error detection. In most applications involving terrestrial (land-based) links, ARQ methods similar to those described in Section 1.3.1 are more efficient than FEC methods, and hence are the most frequently used. Such methods rely on a return path for acknowledgment purposes. However, in most entertainments applications, a return path is simply not available or, even if one was available, the round-trip delay associated with it may be very long compared with the data transmission rate of the link. For example, with many satellite links the propagation delay may be such that several hundred megabits may be transmitted by the sending station before an acknowledgment could be received in the reverse direction. In such applications, FEC methods are used. The aim of this appendix is to give an introduction to the techniques most widely used with FEC methods.

C.2 Block codes

An example of a block code is the Hamming single-bit code. In practice, this FEC method is of limited use for digital transmission. Nevertheless, we shall look at it briefly to introduce the subject of block codes and some of the terms associated with coding theory. Clearly, a comprehensive description of the subject of coding theory is beyond the scope of this book and hence the aim here is simply to give a brief introduction. If you have an interest in coding theory and would like to gain a more extensive coverage, consult some of the references given in the bibliography at the end of the book.

Recall that the term used in coding theory to describe the combined message unit, comprising the useful data bits and the additional check bits, is **codeword**. The minimum number of bit positions in which two valid codewords differ is known as the **Hamming distance** of the code. For example, consider a coding scheme that has seven data bits and a single parity bit per codeword. Assuming even parity is being used, consecutive codewords in this scheme are as follows:

0000000   0
0000001   1
0000010   1
0000011   0

We can see from this list that such a scheme has a Hamming distance of 2, as each valid codeword differs in at least two bit positions. This means that it does not detect 2-bit errors since the resulting (corrupted) bit pattern will be a different but valid codeword. However, it does detect all single-bit errors since, if a single bit in a codeword is corrupted, an invalid codeword will result.

In general, the error-detecting and error-correcting properties of a coding scheme are both related to its Hamming distance. It can be shown that to detect n errors, we must use a coding scheme with a Hamming distance of $n + 1$, while to correct for n errors, we must use a code with a Hamming distance of $2n + 1$.

The simplest error-correcting coding scheme is the Hamming single-bit code. Such a code detects not only when a single-bit error is present in a received codeword but also the position of the error. The corrected codeword is derived by inverting the identified erroneous bit. This type of code is known as a block code, since the original message to be transmitted is treated as a single block (frame) during the encoding and subsequent decoding processes. In general, with a block code, each block of k source digits is encoded to produce an n-digit block (n greater than k) of output digits. The encoder is said to produce an (n, k) code. The ratio k/n is known as the **code rate** or **code efficiency** while the difference $1 - k/n$ is known as the **redundancy**.

To illustrate this, consider a Hamming code to detect and correct for single-bit errors assuming each codeword contains a 7-bit data field – an ASCII character, for example. Such a coding scheme requires four check bits since, with this scheme, the check bits occupy all bit positions that are powers of 2. This code is known as an $(11, 7)$ block code with a rate of $7/11$ and a redundancy of $1 - 7/11$. For example, the bit positions of the value 1001101 are as follows:

11 10 9 8 7 6 5 4 3 2 1
 1 0 0 x 1 1 0 x 1 x x

The four bit positions marked 'x' are used for the check bits, which are derived as follows. The 4-bit binary numbers corresponding to those bit positions with a binary 1 are added together using modulo-2 arithmetic and the four check bits are the following 4-bit sum:

$$11 = 1\ 0\ 1\ 1$$
$$7 = 0\ 1\ 1\ 1$$
$$6 = 0\ 1\ 1\ 0$$
$$3 = \underline{0\ 0\ 1\ 1}$$
$$= \underline{1\ 0\ 0\ 1}$$

The transmitted codeword is thus:

$$11\ 10\ 9\ 8\ 7\ 6\ 5\ 4\ 3\ 2\ 1$$
$$1\ \ \ 0\ 0\ \textit{1}\ 1\ 1\ 0\ \textit{0}\ 1\ 0\ \textit{1}$$

Similarly, at the receiver, the 4-bit binary numbers corresponding to those bit positions with a binary 1, including the check bits, are again added together. If no errors have occurred, the modulo-2 sum is zero:

$$11 = 1\ 0\ 1\ 1$$
$$8 = 1\ 0\ 0\ 0$$
$$7 = 0\ 1\ 1\ 1$$
$$6 = 0\ 1\ 1\ 0$$
$$3 = 0\ 0\ 1\ 1$$
$$1 = \underline{0\ 0\ 0\ 1}$$
$$= \underline{0\ 0\ 0\ 0}$$

Now consider a single-bit error: say bit 11 is corrupted from 1 to 0. The new modulo-2 sum is now:

$$8 = 1\ 0\ 0\ 0$$
$$7 = 0\ 1\ 1\ 1$$
$$6 = 0\ 1\ 1\ 0$$
$$3 = 0\ 0\ 1\ 1$$
$$1 = \underline{0\ 0\ 0\ 1}$$
$$= \underline{1\ 0\ 1\ 1}$$

Firstly, the sum is nonzero, which indicates an error, and secondly, the modulo-2 sum, equivalent to decimal 11, indicates that bit 11 is the erroneous bit. The latter is inverted to obtain the corrected codeword and hence data bits.

It can also be shown that if two bit errors occur, the modulo-2 sum is nonzero, thus indicating an error, but the positions of the errors cannot be determined from the sum. The Hamming single-bit code can correct for single-bit errors and detect two-bit errors but other multiple-bit errors cannot be detected.

As we saw in Section 1.3.1, the main types of error in many data communication networks are error bursts rather than, say, isolated single or double-bit errors. Hence, although the Hamming coding scheme in its basic form appears to be inappropriate for use with such networks, a simple technique called interleaving is often used to extend the application of such a scheme.

Consider, for example, a requirement to transmit a block of data, comprising a string of, say, eight ASCII characters, over a simplex channel that has a high probability of an error burst of, say, seven bits. The controlling device first converts each ASCII character into its 11-bit codeword form to give a block of eight 11-bit codewords. Then, instead of transmitting each codeword separately, the controlling device transmits the contents of the block of codewords a column at a time. Thus the eight, say, most significant bits are transmitted first, then the eight next most significant bits and so on, finishing with the eight least significant bits. The controlling device at the receiver then performs the reverse operation, reassembling the transmitted block in memory, prior to performing the detection and, if necessary, correction operation on each codeword.

The effect of this approach is that if an error burst of up to seven bits does occur, it affects only a single bit in each codeword rather than a string of bits in one or two codewords. This means that, assuming just a single error burst in the 88 bits transmitted, the receiver can determine a correct copy of the transmitted block of characters.

Although the approach just outlined provides a way of extending the usefulness of this type of encoding scheme, Hamming codes are used mainly in applications that have isolated single-bit errors; an example is in error-correcting semiconductor memory systems. As we showed in Figure 5.20, the preferred method of achieving FEC in most digital communication systems is based on a combination of a Reed–Solomon block code and a convolutional coder. We shall now briefly describe the operation of convolutional coders.

C.3 Convolutional codes

Block codes are *memoryless* codes as each output codeword depends only on the current *k*-bit message block being encoded. In contrast, with a convolutional code, the continuous stream of source bits is operated upon to produce a continuous stream of output (encoded) bits. Because of the nature of the encoding process, the sequence of source bits is said to be convolved (by applying a specific binary operation on them) to produce the output bit sequence. Also, each bit in the output sequence is dependent not only on the current bit being encoded but also on the previous sequence of source bits, thus implying some form of memory. In practice, as we shall see, this takes the form of a shift register of a finite length, known as the **constraint length**, and the convolution (binary) operation is performed using one or more modulo-2 adders (exclusive-OR gates).

C.3.1 Encoding

An example of a convolutional encoder is shown in Figure C.1(a). With this encoder, the three-bit shift register provides the memory and the two modulo-2 adders the convolution operation. For each bit in the input sequence, two bits are output, one from each of the two modulo-2 adders. The encoder shown is thus known as a rate $1/2(k/n)$ convolutional encoder with a constraint length of 3.

Because of the memory associated with a convolutional encoder, we must have a convenient means of determining the specific output bit sequence generated for a given input sequence. Three techniques can be used, each based on a form of diagrammatic representation: a tree diagram, a state diagram, and a trellis diagram. In practice, the last is the most frequently used method because it is the most useful for demonstrating the decoding operation. However, before we can draw this, we must determine the outputs for each possible input sequence using either the tree or state diagram.

As an example, Figure C.1(b) shows the **tree diagram** for the encoder in Figure C.1(a). The branching points in the tree are known as nodes and the tree shows the two possible branches at each node; the upper of the two branches corresponds to a 0 input bit and the lower branch to a 1 bit. The pair of output bits corresponding to the two possible branches at each node are shown on the outside of each branch line.

As we can see, with a tree diagram the number of branches in the tree doubles for each new input bit. However, the tree is repetitive after the second branch level since, after this level, there are only four unique branch nodes. These are known as *states* and are shown as *A*, *B*, *C* and *D* in the figure.

As we can see, from any one of these nodes the same pair of output bits and new node state occurs, irrespective of the position of the node in the tree. For example, from any node *C* the same pair of branch alternatives occur: 10 output and new state *A* for a 0 input, or 01 output and new state *B* for a 1 input.

Once we have identified the states for the encoder using the tree diagram, we can draw the **trellis diagram**. As an example, the trellis diagram for the same encoder is shown in Figure C.2(b). As we can see, after the second branch level, the repetitive nature of the tree diagram is exploited by representing all the possible encoder outputs in a more reduced form.

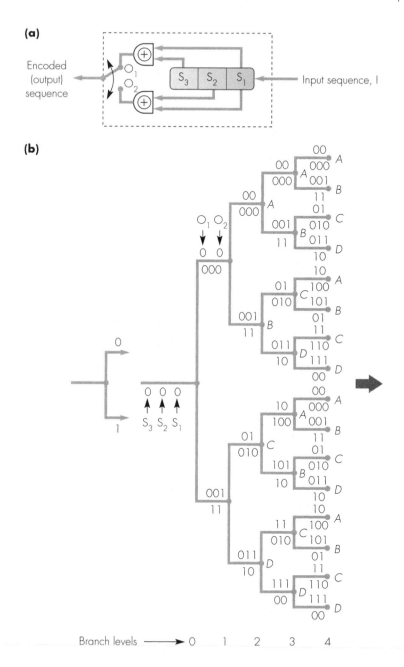

(a)

(b)

Branch levels ⟶ 0 1 2 3 4

Figure C.1 Convolutional coder principles: (a) example encoder circuit; (b) tree diagram representation of the encoder.

(a)

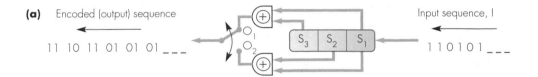

Input sequence	Shift register contents			Output sequence	
I	S_1	S_2	S_3	O_1	O_2
1	1	0	0	1	1
1	1	1	0	1	0
0	0	1	1	1	1
1	1	0	1	0	1
0	0	1	0	0	1
1	1	0	1	0	1

(b)

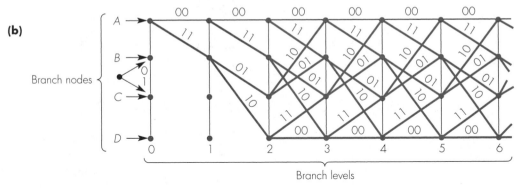

(c)

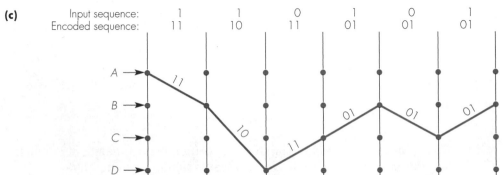

Figure C.2 Convolutional encoder output derivation: (a) circuit; (b) trellis diagram; (c) example output.

The trellis diagram shows the outputs that result from this encoder for all possible input bit sequences. Then, for a specific input sequence, a single path through the trellis – and hence sequence of output bits – results. As an example, Figure C.2(c) shows the path through the trellis, and hence the output sequence, corresponding to the input sequence 110101... .

Initially, we assume that the shift register is cleared, that is, it is set to all 0s. After the first bit in the input sequence has been shifted (entered) into the shift register, its contents are 001. The outputs from the two modulo-2 adders are $0 + 1 = 1$ (adder 1) and $0 + 1 = 1$ (adder 2). Thus, the first two output bits are 11 and these are output before the next input bit is entered into the shift register. Since the input bit was a 1, the lower branch path on the trellis diagram is followed and the output is 11, as derived.

After the second input bit has been entered, the shift register contains 011. The two adder outputs are $0 + 1 = 1$ (adder 1) and $1 + 1 = 0$ (adder 2). Thus, the two output bits are 10 and again these are output before the next input bit is processed. Again, since the input bit was a 1, the lower branch on the trellis diagram is followed and the output is 10, as derived. Continuing, the third input bit makes the shift register contents 110 and hence the two output bits are 11: $1 + 0 = 1$ (adder 1) and $1 + 0 = 1$ (adder 2). Also, since the input bit was a 0, the upper branch path on the trellis diagram is followed. This process then continues.

C.3.2 Decoding

The aim of the decoder is to determine the *most likely* output sequence, given a received bitstream (which may have errors) and a knowledge of the encoder used at the source. The decoding procedure is equivalent to comparing the received sequence with all the possible sequences that may be obtained with the respective encoder and then selecting the sequence that is closest to the received sequence. Recall that the Hamming distance between two codewords is the number of bits that differ between them. Therefore, when selecting the sequence that is closest to the received sequence, the Hamming distance between the received sequence and each of the possible sequences is computed, and the one with the least distance is selected. Clearly, in the limit this necessitates comparing the complete received sequence with all the possible sequences, and hence paths through the trellis. This is impractical in most cases and hence we must compromise.

Essentially, a running count is maintained of the distance between the actual received sequence and each possible sequence but, at each node in the trellis, only a single path is retained. There are always two paths merging at each node and the path selected is the one with the minimum Hamming distance, the other is simply terminated. The retained paths are known as **survivor paths** and the final path selected is the one with a continuous path through the trellis with a minimum aggregate Hamming distance. This procedure is known as the **Viterbi algorithm**. The decoder, which aims to find the most likely path corresponding to the received sequence, is known as a **maximum-likelihood decoder**. Example C.1 describes the Viterbi algorithm.

Example C.1

Assume that a message sequence of 1001110 ... is to be sent using the encoder shown in Figure C.1(a). From the trellis diagram for this encoder, we can deduce that this will yield a transmitted (output) sequence of:

11 01 10 11 10 00 11 ...

Now assume a burst error occurs so that two bits of this encoded sequence are corrupted during transmission. The received sequence is as follows:

11 01 00 11 11 00 11 ...
       ↑   ↑

Use the Viterbi algorithm to determine from this the most likely transmitted sequence.

Answer.

The various steps associated with the encoding and decoding procedures are shown in Figure C.3 at the end of this appendix. Part (a) shows the path through the trellis corresponding to the original output from the encoder and part (b) shows how the survivor paths are chosen. The number shown by each path merging at a node in Figure C.3(b) is the accumulated Hamming distance between the path followed to get to that node and the actual received sequence.

If the path chosen is that starting at the root node (branch level 0), the received sequence is 11 and the Hamming distances for the two paths are 2 for path 00 and 0 for path 11. These two distance values are added to the paths emanating from these nodes. Thus, at branch level 1, the received sequence is 01 and the two paths from node *A* have Hamming distances of 1 for path 00 and 1 for path 11. The accumulated distances are thus 2 + 1 = 3 for each path. Similarly, the two paths emanating from node *B* have Hamming distances of 0 for path 01 and 2 for path 10, and hence the accumulated distances are 0 + 0 = 0 and 0 + 2 = 2, respectively. A similar procedure is repeated at branch level 2.

At branch level 3 and onwards, however, the selection process starts. Thus, the two paths merging at node *A* (at branch level 3) have accumulated distances of 3 and 1, of which the latter is selected to be the survivor path for this node – this is shown as a bold line on the trellis diagram. A similar selection process is followed at nodes *B*, *C*, and *D*. At node *C*, however, we can see that the two merging paths both have the same accumulated distance of 4. In such cases, the upper path is selected. Also, after the selection process, all subsequent distances are calculated relative to the accumulated distance associated with the selected path.

It now remains to select the most likely path and hence the output sequence. Although the decoding procedure continues, by inspection of the portion of the trellis shown, we can see that:

■ only four paths have a continuous path through the trellis;
■ the distance corresponding to the path *ABCABDDC* is the minimum.

Thus, this is the path that is selected, the corresponding output sequence being 11 01 10 11 10 00 11 ..., which corresponds to the original encoded (and hence transmitted) sequence.

Finally, note that no FEC method can identify all errors. In general, codes like the convolutional code are used primarily to reduce the error probability (bit error rate) of a link to a more acceptable level. A typical reduction with a rate 1/2 convolutional coder is between 10^2 and 10^3. Hence when used with a Reed–Solomon (block) coder, the number of residual bit errors after the block decoding process is reduced to a level that is acceptable for most entertainment applications involving audio and video streams.

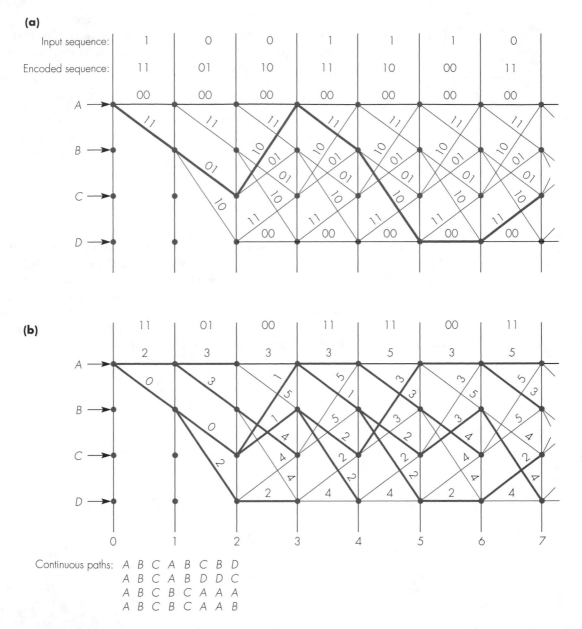

Figure C.3 Convolutional decoder output derivation: (a) actual decoder output; (b) derived survivor paths.

Appendix D Radio propagation and transmission basics

Wireless networks now form an increasingly important part of the Internet. As we saw in the introduction to Chapter 4, wireless networks include ad-hoc piconets, wireless LANs and cellular radio networks. As we saw, the user devices associated with these networks – pocket PCs, notebook computers, mobile phones, etc. – communicate with the network using radio transmissions instead of fixed wiring. Hence although the subject of radio propagation and transmission is outside the scope of this book, the importance of wireless networks means it is useful to have a basic understanding of these topics. That is the aim of this appendix.

D.1 Radio propagation

In free space, radio-frequency waves propagate/travel at the speed of light, that is, 3×10^8 meters per second. They have a frequency of between 10^4 and 10^{12} hertz (Hz) and are used extensively in many applications including wireless LANs, cellular phone networks, and radio and television broadcasting. Frequencies above 10^8 Hz are known as **microwave frequencies** and these are used, in addition to the applications we have just listed, in applications such as microwave ovens and high-power heating equipment.

In general, the cables used in fixed-wire networks have one or more central conductors that carry the signals and an outer shield to minimize the attenuation of the signal and to screen the conductors from external interference. In contrast, radio waves are simply broadcast using a suitable transmitter and hence can be received by any device within the field of coverage of the transmitter. The waves can readily propagate through walls, doors and windows and, because of this, tight controls are applied to the use of the radio spectrum. The wide range of usage of radio also means that radio bandwidth is scarce and, for a particular application, a specific frequency band must be officially allocated. Historically, this has been done on a national basis but increasingly, international agreements are now made that set aside selected frequency bands for those applications that have international relevance.

The requirement to confine radio emissions to a specific frequency band and for the related receivers to select only those signals within this band means that, in general, the circuitry associated with radio-based systems is more sophisticated than that used in fixed-wire systems. Nevertheless, the widespread use of radio – particularly in high-volume consumer products – means that sophisticated radio system designs can be implemented at reasonable costs.

Path loss

All radio receivers are designed to operate to a specified signal-to-noise ratio (SNR); that is, the ratio of the power of the received signal to the power of the receiver noise signal must not fall below the specified value. In general, the complexity – and hence cost – of the radio receiver increases as the specified SNR decreases. The falling cost of portable and hand-held devices, however, means that the acceptable cost of the radio interface unit of these devices must be comparable with that of a fixed-wire interface unit. This means, therefore, that the SNR of the radio receiver must be set at as high a level as possible.

In practice, the SNR is dependent on a number of interrelated parameters and each of these must be considered in relation to the design of the radio receiver. The receiver noise figure is a function of both the ambient temperature – which gives rise to thermal noise – and the bandwidth of the received signal; the larger the bandwidth or temperature, the larger the noise figure. Hence for a specific application, the receiver noise figure is essentially fixed.

The signal power at the receiver is a function not only of the power of the transmitted signal but also of the distance between transmitter and receiver. In free space, the power of a radio signal decays inversely with the square of the distance from the transmitter. In addition, in an indoor environment, the decay is increased further, firstly because of the presence of objects such as furniture and people and, secondly, because of destructive interference of the transmitted signal caused by the reflected signals from these objects. These combine to produce what is called the **path loss** of the radio channel.

As we can deduce from this, in order for the radio receiver to operate with an acceptable SNR, it must operate with as high a transmitter power level as possible and/or with a limited range of coverage. In practice, with most portable devices, the power of the transmitted signal is limited by the power consumption of the radio interface unit since this leads to an increase in the load on the device's battery. It is for these reasons that the range of coverage of an ad-hoc LAN is normally shorter than that of an infrastructure/wireless LAN.

Adjacent channel interference

Since radio waves propagate through most objects with only modest attenuation, it is possible to get interference from other adjacent transmitters that are operating in the same frequency band and are located either in adjacent rooms within the same building or in other buildings. With wireless LANs, therefore, since multiple such LANs may be set up in adjacent rooms/buildings, techniques must be adopted that allow several users of the same frequency band to coexist. We shall describe a number of transmission schemes that allow this in the next section.

Multipath

Radio signals are affected by multipath; that is, at any point in time the receiver receives multiple signals that originate from the same transmitter, each of which has followed a different path between the transmitter and receiver. This is known as **multipath dispersion** or **delay spread** and causes the signals relating to a previous bit/symbol to interfere with the signals relating to the next bit/symbol. This is known as **intersymbol interference** (**ISI**) and is shown in Figure D.1(a). As we can deduce from this, the higher the bit rate – and hence the shorter each bit cell period – the larger the level of intersymbol interference.

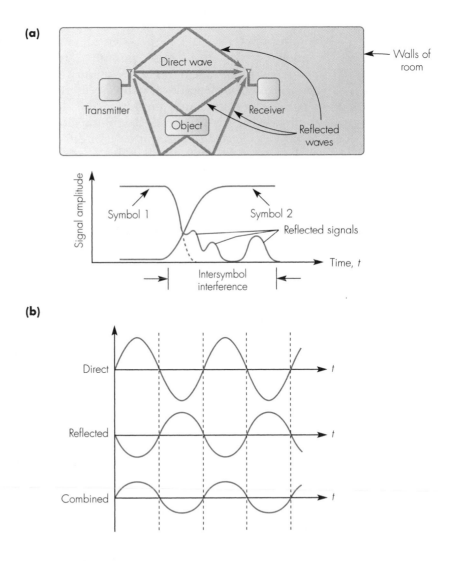

Figure D.1 Radio propagation impairments: (a) intersymbol interference; (b) Rayleigh fading.

In addition, an impairment known as **frequency-selective fading** is caused by the variation in path lengths of the different received signals. This gives rise to relative phase shifts between them which, at radio frequencies, can cause the various reflected signals to significantly attenuate the direct path signal and, in the limit, to cancel each other out. This is known as **Rayleigh fading** and is illustrated in Figure D.1(b). In practice, the amplitude of the reflected wave is a fraction of the direct wave, the amount of attenuation being determined by the reflecting material. One solution to this problem is to exploit the fact that the wavelength of radio frequency signals is very short – a fraction of a meter – and hence is sensitive to small variations in the location of the antenna. To overcome this effect two antennas are often used with a physical separation between them of one-quarter wavelength. The signals received from both antennas are then combined to form the composite received signal. This technique is known as **space diversity**.

An alternative solution is to use a technique known as **equalization**. Delayed and attenuated images of the direct signal – equivalent to the multipath reflected signals – are subtracted from the actual received signal. Since the reflected signals will vary for different locations of the transmitter and receiver, the process has to be adaptive. The circuit that is used, therefore, is known as an **adaptive equalizer** and clearly, the use of such circuits adds cost to the receiver implementation.

D.2 Transmission schemes

There are a number of different transmission schemes used with wireless LANs. With ad-hoc networks such as Bluetooth, for example, the transmission scheme used is called frequency-hopping spread spectrum (FHSS). With wireless LANs, three schemes are used: direct sequence spread spectrum (DSSS), FHSS, and coded orthogonal frequency division multiplexing (COFDM), also known as multi-carrier modulation (MCM). We shall describe the principle of operation of each of these schemes.

Frequency-hopping spread spectrum

As we indicated in Chapter 4, the majority of wireless LANs operate in the ISM bands. Hence in order to coexist with the other applications that use these bands, as we indicated earlier, it is essential that the transmission scheme used has a high level of co-channel interference rejection. For wireless LAN applications one approach is to use a technique called **spread spectrum**. There are two forms of spread spectrum: frequency-hopping and direct sequence. We shall discuss the first in this subsection and the second in the following subsection.

The principle of operation of FHSS is shown in Figure D.2(a). The allocated frequency band is divided into a number of lower frequency subbands called **channels**. Each channel is of equal bandwidth and this is determined by the data bit rate and the modulation method used. For example, both Bluetooth and one type of IEEE802.11 wireless LAN use 79 hopping channels each with a bandwidth of 1 MHz. Each channel is then modulated using FSK to yield 1 or 2 Mbps per channel. A transmitter then uses each channel for a short period of time before moving/hopping to a different channel. When a channel is being used, a carrier frequency at the center of the channel is modulated with the bit(s) being transmitted at that time. The pattern of usage of the channel is pseudorandom and is known as the **hopping sequence**, the time spent on each channel the **chip period**, and the hopping rate the **chipping rate**.

There are two modes of operation of frequency-hopping that are determined by the ratio of the chipping rate to the source data rate. These are shown in Figure D.2(b) and (c). When the chipping rate is higher than the data rate the operational mode is known as **fast frequency-hopping,** while if the chipping rate is lower than the data rate the operational mode is known as **slow frequency-hopping**. In both cases, a carrier frequency in the center of each channel is used.

An advantage of frequency-hopping is its ability to avoid using selected (narrowband) channels within the overall allocated frequency band. This can be particularly useful with the ISM bands because of the possible presence of one or more high-power narrowband interference sources within the field of coverage of the wireless network. Hence with FHSS, if an interference source that operates at a specific frequency is known to be present, then it is possible to eliminate the use of that frequency from the hopping sequence.

This technique is particularly useful with slow frequency-hopping since, with fast frequency-hopping, multiple frequency hops per data bit are used and hence only a single chip will be affected. A majority decision can then be used to determine the most likely data bit transmitted, 0 or 1. However, fast frequency-hopping systems are more costly than slow frequency-hopping systems. Also, since both transmitter and receiver must be in synchronism – that is, must hop together – slow frequency-hopping systems are easier to synchronize. Hence slow frequency-hopping systems provide a lower cost alternative for use in wireless LANs.

Direct sequence spread spectrum

The principle of operation of direct sequence spread spectrum (DSSS) is shown in schematic form in Figure D.3. The source data to be transmitted is first XORed – exclusive-ORed – with a **pseudorandom binary sequence**; that is, the randomness of the sequence is constrained to a defined cycle length. As we can see in the figure, each pseudorandom value is made much larger than the data bit rate. Hence when the XORed signal is modulated and transmitted, it occupies – and is said to be spread over – a proportionately wider frequency band than the original source data bandwidth, making the signal appear as (pseudo) noise to other users of the same frequency band.

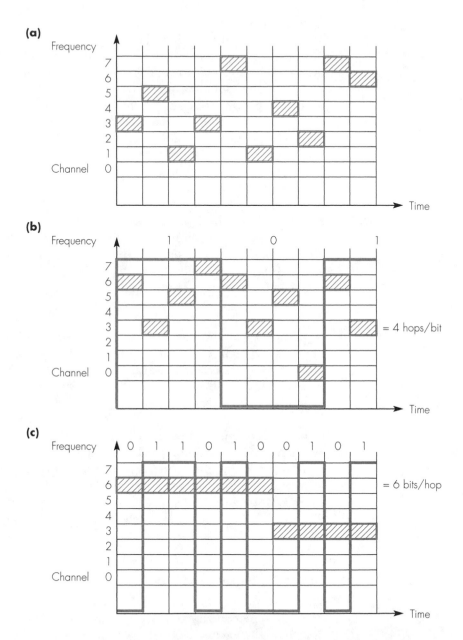

Figure D.2 Frequency hopping spread spectrum: (a) principle of operation; (b) fast frequency hopping; (c) slow frequency hopping.

All the members of the same wireless LAN know the pseudorandom binary sequence that is being used. All data frames being transmitted are preceded by a preamble sequence followed by a start-of-frame delimiter.

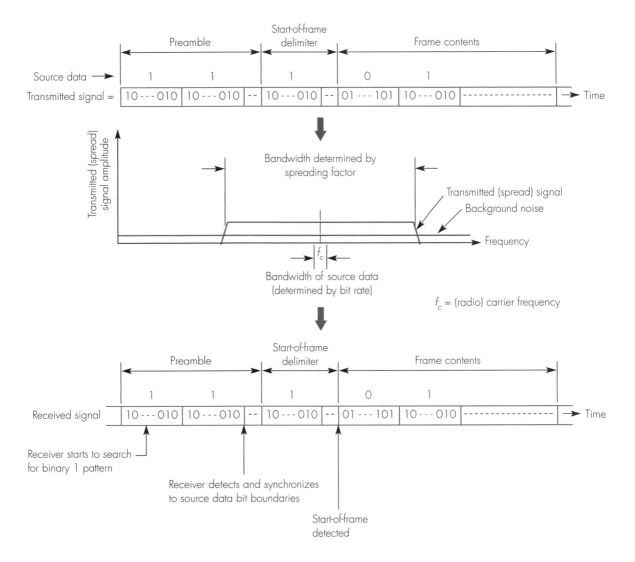

Figure D.3 Direct sequence spread spectrum – principle of operation.

Hence after demodulating the transmitted signal, all receivers first search for the known preamble sequence – normally a string of all binary 1s – and, once the sequence has been found, the receivers start to interpret the received bitstream on the correct source data bit boundaries. They then wait for the start-of-frame delimiter to be received and then proceed to receive the frame contents. The intended recipient(s) is (are) determined by the destination address at the head of the frame in the normal way.

Clearly, since all the stations belonging to the same wireless LAN occupy the same allocated frequency band and use the same pseudorandom binary sequence, their transmissions will interfere with one another. Hence, as we indicated in Sections 4.2.3 and 4.3.2, an appropriate MAC method must be used to ensure only one transmission takes place at a time.

In practice, the generation of a pseudorandom binary sequence is relatively straightforward since it can be produced digitally using only a number of shift registers and a set of exclusive-OR gates connected in a feedback loop. The principle is shown in Figure D.4(a). In this example a single 3-bit shift register and a single exclusive-OR gate are used and this produces the seven pseudorandom 3-bit codes – also known as (shift register) states – before it repeats. Note that the 000 state is not present since the shift register contents would then remain unchanged after each successive clock pulse. In general, there are a maximum of 2^{n-1} states for an n-bit shift register and, if the feedback combination produces all 2^{n-1} states, it is known as a **maximal-length shift register**. The output from the most significant element of the shift register is used as the pseudorandom binary sequence which, in this case, is equal to the 7-bit binary pattern 1110010.

The pseudorandom sequence is used by performing an exclusive-OR operation between the sequence and each data bit to be transmitted. As an example, if we assume the 7-bit pseudorandom pattern derived in Figure D.4(a), then part (b) illustrates the transmitted bit pattern corresponding to a set of four data bits. Note that for each data bit seven bits are transmitted, and that for any data bit position, the transmitted bit sequence for a binary 0 is simply the inverse of that for a binary 1. The pseudorandom binary sequence is known also as the **spreading sequence**, each bit in the sequence a **chip**, the resulting transmission bit rate the **chipping rate**, and the number of bits in the sequence the **spreading factor**.

The spreading factor determines the performance of a spread spectrum system. Normally, it is expressed in decibels (dB) and is then known as the **processing gain**; that is, the processing gain is the logarithm of the spreading factor. For example, a spread spectrum system with a spreading factor of 10:1 has a processing gain of 10 dB, 100:1 of 20 dB, and so on. In terms of the signal-to-noise ratio (SNR) – also expressed in dB – the processing gain effectively subtracts from this. Hence for a non-spread-spectrum system that requires a SNR of, say, 10 dB – that is, the signal power must be ten times the noise power for satisfactory operation – then with spread spectrum and a processing gain of 10 dB, the system will operate satisfactorily even when the signal power is equal to the noise power.

A schematic diagram of a simple direct sequence radio transmitter and receiver is shown in Figure D.4(c). After each data bit has been exclusive-ORed with the pseudorandom sequence, the resulting high bit rate binary signal is transmitted by modulating a carrier signal. The frequency of the resulting signal is then increased – using a **mixer circuit** – so that the transmitted signal is in the defined frequency band. Typical modulation schemes used are binary phase shift keying (BPSK) and quadrature PSK (QPSK), the principles of which we described earlier in Section 2.2.2 when we studied modems.

We can deduce from the foregoing that the receiver must operate in synchronism with the received signal so that the results of performing the

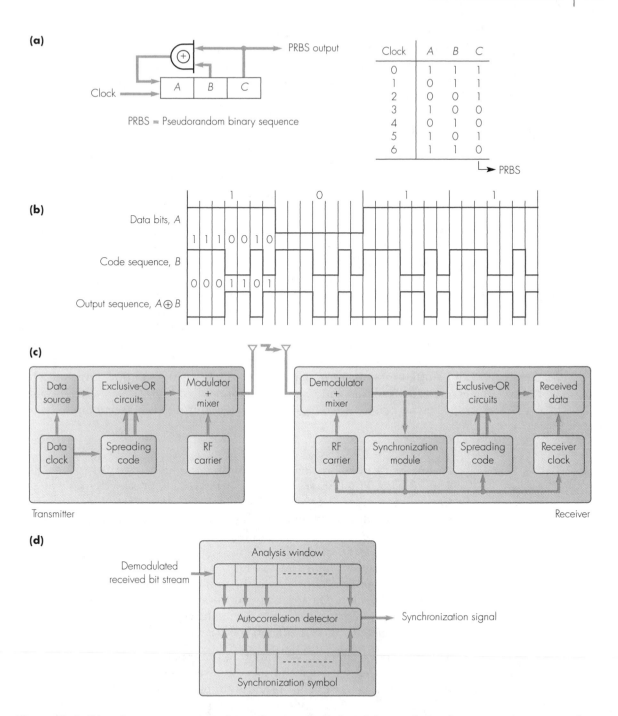

Figure D.4 Direct sequence spread spectrum principles: (a) pseudorandom sequence generator; (b) spread sequence generation; (c) transmitter and receiver schematic; (d) synchronization module schematic.

exclusive-OR operation are interpreted on the correct data bit (symbol) boundaries. To achieve this, a known binary pattern is transmitted at the beginning of each frame – the preamble – and the receiver uses this to achieve both clock/bit and symbol synchronization. A schematic diagram of the synchronization module is shown in Figure D.4(d).

Clock synchronization (at the chipping rate) is achieved using one of the standard methods we described in Section 1.3.3. To achieve symbol synchronization – at the data rate – each transmitted frame is preceded by a preamble that comprises a string of binary 1 symbols (data bits). As the spread preamble is received, it is passed through an n-bit shift register – where n is the number of bits in the spreading sequence – and compared on a chip-by-chip basis with the known sequence corresponding to a 1 data bit. If the two bits in a particular chip position are the same, then an agreement (A) is said to occur, while if they are different, a disagreement (D) occurs. A measure of the difference between the two symbols is then computed by subtracting the number of Ds from the number of As and this is known as the **autocorrelation function**. Clearly, when the known symbol is located then the autocorrelation function will be a maximum positive value equal to the number of chips in the spreading sequence. The receiver is then in symbol synchronization. The reliability of the synchronization process is determined by the autocorrelation between the chosen spreading sequence and shifted versions of it. This becomes increasingly important when chip errors are present in the received (demodulated) spread sequence because of excessive noise, for example. This is best illustrated by an example.

Example D.1

A typical spreading sequence used in direct sequence spread spectrum systems is the 11-bit binary sequence 10110111000. It is an example of a **Barker sequence**. Determine and plot the autocorrelation for this sequence for plus and minus 10 bits (chips) either side of it.

Answer:

The solution is summarized in Figure D.5. In part (a) the received bit/chip sequence is shown with the analysis window coinciding with the spreading sequence – synchronization symbol – together with an additional sequence either side of it. Clearly, in this position, all bit positions will be in agreement and the autocorrelation equal to +1.

The two other examples correspond to the situation plus or minus 1 bit of the spreading sequence and, as we can see, this yields an autocorrelation of –1. In fact, with this pseudorandom sequence all bit positions either side of it yield an autocorrelation of –1. The autocorrelation plot of this is therefore as shown in Figure D.5(b) and, as we can see, the signal output by the synchronization module will be positive only when the synchronization symbol is received.

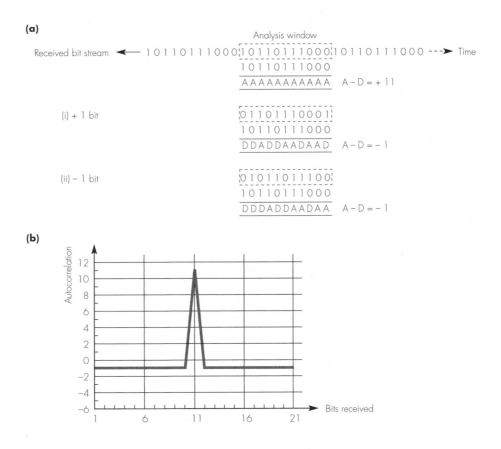

Figure D.5 Synchronization principle: (a) autocorrelation example; (b) autocorrelation graph.

COFDM principles

The principle of operation of the COFDM scheme is shown in Figure D.6(a).

Using COFDM, instead of just a single carrier signal, multiple orthogonal (equally-spaced) carriers are used, each of which is independently modulated by one or more bits from the bitstream to be transmitted. In the simple example shown in Figure D.6(a), five carriers are used, each of which is modulated by a single bit from the transmitted bitstream using on–off keying. The first carrier is a DC level, while the remaining four carriers are all sinusoidal signals of frequencies f_s, $2f_s$, $3f_s$ and $4f_s$ respectively. The period T_s is called the symbol period and, since on–off keying is being used, is equal to the time to transmit five bits from the bitstream being transmitted. Alternatively, if N carriers were used, each modulated using, say, QPSK, then T_s would be the time to transmit $2 \times N$ bits from the bitstream. During each symbol period, the five modulated signals are added together to form the signal/symbol that is transmitted.

At the receiver, before starting to process each received symbol, the receiver waits for a short time interval known as the **guard interval** to ensure that all delayed versions of the direct-path signals that make up the symbol have been received. In this way, instead of the delayed signals interfering with the direct-path symbol, since the same signals make up the symbol, they simply increase the power in the received symbol before it is processed. The processing involves determining which of the five carrier signals are present in the symbol and, based on this (and knowledge of the modulation method that has been used) the receiver can determine the original bitstream that was transmitted. As we show in Figure D.6(b), by using a set of carriers that are orthogonal, there is a fixed spacing of $1/T_s$ between adjacent carriers, which simplifies the processing that is required to determine which of the carriers are present in each received symbol.

In practice, the generation of each symbol is carried out digitally using a mathematical technique called the **inverse discrete Fourier transform (IDFT)**. The digital symbol output by the IDFT is converted into an analog symbol using a digital-to-analog converter prior to transmission. Similarly, the received symbol is first converted into a digital form – using an analog-to-digital converter (ADC) – before the symbol is processed using the DFT to determine the carriers that are present.

Although adding a guard interval avoids intersymbol interference, it also influences the maximum bit rate that can be supported; the longer the guard interval, T_g, the lower the maximum bit rate. Typically, therefore, T_g is limited to a maximum value of $T_s/4$. Hence, in the IEEE802.11a wireless LAN application, the number of carriers used is 52.

As with the other two schemes, it is necessary for the receiver to detect reliably the start of each new symbol that is received; that is, for the receiver to obtain and maintain symbol synchronization. In order to do this, the 52 orthogonal subcarrier frequencies in each block are made up of 48 for information frames and four for synchronization functions. Each of the 48 subcarriers in an information frame is modulated using BPSK (yielding up to 9 Mbps), QPSK (up to 18 Mbps), 16-QAM (up to 36 Mbps) and 64-QAM (up to 54 Mbps).

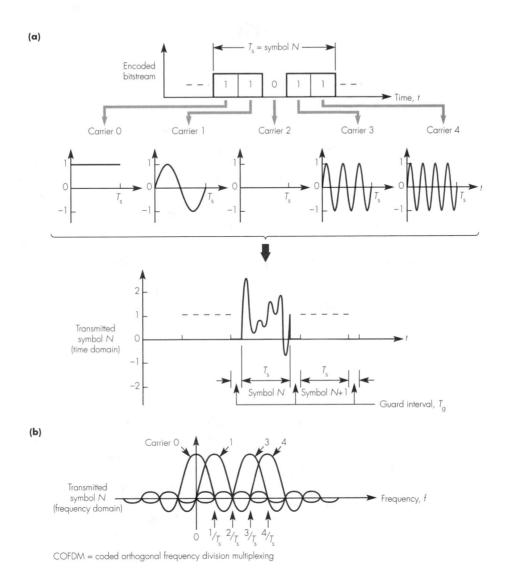

(a)

(b)

COFDM = coded orthogonal frequency division multiplexing

Figure D.6 COFDM principles: (a) symbol generation (time domain); (b) frequency domain symbol.

Appendix E ATM networks in the Internet backbone

As we indicated in Section 1.2.3, asynchronous transfer mode (ATM) networks are used extensively in the backbone switching networks relating to the PSTN/ISDN and the public Internet. The main reason for this is that once a virtual path/circuit between any pair of switching nodes that make up the total network has been established – for example edge routers in the case of the Internet backbone – the switching of the related data flows over this path/circuit can be carried out at very high rates. In the ISP backbone networks that we identified in Figure 2.35, for example, all-optical transmission lines operating at very high bit rates are used to interconnect the set of core routers that make up the backbone. Hence in order to switch the data flows that are arriving at the interface to each core router at these rates, ATM switches are used instead of conventional packet switches. The general arrangement is as shown in Figure E.1 and we shall use this application to describe also the operational mode of ATM networks in general.

E.1 Cell switching principles

In order to achieve the very high switching rates that are necessary, the packet flows relating to each virtual path/circuit are first fragmented at the network interface – in the edge routers, for example – into small fixed-sized packets called **cells**. In addition, since the rate of arrival of the packets relating to each packet flow varies, so the rate of entry of cells into (and through) the ATM switching network also varies. Hence instead of allocating a fixed portion of transmission bandwidth per virtual path/circuit, the cell streams relating to different packet flows are multiplexed together on a statistical basis. The switching units then operate using a form of packet switching called **cell switching**.

The adoption of a small fixed-sized cell means that cell switches can operate at a much higher rate than conventional packet switches that switch/route variable-length packets. As a result, cell switching is known also as **fast packet switching**. In addition, because the cells relating to different packet flows have varying time intervals between them during both transmission and switching, this mode of operation is known as the asynchronous transfer mode (ATM) and networks that operate in this way as (broadband) ATM networks.

Having adopted a small cell size and a cell-switching mode of operation, the next decision to be made was whether the network should operate in a connection-oriented (CO) or a connectionless (CL) mode. As we explained

(a)

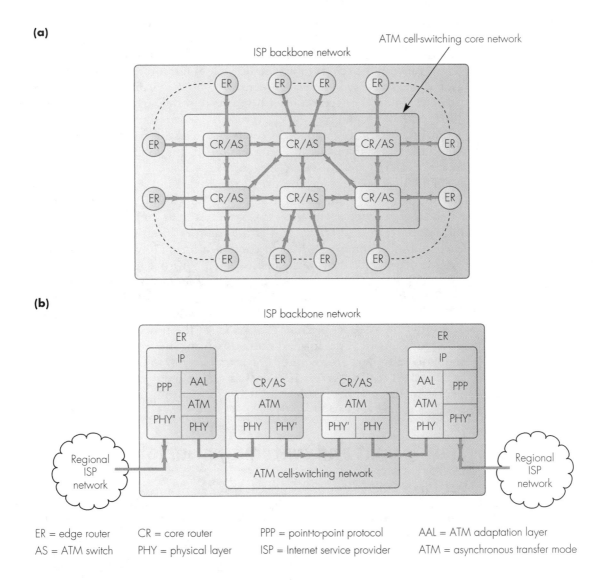

(b)

Figure E.1 ATM switching in ISP backbone networks: (a) application schematic; (b) ATM protocol stacks.

ER = edge router   CR = core router   PPP = point-to-point protocol   AAL = ATM adaptation layer
AS = ATM switch   PHY = physical layer   ISP = Internet service provider   ATM = asynchronous transfer mode

in Section 1.2.3, in a CL mode network each packet requires the full network-wide address of both the source and destination end systems in its header. The adoption of a small cell size, however, meant that the header would then be disproportionately large compared with the actual cell contents. Hence in order to keep the header small, the CO mode of operation was chosen. In a packet-switched network this involves a path/route through the network being established prior to the transfer of any data packets and, on completion of the session, the path being closed down. The resulting path is called a virtual circuit and, in order for each packet-switching exchange to relate incoming packets to a specific virtual circuit, a unique identifier is assigned to the session on each line making up the virtual circuit as this is set up. The identifier used on each line is called the virtual circuit identifier (VCI) and, by assigning a new VCI for each line, a reduced set of identifiers is required to identify the packets relating to the different sessions on each line/link rather than the different sessions in the total network. This same mode of operation is used in ATM networks.

The final decision was the size of the payload of a cell. Small cells have advantages for constant bit rate traffic since only a short delay is experienced as successive bytes relating to the same data stream are assembled and disassembled into and from cells at the network interface. Conversely, since each cell must contain additional routing information, small cells have the disadvantage that the overheads associated with each cell (in terms of transmission and switching) are higher. A compromise was reached by the various international standards bodies and a cell size of 53 bytes was chosen. This comprises a 48-byte payload (data) field with a 5-byte header for the VCI and other fields. Also, because the quality of the transmission lines is good, no error control is performed on cells within the network and hence no sequence numbers are required for retransmission purposes. However, the header does contain error check bits to detect the presence of transmission errors in the various header fields in order to minimize the number of wrongly routed cells.

E.2 Cell format and switching principles

As we have outlined, prior to any cells being sent, a virtual circuit/path is first established. Each virtual path/circuit is a series of links and ATM switches between the source and destination edge routers. In an ATM network, the virtual circuit identifier used on each link is known as the **protocol connection identifier** (**PCI**) and this is assigned when the virtual circuit/path is set up. In this application, a **permanent virtual circuit** (**PVC**) is set up between each pair of edge routers. Then, on receipt of each packet the network part of the source and destination IP addresses are used to determine the VPI that should be assigned to the related set of cells in the stream. The principle of the routing scheme used is shown in Figure E.2(a).

Associated with each incoming link/port is a routing table that contains, for each incoming PCI, the corresponding outgoing link/port and the new PCI to be used. The routing of cells in both directions along a route is thus very fast as it involves a simple look-up operation. As a result, cells from each link can be switched independently and at very high rates. This allows parallel switch architectures to be used and high bit rate transmission lines in the gigabit range, each operating at its maximum rate.

In practice, the PCI is made up of two subfields: a **virtual path identifier** (**VPI**) and a **virtual channel identifier** (**VCI**). Routing can be performed using either one or a combination of the two. Two examples are shown in Figure E.2. In part (b), switching is performed on virtual paths and the VCIs within each virtual path remain unchanged. In part (c), switching is performed on the virtual channels within each virtual path independently and the virtual paths simply terminate at each switch port.

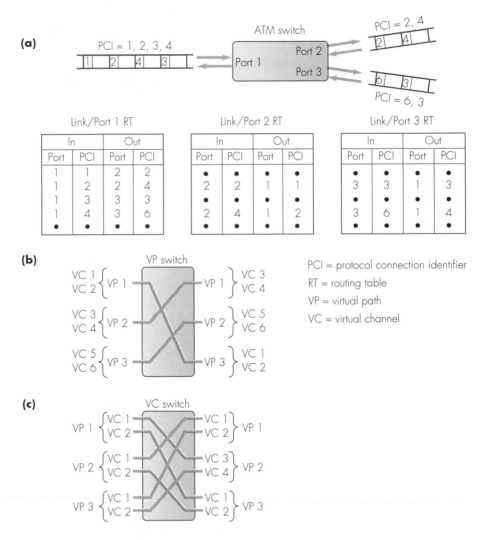

Figure E.2 Cell switching principles: (a) routing schematic; (b) VP routing; (c) VC routing.

An example of the use of virtual path switching is when multiple user-to-user packet flows originating at the same network entry point are all intended for the same destination exit point as is the case in our application. Each individual flow is assigned a separate VCI and the cells relating to each flow are multiplexed together at the source interface onto the same virtual path. The multiplexed set of cells relating to each flow are then switched using the VPI field only and hence all follow the same path through the ATM switching network. In this way, the set of VCIs remain unchanged and are used at the destination to identify and demultiplex the individual packet flows.

The format of each cell is shown in Figure E.3, as we can see, the header is made up of five fields. Their functions are as follows:

■ **Virtual path identifier (VPI)**: this is a 12-bit field and, as we described, it is used for identification/routing purposes within the networks.

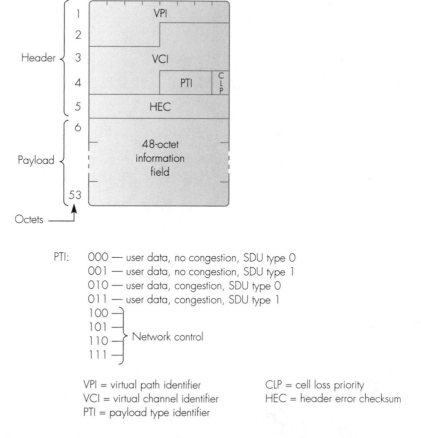

Figure E.3 **ATM cell format within the core network.**

- **Virtual channel identifier** (**VCI**): this is a 16-bit field and is also used for identification/routing purposes within the network.

- **Payload type indicator** (**PTI**): this indicates the type of data carried in the cell payload. All cells containing user data have a zero in the most significant bit. The next bit indicates whether the cell has experienced excessive delay/congestion or not, and the third bit the service data unit (SDU) type – 0 or 1. We shall discuss its use later in Section E.3.1 when we describe the AAL5 protocol. The four remaining cell types are used for network control purposes such as for setting up PVCs.

- **Cell loss priority** (**CLP**): within the network the statistical multiplexing of cells on each link may occasionally result in some cells having to be discarded during heavy load conditions. This field has been included to enable the user to specify a preference as to which cells should be discarded: CLP = 0 high priority, CLP = 1 low priority and hence discard first.

- **Header error checksum** (**HEC**): this is generated by the physical layer and is an 8-bit CRC on the first four bytes of the cell header.

E.3 ATM protocol stack

In this application, as we showed in Figure E.1(b), there are three protocols associated with the switching of data packets over the ATM cell-switching network. These are as follows:

- **ATM adaptation layer** (**AAL**): as its name implies, the AAL performs an adaptation (convergence) function between the IP layer and the cell-based service provided by the ATM layer. Hence at the source edge router this is concerned with the fragmentation of each IP packet it receives into a stream of 48-byte segments and, at the destination edge router, the reassembly of the 48-byte segments back into the original IP packet. As we indicated earlier, a separate VCI is allocated to each new packet flow and the VCI is used to relate each segment to a particular packet stream.

- **ATM layer**: this performs all the functions relating to the routing/switching and multiplexing of cells over the cell-switching network. In the source edge router, its main function is to assign values to the fields in the 5-byte header of each 48-byte segment generated by the AAL for this PVC. Similarly, at the destination edge router, on receipt of each cell relating to this PVC, it removes the 5-byte header and passes the 48-byte payload/segment to the AAL together with the VCI that has been allocated for this packet flow. Within each core router (ATM switch) in the cell-switching network, the ATM layer performs the switching of cells based on the VPI field only.

- **ATM physical layer**: this is made up of two sublayers, the **physical medium dependent** (**PMD**) sublayer and the **transmission convergence** (**TC**) sublayer. The PMD sublayer forms the physical interface to the transmission line/cable. Normally, as we showed in Figures 2.17 and 2.19 the transmission line is composed of one or more channels from either a PDH or a SDH/SONET digital multiplexing hierarchy. In this application, typical bit rates range from 139.264 Mbps (E4) to 622.08 Mbps (STM-4) or higher. The TC sublayer then performs the convergence function between the stream of ATM cells generated by the ATM layer and the related bitstream to be transmitted by the PMD sublayer. Similarly, at the receiving end, it converges the received bitstream from the PMD sublayer into (ATM) cells ready for processing by the ATM layer. In addition, the TC sublayer generates the HEC byte for each cell and, at the destination, processes the received HEC byte to determine the presence of errors in the cell header.

E.3.1 AAL5

In this application, the AAL layer used for the transfer of IP packets over an ATM network is AAL5. It is called the **simple and efficient adaptation layer** (**SEAL**). It is composed of two sublayers: the **convergence sublayer** (**CS**) that provides the interface with the IP layer, and the **segmentation and reassembly** (**SAR**) sublayer that performs the segmentation and reassembly of IP packets into/from the 48-byte segments that are sent/received over the ATM switching network. The formats of the PDUs associated with both the CS and SAR protocols are shown in Figure E.4.

The IP packet to be transferred is called the AAL user service data unit (AAL user SDU) and, as we can see, with AAL5 there is no header associated with the constructed CS-PDU. The use of the various fields is as follows:

- The *pad* field in the trailer is 0–47 bytes so that the length of each CS-PDU can be an integral number of complete 48-byte segments. This has the advantage that the fields in the trailer of the CS-PDU are always the last 8 bytes of the last segment, which leads to faster processing at the destination.

- The AAL *user-to-user* (*UU*) *identifier* enables the two correspondent user layers to relate the AAL SDU to a particular service access point (SAP) and hence packet stream.

- The use of the *CPI* field has yet to be defined. It is included to support future functions and currently to make the tail an even number of bytes.

- The *length* field indicates the number of bytes in the user data field and is an integer value in the range 0 to 65 535.

- The *CRC* field detects the presence of any transmission errors in the reassembled CS-PDU. If errors are detected, then the user layer above is

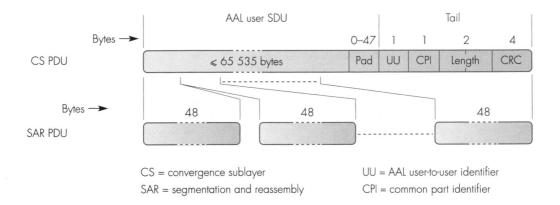

Figure E.4 AAL5: CS and SAR PDU formats.

informed when the SDU (IP packet) contained within the PDU is delivered. In this way it is left to the user layer to decide what action to take; in some instances this will be to discard the packet – for example if it contains normal data – while in others, it will be to accept it and take appropriate recovery steps – for example if the packet contents relate to a video or audio stream.

As we can see, there is no head or tail associated with the SAR PDU. Each comprises the full 48 bytes and the SAR protocol is said to be null. The lack of a header means that the segments relating to the same CS-PDU are identified using the fields in the header of the ATM cell that is used to transport the segment. With AAL5, the SDU type bit in user data cells – also known as **ATM-layer user-to-user** (**AUU**) cells – is used to indicate whether the cell contents form the beginning or continuation of the CS-PDU (binary 0) or the end (binary 1). Although this means that the operation of the AAL layer is now linked with that of the ATM layer, it is done to improve the efficiency of the segmentation process.

AAL5 is also used as the AAL layer for the segmentation and reassembly of messages associated with the signaling protocol. It is known as the **signaling AAL** or **SAAL**. Signaling messages are used, for example, to set up and tear down permanent and semi-permanent virtual circuits/paths through the ATM switching network such as the virtual circuits/paths linking each pair of edge routers in this application.

Bibliography and further reading

In order to keep abreast of developments in the communications and networking fields, you should try to read on a regular basis the journals and magazines published in these fields by the major institutions. The journals include *IEEE Transactions on Communications, IEEE Journal on Selected Areas in Communications, Communications of the ACM* and *IEE Proceedings on Communications.*

The magazines include *IEEE Network, IEEE Communications, IEEE Internet Computing* and *IEEE Multimedia,* all of which contain articles relating to state-of-the-art developments in their related fields.

The listing of titles within this bibliography reflects the order in which the related topic is discussed in the text.

Chapter 1

Halsall F. (1996). *Data Communications, Computer Networks and Open Systems* 4th edn. Addison-Wesley

Black U.D. (1993). *Data Link Protocols.* Prentice Hall

Marano K. et al. (1990). Echo cancellation and applications. *IEEE Communications Magazine,* January

Pearson J.E. (1992). *Basic Communication Theory.* Prentice Hall

Ramabadroan T. (1988). A tutorial on CRC computations. *IEEE Micro Magazine,* August

Choi T.Y. (1985). Formal techniques for the specification of protocols. *IEEE Communications Magazine,* January

Conrad J. (1980). Character-oriented data link control protocols. *IEEE Transactions on Communications,* April

Carlson D.E. (1980). Bit-oriented data link control procedures. *IEEE Transactions on Communications,* April

Danthine A.A.S. (1980). Protocol representation with finite-state models. *IEEE Transactions on Communications,* April

Pouzin L. and Zimmerman H. (1978). A tutorial on protocols. *IEEE Proceedings,* November

Storer J.A. (1988). *Data Compression: methods and theory.* Computer Science Press

ISO (1994). *Digital Compression and Coding of Continuous Tone Still Images (JPEG).* ISO 10918-1

Clark R.J. (1995). *Digital Compression of Still Images and Video.* Academic Press

Benoit H. (1997). *Digital Television: MPEG-1, MPEG-2 and DVB.* Arnold

Halsall F. (2000). *Multimedia Communications.* Addison-Wesley

Chapter 2

Bellamy J. (2000). *Digital Telephony* 3rd edn. Wiley

Azzam A.A. and Ransom N. (1999). *Broadband Access Technologies.* McGraw-Hill

Halsall F. (2000). *Multimedia Communications.* Addison-Wesley

Carlson J. (2001). *PPP Design Implementation and Debugging* 2nd edn. Addison-Wesley

Ericsson (1987). *Telecommunications: telephone networks 1 and 2*. Chartwell-Black

Nortel (1992). *Synchronous Transmission Systems*. Northern Telecom Europe

Lechleider J.W. (1989). Line codes for digital subscriber lines. *IEEE Communications Magazine*, September

Held G. (1994). *The Complete Modern Reference* 2nd edn. Wiley

Ibe O.C. (1997). *Essentials of ATM Networks and Services*. Addison-Wesley

EIA (1987). *Standard Interface Between a DTE and DCE for Serial Data Interchange* (EIA-232D)

Metz C. (2001). Interconnecting ISP networks. *IEEE Internet Computing*, May

Shepard S. (2001). *SONET/SDH Demystified*. McGraw-Hill

Summers C.K. (1999). *ADSL: standards, implementation and architecture*. CRC Press

Vetter R.J. et al. (2000). Systems aspects of APON/VDSL deployment. *IEEE Communications Magazine*, May

Chapter 3

Metcalf R.M. and Boggs D.R. (1976). Ethernet: distributed packet switching for local computer networks. *Communications of the ACM*, July

IEEE (1983). *CSMA/CD Access Method and Physical Layer Specifications* (IEEE Standard 802.3)

Stuck B.W. (1983). Calculating the maximum throughput of LANs. *IEEE Computer*, May

Backes F. (1988). Transparent bridges for the interconnection of IEEE 802 LANs. *IEEE Network Magazine*, January

Perlman R. (2000). *Interconnections* 2nd edn. Addison-Wesley

Hart J. (1988). Extending the IEEE802.1 bridge standard to remote bridges. *IEEE Network Magazine*, January

IEEE (1995). *MAC and Physical Layer Parameters for 100BaseT* (IEEE Standard 802.3u)

Breyer R. and Riley S. (1999). *Switched, Fast and Gigabit Ethernet*. New Riders

Cisco (1998). *Designing Switched LAN Interconnections*. Cisco Systems

Molle M. (1997). Frame bursting: a technique for scaling CSMA/CD to gigabit speeds. *IEEE Network Magazine*, July

Frazier H. and Johnson H. (1999). Gigabit Ethernet: from 100 to 1000 Mbps. *IEEE Internet Computing*, January

Izzo P. (2000). *Gigabit Networks*. Wiley

IEEE (1985). *Logical Link Control Protocol* (IEEE Standard 802.2)

Brown S. (1999). *Implementing Virtual Private Networks*. McGraw-Hill

Smith P. (1993). *Frame Relay*. Addison-Wesley

Chapter 4

Schiller J. (2003). *Mobile Communications* 2nd edn. Addison-Wesley

Bhagwat P. (2001). Bluetooth: technology for short-range wireless applications. *IEEE Internet Computing*, May–June

Bisdikian C. (2001). An overview of the Bluetooth wireless technology. *IEEE Communications Magazine*, December

Bray J. and Sturman C.F. (2002). *Bluetooth 1.1: connect without cables* 2nd edn. Prentice Hall

Chen K.C. (1994). Medium Access Control of wireless LANs for mobile computing. *IEEE Network Magazine*, September–October

Bluetooth (2001). *Specification of the Bluetooth System Vol. 2.* Bluetooth Special Interest Group (SIG), version 1.1

Bluetooth (2002). *Bluetooth Special Interest Group. http://www.bluetooth.com/*

Crow B.P. et al. (1997). IEEE.802.11 Wireless local area networks. *IEEE Communications Magazine*, September

Doufexi A. et al. (2002). A comparison of the Hiperlan/2 and IEEE802.11a wireless LAN standards. *IEEE Communications Magazine*, May

Kapp S. (2002). 802.11: leaving the wire behind. *IEEE Internet Computing*, January–February

Lansford J. et al. (2001). WiFi (802.11b) and Bluetooth: enabling coexistence. *IEEE Network Magazine*, September–October

Perkins C.E. (2001). *Ad Hoc Networking.* Addison-Wesley

Ohara B. and Petrick A. (1999). *802.11 Handbook: a designers companion.* IEEE Press

GSM Association (2002). *http://gsmworld.com/*

ETSI (1997). *High-speed Circuit Switched Data (HSCSD), Stage 1.* European Telecommunications Standards Institute (ETSI) (GSM 02.34, V5.2.1)

Brasche G. et al. (1997). Concepts services and protocols of the new GSM phase2+ General Packet Radio Service (GPRS). *IEEE Communications Magazine*, 35(8)

Collins D. and Smith C. (2001). *3G Wireless Networks.* McGraw-Hill

Ahmavara K. et al. (2003). Interworking architecture between 3GPP and WLAN systems. *IEEE Communications Magazine*, November

Wong K.D. et al. (2003). Supporting real-time IP multimedia services in UMTS. *IEEE Communications Magazine*, November

Chapter 5

IEEE (1997). *IEEE Network: special issue on broadband services over residential networks*, January

Bisdikian C. et al. (1996). Residential broadband data services over HFC networks. *IEEE Comunications Magazine*, November

Pugh W. and Boyer G. (1995). Broadband access: comparing alternatives. *IEEE Communications Magazine*, August

Khasnabish B. (1997). Broadband to the home: architectures and access methods. *IEEE Network Magazine*, January

Lin Y-D. (1998). The IEEE802.14 MAC protocol. *IEEE Communications Surveys*, October

Cable Television Laboratories Inc. *Data-over-cable Service Interface Specification. http://www.cablemodem.com*

Kiniry J.R. and Metz C. (1998). Cable modems: cable TV delivers the Internet. *IEEE Internet Computing*, May

Droms R. (1997). *Dynamic Host Configuration Protocol (DHCP)*, March (RFC 2131)

Paff A. (1995). Hybrid fiber/coax in the public telecommunications infrastructure. *IEEE Communications Magazine*, April

Benoit H. (1999). *Satellite Television: techniques of analog and digital television.* Arnold

Donaldson G. and Jones D. (2001). Cable television network architectures. *IEEE Communications Magazine*, June

Chapter 6

Postel J. (1980). *The Internet Protocol*, September (RFC 791)

Huitema C. (1995). *Routing in the Internet.* Prentice Hall

Dutcher B. (2001). *The NAT Handbook.* Wiley

Braden R.T. et al. (1998). *Computing the Checksum for the IP Protocols,* September (RFC 1071)

Plummer D.C. (1992). *An Ethernet Address Resolution Protocol,* November (RFC 826)

Finlayson R. et al. (1984). *A Reverse Address Resolution Protocol,* June (RFC 903)

Hendrick C.L. (1988). *Routing Information Protocol,* June (RFC 1058)

Waitzman D. et al. (1988). *Distance Vector Multicast Routing Protocol,* November (RFC 1075)

Moy J. (1991). *OSPF Version 2,* July (RFC 1247)

Moy J. (1994). *Multicast Extensions to OSPF,* March (RFC 1584)

Solomon J.D. (1998). *Mobile IP: the Internet unplugged.* Prentice Hall

Davie B. and Rekhter Y. (2000). *MPLS Technology and Applications.* Morgan Kaufmann

Lin Y.D. et al. (2002). QoS routing granularity in MPLS networks. *IEEE Communications Magazine*

Floyd S. and Jacobson V. (1993). Random early detection gateways for congestion avoidance. *IEEE Transactions on Networking,* August

Jain R. (1990). Congestion control in computer networks: issues and trends. *IEEE Network Magazine,* May/June

Metz C. (2000). Differentiated Services. *IEEE Multimedia Magazine,* July/September

Wang Z. (2001). *Internet QoS.* Morgan Kaufmann

Zhang L. (1993). RSVP: a new Resource ReSerVation Protocol. *IEEE Network Magazine,* September–October

Metz C. (1999). RSVP: general purpose signaling for IP. *IEEE Internet Computing,* May

Braden R. (1997). *RSVP Version 1 Functional Specification,* September (RFC 2205)

Blake S. et al. (1998). *An Architecture for Differentiated Services,* December (RFC 2475)

Deering S. and Hinden R. (1995). *IPv6 Specification,* December (RFC 1883)

Hinden R. and Deering S. (1995). *IPv6 Addressing Architecture,* December (RFC 1884)

Huitema C. (1997). *IPv6: the new Internet protocol.* Prentice Hall

Chapter 7

Socolofsky T. and Kale C. (1991). *A TCP/IP Tutorial,* January (RFC 1180)

Stevens W.R. (1994). *TCP/IP Illustrated, Vol. 1.* Addison-Wesley

Comer D.E. (2000). *Interworking with TCP/IP, Vol.1* 4th edn. Prentice Hall

Postel J.B. (1981). *The Transmission Control Protocol (TCP),* September (FRC 793)

Nagel J. (1984). *Congestion Control in TCP/IP Internetworks,* January (RFC 896)

Clark D.D. (1982). *Window and Acknowledgment Strategy in TCP,* July (RFC 813)

Mogel J.C. and Deering S.E. (1990). *Path NTU Discovery,* April (RFC 1191)

Jacobson V. et al. (1992). *TCP Extensions for High Performance,* May (RFC 1323)

Stevens W. (1997). *TCP Slow Start, Congestion Avoidance, Fast Retransmit and Fast Recovery Algorithms,* January (RFC 2001)

Mathis M. et al. (1996). *TCP Selective Acknowledgment Options,* October (RFC 2018)

Allman M. et al. (1999). *TCP Congestion Control,* April (RFC 2581)

Postel J.B. (1980). *The User Datagram Protocol (UDP),* August (RFC 768)

Schultzrinne H. et al. (1989). *RTP: a transport protocol for real-time applications,* also includes specification of RTCP (RFC 1889)

Clark D.D. et al. (1989). An analysis of TCP processing overhead. *IEEE Communications Magazine,* June

Perkins C.E. (2002). *RTP: audio and video for the Internet.* Addison-Wesley

Huston G. (2001). TCP in a wireless world. *IEEE Internet Computing,* March–April

Xylomenos G. et al. (2001). TCP performance issues over wireless links. *IEEE Communications Magazine,* April

Chapter 8

Mockapetris P.V. (1983). *Domain Names: implementation specification*, November (RFC 833)

Mockapetris P.V. (1987). *Domain Names: concepts and facilities*, November (RFC 1034)

Reynolds J. and Postel J. (1994). *Assigned Numbers*, October (RFC 1700)

Kille S. (1995). *A String Representation of Distinguished Names*, March (RFC 1779)

Postel J.B. (1982). *Simple Mail Transfer Protocol (SMTP)*, August (RFC 821)

Crocker D.H. (1982). *Standard Format for Internet Text Messages*, August (RFC 822)

Myers J. and Rose M. (1996). *Post Office Protocol Version 3 (POP3)*, May (RFC 1939)

Freed N. and Borenstein N. (1996). *Multipurpose Internet Mail Extensions*, November (RFC 2045/8)

Postel J. and Reynolds J. (1985). *The File Transfer Protocol (FTP)*, October (RFC 959)

Davidson J. and Peters J. (2000). *Voice-over IP Fundamentals*, Cisco Press

Deering S.E. (1993). SIP: Simple Internet Protocol. *IEEE Network Magazine*, May–June

Kumar V. et al. (2001). *IP Telephony with H.323*. Wiley

Wright D.J. (2001). *Voice Over Packet Networks*. Wiley

Morgan S. (1998). The Internet and the local telephone network: conflicts and opportunities. *IEEE Communications Magazine*, January

Stallings W. (1993). *SNMP, SNMPv2, and CMIP*. Addison-Wesley

McCloghrie K. and Rose M.T. (1991). *MIBII for Network Management of TCP/IP Internets*, March (RFC 1213)

Chapter 9

Berners-Lee T. et al. (1994). The World Wide Web. *Communications of the ACM*, Vol. 37, August

Vetters R.J. et al. (1994). Mosaic and the World Wide Web. *IEEE Computer*, October

World Wide Web Consortium home page: *http://www.w3.org*

Khare R. (1999). Anatomy of a URL. *IEEE Internet Computing*, September

Berners-Lee T. et al. (1996). *Hypertext Transfer Protocol, HTTP/1.0*, May (RFC 1945)

Fielding R. et al. (1997). *Hypertext Transfer Protocol, HTTP/1.1*, January (RFC 2068)

Cheswick W.R. and Bellovin S.M. (1994). *Firewalls and Internet Security*. Addison-Wesley

Baentsch M. et al. (1997). Web caching: the application-level view of the Internet. *IEEE Communications Magazine*, June

Luotoren A. and Altis K. (1994). World Wide web proxies. *Computer Networks and ISDN*, November

Berghel H.L. (1996). The client side of the Web. *Communications of the ACM*, January

Kwan T.T. et al. (1995). NCSA's WWW server: design and performance. *IEEE Computer*, November

Meyers P. (1998). *The HTML Web Classroom*. Prentice Hall

Bryan M. (1997). *SGML and HTML Explained*. Addison-Wesley

Rule J. (1999). *Dynamic HTML*. Addison-Wesley

Castro E. (1997). *Perl and CGI for the World Wide Web*. Addison-Wesley

Schulzrinne H. et al. (1998). *Real-time Streaming Protocol (RTSP)*, April (RFC 2326)

Campione M. and Walrath K. (1996). *The Java Language Tutorial*. Addison-Wesley

Arnold K. and Gosling J. (1996). *The Java Programming Language*. Addison-Wesley

Van der Linden P. (1996). *Just Java*. Prentice Hall

Chapter 10

Kaufman C. et al. (2002). *Network Security* 2nd edn. Prentice Hall

Netscape (1998). *Introduction to Public Key Cryptography*. Netscape Communications Corporation

Kaufman C. et al. (1995). *Networking Security: private communications in a public world.* Prentice Hall

Kummert H. (1998). *The PPP Triple-DES Encryption Protocol,* September (RFC 2420)

Rivest R.L. et al. (1978). On a method for obtaining digital signatures and public key cryptosystems. *Communications of the ACM,* February

Rivest R.L. (1992). *The MD5 Message Digest Algorithm,* April (RFC 1321)

Kohl J. and Neuman B.C. (1993). *The Kerberos Network Authentication Service,* September (RFC 1510)

Maughan D. et al. (1998). *Internet Security Association and Key Management Protocol (ISAKMP),* November (RFC 2408)

Kent S. (1993). *Certificate-based Key Management,* February (RFC 1422)

Mullins J. (2002). Making unbreakable code. *IEEE Spectrum,* May

Nichols R.K. and Lekkas P.C. (2002). *Wireless Security.* McGraw-Hill

Perlman R. and Kaufman C. (2000). Key exchange in IPSec. *IEEE Internet Computing,* November–December

Schneier B. (1996). *Applied Cryptography* 2nd edn. Wiley

Schneier B. (1995). *E-Mail Security.* Wiley

Zimmermann P.R. (1995). *The Official PGP User Guide.* MIT Press

Ziv J. and Lempel Z. (1997). A universal algorithm for sequential data compression. *IEEE Transactions on Information Theory,* Vol. IT-23, May

Stinson D.R. (2002). *Cryptography Theory and Practice* 2nd edn. CRC Press

Index